New Immigrants in
the United States

CAMBRIDGE LANGUAGE TEACHING LIBRARY

A series covering central issues in language teaching and learning, by authors who have expert knowledge in their field.

In this series:

New Immigrants in the United States

Readings for Second Language Educators

Edited by

Sandra Lee McKay

San Francisco State University

Sau-ling Cynthia Wong

University of California at Berkeley

CAMBRIDGE
UNIVERSITY PRESS

PUBLISHED BY THE PRESS SYNDICATE OF THE UNIVERSITY OF CAMBRIDGE
The Pitt Building, Trumpington Street, Cambridge, United Kingdom

CAMBRIDGE UNIVERSITY PRESS
The Edinburgh Building, Cambridge CB2 2RU, United Kingdom   http://www.cup.ac.uk
40 West 20th Street, New York, NY 10011-4211, USA   http://www.cup.org
10 Stamford Road, Oakleigh, Melbourne 3166, Australia
Ruiz de Alarcón 13, 28014 Madrid, Spain

© Cambridge University Press 2000

First published 2000

Printed in the United States of America.

Typeface Sabon 10^1/$_2$/12pt.   [SB]

Library of Congress Cataloguing in Publication data
New immigrants in the United States : readings for second language education /
[compiled by] Sandra Lee McKay, Sau-ling Cynthia Wong.
p.   cm. – (Cambridge language teaching library)
ISBN 0-521-66087-4 – ISBN 0-521-66798-4 (pbk.)
1. English language – Textbooks for foreign speakers. 2. United States – Emigration and
immigration – Problems, exercises, etc. 3. Immigrants – United States – Problems,
exercises, etc. 4. Readers – Emigration and immigration. 5. Readers – Immigrants.
I. Series.   II. McKay, Sandra.   III. Wong, Sau-ling Cynthia.

PE1128 N384 2000
428′.007 21 – dc21
                                                                          99-043715

*A catalogue record for this book is available from
the British Library*

ISBN 0 521 660874 hardback
ISBN 0 521 667984 paperback

Contents

Contents

Part III   Investing in English language learners   393

Contributors

Chuong Hoang Chung, San Francisco State University, California
Joan May T. Cordova, Wheelock College, Boston, Massachusetts
Ofelia García, Long Island University, Brooklyn, New York
Eli Hinkel, Seattle University, Washington
John M. Lipski, University of New Mexico, Albuquerque
M. G. López, New York University, New York
Reynaldo F. Macías, University of California, Los Angeles
Sandra Lee McKay, San Francisco State University, California
Pyong Gap Min, Queens College of the City University of New York
Rachel F. Moran, University of California, Berkeley
Bonny Norton, University of British Columbia, Canada
Ricardo Otheguy, City College of the City University of New York
Ana Roca, Florida International University, Miami
Kamal K. Sridhar, State University of New York at Stony Brook
S. N. Sridhar, State University of New York at Stony Brook
Guadalupe Valdés, Stanford University, California
Calvin Veltman, University of Quebec, Montreal, Canada
Sau-ling C. Wong, University of California, Berkeley
Ana Celia Zentella, Hunter College of the City University of New York

To the reader

Throughout this book we generally use the term *English language learner* to refer to individuals who actively use a language other than English in their home. The term *limited English proficient (LEP) student*, though commonly used in educational research and policy guidelines, has been avoided because it has negative connotations and minimizes the value of the learners' other language. (See Chapter 1, however, for objections to the term *English language learner* as well.)

We use the term *Latino* rather than *Hispanic* since the connotations of *Latino* include the African and indigenous heritage as well as the Spanish heritage of these people. We avoid using the term *Anglo-American* unless specifically referring to those of English heritage. Otherwise we use the term *European American*. Finally, we use the terms *White* and *Black American* when highlighting issues of race and use terms such as *African American* or *Haitian* when ethnicity or culture is being discussed. Individual contributors have also clarified their use of particular terminology. For example, Joan May T. Cordova has chosen to use the term *Filipina/o* to emphasize the presence of women in Filipina/o history, and M. G. López, because of his focus on the Hmong, Khmer, and Laotian communities, has chosen to use the term *Southeast Asian* to refer to individuals originally from Cambodia and Laos.

The term *mother tongue* is used in the text because of its common usage in the field; we intend no sexist bias in its use.

Acknowledgments

We thank the contributors to this volume for their thoughtful and thoroughly researched portraits of new immigrants to the United States, and Debbie Goldblatt and Mary Carson of Cambridge University Press for their encouragement and constructive feedback. Thanks also to Olive Collen and Ellen Garshick for their careful work in editing.

Finally, we are grateful to our families for their understanding and support throughout the project.

Introduction

Sandra Lee McKay
Sau-ling C. Wong

The language situation of the United States is fraught with contradictions. The English language is so universally recognized that many Americans believe it to be the official language – and certainly most act as if it already were – but nothing in the Constitution designates it as such. When the nation opens its borders to immigrants and refugees from all over the world, proficiency in English is not stipulated as a condition for entry; once admitted, however, the newcomers often find themselves facing social, economic, and political consequences of their lack of mastery of the language. Many in the United States today claim to espouse cultural pluralism; at the same time linguistic pluralism, its twin, is frequently treated as if it were a problem created for the Anglophone majority by burdensome language minorities. As a nation without an explicitly articulated language policy, the United States generally looks to the schools as the major vehicles for language planning; yet the United States provides few resources for developing effective language programs for English language learners.

These contradictions have become more acute during the years since the liberalization of immigration law in 1965, which, by eliminating an earlier bias in favor of European (especially northwest European) immigration, has dramatically altered the makeup of the U.S. population. Not only have the demographic changes resulted in classrooms of great ethnic, cultural, and linguistic diversity, rendering the teacher's task ever more daunting, but the Asian and Latino backgrounds of many post-1965 immigrants have exacerbated White-nativist sentiments and turned English monolingualism into a litmus test of patriotism. In an era of globalization, the United States, a world power, has become more rather than less myopic and intolerant in its treatment of language minorities. As demonstrated by the 1998 passage of Proposition 227 (banning bilingual education) in California, English language learners in the public schools frequently bear the brunt of the mainstream population's anxieties over the changing face of America.

As educators, we have attempted before to provide a social and educational perspective on language diversity in the United States (McKay & Wong, 1988). However, a number of factors have made it imperative that we revisit the issues now. In terms of demographics, the decennial census of 1990 and other surveys have provided much new information on the current composition of English language learners in the United States. The percentage of speakers of other languages in the school population, as a proportion of the total population, has increased significantly during the 1990s. Whereas one in ten school-age children in the 1980s was from a non-English-speaking background, by the early 1990s this number had increased to one in seven. The growth in the number of speakers of non-European languages is particularly striking. For example, the number of Asian Indian speakers increased by 165 percent, Vietnamese speakers by 161 percent, and Thai and Laotian speakers by 143 percent (Waggoner, 1993). In terms of scholarship, the 1990s have witnessed immense growth in research in second language acquisition, language use within language minority communities, and effective English education programs.

But these factors are not merely factual: They have an unavoidable political dimension that makes examining present-day linguistic diversity in the United States all the more important. Although demographic changes are in themselves threatening to the established population, the contemporary debates on language carry noticeable racial subtexts. A frequently heard opinion is that today's immigrants are different – worse – than those who came earlier. Compared with the latter (meaning European immigrants), Asians and Latinos, who constitute the majority of post-1965 language minorities, are portrayed as being lazy and clannish, uncommitted to their new country and unwilling to make the extra effort to learn English: in short, unassimilable. As Chapters 1 and 2 and others in this volume demonstrate, the language shift undergone by today's English language learners differs little from historical patterns. It is continued immigration that has created the impression of unassimilability, masking the interest, effort, and success in English learning on the part of Asian and Latino immigrants. Although we are aware that even the most scrupulous, persuasive research in the world may not influence policy makers or voters when the larger political climate is hostile to its findings, we are committed to bringing such research to those who are concerned about the English learners in our midst.

In putting together this volume with a sense of urgency and responsibility, we proceed from several assumptions. First, we believe that the linguistic diversity of the United States is a valuable resource rather than a problem and that the emphasis in current U.S. language education practices – curtailing mother-tongue maintenance among immigrants and then providing foreign language programs for Anglophone monolinguals (many of whom are former bilinguals) – is, to say the least, wasteful. Language resources, like natural resources, should be wisely conserved and developed. Second, we believe that English language learners, regardless of their ethnic origin and length of residence in the

United States, have a dual right: to gain proficiency in English through effective educational programs and to maintain their mother tongue in their family and community life and, if possible, in their educational setting. Further, an enlightened language education policy should recognize that these two processes, rather than being antagonistic, are in fact interdependent. Finally, we believe that although schools can do a great deal to help English language learners attain their potential for participation in American society, there are limits to the power of education. The philosophical commitment of the entire community to a language-as-resource perspective, accompanied by economic support, is necessary before a more coherent and farsighted language policy can be implemented through the schools. At the moment, when the national mood is dominated by nativist sentiments, as evidenced in the growing English-only movement, whether such a reorientation is forthcoming may be doubtful, but it is worth bearing in mind and working for.

We are fully convinced that language teaching and learning are not simply issues of pedagogy or individual endeavor. The liberalization of immigration law in 1965 created dramatic changes in both the size and makeup of language minorities in the United States, resulting in more diverse language classrooms. As schools all over the country experience an influx of English language learners, it becomes increasingly apparent that what happens in schools is intimately related to what happens in the surrounding community. Without a clear understanding of the social context in which English language learners operate, efforts to aid these learners in their English language education may well prove misdirected or even counterproductive. Thus this volume is designed to go beyond what is provided by many resource handbooks for teachers, such as those prepared by state departments of education or local school districts: a list of features in the learners' native language that contrast with those of English and an inventory of the learners' cultural values and practices. We believe that, in order to make pedagogical decisions that will benefit the learner, educators must have an understanding of language learners as members of complex social networks encompassing both the language minority community and the larger society. In addition to the usual linguistic and cultural background information, we seek to raise questions such as: Why have these learners come to the United States? How do these learners use English and their first language in their homes and communities? What personal investments do they have in learning English, and how do these investments change over time? What legal and educational policies currently exist regarding the rights of these individuals to use their first language as well as to receive adequate English education? What educational programs are there for English language learners, and how effective are they?

3

To address these questions, this volume features chapters organized into three parts. In Part I, "Historical and Contemporary Overviews on English Language Learners in the United States," Reynaldo Macías describes the makeup of previous generations of English language learners in the United States and provides current demographic data on English language learners, paying special attention to methodological problems in determining their numbers. In Chapter 2, Calvin Veltman examines the process whereby immigrants come to adopt English and lose their mother tongue, demonstrating how very rapidly immigrants – including the much-criticized Spanish speakers – by and large – have learned English.

Part II, "New Immigrants in the United States: History, Language Background, and Community," provides teachers with information on the immigration background, language characteristics, and language use patterns of the most numerous groups of present-day English language learners. Specifically, each of these chapters includes the following information:

- an overview of the immigration history of the group
- current demographics of the group
- a summary of research on language use within the community, typically with a description of the linguistic features of the native language and relevant values of the native culture
- suggestions for educational programs for this group of learners
- an annotated list of further readings that would be helpful to language teachers

Part III, "Investing in English Language Learners," explores three types of investment necessary for successful language learning – educational investment, legal and policy investment, and individual investment. Sandra McKay (Chapter 14) describes prevalent models of educational programs for English language learners, summarizes existing research on the experience of English language learners in schools and their communities, and suggests some characteristics of effective programs for English language learners. Rachel Moran (Chapter 15) considers the implications of the current federal policy of allowing state and local initiatives to meet the needs of English language learners, examining California and New York as examples. Finally, Bonny Norton reconsiders the adequacy of current notions of motivation in second language acquisition research and offers an alternative perspective of investment that is sensitive to social power differentials and to the multiple social identities of an individual learner.

To help us select language minority groups to include in this volume, we consulted a study conducted by the U.S. Department of Education (Fleischman & Hopstock, 1993), whose mail survey of 745 school dis-

TABLE I. MOST POPULOUS LANGUAGE GROUPS AMONG
ENGLISH LEARNERS, U.S. PUBLIC SCHOOLS, 1993

Language group	English learners	
	No.	%
Spanish	1,682,560	72.9
Vietnamese	90,922	3.9
Hmong	42,305	1.8
Cantonese	38,693	1.7
Cambodian	37,742	1.6
Korean	36,568	1.6
Laotian	29,838	1.3
Navajo	28,913	1.3
Tagalog	24,516	1.1
Russian	21,903	0.9

Source: Fleischman and Hopstock (1993).

tricts nationwide yielded a list of the most populous language groups represented among English learners in public schools. The ten most populous groups are given in Table 1. These data became the basis for our decisions on group-specific chapters. Regrettably, practical constraints prevent us from including all the groups on which language educators might need information. Also, the nationwide figures do not address local concentrations and are likely to be less useful to teachers in private institutions catering to different student groups than public institutions do.

Except for the Navajo (see below), we have included chapters on all the groups in the table, with the following modifications:

- Because of the size of the Spanish group, the text includes four chapters on Spanish-speaking learners of English, focusing on learners of Mexican (Chapter 3, by Guadalupe Valdés), Puerto Rican (Chapter 4, by Ana Celia Zentella), Cuban (Chapter 5, by Ofelia García, Ricardo Otheguy, and Ana Roca), and Central American (Chapter 6, by John Lipski) background. These chapters illustrate the tremendous diversity within the Spanish-speaking population in the United States.
- Because of similarities in the immigration history of the Hmong, Cambodians, and Laotians and because of the relative scarcity of research on these communities, these groups are discussed in one chapter (Chapter 8, by Miguel López). The Vietnamese group is discussed separately in Chapter 7 (by Chuong Hoang Chung).
- Chinese speakers, who are listed separately in the Department of Education's statistics (Cantonese speakers are ranked fourth; Mandarin

speakers, seventeenth) are covered in a single chapter (Chapter 9, by Sau-ling C. Wong and Miguel López).

- In Chapter 11, Joan May Cordova examines Filipino learners of English as a whole, though Tagalog speakers constitute the majority in that group.
- English language learners of Korean and Russian backgrounds take up a chapter each (Chapter 10, by Pyong Gap Min, and Chapter 12, by Eli Hinkel, respectively).
- We include a group not among the top ten: Asian Indians, who experienced the highest percentage of growth (165%) in the 1990s (Waggoner, 1993), are the focus of Chapter 13, by Kamal Sridhar and S.N. Sridhar.
- Given the immigrant focus of this volume, we have not included a chapter on the Navajo. This does not imply that there are no similarities between Navajo speakers and other language minorities in terms of their language-learning experiences in the American educational system; nor are we suggesting that the Navajo speakers are less important than immigrant groups. We do believe, however, that as a Native American group with a distinct history on North American soil and in relation to the nation-state of the United States, English language learners of Navajo background should receive a distinct analysis as well, one best left to a different kind of book.
- By a similar logic, we do not examine speakers of African-American vernacular in this volume, even though they are also a populous language – or more accurately dialectal – minority in the United States. We believe that the historical and contemporary racialization of Black people in the United States would make their educational experiences and relationship to the English language unique and that their language minority status would be more appropriately considered on its own terms rather than as part of this volume.

This book aims to provide a social and educational perspective on contemporary English language learners, especially those large, fast-growing Hispanic and Asian groups whose presence is felt strongly in U.S. schools. It is addressed to preservice and in-service teachers of English in language arts, bilingual education, or English as a second language (ESL) classrooms. It also provides information that would be of interest to those involved in the administration of ESL and content classes. The text is appropriate for use in undergraduate and graduate teacher education courses that focus on the special language needs of nonnative speakers of English, whether for mainstream content class teachers, bilingual education teachers, or ESL teachers. Although the book is primarily addressed to preservice and in-service teachers in the United States, it is also relevant to educators in other countries with large immigrant populations, as the situations and issues can be fruit-fully compared and contrasted. We hope that the information and per-spective offered in this book can help create a better understanding of English language learners in a context larger than the classroom or school.

References

Fleischman, H. L., & Hopstock, P. J. (1993). *Descriptive study of services to limited English proficient students.* Arlington, VA: Development Associates.

McKay, S. L., & Wong, S. C. (Eds.). (1988). *Language diversity: Problem or resource?* New York: Newbury House.

Waggoner, D. (1993). The growth of multilingualism and the need for bilingual education: What do we know so far? *Bilingual Research Journal, 17,* 1–12.

I *Historical and contemporary overviews on English language learners in the United States*

The two chapters in Part I document the linguistic diversity of the United States and the rapid shift to English that occurs among those who come to the United States speaking other languages. In "The Flowering of America: Linguistic Diversity in the United States," Reynaldo Macías provides an overview of past and present linguistic diversity in the United States. Beginning with a brief discussion of the ways in which language and literacy data can be collected, Macías summarizes linguistic diversity from the colonial era through the 1990s. He then provides a comprehensive overview of present-day linguistic diversity in the United States, including information on the English-speaking ability of non–English speakers in the United States. In closing, he highlights some of the population projections made by the U.S. Census Bureau that suggest that the numerical dominance of the White population is decreasing and that, within one generation, Latinos may contribute more net growth to the United States than all other groups combined. As he points out, such projections imply "that diversity is here to stay, it reflects the rest of the world, and it should be a hallmark of the educational and language policy and planning that is done."

In "The American Linguistic Mosaic: Understanding Language Shift in the United States," Calvin Veltman demonstrates "the process whereby immigrants and their children come to learn and adopt the English language." Drawing on data from the 1976 Survey of Income and Education and on 1990 census data, Veltman establishes that immigrant groups, regardless of their origin, learn English use it as the preferred language very rapidly. The majority of the chapter is devoted to analyzing language shift among Latinos, a group frequently stereotyped as excessively slow in acquiring English and targeted by English-only proponents. Veltman demonstrates that this impression derives from continued immigration rather than from any unusual retention of the mother tongue. In addition, he examines language shift among several Asian groups, concluding that in every group the "rates of language shift to English are so high that all minority languages are routinely abandoned, depriving the United States of one type of human resource that it may be economically and politically desirable both to maintain and develop." In closing, he urges language educators to allow immigrants the necessary time to gain proficiency in English while encouraging them to maintain the linguistic resources they have. Veltman's findings in language shift are echoed in most of the chapters in Part II.

These two chapters have several implications for second language educators. First, Chapter 1 makes it clear that linguistic diversity will be a central feature of U.S. schools during the twenty-first century. Furthermore, the immigrant population, unlike earlier generations, will be largely of non-European backgrounds and primarily of Hispanic and Asian origin. Thus, second language educators will need to become familiar with the linguistic and cultural background of this new immigrant population. Second, although, as Veltman points out in Chapter 2, the shift to English will occur rapidly among the immigrant population, first-generation immigrants and their children will face special challenges. The children may acquire English fairly rapidly, but this will not necessarily be the case for their parents. This difference may create tensions in the home since parents who are unfamiliar with English may come to depend on their children for their language needs, a situation that can undermine parental authority. Indeed, several chapters in Part II highlight the negative effect that language shift has on individual family dynamics. Finally, the rapid shift to English that Veltman documents can result in the loss of a major linguistic resource unless measures are taken to support the maintenance of immigrant languages. Hence, second language educators need to support efforts to maintain community languages while helping new immigrants acquire English; they also need to recognize that, for first- and second-generation immigrants, attaining full proficiency in English is a challenging and arduous task.

1 The flowering of America

Linguistic diversity in the United States

Reynaldo F. Macías

Introduction

The North American area that is now the United States has had a linguistically diverse population since before the first European contacts. Whether one considers the 500-plus indigenous languages, the various colonial languages, or the subsequent numbers of immigrant languages and creoles developed within the current national borders, the area has seen substantial numbers of speakers of different languages. During this period of U.S. history, English speakers have increased to numerical dominance. Although specific language studies have been done of many of these languages, a broad-gauge identification and description of the country's language history and current resources is lacking. In this chapter I briefly review some of the history of language diversity in the United States, then describe language diversity in the nation in the late 1990s including oral ability and literacy. I complete this survey of language diversity by addressing the implications of these data for schooling.

Background: Language statistics

Language and literacy data can be collected in several ways. The ideal way of collecting data on the languages and literacies of a population is with direct measures or assessments (e.g., tests, observations). Another way of collecting this information is to use indirect measures (e.g., ask people what they speak, read, or write). Asking people openly about their language abilities is considered an indirect measure, because no specific independent evidence of the accuracy of the responses is collected, but the measures or questions still specifically address the oral language abilities or literacies of interest. The third way of collecting data is to use surrogate measures, or substitutes for direct measures of language ability and literacy. The most commonly used surrogate measure for literacy, for example, is the number of years of schooling completed by a person. A surrogate measure is often based on a logical relationship between the measure and the language variables of interest (see

I thank Juan Venegas, Research Associate for the University of California's Linguistic Minority Research Institute, for the research assistance he provided in the preparation of this chapter.

11

Table 1 as an example of national-origin data used to indicate language diversity). Sometimes this relationship is reversed, and language questions are used as surrogates for other variables.

Language diversity during the colonial period in the area that became the United States is known only in its broad profiles. Estimates of the number of indigenous, or American Indian, languages at the eve of European contact range as high as 500. European languages were much fewer in number but came to dominate in numbers of speakers by the nineteenth century. In an attempt to document some of this language diversity, Kloss (1998), relying on the American Council of Learned Societies (1932) reprint of the *Report of the Committee on Linguistic and National Stocks in the Population of the United States,* used population (colonial settlement) counts, data on foreign birth, and immigration data to describe the language diversity of the colonial and early national periods (see Table 1). These figures are estimates of single large contributions of so-called foreign stock to areas that have become part of the United States. The data are not comprehensive, nor are they cumulative across time, and they seriously underestimate specific population subgroups (see Macías, in press, for a discussion of Spanish speakers). The estimated total national population is included in Table 1 as a benchmark comparison to the numbers provided by Kloss (1977). In studies done closer to the present, the quality, scope, comprehensiveness of the data are improved, and data collection is more systematic. The most important of these more current data collection activities are the national decennial census undertaken by the U.S. government and large, national surveys often undertaken by the statistics-gathering agencies of the U.S. government.

The U.S. decennial census has included various language and literacy questions since the nineteenth century. These questions were generally few in number and asked whether or not respondents could read or write in any language, whether they could speak English, and what the mother tongue of each respondent was.[1] These questions were not always asked in the same census. Questions on literacy, for example, were first asked by the Census Bureau in 1840.

Efforts to obtain data on language characteristics of persons in the United States began with questions on the ability of those aged 20 and older to read and write in any language in the decennial censuses of 1840, 1850, and 1860. Statistics on literacy were obtained for the first time for the population 10

---

1 Questions on language have focused on different aspects: (1) language acquisition and mother tongues; (2) language ability or proficiency, especially distinguishing between orality and literacy; (3) the language used for particular purposes or in particular domains; and (4) household languages or languages used in other environments (as opposed to personal languages).

TABLE I. NUMERICAL STRENGTH OF ORIGINAL SETTLERS AT ANNEXATION,
NORTH AMERICAN COLONIES AND THE UNITED STATES, 1664–1899

Year	Language group	No.	Event and comments
1664	Total population	75,058	
	Dutch	6,000	Annexation of New Netherlands, New York, and nearby area
1763	Total population	1,593,625	
	French	5,000	Annexation of Midwest, east of the Mississippi River
1790	Total population	3,929,000	
	German	279,200	
1803	Total population	5,872,000	
	French	38,000	Annexation of Louisiana (20,000 Negroes and 15,000 Whites); annexation of Missouri (3,000)
1821	Total population	9,939,000	
	Spanish	3,000–5,000	Purchase of Florida (Spaniards)
1845	Total population	20,182,000	
	Spanish	6,000	Annexation of Texas
	German	13,000	
1848	Total population	22,018,000	
	Spanish	30,000	Mexican cession (25,000 Spaniards in New Mexico; 5,000 Spaniards in California)
1850	Total population	23,261,000	
	German	584,000	From Germany
	French	94–104,000	40,000–50,000 from French Canada; 54,000 from France
	Spanish	13,000	From Mexico
	Total non-English	800,000	Immigrants to the United States born outside the United Kingdom
1867	Total population	37,376,000	
	Russian	500	Alaska purchase (500 Russians, 1,000 Creoles, 10,000 Eskimos, and 5,000 Indians)
	Amerindian	15,000	
1880	Total population	50,262,000	
	German	2,000,000	From Germany
	French	307,000	200,000 from French Canada; 107,000 from France
	Swedish	194,000	From Sweden
	Norwegian	182,000	From Norway
	Spanish	68,000	From Mexico
	Total non-English	3,400,000	Immigrants to the United States born outside the United Kingdom

TABLE I. Continued

Year	Language group	No.	Event and comments
1898	Total population	73,494,000	
	Hawaiian	39,000	Annexation of Hawaii; Hawaiians, including 10,000 of mixed lineage
	Japanese	25,000	
	Spanish	885,000	Puerto Rican conquest (includes 380,000 Mulattoes and Negroes)
	Filipino	7,000,000	In Philippine Islands
	Chamorro	9,000	In Guam
1899	Samoan	5,000	In East Samoa

Source: For 1664–1898, see Kloss (1998, pp. 10–11), especially Tables 1–2 and 1–3. Total national population is from U.S. Bureau of the Census (1975), Vol. 1, p. 8; Vol. 2, p. 1168).

years of age and older in 1870. This effort was continued thereafter in the decennial census through 1930 and in sample surveys in 1947, 1952, 1959, and 1969. (Waggoner, 1981, p. 486)

Questions on English language ability mainly sought to identify the foreign born and their progeny.

Information on speaking ability in English was sought for the native- and foreign-born White population aged 10 and older beginning in 1890. In that year, enumerators were instructed to record persons who were unable to speak English "so as to be understood in ordinary conversation." They were instructed to record the name of the non-English language or dialect spoken. (Waggoner, 1981, p. 486)

Even though the Census Bureau has gathered this information on the population's literacy, non-English languages spoken, and English language ability, it has not always made use of the information.

Unfortunately for the student of non-English language usage in the United States, the non-English language responses were not tabulated [in 1890]. In 1900, when this information was compiled for the foreign White stock (foreign-born White persons and native-born White persons of foreign or mixed parentage), enumerators were only expected to record whether or not the persons being counted could speak English. As with the literacy question, a question on English-speaking ability was asked in the successive decennial censuses through 1930. In 1930, when the statistics were compiled only for the foreign-born, data for foreign-born White persons 10 years of age and older were tabulated for the first time by country of birth and by literacy, but not by mother tongue. (Waggoner, 1981, p. 486)

The Census Bureau added a "mother-tongue" language question to the decennial census for the first time in 1910, again as a surrogate identifier for the foreign born and their children.

> In [1910] and in 1920, enumerators gathered data for the foreign White stock. In 1930, the [mother-tongue] question was asked of all persons of foreign birth, but data were tabulated only for White persons. Not until 1940 was the question asked for a sample of the entire population, including native-born children of native-born parents. At that time three out of five of the non-English mother-tongue claimants among the White population for whom data were published, were born in the United States. In 1960, the mother-tongue question was again asked only for the foreign born. (Waggoner, 1981, p. 487)

Though called a "mother-tongue" question, the question in the 1940 census asked about the childhood language, and it really concerned household languages rather than personal language ability and use. In the 1970 census, a mother-tongue question asked the (male) head of the respondent household in a sample of the entire national population whether a non-English language had been spoken in his home when he was a child.[2] One can readily see that the question did not ask about what languages he had learned or used when he was a child. Nor did it ask about his current language abilities or uses. The assumption was that if a non-English language had been spoken in his childhood household, then either this household had been in a foreign country (e.g., he grew up outside the United States), or native speakers of the language in the U.S. household still had ties to the "old country" (e.g., though the respondent may have been native born, his parents or grandparents still spoke the foreign language). This question was often used as an indicator of group assimilation.

These census data are more reliable than previously collected data in that similar indirect measures were used for each data collection effort, the data collection was systematic, and the data collected were relatively more comprehensive than in earlier years. About 24% of the national population in 1910 reported a non-English mother tongue (see Table 2). By 1920, this figure had decreased to 15% of the national population; in 1940, to 16.5%; in 1960, to 10.2%. However, by 1970 the percentage had doubled to 20.9% of the national population. This pattern and the dramatic increase in 1970 reflect several changes in the reporting of the data and in the composition of the national population. For most of the period between 1900 and 1960, the data on mother tongue were collected and reported only for foreign-born Whites and native-born Whites of foreign-born or mixed parentage within the U.S. states and the District of Columbia. No data were collected in U.S. territories

2 Until 1970, the definition of *head of household* identified that person as a male.

TABLE 2. IMMIGRANTS BY COUNTRY OF ORIGIN OR BIRTH, UNITED STATES, SELECTED DECADES, 1901–1990

Country of origin or birth	1901–1910		1911–1920		1921–1930		1971–1980		1981–1990	
	No.	%	No.	%	No.	%	No.	%	No.	%
All non-U.S.	8,795,386	100.0	5,735,811	100.0	4,107,209	100.0	4,493,300	100.0	7,338,100	100.0
Europe	8,136,016	92.5	4,376,564	76.3	2,477,853	60.3	801,300	17.8	705,600	9.6
Canada	179,226	2.0	742,185	12.9	924,515	22.5	114,800	2.6	119,200	1.6
Mexico	49,642	0.6	219,004	3.8	459,287	11.2	637,200	14.2	1,653,300	22.5
Central America	8,192	0.1	17,159	0.3	15,769	0.4	132,400	2.9	251,800	3.4
South America	17,280	0.2	41,899	0.7	42,215	1.0	284,400	6.3	455,900	6.2
Caribbean	107,548	1.2	123,424	2.2	74,899	1.8	759,800	16.9	892,700	12.2
Asia	243,567	2.8	192,559	3.4	97,400	2.4	1,633,800	36.4	2,817,400	38.4

Source: U.S. Bureau of the Census (1945, p. 111, Table 117; 1994, p. 11, Table 8).

(Puerto Rico, Guam, and the Philippines, and Hawaii and Alaska before they became states).

Another reason for these changes is the control over immigration during the early part of the twentieth century, when a national quota system favored northern and western European nations and exempted the Americas. In 1965, the national quota system was revised. The new, more equitable system covered most countries in the world, including many of the new nations in decolonized areas, like Africa, and removed restriction on immigration from Asian countries. Such restrictions had been established in the late nineteenth and early twentieth centuries. These national quotas and restrictions kept immigration from most of the world at bay, overwhelmingly favoring immigration from Europe (see Table 2 and Figure 1). Between 1901 and 1910, 92.5% of the immigrants to the United States came from Europe. Between 1981 and 1990, this figure was only 9.6%. Immigration from Asian countries, on the other hand, rose from 2.8% in the first decade of the twentieth century to 38.4% from 1980 to 1990.

The proportion of the national population that was foreign born was highest in the early part of the twentieth century (13.7% in 1900 and 14.8% in 1910) and lowest in 1970 (4.7%). By 1990 it had increased to 7.9% (U.S. Immigration and Naturalization Service, 1997a). The number of foreign-born residents in 1990 (19,767,000), however, surpassed the number in 1900 (10,445,000). Even though the proportion of foreign-born residents has declined, the numbers almost doubled in the twentieth century. Because the foreign born are concentrated in certain regions of the country, such as the West, the numbers and proportions take on greater dimensions for those regions.[3] Of foreign-born residents in 1996, one quarter entered the country between 1990 and 1996, and another 34.3% entered between 1980 and 1990, so that more than half of the foreign-born population had relatively arrived recently. Even so, of the total foreign-born population in 1996, almost a third (32.2%) were naturalized citizens (Hansen & Faber, 1997).

German, Italian, Polish, and French were the four most widely spoken non-English languages in the United States in 1910. By 1970, the most widely spoken non-English languages were Spanish, German, Italian, French, and Polish (see Table 3). The three-generation model of language shift from the immigrant language to English was established during the

---

3 An interesting note is that the equivalent of almost a third (31%) of the immigration between 1900 and 1990, about 11,882,000 persons, emigrated from the United States to other parts of the world. Many of these persons were immigrants to the United States who decided not to stay. Between 1931 and 1940, a decade with a low number of immigrants, the emigrants were equivalent to 123% of the immigrants and the net immigration was a negative 121,000 persons. That is, more people left the country than entered it as immigrants (U.S. Immigration and Naturalization Service, 1997b).

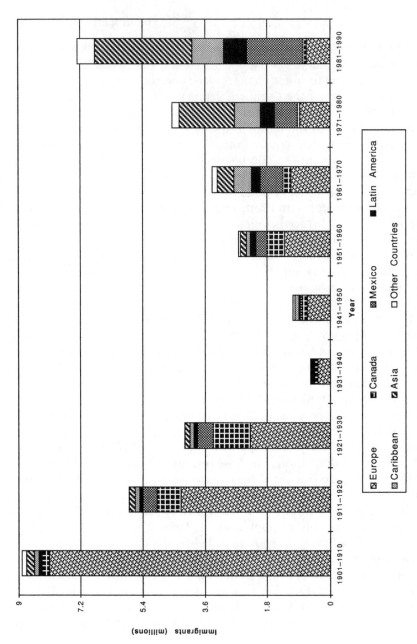

Figure 1   Immigration to the United States, by Region, 1900–1990.

18

TABLE 3. NON-ENGLISH LANGUAGE SPEAKERS IN THE UNITED STATES
1910–1970

Year	Language group	No.	%	Comments
1910	Total population	92,407,000		
	French	1,357,169	6.1	Mother tongue of white foreign born and of White native born of foreign or mixed parentage
	German	8,817,271	39.7	
	Polish	1,707,640	7.7	
	Italian	2,151,422	9.7	
	Spanish	448,198	2.0	
	Total non-English	22,205,962	100.0	
1920	Total population	106,461,000		
	French	1,290,110		Mother tongue of White foreign born and of White native born of foreign or mixed parentage
	German	8,164,111	51.1	
	Polish	2,436,895	15.3	
	Italian	3,365,864	21.1	
	Spanish	850,848	5.3	
	Total non-English	15,964,771	100.0	
1940	Total population	132,122,000		
	French	1,412,060	6.5	Estimates by Fishman et al. (1966) for non-English mother tongues of White foreign born and White native born of foreign or mixed parentage
	German	4,949,780	22.7	
	Polish	2,416,320	11.1	
	Italian	3,766,820	17.3	
	Spanish	1,861,400	8.5	
	Total non-English	21,786,540	100.0	Does not include all non-English languages and speakers
1960	Total population	180,671,000		
	French	1,043,220	5.7	Estimates by Fishman et al. (1966) for non-English mother tongues of White foreign born and White native born of foreign or mixed parentage

Reynaldo F. Macías

TABLE 3. Continued

Year	Language group	No.	%	Comments
	German	3,145,772	17.1	
	Polish	2,184,936	11.9	
	Italian	3,683,141	20.1	
	Spanish	3,335,961	18.2	
	Total non-English	18,352,351	100.0	Does not include all non-English languages and speakers
1970	Total population	203,210,158		
	French	2,598,408	6.1	Mother tongue of foreign born and native born of foreign or mixed parentage
	German	6,093,054	14.3	
	Polish	2,437,938	5.7	
	Italian	4,144,315	9.8	
	Spanish	7,823,583	18.4	
	Total non-English	42,493,045	100.0	Includes 9.3 million who did not report language

Source: For 1910–1960, see Fishman et al. (1966, pp. 36, 38, 44). For 1970, see U.S. Bureau of the Census (1973, p. 492, Table 19). Total national population is from U.S. Bureau of the Census (1975, Vol. 1, p. 8, Vol. 2, p. 1168).

1950s and 1960s by studying principally European immigrants during the period 1900–1960. The nature of language shift before 1900, and for other groups during the twentieth century, has been less studied.

In the mid-1970s, concerned with better estimating the need for bilingual education services,[4] the federal government began a series of projects and national surveys that have had a profound impact on the collection of national, survey language data (for a detailed review of these efforts during the 1970s and early 1980s, see Macías with Spencer, 1984).

The National Center for Education Statistics developed a set of protocols for language abilities and use, including survey questions that one could have confidence in and that would reflect the school practices of identifying and classifying students who were from non-English-language backgrounds and who had limited English-speaking abilities.

4 The Federal Bilingual Education Act was signed into law in 1968. The congressional finding that estimated the need for these services placed it at approximately five million students.

20

These protocols and questions became known as the Measure of English Language Proficiency (MELP). This series of questions was concurrently validated with school classification practices in bilingual programs. Like many of the other projects during this period, these questions focused primarily on the English language abilities of the population. The collection and analysis of data on non-English languages, however, were seen as incidental to the main task of identifying the population with limited-English-speaking abilities – specifically, identifying the pool within which these limited-English-speaking students could be found. The questions on non-English language background were then used in the Current Population Study conducted by the Census Bureau in July 1975 and were analyzed for their utility. These questions asked about the current language use and English language ability of individuals in the households in order to yield a picture of the U.S. population with a non-English language background.

The following year, a congressionally mandated study on children in poverty (the Survey on Income and Education) was undertaken. The study was large enough (over 500,000 persons) to be touted as a mid-decennial census. The language questions added to this survey provided the first comprehensive picture of current language diversity of individuals within the United States. This population survey, which was large enough to report the data at the state level, gave a clearer picture of language and its relationship to many demographic and social variables, but it did not have a direct measure of English proficiency. Therefore, in 1978 and 1979, the National Center for Education Statistics and the National Institute of Education, with support from the Office for Bilingual Education, undertook the Children's English and Services Study (CESS), which was designed to sample households with language minority families that included a child between the ages of 5 and 14 years. These children were given a direct measure of English proficiency, including proficiency in reading and writing, specifically developed for the CESS. However, the survey included no direct measure of their non-English proficiencies. By estimating the number of limited English proficient (LEP) children and youth (aged 5 to 14 years) in the United States, the Survey on Income and Education and the CESS allowed for the first empirically derived estimate of the need for bilingual services in the country.[5]

5 The CESS advisory committee, made up of researchers and school personnel, recommended that the English language assessment include reading and writing as well as speaking and understanding because literacy was so central to academic achievement and effective schooling. In the 1978 amendments to the Bilingual Education Act, the definition of children and youth in need of services was changed to include reading and writing. The terms *non-English-speaking* and *limited English speaking* (NES and LES) were changed to *non-English proficient* and *limited English proficient* (*NEP* and *LEP*) to reflect this change.

The developmental work of the Survey of Income and Education and the CESS was very important in that it provided information on the national population's language abilities that could guide other surveys in drawing their samples for data collection and policy development. For example, one project linked information from these data sets to the Census Bureau's regular population projections. The results provided the basis for a study that projected the age, language, and region of language minority and LEP youth and adults to the year 2000 (see Macías with Spencer, 1984).

In preparation for the 1980 census, the Bureau wondered whether or not the old mother-tongue question was still useful to policy makers and researchers. After several discussions and a review of the decade's work in this area, the Bureau exchanged the mother-tongue question for three new ones: (1) "Does . . . speak a language other than English?" (2) "What is that language?" and (3) "How well does . . . speak English?" The latter question was to be answered: "very well," "well," "not well," or "not at all." All of these questions centered on oral language abilities and not on reading or writing and can be considered indirect language ability measures (as indicated above).[6] These same questions were asked again in the 1990 census.

The 1980 census provided a significant, broad view of the current language abilities of the U.S. population. It indicated that over one in ten persons in the country (25,621,850) spoke a language other than English, with Spanish, German, Italian, French, and Polish the most commonly spoken of these languages (see Table 4). Spanish was spoken by 49% of non-English language speakers, and German by 6.7%. Almost 82% of non-English speakers also reported speaking English very well or well, indicating a high proportion of bilinguals.

In the early 1990s, there was an attempt to change this nomenclature again. This time, the identifier *English language learners* was promoted as a way of reducing the alleged stigma attached to the term LEP since being limited was seen as an obstacle to a positive identity for the student and as promoting a negative image on the part of teachers. Critics of the change indicated that it created an exclusive focus on English (diminishing the values of the non-English language), that all students were English learners whether they were native speakers of the language or not, and that the stigmas on language minority students were less a function of labels than they were of other stereotypes operating within the teacher preparation and school communities. These critics also pointed out that the use of the term *English language learners* ignored the history of the legal and technical definition of NEP and LEP. Not until 1998 did any legislation or official rules seem to use the newly promoted term: California's Proposition 227, mandating English language instruction for these students, used the term *English language learners,* with a narrowed definition of the students involved.

6 On the questionnaire that went to 100% of the population, the 1980 census also asked a question on Latino identification – the first time that Latino ethnicity or identification was included in this way. Prior to 1980, various techniques were used to estimate this population, including doing Spanish surname matches and asking about this identification only in certain states.

In a two-year follow-up to the 1980 census, the English Language Proficiency Study (ELPS) was designed to identify a sample of the language minority population, verify their answers to the 1980 census, and administer a direct measure of English proficiency – the CESS instruments for those 5 through 18 years of age and another measure, called the Measure of Adult English Proficiency (MAEP). The results of this study became mired in political territorial struggles and were never fully developed or released. These English proficiency measures tended to be discrete-point tests with cutoff scores that indicated whether or not the respondent was proficient in English.

About 1986, the literacy field and the federal government supported a national literacy assessment for young adults. This assessment used a new approach to the measurement of literacy, eschewing the single cutoff scores of discrete-point tests that placed respondents in the categories of literate, functionally literate, and illiterate. Instead, it used what has become known as a *profiles approach* to literacy assessment along three text-driven literacy probability scales:[7] prose, document, and quantitative literacy. These scales range from 0 to 500 points and were later divided into five levels. The literacy assessment included a background questionnaire that was translated into Spanish; data collection and translator protocols were established for other languages, too. Questions on language use and ability were included in this background questionnaire for those respondents identified as having a non-English language background. A short set of screening questions was also used to identify people whose English literacy or English oral proficiencies were so limited that they could not take the direct literacy assessment. About 2% of the population was screened out on this basis, around 1% each for low English literacy and limited English proficiency.

In 1992, the National Adult Literacy Survey mandated by Congress, in part to monitor the nation's progress in meeting the National Education Goal of eliminating illiteracy by the year 2000, was in the field collecting data. Like the Young Adult Literacy Survey of 1986, it included a background questionnaire with questions on languages spoken in the home and learned in the home before entering school and on how well the respondent spoke, understood, read, and wrote the English language and the non-English language. The survey, designed to report

---

7 In *probability scaling,* a score for an individual is interpreted as meaning that the person has an 80% probability of getting the items at that level and below correct. It also means that a person who scores at one level can still successfully undertake tasks at a higher level but with a lower probability of success (50% in the next highest level, 15% two levels above). Probability scaling avoids the dichotomous definition of *literate* versus *illiterate* and takes into account the possibility of task familiarity and the need to perform tasks higher on the scale, as well as task complexity and text type. This method is not unlike the use of probabilities to describe language use in early sociolinguistic variation theories.

23

TABLE 4. LANGUAGE SPOKEN AT HOME AND ABILITY TO SPEAK ENGLISH, BY LANGUAGE GROUP, UNITED STATES, 1980

Rank	Group	No.	Persons under 5 years old	Ability to speak English, persons aged 5 years and over				
				Total	Very well	Well	Not well	Not at all
	Total population	226,360,983	16,113,528	210,247,455	12,879,004	5,957,544	3,005,503	1,217,989
	Speak English only at home	200,739,133	13,551,718	187,187,415	—	—	—	—
	Speak a non-English language	25,621,850	2,561,810	23,060,040	12,879,004	5,957,544	3,005,503	1,217,989
1	Spanish	12,653,651	1,537,457	11,116,194	5,534,875	2,873,539	1,770,047	937,733
2	German	1,706,099	119,506	1,586,593	1,169,055	339,884	72,396	5,258
3	Italian	1,704,723	86,379	1,618,344	996,551	407,136	183,708	30,949
4	French	1,697,816	147,065	1,550,751	1,106,586	332,996	100,529	10,640
5	Polish	851,825	31,178	820,647	537,240	198,309	75,249	9,849
6	Chinese	688,403	57,597	630,806	253,059	190,653	131,246	55,848
7	Philippine languages	543,745	69,595	474,150	274,235	155,837	39,504	4,574
8	Greek	434,668	33,225	401,443	243,767	97,040	50,444	10,192
9	Amerindian and Alaskan languages	387,139	54,119	333,020	169,790	114,502	33,596	15,132
10	Portuguese	386,334	34,459	351,875	166,018	89,144	63,266	33,447
11	Japanese	362,710	26,392	336,318	161,238	109,428	58,245	7,407

12	Yiddish	332,014	16,061	315,953	222,034	74,942	16,795	2,182
13	Korean	306,177	39,897	266,280	90,157	99,145	63,955	13,023
14	Asian Indian languages	284,550	41,148	243,402	167,634	55,377	16,292	4,099
15	Arabic	249,944	32,415	217,529	122,304	66,385	23,528	5,312
16	Vietnamese	221,334	26,746	194,588	47,643	73,414	57,023	16,508
17	Hungarian	186,566	7,571	178,995	109,234	53,149	15,248	1,364
18	Russian	182,814	9,588	173,226	75,622	50,072	35,774	11,758
19	Dutch	161,390	13,344	148,046	109,840	32,882	4,871	453
20	Serbo-Croatian	160,219	9,964	150,255	82,677	44,998	19,632	2,948
21	Ukrainian	127,164	5,872	121,292	70,773	33,520	15,398	1,601
22	Czech	127,016	4,660	122,356	83,948	31,164	6,823	421
23	Persian	117,229	10,237	106,992	52,480	40,454	11,685	2,373
24	Norwegian	117,175	4,710	112,465	86,299	22,459	3,557	150
25	Armenian	106,262	5,628	100,634	52,772	27,063	15,490	5,309
26	Swedish	104,786	4,723	100,063	76,993	19,329	3,572	169
27	Thai	101,961	17,000	84,961	24,357	30,407	21,513	8,684
28	Slovak	89,272	1,611	87,661	59,237	21,416	6,657	351
29	Lithuanian	75,171	2,321	72,850	46,423	17,839	7,950	638
30	Finnish	72,061	3,003	69,058	50,263	14,389	4,183	223
31	Other specified languages	733,762	79,716	654,046	399,344	175,995	62,078	16,629
32	Unspecified languages	347,870	28,623	319,247	236,556	54,677	15,249	2,765

Source: U.S. Bureau of the Census (1984a, Table 256).

more accurately on Blacks and Latinos, included a sample of the incarcerated population and weighted the findings to adjusted population estimates from the 1990 census.[8] This important survey directly assessed English literacy and indirectly measured language and literacy acquisition, language use, and language abilities in several languages.

I note that data collection could still be improved in several ways. For example, none of the above-mentioned surveys and projects collected data or reported on U.S. territories (e.g., Puerto Rico, Guam) or American Indian reservations. The inclusion of these jurisdictions is important in obtaining information on the language or literacy diversity of the nation. Also, although the decennial census asks questions about literacy in the outlying territories, these indirect measures differ from each other, and there is no similar question on the sample questionnaire for the fifty states. The reporting of the data also differs for these jurisdictions, making it more difficult to compile and compare the data. Last, few of the questionnaires or surveys use non-English versions of their data collection instruments, and none includes a measure of language proficiency or literacy in non-English languages (including foreign languages).

Data on languages from the U.S. decennial census

The most comprehensive information available on the language diversity of the United States comes from the decennial census of population. Although census data do not provide much information on language (other than non-English languages spoken at home and the English language ability of persons with a non-English language background), they can be related to a large number of other individual, group, and household variables to yield a profile of language minorities that would not otherwise be available.

The U.S. population increased 10% between 1980 and 1990, from 226 million to 248 million persons. The number of persons who spoke a language other than English increased almost four times more than this figure (38.6%) during this same decade (see Table 5). More than 31.8 million people (14% of the nation's population five years old and over) said that they spoke a language other than English in 1990, com-

---

8 The 1990 census included a follow-up study that estimated the undercounting of hard-to-count groups, including racial minorities, immigrants, the homeless, and rural groups. This study was used to adjust the results of the census enumeration results to more accurately estimate the national population and the population of selected subgroups. The federal government did not adopt the adjusted numbers as official figures for the purpose of congressional district reapportionment, so they were not released. The National Adult Literacy Survey was the first national survey to release results that matched the adjusted population figures rather than the official ones in order to better reflect the distribution of literacy in the U.S. population.

pared with 23.1 million (11 percent) a decade earlier. After English, Spanish was the most common language spoken in the United States. Over half (54.4%; 17.3 million) of those who said they spoke a language other than English in 1990 reported that they spoke Spanish. In 1980, about 11.1 million persons spoke Spanish, 48% of all those who spoke a language other than English.

The non-English language speakers, with the possible exception of Spanish speakers, were also distributed unevenly throughout the country. In all four census regions, Spanish was the most frequently spoken non-English language. The next most widely used language varied by region – Italian and German spoken more frequently in the Northeast and Midwest, and French and Chinese in the South and West, respectively. Among those who used a language other than English, Spanish was the prevailing language in thirty-nine states and the District of Columbia; French was the most used in Louisiana, Maine, New Hampshire, and Vermont; and German was the most used in Montana, Minnesota, and North and South Dakota. In Rhode Island, Portuguese was used more than any other non-English language; in Alaska, Yupik; and in Hawaii, Japanese. In 1990, more than half of all non-English language speakers lived in three states: California (8.6 million), New York (3.9 million), and Texas (4.0 million) (see Table 6). New Mexico had the largest percentage of non-English language speakers at 36%, followed by California with 32% (see Figure 2). In eighteen states, 10% or more of the population spoke a non-English language.

Spanish was ten times more widely spoken than French, which was spoken at home by 1.7 million in 1990 (see Table 6). The next most widely spoken language was German, at 1.5 million speakers, followed by Italian at 1.3 million and Chinese at 1.2 million. About 4.5 million persons spoke an Asian or Pacific Island language, and nearly 332,000 spoke a Native North American language. The Census Bureau tabulations provided 380 language codes in the 1990 census, of which 170 were for Native North American languages and 53 were for languages with no reported speakers.

Profiles of bilingualism

In addition to asking about speaking a non-English language, the 1990 census included a question on the English-speaking ability of non-English language speakers aged 5 years and older. The answers to this question can be used construct profiles of bilingualism for the national population.

English-speaking ability was rated "very well," "well," "not well," or "not at all." Dividing these answers into two groups ("very well" and "well" in one group,"not well" and "not at all" in the other) and com-

TABLE 5. CHANGES IN THE NON-ENGLISH-SPEAKING POPULATION BETWEEN 1980 AND 1990, UNITED STATES, BY LANGUAGE AND AGE GROUP

Language and age group	1980		1990		Net Change		
	No.	%	No.	%	No.	% change	% increase
Non-English	22,973,410	100.0	31,844,979	100.0	8,871,569	100.0	38.6
5–17 Years	4,529,098	19.7	6,322,934	19.9	1,793,836	20.2	39.6
18+ Years	18,444,312	80.3	25,522,045	80.1	7,077,733	79.8	38.4
Spanish	11,117,606	100.0	17,345,064	100.0	6,227,458	100.0	56.0
5–17 Years	2,947,051	26.5	4,167,653	24.0	1,220,602	19.6	41.4
18+ Years	8,170,555	73.5	13,177,411	76.0	5,006,856	80.4	61.3
Other	11,855,804	100.0	14,499,915	100.0	2,644,111	100.0	22.3
5–17 Years	1,582,047	13.3	2,155,281	14.9	573,234	21.7	36.2
18+ Years	10,273,757	86.7	12,344,634	85.1	2,070,877	78.3	20.2

Source: Macías (1993).

28

TABLE 6. LANGUAGE SPOKEN AT HOME, U.S. POPULATION AGED 5 YEARS AND
OVER, BY STATE, 1990

State	Total population	Language spoken at home		
			non-English language	
		English only	No.	%
All	230,445,777	198,600,798	31,844,979	13.8
Alabama	3,759,802	3,651,936	107,866	2.9
Alaska	495,425	435,260	60,165	12.1
Arizona	3,374,806	2,674,519	700,287	20.8
Arkansas	2,186,665	2,125,884	60,781	2.8
California	27,383,547	18,764,213	8,619,334	31.5
Colorado	3,042,986	2,722,355	320,631	10.5
Connecticut	3,060,000	2,593,825	466,175	15.2
Delaware	617,720	575,393	42,327	6.9
District of Columbia	570,284	498,936	71,348	12.5
Florida	12,095,284	9,996,969	2,098,315	17.3
Georgia	5,984,188	5,699,642	284,546	4.8
Hawaii	1,026,209	771,485	254,724	24.8
Idaho	926,703	867,708	58,995	6.4
Illinois	10,585,838	9,086,726	1,499,112	14.2
Indiana	5,146,160	4,900,334	245,826	4.8
Iowa	2,583,526	2,483,135	100,391	3.9
Kansas	2,289,615	2,158,011	131,604	5.7
Kentucky	3,434,955	3,348,473	86,482	2.5
Louisiana	3,886,353	3,494,359	391,994	10.1
Maine	1,142,122	1,036,681	105,441	9.2
Maryland	4,425,285	4,030,234	395,051	8.9
Massachusetts	5,605,751	4,753,523	852,228	15.2
Michigan	8,594,737	8,024,930	569,807	6.6
Minnesota	4,038,861	3,811,700	227,161	5.6
Mississippi	2,378,805	2,312,289	66,516	2.8
Missouri	4,748,704	4,570,494	178,210	3.8
Montana	740,218	703,198	37,020	5.0
Nebraska	1,458,904	1,389,032	69,872	4.8
Nevada	1,110,450	964,298	146,152	13.2
New Hampshire	1,024,621	935,825	88,796	8.7
New Jersey	7,200,696	5,794,548	1,406,148	19.5
New Mexico	1,390,048	896,049	493,999	35.5
New York	16,743,048	12,834,328	3,908,720	23.3
North Carolina	6,172,301	5,931,435	240,866	3.9
North Dakota	590,839	543,942	46,897	7.9
Ohio	10,063,212	9,517,064	546,148	5.4
Oklahoma	2,921,755	2,775,957	145,798	5.0
Oregon	2,640,482	2,448,772	191,710	7.3

TABLE 6. Continued

State	Total population	English only	Language spoken at home non-English language No.	%
Pennsylvania	11,085,170	10,278,294	806,876	7.3
Rhode Island	936,423	776,931	159,492	17.0
South Carolina	3,231,539	3,118,376	113,163	3.5
South Dakota	641,226	599,232	41,994	6.5
Tennessee	4,544,743	4,413,193	131,550	2.9
Texas	15,605,822	11,635,518	3,970,304	25.4
Utah	1,553,351	1,432,947	120,404	7.8
Vermont	521,521	491,112	30,409	5.8
Virginia	5,746,419	5,327,898	418,521	7.3
Washington	4,501,879	4,098,706	403,173	9.0
West Virginia	1,686,932	1,642,729	44,203	2.6
Wisconsin	4,531,134	4,267,496	263,638	5.8
Wyoming	418,713	394,904	23,809	5.7

Source: U.S. Bureau of the Census (1993b).

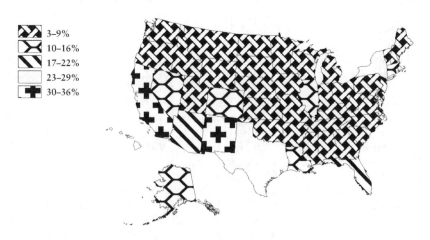

3–9%
10–16%
17–22%
23–29%
30–36%

Figure 2   Persons aged 5 years and over speaking a language other than English, U.S. states, 1990 (%).

bining them with the information on non-English language speakers yields a rough idea of the group bilingualism in the United States.[9] Most language groups had a high degree of bilingualism, some as high as 90% (see Table 7). In twenty-one of the top fifty non-English language groups, more than 90% of the group members spoke English very well or well. Most spoke European languages (e.g., Danish, Dutch, Swedish, Hebrew, Norwegian, Pennsylvania Dutch, Finnish, Czech, German). Some of the non-European languages included in this group were Cajun, Tagalog, Bengali, and Hindi.

Language groups with a low percentage of bilinguals and a high percentage of non-English monolinguals (who spoke English not well or not at all) included Miao (Hmong), Cambodian, Korean, Chinese, Vietnamese, Thai, Russian, Spanish, and Armenian. More than 25% of the members of these groups were monolingual in these languages. These groups tend to be Asian in origin, partly because they reflect a high number of recent immigrants to the United States.

Among the non-English-language-speaking population aged 5 years and older, nearly six in ten spoke English very well, whereas two in ten spoke English either not well or not at all. For example, among the nation's Mon-Khmer (Cambodian) and Miao (Hmong) speakers, more than four in ten spoke English not well or not at all. Among the Chinese, Korean, Vietnamese, Russian, and Thai language populations, the proportion was roughly three in ten.

In 1992, the U.S. Department of Education collected data for the National Adult Literacy Survey. The background data questionnaire included questions about non-English language background, acquisition, use, and abilities. The following is a partial profile of the self-reported oral bilingualism of the U.S. population aged 16 and older in 1992. The distribution of language resources was consistent with that found in other sources. Of the national adult population (191.2 million), about 10% (about 19.1 million) were bilingual, 87% (166.3 million) were English monolingual; and about 3% (5.7 million) were monolingual in a non-English language (see Table 8).

Of adults who live in a household where a non-English language is spoken (28.3 million), about 50.5% (14.3 million) had a Spanish language background, 30.1% (8.5 million) were of other European lan-

---

9 The federal government has twice used this self-reported ability to speak English to establish limited English proficiency, including in reading and writing. Reading and writing ability is imputed by taking a higher level of self-reported speaking ability in English. In this case, persons were classified as LEP (U.S. General Accounting Office, 1994) or not literate in English (Kominski, 1985, 1989) if they answered "well," "not well," or "not at all" to the question (see Macías, 1993). This procedure was statistically rationalized in both cases by comparing the results with other counts of limited English proficiency.

TABLE 7. LANGUAGE SPOKEN AT HOME AND ABILITY TO SPEAK ENGLISH, PERSONS AGED 5 YEARS AND OVER, UNITED STATES, 1990

Rank	Language group	No.	%	Percent of NEL speakers who speak English			
				Very well	Well	Not well	Not at all
	All	230,445,777	100.0				
	English only	198,600,798	86.2				
	Non-English Language	31,844,979	100.0				
1	Spanish	17,339,172	54.4	56.1	23.0	15.2	5.8
2	French	1,702,176	5.3	72.0	18.7	8.8	0.5
3	German	1,547,099	4.9	75.1	18.4	6.3	0.3
4	Italian	1,308,648	4.1	66.8	21.7	10.2	1.3
5	Chinese	1,249,213	3.9	39.7	30.4	21.2	8.7
6	Tagalog	843,251	2.6	66.0	26.6	6.9	0.6
7	Polish	723,483	2.3	63.0	23.4	11.8	1.8
8	Korean	626,478	2.0	38.8	31.1	24.7	5.4
9	Vietnamese	507,069	1.6	36.7	35.0	23.3	4.9
10	Portuguese	429,860	1.4	54.7	22.4	16.6	6.3
11	Japanese	427,567	1.3	47.5	31.2	19.5	1.8
12	Greek	388,260	1.2	68.5	20.1	10.0	1.3
13	Arabic	355,150	1.1	66.3	23.1	8.9	1.7

14	Hindi (Urdu)	331,484	1.0	70.8	20.3	7.4	1.5
15	Russian	241,798	0.8	45.6	27.3	20.8	6.2
16	Yiddish	213,064	0.7	71.0	20.8	7.2	1.0
17	Thai (Laotian)	206,266	0.6	37.9	34.0	23.0	5.1
18	Persian	201,865	0.6	62.0	25.5	9.8	2.7
19	French Creole	187,658	0.6	47.5	30.2	19.0	3.3
20	Armenian	149,694	0.5	49.8	24.3	17.0	8.9
21	Navaho	148,530	0.5	55.4	29.9	9.5	5.1
22	Hungarian	147,902	0.5	65.0	25.6	8.6	0.8
23	Hebrew	144,292	0.5	76.5	18.5	4.5	0.5
24	Dutch	142,684	0.4	76.3	19.5	3.8	0.3
25	Mon-Khmer (Cambodian)	127,441	0.4	26.7	30.4	32.1	10.8
26	Gujarathi	102,418	0.3	66.1	22.1	8.8	3.0
27	Ukrainian	96,568	0.3	63.1	23.3	12.3	1.3
28	Czech	92,485	0.3	70.6	23.2	5.9	0.3
29	Pennsylvania Dutch	83,525	0.3	56.8	37.5	4.9	0.8
30	Miao (Hmong)	81,877	0.3	22.4	31.3	32.4	13.9

Source: U.S. Bureau of the Census (1993b).

guage backgrounds, 6.8% (1.9 million) were of Asian language backgrounds, and 12.3% (3.5 million) were of other language backgrounds. Of these groups, the Spanish language group had the largest proportion of non-English monolinguals at 31.2%, followed by the Asian language group at 27.8% (see Table 12 in the section "Profiles and Shadows of Biliteracy"). The largest proportions of bilinguals were found in the "other" language group (87%) and the European language group (73.8%). The largest proportion of English monolinguals (22.9%) was found in the European language group.

Outlying jurisdictions

In addition to the numbers of different languages spoken in the mainland United States, the outlying jurisdictions of the country exhibit language diversity. Notable examples are Puerto Rico, which has over three million persons, and Guam, which has a population of over 100,000 (other jurisdictions include the U.S. Virgin Islands, American Samoa, the Marshall Islands, Palau, the Federated States of Micronesia, Wake Island, and the Commonwealth of the Northern Marianas). These jurisdictions are part of the United States, and persons born there are U.S. citizens and are free to move between these territories and the mainland. Many Puerto Ricans and Guamanians, especially, regularly migrate between the islands and the mainland.

Each of these island possessions has a history of conflict over language policies. Puerto Rico has adopted both English and Spanish for official, governmental purposes, and Guam has a Chamorro (the indigenous language of Guam) Language Commission.

The population of Puerto Rico in 1990 was 3.5 million (U.S. Bureau of the Census, 1993a). Over 98% of the population aged 5 years and older spoke Spanish, with 75% of the total population being monolingual in Spanish (see Table 9). About 23% were bilingual, speaking Spanish and English easily. Between 1980 and 1990, the increase in the percentage of people learning English (38.1%) was greater than the general increase in population (13.8%).

Guam, on the other hand, has had a much smaller indigenous population than Puerto Rico and has been governed by various powers during the twentieth century (including Spain, Japan, and the United States). The United States has developed a strong military presence in Guam, and as the United States' westernmost point in the Pacific, the island has become a popular tourist attraction for travelers from Asian countries. It has also attracted immigration from the surrounding islands. Its total population grew 25% between 1980 and 1990 (see Table 10). Over a third of the population aged 5 years and older speaks only English at home, and the rest (62.7%) speak a non-English language at

TABLE 8. BILINGUALISM BY RACE OR ETHNICITY, PERSONS AGED 16 YEARS AND OLDER, UNITED STATES, 1992

| | Language ability | | | | | | |
| | English monolingual | | Bilingual | | Monolingual in non-English language | | Total |
Race or ethnicity[a]	No.	%	No.	%	No.	%	
White	137,693,000	95.9	7,247,000	5.0	0	0.0	144,940,000
Black	20,546,540	97.0	635,460	0.0	0	3.0	21,182,000
Asian/Pacific Islander	1,070,160	26.0	2,428,440	59.0	617,400	15.0	4,116,000
Other	1,628,900	65.0	726,740	29.0	150,360	6.0	2,506,000
Latino	4,615,500	25.0	9,231,000	50.0	4,615,500	25.0	18,462,000
Mexican	2,562,250	25.0	4,919,520	48.0	2,767,230	27.0	10,249,000
Puerto Rican	438,000	20.0	1,445,400	66.0	284,700	13.0	2,190,000
Cuban	28,080	3.0	514,800	55.0	383,760	41.0	936,000
Central and South American	251,680	11.0	1,189,760	52.0	846,560	37.0	2,288,000
Other Latino	1,371,510	49.0	1,063,620	38.0	363,870	13.0	2,799,000
Total	166,349,220	87.0	19,120,600	10.0	5,736,180	3.0	191,206,000

Source: Data was run from the National Adult Literacy Survey (1992). The data set is available from the National Center for Educational Statistics.

[a]Racial categories are mutually exclusive.

TABLE 9. LANGUAGE ABILITY OF PERSONS AGED 5 YEARS AND OLDER, PUERTO RICO, 1980 AND 1990

| Ability | All, 1980 | Year and age group 1990 | | | | Change, 1980–1990 (%) |
		All	5–17 years	18–64 years	65+ years	
All	2,855,868	3,249,495	851,344	2,026,092	372,059	13.8
Speak Spanish	2,805,444	3,192,310	833,499	1,997,197	361,614	13.8
Speak English easily	541,160	747,480	105,850	581,134	60,496	38.1
Speak English with difficulty	643,873	792,032	162,332	531,680	98,020	23.0
Unable to speak English	1,620,411	1,652,798	565,317	884,383	203,098	2.0
Unable to speak Spanish	50,424	57,185	17,845	28,895	10,445	13.4
Speak English easily	10,929	12,679	2,089	9,705	885	16.0
Speak English with difficulty	2,910	3,361	1,724	1,288	349	15.5
Unable to speak English	36,585	41,145	14,032	17,902	9,211	12.5

Source: U.S. Bureau of the Census (1984a, p. 24, Table 45; 1993a, p. 35, Table 8, and p. 46, Table 19).

TABLE 10. LANGUAGE ABILITY AND LITERACY, GUAM, 1980 AND 1990

Group	1980	1990	Change (%)
All	105,979	133,152	25.6
Aged 5 years and older	92,977	118,055	27.0
Speak only English at home	33,182	44,048	32.7
Unable to read or write in any language	2,823	—	—
Speak a non-English language at home	59,795	74,007	23.8
Speak English more frequently	16,663	19,710	18.3
Unable to read and write	725	—	—
Speak English and other language			
equally often	18,720	26,789	43.1
Unable to read and write	347	—	—
Speak English less frequently	24,004	26,331	9.7
Unable to read and write	830	—	—
Do not speak English	408	1,777	188.5
Unable to read and write	92	—	—

Source: U.S. Bureau of the Census (1984b, p. 13, Table 29; 1992, pp. 21–24, Tables 12, 13).

home. The English language questions in the census focused on the frequency of use in comparison with the non-English language. No questions asked about ability or the number of languages a person spoke. If non-English speakers who used English more frequently than or equally as frequently as they used the non-English language are regarded as bilinguals, then 39.4% of the non-English language population aged 5 years and older was bilingual in 1990. Another 23.3% non-English speakers spoke English less frequently than they spoke the non-English language or did not speak English at all.

Profiles and shadows of biliteracy

Describing the biliteracy of the population was formerly not possible. Even the notion of *biliteracy* (the ability to read and write in two or more languages) has not taken root in many educational and linguistic circles. There is a much greater concern in the United States for second language literacy[10] in English, especially reading, for school-age stu-

10 The ability to read and write in a second language does not imply literacy in the first language, which can be referred to as *native language* or *mother-tongue literacy*. Since children in many speech communities in the world acquire more than one oral language before school, these sequential terms should be taken to reflect the various possible relationships between oral and literate language rather than a fixed sequence of oral and literacy acquisition.

dents and adult ESL learners. The Young Adult Literacy Survey in 1986 and the National Adult Literacy Survey in 1992 allowed analysts to describe the self-reported literacy and biliteracy of the nation's population with a non-English language background. The partial results on (bi)literacy presented here, however, are more like shadows. They pretend to be profiles, yet they may be distorted since no other large-scale sources of data exist with which to compare them. As an incremental and initial description of biliteracy, they are reliable descriptions of the diverse types of literacy found in the U.S. population. The following reflects only the analysis of the background questionnaire data for the 1992 National Adult Literacy Survey.

- Of the total U.S. population aged 16 years and older (191.2 million), 89% (170.2 million) indicated that they were literate only in English; about 7% (13.4 million) claimed to be biliterate; about 3% (5.7 million), literate only in the non-English language; and about 1% (1.9 million), not literate at all (see Table 11).
- Of those who indicated that they spoke a non-English language (24.7 million), about 43.8% (10.8 million) claimed to be biliterate; 27% (6.7 million), literate only in English; about 25% (6.0 million), literate only in the non-English language; and about 5% (1.2 million), not literate at all (see Table 12).
- Of those who were bilingual (20.0 million), about 62% (12.4 million) indicated that they were also biliterate; 27% (5.4 million), English monoliterate; 8% (1.6 million), literate only in the non-English language; and 3% (600,630), not literate at all. Of those who were biliterate (12.8 million), about 96% (12.3 million) indicated that they were also bilingual.
- The subgroups with the highest average prose scale score of 281 were the English monolinguals and English monoliterates, followed by the biliterate group at 251 and the bilinguals at 240; the nonliterate and non-English monoliterate groups scored 155 and 133 on average, respectively. All subgroups scored in the lower two levels of the scale (Level 1 = 0–225; Level 2 = 226–275) except for the English monolingual and monoliterate groups, which scored in the third level of the scale (276–325). The average score for the total population was 272.

The proportion of biliterates did not differ greatly among persons of various non-English language backgrounds, ranging from 40% of those of European language background to 56.8% of persons with language backgrounds other than European, Spanish, and Asian (see Table 12). About 46% of persons of Asian and Spanish language backgrounds were biliterate. The proportion who were literate only in one language was more striking. Of persons of European language background, for example, 50% were monoliterate in English, and only 6.6% were liter-

TABLE 11. LITERACY BY RACE OR ETHNICITY, PERSONS AGED 16 YEARS OR OLDER, UNITED STATES, 1992

Race or ethnicity	English monoliterate		Biliterate		Non-English languge monoliterate		Nonliterate		Total
	No.	%	No.	%	No.	%	No.	%	
White	140,579,190	97	4,347,810	3	0	0	0	0	144,927,000
Black	20,765,220	98	423,780	2	211,890	1	0	0	21,189,000
Asian/Pacific Islander	1,481,760	36	1,934,520	47	617,400	15	82,320	2	4,116,000
Latino	6,098,730	33	6,468,350	35	4,989,870	27	1,108,860	6	18,481,000
Mexican	3,488,060	34	3,077,700	30	2,975,110	29	718,130	7	10,259,000
Puerto Rican	591,300	27	1,116,900	51	350,400	16	131,400	6	2,190,000
Cuban	84,240	9	421,200	45	393,120	42	37,440	4	936,000
Central or South American	321,580	14	964,740	42	872,860	38	137,820	6	2,297,000
Other Latino	1,623,420	58	783,720	28	363,870	13	27,990	1	2,799,000
Other	1,979,740	79	300,720	12	175,420	7	50,120	2	2,506,000
Total	170,185,800	89	13,385,400	7	5,736,600	3	1,912,200	1	191,220,000

Source: Data was run from the National Adult Literacy Survey (1992). The data set is available from the National Center for Education Statistics.

TABLE 12. LITERACY BY LANGUAGE BACKGROUND, ALL NON-ENGLISH SPEAKERS AGED 16 AND OLDER, UNITED STATES, 1992

Language background	English monoliterate		Biliterate		Non-English language monoliterate		Non-literate		Total
	No.	%	No.	%	No.	%	No.	%	Total
Spanish	1,993,000	13.9	6,519,000	45.5	4,935,000	34.4	883,000	6.2	14,330,000
European	4,327,000	50.7	3,443,000	40.3	566,000	6.6	201,000	2.4	8,537,000
Asian	359,000	18.7	886,000	46.2	596,000	31.1	75,000	3.9	1,916,000
Other	1,163,000	33.4	1,974,000	56.8	233,000	6.7	107,000	3.1	3,477,000
Total	6,679,000	27.0	10,848,000	43.8	6,097,000	24.6	1,159,000	4.7	24,783,000

Source: Data was run from the National Adult Literacy Survey (1992). The data set is available from the National Center for Education Statistics.

ate only in the European language. This pattern contrasted with that for persons of Asian and Spanish language backgrounds, whose English-only literacy stood at 18.7% and 13.9%, respectively, and which evidenced much higher proportions of literacy only in the non-English language (31% and 34%, respectively).

Although self-report data were collected for the outlying territories as part of the decennial census, these data are not comparable to those from the young Adult Literacy Survey and the National Adult Literacy Survey. The census question was not language specific; it merely asked "Does . . . . read or write in any language?" The Census Bureau reported this question generally for persons aged 10 years and older in the 1990 census. For 1980, it reported on children as young as 5 years old as well (see Tables 10 and 13). The information collected did not identify the language(s) of literacy, nor did it distinguish between reading and writing. Thus there is no way of constructing a biliteracy classification for analysis from census data for the outlying territories. In 1990, 89.4% of the population aged 10 years and older in Puerto Rico reported being able to read and write in a language. Similar data were not reported for Guam in 1990.

Language diversity and schooling

The language diversity in the United States has several implications for schooling. First, the language and educational needs of those students who have limited English proficiency require some attention. Second, the development of second or foreign language competencies among the national population, for both the language minority populations and native English monolinguals, should be explored.

LEP students

One clear point made by the demographic research is that the enrollment of LEP students in the public schools has continued to increase. The language needs of many LEP students are not being addressed, most are taught entirely in English, and there are not enough qualified teachers for either bilingual or English as a second language instruction. In addition, the linguistic diversity of the United States is likely to increase as the racial and ethnic diversity of the nation increases in the first half of the twenty-first century. Addressing and resolving these policy and cultural issues will become increasingly important.

The identification of NEP and LEP students follows a path similar to that described for the surveys that identified persons of non-English language background. Most states have a home language survey that families must complete when they first enroll their children in school. If the

41

TABLE 13. LITERACY, PERSONS AGED 10 YEARS AND OLDER, PUERTO RICO, 1980
AND 1990

Age group and literacy	1980	1990	Change (%)
All	3,196,520	3,522,037	10.2
10+ Years	2,524,558	2,904,455	15.0
Able to read and write in a language	2,265,119	2,596,540	14.6
Unable to read and write in any language	259,439	307,915	18.7
10–17 years	551,437	536,304	−2.7
Able to read and write in a language	518,457	473,680	−8.6
Unable to read and write in any language	32,980	62,624	89.9
18–64 Years	1,720,540	2,026,092	17.8
Able to read and write in a language	1,568,990	1,862,233	18.7
Unable to read and write in any language	151,550	163,859	8.1
65+ years	252,581	342,059	35.4
Able to read and write in a language	177,672	260,627	46.7
Unable to read and write in any language	74,909	81,432	8.7

Source: U.S. Bureau of the Census (1984a, p. 24, Table 45; 1993a, p. 35, Table 4, and p. 46, Table 19).

survey reveals any non-English language in the family's home, then the student is often directly assessed in the non-English language as well as in English. Those students who are not proficient enough in English to participate effectively in an English-only classroom are considered to be LEP and are entitled to have their language and educational needs attended to by the school district. Although this process varies somewhat from state to state, and although the survey questions or language proficiency instruments may be different, some commonalities exist. A pool larger than the student population is initially identified, in most cases the households in which the students live (see Table 14 for the variables often used to identify this pool). Students who may be limited in their English proficiency are identified, and their language proficiency is more specifically assessed. This assessment may be direct or indirect, or it may even use surrogate measures to identify limited English proficiency.

The differences between identifying students as having a non-English language background or as LEP for schooling purposes and identifying them for population estimates lead to varying results (see the possible definitions of *universe* in Table 14). Since states vary in their definition and operationalization of LEP, data are not comparable from state to

TABLE 14. VARIABLES USED IN CONCEPTUALIZING STUDENTS OF
NON-ENGLISH LANGUAGE BACKGROUND AND STUDENTS IN NEED OF
SPECIAL LANGUAGE SERVICES

Non-English language background or language minority students	*Students with no or limited English abilities*

Universe
Total population
Public school enrollment
Age band
  5–14 years
  6–18 years
  5–17 years
  K–12
 	
Pool (screening) factors
Mother tongue
Household language 1 (usually used)
Household language 2 (often used)
individual language 1 (usually used)
Individual language 2 (often used)
National origin
	Need factors
	Direct measures of English
	  Reading
	  Writing
	  Speaking
	  Understanding
	Indirect measures of English
	  proficiency
	  Standardized reading achievement
	    test
	  Reported ability to speak English
	  Reported ability to understand
	    English
	  Family income
	Language dominance
	  Relative frequency of use
	  Relative proficiency or ability

Source: Macías (1984).

state. Although aggregating the different state counts could give rise to some methodological concerns (given the lack of uniformity in the definitions of LEP across the states), it is the principal method of estimating the LEP student enrollment nationally.[11] In the 1996–1997 school year, forty-eight states and the District of Columbia reported a total of 3,378,846 LEP students in public and private schools in kindergarten through the twelfth grade. Six of the nine outlying territories and jurisdictions reported another 73,212 LEP students for the same year (see Table 15). This estimate, which did not include all states or outlying jurisdictions, represented about 7% of the more than 46 million students reported enrolled in those states and jurisdictions.

Additional characteristics of the LEP student enrollment are not always easy to come by. An earlier study (Fleischman & Hopstock, 1993) indicated that about a third of LEP students enrolled in U.S. public

11 To identify and estimate the number of LEP students, the services they receive, and other information about this population, the U.S. Office for Bilingual Education and Minority Languages Affairs undertakes a yearly survey of the states that receive monies from the office. (see Macías, Nishikawa, Alegría, & Venegas, 1998, for a copy of this annual report).

schools were native born. This proportion was much greater than most educators had believed, given the strong association in the public mind between lack of proficiency in English and immigrant status. The study attributed other characteristics to the LEP enrollment (e.g., 73% spoke Spanish; 77% were entitled to meal programs under poverty criteria). Individual states can also describe their LEP student enrollment more specifically. However, national studies that can help characterize this group of students are lacking.[12]

Predicting future numbers and percentages of language minority and LEP students in the schools is also difficult. However, if we use ethnic data as a surrogate measure, there are population projections developed by different governmental agencies that are reported by race and ethnicity. Generally, the finding is that racial categories with higher proportions of LEP children, youth, and adults will continue to increase (see Table 16 for a set of population projections by race developed by the U.S. Bureau of the Census).

Selected highlights of the population projections made by the U.S. Bureau of the Census in 1996 are instructive of the compositional changes of the U.S. population through the first half of the twenty-first century.

- In the middle series, the population was projected to reach 275 million by 2000 – a growth of 12 million or 4.5% since 1995. Only during the 1930s did the U.S. population ever grow more slowly. The population may top 300 million shortly after 2010, and by the middle of the twenty-first century the population may increase to 394 million – a 50% increase from the population in 1995.
- Although nearly three quarters of the population was non-Hispanic White in 1995, this group will contribute only about one quarter of the total population growth between 1995 and 2005. From 2030 to 2050, the non-Hispanic White population will contribute nothing to U.S. population growth because it will be declining in size.
- The non-Hispanic White share of the U.S. population will steadily fall from 74% in 1995, to 72% in 2000, 64% in 2020, and 53% in 2050.
- Every year from 1996 to 2050, the race or ethnic group adding the largest number of people to the population was projected to be the Hispanic-origin group. In fact, after 2020, the Hispanic population of the United States is projected to grow by more every year than will all

---

12 At this writing, the federal government is in the process of changing the questionnaire used in the annual Survey of State Educational Agencies, which collects data on LEP students, in order to collect a greater, more diverse, and more specific set of background characteristics. This new survey questionnaire was expected to be in the field in 1999 or 2000, and reports based on this questionnaire should be available shortly thereafter.

other races or ethnic groups combined. By 2010, the Hispanic-origin population may become the second largest race or ethnic group.

- By 2030, less than half of the U.S. population under age 18 will be non-Hispanic White. In that year, this group will still constitute three quarters of the population aged 65 and over.
- In 1995, nearly two thirds of all births were non-Hispanic White, about one in six was Black, and one in six was of Hispanic origin. By the middle of the twenty-first century, about two of every five births will be non-Hispanic White, one in three will be Hispanic, one in five will be Black, and one in ten will be Asian and Pacific Islanders.
- The middle series assumes that, every year, four of every ten people added to the population through net immigration will be Hispanic, three of every ten will be Asian and Pacific Islanders, two in ten will be non-Hispanic White, and one in ten will be Black (Day, 1996, pp. 1–2).

These conservative Census Bureau projections reveal several characteristics of the composition of the U.S. population. The numerical dominance of the White population is decreasing, and Whites may constitute less than half of the total school-age population by 2030. Net immigration may continue, with an 80% non-White contribution to population growth. After 2020, within one generation, Latinos may contribute more net growth to the U.S. population than all other groups combined will. The Census Bureau projections indicate a continued disproportionate concentration of foreign-born residents in California over the next two generations. In 1995, 40% of the foreign-born persons in the nation resided in California. The implications for language diversity are staggering. In the late 1990s, about half of the Latino enrollment and almost half of the Asian and Pacific Islander enrollment in California was LEP. If this proportion holds steady until 2025 or 2040, then the need to address the English language proficiency of these students will continue to be an important policy and educational issue for several more generations.

Given this brief description of the linguistic diversity enrollment, the debate over bilingual education can be seen, in part, as a battle over the demographic composition of the nation. The culturally conservative argument states, "If we can control our borders, reduce immigration, and assimilate those immigrant children, youth, and adults already in the country, then everything will be all right" and that "in a controlled immigration situation, with adequate time, a focus on English, and sufficient effort, the right situation will prevail." The other argument, more culturally liberal, simply put, is, "Diversity is here to stay, it reflects the rest of the world, and it should be a hallmark of the nation's educational and language policy and planning.

TABLE 15. K–12 ENROLLMENTS, UNITED STATES, BY TYPE OF SCHOOL AND BY STATE, 1996–1997

Jurisdiction	Total enrollment			LEP enrollment			LEP as % of total enrollment		
	Public	Nonpublic	Total	Public	Nonpublic	Total	Public	Nonpublic	Total
Alabama	717,846	—	717,846	5,565	—	5,565	0.8	—	0.8
Alaska	126,244	3,835	130,079	34,942	—	34,942	27.7	—	26.9
Arizona	783,547	32,330	815,877	93,528	—	93,528	11.9	—	11.5
Arkansas	323,746	—	323,746	5,282	—	5,282	1.6	—	1.6
California	5,612,965	615,071	6,228,036	1,381,393	—	1,381,393	24.6	—	22.2
Colorado	333,880	—	333,880	24,675	—	24,675	7.4	—	7.4
Connecticut	527,184	75,230	602,414	19,819	—	19,819	3.8	—	3.3
Delaware	110,549	22,119	132,668	1,928	—	1,928	1.7	—	1.5
District of Columbia	78,847	15,270	94,117	4,911	171	5,082	6.2	1.1	5.4
Florida	2,356,369	—	2,356,369	288,603	—	288,603	12.2	—	12.2
Georgia	1,321,239	101,633	1,422,872	14,339	—	14,339	1.1	0.0	1.0
Hawaii	188,485	32,600	221,085	12,349	151	12,500	6.6	—	5.7
Idaho	209,340	5,798	215,138	12,210	47	12,257	5.8	—	5.7
Illinois	1,973,040	320,880	2,293,920	118,246	—	118,246	6.0	—	5.2
Indiana	977,535	102,471	1,080,006	9,195	—	9,195	0.9	—	0.9
Iowa	505,523	44,302	549,825	7,304	263	7,567	1.4	0.6	1.4
Kansas	466,367	31,888	498,255	12,843	566	13,409	2.8	—	2.7
Kentucky	625,531	109,428	734,959	3,194	121	3,315	0.5	0.1	0.5
Louisiana	712,598	154,336	866,934	6,494	520	7,014	0.9	0.3	0.8
Maine	229,770	13,223	242,993	2,386	172	2,558	1.0	1.3	1.1
Maryland	798,944	125,581	924,525	16,186	155	16,341	2.0	0.1	1.8
Massachusetts	935,623	127,305	1,062,928	44,394	—	44,394	4.7	—	4.2
Michigan	1,673,879	—	1,673,879	25,988	—	25,988	1.6	—	1.6

Minnesota	837,723	83,955	921,678	28,237	—	28,237	3.4	—	3.1
Mississippi	504,792	47,110	551,902	1,594	1,630	3,224	0.3	3.5	0.6
Missouri	893,241	103,559	996,800	6,514	234	6,748	0.7	0.2	0.7
Montana	164,627	11,917	176,544	8,846	175	9,021	5.4	1.5	5.1
Nebraska	291,967	41,696	333,663	6,252	66	6,318	2.1	0.2	1.9
Nevada	282,131	12,970	295,101	27,977	—	27,977	9.9	—	9.5
New Hampshire	—	—	0	1,590	108	1,698			
New Jersey	1,218,578	214,830	1,433,408	49,300	—	49,300	4.0	—	3.4
New Mexico	325,384	3,323	328,707	78,107	374	78,481	24.0	11.3	23.9
New York	2,812,031	478,119	3,290,150	220,840	26,247	247,087	7.9	5.5	7.5
No. Carolina	1,247,144	77,647	1,324,791	24,771	—	24,771	2.0	—	1.9
No. Dakota	118,654	9,524	128,178	6,340	1,255	7,595	5.3	13.2	5.9
Ohio	1,817,150	242,421	2,059,571	12,391	—	12,391	0.7	—	0.6
Oklahoma	620,695	12,836	633,531	31,941	180	32,121	5.1	1.4	5.1
Oregon	541,175	38,764	579,939	33,559	—	33,559	6.2	—	5.8
Pennsylvania	—	—	—	—	—	—			
Rhode Island	150,556	20,127	170,683	10,009	—	10,009	6.6	—	5.9
So. Carolina	640,490	49,453	689,943	3,202	171	3,373	0.5	0.3	0.5
So. Dakota	125,577	15,235	140,812	6,515	4,300	10,815	5.2	28.2	7.7
Tennessee	962,645	85,321	1,047,966	7,223	190	7,413	0.8	0.2	0.7
Texas	3,828,975	202,053	4,031,028	513,634	—	513,634	13.4	—	12.7
Utah	478,028	—	478,028	35,286	—	35,286	7.4	—	7.4
Vermont	103,693	9,448	113,141	750	45	795	0.7	0.5	0.7
Virginia	—	—	—	—	—	—			
Washington	971,903	78,358	1,050,261	55,773	—	55,773	5.7	—	5.3
West Virginia	—	—	—	—	—	—			
Wisconsin	879,259	150,140	1,029,399	23,270	—	23,270	2.6	—	2.3
Wyoming	98,777	2,229	101,006	1,850	160	2,010	1.9	7.2	2.0
Subtotal, states	41,504,246	3,924,335	45,428,581	3,341,545	37,301	3,378,846	8.1	1.0	7.4

TABLE 15. Continued

Jurisdiction	Total enrollment			LEP enrollment			LEP as % of total enrollment		
	Public	Nonpublic	Total	Public	Nonpublic	Total	Public	Nonpublic	Total
American Samoa	25,737	—	25,737	4,765	—	4,765	18.5	—	18.5
Guam	10,878	5,008	15,886	10,878	4,758	15,636	100.0	95.0	98.4
Marshall Islands	29,259	3,421	32,680	28,089	3,284	31,373	96.0	96.0	96.0
Micronesia									
Northern Marianas	—	—	—	—	—	—	—	—	—
Palau[a]	2,901	842	3,743	2,756	800	3,556	95.0	95.0	95.0
Puerto Rico	618,861		618,861	16,618	—	16,618	2.7	—	2.7
U.S. Virgin Islands	21,908	6,255	28,163	1,264	—	1,264	5.8	—	4.5
Wake Island	—	—	—	—	—	—	—	—	—
Subtotal, territories	709,544	15,526	725,070	64,370	8,842	73,212	9.1	57.0	10.1
Total	42,213,790	3,939,861	46,153,651	3,405,915	46,143	3,452,058	8.1	1.2	7.5

Note: Empty cells represent missing data or no report from that state.
[a]Data are for limited Spanish proficient students instead of LEP students.
Source: Macías et al. (1998).

48

TABLE 16. U.S. POPULATION, BY RACE, 1990–2010

Race or ethnicity	July 1, 1990[a]		July 1, 2000[b]		July 1, 2010[b]	
	No.	%	No.	%	No.	%
All	249,402,000	100.0	274,634,000	100.0	297,716,000	100.0
White	188,601,000	75.6	197,061,000	71.8	202,390,000	68.0
Black	29,374,000	11.8	33,568,000	12.2	37,466,000	12.6
Asian and Pacific Islander	7,076,000	2.8	10,584,000	3.9	14,402,000	4.8
AmerIndian, Aleut, and Eskimo	1,802,000	0.7	2,054,000	0.7	2,320,000	0.8
Latino	22,549,000	9.0	31,366,000	11.4	41,139,000	13.8

Note: Racial categories are mutually exclusive.
[a]Estimated.
[b]Projected.
Source: Day (1996, p. 12, Table I).

Foreign language learning

This debate over the demographic and linguistic composition of the United States focuses on immigrants and language minorities; it does not often address the learning of foreign languages in the schools. Estimates of the number of students engaged in foreign language study are difficult to interpret. One measure is the number of students who register for a foreign language class at any one time. Using this registration measure, the Association of Departments of Foreign Languages tracks the changes in higher education foreign language study in the United States. From 1960 through 1990, the number of fall registrations generally increased (see Table 17), although the number in 1990 was not that different from the number in 1970. One pattern of change during this thirty-year period is the languages being studied. In 1960, the most studied languages were French (35.4%), Spanish (27.6%), German (22.6%), Russian (4.7%), and Latin (4%). In 1990, the most studied languages were Spanish (45.1%), French (23%), German (11.3%), Italian (4.2%), and Japanese (3.9%).

The average length of time spent studying these languages was fairly short. Little information was available on completion of these courses (as opposed to registrations), and most of the increase in registrations during the 1980s reflected the initial offering of foreign languages in community colleges. In 1990, foreign language enrollments constituted 8.5% of total college undergraduate enrollments, almost half of the fig-

TABLE 17. REGISTRATION IN FOREIGN LANGUAGE CLASSES AT U.S. INSTITUTIONS OF HIGHER EDUCATION, FALL 1960–1990

Language	1960		1970		1980		1990	
	No.	%	No.	%	No.	%	No.	%
All	647,100	100.0	1,111,500	100.0	924,800	100.0	1,184,100	100.0
French	228,800	35.4	359,300	32.3	248,400	26.9	272,500	23.0
Spanish	178,700	27.6	389,200	35.0	379,400	41.0	533,900	45.1
German	146,100	22.6	202,600	18.2	126,900	13.7	133,300	11.3
Russian	30,600	4.7	36,100	3.2	24,000	2.6	44,600	3.8
Latin	25,700	4.0	27,600	2.5	25,000	2.7	28,200	2.4
Ancient Greek	12,700	2.0	16,700	1.5	22,100	2.4	16,400	1.4
Italian	11,100	1.7	34,200	3.1	34,800	3.8	49,700	4.2
Hebrew	3,800	0.6	16,600	1.5	19,400	2.1	13,000	1.1
Chinese	1,800	0.3	6,200	0.6	11,400	1.2	19,500	1.6
Japanese	1,700	0.3	6,600	0.6	11,500	1.2	45,700	3.9
Portuguese	1,000	0.2	5,100	0.5	4,900	0.5	6,200	0.5
Arabic	500	0.1	1,300	0.1	3,500	0.4	3,500	0.3
Others	4,600	0.7	10,000	0.9	13,500	1.5	17,600	1.5

Source: Brod & Huber (1992).

ure in 1965 (16.5%; Starr, 1994). The general increase in foreign language enrollments belies a fairly small increase within much faster growth in the total number of undergraduates between 1960 and 1990. In other words, foreign language enrollments did not keep pace with undergraduate student enrollment. Without major changes in foreign language education policies and a better sense of the foreign language proficiency of those who study foreign languages, such courses will contribute little to language diversity in the United States. High school and college graduates often complain that they did not learn to speak or use a foreign language very well despite having studied it in school. Since no survey of the foreign language competencies of the U.S. population ties those competencies to the formal study of foreign languages, such study does not seem to be a significant contemporary source of language diversity in the United States.

In 1979 the President of the United States appointed a commission to study foreign languages and international studies in the country. Although the commission's reports presented strong arguments for the desirability of promoting foreign language study and even preserving the non-English language resources of the nation, Congress appropriated little funding for foreign language study in the almost two decades following the reports (see Simon, 1980, for a succinct and informative review of these arguments and suggested strategies for achieving foreign language competencies in the nation). There is, however, an independently supported national foreign language center established to study and promote foreign language competencies in the nation,[13] but little else has been done to strongly promote the widespread study of foreign languages in the nation (see Lambert, 1994, for a review of U.S. foreign language policy needs and Adelman, 1994, for a review of the benefits of foreign language study).

A 1987 study of foreign language teaching in elementary and secondary schools indicated that only 22% of elementary schools taught foreign languages whereas 87% of secondary schools did so (Thompson, Christian, Stanfield, & Rhodes, 1990). However, the majority of these schools reported that less than half their students were enrolled in foreign language classes. Only 10% of the schools offered intensive language courses. In about 56% of the elementary schools and 37% of the secondary schools, the foreign language teachers were native speakers of the languages being taught, and most had had no in-service training during the year prior to the survey. Half of the foreign language elementary school teachers were not certified to teach foreign languages. The

---

13 The National Foreign Language Center, currently housed at the Johns Hopkins University, Washington, DC, campus, publishes a quarterly newsletter, entitled *NFLC Perspectives*, which keeps the foreign language field and the general public apprised of its activities.

study noted as well a critical articulation problem between elementary and secondary schools in foreign language teaching. "With regard to articulation, one-third of the elementary schools reported that students who began the study of a foreign language in elementary school had to start the sequence over in secondary school because there were no special classes for those who had been enrolled in a FLES [foreign language in elementary school] program" (Thompson et al., 1990, p. 32).

In a 10-year follow-up survey, a number of changes were noted, some of which paralleled those at the college level: (1) Elementary school foreign language instruction was up 10% over 1987 (22% of elementary schools in 1987 taught foreign languages, whereas 31% did so in 1997), but secondary schools remained stable during the decade (87% in 1987 and 86% in 1997). (2) Spanish language instruction increased from 68% of elementary schools offering foreign language instruction in 1987 to 79% in 1997; Spanish language instruction at secondary schools increased from 86% to 93%; all other languages decreased in elementary schools except for Japanese, Italian, and Sign Language, and remained fairly stable in secondary schools except for the increase of Russian. (3) Language classes for native speakers increased dramatically at both elementary and secondary levels (up to 8% from 1% in 1987 in elementary schools, and up to 9% from 1% in 1987 in secondary schools). (4) Staff development and in-service training increased significantly at both the elementary and the secondary school levels. (5) Teachers at the secondary level are using the target language more in their classrooms (22% of secondary school teachers in 1997 reported using the target language more than 75% of the time, as opposed to 18% of the teachers in 1987). Articulation between elementary and secondary school instruction of foreign languages continued to be a major problem in 1997, with 26% of elementary schools (down from 31% in 1987) reporting that their districts place students who have studied foreign languages in elementary school in level one classes in secondary schools with students who have no prior knowledge or study of the language (cf. Branaman & Rhodes, 1997).

Summary

The U.S. population is overwhelmingly English monolingual. Yet U.S. history has involved and the U.S. population includes a significant number of non-English speakers. Although the profile of these non-English speakers has improved since 1980, much remains to be learned about this group and about the foreign language abilities of the U.S. population. Both non-English speakers and foreign language study contribute to national linguistic diversity. Like flowers in the process of blooming, the full linguistic beauty of the U.S. human bouquet has yet to be seen.

Suggestions for further reading

August, D., & Hakuta, K. (Eds.). (1998). *Educating language minority children*. Washington, DC: National Academy Press.
> A general research synthesis of bilingualism, cognitive and social aspects of schooling, assessment, and program evaluation. Well written and based on recent research reviews written by a committee of scholars in various fields.

Barkin, E. (1996). *And still they come: Immigrants and American society, 1920 to the 1990s* (American History Series). Wheeling, IL: Harlan Davidson.
> General history of immigrants and immigration to the United States during the larger part of the twentieth century. Provides clear comparisons of various time periods, groups, and transnational movement of peoples, cultural adaptations, and ethnicity. Covers major immigration reform policies of the 1980s and the 1990s through 1995.

Barrett, R. (1994). *Using the 1990 U.S. census for research* (Guides to Major Social Science Data Bases 3). Thousand Oaks, CA: Sages.
> Brief introduction to the census, its purpose, organization, implementation, and reporting. Allows novices who are not statisticians to become familiar with some of the technical aspects of this demographic and political activity. Major purpose is description of the 1990 census database and sources (including multimedia formats) for research purposes.

Crawford, J. (Ed.). (1992). *Language loyalties: A sourcebook on the official English controversy*. Chicago: University of Chicago Press.
> Major compilation of portions of original documents and a few original essays on various historical and contemporary issues in the English-only movement. Little analysis, good as a reference and source book.

Kloss, H. (1998). *The American bilingual tradition* (2nd ed.). McHenry, IL: Delta Systems and Center for Applied Linguistics. (Original work published 1977)
> Second printing of this classic summary of the history of U.S. language policies. A new introduction by Reynaldo F. Macías and Terrence Wiley places the book within the larger sociolinguistic history of the nation.

Lambert, R. (Ed.). (1994, March). Foreign language policy – An agenda for change [special issue]. *Annals of the American Academy of Political and Social Science, 532.* Thousand Oaks, CA: Sage.

> Good collection of fifteen essays grouped into three sections (planning processes, institutional levels and clienteles, and priority planning domains). Includes analyses of foreign language policies, foreign languages in elementary through higher education, and assessment issues.

Leibowitz, A. (1970). The imposition of English as the language of instruction in American schools. *Revista de Derecho Puertorriqueño, 38,* 175–224. Also published as Leibowitz, A. (1971). *Educational policy and political acceptance: The imposition of English as the language of instruction in American schools.* (ERIC Document Reproduction Service No. ED 047 321)

> This essay is generally found in its ERIC version. Although it has been published in a law review, it is not easily obtained. Only referenced work on how English was made the almost universal language of instruction in U.S. flag schools.

Nakanishi, D., & Nishida, T. Y. (Eds.). (1995). *The Asian American educational experience: A Sourcebook for teachers and students.* New York: Routledge.

> Very well edited and organized collection of twenty-four essays grouped into four areas: history, academic achievement, challenges of growth and diversity, and higher education.

Population Reference Bureau, 1875 Connecticut Ave., NW, Suite 520, Washington, DC 20009-5728. ⟨http://www.prb.org⟩.

> An educational organization dedicated to collecting, analyzing, and disseminating demographic materials to the public and educators. Various publications, including a newsletter, population bulletins and maps. Aside from the very good quality of its materials, the Bureau focuses on educators and their need to make demographic data useful and understandable in the classroom.

Spener, D. (Ed.). (1994). *Adult biliteracy in the United States.* McHenry, IL: Center for Applied Linguistics and Delta Systems.

> Ten very readable essays on various aspects of language diversity, literacy, bilingualism, and adults, and schooling.

Spring, J. (1996). *The cultural transformation of a Native American family and its tribe: 1763–1995 – A basket of Apples.* Mahwah, NJ: Erlbaum.

> Broad historical review of cultural changes within the Choctaw nation, including a focus on education and schooling, language, and other aspects of social and cultural organization.

U.S. Bureau of the Census (1989). *200 years of U.S. census taking: Population and housing questions, 1790–1990.* Washington, DC: U.S. Government Printing Office.

Historical review of the decennial census of the United States based on the questionnaires used in each census since its inception in 1790.

Valdés, G., & Figueroa, R. (1994). *Bilingualism and testing: A special case of bias.* Norwood, NJ: Ablex.

Major synthesis of research and policy analyses of testing and language issues. Introduces various concepts related to bilingualism and assessment that any teacher should understand.

Weinberg, M. (1996). *A chance to learn: A history of race and schooling in the United States* (2nd ed.). Long Beach: University Press for California State University, Long Beach.

Comprehensive history of race and schooling, covering the period from the colonial period to the present for Blacks, Asians, Latinos (Mexicans and Puerto Ricans), and American Indians. Covers not only elementary and secondary schooling but higher education as well. Also pays attention to the impact of race in schooling on dominant White students.

Wiley, T. (1996). *Literacy and language diversity.* McHenry, IL: Center for Applied Linguistics/Delta Systems.

Noteworthy synthesis of the literature on literacy, schooling, bilingualism, and diversity among K–12 students and adults as well as for literacy in the dominant language and minority languages. Brings together research literature not often referenced in singular works.

References

Adelman, C. (1994). The empirical evidence of foreign language study. *Annals of the AAPSS, 532*, 59–73.

American Council of Learned Societies (1932). *Report of the committee on linguistics and national stocks in the population of the United States.* Washington, DC. Reprinted from the *Annual Report of the American Historical Association for 1931.* (1932) Washington, DC.

Branaman, L., & Rhodes, N. (1997). *A national survey of foreign language instruction in elementary and secondary schools – A changing picture: 1987–1997. Executive summary.* Washington DC: Center for Applied Linguistics. ⟨http://www.cal.org/public/results.htm⟩.

Brod, R., & Huber, B. (1992). Foreign language enrollments in U.S. institutions of higher education, fall 1990. *ADFL Bulletin, 23*(3).

Day, J. (1996). *Population projections of the United States by age, sex, race, and Hispanic origin: 1995 to 2050* (Current Population Reports No. 25–1130). Washington, DC: U.S. Bureau of the Census.

Fishman, J., et al. (1966). *Language loyalty in the United States: The maintenance and perpetuation of non-English mother tongues by American ethnic and religious groups.* The Hague, Netherlands: Mouton.

Fleischman, H., & Hopstock, P. (1993). *Descriptive study of services to limited*

English proficient students, Vol. 1 (Report prepared for the Office of the Under Secretary, U.S. Department of Education). Arlington, VA: Development Associates.

Kloss, H. (1998). *The American bilingual tradition* (2nd ed.). McHenry, IL: Delta Systems and Center for Applied Linguistics. (Original work published 1977)

Kominski, R. (1985, February 4). *Final report – Documentation of Voting Rights Act determinations.* (Unpublished memorandum to Paul Siegel, U.S. Bureau of the Census).

Kominski, R. (1989). *How good is "How well"? An examination of the Census English speaking ability question.* Paper presented at the annual meeting of the American Statistical Association, Washington, DC.

Lambert, R. (1994). Problems and processes in U.S. foreign language planning. *Annals of the AAPSS, 532,* 47–58.

Macías, R. F. (1993). Language and ethnic classification of language minorities: Chicano and Latino students in the 1990s. *Hispanic Journal of Behavioral Sciences, 15,* 230–257.

Macías, R. F. (1999). Language politics and the sociolinguistic historiography of Spanish in the United States. In P. Griffin, J. Peyton, W. Wolfram, & R. Fasold (Eds.), *Language in action: New studies of language in society* (pp. 53–84). Cresskill, NJ: Hampton Press.

Macías, R. F., Nishikawa, S., Alegría, A., & Venegas, J. (1998). *Summary report of the Survey of the States' Limited English Proficient Students and available educational programs and services, 1995–96.* Washington, DC: National Clearinghouse for Bilingual Education.

Macías, R. F., with Mary Spencer. (1984). *Estimating the number of language minority and limited English proficient persons in the U.S.: A comparative analysis of the studies.* Los Alamitos, CA: National Center for Bilingual Research.

Simon, P. (1980). *The tongue-tied American: Confronting the foreign language crisis.* New York: Continuum.

Starr, S. F. (1994). Foreign languages on the campus: Room for improvement. *Annals of the AAPSS, 532,* 138–148.

Thompson, L., Christian, D., Stanfield, C., & Rhodes, N. (1990). Foreign language instruction in the United States. In A. Padilla, H. Fairchild, & C. Valadez (Eds.), *Foreign language education: Issues and strategies* (pp. 13–35). Newbury Park, CA: Sage.

U.S. Bureau of the Census. (1945). *Statistical abstract of the United States 1944–45.* Washington, DC: U.S. Government Printing Office.

U.S. Bureau of the Census. (1973). *1970 census of population, national origin and language.* Washington, DC: U.S. Government Printing Office.

U.S. Bureau of the Census. (1975). *Historical statistics of the U.S. – Colonial times to 1970.* Washington, DC: U.S. Government Printing Office.

U.S. Bureau of the Census. (1984a). *1980 census of population: Vol. 1, Chapter C, Part 53A – Puerto Rico* (PC80-1-C53A). Washington, DC: U.S. Government Printing Office.

U.S. Bureau of the Census. (1984b). *1980 census of population: Vol. 1, Chapter C/D, Part 54 – Guam* (PC80-1-C/D54). Washington, DC: U.S. Government Printing Office.

U.S. Bureau of the Census. (1984c). *1980 census of population: Vol. 1, Chapter*

D, *Part 1 – United States Summary* (PC80-1-D1-A). Washington, DC: U.S. Government Printing Office.

U.S. Bureau of the Census. (1992). *1990 census of population and housing – Guam* (1990 CPH-6-G). Washington, DC: U.S. Government Printing Office.

U.S. Bureau of the Census. (1993a). *1990 census of population – Puerto Rico* (1990 CP-2-53). Washington, DC: U.S. Government Printing Office.

U.S. Bureau of the Census. (1993b). *Language spoken at home and ability to speak English for the United States, regions and states: 1990* (Special tabulation of 1990 Census of Population, 1990 CPH-L-133). Washington, DC: U.S. Bureau of the Census, Education and Social Stratification Branch.

U.S. Bureau of the Census. (1994). *Statistical abstract of the United States 1994*. Washington, DC: U.S. Government Printing Office.

U.S. General Accounting Office. (1994). *Limited English proficiency: A growing and costly educational challenge facing many school districts* (Report to the Chairman, U.S. Senate Committee on Labor and Human Resources, GAO/HEHS-94-38). Washington, DC: Author.

U.S. Immigration and Naturalization Service. (1997a). *Immigration and emigration by decade: 1901–90.* ⟨http://www.ins.usdoj.gov/stats/300.html⟩.

U.S. Immigration and Naturalization Service. (1997b). *Total and foreign born U.S. population: 1900–1990.* ⟨http://www.ins.usdoj.gov/stats/308.html⟩.

Waggoner, D. (1981). Statistics on language use. In C. Ferguson & S. Heath (Eds.), *Language in the USA* (pp. 486–515). Cambridge: Cambridge University Press.

2 The American linguistic mosaic

Understanding language shift in the United States

Calvin Veltman

Introduction

The objective of this chapter is to help readers understand the *process* whereby immigrants and their children come to learn and adopt the English language in the United States. Using data compiled by the U.S. Bureau of the Census, I show that the learning of English occurs very rapidly among immigrants; that large numbers come to adopt English as their primary, preferred language; that many will give birth to children having English for their first language (mother tongue); and, finally, that the entire first generation of native-born children who do not have English for their mother tongue will come to speak English on a regular basis. In fact, the vast majority of the native born will make English their primary, preferred language, and many of them will abandon the regular use of their mother tongue.

Further, I show this to be true for all minority language groups. Consequently, public authorities, including teachers and school administrators, need not take repressive measures to further promote the use and adoption of English by immigrants and their children; the desire of immigrants in all minority language groups to learn English and make this language their own is sufficiently high to produce the kind of outcome that most Americans cherish, that is, that immigrants become English-speaking people. I unequivocally demonstrate that rates of language shift to English are so high that all minority languages are routinely abandoned, depriving the United States of one type of human resource that may be economically and politically desirable both to maintain and to develop.

Language maintenance and language shift

This chapter does not generally deal with the total size of minority language groups, that is, with the demographic factors that are fueling population growth among immigrant groups. Such topics are covered in Chapter 1. It is nonetheless important to summarily address this topic so that readers are clear about what I hope to accomplish in this chapter.

For example, census data show that the number of Spanish-speaking people living in the United States has been steadily rising throughout the twentieth century. The 1970 census reported the presence of some 7.8 million persons who as children lived in homes where Spanish was spoken. Some 14.6 million people reported Hispanic ancestry in 1980; the number had grown to more than 20 million by 1990 and is projected to reach more than 30 million by the turn of the century.[1] Obviously, much of this growth is due to continuing high levels of immigration; equally obviously, immigrants from Latin America speak Spanish, causing the number of Spanish-speaking people resident in the United States to grow rapidly as well.[2]

The concern in this chapter is not, however, the documentation of the rise in the numbers of Hispanic Americans and the corresponding growth of the Spanish-speaking population, nor with the growth of other immigrant groups and their associated immigrant languages. Rather, this chapter focuses on the linguistic trajectory of immigrant groups after they arrive in the United States. How rapidly do they learn English? How quickly do they adopt it as their preferred language? What consequences does this adoption have for the next generation? In the event that native-born children do not speak English as a native language, how rapidly do they learn English, how many adopt it as their personal language, and how many cease to use their mother tongue on a regular basis? Is this process of movement from the minority language to the majority language a two- or a three-generational process? Or can some minority language groups, most notably Hispanics, be expected to perpetuate their language indefinitely into the future because they enjoy very high rates of language maintenance?

Factors related to language maintenance

Much of the literature dealing with language maintenance and shift has been based on case studies of individual groups or on the use of indirect indicators of language maintenance and/or loss,[3] such as those relating to the presence of an ethnic press, ethnic media, ethnic schools, ethnic religious and social organizations, and an autonomous ethnic economy

1 The Census Bureau reports 22.4 million persons of either principal or secondary Hispanic origin (U.S. Bureau of the Census, 1995, Table 12). However, the 5% Public Use Microdata Sample reveals the presence of only 20.3 million such persons, of whom 19.2 million declared Hispanic origin for their primary ancestry.
2 Birthrates are also substantially higher among Hispanic women and are expected to remain so (U.S. Bureau of the Census, 1997, Table 94).
3 Data obtained from the U.S. census remain sketchy at best. For example, the 1980 and 1990 censuses contain no data on the mother tongue of the American population, nor do they provide information on the relative dominance of English or the minority language. In the 1970 census, the question relating to mother tongue was so poorly defined that approximately half of the population identified as belonging to a minority language group had English for their mother tongue (Veltman, 1983).

Calvin Veltman

(Fishman et al., 1966). Similarly, Breton (1964), a leading Canadian theoretician, proposes that ethnic groups characterized by *institutional completeness* are better able to preserve their languages and cultures than those which are apparently not so fortunate.

In their analysis of this topic, Conklin and Lourie (1983) list nine political, social, and demographic factors, seven "cultural factors," and five "linguistic factors" (p. 175) that may be related to language maintenance or loss.[4] Unfortunately, an examination of such a large number of factors cannot be carried out in the absence of a sufficiently large sample of minority language groups having a wide variety of differing values on the variables being studied. The current state of knowledge does not, therefore, permit definitive conclusions regarding the relative importance of each factor or any combination of factors contributing to language maintenance or shift.

Furthermore, even a cursory study of the history of immigration to the United States reveals that no immigrant group has been able to preserve its minority language longer than two or three generations.[5] Consequently, the potential role of either institutional completeness or the twenty-one factors advanced by Conklin and Lourie is likely to be exceedingly limited or, at the very least, without long-term significance. In the absence of continuing immigration, history teaches that all minority languages will eventually be lost.

In fact, many U.S. immigrant groups have shown characteristics that should have been favorable to the maintenance of ethnic languages on U.S. soil. For example, between 1820 and 1850, 5.2 million Germans arrived in the United States. Their numerical dominance and geographic concentration in urban settings or in rural, isolated settings, together with favorable cultural conditions and the presence of German language institutions of all types, are among the factors identified as being favorable to ethnic language retention (Molesky, 1988, p. 42). Nonetheless, in the 1990 census, of the 222 million Americans who reported their ethnic ancestry, 58 million people claimed German ancestry in

---

4 Among the political, social, and demographic variables favoring language maintenance, Conklin and Lourie (1983) mention, e.g., the large size and high concentration of the group, recent arrival or continued immigration, close proximity to the homeland, a high rate of return migration, the presence of ethnic economic niches, low social and economic mobility, and the presence of nativist feelings in the larger population with respect to the group; cultural factors include the presence of mother-tongue institutions of all types, the grounding of ethnic identity in the language itself, the presence of strong family ties and kinship networks, and important cultural differences relative to Anglo-American society. Linguistic factors emphasize the characteristics of the mother tongue itself: According to the authors, the fact that the language is a standard, written variety enjoying international status as opposed to a dialect, that it uses the Latin alphabet, and that literacy is widespread within the group supposedly favors language maintenance.

5 Possible exceptions are marginal religious groups such as the Hassidim or the Amish.

whole or in part whereas German was spoken at home only by 1.5 million people (U.S. Bureau of the Census, 1995). Clearly, if any linguistic group could have been expected to survive on U.S. soil, this one should have – but it did not.

Similarly, between 1880 and 1920, 23 million immigrants from southern and eastern European nations came to the United States. In 1920, most of the Jewish population of the United States, which stood at just under 3 million, spoke Yiddish, lived in ethnic enclaves in the larger cities, faced economic discrimination in the United States, and had a strong commitment to a special religion. These factors, identified as those which are favorable to language maintenance, did not permit Yiddish to survive as an American language. According to the 1990 census, only 213,000 people, most of whom were undoubtedly elderly, reportedly spoke Yiddish at home (U.S. Bureau of the Census, 1995). Similarly, French was spoken by fewer than 1.9 million of the 13.2 million persons of Cajun, French, or French Canadian origin in 1990; only 1.3 million of the 14.7 million people claiming Italian origin in whole or in part spoke Italian; and some 723,000 of the 9.4 million people of Polish origin spoke Polish (U.S. Bureau of the Census, 1995).

I conclude, therefore, that the presence of large, economically deprived, immigrant minority (language) groups characterized by high degrees of institutional completeness has been insufficient to produce the maintenance of ethnic languages in the United States, either extensively or even minimally. All large immigrant groups that arrived prior to the 1960s were successfully integrated into the English language majority, irrespective of the degree of resistance that they may have offered. Most authors conclude that the process is generally completed within two to three generations (Conklin & Lourie, 1983; Fishman et al., 1966; Glazer, 1978; Veltman, 1988).

Do the newer minority language groups resist the adoption of English?

Given this historical overview of the integration of the largest minority language groups into the English language majority in the more distant past, is there is any reason to believe that the factors producing such extensive language shift in the past are still operative? Or has there been such a substantial change in the factors that structure language shift and maintenance that newer immigrant groups may be expected to better resist pressures to learn and adopt the English language?

Proponents of English language amendments tend to assume that such changes have occurred. In particular, they hold that Hispanics, unlike the French Canadians, Germans, Italians, Poles, and Yiddish speakers of previous generations, are successfully resisting integration into the English language group. In fact, the argument is sometimes made that Latinos are so successful in retaining their language that the dominance of English is threatened. Consequently, the argument goes, English-speaking people, in order to provide for the long-term economic well-being of their children, should learn Spanish or, alternatively, legislative bodies should prohibit or severely restrict the use of Spanish.

Many Americans, including some scholars, share the belief that the growth of the Spanish language group is at least partly explained by the ability of Spanish-speaking people to maintain their language. Molesky (1988) observes that "it is . . . true that taken as a group, Spanish speakers have been *very language retentive*" [italics added] (p. 61). She then cites a number of factors that may be thought to contribute to higher degrees of language maintenance among Hispanics: (1) Many are "sojourners and . . . cyclical immigrants"; (2) "concentration (of Hispanics) in 'barrios' or ethnic enclaves is widespread"; (3) because of severe exclusion from economic participation, "shift to English has been retarded by low social mobility and limited economic rewards"; (4) "consciousness of being a minority discriminated against by a hostile, English-dominant world reinforces the retention of Spanish"; and (5) "for political refugees, the ethnic language is a symbol of their past and their struggles and therefore tends to be retained; this is particularly true if they have any hope of returning to their homeland" (p. 61).

As a matter of fact, a significantly higher degree of language maintenance cannot account for the increased presence of Spanish; most of this presence is explained by a large, continuous stream of new Spanish-speaking immigrants to the United States. For example, the 1990 census found that 8 million people aged 5 and over were born in Spanish-speaking countries; nearly half had entered the United States during the preceding 10-year period. Thus, Hispanic immigration is by and large relatively new, as is the immigration of Asian groups. If movement to English may be expected to occur over two or three generations, then it is obviously too early to conclude that these newer immigrant groups are resisting the adoption of English with greater success than did the large immigrant groups that arrived in the late nineteenth or early twentieth century. As I shall demonstrate, the evidence does not support the conclusion that any minority language group is "resisting" the learning and adoption of the English language.

The Plan of Analysis

I begin my examination of the language shift process by considering the quality of the data available to carry out the analyses, and discussing the methods by which such data may be correctly interpreted. In the next section, I examine data from the 1976 Survey of Income and Education (SIE; U.S. Bureau of the Census, 1976). Since no other nation-wide data set contains satisfactory information on mother tongue, the SIE is the only database that permits a direct examination of the process of language shift and language maintenance for specific minority language groups.

After completing the methodological discussion, I then examine the process whereby Hispanic immigrants adapt to the U.S. environment, since this group is the one most frequently identified as resisting integration into the English language group. This analysis is followed by an examination of the language shift patterns of native-born people of Spanish mother tongue, including data showing that native-born Hispanics in the late twentieth century adopt English in greater numbers than did Hispanics 20, 30, or 40 years before. I then examine the cumulative, intergenerational effects of language shift on the Spanish language group.

Having established the basic parameters of the integration of the Spanish language group into the larger English-speaking society, I then examine the ability of specific, non-Hispanic minority language groups to survive in the United States, using once again data from the SIE.

Since the SIE data are more than twenty years old at this writing, I then see what information from the 1990 census may be useful for determining whether immigrant groups that arrived during the 1975–1990 time period continue to integrate into the English language group. This discussion also permits the disaggregation of the Spanish language group into its most important national-origin groups.

The 1976 Survey of Income and Education

Questionnaire content and quality of the data

According to Chapter 1 of the volume, although the "ideal way of collecting data on the languages . . . used by a population is with direct measures or assessments (e.g., tests, observations) . . . , another way of collecting this information is to use indirect measures (e.g., asking people what they speak, read, or write)" (p. 11). This is the general procedure that social scientists, including those employed by the U.S. Bureau of the Census, have used to obtain data on language origins and practices in the U.S. population. However, only once has the Bureau collected a data set that permits the calculation of rates of language shift to English for minority language groups: the 1976 Survey of Income and Education. The SIE presents several important advantages over data derived from the U.S. decennial censuses.

First, the decennial census has never included a question that adequately ascertained the mother tongue of U.S. residents. Calling a census item a "mother tongue" question is meaningless when the question used is vague, ambiguous, or deliberately designed to gather as large a minority language population as possible.[6] However, the presence of a good question to ascertain mother tongue is exceedingly important because it is impossible to accurately calculate rates of language shift without initially knowing the size of the minority language population. The SIE is the only large-scale U.S. study that has reasonably ascertained the mother tongue of most of the U.S. population.[7] The appropriate question read: "What language was usually spoken in this person's home when he (she) was a child?" Though not directly determining the mother tongue of the individual, the correspondence between the "language usually spoken" in the childhood home and the "mother tongue" of the children raised in the home should be quite high.

Secondly, the decennial census is severely limited in the scope and number of questions that can be asked regarding current language practice. Since the SIE contained a number of language-use questions, four categories of language use among people of any given minority language group can be distinguished with some certainty. These categories are established by comparing responses to the questions on the language usually spoken by the individual and on the presence or absence of a second language.[8] The first two categories refer to people who normally maintain their mother tongue as their primary language, that is to say, they speak it more often than they do English:

1. Effective *non-English monolingualism:* The person is reported to usually speak a language other than English and does not often speak English;
2. *Non-English-dominant bilingualism:* The person usually speaks a language other than English but often speaks English.

The second set of categories reference significant language shift from the minority language to English, since English has been adopted as the primary language. The mother tongue is either relegated to the status of a

6 See the detailed discussion in Veltnam (1983, pp. 3–6).
7 Nonetheless, persons born in the United States and living in English-only households were not required to furnish data concerning their mother tongue. Given the rates of the abandonment of minority languages, it is clear that many such persons now live in monolingual English households. Had their mother tongue been correctly ascertained, the rates of adoption of English and the abandonment of minority languages among the native born would undoubtedly be substantially higher than the rates presented in subsequent sections of this chapter.
8 The primary language of the individual was obtained by asking, "What language does this person usually speak?" The presence of a frequently used second language was determined by the response to the following question: "Does this person often speak another language?" If the response was affirmative, the respondent was asked to identify the specific language so used.

second, frequently spoken language or is not used on a regular basis. When the mother tongue is no longer used on a regular basis, I characterize this situation as one of the *abandonment* of the minority language in favor of English.

3. *English-dominant bilingualism:* The person usually speaks English and continues to speak his or her mother tongue often;
4. *English monolingualism:* The person usually speaks English and does not often speak his or her mother tongue.

Although it is undoubtedly true that some people may have had difficulty distinguishing which language they usually speak and that others may have had difficulty ascertaining whether they often spoke another language, the presence of four types of current language practice permits the analyst to distinguish different degrees of language shift from a minority language to English.

In addition to the presence of excellent questions with respect to mother tongue and current language practice, the SIE also is characterized by very large sample sizes. This permits us rather refined analyses of the process of language shift in the United States, particularly for the Spanish language group. For most other groups, patterns of language shift for native- and foreign-born groups can be established with some accuracy; within foreign-born groups, it is possible to distinguish the impact of having migrated prior to 1960, during the 1960s, or during the 1970s, i.e., prior to the collection of data during the spring of 1976. For the purposes of this chapter, this degree of detail is sufficient.

Methodological considerations in the analysis of language shift

It is extremely important to avoid comparing the rates of language shift of different minority language groups, unless, of course, one is certain that they are identical in composition and structure. When one group is composed almost entirely of the native born, for example, persons in the French or Yiddish minority language groups, and another is composed nearly entirely of foreign-born persons, for example, the Vietnamese, it stands to reason that the two former groups are characterized by much higher rates of the adoption of English and the abandonment of the mother tongue than are the Vietnamese. In short, the analyst needs to be absolutely certain that minority language groups are indeed comparable before comparing them; doing otherwise may lead to the erroneous conclusion that one group maintains its mother tongue better than another when such is not really the case.

Consequently, proper method in the study of language shift requires that immigrants and native-born persons be studied separately. Moreover, rates of language shift should not be compared across minority language groups, either for the foreign born or the native born, unless it is equally certain that the internal structure of the groups being compared is similar. For example, the average length of residence in the United States for a French-speaking immigrant is longer than that observed for Hispanics; the latter are more recent immigrants. It follows, accordingly, that language maintenance should be higher among Hispanics than among French-speaking immigrants, independently of whether or not Hispanics are more likely to maintain their language as a group than are French-speaking immigrants.

The same logic applies to the analysis of language shift among native-born members of minority language groups. As I show, the elderly and very young children are less likely to speak and adopt English than are teenagers, young adults, and middle-aged adults. Unless two native-born groups are similar in age structure, direct comparisons should be avoided.[9]

Consequently, I study the process of the integration of immigrants in terms of their age at time of arrival in the United States and their length of residence there. Very young immigrant children may be expected to enter the educational system in the same manner as young native-born children in the same minority language group, experiencing the same pressures and enjoying the same opportunities. Older immigrants, however, frequently enter the host country as a family unit. Although they may learn and use English in conjunction with their general integration into American life, they are unlikely to be as profoundly influenced in terms of their personal identity as are the youngest immigrants. In each case, longer residence in the United States is associated with greater language shift. The language shift process of native-born members of minority groups is examined simply as a function of their age.[10]

Language shift in the Spanish minority language group

LANGUAGE SHIFT AMONG IMMIGRANTS

My analysis begins with Figures 1, 2, and 3, each of which examines the evolution of a particular type of language shift for immigrants as a function of two factors: their age on arrival in the United States and their length of residence there. The latter variable is conceived of in terms of 5-year time periods.[11] All three figures refer to exactly the same immi-

---

9 The use of standardization techniques can circumvent this problem to a great extent.
10 Actually, the principles of analysis are the same. Since all of the native born arrived in the United States at zero years of age, one need only take into account their length of residence, i.e., their current age.
11 The original data are presented in Veltman (1988, Figures 5.2–5.6). I have fit curves to the raw data in order to develop 5-year time sequences depicting both the rates and types of language shift observed in the SIE (Veltman, 1988, Table A2–3); these

grant population. The first, however, simply represents the extent to which English is used on a regular basis, whether or not Spanish is still spoken more frequently, has been replaced by English as a primary language, or has simply been abandoned.[12] Figure 2 represents the extent to which English has been appropriated as a personal, preferred (primary) language, and Figure 3 presents the extent to which Spanish has been, to all intents and purposes, abandoned in daily use.

Learning and using English on a regular basis

Data on the extent to which English is reportedly often spoken are presented in Figure 1. This figure shows that younger immigrants made extremely rapid progress in learning English and using it on a regular basis; in fact, most of the mobility observed for the three youngest groups of immigrants occured within the first 5 years of residence in the United States. Within this very short time period, more than half of the youngest immigrants, three-fourths of those aged 5 to 9 years, and two thirds of those aged 10 to 14 years at time of arrival reportedly spoke English on a regular basis. After 5 to 10 years of residence in the United States, approximately 80% of the immigrants aged 0–4 and 10–14 frequently spoke English, and 90% of those aged 5–9 at time of arrival adopted that language for use on a regular basis. After 15 to 20 years of residence, nearly all of the youngest groups of immigrants frequently spoke English, a finding that makes intuitive sense since these immigrant children received most or all of their schooling in the United States.

Figure 1 also reveals a certain rupture in the pattern of the data, at least for the first 5- to 10-year period, when immigrants aged 15–19 upon arrival seem to resemble adults rather than children. The rate of the frequent use of English is approximately 45% for the 15–19 year-olds after 5 years of residence; the use of English declines progressively with increasing age at time of arrival. Further, this figure shows that it took longer for immigrants aged 15 and over at time of arrival to begin to use English on a regular basis. That is to say, the upper three regions of the graph occupy considerably more space for this group than they do for the younger immigrants; this suggests that some immigrants in the older age groups will take at least 5 years to begin using English on a regular basis; others, 10 years; still others, at least 15 years. After 15 to 20 years of residence in the United States, a majority of immigrants in every age group frequently spoke English, except for those who were at

interpolated data were used in my linguistic projections of the size and composition of the Spanish language group for the period 1976–2001.

12 In other words, the figure shows the extent to which monolingualism in Spanish has been abandoned.

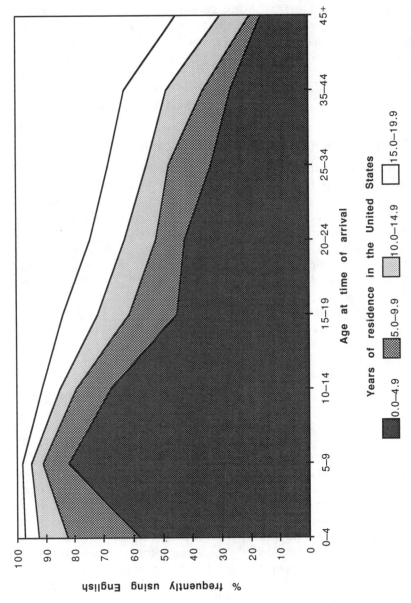

Figure 1   Frequent use of English by immigrants of Spanish mother tongue, United States, 1976.

least 45 years of age when they arrived in the United States. Since these oldest immigrants bore no children after arrival in the United States, their maintenance of Spanish is relatively immaterial from a purely demographic viewpoint.

Adopting English as primary language

Although the use of English on a regular basis is a first indicator of the extent of the integration of Hispanic immigrants into U.S. society, the adoption of English as the primary, preferred language represents a significant transformation of the language practices of immigrants, most of whom spoke little or no English on their arrival in the United States. Nonetheless, some immigrants choose to make English their primary, preferred language, most often relegating Spanish to the status of a second, frequently used language. The adoption of English by these immigrants is extremely important because their children will have English, not Spanish, for their first language. This feature of the language shift process may come as a surprise for many readers. Logically, however, if parents normally speak English, their children will normally have English for their first language.

As can be readily observed from Figure 2, after 0 to 5 years of residence in the United States, approximately 20% of immigrants aged 0 to 14 years at time of arrival had already adopted English as their preferred, usual language. After 5 additional years of residence, over 40% of the two younger groups had so adopted English; 10 years later, approximately two thirds had made English the language they usually spoke.

The rhythm with which the process of adopting English as the personal, preferred language occurred is also worthy of attention: Approximately one third of the total amount of language shift for the two younger groups was attained during the first 5 years of residence, another third during the second 5-year period, and most of the remainder during the third 5-year period. That is to say, after 10 to 15 years of residence in the United States, little further language shift is observed; the entire process is generally completed after 15 to 20 years of residence.

Figure 2 also shows that the older the immigrants at time of arrival, the less likely they were to become predominantly English speaking. The final rate of adoption of English, which is greater than 65% in the two younger groups, drops to approximately 40% of those who were 10 to 14 years of age at time of arrival and to 25% for those aged 15–19 when they arrived in the United States. The final rate of the adoption of English, which is associated with increasing age at time of arrival, then declined slowly. The rate is less than 10% for immigrants who were over 45 years of age when they came to the United States.

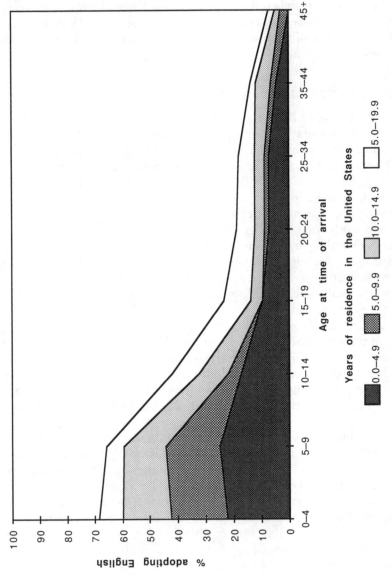

Figure 2 Immigrants of Spanish mother tongue, with English as the dominant language, United States, 1976.

Since approximately one third of Hispanic immigrants are less than 15 years of age when they arrive in the United States (Veltman, 1988, Table 10.7) and since the adoption of English is most extensive in the younger age groups, many of their children will probably learn English rather than Spanish as their first language. The adoption of English by members of the immigrant generation itself is already, therefore, associated with significant erosion of the capacity of the Spanish language group to perpetuate itself on U.S. soil.

The abandonment of Spanish

If adopting English as one's primary, preferred language represents a significant step in the integration of immigrants, the abandonment of the daily use of Spanish signifies a much more radical, profound type of integration into the English-language group. Figure 3 presents the total proportion of immigrants in each age group who reportedly no longer speak their mother tongue on a frequent basis.[13]

On the whole, the abandonment of Spanish is a negligible phenomenon among immigrants who arrived in the United States when they were at least 15 years old. The figure ranges from approximately 2% among the 15–19 year-olds to almost zero among those aged 45 or more at time of arrival. On the other hand, more than 10% of those in the three younger age groups eventually ceased to use Spanish on a regular basis. Nearly all of this language loss occurred after 10 years of residence in the United States, that is, when these people had attained adolescence or their early adult years.

In fact, it seems reasonable to associate the abandonment of Spanish with the emancipation of highly anglicized, younger immigrants from parental constraints, that is, with their setting up their own households or attending college away from home. Since these environments are more likely to be ethnically heterogeneous than the parental home or local community is, the opportunity to use Spanish on a regular basis undoubtedly diminishes, leading to the progressive deterioration of Spanish language skills and the opportunity or motivation to use it.

It goes without saying that since their parents no longer speak Spanish on a regular basis, the children of these immigrants will likely not learn Spanish in their childhood homes. Such language loss is, therefore, already permanent.

---

13 This is not to say that such individuals never speak Spanish; they may still do so with some individuals and within some situations. On the other hand, by their own admission, they no longer speak Spanish frequently. They may, however, speak it sufficiently frequently to qualify as a Spanish-speaking person in the 1980 or 1990 U.S. census (see the discussion in the section "Corroborating Evidence").

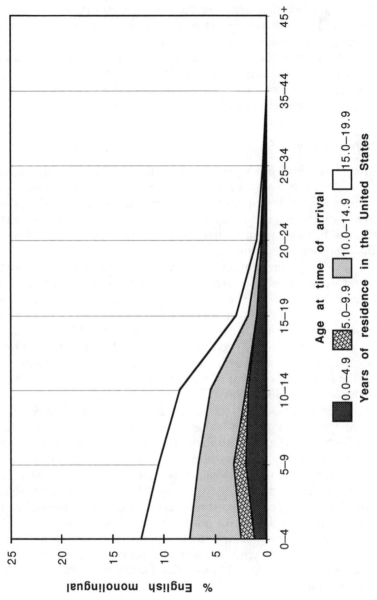

Figure 3   English monolingualism among immigrants of Spanish mother tongue, United States, 1976.

Trends in language shift among native-born persons of Spanish mother tongue

OBSERVED PATTERNS OF LANGUAGE SHIFT

Having established that movement from Spanish to English is both rapid and very extensive among Hispanic immigrants, particularly the youngest ones, I turn to language shift among the native born of Spanish mother tongue. For the moment, I pay no attention to the children of Hispanic immigrants who were given English for their first language. To all intents and purposes, their children were already lost to the Spanish language group, either because they never learned Spanish or because, having learned it as a second language, they generally abandoned it as they grew up.[14]

Figure 4 presents rates of language shift for the native born as a function of age. Since no information on age at time of arrival is necessary for the native born, all three types of language shift may be represented on a single figure:

- The lower area represents the extent of English monolingualism observed in the native-born population for each age group.[15]
- The next-highest area represents the extent of the adoption of English as a primary, preferred language, including both its abandonment (the blackened, lower area) and the retention of Spanish as a second language (English-dominant bilingualism), represented by the second layer from the bottom.
- The line near the top of the figure represents the percentage of persons who spoke English on a regular basis, including those who adopted English as a primary language and those who used English as a second, frequently used language. The area above this line, at the top of the figure, represents the extent of monolingualism in Spanish.

Several features of Figure 4 are of great interest. First, nearly all native-born persons of Spanish mother tongue under 50 years of age at the time of the study spoke English on a regular basis. In fact, except for the youngest children, approximately 95% of people in all age groups under 40 years of age regularly spoke English. This figure declines with increasing age. Slightly more than half of those aged 70 and over in 1976 regularly spoke English.

The line representing the percentage of people in each age group who adopted English as a primary, preferred language has a similar shape. The 4–9 year-olds were less likely to have adopted English than their older peers. The figure exceeds 60% among 10–14 and 15–19 year-olds

14 See Veltman, 1988 (p. 94) for a fuller discussion of this issue.
15 Or, alternatively, the effective abandonment of Spanish.

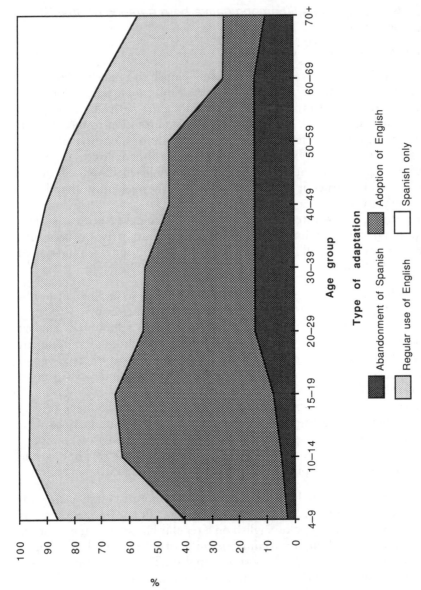

Figure 4 Language shift among the native born, Spanish mother tongue, United States, 1976.

and then drops progressively for each succeeding age group. Less than 30% of those aged 70 or more at the time of the study usually spoke English. In other words, their rates of language maintenance are higher than in the younger groups.

On the other hand, the line that represents the extent to which native-born persons abandoned the frequent use of their mother tongue appears to be relatively constant at approximately 12% – except in the very youngest groups. Their rates may, however, be expected to rise as they leave the parental home. While still living at home, they are in constant contact with Spanish-speaking people (i.e., their parents) so that it is unlikely that they would (or could) abandon the regular use of Spanish.

TREND ANALYSIS OF LANGUAGE SHIFT

The most important issue in interpreting Figure 4 concerns the meaning to assign to the observation that the young were more likely to use English and to adopt it than their elders were. Some observers have proposed that Hispanics who have once adopted English will one day return to the dominant use of Spanish as they grow older (Cardenas, 1980). However, prevalent theory in the area of linguistic demography requires that the interpretation of this figure in a somewhat different manner, i.e., that it furnishes evidence about events that occurred in a more distant past.[16]

In fact, the analysis of language shift based on census-type data is similar to the demographic analysis of trends in birthrates. Since very few births are recorded for women over 45 years of age, the average number of children born by 45–49-year-old women can be compared with the average number born to 50–54-year-old women, to 55–59-year-old women, etc. If the birthrate decreases over time, then the 45–49 year-olds should have smaller average family size than the 50–54 year-olds, who in turn may be expected to have a smaller family size than the 55–59 year-olds . . .

Since language shift among the native born appears to stop when minority language children leave the family home and make independent life decisions on a wide variety of matters, the average rate of the adoption of English for 20–24 year-olds can be compared with that of 25–29 year-olds, whose rate can in turn be compared with that of 30–34 year-olds, and so forth – in the same manner as trends in birthrates can be interpreted from census data. As Figure 4 clearly shows, the rate of adoption of English for people aged 70 and over in 1976 was approximately 27%. Since these people were most likely in their twenties during the

16 See Veltman (1983, pp. 20–26; or 1988, Chapter 6) for a fuller treatment of the methodological aspects of this approach.

1920s, the 27% figure testifies to the attractiveness of the English language at that time, or, alternatively, it measures the need felt by these members of the Spanish minority language group to become English-speaking when they were young.

On the other hand, approximately 45% of the 50–59 year-olds adopted English as their principal language of use; these people came to maturity during the 1940s. Similarly, approximately 56% of the 20–29 year-olds have made English their primary language; these people were just completing the language shift process during the 1970s. Already, however, the 10–14 and 15–19 year-olds adopted English at rates exceeding those of the 20–29 year-olds and exceeding 60%.

All these data suggest that younger, native-born members of the Spanish language group are more likely to adopt English today than their older peers did when they were young. In fact, the ability of Hispanics to maintain the dominant use of Spanish has receded significantly as time has gone on; the closer ones to 1976, the greater the rates of language shift observed. The power of the English language to attract new primary users from among native-born speakers of Spanish is stronger than ever and appears to be continually increasing. One may readily assume, without too much danger, that some 70% of those aged 10–14 and 4–9 in 1976 have by now adopted English and that the rates should continue to rise as the twenty-first century approaches.

This finding is not unusual within the field of linguistic demography. Rising rates of language shift have also been documented for Franco-Americans, both nationally and in the New England and Louisiana areas (Veltman, 1983, 1987), among Hispanics in all areas of the United States for which data were available (Veltman, 1983, 1989), and among English- and French-speaking minorities in both English Canada and Quebec (Castonguay, 1976; Lachapelle & Henripin, 1980). In short, it appears that everywhere in North America, minority language groups have been subjected to increasingly greater pressures to adopt the language of the dominant group, a finding I attribute to greater urbanization; universal mass education; the development of mass communications, including radio, television, and multimedia industries; and greater regional integration into the national economy, among other factors.

DEMOGRAPHIC MODELING OF THE LANGUAGE SHIFT PROCESS

The information presented in the preceding sections of this chapter allows a simulation of the transformations that occur when a typical group of Spanish language immigrants arrives in the United States (Veltman, 1989). Table 1 presents the language characteristics of the immigrant group itself after 20 years' residence in the United States, together

TABLE I. MOTHER TONGUE AND LANGUAGE PRACTICE OF SPANISH-LANGUAGE
IMMIGRANTS, THEIR CHILDREN, AND THEIR GRANDCHILDREN, UNITED STATES,
1976 (%)

Language characteristic	Immigrants	Their children	Their grandchildren
Spanish mother tongue			
Spanish only	22	2	0
Spanish-dominant bilingual	44	20	4
English-dominant bilingual	26	34	16
English only	8	14	5
Subtotal	100	70	25
English mother tongue			
English-dominant bilingual	0	5	10
English only	0	25	65
Subtotal	0	30	75
Summary statistics			
Spanish only	22	2	0
Spanish-dominant bilingual	44	20	4
Total, English-dominant bilingual	26	39	26
Total, English only	8	39	70

Source: Veltman (1988, 1989).

with those of their children and their grandchildren when they reach
their twenty-fifth birthdays.

As the table readily shows, two thirds of the original immigrant
group continue to speak Spanish as their primary, preferred language;
however, only 22% do not speak English on a regular basis. Among
those who make English their preferred language, most continue to use
Spanish on a regular basis. Only 8% of the original immigrants have
abandoned Spanish as a frequently spoken language.

Given the observed patterns of language shift among the immigrant
generation, 30% of their native-born children, most of whom will not
speak Spanish on a regular basis as adults will have English for a first
language. Only 2% of the native-born children of the original immigrant group will remain essentially monolingual in Spanish, and only
22% will speak Spanish as their preferred, primary language. As can be
seen from the summary statistics in the lower panel of Table 1, 39% of
the first generation of native-born children will be effectively monolingual in English. Another equally important group will speak English as
their primary language but will maintain Spanish as a second language.

As for the grandchildren of the original immigrant group, only 25%

may be expected to have Spanish for a first language. All speak English on a regular basis, and only 4% speak Spanish as their primary, preferred language. Should all such people intermarry, which is highly unlikely, 4% of the third generation born on American soil would have Spanish for their mother tongue. According to the summary statistics, fully 70% of the grandchildren of the original immigrant group will be monolingual in English, whereas 26% will normally speak English but continue to use Spanish as a second language.

This model of the transformation of the Spanish language group over time provides a clear idea of the extent to which it is possible to maintain a minority language in the United States at the end of the twentieth century; it also provides a good impression of the extent to which minority languages are abandoned in the normal course of events. After two native-born generations, Spanish is to all intents and purposes lost as a primary language and is only maintained by a minority as a second language, a language their children will likely not learn or likely not maintain. The observed patterns of language shift are, therefore, consistent with a two- to three-generational model of language shift, depending on how the generations are defined and counted. Furthermore, since the trend toward greater language shift and lower language maintenance appears to be rising, it is likely that none of the grandchildren of the original immigrants, rather than 4%, will maintain Spanish as their principal language at the beginning of the twentieth century.

Language shift among immigrants in other minority language groups

Whether the observed patterns of language shift for Hispanics applies equally well to other minority language groups remains to be seen, however. I approach this topic by presenting data from the SIE that indicate the extent of both the adoption of English and the abandonment of the minority language as a function of the period during which members of the minority language group arrived in the United States. Unfortunately, sample sizes do not permit refining the analysis by including data for age at time of arrival, a factor that has been found to be important among Spanish language immigrants.[17]

In addition, I note that the data presented in Table 2 refer to persons aged 14 and over in 1976; consequently, the language shift of those

---

17 For example, most members of the French, German, Italian, Polish, and Yiddish language groups are native born and are themselves relatively elderly; there are few immigrants and few children of minority mother tongue present in the SIE sample. On the other hand, sample sizes tend to be small for the newer immigrant groups; often there are very few children who were born in the United States and virtually no older people.

children who arrived during the late 1960s and the 1970s but who have not yet attained 14 years of age is excluded from analysis. Since their mobility is likely to be extensive, the data presented in Table 2 are, therefore, rather conservative estimates of the mobility actually characterizing these most recent groups of immigrants.[18] Given the fact that the regular use of English is universal in the non-Spanish language groups present in the SIE, my discussion is limited to the adoption of English and the abandonment of minority languages.

First, Table 2 permits a direct comparison of the rates of the adoption of English and the abandonment of minority languages by the Spanish and non-Spanish immigrant groups having lived in the United States for varying amounts of time. The differences observed are important. Whereas only 12.2% of the most recently arrived Spanish language immigrants adopted the English language, 43.5% of the non-Spanish language immigrants who arrived during the 1970s did so; among immigrants having arrived during the 1960s, the rate is 60.4% in the non-Spanish group as opposed to 29.1%; for immigrants having arrived prior to 1960, the rate is 80.1% as opposed to 41.9% for the Spanish language group. If Hispanic rates of language shift to English are considered high and rising, then the overall rate of language shift for the non-Hispanic groups taken as a whole may be considered extremely high. There is, therefore, some foundation to the prevalent theory that Hispanics are better able to maintain their language than are other minority language groups.

Second, Table 2 shows that no other group consistently rivals the Spanish language group in its ability to maintain the predominant use of a minority language. Only immigrants of Chinese-language origins appear to be somewhat more successful than most other groups in maintaining the predominant use of the minority language in all three time periods examined.[19] Even they, however, are not as likely as Spanish language immigrants to speak their mother tongue as their principal language of daily use.

Third, with respect to the abandonment of minority languages, several groups seem to be characterized by extremely low rates of abandonment for the most recent time periods; however, no group except the Spanish language group has overall rates of abandonment under 10%. On the average, among immigrants having arrived prior to 1960, 43.7% of those in the non-Spanish minority language groups have

18 See Veltman (1983, pp. 48–58) for a fuller discussion of language shift among the foreign born.
19 Although immigrants of Portuguese mother tongue who arrived during the 1960s and 1970s showed very low rates of adoption of English, those who have resided in the United States for a much longer period have adopted English at rates similar to those observed in other, non-Spanish minority language groups.

TABLE 2. ADOPTION OF ENGLISH AND ABANDONMENT OF MINORITY LANGUAGES, BY PERIOD OF ARRIVAL IN THE UNITED STATES, 1976 (%)

Language group	Adopted English			Abandoned minority language		
	Arrived in 1970s	Arrived in 1960s	Arrived before 1960	Arrived in 1970s	Arrived in 1960s	Arrived before 1960
Arabic	60.5	68.7	88.7	4.1	5.2	27.3
Chinese	26.3	34.6	43.4	4.1	3.4	11.5
Filipino	51.9	71.5	69.7	8.9	27.1	14.7
French	54.7	59.2	85.7	10.5	15.9	48.2
German	71.3	89.2	94.0	31.9	37.7	52.8
Greek	27.0	29.7	64.2	0.9	1.0	18.5
Italian	34.3	53.4	71.9	1.8	8.3	35.5
Japanese	43.6	78.8	50.0	15.9	24.3	23.0
Korean	38.3	69.3	86.0	8.2	33.2	82.7
Polish	28.8	47.4	69.0	7.3	4.8	31.9
Portuguese	15.8	29.9	64.3	2.7	3.1	27.3
Russian	—	87.0	88.1	—	33.8	66.5
Scandinavian	59.5	99.8	96.1	18.2	31.8	72.3
Vietnamese	30.8	100.0	—	7.6	2.3	—
Yiddish	—	91.9	91.9	—	0.0	62.4
All others	54.6	66.0	78.5	14.0	17.7	42.1
All non-Spanish	43.5	60.4	80.1	9.2	16.1	43.7
Spanish	12.2	29.1	41.9	0.4	2.9	6.5

Source: U.S. Bureau of the Census (1976).

TABLE 3. ADOPTION OF ENGLISH AND ABANDONMENT
OF MINORITY LANGUAGES, NATIVE-BORN PERSONS AGED
14 AND OVER, UNITED STATES, 1976 (%)

Language group	Adopted English	Abandoned mother tongue
Arabic	97.7	70.0
Chinese	90.0	29.3
Filipino	97.0	67.9
French	87.0	54.3
German	96.4	85.4
Greek	97.5	48.2
Italian	98.6	75.4
Japanese	90.3	54.9
Polish	97.7	73.4
Portuguese	96.5	59.9
Russian	99.0	77.2
Scandinavian	99.6	87.7
Yiddish	96.7	79.1
All others	93.1	71.0
All non-Spanish	94.3	71.5
Spanish	64.8	13.8

Source: U.S. Bureau of the Census (1976).

abandoned the frequent use of their mother tongue, as opposed to only 6.5% for the Spanish language immigrants who arrived during the same time period.

The data presented in Table 2 lead to the conclusion that, although some groups undergo more rapid integration into the English language group or abandon more readily the use of the immigrant language, no individual minority language group presents a pattern of language shift that is more conductive to the preservation of the mother tongue than that already observed for Spanish language immigrants.

Language shift among native-born members of non-Spanish language minorities

If language shift is both extensive and rapid among non-Hispanic immigrants, their native-born children undergo rates of language shift that I would classify as epidemic. Table 3 shows that the rate of adoption of English is generally over 90% in the non-Spanish minority language groups, compared with only 64.8% in the Spanish language group.[20] Further, in the non-Hispanic minority language groups, the mother

20 The data continue to refer to persons aged 14 or over at the time of the study.

tongue is abandoned by 71.5% of the native-born population as a frequently used language; in all groups except for the Chinese and Greeks,
the native born are more likely to abandon their mother tongue than to
retain it as a frequently spoken, second language. The rate of abandonment of the mother tongue is, however, substantially higher among
speakers of Chinese (29.3%) and Greek (48.2%) than among those of
Spanish mother tongue (13.8%). No other minority language group is,
therefore, able to retain such a large proportion of the native born either as principal speakers or as second language users of a minority language as is the Spanish language group.

It is, therefore, abundantly clear that all minority language groups
undergo more rapid integration into the English-speaking population
than does the Spanish language group, both in the immigrant generation and among the native born. Consequently, the model of language
shift presented in Table 1 for the Spanish language group may be viewed
as universally applicable to all minority language groups, that is, as
defining the maximum length of time that a minority language is likely
to survive in the United States. In fact, the data presented in this section
make it abundantly clear that no non-Spanish minority language will
endure for such a long time period; indeed, most grandparents in all
groups will not be able to communicate with their grandchildren in any
language other than English.

Corroborating evidence of the extent of language shift from the 1990 U.S. census

Methodological considerations

In this section, I look at fragmentary information derived from the 1990
U.S. census with respect to the language shift patterns of immigrant
groups. As I have already observed, decennial census questionnaires do
not seek information on the mother tongue of individuals. Some other
fundamental characteristic therefore must be found against which to
compare current language practice. I have resolved this issue by examining the language characteristics of individuals within specific ancestry
groups,[21] since this procedure permits the analyst to ascertain the presence of English monolingualism, i.e., when member's of the group declared that they spoke no language other than English at home.[22]

21 Data were obtained from the 5% Public Use Microdata Sample via the Data Extrac-
tion Service of the U.S. Bureau of the Census. Totals for ancestry groups in Table 4
differ from those published by the Bureau of the Census because I did not search for
persons declaring multiple origins.
22 The data were obtained using three questions: "Does this person speak a language
other than English at home?" If the answer was affirmative, the respondent was then

Since the census made no effort to determine the relative dominance of the English language, there is no way of knowing how many of the people who reported that they spoke English very well had in fact made English their primary, preferred language. It should, however, be clear to everyone that people do not come to speak English very well without engaging in extensive conversations with English-speaking people. There is, therefore, a high probability that people who speak English very well have adopted English as their personal, preferred language.[23] This is less likely to be the case for those who report that they speak English well; such people are more likely to retain their mother tongues either as a primary language or a regularly used second language. Most likely, people who do not have good English skills normally speak their mother tongues and do not use English extensively, if at all.

This use of 1990 census data is clearly satisfactory for examining the linguistic characteristics of the foreign born, since one can safely assume that, in most cases, the foreign born have a minority language for their mother tongue. Census data are less satisfactory for the examination of the language shift patterns of the native born, unless one can presume that nearly all of the native born are the children of immigrants. Although this is undoubtedly the case for a good many of the groups I examine, it is clearly not so for people of Japanese, Mexican, or other Hispanic ancestries, the vast majority of whom were born in the United States. In such cases, the extent of English monolingualism is the cumulative result of the language shift of more than one generation, which renders interpretation of the data somewhat more difficult.

Before proceding to the presentation of results, I note that the U.S. Bureau of the Census has published data from the 1990 census that differ from the data I have assembled. First, ancestry data published by the Bureau of the Census normally include people declaring a given origin either as their first ethnic ancestry or as their second. For example, the census has indicated that some 22.4 million Americans reported either a primary or a secondary Hispanic origin. However, only 19.2 million Americans claimed Hispanic origin as a first origin. Although a significant number of persons of Afro-American, English, Irish, Italian, French, German, and other origins also claimed a secondary Hispanic origin, it is clear that these people are not members of the Hispanic group in the same way as are people who claim Puerto Rican or Cuban origin, for example. If these claims of mixed origin are to be taken at

---

asked, "What is that language?" and "How well does this person speak English?" Four response categories were provided: "Very well," "Well," "Not very well," and "Not at all."

23 Cross-tabulations from the SIE comparing the relationship between the four language shift categories and the ability to speak English tend to support this line of thought.

face value, they indicate that some ethnic intermarriage has occurred in the past between Hispanics and non-Hispanics, the Hispanics having with few exceptions abandoned the use of Spanish, if indeed that they still spoke it at the time of such intermarriages.

Similarly, census reports of the number of people speaking a minority language at home appear to be somewhat exaggerated. For example, 428,000 people reportedly spoke Japanese at home; however, only 340,000 are of Japanese ancestry.[24] These data suggest that many of those declaring that they spoke Japanese at home likely did not do so. Since such persons are not of Japanese origin, they should be excluded when considering the linguistic characteristics of the Japanese minority group.

Similarly, too, only 13.6 million of the 17.3 million speakers of Spanish aged 5 and over came from Hispanic ancestry groups. An additional 150,000 Spanish speakers were found among those who declared a second (Hispanic) ancestry. This leaves some 3.5 million Americans with no Hispanic ancestry who – probably erroneously – reported speaking Spanish at home. My analysis is, consequently, not based on language groups but restricted to the principal ethnic ancestry groups from which minority languages have come and may continue to be frequently used.

Linguistic characteristics of selected minority groups

IMMIGRANTS

Table 4 is divided into two panels: The upper half presents the linguistic characteristics of Asian immigrants in the United States, and the bottom half presents those of Hispanic ancestry groups.[25] Within Asian and Hispanic categories, the data are ordered by the percentage of all immigrants aged 5 and over in 1990 who arrived during the 1980s. The total foreign-born presence in each ancestry group is presented in the last col-

24 Some 39,000 declared European ancestry, 14,000 declared Afro-American and "American" ancestry, 18,000 did not declare their ancestry, and the remainder belonged to smaller non-European, non-American groups.
25 People claiming Latin American, Spanish (Spaniard), and Other Hispanic ancestry appear in fact to be offshoots of the mainline national origin groups. Among 'Latin Americans' 4.8% were born in Puerto Rico, 25.4% in Central American countries, and 6.5% in South American countries. Only 8.9% of persons in the Spaniard ancestry group (all Spanish from Spain's regional and national origin groups) were born in Spain as opposed to 16.6% in Cuba, 5% in Central America, and 5.2% in South America. As for other Hispanics, 39.5% declared Hispana or Hispano origin as opposed to 60.5% of Spanish origin; this latter category presumably includes the California, Tejano, Tejana, Nuevo Mexicano, and Spanish American categories, which are not separately identified in the Public Use Microdata Sample. Although most were born in the United States (73.4%), 5.9% were born in Puerto Rico, 10.2% in Central America (mostly Mexico), 3.5% in Cuba, and 2.8% in South America.

84

TABLE 4. SELECTED CHARACTERISTICS OF THE FOREIGN BORN IN SELECTED ANCESTRY GROUPS, UNITED STATES, PERSONS AGED 5 AND OVER, 1990

Principal ancestry group	Arrived in the 1980s (%)	Period of immigration (%)					Are English monolingual (%)	Speak English well (%)	Total with good English skills (%)	Total immigrant population	
		1986–1990	1981–1985	1975–1979	1970–1974	<1970				No.	%
Cambodian	87.7	27.4	60.3	11.0	0.1	1.2	2.5	55.2	57.7	107,816	88.4
Laotian	78.4	27.0	51.5	20.8	0.6	0.2	2.0	58.0	60.1	116,197	88.6
Hmong	73.5	38.8	34.7	26.0	0.4	0.1	2.6	49.9	52.5	50,091	77.3
Chinese	59.8	31.5	28.3	18.0	10.6	11.5	5.2	56.9	62.1	1,128,764	74.3
Vietnamian	59.2	24.2	35.0	35.2	4.3	1.3	4.8	66.5	71.4	465,999	89.0
Asian Indian	58.7	32.7	26.0	17.3	15.0	9.0	15.2	76.0	91.2	514,250	81.4
Korean	55.1	28.8	26.3	22.2	15.2	7.5	16.2	56.2	72.5	613,175	84.8
Japanese	49.0	40.2	8.8	6.8	9.7	34.5	20.3	57.2	77.5	298,786	35.1
Filipino	47.6	25.2	22.4	17.7	16.3	18.3	14.3	78.9	93.2	814,374	66.1
Thai	40.4	21.2	19.2	23.2	26.3	10.2	17.7	67.7	85.4	76,548	78.9
Central American	70.1	37.9	32.2	13.0	7.4	9.5	4.7	52.4	57.1	870,996	86.5
Latin American	55.5	25.2	30.3	11.6	10.3	22.6	9.2	58.3	67.5	15,730	44.3
Dominicans	52.6	29.0	23.6	14.4	12.6	20.4	4.2	50.5	54.7	336,201	77.1
South American	51.6	28.4	23.2	13.5	13.5	21.4	6.1	63.5	69.6	631,084	80.4
Mexican	48.0	27.3	20.7	18.4	13.8	19.8	4.2	47.6	51.8	3,949,580	39.9
Other Hispanic	40.4	21.2	19.2	12.1	11.9	35.6	8.9	62.8	71.7	695,520	28.9
Puerto Rican	29.8	17.2	12.6	9.2	9.4	51.6	5.6	70.1	75.7	806,261	49.8
Spaniard	28.5	14.3	14.2	8.2	13.0	50.3	6.4	63.7	70.1	146,452	48.9
Cuban	27.2	6.6	20.6	3.9	15.4	53.5	4.3	55.8	60.1	553,462	73.5
All Hispanic groups	46.6	25.4	21.2	14.6	12.5	26.3	5.0	54.0	59.0	8,005,286	46.4

Source: U.S. Bureau of the Census (1990).

umn, which reveals that only the Japanese are predominantly native born among the Asian groups. Roughly two thirds to nine tenths of people in all other Asian groups were foreign born, indicating the recency of arrival of nearly all Asian groups. Further, more than 40% of the immigrants in all Asian groups arrived during the 10-year period preceding the 1990 census, ranging from a low of 40.4% among Thai ancestry immigrants to more than 70% among the Hmong, Laotian, and Cambodian groups.

Table 4 reveals that, in the Asian ancestry groups, the percentage of immigrants who reportedly no longer spoke a language other than English tends to rise as the percentage of those who arrived in the 1980s declines. Rates of English monolingualism are exceedingly low among the Cambodian, Laotian, and Hmong ancestry groups, in which nearly all immigrants arrived after 1975. Similarly, the total percentage having good English language skills, i.e., speaking only English at home or, among those who continue to use their mother tongue at home, speaking English either well or very well varies from a low of 52.5% in the Hmong group to 60.1% in the Laotian group. These data, though not absolutely conclusive, lead to the inference that English has already made serious inroads in these three groups. The fact that such recent arrivals have ceased to speak their mother tongue is already telling, as is the fact that such important majorities already speak English so well. Note also that the linguistic situation is relatively similar among immigrants of Chinese and Vietnamese ancestry, although the rate of English monolingualism already hovers around 5%.

In the remaining five groups (Asian Indian,[26] Korean, Japanese, Filipino, and Thai), English monolingualism varies from a low of 14.3% among Filipino immigrants to 20.3% among the Japanese, and the ability to speak English with some ease ranges from a low of 72.5% among Korean immigrants to 93.2% among persons of Filipino ancestry. These data lead to the conclusion that the adoption of English has been extremely rapid in these five groups, even though the percentage of very recent immigrants tends to be rather high.

As is evident from the first column in Table 4, no Hispanic group is as recently arrived as the Cambodian, Laotian, and Hmong ancestry groups. Approximately three fourths or more of the people in the Cuban, Dominican, South American, and Central American national origin groups were foreign born. However, only 27.2% of the Cuban immigrants arrived during the 1980s, as opposed to a majority of immigrants in the three other groups. People in the Other Hispanic ancestry groups are the least likely to have been born abroad, although 40.4% of the foreign born arrived during the 1980s. Although approximately half

---

26 Includes immigrants of Pakistani and Bengladeshi origins.

of Puerto Ricans were born abroad, the majority arrived in the United States prior to the 1970s. Most Mexican-Americans are native born, but nearly half of all immigrants arrived in the 10-year period prior to the census. On the whole, then, the Hispanic ancestry groups tend to have arrived in the United States at a somewhat earlier time than did most of the Asian ancestry groups.

In spite of their relatively longer period of residence in the United States, the extent of English monolingualism tends to hover around 5% in most Hispanic ancestry groups, attaining 8.9% among the Other Hispanic group and 9.2% among those claiming Latin American ancestry. These figures remain somewhat lower than those observed in the Asian groups, in which the composition in terms of time of arrival is relatively comparable. Similarly, the percentage of immigrants having good English language skills tends to be lower than that observed for most Asian groups. For example, only 60.1% of the immigrants of Cuban ancestry have good English language skills although more than half of them arrived prior to 1970. Again, 75.7% of foreign-born Puerto Ricans had good English language skills, a figure substantially below that for persons of Filipino, Japanese, or Thai ancestry, even though the latter were much more likely to have arrived in the United States recently.

Nevertheless, the census data confirm the SIE findings: Even in the immigrant generation, some Hispanics apparently abandon the use of Spanish in favor of English. Similarly, census data tend to confirm the proposition that language shift to English occurs very rapidly in immigrant groups and more rapidly in the non-Hispanic groups than in the Hispanic groups as a whole. Even the most recently arrived groups are characterized by patterns of language use that tend to suggest that the adoption of English is well under way.

Further, the same forces that structure the linguistic integration of Hispanic immigrants are observable in 1990 census data for both Asian and Hispanic groups, namely, that younger immigrants undergo more profound integration into the English language group than do older ones.[27] It is, therefore, highly probable that some of the younger immigrants who speak English very well have already made that language their principal language of use.

THE NATIVE BORN

Table 5 presents the linguistic characteristics of the native born of various ancestry groups ranked by the percentage of each group that was native born. As mentioned, the greater the percentage of the native

---

27 The presentation of time-of-arrival and length-of-residence data is not possible given the limited objectives and the space available here.

TABLE 5. SELECTED CHARACTERISTICS OF THE NATIVE BORN IN SELECTED
ANCESTRY GROUPS, UNITED STATES, PERSONS AGED 5 AND OVER, 1990

Principal ancestry group	Native born (%)	Are English monolingual (%)	Speak English well (%)	Total with good English skills (%)	Native born population
Japanese	64.9	79.7	12.5	92.2	551,367
Chinese	30.2	50.4	35.7	86.1	390,032
Filipino	29.0	81.8	13.8	95.7	416,790
Asian Indian	24.4	51.3	39.6	90.9	119,095
Hmong	22.7	2.8	21.6	21.6	14,708
Thai	21.2	61.2	27.8	89.0	20,469
Korean	15.2	51.7	34.6	86.3	109,518
Vietnamian	12.4	21.5	43.8	65.3	57,784
Cambodian	11.6	12.7	32.2	44.8	14,094
Laotian	11.4	6.1	37.6	37.6	14,938
Other Hispanic	71.1	49.1	47.2	96.3	1,714,962
Mexican	60.1	32.7	61.3	94.0	5,948,133
Latin American	55.7	31.6	60.9	92.5	19,804
Spaniard	51.1	52.5	44.9	97.4	153,290
Puerto Rican	50.2	27.3	67.9	95.2	814,262
Cuban	26.5	26.2	70.9	97.1	199,672
Dominicans	22.9	13.2	78.8	92.0	99,829
South American	19.6	28.1	68.1	96.2	154,051
Central American	13.5	26.2	65.1	91.3	135,374
All Hispanic groups	58.6	35.1	59.6	94.6	9,239,377

Source: U.S. Bureau of the Census (1990).

born, the more likely that the language patterns observed represent the cumulative effects of movement to English over two or more native-born generations. For example, the community of Japanese origin was sufficiently large that it was viewed as a potential threat during World War II. Many members of the current group of the native born of Japanese ancestry are likely to be the children and grandchildren of those interned at that time. If the grandparents adopted English, it follows that both their children and grandchildren would be English speaking, i.e., of English mother tongue and most likely monolingual in English. That nearly 80% of the people of Japanese ancestry are English monolinguals is therefore not surprising. Similarly, since more than 50% of the people in five Hispanic groups were native born, the levels of English monolingualism observed can likely be attributed at least partly to the adoption of English by successive generations.

Briefly, Table 5 shows that English monolingualism was a characteristic feature of the native-born generation. More than 25% of the native-born people in each Hispanic ancestry group except Dominicans did not speak Spanish at home; similarly, more than 90% of the people in each group had good English skills. Among the Asian groups, natives of Cambodian, Hmong, and Laotian ancestry were less likely to be English monolinguals; less than half of the people had good English skills. Natives of Vietnamese origin were also somewhat less integrated into the English language group than were those of Japanese, Chinese, Filipino, Asian Indian, Thai, or Korean ancestry. More than half of the natives in each of these latter groups did not speak a minority language at home, and at least 85% had good English language skills. These figures are particularly striking since most of the native born in these groups are the children of relatively recent immigrants, confirming once again the rapidity with which immigrant groups become English speaking in the United States.

With respect to the four groups showing the lowest levels of English monolingualism, most of the native-born Dominicans still lived in the parental home, a situation that is not conducive to exclusive use of English. In fact, three fourths were under 19 years of age in 1990. This situation was even more prevalent among natives of Cambodian, Hmong, and Laotian ancestry, of whom 82–83% were aged 5–9; children under 15 years of age accounted for no fewer than 95% of the native born.[28] Clearly, under these circumstances the disappearance of the minority language is unlikely; similarly, these young children had not had time to develop the excellent English language skills that are required for an eventual move toward English monolingualism. Nonetheless, the presence of English monolingualism among the native born in these three groups may be expected to increase rapidly as these children move out of the parental home and as the maturing youngest immigrants begin to bear English-speaking children.

Conclusion

Although some readers think that the world has dramatically changed since 1976, the principal forces driving language shift to English are unlikely to have diminished in strength.[29] The data presented in the last part of this chapter from the 1990 census furnish no indication that nei-

28 These figures exclude children aged 0–4 years since no language data are available for them. In all three Asian groups, these children account for half of the entire native-born population.

29 The conditions that seem most related to the preservation of the mother tongue include the establishment of tightly knit, self-sufficient, and, probably, religious-based communities similar to those of the Hassidim or the Amish. By definition, most immigrants do not seek the level of isolation required to establish such communities.

ther the immigrant generation nor the native born among the newer Asian and Hispanic groups are successfully maintaining their respective minority languages. In fact, given the rapidity of the movement to English and the presence of English monolinguals in all groups, one would have to conclude that the maintenance of the minority language does not appear to be an important priority for many members of the newer immigrant groups.

It should also be remembered that extremely important minority language groups that were highly concentrated in specific regions of the country – the French, German, Italian, Polish, and Yiddish, to name but the largest – were unable to resist the integration of their members into the English language majority, not even in rural areas where they were clearly dominant, controlled their own schools, and were characterized by what today we would call *institutional completeness*.[30] It would seem highly unlikely that members of the newer immigrant groups, almost all of whom seek to live in major metropolitan areas, could resist the pressures leading to the adoption of English. If the Spanish language group has become increasingly unable to do so, as Table 1 shows, it would seem most unlikely that other groups might do significantly better, as observed in the analyses of Tables 2–5. The pressures on minority language groups to adopt English appear to be rising rather than relenting as the twenty-first century approaches.

This leads to two major types of conclusions. First, at the political level, there is no evidence that continued immigration poses any threat to the linguistic integrity of the United States. The learning of English and its adoption as a personal, preferred language occur very rapidly in immigrant groups and even more rapidly among the children of immigrants. Those who dread the rise of autonomous little Quebecs within the United States or the balkanization of the country clearly have no understanding of the linguistic and political situation prevailing in other parts of the world.[31] The data examined in this chapter provide no basis for this fear.

From the educational perspective, teaching minority language children in English no doubt imposes a greater burden on teachers than would a classroom full of English-speaking children. This being said, the data show extreme willingness on the part of new immigrants, par-

---

30 See Fishman (1966) for what continues to be the best overall portrait of the largest immigrant groups that came to the United States prior to World War II.

31 In Quebec, for example, persons of French mother tongue compose nearly 85% of the population. Their net rate of loss to English is entirely compensated by the integration of third-language immigrants, leading to an essentially stable demographic situation. In addition, provinces enjoy greater powers than do U.S. states, such that the French-speaking province has greater autonomy to pursue a wider range of objectives.

ticularly those in their prime years of schooling, not only to learn English rapidly but also to make it their principal language of communication. Although this willingness does not enable their parents to communicate easily with teachers and administrators or to help their children with homework, it does represent a very positive basis for integration into the English language group. While helping them move in this direction, it is important that teachers and administrators allow new immigrants the time necessary to master basic English language skills, after which the vast majority of younger immigrants will begin the process of adopting English as their principal, preferred language of use.

Suggestions for further reading

Fishman, J. (1966). *Language loyalty in the United States*. The Hague: Mouton.

> A seminal work in the area of language shift, this book makes use of data from the 1940 U.S. census, supplemented by the analysis of a series of indirect indicators of language retention and loss. Particular attention was paid to the presence of minority language media, educational institutions, parishes, social organizations, and other factors.

Gordon, M. (1964). *Assimilation in American life: The role of race, religion and national origins*. New York: Oxford University Press.

> This book provides an important reminder that the adoption of the English language by members of minority language groups is simply a first step in the process of integration into U.S. society. A variety of indicators of integration are discussed, together with a summary analysis of the position of different groups in U.S. society.

Veltman, C. (1983). *Language shift in the United States*. Berlin: Mouton.

> Following a discussion of methodological issues in the study of language shift, the first half of this book presents the language shift characteristics of people in the fifteen largest minority language groups as derived from the 1976 Survey of Income and Education. The Spanish language group is further subdivided into Mexican, Cuban, Puerto Rican, and Other Hispanic origin groups. Data are presented separately for native-born adults and for foreign-born adults who arrived before 1960, during the 1960s, or during the 1970–1976 period. Trend analysis indicates that rates of language shift in minority language groups had risen steadily over the preceding 40 years, most notably in the Spanish language group. Two other chapters document language shift among children and

teenagers in these same minority language groups, the latter chapter drawing heavily on data from the 1980 High School and Beyond Survey. The remainder of the book is dedicated to the analysis of the impact of learning and adopting English on educational and occupational achievements.

Veltman, C. (1988). *The future of the Spanish language in the United States*. Washington, DC: Hispanic Policy Development Project.

This book presents a complete demographic model of the future of the Spanish language group, assuming that future rates of language shift are similar to those developed from the 1976 Survey of Income and Education. The language shift patterns of native-born children are first examined, then those of a typical group of Spanish-speaking immigrants. Rates of intergenerational language loss are also developed. These rates are then integrated into a complete population model, including estimated birth and mortality rates and various levels of international migration.

Veltman, C. (1991). Theory and method in the study of language shift. In J. Dow (Ed.), *Language and ethnicity,* (pp. 145–168). Amsterdam: John Benjamins.

This article discusses the appropriate methodology to be used in the study of language retention and loss, including information drawn from Canadian and U.S. sources.

References

Breton, R. (1964). Institutional completeness of ethnic communities and the personal relations of immigrants. *American Journal of Sociology, 70,* 193–205.

Cardenas, R. (1980). Critique. In *The retention of minority languages in the United States* (pp. 47–48). Washington, DC: National Center for Education Statistics.

Castonguay, C. (1976). Les transferts linguistiques au foyer [Language transfer in the home]. *Recherches sociographiques, 18,* 431–450.

Conklin, N. F., & Lourie, M. A. (1983). *A host of tongues.* New York: Free Press.

Fishman, J. A., et al. (1966). *Language loyalty in the United States.* The Hague: Mouton.

Glazer, N. (1978). The process and problems of language maintenance: An integrative review. In M. A. Lourie and N. F. Conklin (Eds.), *A pluralistic nation: The language issue in the United States* (pp. 32–42). Rowley, MA: Neubury House.

Lachapelle, R., & Henripin, J. (1980). *La situation démolinguistique au Canada: Évolution passée et prospective* [The demolinguistic situation in Canada: Past, present and future]. Montréal, Canada: Institute for Research on Public Policy.

Molesky, J. (1988). Understanding the American linguistic mosaic. In S. McKay

& S. C. Wong, *Language diversity: Problem or resource?* (pp. 29–68). New York: Harper & Row.

U.S. Bureau of the Census. (1976). *Survey of income and education* [Computer file]. Washington, DC: Author.

U.S. Bureau of the Census. (1979). *Ancestry and language in the United States: November 1979.* (Current Population Reports, Special Studies, Series P-3, No. 116). Washington, DC: U.S. Government Printing Office.

U.S. Bureau of the Census. (1990). *1990 census of population: 5% public use microdata sample* [Computer file]. Washington, DC: Author.

U.S. Bureau of the Census. (1995). Population. In *Statistical abstract of the United States 1995.* Washington, DC: U.S. Government Printing Office. ⟨http:www.census.gov/prod/1/gen/95 statab/pop.pdf⟩

U.S. Bureau of the Census. (1997). Vital statistics. In *Statistical abstract of the United States 1997.* Washington, DC: U.S. Government Printing Office. ⟨http://www.census.gov/prod/3/97 pubs/97 statab/vitstat.pdf⟩.

Veltman, C. (1983). *Language shift in the United States.* The Hague: Mouton.

Veltman, C. (1987). *L'avenir du français aux États-Unis* [The future of French in the United States]. Québec, Canada: Conseil de la langue française.

Veltman, C. (1988). *The future of the Spanish language in the United States.* Washington, DC: Hispanic Policy Development Project.

Veltman, C. (1989). Croissance et anglicisation de la population hispano-américaine [The growth and anglicization of the Hispanic-American Population]. In P. Pupier and J. Woehrling (Eds.), *Langue et droit* [Language and law] (pp. 487–495). Montréal, Canada: Wilson & Lafleur.

II *New immigrants in the United States: History, language background, and community*

The chapters in Part II examine new immigrants in the United States. By using the term *new immigrants*, we mean to suggest not only that these immigrants are recent arrivals to the United States, but also that they differ significantly in their overall racial makeup from the immigrants arriving before 1965, being much more racially diverse and including far fewer immigrants from Europe. Clearly, many of the immigrant groups examined in this section have a long history in the United States (e.g., Chinese, Puerto Ricans, and Mexicans). Yet in some instances their reasons for immigration have changed, thus affecting the overall educational and economic background of the group. For example, whereas some groups initially immigrated to the United States as a result of colonization (e.g., Puerto Ricans and Filipinos) or labor importation (e.g., Chinese), many recent immigrants from such groups come today out of a motivation to attain better educational and economic opportunities. In other instances (e.g., Koreans and Asian Indians), despite a long history of immigration to the United States, it is only after 1965 that the group's numbers have grown dramatically. Finally, we also use the term new immigrant for groups that initially entered the United States as a result of the Vietnam War; the refugee aspect of these groups' experiences are examined in Chapters 7 and 8, on the Vietnamese and the Hmong, Khmer, and Laotian communities.

The chapters in this section all begin with an overview of the immigration history of the group in question, often delineating various phases of immigration. The existence of such phases demonstrates that the reasons for immigration and the type of immigrant who comes to the United States in any group can change significantly during the course of history. The chapters in this section also provide current demographic data on each immigrant group: overall educational and economic background, age, and settlement patterns. Finally, included in each chapter is information on the linguistic features of the group's mother tongue and salient features of the native culture as well as a description of how the use of English and the mother tongue has been influenced by the immigrants' bilingualism in the midst of an English-speaking environment. In general, the chapters illustrate the tremendous diversity that exists among new immigrants to the United States.

To begin, Chapters 3, 4, 5, and 6, on the Hispanic community, demonstrate the diversity between Spanish-speaking groups and within the groups themselves. In Chapter 3, Guadalupe Valdés emphasizes how the Mexican American community differs in terms of individual members' length of residence in the United States, educational level, class, and language ability in English and Spanish. In Chapter 4, Ana Celia Zentella draws on her research in the Puerto Rican community to demonstrate the differences in the language patterns found in the home environment of Puerto Ricans. Who speaks English and who speaks Spanish to whom differs from family to family, reflecting the influence of language shift on individual immigrant families. This difference in language use within the family, which is typical of many recent immigrant groups, clearly affects family dynamics. In Chapter 5, Ricardo Otheguy, Ofelia García, and Ana Roca identify the distinctive characteristics of Cuban Americans relative to other Hispanic groups in terms of immigration history, nativity, age, income, and language use. The authors argue that the process of *transculturation* has resulted in a unique pattern of bilingualism among Cuban Americans. Next, John Lipski, (Chapter 6) traces how the political turmoil in Central America during the 1980s resulted in new waves of immigrants coming to the United States not only from the privileged class, from which Central American immigrants traditionally had come, but also from the lower middle and lower working class. He outlines the immigration history, demographics, variety of Spanish spoken, and special educational needs of Salvadorans, Nicaraguans, and Guatemalans. Taken together, the four chapters clearly demonstrate that although Hispanic Americans have a common Spanish-speaking heritage, they differ greatly in their cultural identity and their experience in the United States, a fact that has tremendous implications for those second language educators who wish to meet the special cultural and language needs of their students.

Chapters 7, 8, 9, and 10, on six Asian American groups, depict an even more diverse community. Chuong Hoang Chung's chapter on the Vietnamese immigrants opens the discussion. After presenting a history of the various waves of Vietnamese refugee immigration from 1975 to the present, Chung emphasizes the special educational needs of Vietnamese Americans that arise from the relatively young age of the population and the different expectations students have regarding classroom behavior. Although the Hmong, Khmer, and ethnic Lao are often described as a singular community, M. G. López (Chapter 8) explores the diversity that exists among these groups in terms of their preimmigration experience and educational level; their settlement patterns in the United States, and their language use, maintenance, and learning in the United States. In keeping with the title of the chapter, "English Language Learners of Chinese Background: A Portrait of Diversity," in Chapter 9 Sau-ling C. Wong and M. G. López discuss the immigration of Chinese from Hong Kong, mainland China, Taiwan, and other Southeast Asian regions. They contend that whereas the pre-1965 Chinese community was fairly homogenous, the present-day Chinese community defies ready generalizations, differing in dialect background, culture, class, and educational level. In contrast, Pyong Gap Min (Chapter 10) points out that the Korean American community is quite homogenous. Sharing a language and culture, many Korean Americans settle in enclaves where they often establish small businesses. Although the homogeneity of the community helps its members maintain ethnic attachments, it presents special challenges in terms of English language learning. The four chapters on the Asian American community present a complex mosaic. Whereas the Vietnamese and Korean communities are fairly homogeneous in terms of language and culture, the Asian American community in general shares few characteristics, differing in culture, language, immigration history, settlement patterns, and most importantly English language needs.

The final three chapters of this section describe three communities that have grown significantly since 1965 – the Filipina/o, the Russian, and the Asian Indian communities. As Joan May T. Cordova points out in Chapter 11, whereas the Filipina/o community has a long history in the United States, from 1980 to 1990 the community increased by 80%. Like the Asian Indian community, Filipina/o Americans come from a linguistically diverse country in which English has an official role. Hence there is often a great deal of code switching in their daily language use, affecting the variety of English used in the Filipina/o community. The immigration of Russians to the United States is a relatively new phenomenon. As Eli Hinkel notes in Chapter 12, because of the nature of earlier Soviet-U.S. relations, many recent immigrants come with little knowledge of U.S. government institutions, culture, and social values, influencing their overall settlement and language learning. In general, the community is well educated and urbanized, having the second-highest levels of education and professional training among immigrant groups, superseded only by immigrants from India. In Chapter 13, Kamal K. Sridhar and S. N. Sridhar draw on their research in the New York Asian Indian community to demonstrate its linguistic and cultural diversity and the manner in which this diversity influences language use within the community. They emphasize the need for language educators to recognize that bilingualism or multilingualism is the norm in most of the world today, affecting the variety of English used in the community and the amount of code switching that occurs.

The chapters in Part II have several implications for second language educators. First, they highlight the importance of second language educators' being aware of the great diversity within and between new immigrant groups. Language learners will each undoubtedly be influenced by their cultural and linguistic background, yet each has a unique immigration, language, and educational history. Second, many of the chapters in this section emphasize the need for mother tongue maintenance as a basis for ethnic identity and a means for promoting communication among family and community members. This suggests the importance of second language educators' support for the development of bilingualism, in which new immigrants achieve full proficiency in English but not at the cost of losing ethnic and family ties. These chapters also clearly demonstrate the widespread use of code switching within immigrant communities – not as a sign of linguistic inadequacy but rather as an indication of a rich linguistic repertoire. This fact may lead second language educators to reflect on their own classroom policies regarding the use of the mother tongue. Finally, these chapters illustrate the fact that many immigrants come to the U.S. classroom with expectations regarding the role of the teacher and learner as well as learning methods. To the extent that their expectations do not match what happens in U.S. classrooms, the learners may be frustrated, resulting in setbacks in language learning. Hence, it is important for second language educators to be aware of differing classroom expectations and allow for a variety of learning styles and strategies. In sum, these chapters illustrate the complexity of teaching English language learners, particularly those within the new immigrant population, in which diversity on many levels is a central factor.

3 Bilingualism and language use among Mexican Americans

Guadalupe Valdés

Mexican Americans in the United States: An overview

Terminology and group Identification

The term *Mexican American* is used to refer to persons of Mexican ancestry who reside in the United States. Segments of this population, however, refer to themselves using a variety of other terms, including *Mexican, mexicano, Chicano, Latino, Hispanic,* and *Spanish American.* Moreover, some segments of this population (e.g., some original residents of northern New Mexico) may claim to have no Mexican (i.e., mixed Indian and Spanish or *mestizo*) ancestry. In this chapter, the term *Mexican American* includes all persons who are of Mexican ancestry and all persons of Spanish origin whose ancestors settled in Mexican-owned territories before 1846.[1]

The heterogeneity of Mexican Americans

Popular stereotypes of Mexican Americans invariably obscure the fact that no one list of qualities and characteristics can be applied to the many different kinds of individuals that the term can refer to. This population includes both recent immigrants and long-term residents; light- and dark-skinned people; educated and uneducated individuals; rural and urban residents; members of single-parent units, nuclear families, and extended families; Catholics and non-Catholics; working-class and middle-class persons; and monolingual Spanish speakers, bilingual speakers of English, and monolingual Spanish and monolingual English speakers. There are Mexican Americans residing in many different U.S. states and working as skilled laborers, university professors, janitors, and engineers; and there are Mexican Americans picking chili and cotton in the fields of the Southwest and enrolled in prestigious universities such as Stanford and Harvard.

---

1 I use the term *Hispanic* when giving population figures because it is used by the U.S. Bureau of the Census. Elsewhere, I use the term *Latino.*

Guadalupe Valdés

The Mexican-origin presence in the United States

The presence of Mexican-origin people in the United States began at a very early point in the history of the European settlement of North America. New Spain, that is, the territory that is now the five southwestern states of New Mexico, Colorado, Arizona, Texas, and California, was first settled during the seventeenth century (1610) and claimed in the name of the King of Spain. In 1821, when Mexico obtained its independence from Spain, the residents of New Spain became residents and citizens of the nation of Mexico.

The Mexican presence, then, predates the settlement of the five southwestern states by European American pioneer families who settled in the Mexican territories. According to a number of scholars who have examined the early history of the Mexican-origin presence in the United States (e.g., McWilliams, 1949; Moore & Pachon, 1985), in the 1820s, when European American settlers began their move westward, Mexican settlements extended over 2,000 miles along the northern border of what is now Mexico. Moore and Pachon (p. 18) estimate that there were approximately 5,000 Mexicans in Texas, 60,000 in New Mexico, 1,000 or fewer in Arizona, and 7,500 in California. In 1848, at the close of the war between Mexico and the United States that resulted in the ceding of all Mexican territories to the United States, the rights of Mexican citizens living in these territories were guaranteed by the Treaty of Guadalupe Hidalgo. Mexican-origin persons, then, unlike other minority groups in the United States, have come to occupy a subordinate position as a result of both the early military conquest of their territories by the United States and the relatively more recent process of immigration.

As might be expected, the presence of Mexican settlements along the border created an unusual situation in that so-called Mexican immigrants moved to an area that formerly belonged to Mexico. Because of these circumstances, Portes and Bach (1985) argue that, in studying early immigration from Mexico to the United States, some scholars confuse "actual population movements with the administrative enforcement of a political border" (p. 76). Portes and Bach point out that until the beginning of the twentieth century, labor flows simply drifted northward, and traffic across the border was commonplace. They further argue that the supposed upsurge of Mexican immigrants in 1910 simply reflects "the imposition of administrative controls on a preexisting inflow" (p. 77).

What appears to be generally clear is that both economic "push" and economic "pull" factors have played a role in the process of immigration. Mexican immigrants to the United States have been primarily what Portes and Rumbaut (1990) have termed *labor migrants* as opposed to *professional immigrants* or *entrepreneurial immigrants*. Political instability in Mexico and low wages have combined with labor demand and higher wages in the United States to attract large numbers of workers to the United States. During certain periods, American growers, the railroad industry, and the mining industry directly recruited labor in Mexico. During other periods, Mexicans have been blamed for domestic unemployment.

Examined over the twentieth century, then, immigration from Mexico to the United States has occurred in what Vernez and Ronfeldt (1991) have called three different phases. The first phase began in the early 1900s. By the 1920s, Mexican-origin individuals made up 11% of all legal immigrants. The second phase occurred after a temporary slowdown during the Depression in the 1930s and led to the importation of large numbers of contract agricultural workers, or *braceros*. Vernez and Ronfeldt estimate that by the end of this period more than 4.5 million Mexicans had come to the United States as temporary workers, a figure that exceeded the number of permanent legal residents eightfold. The third phase, ongoing in the late 1990s, began with the passage of the 1965 Immigration Reform Act, which placed the first ceiling on immigration from the Western Hemisphere. Until the 1970s, however, permanent Mexican legal immigration to the United States grew more rapidly than total legal immigration did. Vernez and Ronfeldt point out that after the 1976 amendment to the 1965 act, which established a quota of 20,000 persons – excluding immediate relatives of U.S. citizens – legal immigration from Mexico stabilized at a yearly average of 66,000. Vernez and Ronfeldt further argue that Mexican immigration has changed in character and that cyclical migration has given way to permanence. Table 1 presents figures on the Mexican-origin population in 1997.

Characteristics of the languages used by Mexican Americans: A description

Mexican American communities

Mexican Americans have settled in both rural and urban areas, among other Latino groups, among other minority groups, and even among

TABLE I. MEXICAN-ORIGIN AND HISPANIC POPULATION OF THE UNITED STATES, 1995

U.S. population	Hispanic-origin population	Mexican-origin population
259,753,000	26,646,000	17,090,000

Source: U.S. Bureau of the Census (1995).

mainstream European Americans. Indeed, in many areas of the country, even those with large numbers of Mexican Americans, there appear to be no neighborhoods or city sections that one would identify as Mexican American exclusively or predominantly. In those areas, then, one might not be able to speak of a Mexican American community; that is, a community primarily settled by Mexican-origin people who have clustered together in much the same way that other immigrant groups have done upon arriving in the United States. In other areas of the country, however, Mexican American communities are alive and well and are growing. In some cases they are made up exclusively of Mexican-origin people, and in other cases they are made up predominantly of Mexican Americans but include other Latinos as well. These Mexican-origin communities are found both in large cities and in small towns in many parts of the United States, and although there are differences among them, they are similar enough that one can generalize about their characteristics and about the use of language among the Mexican Americans who live there. The communities described here, then, are representative of many Mexican American communities, both large and small.

Mexican American bilinguals

Mexican American bilinguals are essentially natural or circumstantial bilinguals as opposed to elite or elective bilinguals. As circumstantial bilinguals, they have acquired their second language in a natural context by having to interact with monolingual and bilingual speakers of English in the work, school, or neighborhood domain. As might be expected, there are many different types of bilinguals in Mexican American communities. Some individuals are clearly Spanish dominant, whereas others are English dominant. Some individuals are biliterate whereas others read and write in only one of their languages. Some individuals are active bilinguals who speak both languages with some ease, whereas other bilinguals are passive in one of their languages and can understand but not speak their "weak" language.

So varied indeed are the different types of English-Spanish bilinguals found in Mexican American communities that it is impossible to conjecture about language strengths or weaknesses based on generation, age, schooling, period of residence in the United States, or any other such criteria. Many first-generation Mexican immigrants acquire English very rapidly, but many do not. Many third- and fourth-generation Mexican Americans are very fluent in Spanish, but many such Mexican Americans no longer even understand their original ethnic language.

Contrary to what is generally put forward by English-only advocates, the Mexican-origin population *is* learning English. Several scholars (e.g., Veltman, 1983, 1988; see also Chapter 2) have clearly established that present-day immigrants to the United States are acquiring English and shifting away from the use of their ethnic languages. In the case of Latinos, Solé (1990) demonstrated that ongoing language shift toward English is unequivocal. One third of the youngest Latinos, for example, have no skills in the ethnic language, and monolingualism in Spanish among Hispanics is weak, encompassing only 16.0% of Puerto Ricans, 12.0% of Mexican Americans, and 1.6% of Cuban Americans.

Similarly, in a careful comparison of the English language skills of the Spanish-speaking foreign-born population in 1980 with the English language skills of the German-speaking foreign-born in 1900, Jasso and Rosenzweig (1990) found that children of the Spanish-speaking population were no less likely to attain English language proficiency than were the children of the German-speaking population.

What emerges clearly from these data, then, is that Spanish-speaking immigrants, like other waves of immigrants before them, are acquiring English and slowly abandoning their mother tongue. What is also clear is that because of the continued influx of new immigrants and because of the spatial concentration of persons speaking the same language especially in border areas, retention of Spanish in Latino communities is often greater than retention of the ethnic language has been among other immigrant groups. The greatest number of Latinos in this country, however, are bilingual; that is, they can function to some degree in *both* English and Spanish. Table 2 presents data from the 1990 census on the English language ability of Mexican-origin persons. Table 3 presents data derived from Table 2 on the bilingual abilities of this population.

TABLE 2. ABILITY TO SPEAK ENGLISH, U.S. MEXICAN-ORI-GIN POPULATION, AGED 5 YEARS AND OLDER, 1990

Ability and age group	No.
Speak a language other than English	9,054,572
5–17 years	2,342,725
18–64 years	6,248,832
65–74 years	299,843
75 years and over	163,172
Do not speak English very well	4,605,389
5–17 years	988,238
18–64 years	3,324,798
65–74 years	178,856
75 years and over	113,497
Total	11,826,999

Source: U.S. Bureau of the Census (1994, Table 115).

TABLE 3. BILINGUAL ABILITIES OF MEXICAN-ORIGIN POPULATION AGED
5 YEARS AND OVER, UNITED STATES, 1990

Ability	No.	%
Speak a language other than English	9,054,572	77
Speak a language other than English but do not speak English very well	4,605,389	39
Speak a language other than English and speak English very well	4,449,183	38
Speak only English	2,772,427	23
Are English monolingual or speak English very well	7,221,610	61
Total	11,826,999	

Note: Persons who reported speaking a language other than English in
Question 15 of the 1990 census were asked to indicate their ability to speak
English based on the categories *very well, not well,* and *not at all.* The
categories *not at all* and *not well* are combined in this table.
Source: U.S. Bureau of the Census (1994, Table 115).

Language use in Mexican American communities

Given the presence of English and Spanish monolinguals as well as
bilinguals in Mexican American communities, if one were to walk down
the street of a typical community and listen closely as people talked to
one another, one could come away with several different impressions
about language and its use among Mexican Americans. If, for example,
one overheard talk among young people as they walked home after
school, one might be convinced that English was the primary language
of the community. On the other hand, if one eavesdropped on two older women, their use of Spanish might persuade one that Spanish clearly
predominated. A different impression might be obtained if one overheard the conversation of second- or third-generation Mexican Americans in their mid-twenties and found that they seemed to use both English and Spanish together, somehow alternating between the two
languages every few words. In that case, one might reach one of two
conclusions: that members of the community speak *both* English and
Spanish, or that members of the community speak *neither* English nor
Spanish (in other words, a hybrid language.)

In fact, the first three of those impressions would be accurate. For
some residents of the community, English would clearly be the dominant and primary language. For other residents of the community,
Spanish would still be the primary means of communication. And for
still others, both English and Spanish would be perceived as necessary
for everyday interaction in the community.

What would soon be apparent to a more trained observer is that, like many other immigrant communities, Mexican American communities are *diglossic*. What this means is that English and Spanish have taken on specialized functions and are associated with certain domains of activity or subject matter. English is the "high" language of prestige; it is the language identified with success and with power. Not only is it the language of the wider surrounding community, but it is also the language of many important domains; banking, the political process, and all the official institutions that affect the lives of the members of the community. Spanish, on the other hand, is the "low" language of intimacy, the language in which casual, unofficial interactions of the home and the in-group are conducted. In some communities, it is also the language of the church and of the surrounding neighborhood stores. In others, English has established itself firmly in every domain outside the home.

The effects of this diglossic relationship can be seen clearly in the ways in which individuals acquire and develop proficiency in each of their two languages. As in monolingual communities, different speakers use different *registers* (language varieties associated with particular contexts) in different situations. According to Biber (1994), registers include very high level varieties of language such as those used in university lectures, the writing of academic articles, and the presentation of evidence before a panel of judges. They also include midlevel varieties such as those used in newspaper reports, popular novels, and interviews as well as low-level registers used in intimate and casual conversation. What is different in bilingual communities, however, is that the high registers of English are used to carry out all formal or high exchanges, whereas Spanish, along with the informal registers of English, is used as the low variety, appropriate primarily for casual or informal interactions.

In addition to being characterized by diglossia and bilingualism, bilingual communities also reflect the social class origins of their residents. In the case of Mexican-origin immigrants, evidence suggests that a large majority of persons who emigrate to the United States do not come from the groups that have obtained high levels of education.[2]

2 Generalizing about the class origins of both early and recent Mexican immigrants gives rise to problems. According to Portes, (1978), McLeod, and Parker Portes and Bach (1985), Jasso and Rosenzweig (1990), and Bean and Tienda (1987), Mexican-origin immigrants are poor and have low levels of educational attainment. However, Durand and Massey (1992) have argued that generalizations about Mexican migration to the United States are inconsistent and contradictory. They maintain that case studies (e.g., Cornelius, 1976a, 1976b, 1978; Mines, 1981, 1984; Dinerman, 1982; Mines & Massey, 1985; Massey, Alarcon, Durand, & Gonzdlez, 1987; Reichert & Massey, 1979, 1980) of Mexican *sending* communities (communities from which large numbers of Mexican nationals have emigrated) have yielded very different views about a number of questions. Among other topics, these studies present contradictory evidence

What is clear is that Mexican immigrants are generally ordinary Mexicans, that is, members of the nonelite strata. The term *ordinary* (following Selby, Murphy, & Lorenzen, 1990, p. 207) excludes the middle and upper sectors, which represent only 10% of the Mexican population, and avoids the use of *working class* or *middle class* and the connotations these terms have for American and European readers.

Some researchers (e.g., Valdés & Geoffrion-Vinci, in press) conjecture that the linguistic repertoires of most ordinary Mexicans who emigrate to the United States are generally made up of the middle to low registers of Spanish. This is important in understanding the Spanish spoken by young Mexican Americans, for it is these registers that serve as models of language as they acquire Spanish in their families and communities.

A further complication in the study of the Spanish spoken in bilingual communities by first-, second-, third-, and fourth-generation Mexicans and Mexican Americans is the fact that over time this minority language – isolated as it is from the broad variety of contexts and situations in which it is used in Mexico – is at risk of undergoing a number of significant changes that do not occur in the same way in nonminority communities. Some researchers (e.g., de Bot & Weltens, 1991; Maher, 1991; Olshtain & Barzilay, 1991; Seliger & Vago, 1991) maintain that the language of immigrants undergoes attrition and structural loss. This attrition, then, results in the transferring by immigrants of their mother tongue in a "mutilated" form (de Bot & Weltens, p. 42) to the next generation of speakers. Even though many researchers would argue with de Bot and Wellen's use of the term *mutilated,* work carried out on tense-mood-aspect simplification by Silva-Corvalán (1994) among Mexican Americans in Los Angeles generally supports the position that patterns of simplification and loss among different generations of bilingual speakers of Spanish do not necessarily reflect the direct influence of English.

In sum, the Spanish that is spoken in bilingual communities in the United States and that is acquired by young bilinguals reflects the class origins of its first-generation speakers. Because in Mexico these speakers did not have access to the range of situations and contexts in which formal high varieties of Spanish are used, their language is characterized by a somewhat narrower range of lexical and syntactic alternatives than is the language of upper-middle-class speakers. More important, perhaps, because in these communities the use of Spanish is restricted to largely low-level functions and private-sphere interactions, over time –

about the class composition of U.S. migration. Durand and Massey (1992) argue that a few community factors, including the age of the migration stream; the geographic, political, and economic position of the community within Mexico; and the distribution and quality of agricultural land affect the class composition of migration. In short, the authors stress the difficulties surrounding attempts at generalization.

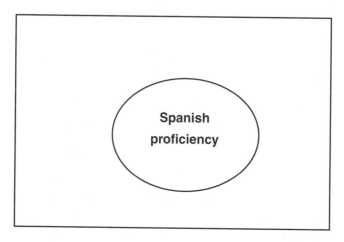

Figure 1   Native speaker of Spanish who acquired Spanish in a monolingual context.

as Huffines (1991) points out – "the immigrant language falls into dis-
use" (p. 125). As a result, many young people in bilingual communities
may not acquire a full mastery of the registers and styles characteristic
of even ordinary Mexican monolinguals.

The Spanish language competencies of monolingual and bilingual speakers of Spanish[3]

In addition to the general inventory of registers and levels of language,
there are other differences between persons who have acquired their
first language in a monolingual context and persons who have acquired
it in a community where two languages are spoken. I illustrate this
graphically by comparing representations of the Spanish language competencies of these two types of speakers. Figure 1 illustrates the Spanish
language proficiency of a native speaker who acquired her first language
in a largely monolingual context. Figure 2, on the other hand, illustrates
the Spanish proficiency of several native speakers of Spanish who acquired their first language in a bilingual environment. The proficiency of
the speakers depicted in Figure 2, who acquire and use Spanish in a
bilingual context (e.g., Catalonia, the United States, Puerto Rico,
Paraguay) is not identical to that of native speakers who have acquired
and used their Spanish in settings in which only Spanish is used for all
interactions. Speakers who acquire their Spanish in bilingual contexts
possess what I represent here as a *smaller* Spanish language proficiency.

3 This section summarizes a perspective initially presented in Valdés (1995).

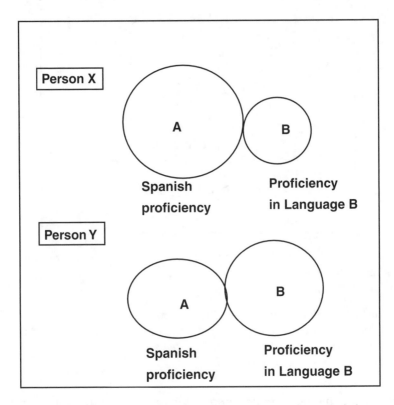

Figure 2   Native speakers of Spanish who acquired Spanish language competence in a bilingual context.

Indeed, several researchers (e.g., Lavandera, 1978) have argued that for bilingual speakers (individuals who acquire and use two languages in their everyday lives) their two linguistic codes together form a unitary whole. The totality of their proficiency and linguistic abilities can be described only by examining the sum of their proficiencies and abilities in the two languages.

Of note also in Figure 2 is that the representations of the proficiencies of different bilingual speakers are different. Person X is represented here as Spanish dominant. This person's ability in Language B is not as great as his or her proficiency in Spanish. Person Y, on the other hand, is dominant in Language B. This person's Spanish, although acquired first, is not his or her strongest language.

According to Bachman (1990), language competence includes a number of different, interacting components, such as grammatical, textual, illocutionary, and sociolinguistic competence. Such competence not only includes the control of vocabulary, morphology, syntax, and phonology but also includes the ability to manipulate interactions; express ideas; and create and imagine when using the language while being sensitive to differences in social and geographical varieties of the language, register differences, naturalness, and cultural references.

Speakers who have acquired their native language in a monolingual context certainly vary in their control and abilities in a number of these areas. Some individuals, for example, claim to be notoriously deaf to differences in style. Nevertheless, all native speakers of a language who have acquired their first language in a monolingual context have developed the competencies necessary in that single language to carry out all of their communicative needs.

The situation is quite different for speakers who acquire their first language in a community in which two language are used. In such cases, speakers may develop very different strengths in each of their languages depending on their opportunities to use each in their everyday lives. It is not unusual to find bilingual individuals with very limited textual competence in one of their two languages because they have not been exposed to reading and writing in that language. Indeed, the language competence of bilingual speakers can be conceptualized as being spread over two languages. Such a conceptualization makes clear that speakers develop different strengths in different components of their language competence. Thus a bilingual individual may have a limited vocabulary in the first language and at the same time have greater sociolinguistic competence in this same language. Bilingual speakers may find themselves groping for terms to discuss school or professional topics in Spanish, for example, while being capable of interpreting every single cultural reference made by fluent monolingual speakers whom they overhear engaged in a heated discussion.

The situation is actually much more complicated. The fact is that even within a single component of competence (grammatical, textual, illocutionary, or sociolinguistic), most bilingual speakers display a great deal of variation in their strengths and limitations. What is important to emphasize is that Mexican American bilingual speakers are not simply imperfect speakers of Spanish who have fallen short of the monolingual norm. They are, rather, complex individuals who are fundamentally different from monolinguals. As opposed to monolingual speakers of Spanish who grow up in societies where Spanish is the sole or primarily societal language, bilingual Mexican Americans are members of communities in which a single language (either English or Spanish) does not suffice to meet all of their communicative needs.

The specific competencies of these speakers are especially difficult to assess and measure because these competencies cannot be easily compared with those of either monolingual English or monolingual Spanish

109

speakers. Indeed, the competence of bilinguals who function on an everyday basis in two languages can perhaps be best understood through the use of the construct of *bilingual range.*

In my attempt to describe functioning bilinguals, I define *bilingual range* as the continuum of linguistic abilities and communicative strategies that an individual may access in one or the other of two languages at a specific moment, for a particular purpose, in a particular setting, with particular interlocutors. From this perspective, at a given moment of interaction, a bilingual is considered to have a particular range in Language A, a particular range in Language B, and a particular range when the languages are used together.

When arguing with a sibling about money, for example, one bilingual's total range might be characterized as follows:

Language A	Language B

This would indicate that the bilingual's momentarily preferred language would be Language B rather than Language A. At a different moment, for other purposes, with other interlocutors, and in a different setting, this same bilingual's range might be characterized as exhibiting greater strengths in Language A than in Language B:

Language A	Language B

Bilingual range encompasses different kinds of competencies in two languages, including, of course, what Bachman (1990) has termed grammatical, textual, illocutionary, and sociolinguistic competence. A bilingual's shifting communicative abilities in different types of interactions and in different settings with both monolingual and bilingual interlocutors are seen to result from the (often momentary) varying availability of these various competencies to the individual.

Currently, much remains to be learned about bilingual range and about why and how communicative abilities and other language competencies in bilinguals appear to shift in unpredictable ways. Even less is known about how to strengthen these abilities and competencies.

The Spanish spoken in Mexican American communities

The Spanish spoken by Mexican Americans in the United States can be classified as a *microvariety* or *microdialect* of Mexican Spanish. This means that Mexican American Spanish is most like the Spanish spoken in Mexico, as opposed to, say, the Spanish spoken in Argentina, in Bolivia, in Guatemala, or in Puerto Rico. It is also a variety of the Spanish spoken in the Americas rather than a variety of the Spanish spoken in Spain. However, just as the English spoken in Texas or Boston is mutually comprehensible with the English spoken in Georgia, Nova Scotia, South Africa, New Zealand, and London, Mexican American Spanish is mutually comprehensible with every other variety of Spanish spoken in both the Americas and the Spanish peninsula.

Since the mid-1970s, linguists and especially sociolinguists have paid a great deal of attention to the study and description of Mexican American Spanish. Early studies (e.g., Elias-Olivares, 1976; Hernández-Chavez, 1975; Peñalosa, 1980; Sanchez, 1982, 1983) focused on describing the characteristics of the Spanish-English bilingual communities and the ways in which Mexican American or Chicano Spanish was different from the Spanish spoken in the rest of the Spanish-speaking world. More recent studies (e.g., Chaston, 1991; Garcia, 1995; Gutierrez, 1996; Gutierrez & Silva-Corvalán, 1993; Jaramillo, 1990; Klee, 1987; Lope-Blanch, 1990; Lozano, 1994; Ocampo, 1990; Silva-Corvalán, 1991, 1994) offer a more sophisticated and refined view of language use patterns as well as of changes that are the result of language contact. These studies have confirmed that, whereas Mexican American Spanish is indeed very similar to Mexican Spanish, it is also different in several key ways. As pointed out, one of the most important differences has to do with the number of social varieties heard in Mexico in contrast to the number heard in Mexican American communities in the United States. Another important difference has to do with the features of Mexican American Spanish that are a result of its contact with English.

I emphasize, however, that when one excludes features that are the product of the influence of English, the similarities between Mexican and Mexican American Spanish are greater than the differences between the two varieties. This perspective is an important one because in writing their descriptions of *Chicano* or Mexican American Spanish, some scholars have not pointed out that the examples they cite (those that reflect no English influence) reflect phenomena also found in the rest of the Hispanic world. This omission has led to many misinterpretations of the nature of Mexican American Spanish. Thus, although reviewing lists of *Chicano* features, such as those found in Peñalosa (1980, p. 99), may be useful, it is important to recall that each of the morphological features and characteristics generally mentioned on the lists is also typical of, at the very least, rural or informal Mexican Spanish.

In each of the cases in Table 4, for example, the items identified as Mexican American are also typical of rural or working-class speakers in many areas of the Spanish-speaking world. The use of archaisms such as

TABLE 4. EXAMPLES OF ITEMS LISTED IN DESCRIPTIONS
OF MEXICAN AMERICAN SPANISH

Item labeled *Mexican American*	*"Standard" Spanish* *equivalent*
vivemos	vivimos
hablates	hablaste
puedemos	podemos
truje	traje
asina	asi
caiba	caía
escrebir	escribir
jeu	fue
pos	pues
haiga	haya

truje, asina, caiba, and *haiga,* for example, has been documented by many Spanish dialectologists (for example, Zamora Vicente, 1970). Variations in verb morphology (*puedemos, vivemos, estábanos, hablates*) are also well documented (Escobar, 1978; Oroz, 1966) as typical of rural speech in many countries.

English influence on Mexican American Spanish may take several forms, some obvious, some subtle. Briefly, contact with English modifies Spanish in three ways: semantic extension, borrowing, and code switching. I emphasize, however, that to say that Mexican American Spanish is influenced by English does not imply that the language in question has ceased to be Spanish.

SEMANTIC EXTENSION

The first type of English influence on Spanish, which I call semantic extension, is rather subtle. Since all the words are in Spanish, there seems at first glance to have been no influence from another language.

1. *Voy a llevar a la niñera a su casa.* (I'm going to take the baby-sitter home.)
2. *A los perros callejeros se los llevan a la perrera.* (Stray dogs are taken to the dog pound.)

However, upon closer examination, it is clear that the Spanish words for *baby-sitter* and *dog pound* have undergone a semantic transformation. Their original meanings were limited to what is normally found in monolingual Spanish-speaking countries. Thus, *niñera* really refers to a servant who lives (or works full-time) in a household and takes care of children, not to a young person of middle-class background who "sits" with children and charges by the hour. *Perrera* refers to a doghouse or even to a female person who takes care of dogs, but not to a dog pound. Few Hispanic countries have such an institution.

BORROWING

A more readily detected form of English influence on Mexican American Spanish is borrowing, which is typical of what happens when speakers of a language come into contact with concepts that are new to them and for which they have no available vocabulary. In the following examples of Mexican American Spanish, new words appear to have been created using English base forms and Spanish inflections: Nouns are given gender, and verbs are conjugated using the complex Spanish morphological system. English borrowings are known as *anglicismos* in the Spanish-speaking world.

3. *Ay te wacho.* [from *watch*] (I'll be seeing you.)
4. *Tengo que taipear esto para la clase.* (I'll have to type this for the class.)
5. *Se está liqueando el rufo.* (The roof is leaking.)

Borrowing is a common result of language contact. For centuries languages have borrowed from one another and have integrated borrowings into their lexical inventory, treating them as if they were native items. For example, English uses terms such as *menu, restaurant,* and *patio* whereas Spanish uses *acequia, film, almohada,* and *canoa.* These examples are all taken from other languages, integrated into the language, and used as if they were originally English or Spanish; in the case of Spanish, the borrowed words listed are accepted by the Real Academia Española. No one suggests that these borrowings distort or seriously threaten either English or Spanish.

CODE SWITCHING

The third way in which English influence on Mexican American Spanish is manifested is code switching, which can be defined as the alternating use of two languages at the word, phrase, clause, or sentence level. In the following examples, stretches of unmodified Spanish alternate with stretches of unmodified English:

6. *Dijo mi mamá* que I have to study. (My mother said that I have to study.)
7. *Tengo la* waist twenty-nine, *tengo que* reduce. (I have a twenty-nine [-inch] waist, I have to reduce.)

113

Code switching is different from borrowing in that the elements from the other language are used in their original form. No attempt is made to adapt them or to integrate them into the system being used. In other words, each switch into Spanish or English consists of unchanged Spanish or English words pronounced by the speakers as a native speaker of that language would pronounce them. There is ordinarily a clean break between the two phonemic systems. Code switching has been studied extensively by many scholars and found to occur commonly between bilingual speakers in many different pairs of languages and in many different parts of the world. Several books on this phenomenon as well as collections of studies have examined this process (e.g., Auer, 1984; Heller, 1988; Jacobson, 1990; Milroy & Muysken, 1995; Myers-Scotton, 1993b).

Both early and more recent work on code switching by English-Spanish bilinguals (Fantini, 1985; Huerta-Macias, 1981; Johnson, 1996; Lavandera, 1981; McClure, 1981; Poplack, 1980, 1981; Valdés, 1976, 1981, 1982; Valdés-Fallis, 1978; Zentella, 1981, 1982, 1997) has made clear that in many ways English and Spanish *together* make up the linguistic repertoire of these speakers. Bilinguals, for example, often switch between languages at the word, phrase, clause, and sentence levels to express a series of different types of meanings. A switch into Spanish, for example, by a Mexican American bilingual who is speaking English to another bilingual of the same background, may signal greater solidarity or a reference to values associated with the ethnic language. A switch might also serve, however, as a simple metaphorical device by means of which a speaker gives emphasis to a particular segment of the utterance (Huerta-Macias, 1981; Valdés-Fallis, 1978; Zentella, 1982). What is important is that the use of two languages by Mexican American bilinguals in many informal interactions results in the fact that most members of the community develop the ability to comprehend spoken Spanish.

The following examples show the contrast between borrowing (8), in which the English element is incorporated into the Spanish system, and code switching (9), in which the English element is used in its original form:

8. *Estábamos jenguiando allí en la esquina.* (We were hanging out there at the corner.)
9. *No tengo tiempo ni para estar hanging out con los amigos.* (I don't even have time to be hanging out with friends.)

Unfortunately, to monolingual speakers of either English or Spanish, code switching suggests that its speakers speak neither language. Nothing, in fact, is further from the truth. As is the case with borrowing, misunderstandings about how language works in bilingual communities have led to unfair judgments about the language strengths of speakers who use their two languages in this manner. Research on bilinguals and bilingual communities has demonstrated, however, that rather than reflecting weakness, complex code switching requires that speakers be very proficient in the two languages used.

The future of Spanish and English in Mexican American communities

Controversies surrounding issues of language maintenance among U.S. Latinos

According to Fishman (1964), immigrant bilingualism in the United States follows a specific pattern that is common to all immigrant groups and that leads to monolingualism by the fourth generation. This pattern can be illustrated as follows:

1. *Initial stage.* Immigrants learn English through their mother tongue. English is used only in those domains (such as work) in which the mother tongue cannot be used.
2. *Second stage.* Immigrants learn more English and can speak to each other in this language or in the immigrant language, although they still depend on the mother tongue.
3. *Third stage.* Speakers function in both languages. English appears to be dominant in more and more domains.
4. *Fourth stage.* English has displaced the mother tongue in all except for the most intimate or private domains. This stage is the exact reverse of the initial stage.

In the case of Mexican Americans, this pattern of transitional bilingualism leading to language shift is often masked by the continuing arrival of new, monolingual Spanish-speaking immigrants into bilingual communities. As I point out in the following paragraphs, however, in spite of the influx of monolinguals into Mexican American communities, the shift toward English among Mexican Americans is unequivocal.

Unfortunately, in the 1990s confusion about the English language proficiency of U.S. Latino populations has been engendered because of the activities of several groups and organizations. Two of these groups, U.S. English and English First, have aggressively promoted the passage of legislation that would establish English as the official language of the United States and prohibit the use of non-English languages in a variety of public and official contexts.

According to the misinformation campaign carried out by U.S. English and English First, Latinos in the United States, as a group, are re-

TABLE 5. OVERALL LANGUAGE ABILITY OF U.S. LATINOS, BY
NATIONAL ORIGIN

| | National origin | | | | | |
| | Mexican | | Puerto Rican | | Cuban | |
Overall language ability	No.	%	No.	%	No.	%
Only Spanish	6	0.6	43	7.3	17	5.3
Better in Spanish	98	11.1	198	33.7	118	37.7
No difference	225	25.9	146	24.9	88	28.2
Better in English	482	54.9	183	31.2	83	26.6
Only English	65	7.4	16	2.8	7	2.2
Total	887	100.0	587	100.0	312	100.0

Source: De la Garza et al. (1992, Table 4.8).

fusing to learn English. Members and supporters of these two organizations claim that Latinos, unlike immigrants in the past, are rejecting the English language and are insisting instead that they deserve special language services, such as bilingual education and bilingual ballots. Concerned about the status of English in this country, English First and U.S. English have mobilized resources to bring about the passage of an English language amendment in each of the fifty states. They have been moderately successful, managing to convince a number of Americans that Congress must pass language legislation that transmits a clear message to the Spanish-speaking population about the importance of English for its citizens.[4]

Reality is quite different. A survey of Latinos carried out by de la Garza, DeSipio, Garcia, Garcia, and Falcon (1992),[5] for example, revealed that the majority of 1,546 Mexican, 589 Puerto Rican, and 682 Cuban respondents polled prefer to be called *American.* Moreover, no more than 10% of respondents from any of the three groups considered themselves monolingual in Spanish or English. This finding is especially noteworthy given that 13% of the Mexican respondents, 66% of the Puerto Rican respondents, and 71% of the Cuban respondents were foreign born.

Tables 5 and 6 summarize data on language ability and home lan-

4 For a thorough discussion of these issues, the reader is referred to Crawford (1992a, 1992b).
5 The Latino National Political Survey was designed to collect basic data describing Latino political values, attitudes, and behavior. Supported by the Ford, Spencer, Rockefeller, and Tinker foundations, the survey was conducted between 1989 and 1990 in forty standard metropolitan statistical areas and involved a sample representative of 91% of the Mexican, Puerto Rican, and Cuban populations of the United States.

TABLE 6. HOME LANGUAGE OF RESPONDENTS BY NATIONAL ORIGIN

| | National origin | | | | | |
| | Mexican | | Puerto Rican | | Cuban | |
Overall language ability	No.	%	No.	%	No.	%
Only Spanish	46	5.2	124	21.1	117	37.7
More Spanish than English	84	9.6	136	23.2	73	23.3
Both languages	234	26.7	175	29.9	78	25.0
More English than Spanish	275	31.3	90	15.3	27	8.6
Only English	238	27.1	61	10.5	17	5.5
Total	878	100.0	586	100.0	312	100.0

Source: De la Garza et al. (1992, Table 4.9).

guage use as presented by de la Garza et al. As the tables show, 772 Mexican American respondents considered themselves to have the same ability in English as in Spanish or to be better in English. At home, 747 of 878 respondents claimed to speak both languages, more English than Spanish, or only English. A small minority, 130 respondents, claimed to speak only Spanish or more Spanish than English at home. These data confirm the information obtained in the 1990 census and presented in Table 2: that 7.2 million of 11.8 million Mexican Americans over 5 years old reported being either monolingual (nearly 2.8 million) or able to speak English very well (over 4.4 million).

Other work on language maintenance and language shift carried out in Mexican American communities (e.g., Bills, 1989; Bills, Hernandez-Chavez, & Hudson, 1995; Hart-Gonzalez & Feingold 1990) coupled with sociolinguistic work carried out among first-, second-, and third-generation speakers of Spanish (e.g., Gutierrez, 1996; Lope Blanch, 1990; Silva-Corvalán, 1994) also provides strong support for the position that Mexican American communities are shifting to English. Hart-Gonzalez and Feingold, for example, in examining the November 1979 Current Population Survey, conclude that there is "a clear overall tendency toward home language shift" (p. 28). Bills, examining the use of Spanish in the Southwest based on the 1980 census, concludes that

there is no evidence in the present study that the Spanish language is being strongly maintained in the United States Southwest. On the contrary, it appears that the Spanish-origin population in the last half of the 20th century is behaving like a "normal" segment of United States society; it seems to be giving up the ethnic language and shifting to English as it becomes exposed to the mainstream of American life. The principal exceptions to this language shift appear to be where there is either isolation from the mainstream or a considerable influx of Spanish speakers from Mexico. (pp. 26–27)

More recently, Bills et al. (1995) examined whether indeed Spanish is maintained better along the U.S.-Mexican border. They concluded that distance from the border contributes to the process of language maintenance and shift in an important, though secondary, way. Locations closer to the border favor maintenance, whereas distance from the border favors shift. However, the authors conclude that

> The Spanish origin persons in the SW most likely to speak Spanish in the home are those born in Mexico and, consequently, among the young, it is their children who are most likely to be SHL [Spanish home language] claimants. Though cities closer to the border tend to have greater Mexican nativity among the Spanish origin population, the retention variable seems to be susceptible to the individual immigrant as a language transmitter and not the community support that Dist [distance] seems to reflect. (p. 26)

Even in cities close to the border, the highest predictor of language shift is education. Only when education is partialed out does distance from the border emerge as a nontrivial, second-order predictor of language loyalty.

Other work carried out in Mexican American communities on the Spanish language itself also supports the position that Spanish is the nondominant language of most third-generation speakers. Research carried out, for example, by Silva-Corvalán (1994) led to the conclusion that, although Spanish is being maintained at the societal level because of the influx of new immigrants, at the individual and family level there is a clear shift to English. In Los Angeles, where Silva-Corvalán carried out her work, speakers of Spanish could be located at very different ends of a continuum of proficiency ranging from fully fluent speakers of Mexican Spanish to users of emblematic Spanish. Silva-Corvalán found clear differences between Group 1 (Los Angeles speakers who were born in Mexico and immigrated to the United States after the age of 11), Group 2 (Los Angeles speakers who were born in the United States or came to the United States before the age of 6) and Groups 2 (Los Angeles speakers born in the United States who had one parent fitting the definition of Group 2). Members of Groups 1 and 2 could converse in Spanish with ease. Speakers in Group 3, however, spoke Spanish with difficulty. More important, however, in the Spanish of Group 3 Silva-Corvalán found clear evidence of simplification of grammatical categories, overgeneralization of forms, and direct and indirect transfer from English. Other, similar work (e.g, Gutierrez, 1996, Lope Blanch, 1990), moreover, supports the position that the Spanish spoken in Mexican American communities is characterized by lexical limitations and morphological insecurities.

For many speakers of Spanish who are concerned about the future of Spanish in the United States, such linguistic changes might be seen as evidence of language shift in progress and impending loss. According to Woolard (1992), commentators have used disease metaphors for the loss of minority languages over time, and many have equated so-called language corruption with eventual demise. What is not clear, as Woolard further argues, is whether linguistic conservatism is a predictor of language maintenance or whether the survival of a language in a minority-majority context requires the acceptance of "interference" phenomena by its speakers. Silva-Corvalán (1994) herself argues that strategies such as simplification, overgeneralization, and regularization "facilitate the maintenance of the less used language, they converge towards rendering communication more efficient" (p. 207). Be that as it may, work on linguistic change undergone by Spanish in Mexican American communities makes it clear that English is very much present there. Indeed, one could argue that for many Mexican Americans, English appears to be dominant in more and more domains. For others, English has displaced the mother tongue in all except for the most intimate or private domains.

In sum, the language situation in Mexican American communities is more or less encouraging depending on one's views about language. Those who worry about Mexican Americans' being left out of the American dream will find it comforting to discover that Mexican Americans *are* learning English and that it is rapidly displacing Spanish. On the other hand, supporters of Spanish language maintenance can also take comfort in the fact that Spanish is still alive although – in the eyes of many – it is not well. Its young speakers, in particular, speak a Spanish that many teachers of Spanish consider unacceptable and incorrect. Like teachers of English, such teachers of Spanish find it difficult to accept the contact variety of Spanish that students bring with them to the classroom. Elaborate debates have taken place concerning how best to "undo the damage that has been done at home." The teaching of the standard language still preoccupies most individuals concerned with designing programs for native speakers.[6] It is unclear whether direct instruction in Spanish can reverse the process of linguistic change, nor is it clear, as Woolard (1992) has argued, that conservatism will lead to language maintenance.

What is encouraging for those who consider immigrant languages to be valuable resources is the fact that Spanish-speaking monolinguals are still present in Mexican American communities. According to data from the 1990 U.S. census (U.S. Bureau of the Census, 1994, Table 115), for example, there are 813,291 *linguistically isolated* households in the United States – those in which no person age 14 years or over speaks only English and no person age 14 or over who speaks a language other

---

6 For a discussion of the teaching of Spanish to Latino bilinguals, see Valdés (1995).

Guadalupe Valdés

than English speaks English very well. Of the 11,567,198 persons in all households in the United States, 2,743,198 live in linguistically isolated households. These persons, then, have personal relationships with individuals with whom they must communicate primarily in Spanish. This is encouraging, because as Woolard (1992) points out,

It is when not just functions, but *personal relationships* order the bilingual repertoire and mandate the use of a particular language that we find evidence of more resistance to language shift. . . . (p. 360)

English in Mexican American communities

In comparison to the research carried out on Spanish as it is used in Mexican American communities, very little work has been undertaken on English as it is spoken among Mexican Americans. Indeed, very little research has been carried out even on the varieties of English spoken among monolingual European Americans in those areas of the country in which there are large numbers of Mexican Americans. Nevertheless, one can safely say that the English spoken in Mexican American communities is a microvariety of American English as opposed to, for example, British English or Australian English. It is more difficult, however, to generalize about the specific regional varieties of American English spoken in these communities and even more difficult to determine to what extent the English spoken by Mexican Americans is truly influenced by Spanish. Put another way, the question is, if one were to walk down the street of a Mexican community in Houston, Texas, for example, would one hear the same Houston, Texas, accent that one hears among European Americans, or would one hear a more general American speech? Would the Houston, Texas, accent be influenced by Spanish? Would the more general American speech also show traces of this influence? To what degree would there be differences among speakers? Would some speak accented English and others not? What would be the difference between individuals who are merely acquiring English and those that are monolingual speakers of the language?

Unfortunately, there are few answers to these questions. The handful of studies that have focused on Mexican American or Chicano English have primarily investigated the speech of young children rather than that of adult Mexican Americans. It is thus difficult to reach conclusions about adult language. In essence, what most existing studies have provided are lists of Spanish-influenced features found in the speech of young Mexican Americans. Metcalf (1979) describes a number of these studies and includes several listings of usually identified "errors" in the areas of pronunciation, intonation, syntax, and vocabulary. Indeed, there appears to be a fascination with what Fishman (1968) has called

120

laundry lists, long presentations of instances where Spanish has "rubbed off" on English.

To some degree, these lists of so-called errors can be useful. For example, some linguists have used them to demonstrate that certain features found in the speech of Mexican Americans are, in fact, not products of Spanish interference or transfer but a direct reflection of the nonstandard local variety of English in use in the surrounding community. These lists are not useful, however, if all or most Mexican Americans are assumed to exhibit these features in their speech. The fact is that the English spoken by some Mexican Americans is indeed a learner's variety and is characterized by many instances of direct transfer from Spanish. The English spoken by other Mexican Americans, however, may be very different indeed. It may show no traces of Spanish influence, a few traces when the speaker is under stress, or even consistent traces at all times.

Not all Mexican Americans can be said to speak English with a Spanish accent, with Spanish intonation, or with elements of Spanish syntax. Indeed, as Gingras (1972) found, Mexican Americans can be classified as belonging to one of four groups: (1) those whose English is indistinguishable from that of monolingual European Americans in the community; (2) those whose speech has slight divergences from the local European American variety, which are probably not detectable by the average person on first contact; (3) those whose speech has moderate divergences from the local variety, all of which are readily apparent to most people; and (4) those whose speech shows clear transfer from the Spanish system and who seem to be in the process of acquiring English. Moreover, members of the first three groups may be monolingual speakers of English, that is, persons whose first language was English and who have never spoken Spanish.

Clearly, the kind of English spoken by different individuals within the same Mexican American community is directly related to the types and kinds of English they are in contact with. If they have contact with the local European variety and American opportunities to interact with a peer group of such speakers, Mexican American children will quickly acquire this variety. If, on the other hand, there is little contact between groups and there are no opportunities to interact with monolingual European American speakers, the result may be quite different. Only other Mexican Americans, who may themselves speak Spanish-influenced varieties of English, will serve as models for those individuals who are acquiring English. It is no wonder, then, that even individuals whose only language is English will speak a variety of this language that seems to suggest they are transferring features from Spanish. No such transfer is occurring, of course, but the impression left with a monolingual European American who hears it is that somehow there is something foreign about Mexican American English.

The fact that large numbers of monolingual English-speaking Mexican Americans live in many communities has led some scholars (e.g., Metcalf, 1979) to suggest that there is a legitimate variety of English that can be called *Chicano English*. For Metcalf, Chicano English is a variety of English identical to the local European American variety, except that it has added a "Spanish accent." He states that it is spoken not by learners of the language but by "people whose native language is a special variety of English with a Spanish sound to it" (p. 1).

Other scholars disagree with this classification entirely. Some would argue that Mexican Americans do not have enough contact with European Americans and therefore do not acquire the local variety of English. Thus, they would maintain that, if anything, Chicano English is a type of general American or Northern Standard English with a Spanish flavor. Other scholars (e.g., Sawyer, 1975) reject the entire concept of the existence of a Mexican American variety of English. They argue that the English spoken by Mexican American bilinguals is an imperfect state in the mastery of English and that it will become more expert from generation to generation.

Until there is more research on the English spoken in Mexican American communities, it will be difficult to defend any of the above positions exclusively. Many unanswered questions remain. For example, to describe Mexican American English or even to decide if it exists requires an understanding how English was acquired by speakers whose English appears to be indistinguishable from that of monolingual Anglos. Did they interact with European Americans? How soon? How frequently? Did this contact continue over a lifetime? Did Mexican American learners make a conscious effort to sound like their European American models? What were the results? Is the English variety spoken by these Mexican Americans truly indistinguishable from European American English in all contexts? Are there limitations? What are these, and where do they appear?

The same types of questions must then be asked about the other three groups of speakers: those whose divergences from European American English are not generally noticeable to lay people, those whose divergences are clearly noticeable, and those whose English is obviously colored by transfers from Spanish. For example, what are the differences between the first two groups? What is the role of English language models in the acquisition process in each case? Are the slight divergences similar in persons of the same social class, educational background, etc.? What other factors appear to influence the acquisition or use of a Spanish-sounding variety?

Clearly, the questions are many and complex. It will take many years before the answers are forthcoming. In the meantime, however, the information available suggests strongly (1) that Mexican Americans from the same community speak different kinds of English, (2) that many Mexican Americans are native speakers of English and are not bilingual, (3) that Mexican Americans can be classified according to the degree to which their English speech diverges from the local European American norm, and (4) that the presence of Spanish language elements in a speaker's English does not indicate that the individual is in the process of learning English.

The question of broken English

As pointed out, for those concerned about the so-called refusal of Mexican-origin people to learn English, the data presented here may be encouraging. The majority of Mexican Americans are bilingual in English and Spanish, and most claim to speak English very well. What the data do not say, however, is that mainstream individuals perceive Mexican Americans as speaking good or adequate English. As recent work on discrimination against bilinguals (Lippi-Green, 1994, 1997; Piatt, 1992; Valdés, 1997) makes clear, the English of non-English-background individuals is always suspect. In schools, as Valdés (1992) points out mainstream teachers often send fluent, functional bilinguals back to the English as a second language (ESL) track if their speech or writing is characterized to any degree by nonnative features. In the workplace, as Lippi-Green (1994, 1997) and Piatt (1992) demonstrate, bilingual speakers are frequently subjected to accent discrimination.

As is the case with the other Englishes around the world (cf. Kachru, 1992), Mexican American or Chicano English is not valued by mainstream speakers of American English. Many see Chicano English as faulty or broken English as opposed to a legitimate variety of the language. As Strevens (1992) argues about nonnative varieties of English,

many native speakers – perhaps the majority – even among teachers of English – overtly or unconsciously despise these varieties. . . . The basic reasons for these native speakers' attitudes is ignorance – a total lack of awareness of the existence of flourishing, effective, functional, sometimes elegant and literary non-native varieties of English. Most NS [native speakers], including teachers of EF/ESL, have not experienced NNS [nonnative speaker] varieties of English in the circumstances of their origins. . . . Consequently, they wrongly equate variations from NS norms with classroom errors and mistakes, or regard NNS varieties as some kind of interlanguage on the path to NS English. (p. 37)

Although the issues surrounding these perceptions are complex in the case of national as opposed to international nonnative varieties of English, it may be worthwhile to hope that in the twenty-first century, more Americans – especially more teachers of English – will be guided

123

by Pennycook's (1994) view that teaching is never neutral. Arguing that to teach is to be caught up in an array of questions concerning power, legitimacy, ownership, inequality, and knowledge, he suggests that speakers of nonnative English should be encouraged to find their own voices in their own varieties of English:

> Thus we need to encourage, what MacCabe (1988) calls, in a positive sense, "broken English," where "breaking" is an attempt to dislodge the central language norms and to recreate other possibilities. . . . I am not, therefore, advocating a *laissez-faire* approach to language forms that encourages students to do as they like, as if English language classrooms existed in some social, cultural and political vacuum. Rather, I am suggesting that first, we need to make sure that students have access to those standard forms of the language linked to social and economic prestige; second, we need a good understanding of the stages and possibilities presented by different standards; third, we need to focus on those parts of language that are significant in particular discourses; fourth, students need to be aware that those forms represent only one set of particular possibilities; and finally, students need to be encouraged to find ways of using the language they feel are expressive of their own needs and desires . . . so that they can start to claim and negotiate a voice in English. (p. 317)

Implications for teachers of English

Language use in Mexican American communities is a complex and fascinating topic. From the study of these communities, much can be learned about the nature of immigrant bilingualism, second language acquisition, and language maintenance and language shift. Much can be learned also about the politics of language, power relationships between communities, and the ways in which perspectives on language can determine access to both political power and economic resources. What does the nature of language use in Mexican American communities mean for English teachers? Clearly, the answer depends on what kind of English teachers they are. In this section, I present a number of suggestions for two different groups of teachers: teachers of English language arts to fluent bilingual or monolingual Mexican Americans and teachers of ESL.

TEACHING FLUENT ENGLISH SPEAKERS WHO ARE
MEXICAN AMERICAN

For teachers who are involved in teaching language arts to supposedly fluent English speakers, the most important task is to learn how to differentiate between actual language limitations and superficial, foreign-sounding features. As noted, Mexican American speakers often have heavy accents in English. Teachers must not confuse pronunciation errors with lack of control of the language and lack of fluency of expression. The fact that speakers have an accent does not imply that their English is imperfectly learned. Teachers must learn to evaluate overall ability to express ideas in English instead of focusing primarily on pronunciation. They must also recall that students bring with them what some scholars have described as a legitimate variety of English, a variety that may have a Spanish flavor but that is as valid as any other. Pronunciation, then, should not be corrected unless the pronunciation of speakers of English from other geographical areas is also being corrected. Pronunciation differences will not interfere with learning to read and write. Teachers do students a grave injustice if they assume that they must correct pronunciation before they can begin instruction in content.

Creating a positive and rich language environment in the classroom is most important. Teachers must be aware that English learners need to hear English from native speakers and interact with European American English-speaking peers. If classes include both European and Mexican Americans, teaching strategies that involve group work and discussion can be most valuable. Teachers should assume that students will profit from being exposed to a large variety of styles and levels of language.

TEACHING ESL

As noted, English is the language of prestige in all Mexican American communities. Clearly, English is considered important, and every child is expected to become an English speaker. The expectations for adults, on the other hand, are not as clear cut. What normally happens is that those individuals who happen to come into contact with English speakers tend to learn at least some English. Those who do not can spend years in the community without learning much English. They depend on other members of the family to interpret or translate for them. This is particularly true of older immigrant women in Mexican American communities.

ESL teachers must remember that Mexican Americans do not lack interest in learning English. Thus older people who after many years decide to take an English class did not refuse to learn English before, but rather for many complex reasons studying English formally may not have been possible or feasible for them. When such older learners enroll in a class, teachers need to be aware that for some of them a formal class setting is a foreign environment. They may have many fears about their own abilities to learn, which may have to do with their ideas about school, the experiences of others in the community in English classes, their children's success or lack of it in both Mexican and American schools, and the like. Moreover, because there are so many myths in the community about what it is to know a language and how languages are learned, these older learners may be afraid that they cannot learn or that they will never be able to speak. Many of these learners probably have attempted at some point to say something in English, but they might have met with ridicule from family members – even their own children, who, like the surrounding majority community, find heavy accents laughable. For this reason, they probably sell themselves short. They do not realize, for example, that the ability to understand is also a valuable skill and part of knowing a language.

The process of teaching such learners clearly begins with sensitivity to fears and scars. If students apparently have very low literacy skills in Spanish, teaching classes in which there is a heavy reliance on written materials makes little sense. It is perhaps important for such students to learn how to read and write well in their own language and in English, but the role of the ESL teacher is to teach these students English, especially oral English. Oral skills will permit students to function in the surrounding European American community. The challenge, then, for the ESL teacher faced with learners who are afraid, who have low literacy skills in their own language, and who may have insecurities about their capacity to learn English is to develop an approach to teaching English that will set students at ease, focus on oral language, and depend minimally on written material.

On the positive side, because English is spoken so widely in Mexican American communities, students are unlikely to have zero familiarity with the language. At the very least they will have learned some phrases (which they may repeat shyly), and they may also have developed some listening comprehension skills. The teacher can build on these to boost students' self-confidence. Of the many approaches and methodologies currently in use for the teaching of English, teachers should choose those that are most appropriate for developing the kinds of skills students need. Therefore, in some cases a heavy grammatical and analytical approach should not be adopted, especially if, when questioned, students state that their goal in learning English is to get a specific job or to communicate in a specific context. As far as possible, instruction should be tailored to students' needs. A topical or notional-functional syllabus may be most effective because it focuses on specific domains and contexts. By teaching phrases to answer the telephone with, for example, and by teaching comprehension of commonly heard telephone talk (e.g., "Is Mary home?" "Is this 555-9879?"), students will quickly be able to use and show off their new skills. This will not be the case if the class has focused on the conjugation of the verb *to be* and has practiced a series of unconnected sentences that cannot be used to say anything real. To keep such learners in class, the teacher must make them feel comfortable, they must sense that the teacher believes that they can learn, and they must feel that they are making some progress.

Not all adult learners in the community will fit this description. Many adult learners from the same community will demand much from the teacher and will feel very comfortable in a class setting. Indeed, they may have selected the class setting because they believe it to be the fastest way of learning English. They will be impatient and will want to progress much faster than is really possible. Teachers can help these students by identifying contexts in the community in which such students can interact with local European Americans and other English speakers. Often such students must be persuaded to set their books aside and attempt to communicate in the real world.

Younger learners present a different picture from that of adult learners. Not only must they acquire English in order to use it in their everyday lives, but they must also acquire the type of school language that will permit them to succeed in an academic setting. I cannot emphasize enough that such learners need to use English for real communication and at the same time be exposed to large amounts of academic language. Fortunately, much is already known about the kinds of English language proficiencies that students must develop to succeed in school. A number of researchers have examined the language demands of all-English classrooms and the effect of particular language teaching practices on academic achievement. Wong Fillmore (1982), for example, found that in order to participate in the life and work of schools and learn academic subject matter, immigrant students must develop two fundamental skills in English: (1) They must be able to comprehend the spoken language of their teachers as they explain and present instruction; and (2) they must comprehend the language of the textbooks from which they are expected to learn.

English language instruction, then, must build on existing research and on current thinking within the ESL profession about what immigrant students need. *ESL Standards for Pre-K–12 Students* (TESOL, 1997), for example, directly addresses the confusion surrounding the goals of English language study by delineating progress indicators of English language development for ESL teachers and administrators. These standards specify the language skills English language learners need in order to have "unrestricted access to grade-appropriate instruction in challenging academic subjects" (pp. 1–2) and stress that learners need to develop English proficiency in order to participate in social interactions as well as to achieve academically in all content areas. Specifically, the three goals of English language learning involve (1) using English to communicate in social settings, (2) using English to achieve academically in all content areas, and (3) using English in socially and culturally appropriate ways. The standards stress that English language learners must develop abilities to request and provide information, paraphrase a teacher's directions, work successfully with partners, negotiate and reach consensus, compare and contrast information, read and get meaning from texts, gather evidence, prepare and participate in debates, and edit and revise written assignments. Moreover, they must be able to choose the language variety, register, and genre as appropriate to the interaction, interlocutors, and setting. They must respond to humor, express anger, make polite requests, engage in small talk, and recognize and use idiomatic speech.

The politics of teaching English[7]

Setting out an unambiguous set of learning objectives for English language learners is an important first step. However, there is much more to consider in implementing programs designed to teach the English language to immigrant students. For example, a number of scholar-practitioners who are part of the ESL and EFL professions (e.g., Bhatt & Martin-Jones, 1992; Corson, 1997; Fairclough, 1989; Kaplan, 1997; Pennycook, 1994; Tollefson, 1991; Wallace, 1992) have attempted to point out to their colleagues around the world that the teaching of English is not neutral. They have argued strongly that the key doctrine of the discourse of ESL teaching – that it is possible to just teach language – is untenable because it is impossible to separate English from its many contexts.

Working within the framework of critical pedagogy and critical language awareness, a number of individuals (e.g., Fairclough, 1992; Pennycook, 1994) have argued that in both English-speaking and non-English-speaking countries, English is one of the "most powerful means of inclusion into or exclusion from further education, employment or social position" (Pennycook, 1994, p. 14). Critiquing the notion of language acquisition as a predominantly psycholinguistic phenomenon, Pennycook (1994), for example, argues that language, rather than being isolated from social, cultural, and educational contexts, is at the center of questions concerning education and inequality. Unfortunately, as Tollefson (1995) has pointed out, most teacher education programs in ESL have focused on second language acquisition, teaching methods, and linguistics without placing these fields in their social, political, and economic contexts. For many scholars (e.g., Tollefson, 1995) applied linguistics and language teaching must undergo a critical

7 This section draws extensively from Valdés (1998).

self-examination. These scholars argue that central concepts in applied linguistics reflect a particular ideological perspective about power relationships. As a result, English language educators adopt uncritical positions about the value of English and about the place of ESL teaching in the schooling of language minority students. They often view language as a formal system for study rather than as something that is located in social action. They do not see that language is always situated within larger discursive frameworks and, as Pennycook (1994) put it, is "part of the cultural and political moments of the day" (p. 34).

From the perspective of theorists working from a critical perspective, ESL classrooms – like all classrooms – are sites of struggle. Auerbach (1995), for example, maintains that if classrooms are seen through an ideological lens, the "dynamics of power and inequality show up in every aspect of classroom life, from physical setting to needs assessment, participant structures, curriculum development, lesson content, materials, instructional processes, discourse patterns, language use and evaluation" (p. 12). Textbooks, for example, often become the curriculum itself, and the teacher's goal is to cover the material, not to uncover what students want to say or what is important to them. Problems are seen to reside in students and not in text materials or in the the teacher's decision to focus on rehearsing correct forms as opposed to generating new meaning and sharing information, opinions, and experiences. Much classroom activity is limited to a focus on the basics, i.e., pronunciation of isolated forms, memorization of vocabulary items, and practice of grammatical structures. The mastery of basics is seen as a prerequisite to creative communication, and there is no acknowledgment that forms and expressions rehearsed in class actually inculcate norms and social relations.

ESL teachers who wish to become effective teachers of Mexican-origin students cannot hope for easy answers. Teaching these students will ideally involve not merely helping students succeed but rather trying to change the ways students understand their lives and the possibilities with which they are presented. As Pennycook (1994) points out, ESL teachers must ask themselves "what sort of vision of society" (p. 209) they are teaching toward. He argues that a critical practice of English language teaching must begin by critically examining and exploring students' knowledges, histories, and cultures in ways that are both affirming and supportive. Teachers must work to help students develop their own voices – not what has been termed the *babble* of communicative language teaching – but voices that are tied to a vision of possibilities. In sum, they must help students to find and create insurgent voices – voices that question the reality that surrounds them.

Suggestions for further reading

The works of Sánchez (1983), Hernández-Chavez (1975), Peñalosa (1975), and Silva-Corvalán (1994) are fundamental to the understanding of Mexican American Spanish. Although slightly dated, the Peñalosa and Hernández-Chavez volumes identify key issues and controversies that continue to arise in discussions about language in Mexican American communities. Sánchez's work is considered a foundational text in the study of Chicano Spanish and presents many examples as well as analyses of Chicano speech. Silva-Corvalán's work with three generations of Mexican-origin immigrants in Los Angeles is considered the most complete study of language change conducted to date.

Several books of readings allow readers to examine Mexican American Spanish in comparison to other Spanish language varieties spoken in the United States and in other areas of the Spanish-speaking world. These volumes include Amastae and Elías-Olivares (1982), Bergen (1990), Klee and Ramos-García (1991), Morgan, Lee, and VanPatten (1987), and Durán (1981). Bergen's volume is one of the several proceedings of the yearly "Español en los Estados Unidos" conferences that have taken place since 1983. Durán's volume is a collection of the papers presented on Latino discourse and communicative behavior and contains a number of seminal papers on English-Spanish code switching. Klee's and Morgan's volumes include a number of articles on Mexican American Spanish as well as on other varieties of Spanish and exemplify more recent concerns in the study of contact varieties of language.

References

Amastae, J., & Elias-Olivares, L. (Eds.). (1982). *Spanish in the United States: Sociolinguistic aspects*. Cambridge: Cambridge University Press.

Auer, P. (1984). *Bilingual conversation*. Amsterdam: John Benjamins.

Auerbach, E. R. (1995). The politics of the ESL classroom: Issues of power in pedagogical choices. In J. W. Tollefson (Ed.), *Power and inequality in language education* (pp. 9–33). Cambridge: Cambridge University Press.

Bachman, L. F. (1990). *Fundamental considerations in language testing*. Oxford: Oxford University Press.

Bean, F. D., & Tienda, M. (1987). *The Hispanic population of the United States*. New York: Russell Sage Foundation.

Bergen, J. (1990). *Spanish in the United States: Sociolinguistic issues*. Washington DC: Georgetown University Press.

Bhatt, A., & Martin-Jones, M. (1992). Whose resource? Minority language, bilingual learners and language awareness. In N. Fairclough (Ed.), *Critical language awareness* (pp. 285–302). London: Longman.

Biber, D. (1994). An analytical frameword for register studies. In D. Biber & E. Finegan (Eds.), *Sociolinguistic perspectives on register.* New York: Oxford University Press.

Bills, G. D. (1989). The US census of 1980 and Spanish in the Southwest. *International Journal of the Sociology of Language, 79,* 11–28.

Bills, G. D., Hernandez-Chavez, E., & Hudson, A. (1995). The geography of language shift: Distance from the Mexican border and Spanish language claiming in the U.S. *International Journal of the Sociology of Language, 114,* 9–27.

Chaston, J. M. (1991). Imperfect progressive usage patterns in the speech of Mexican American bilinguals from Texas. In C. A. Klee & L. Ramos-García (Eds.), *Sociolinguistics of the Spanish-speaking world: Iberia, Latin American, United States* (pp. 299–311). Tempe, AZ: Bilingual Press.

Clyne, M. G. (1987). Constraints on code-switching: How universal are they? *Linguistics, 25,* 739–764.

Cornelius, W. A. (1976a). *Mexican migration to the United States: The view from rural sending communities.* (Migration and Development Monograph C/76-12). Cambridge: Massachusetts Institute of Technology, Center for International Studies.

Cornelius, W. A. (1976b). Outmigration from rural Mexican communities. *Interdisciplinary Communications Program Occasional Monograph Series, 5*(2), 1–39.

Cornelius, W. A. (1978). *Mexican migration to the United States: Causes, consequences, and U.S. responses* (Migration and Development Monograph C/78-9). Cambridge: Massachusetts Institute of Technology, Center for International Studies.

Corson, D. (1997). Social justice in the work of ESL teachers. In W. Eggington & H. Wren (Eds.), *Language policy: Dominant English, pluralist challenges* (pp. 149–163). Amsterdam: John Benjamins.

Crawford, J. (1992a). *Hold your tongue.* Reading, MA: Addison Wesley.

Crawford, J. (Ed.). (1992b). *Language loyalties: A source book on the official English contoversy.* Chicago: University of Chicago Press.

de Bot, K., & Weltens, B. (1991). Recapitulation, regression, and language loss. In H. W. Seliger & R. M. Vago (Eds.), *First language attrition* (pp. 31–51). New York: Cambridge University Press.

de la Garza, R. O., DeSipio, L., Garcia, F. C., Garcia, J., & Falcon, A. (1992). *Latino voices: Mexican, Puerto Rican, and Cuban perspectives on American politics.* Boulder, CO: Westview Press.

Dinerman, I. R. (1982). *Migrants and stay-at homes: A comparative study of rural migration from Michocan, Mexico* (Monographs on U.W.-Mexican Studies No. 5). La Jolla: University of California at San Diego, Program in United States – Mexican Studies.

Durán, R. (Ed.). (1981). *Latino language and communicative behavior.* Norwood, NJ: Ablex.

Durand, J., & Massey, D. S. (1992). Mexican migration to the United States: A critical review. *Latin American Research Review, 27*(2), 3–42.

Elias-Olivares, L. (1976). *Ways of speaking in a Chicano community: A sociolinguistic approach.* Unpublished doctoral dissertation, University of Texas, Austin.

Escobar, A. (1978). *Variaciones sociolingüísticas del castellano en el Perú* [Sociolingulistic variations in the Spanish of Peru]. Lima, Peru: Instituto de Estudios Peruanos.

Fairclough, N. (1989). *Language and power.* London: Longman.

Fantini, A. E. (1985). *Language acquisition of a bilingual child: A sociolinguistic perspective.* Clevedon, England: Multilingual Matters.

Fishman, J. A. (1964). Language maintenance and language shift as fields of inquiry. *Linguistics, 9,* 32–70.

Fishman, J. A. (1968). Sociolinguistic perspective on the study of bilingualism. *Linguistics, 39,* 21–49.

Garcia, M. E. e. a. (1995). Postnuclear /-s/ in San Antonio Spanish: Nohotros no aspiramos. *The Georgetown Journal of Languages and Linguistics, 3,* 139–162.

Gingras, R. C. (1972). *An analysis of the linguistic charcteristics of the English found in a set of Mexican-American child data.* Los Alamitos, CA: Southwest Regional Laboratory of Educational Research and Development. (ERK Document Reproduction Service No. ED 111 002)

Gutierrez, M. (1996). Tendencias y alternancias en la expresión de condicionalidad en el español hablado en Houston [Tendencies and alternatives in conditional expressions in spoken Spanish in Houston]. *Hispania, 79,* 567–577.

Gutierrez, M. J., & Silva-Corvalán, C. (1993). Clíticos el español en una situación de contacto [Spanish clitics in a contact situation]. *Revista Española de Lingüística, 23,* 207–220.

Hart-Gonzalez, L., & Feingold, M. (1990). Retention of Spanish in the home. *International Journal of the Sociology of Language, 84,* 5–34.

Heller, M. (1998). *Code-switching: Anthropological and sociolinguistic perspectives.* Berlin: Mouton de Gruyter.

Hernández-Chávez, E. (Ed.). (1975). *El lenguaje de los chicanos* [The language of the Chicanos]. Arlington, VA: Center for Applied Linguistics.

Huerta-Macias, A. (1981). Codeswitching – all in the family. In R. Durán (Ed.), *Latino language and communicative behavior* (pp. 153–168). Norwood, NJ: Ablex.

Huffines, M. L. (1991). Pensylvania German: Convergence and change as strategies of discourse. In H. W. Seliger & R. M. Vago (Eds.), *First language attrition* (pp. 127–137). New York: Cambridge University Press.

Jacobson, R. (1990). *Codeswitching as a worldwide phenomenon.* New York: Peter Lang.

Jaramillo, J. A. (1990). Domain constraints in the use of *tú* and *usted.* In J. Bergen (Ed.), *Spanish in the United States: Sociolinguistic issues* (pp. 14–22). Washington, DC: Georgetown University Press.

Jasso, G., & Rosenzweig, M. R. (1990). *The new chosen people: Immigrants in the United States.* New York: Russell Sage Foundation.

Johnson, M. G. (1996). *Discourse markers in Tejano speaking: Code-switching as a resource in Spanish-English conversation.* Unpublished doctoral dissertation, University of Texas, Austin.

Kachru, B. B. (1992). *The other tongue: English across cultures.* Urbana: University of Illinois Press.

Kaplan, R. B. (1997). Foreword: Palmam qui meruit ferat. In W. Eggington &

H. Wren (Eds.), *Language policy: Dominant English, pluralist challenges* (pp. xi–xxiii). Amsterdam: John Benjamins.

Klee, C. (1987). Differential language usage patterns by males and females in a rural community in the Rio Grande Valley. In T. A. Morgan, J. F. Lee, & B. VanPatten (Eds.), *Language and language use: Studies in Spanish dedicated to Joseph H. Matluck* (pp. 125–145). Lanham, MD: University Press of America.

Klee, C. A., & Ramos-García, L. A. (Eds.). (1991). *Sociolinguistics of the Spanish-speaking world.* Tempe, AZ: Bilingual Press.

Lavandera, B. (1981). Lo quebramos, but only in performance. In R. Durán (Ed.), *Latino language and communicative behavior.* Norwood, NJ: Ablex.

Lavandera, B. A. (1978). The variable component in bilingual performance. In J. E. Alatis (Ed.), *Georgetown University Round Table on languages and Linguistics 1978* (pp. 391–409). Washington, DC: Georgetown University Press.

Lippi-Green, R. (1994). Accent, standard language identity and discrimination pretext in the courts. *Language in Society, 23,* 163–198.

Lippi-Green, R. (1997). *English with an accent.* London: Routledge.

Lope Blanch, J. M. (1990). *El español hablado en el suroeste de los Estados Unidos: Materiales para su estudio* [The Spanish spoken in the United States Southwest: Materials for its study]. Mexico DF: Universidad Nacional Autónoma de Mexico.

Lozano, A. G. (1994). San Luis Valley lexicon: Relics and innovations. *Confluencia: Revista Hispanica de Cultura y Literatura, 9*(2), 121–127.

Maher, J. (1991). A crosslinguistic study of language contact and language attrition. In H. W. Seliger & R. M. Vago (Eds.), *First language attrition* (pp. 67–84). New York: Cambridge University Press.

Massey, D. S., Alarcon, R., Durand, J., & Gonzalez, H. (1987). *Return to Aztlan: the social process of international migration from western Mexico.* Berkeley: University of California Press.

McWilliams, C. (1949). *North from Mexico.* Philadelphia: Lippincott.

Metcalf, A. A. (1979). Chicano English. *Language in Education: Theory and Practice, 21.*

Milroy, L., & Muysken, P. (Eds.). (1995). *One speaker, two languages: Cross-disciplinary perspectives on code-switching.* Cambridge: Cambridge University Press.

Mines, R. (1981). *Developing a community tradition of migration: A field study in rural Zacatecas, Mexico and California settlement areas* (Monographs in U.S.-Mexican Studies No. 3). La Jolla: University of California at San Diego, Program in United States – Mexican Studies.

Mines, R. (1984). Network migration and Mexican rural development. In R. C. Jones (Ed.), *Patterns of undocumented migration: Mexico and the United States.* Totowa, NJ: Rowman & Allanheld.

Mines, R., & Massey, D. S. (1985). Patterns of migration to the United States from two Mexican communities. *Latin American Research Review, 20,* 104–124.

Moore, J., & Pachon, H. (1985). *Hispanics in the United States.* Englewood Cliffs, NJ: Prentice Hall.

Morgan, T. A., Lee, J. F., & VanPatten, B. (Eds.). (1987). *Language and lan-*

guage use: Studies in Spanish dedicated to Joseph H. Matluck. Lanham, MD: University Press of America.

Myers-Scotton, C. (1993a). *Dueling languages: Grammatical structure in code-switching.* Oxford: Clarendon Press.

Myers-Scotton, C. (1993b). *Social motivations for code-switching: Evidence from Africa.* Oxford: Clarendon Press.

Ocampo, F. (1990). El subjuntivo en tres generaciones de hablantes bilingües [The subjunctive in three generations of bilingual speakers]. In J. Bergen (Ed.), *Spanish in the United States: Sociolinguistic issues* (pp. 39–48). Washington, DC: Georgetown University Press.

Olshtain, E., & Barzilay, M. (1991). Lexical retrieval difficulties in adult language attrition. In H. W. Seliger & R. M. Vago (Eds.), *First language attrition* (pp. 139–150). New York: Cambridge University Press.

Oroz, R. N. (1966). *La lengua castellana en Chile* [The Spanish language in Chile] Santiago: Universidad de Chile.

Peñalosa, F. (1980). *Chicano sociolinguistics.* Rowley, MA: Newbury House.

Pennycook, A. (1994). *The cultural politics of English as an international language.* London: Longman.

Pfaff, C. W. (1979). Constraints on language mixing. *Language, 55,* 291–213.

Piatt, B. (1992). *Language on the job.* Albuquerque: University of New Mexico Press.

Poplack, S. (1980). Sometimes I'll start a sentence in Spanish y termino en español: Toward a typology of code-switching. *Linguistics, 18,* 581–618.

Poplack, S. (1981). Syntactic structure and social funcion of code-switching. In R. Duran (Ed.), *Latino language and communicative behavior* (pp. 169–184). Norwood, NJ: Ablex.

Portes, A., McLeod, S. A., & Parker, R. N. (1978). Immigrant aspirations. *Sociology of Education, 51,* 241–260.

Portes, A., & Bach, R. L. (1985). *Latin journey: Cuban and Mexican immigrants in the United States.* Berkeley: University of California Press.

Portes, A., & Rumbaut, R. G. (1990). *Immigrant America: A portrait.* Berkeley: University of California Press.

Reichert, J. S., & Massey, D. A. (1979). Patterns of U.S. migration from a Mexican sending community: A comparison of legal and illegal migrants. *International Migration Review, 14,* 475–491.

Reichert, J. S., & Massey, D. S. (1980). History and trends in U.S.-bound migration from a Mexican town. *International Migration Review,* 475–491.

Sánchez, R. (1982). Our linguistic and social context. In J. Amastae & L. Elias-Olivares (Eds.), *Spanish in the United States: Sociolinguistic aspects* (pp. 9–46). Cambridge: Cambridge University Press.

Sánchez, R. (1983). *Chicano discourse.* Rowley, MA: Newbury House.

Sawyer, J. B. (1975). Spanish English bilingualism in San Antonio, Texas. In E. Hernandez-Chavez, A. Cohen, & A. Beltramo (Eds.), *El lenguaje de los chicanos* [The language of the Chicanos] (pp. 77–98). Arlington, VA: Center for Applied Linguistics.

Selby, H. A., Murphy, A. D., & Lorenzen, S. A. (1990). *The Mexican urban household.* Austin: University of Texas Press.

Seliger, H. W., & Vago, R. M. (1991). The study of first language attrition. In H. W. Seliger & R. M. Vago (Eds.), *First language attrition* (pp. 3–15). New York: Cambridge University Press.

Silva-Corvalán, C. (1994). *Language contact and change: Spanish in Los Angeles.* New York: Oxford University Press.

Silva-Corvalán, C. (1991). Spanish language attrition in a contact situation with English. In H. W. Seliger & R. M. Vago (Eds.), *First language attrition* (pp. 151–171). New York: Cambridge University Press.

Solé, Y. R. (1990). Bilingualism: Stable or transitional? The case of Spanish in the United States. *International Journal of the Sociology of Language, 84,* 35–80.

Strevens, P. (1992). English as an international language: Directions in the 1990's. In B. B. Kachru (Ed.), *The other tongue* (pp. 27–47). Urbana: University of Illinois Press.

TESOL (1997). *ESL Standards for Pre-K–12 Students.* Alexandria, VA: Author.

Tollefson, J. W. (1991). *Planning language, planning inequality: Language policy in the community.* London: Longman.

Tollefson, J. W. (Ed.). (1995). *Power and inequality in language education.* Cambridge: Cambridge University Press.

U.S. Bureau of the Census. (1995, February 9). March 1994 CPS: Population by ethnicity and nativity. ⟨http://www.census.gov/population/socdemo/hispami/hnatvy95.txt⟩.

U.S. Bureau of the Census. (1994). 1990 census of population – Social and economic characteristics: United States summary. Washington, DC: U.S. Government Printing Office.

Valdés, G. (1992). Bilingual minorities and language issues in writing: Toward professionwide responses to a new challenge. *Written Communication, 9,* 85–136.

Valdés's, G. (1976). Code switching and language dominance: Some initial findings. *General Linguistics, 18,* 90–104.

Valdés, G. (1981). Codeswitching as a deliberate verbal strategy: A microanalysis of direct and indirect requests among bilingual chicano speakers. In R. Durán (Ed.), *Latino language and communicative behavior* (pp. 95–107). Norwood, NJ: Ablex.

Valdés, G. (1982). Social interaction and code-switching patterns: A case study of Spanish/English interaction. In J. Amastae & L. Elias-Olivares (Eds.), *Spanish in the United States: Sociolinguistic aspects* (pp. 209–229). Cambridge: Cambridge University Press.

Valdés, G. (1995). The teaching of minority languages as "foreign" languages: Pedagogical and theoretical challenges. *Modern Language Journal, 79,* 299–328.

Valdés, G. (1997). Bilinguals and bilingualism: Language policy in an anti-immigrant age. *International Journal of the Sociology of Language, 127,* 25–52.

Valdés, G. (1998). The world outside and inside schools: Language and immigrant Children. *Educational Researcher, 27*(6), 1–15.

Valdés, G., & Geoffrion-Vinci, M. (in press). Chicano Spanish: The problem of the "underdeveloped" code in bilingual repertoires. *Modern Language Journal.*

Valdés-Fallis, G. (1978). *Code-switching and the classroom teacher.* Arlington, VA: Center for Applied Linguistics.

Veltman, C. (1988). *The future of the Spanish language in the United States.* New York: Hispanic Policy Development Project.

Veltman, C. J. (1983). *Language shift in the United States*. Berlin: Mouton.

Vernez, G., & Ronfeldt, D. (1991). The current situation in Mexican immigration. *Science, 251,* 1189–1193.

Wallace, C. (1992). Critical literacy awareness in the EFL classroom. In N. Fairclough (Ed.), *Critical language awareness* (pp. 59–92). London: Longman.

Wong Fillmore, L. (1982). Language minority students and school participation: What kind of English is needed? *Journal of Education, 164,* 143–156.

Woolard, K. A. (1992). Language convergence and language death as social processes. In N. C. Dorian (Ed.), *Investigating obsolescence: Studies in language contraction and death* (pp. 365–367). Cambridge: Cambridge University Press.

Zamora Vicente, A. (1970). *Dialectología española* [Spanish dialectology]. Madrid: Editorial Gredos.

Zentella, A. C. (1981). Ta bien, you could answer me en cualquier idioma: Puerto Rican codeswitching in bilingual classrooms. In R. Duran (Ed.), *Latino language and communicative behavior* (pp. 109–131). Norwood, NJ: Ablex.

Zentella, A. C. (1982). Code-switching and interactions among Puerto Rican children. In J. Amastae & L. Elias-Olivares (Eds.), *Spanish in the United States: Sociolinguistic aspects* (pp. 351–385). Cambridge: Cambridge University Press.

Zentella, A. C. (1997). *Growing up bilingual.* Oxford: Blackwell.

4 Puerto Ricans in the United States

Confronting the linguistic repercussions of colonialism

Ana Celia Zentella

In 1998 Puerto Rico, an island in the Caribbean that is about the size of Connecticut and has a population of 3.8 million, completed a century of belonging to the United States. Uninterrupted U.S. jurisdiction in their homeland since 1898 distinguishes Puerto Ricans from immigrants in unique ways, with significant repercussions for the educational and socioeconomic progress of Puerto Ricans in general and for the development of their English, Spanish, and bilingualism in particular. Puerto Rico had been a colony of Spain for more than 400 years until the invasion by General Miles on July 25, 1898. The Spanish language, religion, racial makeup, and way of life of Puerto Ricans today were influenced first by the indigenous Taino people – who were virtually extinguished in 60 years – and then by the thousands of enslaved Africans who were brought to the island for more than two centuries. As a colony of the United States from 1898 until 1952 and since then as a commonwealth, Puerto Ricans have been subject to intense Americanization via U.S. laws that are the ultimate arbiters of their nationality and of the official language(s) of their legal and educational systems.

Under U.S. governors appointed in Washington, DC, English was imposed on the island's legal and educational system for the first half of the twentieth century. The Americanization of the school system and the displacement of Puerto Rican teachers, clergy, business leaders, and politicians produced an alarming number of dropouts instead of fluent English speakers (Negrón de Montilla, 1970). When the nationalist movement opposed U.S. rule in favor of independence, it was systematically devastated by the incarceration or murder of its leaders, and by policies and practices that solidified Puerto Rican dependency on the United States. These measures included making Puerto Ricans citizens of the United States, drafting Puerto Rican males into the U.S. armed services (many into the Black battalions until the army was desegregated), experimenting with high-estrogen contraceptives on Puerto Rican women, promoting sterilization for birth control, and recruiting hundreds of thousands of immigrants to work in the United States (Maldonado-Denis, 1972). At the turn of the twenty first century, Puerto Ricans constitute the second largest group of Latinos in the United States (approximately two million), and in many northeastern school districts – where they were the first mixed racial immigrants that communities of European origin had encountered – the majority of the children are of Puerto Rican background.

An adequate analysis of the language and education nexus in U.S. immigrant communities must take into account the formative experiences of each community, including the political and economic conditions of the homeland that precipitated immigration and the nature of the migration patterns that ensued. Because language reflects, transmits, and creates the collective experiences and ways of being of its speakers, massive population movements affect what and how immigrants speak, read, and write. The language skills and attitudes of Puerto Ricans are the product of their island's status as a territory of the United States, its proximity to the U.S. mainland, and the circular migration pattern that resulted from the push-pull of economic and political forces.

Push-pull migration

When the first groups of Puerto Ricans emigrated to the United States at the turn of the twentieth century, the boat trip could take up to 9 days. In 1910 the U.S. census first recorded the presence of approximately a thousand Puerto Ricans on the mainland. After U.S. citizenship was conferred on Puerto Ricans in 1917 – a few weeks before the United States entered World War I – emigration increased and did so once again during the Depression years of the late 1920s and the 1930s. It reached its highest point in the post–World War II decade (1945–1955), when over 50,000 Puerto Ricans left the island annually in an attempt to escape the arduous conditions, which, ironically, were due to the increasingly pervasive U.S. control of their island's economy. The airline service that was established in 1946 between San Juan and New York City to provide cheap labor for New York's businesses, particularly the garment industry, shortened the 9-day boat trip to 9 hours. More than 80% of the Puerto Ricans who emigrated during the first half of the twentieth century took up residence in New York City, but in the second half the trend was away from the megalopolis in favor of other cities in the Northeast and West, e.g., in New Jersey, Pennsylvania, Connecticut, Ohio, Illinois, and California. In the 1970s major budget cuts and layoffs in New York pushed the poor out of that city, and the hope of a second chance pulled many back to their homeland; for the first time, return migration to Puerto Rico was greater than outmigration from the island. The continual push-pull – between hardship conditions, which push Puerto Ricans out of either the United States or Puerto Rico, and the promise of better opportunities, which pulls them toward the other shore – responds to powerful economic interests in the

United States, which create favorable or unfavorable working and living conditions in the metropolis and the territory (Bonilla, 1985).

Many of the early Puerto Rican arrivals left small pueblos, and significant numbers of them had learned trades and had strong literacy skills in Spanish. After World War II, the extended families of former soldiers and residents of the poor barrios and notorious shantytowns of the capital area arrived in the United States displaying the ravages of an inferior educational experience and the disruption of traditional ways. More recently, those who hop a jet and make the move in $3^1/_2$ hours include many Puerto Ricans who are disgruntled with the inflated cost of living (25% higher than that of the United States), low wages (more than half earn less than $5,000 per year), escalating poverty (almost two thirds live at or below the poverty line), and the terrifying incidence of drug addiction, crime, and murder. The exodus of the well-educated elite constitutes a brain drain of engineers, scientists, and other professionals, which exacerbates the island's problems. At the end of the twentieth century, the class background, education, and skills of new arrivals are more diverse than they have ever been, and they take up residence in more diverse regions of the United States. New York remains the city with the greatest Puerto Rican concentration (in 1990 it was home to 896,763 of the country's 2.5 million Puerto Ricans), but in the early 1990s the fastest-growing cities in terms of Puerto Rican population were Lawrence, Massachusetts, Tampa, Florida, and Allentown, Pennsylvania (Rivera-Batiz & Santiago, 1994).

Despite the differences in migration eras, backgrounds, reasons for emigrating, and areas of settlement, and despite the increasing Americanization of Puerto Rico, all who leave the island for the United States continue to share linguistic and cultural patterns of behavior that conflict with those of the mainstream United States. After having been part of a cultural majority all their lives, many undergo culture shock when they realize that they become a racially defined minority as soon as they step on the mainland. Every Puerto Rican is born a citizen of the United States, but the distance between the promises of citizenship and the harsh realities of their working-class ghettoes makes their situation more like that of other "castelike" groups who were forcibly incorporated into the United States (Native Americans, African Americans, and Mexicans) than that of immigrants from other Spanish-speaking parts of the world (Ogbu, 1988). Ogbu attributes the fact that these four groups rank lowest on major indicators of educational, economic, and social well-being to their long history as unwilling and oppressed internal colonies of the United States, which he believes fosters an "oppositional identity" that rejects, among other things, learning standard English. Ogbu's (1988) distinction between "involuntary caste-like minorities" and "voluntary immigrants" with "non-oppositional identities" has been criticized for obscuring the fact that members of both groups can be oppositional or non-oppositional (Trueba, 1988), and I found that individual Puerto Rican teenagers in New York manipulated multiple identities easily (Zentella, in press). What, then, are the repercussions of the similar linguistic exploitation that the castelike groups have endured? The extermination and containment of Indians, the enslavement of Africans, the takeover of vast parts of Mexico's territory, and the colonization of Puerto Rico were all accomplished with the aid of governmental and educational policies that denied the people their native languages and imposed English, sometimes brutally (Molesky, 1988). The Puerto Rican experience proves that the legacy of subtractive policies has continued to take a grave toll on the residents of Puerto Rico and on Puerto Rican residents in the United States.

The "language problem"

When island Puerto Ricans debate the language problem – as they have for a century – it is always in relation to three status alternatives. Statehood is associated with English, and independence with Spanish; as a territory and commonwealth of the United States (the third status alternative), Puerto Rico has never had a consistent language policy. A law passed in 1902 allowed for the local government's "indiscriminate" use of either language with translations when necessary, but it was contradicted by policies that made English the language of the schools and the legal system. Puerto Rico's first U.S. commissioner of education claimed these policies did Puerto Ricans a favor because, in his unenlightened opinion, Puerto Rican Spanish was a "patois," "almost unintelligible," with "no literature," and "little value as an intellectual medium" (Commissioner Brumbaugh, cited in Osuna, 1949, p. 324). The first half of the twentieth century was marked by legal, educational, and political struggles – including armed conflict – over Puerto Rico's right to maintain its language, among other demands. The U.S. Congress refused to consider statehood for Puerto Rico, in part on racial grounds against another non-White state, but it also rejected any movement for independence. To defuse separatist fervor, the United States allowed Puerto Ricans to elect their own governor in 1948, and Spanish became the language of instruction in the schools (with compulsory English courses in every grade). Furor over the language problem died down, although intellectuals never stopped denouncing the encroaching power of English.

The language problem resurfaced with increased intensity in 1981, when Senator S. I. Hayakawa (Republican of California) introduced an amendment of the Constitution to make English the official language of the United States, including Puerto Rico. Reaction on the island was so strong that the 1902 bilingual law was overturned, and Spanish became the official language of Puerto Rico in 1991. A year and a half later, a change in the party in power resulted in the reenactment of the 1902 bilingual law, but a proposed referendum to decide the island's political status may result in another shift in language policy before the year 2000. Despite these unpredictable twists and turns in language policy and the magnitude of the U.S. presence, Spanish continues to be the language of daily life in Puerto Rico. Less than 50% of the population evaluated themselves as bilingual for the 1990 census, and child rearing in Spanish is the norm.

Puerto Rican in-migrants[1]

The linguistic insecurity caused by sanctioned ideologies of English superiority and Spanish inferiority is part of the baggage that accompanies Puerto Ricans who move to the United States; no other in-migrant group is weighed down by similar baggage. In the United States the language problem becomes synonymous with the education problem, i.e., the widespread educational failure in working-class Puerto Rican communities is blamed on limited English proficiency. Conventional explanations for why New York Puerto Ricans have the lowest high school completion rates for persons 25 years of age and older ("45% in 1991, compared with 56% of other Latinos, 66% of Blacks and 72% of Whites," Institute for Puerto Rican Policy, 1992 p. 8) often cite language. Puerto Rican children are assumed to drop out because they do not know English, because they know the wrong kind of English, or because their bilingualism is cognitively confusing.

The truth is that whereas the majority of every other Spanish-speaking group in the nation was born in Latin America, more than half of the Puerto Ricans in the United States were born on the mainland. As a result, most were raised hearing English in and out of the home and are English dominant or monolingual in English. Despite their greater knowledge of English when compared to other Latinos in New York City, Puerto Ricans there have the highest poverty rate of any group: 55% compared with 33% for African Americans, 32% for other Latinos, and 12% for Whites (Institute for Puerto Rican Policy, 1992). The youthfulness of Puerto Ricans in the United States (over one third are of school age) makes education, the traditional hope for a way out of the ghetto, a burning issue.

1 The term *in-migrant* includes immigrants from separate nations and new arrivals from colonies or territories of the receiving nation (Baker, 1996).

Ana Celia Zentella

Language research of pedagogical value

I have stressed the historical, political, and socioeconomic aspects of the Puerto Rican experience because they must be addressed, not merely understood, by those who strive to make the promise of education a reality for all Puerto Ricans. Fortunately, over two decades of research on language and Puerto Ricans in the United States is available to help educators "teach from strengths" (McGowan, 1987, p. 1), i.e., to adopt a philosophy and methodology that build upon the linguistic resources that students and teachers bring to the classroom from their homes and communities. The best studies avoid vacuous generalizations such as "Puerto Ricans speak Spanish/English/Spanglish" and base their findings on empirical analyses of real – not idealized or experimentally contrived – language use. By incorporating the theories and methods of sociolinguistics (Labov, 1972), researchers from a variety of disciplines, many of whom are of Puerto Rican background themselves, have provided an insider's view of language structures, attitudes, and behavior among diverse groups of Puerto Ricans in diverse settings. Their work effectively shatters myths concerning the existence of ideal or perfectly balanced bilinguals, the cognitive disadvantages of bilingualism, and the destructive nature of code switching, or so-called Spanglish. It also documents the wealth of linguistic knowledge and skills schools can tap in order to "teach from strengths" (p. 1).

Most of the research on the language varieties, attitudes, and language use of Puerto Ricans in the United States has been conducted in New York City and its environs, where the majority of Puerto Ricans live. But studies of smaller communities in Indiana (Attinasi, 1985), Pennsylvania (Micheau, 1990), and Massachusetts (Walsh, 1991), also prove that the vitality of Spanish, English, and bilingualism in each community is influenced by the political, social, demographic, cultural, and linguistic factors that result from the unique history of U.S. – Puerto Rico relations documented here, and by their local manifestations of the factors listed by Conklin and Lourie (1983).

The Language Policy Task Force (LPTF) of the Centro de Estudios Puertorriqueños (Center for Puerto Rican Studies) in New York City conducted ethnographic and sociolinguistic research with one block's residents in *El Barrio* (the neighborhood), sometimes referred to as Spanish Harlem. For almost 10 years beginning in 1975, members of the LPTF provided qualitative and quantitative analyses that proved that code switching was not haphazard but rule governed (Poplack, 1980), that the verbal system of Puerto Ricans in New York had not departed significantly from Golden-Age Spanish (Pousada & Poplack, 1982), that the gender assignment of loan words imported into Spanish followed Spanish rules (Poplack, Pousada, & Sankoff, 1982), and that

142

the narratives of Spanish- and English-dominant bilinguals made effective and strategic use of both languages (Alvarez, 1989). Most important, they challenged Fishman's (1991) prediction that a nondiglossic community like *El Barrio* loses its heritage language because its functions overlap with those of the dominant language instead of being preserved for and by particular domains. According to the Centro's life-cycle model, *El Barrio's* second-generation Puerto Ricans revived their latent childhood Spanish skills when they became members of adult Spanish-dominant networks, (Pedraza, Attinasi, & Hoffman, 1980). Other seminal articles documented the extent to which community members as well as teachers of Puerto Rican background advocated Spanish maintenance and English proficiency (Attinasi, 1979) and the extent of intergenerational support for bilingual education (Language Policy Task Force, 1982).

Language patterns at home

My work in *El Barrio* focused on twenty families with children who were born and raised in a community (*El Bloque*, or the block) not far from the one studied by the Centro's LPTF. I wrote a book-length analysis of the bilingualism of five second-generation New York Puerto Rican girls over a decade – from their first-generation caregivers' language use to the early language acquisition of their third-generation toddlers (Zentella, 1997a). The varied patterns of Spanish and English adult-adult, child-child, and child-adult interactions in which the girls were immersed were described in Zentella (1988), but not until I collected data that spanned their adolescence and young adulthood was I able to appraise the relevance of the early family patterns to the girls' academic progress and to the development of their language skills in later life.

The number of possible communication patterns that can exist in a family grows exponentially with each member. In principle, every bilingual speaker may choose to speak to another member of the family in Spanish, English, or both, and each bilingual interlocutor has the same choices. In practice, not every family member is bilingual, and not every bilingual exercises all three choices at home. The four principal patterns that emerged in *El Bloque* (see Figure 1) are characteristic of many ethnolinguistic minority communities, although many variations exist.

In the majority of the families (fifteen of twenty), the children heard their parents speak Spanish at home to each other and were always spoken to in Spanish by at least one principal caregiver (Patterns I and II). The parents in these families had emigrated to the United States after spending their youth, including early adolescence, in Puerto Rico. Their homes most closely approximated the one language – one environment

143

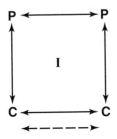

I.

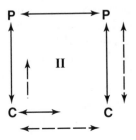

II.

I.

The parents speak only Spanish to each other and the children, who respond to them in Spanish but speak English and Spanish to each other.

II.

The parents speak Spanish to each other and the children; one of them sometimes speaks English as a second language to them. The children respond in both languages, preferring Spanish for their parents and English for each other.

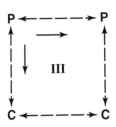

III.

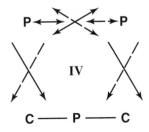

IV.

III.

The parents speak English to each other and to the children; one speaks some Spanish to them. The children respond in English and speak it to each other.

IV.

The parents code switch frequently among themselves and to the children, who are too young to speak yet.

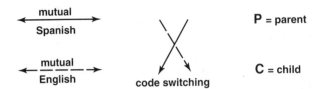

Figure 1   Communication patterns in the home.
Source: Zentella, (1985), p. 50.

principle favored by researchers on bilingualism (see Romaine, 1989, for a summary) because the children had to speak Spanish at home to one adult at least, and they had to speak English outside the home. The effectiveness of the principle was corroborated by the fact that the highest percentage of bilingual children came from these families but that the families also produced children who were not proficient in Spanish.

Parents who were born and raised in New York City, who left Puerto Rico before late adolescence, or who married a monolingual English speaker (one mother) spoke mainly English to each other and to their children (Pattern III). As expected, those families raised English-dominant and even English-monolingual offspring primarily, but some also raised fluent bilinguals. Two young couples in their early twenties were the only caregivers who frequently alternated English and Spanish with each other and their toddlers (Pattern IV). The incipient vocabulary of the children consisted of words from both languages.

Even this brief overview reveals that it is impossible to make accurate predictions about the bilingual fluency of children based on the predominant communication patterns of the home. This is because families in working-class communities around the world, including *El Bloque,* do not raise their children in nuclear units isolated from their neighbors; they count on the support of dense and multiplex network structures (Milroy, 1980). *Density* refers to the fact that everyone knows everyone else, whereas *multiplexity* is achieved because residents relate to each other in a variety of roles: as kin, coworkers, coreligionists, friends, neighbors. In *El Bloque,* for example, nine of the twenty households belonged to the same family, related by blood, marriage, or *compadrazgo* (ritual kinship). Two other households linked four more families to each other. Several residents worked together fixing cars, in the local numbers parlor, in a housekeeping program, or in the *bodega* (grocery store). In dense and multiplex communities, there is constant and impromptu visiting, exchanging, and sharing. Older children from one family baby-sit for the infants of another, and all the children have the run of most apartments. As a result, children are exposed to a variety of communication patterns in addition to the one in their home, all of which influence their language development. Once they are out on the streets of such tightly knit urban communities, their immersion in diverse language varieties increases.

Linguistic diversity in Puerto Rican *bloques*

Children participate in activities that require English, Spanish, or both. Girls as well as boys take part in sports, dancing, games, contests, etc. in full view of members of distinct community networks. Most of the in-

TABLE I. NETWORKS AND CODES OF *EL BLOQUE*

Network	Primary code	Other codes
Children	PRE	PPRS, AAVE
Teens	PRE	PPRS, SE, EDS
Young dudes	AAVE	PRE, PPRS, SE, EDS
Young mothers	PRE	PPRS, SE, AAVE
Mature females	PPRS	SPRS, HE
Mature males	PPRS	SPRS, HE, SE

Note: Abbreviations are as follows:

Spanish codes

English codes

EDS: English-dominant Spanish
PPRS: Popular Puerto Rican Spanish
SPRS: Standard PR Spanish

AAVE: African American Vernacular
  English
HE: Hispanized English
PRE: Puerto Rican English
SE: Standard (New York City)
  English

teraction among children who were born and raised in the United States takes place in English. Spanish, however, is always in the background, particularly during good weather when dozens of people gather out on the street; in *salsa* music from car radios and boom boxes, the comments of domino players, exchanges between *bodegueros* (grocery store owners) and their clients, older women's chats and their admonitions to children, the hawking of wares by itinerant street vendors and hustlers, and the thrice-daily lamenting over the *bolita* (illegal lottery). No activity is the impenetrable domain of either Spanish or English; each language is likely to be invaded by the other because speakers who are monolingual in English interrupt or partake in a Spanish activity and vice versa, or because bilinguals switch languages momentarily.

My references to English and Spanish give the false impression that they are two distinct and unified entities with clearly defined boundaries, which does not capture the reality of most working-class Puerto Rican *bloques* (Urciuoli, 1985). Life as a second-generation member of a *bloque* is not only a bilingual experience, it is also a multidialectal experience. For example, each of *El Bloque's* social networks – based on birthplace, age, and gender – was identified with or by the one or more dialects of English and Spanish its members spoke (see Table 1). Those dialects reflected the community's diverse regional, ethnic, and class identifications with Puerto Rico's past and with New York City's present.

Each social network usually is identified by one code more than another, but its members rarely speak only one. In *El Bloque*, older males and females were more likely to communicate in standard or popular Puerto Rican Spanish (SPRS or PPRS), young males ("dudes") preferred African American Vernacular English (AAVE) on the street, and elementary-school children spoke Puerto Rican English (PRE). Similar configurations are likely in most working-class *bloques*. But members of each network live and interact frequently with members of other networks, which expands their verbal repertoire. Thus, except for the small middle class that has left the *bloques*, second-generation Puerto Ricans in the United States usually are bidialectal as well as bilingual. Often, their verbal repertoire is larger than that of their teachers, particularly those teachers who know standard English only.

Varieties of Spanish

First-generation adults who come from the island's larger towns and who were able to pursue education beyond the elementary grades speak the standard Spanish of Puerto Rico, but most speak PPRS, which shares most of its features with all other varieties of Spanish in Latin America and Spain. It is most similar to the Spanish of the other Spanish-speaking nations in the Caribbean, Cuba, and the Dominican Republic. The Caribbean was the cradle of Spanish in the New World, and it remains one of the principal dialect zones of Latin American Spanish (Cotton & Sharp, 1988).

The pronunciation of Latin American Spanish differs from that of Spain's Castilian dialect primarily in intonation and in a few consonants that changed centuries ago. Most distinctive is the Latin American pronunciation of ⟨z⟩ and ⟨c⟩ before ⟨i⟩ or ⟨e⟩ as /s/, e.g., *cinco zapatos* (five shoes) would be pronounced /sinko sapatos/. Castilian distinguishes between ⟨c⟩ and ⟨z⟩, pronounced like the soft ⟨th⟩ in *thin* (symbolized by θ), and ⟨s⟩, e.g., /θinko θapatos/. Just as English speakers have difficulty pronouncing the vowels and ⟨rr⟩ of Spanish, all first-generation Spanish speakers have trouble with the English phonemes that are not part of their native language's phonological inventory: ⟨v⟩ in an English word may be pronounced like a ⟨b⟩, ⟨sh⟩ like ⟨ch⟩, ⟨z⟩ like ⟨s⟩, and the "soft" and "hard" ⟨th⟩ sounds may be realized as ⟨t⟩ and ⟨d⟩, respectively. Every learner of a new language tends to produce the consonants and vowels of the native language that most closely approximate those of the new language (cf. contrasting pronunciations summarized in Spanish-English dictionaries, e.g., Castillo & Bond, 1981). The fourteen vowels and diphthongs of English constitute a major challenge because Spanish has only five vowels. For example, "She is very pretty and good" may sound closer to "Chee ees bery preety en guud." The fact that Hispanized English of first-generation Latinos in the United States has become the stereotypical butt of many jokes whereas French-

147

accented English communicates sophistication – even elegance – reflects the inferior status unfairly accorded to Spanish-speaking immigrants.

Puerto Ricans and other speakers of Caribbean Spanish distinguish themselves from their Cuban, Dominican, and Mexican neighbors and coworkers by a few pronunciations – most notably in two additional realizations of /s/ in syllable-final position, e.g., in *costas* (coasts). Particularly in informal styles, that /s/ can be realized in Caribbean Spanish as an /h/ (/kohtah/), or it may be dropped (/kota/), even by speakers with university educations. These options are found in the Andalusian and Canary Island varieties of Spanish, which were spoken by the principal colonizers of the Caribbean. Another shared feature, one that is characteristic of the Caribbean poor and stigmatized accordingly, is the alternation of syllable final ⟨r⟩ and ⟨l⟩, e.g., *cortar* (to cut) may be realized as /koltal/. The only feature that distinguishes PPRS from its Caribbean neighbors – besides its intonation patterns and some regional vocabulary items – is the velar version of the trilled ⟨rr⟩ in the middle of words and word-initial ⟨r⟩, e.g., *corren rápido* (they run fast). In addition to the widespread apico-alveolar version that is customary in Spanish, Puerto Ricans may produce a French-like /r/ or a devoiced version that sounds like the German ⟨ch⟩ in Bach. Vestiges of the variations of trilled ⟨rr⟩ and of syllable-final /s/ and /r/ appear in the English pronunciation of students who were born and raised in Puerto Rico. Additionally, contradictory graphemic labels (e.g., the name of the letter ⟨e⟩ in English is the name of the letter ⟨i⟩ in Spanish) are likely to confuse learners of English and Spanish.

Educators must be aware of phonological and graphemic discrepancies in both languages as well as the fact that the traditional Spanish alphabet includes ⟨ch⟩, ⟨ll⟩, ⟨ñ⟩, and ⟨rr⟩ after ⟨c⟩, ⟨l⟩, ⟨n⟩ and ⟨r⟩, respectively.[2] Educators, speech therapists, evaluators, and other professionals must avoid misinterpreting normal examples of transfer as signs of learning problems or speech impediments. Sadly, incorrect evaluations of Spanish speakers in New York City have increased the number of misplacements in special education classes for language disability at alarming rates (special education supervisor for New York City School District 32, personal communication, 1997).

Differences among Spanish dialects sometimes become the focus of ignorant declarations about the superiority of one dialect or another, e.g., the claim that Puerto Rican Spanish (PRS) is not real Spanish. Such claims are particularly damaging when made by teachers who contrib-

---

2 In early 1998, Spain's Real Academia, which sets official Spanish language rules, declared that Spanish would adhere to the twenty-six-letter Roman alphabet, but dictionaries and alphabetical listings that predate the change are organized on the basis of thirty letters.

ute unwittingly to Puerto Rican students' linguistic insecurity, which impedes their acquisition of excellent oral and written skills in Spanish and English. The detractors of PRS are unaware of basic facts about dialectal variety and its regional and social correlates. Everyone in the world speaks a dialect of a language, including the King of Spain and the Queen of England. Nothing in the pronunciation or grammar of one code is superior intrinsically to another, although historical, economic, and political circumstances bestow the highest status on the dialect of the powerful elite.

Varieties of English

The majority of Puerto Ricans in mainland schools were born in the United States, and their fellow students often include many African Americans. Consequently, their oral and written English skills are likely to reflect the influence of AAVE. This influence is most obvious among the youth – particularly males – who speak AAVE in ways that usually are indistinguishable from those of their Black friends (Wolfram, 1974). Many of the nonstandard features that AAVE shares with various dialects of English (Wolfram & Fasold, 1974) appear in the writing of *El Bloque*'s children, including lack of subject-verb agreement ("when she have the baby"), zero copula ("she Jewish"), and unmarked past tenses ("J. move out"). They are typical of PRE, the principal linguistic code shared by Puerto Ricans and other young Latinos who were born or raised in New York City and who share the complex and dense networks of working-class *bloques*. Among the grammatical aspects that may distinguish PRE from both standard New York City English and AAVE is the resumptive pronoun in relative clauses, e.g., "You know that thing, that it gots points on it?" (Urciuoli, 1980). Primarily distinguished by its vowels, consonants, and syllable timing, PRE includes some unique vocabulary, word formations, and grammatical rules – in addition to those borrowed from AAVE – all of which deserve to be studied in depth.

English enjoys a favored position in Puerto Rican communities because of the symbolic domination (Bourdieu, 1991) it exerts in the United States and Puerto Rico and because of its international prestige. Also, as the children grow, so does the number of activities beyond the confines of their *bloques:* schooling, jobs, sports, movies, dancing. These activities and the popular English media further enhance the status of English; it is considered more valuable because it enables the children to communicate with more – and more varied – people. It is linked to prosperity because every affluent person they see or meet speaks English whereas the Spanish-speaking immigrants traditionally are the poorest families in their neighborhood. No educator has to convince Puerto Ricans of the importance of learning English. Unfortunately, negative attitudes toward the varieties of Spanish and English that Puerto Ricans speak and methodologies that fail to capitalize on the verbal repertoire of students provoke high dropout rates.

Spanglish

One of the most misunderstood and belittled skills of bilinguals is their ability to switch from one language to another. The pejorative designation of Spanish-English code switching as *Spanglish* communicates the notion that switchers are semi- or alingual, incapable of clear speech or thought. Unfortunately, the teacher in Massachusetts who disparaged her Puerto Rican students' language abilities as follows is not alone in her beliefs:

These poor kids come to school speaking a hodge podge. They are all mixed up and don't know any language well. As a result, they can't even think clearly. That's why they don't learn. It's our job to teach them language – to make up for their deficiency. And, since their parents don't really know any language either, why should we waste our time on Spanish? It is "good" English which has to be the focus. (Walsh, 1991, p. 107)

More than three decades of research on code switching in Mexican as well as Puerto Rican communities and educational settings refute these views. Code switching is not a "hodge podge" but a way of alternating languages that follows complex rules and accomplishes many important discourse strategies, such as emphazing, clarifying, or highlighting a change in topic, focus, or role (Alvarez, 1989; Genishi, 1976; Gumperz & Hernández-Chávez, 1975; Huerta, 1978; Olmedo-Williams, 1979; Pfaff, 1975; Poplack, 1980; Sankoff & Poplack, 1981; Torres, 1997; Valdés, 1976, 1981; Zentella, 1981, 1990, 1997a). The children of *El Bloque* learned to code switch initially because they had to switch languages when they spoke to monolinguals in English or Spanish. Accustomed to moving from one phonological and syntactic system to another with ease, they extended this facility to their conversations with fellow bilinguals to manage their discourse effectively and to signal their dual identity as Puerto Ricans and New Yorkers. The definition of the *ideal bilingual* proposed by Weinreich (1953/1968) – one who never switches in the same situation with the same speaker – is rebutted by fluent bilingual Latinos who switch in the same situation, with the same speaker, and even within sentence boundaries, but in accordance with the grammars of both languages. Code switchers can be, or can develop into, excellent speakers of English and Spanish, but the stigma attached to Spanglish in their communities and the dominant society causes some to abandon Spanish altogether.

Individual differences in English and Spanish proficiency

Differences in bilingual proficiency between children of different families are to be expected, but differences within families may be more surprising, particularly to teachers who teach siblings over the years. Numerous situational, educational, or cultural variables may account for the dissimilar language abilities of brothers and sisters (Zentella, 1997a); of particular interest is the socialization of young Puerto Rican children into appropriate male and female roles (Zentella, 1987). Daughters receive more exposure to Spanish than sons, e.g., more restriction to the house and mother; play and friendships with girls; caregiving responsibilities for infants; attendance at Spanish religious services; and inclusion in female discussions and activities, such as cooking, sewing, cleaning, washing clothes, communicating with family members in Puerto Rico, and watching the *novelas* (soap operas). In communities like *El Bloque*, females who were born in the United States are expected to maintain Spanish more than males, but they also must be capable of representing themselves and others – in English – in dealings with the bureaucracies of schools, hospitals, social security offices, etc. Often, as a result, girls are better bilinguals than their brothers.

Despite the immersion of females in activities conducted in Spanish, not all second-generation males speak less Spanish or more English than their sisters. One or more members of each family are subjected to one or more Spanish or English influences to varying degrees and at different stages of their lives, modifying each child's personal language development. These include visits to and from Puerto Rico and the length of these visits; enrollment in a bilingual or monolingual program; the amount of time a family member is confined to the home or allowed to roam; contact with African Americans or other Latinos; religious services that do or do not require Spanish or English literacy; and participation in after-school, dance, or theater programs conducted in English or Spanish. The positive or negative quality of these experiences shapes each person's identity in ways that help determine the commitment to learn and develop Spanish, English or both. Children may identify culturally as Puerto Rican, American, Nuyorican, Rochesterican, etc. and racially as Black, White, *trigueño* (olive skinned), *jabao* (fair haired and skinned with black features), or another mixed Puerto Rican color category. Often, these identities are not in opposition to each other but complementary, and as such they challenge the boundaries of classifications in the United States as well as in Puerto Rico.

As if the variety of situational and identity variables were not enough, they interact with cognitive and social variables involved in language learning. Wong Fillmore's (1976) 2-year school study of Chinese and Mexican kindergartners identified the relevant cognitive abilities as follows: discerning the patterns of the units, the structure, and the meanings that make up language including memory; inductive reasoning; mental flexibility; and pattern recognition. The social abilities of successful English language learners facilitate adequate language learning practice: sociability, outgoingness, and talkativeness. Wong Fillmore found that high ratings in cognitive and social abilities were characteristic of children who picked up English easily, but some children with these abilities did not learn English easily. Her most important finding, which has been corroborated many times since her study, was that variation in language learning ability is the norm. What some children learned in 8 months took others who were evaluated as brighter 2–3 years to learn.

Language shift

Many U.S. Americans believe that Spanish speakers are not learning English as quickly as earlier immigrants did, but Veltman (1983; see also Chapter 2) found that Spanish is being lost rapidly, even before the third generation. The great majority of Latinos in the United States know English, and only recent immigrants or those who left their homelands as adults may be monolingual. Birthplace is the most significant determinant of language loss or maintenance. Children born in the United States are more likely to become English monolinguals than those born in the homeland, although those who emigrate as youngsters make the transition from Spanish monolinguals to English-dominant bilinguals within a few years, precipitated by schooling and furthered by their devotion to English TV, movies, radio.

As shown by data beginning with the 1980 census and escalating in 1990 census data, more than half of all Puerto Ricans in New York City were born in the United States (Rivera-Batiz & Santiago, 1994). The English language ability of Puerto Ricans also improved over the decade: "sixty-three percent of all Puerto Ricans aged five and over reported a "strong" command of English in 1990, up from 53 percent in 1980" (Department of City Planning, 1993, p. 4). The increase in English proficiency extended to the island born, whose percentage of strong English speakers increased from 37% to 46% in 10 years. Improved English proficiency need not be at the expense of Spanish, but that was the unfortunate outcome for almost all the youth of *El Bloque*. Figure 2 demonstrates the language shift I observed in *El Bloque* between 1980 and 1993 (Zentella, 1997a). When I first went to the community, there were twenty Puerto Rican families with twenty-six children between 3 and 20 years old – four of whom had been born in Puerto Rico but had been moved to New York City before they were eight years old. Most of the children were more proficient in English than Spanish (in Figure 2, *EB, ED,* and *EM* total 61%), but only one was an English monolingual, and 39% had very strong Spanish skills. By 1993, 93% of the original twenty-six children and thirty-six more – mainly siblings and children of the first group – had moved conclusively toward the English end of the language proficiency spectrum. In 13 years, the rate of English monolinguals had risen 13% among those I was able to interview, and those who had moved away were rated either English dominant or monolingual in English by their relatives. There was no longer anyone more proficient in Spanish than in English, and the percentage of bilinguals who were at ease in both languages (*BB*) had decreased threefold. The loss of fluency in Spanish did not translate into higher graduation rates: Only ten of the twenty-three members of *El Bloque* who were 20 years old or older had earned a high school diploma. That rate (43%) was 11% below the national average for Puerto Ricans (54%), 17% below the average for Latinos (60%), and 40% below the average for all 19- and 20-year-olds (83%) (De Witt, 1991). I found it significant that the most fluent bilinguals – mainly those who had studied some in Puerto Rico or in bilingual programs in New York City – were among the high school graduates.

The shift to English begins as soon as children enter school; even a 3-year-old said, "I can't," when asked to respond in Spanish after a few months in a bilingual Head Start program. If children know that adult caregivers understand English even if they do not speak it, a nonreciprocal pattern of communication begins, i.e., the child speaks English, and the adult speaks Spanish. None of the parents of *El Bloque* insisted that their children respond in Spanish, and as the parents' own English improved, they began to speak English to their children. At best, their children grow up to be passive bilinguals, with an ability to comprehend Spanish that far outstrips their ability to speak it.

After studying language maintenance efforts all over the world, Fishman (1991) concludes that nothing "can substitute for the re-establishment of young families of child-bearing age in which Xish is the normal medium or co-medium of communication and/or of other culturally appropriate home, family, neighborhood and community intergenerational activity" (p. 91). In 1993, the young second-generation parents I observed were raising their children primarily in English, and their own Spanish was limited to several tenses. Spanish was part of their chil-

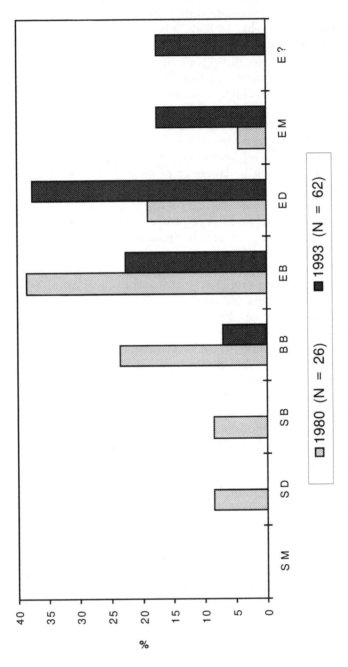

Note: SM: Monolingual in Spanish, limited English comprehension; SD: Spanish dominant, weak English (limited vocabulary tenses); SB: Spanish dominant bilingual, fluent English; BB: Balanced bilingual, near-equal fluency in both languages; EB: English dominant bilingual, fluent Spanish; ED: English dominant, weak Spanish (limited vocabulary tenses); EM: English dominant, limited Spanish comprehension; E?: Either English dominant or English monolingual (based on the evaluation of others).

Figure 2 Language shift, 1980 and 1993 (%).

dren's lives because poverty kept them living with or near Spanish-dominant grandparents in Spanish-speaking neighborhoods. Visits to Puerto Rico were rare, but some visitors from the island brought the children in contact with relatives who were monolingual in Spanish, and local schools had increasing numbers of Mexican and Dominican children whose parents spoke to them in Spanish. Most of the third-generation offspring of *El Bloque* understood a little basic Spanish, but they would not be able to raise a fourth generation of bilinguals unless they went to school in Puerto Rico or married a newcomer.

Often, parents are chastised for not staving off language shift, especially since their choice of child-rearing language is so crucial. But few critics stop to consider the experiences, and the pressures beyond parental control, that lead caregivers to stress English at the expense of Spanish even when their proficiency in English is limited. Macro social and economic issues play decisive roles, for example, employment opportunities that determine the rate and residential patterns of the migration flow to and from Puerto Rico, outmarriage rates, availability of jobs for women or men, number and type of housing units and tenant selection practices, number of Puerto Rican families and businesses in the neighborhood, urban renewal and dislocation, and the quality of local bilingual education programs. During the initial phase of my study of *El Bloque* (1979–1981), the prevalent configurations of these factors favored the continued presence of Spanish, but the city took over the tenements to renovate them, and residents were displaced. "The end of *El Bloque*," as members referred to it, came when the empty buildings undergoing renovation were occupied by drug dealers, homeless vagrants, and Cuban immigrant squatters. When the apartments finally became available, most of the former residents did not return, and the city brought in formerly homeless families – some of whom were African Americans who had never lived in *El Barrio*. The dense and multiplex networks of *El Bloque* were disrupted, with negative repercussions for the maintenance of Spanish. And nationwide, the insidious Hispanophobia fomented by the English-only movement eliminated protections for Spanish speakers (Zentella, 1997b).

Even the most committed supporters of bilingualism for ethnolinguistic minorities feel impotent against the powerful national forces in opposition. With guns leveled at immigration, health and education services for legal residents, bilingual education, bilingual ballots, and affirmative action, self-proclaimed protectors of the American dream call for unity at the expense of diversity, and in English only (Crawford, 1992). By the end of 1998, twenty-three states had passed legislation – most introduced since the mid-1980s – that requires official business to be conducted in English only. Supporters insist that the laws are meant to help immigrants learn English, but they do not provide classes for the thousands on waiting lists. Instead, they create a climate of linguistic and cultural intolerance that fosters harassment and even racial and ethnic violence. Nationwide, the support of the Equal Employment Opportunity Commission for the right of employees to speak a language other than English on the job (except to ensure safety) has eroded, and the number of complaints is increasing (Valdés, 1997). Personally, after a lifetime in New York City, I have been dismayed by the "speak English" comments directed at me recently. In 1994, at least one New York City candidate for the State Assembly campaigned on an English-only platform.[3] In 1997, the only bilingual community college in the city was relentlessly attacked by the media, and its (New York Puerto Rican) president was forced to resign. Parents from immigrant backgrounds who strive to do what they are told is best for their children are not immune to the insistent messages of English superiority and the so-called problems with bilingualism and bilingual education. As a result, the children of ethnolinguistic minorities – who should have the best chance to develop bilingual skills – become monolingual, often in stigmatized English dialects. Middle- and upper-class children, on the other hand, are given the advantages of au pairs, lessons via computer or private tutors, language camps, and study abroad in order to learn the languages that will safeguard their status in the twenty-first century.

Implications for educational practice

Puerto Rican parents are strong supporters of bilingualism; as one father told me: "*Un hombre que habla dos idiomas vale por dos*" (A man who speaks two languages is worth two men). They want their children to learn English but wish it did not have to be at the expense of Spanish. Those who dream of returning to Puerto Rico count on their children being able to get along in Spanish, and everyone desires access to jobs that require skills in English and Spanish. Most are unaware of what it takes to ensure that a child acquires excellent oral and literate skills, and too many are advised – by educators, therapists, or pediatricians with no bilingual training – that bilingualism is cognitively confusing. Puerto Rican parents in New York City were in the vanguard of the struggle to make bilingual education a reality in 1974, "for students whose English language deficiency prevents them from effectively participating in the learning process and who can more effectively participate in Spanish" (consent decree cited in *Facts and Figures 1993–1994.*

---

3 Frank Borzellieri, the Republican challenger in the thirty-eighth District, Queens, where "Hispanics are the largest minority with 26% of the population," campaigned for "eliminating foreign languages from government-issued documents and banning from public schools books he considered anti-American, like biographies of Martin Luther King, Jr." (Onishi, 1994, p. 9).

As the century ends, however, some Puerto Ricans and other Latinos are being convinced by negative media reports that bilingual education does not work and that it will stigmatize their child (Del Valle, 1997). Partnerships among parents, schools, and community organizations, which could counter negative arguments with sound research and work together to foster widespread bilingualism, are rare despite common goals (Hidalgo & Nevárez-La Torre, 1997).

The most thorough research on the relationship between bilingualism and higher order cognitive skills in lower working-class Puerto Rican students was conducted in Connecticut schools (Hakuta, 1986). This large (392 children) longitudinal (3 years, K–6) study documents the positive influence of bilingualism on cognitive ability in children who were dominant in one of their languages, or *nonbalanced* bilinguals. Regardless of proficiency level, the cognitive skills demonstrated by the children's metalinguistic ability, nonverbal intelligence, and spatial relations were significantly related to bilingualism. As for language learning, students who were initially more capable in Spanish tended to become more capable in English as they moved up through the grades.

But bilingual education is under siege nationwide. Undoubtedly, reforms in administration, teacher training, placement, and evaluation are needed, but the conviction that children can be and are being well educated in two languages must not be abandoned. In New York City, 15% of the 1,015,756 students enrolled in public schools in 1993–1994 were identified as limited English proficient (LEP), 68% of whom were Spanish speakers.[4] A large national research effort concluded that New York City had some outstanding bilingual programs in which there was "a direct and consistent correlation between Spanish-language development and student gains" in English language, reading, and math (Crawford, 1992, p. 230). No newspaper publicized these results, but when a report based on unsound methodology unfavorably compared the city's bilingual education with English as a second language, it enjoyed extensive coverage (Dillon, 1994; Leo, 1994; "Talking Turkey About English," 1994). Amidst the anti–bilingual education storm, groups of Puerto Rican and other Latino educators have organized alternative, new-vision schools against great odds and with limited financial support from the New York City Board of Education. Another encouraging sign is the increasing interest in two-way or dual bilingual programs, in which language minority children and English monolinguals learn each other's language as well as their own. The success of the early efforts is slowly becoming known as middle-class parents who are monolingual

---

4 The label *LEP* has been criticized because it conjures up leprous images. Casanova (1991) offers *SOL* (speakers of other languages) as a substitute.

in English join forces with working-class, Spanish-speaking parents (Morison, 1990).

Communities as poor and politically weak as most Puerto Rican communities in the United States deserve the support of a broad spectrum of enlightened citizenry and legislators – with educators in the forefront – because the struggle over language rights and bilingual education is in the best interests of the entire nation. Without mainstream support for a new vision of a linguistically competent society, other ethnolinguistic minorities who lose their native language will follow in the footsteps of many American Indians and African Americans, i.e., they will end up without their heritage language and without a high school diploma. Concerning New York Puerto Ricans specifically, "about half of those who enter the school system deficient in both Spanish and English eventually lose their Spanish skills and gain no skills in English" (Willner, 1985, p. 3). The United States must abandon pedagogical approaches that stress English at the expense of the heritage language; they do not produce proficient English speakers, and they prevent the children of Puerto Ricans and other ethnolinguistic minorities from helping the rest of the nation mature culturally and linguistically.

A recent review of effective programs for Latino students in elementary and middle schools is encouraging; it describes programs that evaluated students in comparison to control groups and that proved replicable. The reviewers are convinced it is possible to change the schools now:

Schools can do a much better job of educating Latino students, using methods and materials that are readily available. There are approaches that are effective and appropriate for bilingual classes, for ESL classes, and for English-dominant Latino students. The existence of these approaches demonstrates that the low achievement of so many Latino students is not inevitable. (Fashola, Slavin, Calderón, & Durán, 1997)

Teachers who do not speak Spanish and cannot count on researchers or model programs for help must understand the crucial role they play in interpreting the dominant society's views for ethnolinguistic minorities. They can regard the bilingual and multidialectal repertoire that Puerto Ricans and others bring to schools as an opportunity for correction and ridicule or for expansion and praise. Too often, neither the Spanish nor the English of Puerto Rican students is considered acceptable: They are criticized for speaking a stigmatized variety of Spanish (PRS or English influenced) or a stigmatized variety of English (PRE or AAVE) and for switching between them. Even in bilingual classes, teachers need to be better informed about the rule-governed nature of nonstandard dialects and the cultural and communicative reasons for code switching. The process of growing up bilingual in communities that experience a cultural, racial, and linguistic push-pull stemming from Puerto Rico's embattled status as a territory of the United States merits special attention. Also, teachers must be made aware of the fact that families may teach their children in ways that differ from those of the classroom, causing children to demonstrate their interest, knowledge, and confusion in culturally specific ways (Heath, 1986; Zentella, 1997a). Moreover, all students' homes have *funds of knowledge* involving local lore and skills that can be tapped for the classroom (Mercado & Moll, 1997). Teachers equipped with cultural and linguistic knowledge are in the best position to teach standard dialects and academic subjects effectively. Students of all ages who are helped to become junior ethnographers – alerted to the varied linguistic abilities they possess and the ones they must acquire for full participation in mainstream society – take part eagerly in their own development. The approach must be additive, not subtractive; the expansion of the linguistic repertoires and ways of learning of the children (and of their teachers), not their reduction, contributes to success in and out of school (Zentella, 1997a).

Of course, language is not the only or even the primary problem in working-class Puerto Rican communities. Educators will be unable to tap into children's language skills in order to expand them if the language issues are isolated from the fundamental problem plaguing the education of ethnolinguistic minorities – a disabling approach. Real change in the teaching of language and other subjects requires a commitment to the four basic principles enunciated by Cummins (1989): (1) strengthening the native language, (2) building upon the first language in teaching of the second, (3) ensuring strong parental inclusion, and (4) having educators and psychologists play an advocacy role. Discriminatory assessments and programs that locate the root of academic failure within the students, their families, or their language must be challenged. Schools and teachers who reject the disabling approach can count on members of the Puerto Rican community for support, especially researchers and organizations devoted to improving education, e.g., Aspira, the Puerto Rican/Latino Education Roundtable, the Puerto Rican Educators' Association, to name just a few. Other strong allies are the local members of the second generation who survived the system, are fluent in English, and are anxious to make the public schools safe and excellent for their children. Together, they will not lose heart at the magnitude of the task or lose sight of the just goal that unites them: crossing linguistic and cultural boundaries to teach and learn from each other – new Americans for the new century.

Suggestions for further reading

Important book-length studies of U.S. Puerto Rican communities analyze language in relation to numerous variables that determine whether and how Puerto Ricans speak Spanish, English, or both. In *Exposing Prejudice,* Urciuoli (1996) presents a compelling analysis of New York Puerto Rican adult experiences with language use and ideologies in the dominant society and explains how the group is racialized via the conflation of its stigmatized racial, class, and ethnic identity. *Puerto Rican Discourse* (Torres, 1997) describes the language attitudes of Puerto Ricans in a suburban Long Island community and examines the Spanish narratives of females who belong to three age or generation groups from a linguistic and feminist perspective. In *Growing up Bilingual* (Zentella, 1997a), I document a New York Puerto Rican *bloque's* bilingualism, by focusing on the languages of the children who were born and raised in the community, including their Spanglish from their elementary school days as the children of in-migrants to their experiences as young mothers raising the third generation.

For the 1980–1989 reports of the Language Policy Task Force and for issues of its journal (*CENTRO*), especially Vol. IX, No. 9, which is devoted to the education of Puerto Ricans, contact the Centro de Estudios Puertorriqueños (Hunter College, City University of New York). Readers interested in Puerto Rican efforts to address educational policies and practices in the United States should contact Aspira of America or the National Puerto Rican Coalition in Washington, DC. (Aspira has local offices in New York and other cities that provide support services to secondary school students and their families.)

References

Alvarez, C. (1989). Code switching in narrative performance. In O. García & R. Otheguy (Eds.), *English across cultures, cultures across English: A reader in cross-cultural communication* (pp. 373–386). Berlin: Mouton de Gruyter.

Attinasi, J. (1979). Language attitudes in a New York Puerto Rican community. In R. Padilla (Ed.), *Bilingual education and public policy in the United States* (pp. 408–446). Ypsilanti: Eastern Michigan University.

Attinasi, J. (1985). Hispanic attitudes in Northwest Indiana and New York. In L. Elías-Olivares, E. Leone, R. Cisneros, & J. Guttiérrez (Eds.), *Spanish language use and public life in the United States* (pp. 27–58). Berlin: Mouton de Gruyter.

Baker, C. (1996). *Foundations of bilingual education and bilingualism.* Clevedon, England: Multilingual Matters.

Bonilla, F. (1985). Ethnic orbits: The circulation of peoples and capital. *Contemporary Marxism, 10,* 148–67.

Bourdieu, P. (1991). *Language and symbolic power.* Cambridge, MA: Harvard University Press.

Casanova, U. (1991). Bilingual education: Politics or pedagogy? In O. García (Ed.), *Bilingual education: Focusschrift in honor of Joshua A. Fishman on the occasion of his 65th birthday* (Vol. 1, pp. 167–180), Philadelphia: John Benjamins.

Castillo, C., & Bond, O. (1981). *The University of Chicago Spanish-English, English-Spanish Dictionary.* New York: Pocket Books.

Conklin, N., & Lourie, M. (1983). *A host of tongues: Language communities in the United States.* New York: Free Press.

Cotton, E. G., & Sharp, J. (1988). *Spanish in the Americas.* Washington, DC: Georgetown University Press.

Crawford, J. (1992). *Hold your tongue: Bilingualism and the politics of "English-only."* Reading, MA: Addison-Wesley.

Cummins, J. (1989). *Empowering minority students.* Sacramento: California Association for Bilingual Education.

Del Valle, S. (1997). *BPO v. Mills* and the struggle for bilingual education. *Centro, 9*(9), 46–57.

Department of City Planning. (1993). *Demographic and socioeconomic profiles, selected tabulations, selected Hispanic origin groups, NYC and boroughs.* Unpublished manuscript.

De Witt, K. (1991, October 1). First report card issued on U.S. education goals. *New York Times,* p. A16.

Dillon, S. (1994, October 20). Report faults bilingual education in New York. *New York Times,* p. A1.

Facts and figures. (1994–1995). New York: New York City Board of Education, office of Bilingual Education.

Fashola, O., Slavin, R., Calderón, M., & Durán, R. (1997). *Effective programs for Latino students in elementary and middle schools.* Baltimore: John Hopkins University, Center for Research on the Education of Students Placed at Risk.

Fishman, J. (1991). *Reversing language shift.* Clevedon, England: Multilingual Matters.

Genishi, C. (1976). *Rules for code switching in young Spanish-English speakers: An exploratory study of language socialization.* Unpublished doctoral dissertation, University of California, Berkeley.

Gumperz, J. J., & Hernández-Chávez, E. (1975). Cognitive aspects of bilingual communication. In E. Hernández-Chávez, A. Cohen, & A. Beltramo (Eds.), *El lenguaje de los Chicanos* (pp. 154–163). Arlington, VA: Center for Applied Linguistics.

Hakuta, K. (1986). *Mirror of language: The debate on bilingualism.* New York: Basic Books.

Heath, S. (1986). Sociocultural contexts of language development. In *Language: Social and cultural factors in schooling and language minority students* (pp. 143–186). Los Angeles: California State University, Evaluation, Dissemination and Assessment Center.

Hidalgo, N., & Nevárez-La Torre, A., (1997). Latino communities: Resources for educational change [Special issue]. *Education and Urban Society, 30*(1).

Huerta, A. (1978). *Code switching among Spanish-English bilinguals: A so-*

ciolinguistic perspective. Unpublished doctoral dissertation, University of Texas, Austin.

Institute for Puerto Rican Policy. (1992). *Puerto Ricans and other Latinos in New York City today: A statistical profile.* New York: Author.

Labov, W. (1972). *Sociolinguistic patterns.* Philadelphia: University of Pennsylvania Press.

Language Policy Task Force. (1982). *Intergenerational perspectives on bilingualism from community to classroom.* New York: Hunter College, Centro de Estudios Puertorriqueños.

Leo, J. (1994, November 2). Some straight talk on a bad bilingual plan. *Daily News.*

Maldonado-Denis, M. (1972). *Puerto Rico: A socio-historic interpretation.* New York: Random House.

McGowan, A. (1987). *Teaching from strengths, a research project funded by the Fund for the Improvement of Secondary Education.*

Mercado, C., & Moll, L. (1997). The study of funds of knowledge: Collaborative research in Latino homes. *Centro, 9(9),* 26–42.

Micheau, C. (1990). *Ethnic identity and ethnic maintenance in the Philadelphia Puerto Rican community.* Unpublished doctoral dissertation, University of Pennsylvania, Philadelphia.

Milroy, L. (1980). *Language and social networks.* Baltimore: University Park Press.

Olmedo-Williams, I. (1983). Spanish-English bilingual children as peer teachers. In L. Elias-Olivares (Ed.), *Spanish in the U.S. setting: Beyond the Southwest* (pp. 89–105). Washington, DC: Inter America Research Associates.

Molesky, J. (1988). Understanding the American linguistic mosaic. In S. McKay & S. C. Wong (Eds.), *Language diversity: Problem or resource?* (pp. 29–68). New York: Harper & Row.

Morison, S. H. (1990). A Spanish-English dual-language program in New York City. *Annals of the American Academy of Political and Social Sciences, 508,* 160–169.

Negrón de Montilla, A. (1970). *Americanization in Puerto Rico and the public school system, 1900–1930.* Río Piedras, PR: Editorial Edil.

Ogbu, J. U. (1988). Cultural diversity and human development. In D. T. Slaughter (Ed.), *Black children and poverty: A development perspective* (pp. 11–28). San Francisco: Jossey-Bass.

Onishi, N. (1994, November 6). An "America-first" challenger is resonating, in English only. *The New York Times,* p. 9.

Osuna, J. J. (1949). *A history of education in Puerto Rico.* Río Piedras, PR: Editorial de la Universidad de Puerto Rico.

Pedraza, P., Attinasi, J., & Hoffman, G. (1980). *Rethinking diglossia* (Language Policy Task Force Working Paper No. 9). New York: Centro de Estudios Puertorriqueños.

Pfaff, C. (1975, December). *Constraints on code switching: A quantitative study of Spanish/English.* Paper presented at the annual meeting of the Linguistic Society of America, Washington, DC.

Poplack, S. (1980). Sometimes I'll start a sentence in Spanish y termino en español: Toward a typology of code-switching. *Linguistics, 18,* 581–616.

Poplack, S., Pousada A., & Sankoff, D. (1982). Un estudio comparativo de la asignación de género a préstamos y nominales. [A comparative study of the assignment of gender to borrowed nouns.] In O. Alba, (Ed.), *El Español del Caribe: Ponencias del VI simposio de dialectología.* [Spanish in the Caribbean: Papers from the VI symposium on dialectology.] Santiago, Dominican Republic: Universidad Católica Madre y Maestra.

Pousada, A., & Poplack, S. (1982). No case for convergence: The Puerto Rican Spanish verb system in a language contact situation. In J. A. Fishman & G. Keller (Eds.), 207–240. New York: Columbia University Teachers College Press.

Riverea-Batiz, F., & Santaigo, C. (1994). *Puerto Ricans in the Unites States: A changing reality.* Washington, DC: National Puerto Rican Coalition.

Romaine, S. (1989). *Billingualism.* Oxford: Basil Blackwell.

Sankoff, D., & Poplack, S. (1981). A formal grammar for code-switching. *Papers in Linguistics, 14,* 3–46.

Talking turkey about English [Editorial]. (1994, October 21). *Daily News,* p. 24.

Torres, L. (1997). *Puerto Rican discourse.* Hillsdale, NJ: Erlbaum.

Trueba, H. (1988). Culturally based explanations of minority students' academic achievement. *Anthropology and Education Quarterly, 19,* 270–287.

Urciuoli, B. (1980, October). *Social Parameters of Language Contact,* paper presented at Spanish in the US: Beyond the Southwest, University of Illinois, Chicago.

Valdés, G. (1976). Social interaction and code switching patterns: A case study of Spanish-English alternation. In G. Keller, R. Teschner, & S. Viera (Eds.), *Bilingualism in the bicentennial and beyond.* Jamaica, NY: Bilingual Press.

Valdés, G. (1997). *Bilingual individuals and language based discrimination: Advancing the state of the law on language rights.* Keynote address given at the American Association of Applied Linguists annual conference, Orlando, FL.

Veltman, C. (1983). *Language shift in the United States.* Berlin: Mouton de Gruyter.

Walsh, C. E. (1991). *Pedagogy and the struggle for voice: Issues of language, power, and schooling for Puerto Ricans.* New York: Bergin & Garvey.

Weinrich, U. (1968). *Languages in contact.* The Hague: Mouton. (Original work published 1953).

Willner, R. (1985). *Ten years of neglect: The failure to serve the language minority students in the New York City public schools* (Report prepared for the Educational Priorities Panel). New York: Educational Priorities Panel.

Wolfram, W. (1974). *Sociolinguistic aspects of assimilation: Puerto Rican English in New York City.* Arlington, VA: Center for Applied Linguistics.

Wolfram, W., & Fasold, R. W. (1974). *The study of social dialects in American English.* Englewood Cliffs, NJ: Prentice Hall.

Wong Fillmore, L. (1976). *The second time around: Cognitive and social strategies in second language acquisition.* Unpublished doctoral dissertation, Stanford University, CA.

Zentella, A. C. (1981). " 'Tá bien, you could answer me en cualquier idioma": Puerto Rican code switching in bilingual classrooms. In R. P. Durán (Ed.) *Latino language and communicative behavior* (pp. 109–132). Norwood, NJ: Ablex.

Zentella, A. C. (1985). The fate of Spanish in the U.S.: The Puerto Rican experience. In N. Wolfson & J. Manes (Eds.), *Language of inequality* (pp. 41–59). New York: Mouton de Gruyter.

Zentella, A. C. (1987). Language and female identity in the Puerto Rican community. In J. Penfield (Ed.), *Women and language in transition* (pp. 167–179). Albany: SUNY Press.

Zentella, A. C. (1988). The language situation of Puerto Ricans. In S. McKay & S. C. Wong (Eds.), *Language diversity: Problem or resource?* (pp. 140–165). New York: Harper & Row.

Zentella, A. C. (1990). Integrating qualitative and quantitative methods in the study of bilingual code switching. *Annals of the New York Academy of Sciences: The Uses of Linguistics, 583*, 75–92.

Zentella, A. C. (1997a). *Growing up bilingual: Puerto Rican children in New York*. Malden, MA: Blackwell.

Zentella, A. C. (1997b). The Hispanophobia of the official English movement in the United States. *International Journal of the Sociology of Language, 127*, 71–86.

Zentella, A. C. (1998). Multiple codes, multiple identities: Puerto Rican children in New York City. In S. Hoyle & C. T. Adger (Eds.), *Kids talk: Strategic language use in later childhood* (pp. 95–112). New York: Oxford University Press.

5 Speaking in Cuban

The language of Cuban Americans

Ricardo Otheguy
Ofelia García
Ana Roca

Transculturación

There is perhaps no better way to develop an understanding of Cuban Americans than to start with the notions of *transculturation* and *neoculturation,* two interrelated theoretical constructs introduced by the Cuban ethnologist Ortiz in his monumental study *Contrapunteo Cubano del Tabaco y del Azúcar* (1940/1978). Though Ortiz's study focused on Cuban society, his two concepts have universal import and are explicitly offered in sharp contrast to the notion of *acculturation* that characterizes European American approaches to the study of ethnolinguistic contact and change:

We understand that the word *transculturation* better expresses the different phases of the transitive process of one culture to another, because this consists of not only acquiring a different culture, which is really what the Anglo-American word *acculturation* means, but the process also necessarily implies the loss or lack of hold of a first culture, that which can be called a partial *deculturation,* and it also points to the consequent creation of new cultural phenomena that could be called *neoculturation.* In effect, as the Malinowski school claims, in all embraces of cultures there is something of what happens in the genetic copulation of individuals: the child always has something of both progenitors, but it is always different from each of them. (p. 96, our translation)

The core of Cubanness adds Ortiz, rests upon a prehistorical as well as historical process of repeated transculturations and their resulting neoculturations. First, there was the transculturation of the paleolithic natives, Ciboneyes and Guanajabibes, into Neolithic Tainos. Then, with incredible speed, Taino culture disappeared in the aftermath of the tumultuous arrival of Europeans from Andalusia, Castile, Galicia, Catalonia, the Basque provinces, Portugal, Genoa, and Florence, who were soon joined by Levantines and Berbers. Soon, Blacks of Guinean and Congo background arrived from Spain. Then, from all over Africa, came waves of Yorubas, Mandingos, Hausas, and Dahomeans. Finally, the English, North Americans, Chinese, and Jews arrived in Cuba. Initially, none of these newcomers, whether White or Black, Spanish speakers or

The title of this chapter mirrors that of *Dreaming in Cuban,* the best-selling novel by Maria Cristina García (1992). The chapter is based on García and Otheguy (1988).

not, were committed to remaining in Cuba, feeling that they were only transients who had been temporarily thrown together in a place that lacked any prior cultural or linguistic definition. In time, however, they all remained and contributed to the waves of Cuban transculturations.

In the prologue to Ortiz's (1940/1978) *Contrapunteo*, the renowned anthropologist Bronislaw Malinowksi explains Ortiz's use of transculturation:

What is essential in the process that we're trying to define is that it is not a passive adaptation to a cultural standard that is rigid and defined. . . . It is a process in which both parts of the equation are modified. A process in which a new reality emerges, compounded and complex; a reality that is not a mechanical aglomeration of characters, *nor even a mosaic,* but a new phenomenom, original and independent (p. 4, our translation)

Transculturation and its attendant neoculturation not only surpass the implications of European American acculturation but even go beyond the more contemporary ideas of *multiculturism* and *pluralism,* a mosaic of cultures, a salad bowl. Ortiz's transculturation implies a new reality that is like neither of the old components but preserves elements of both. Cubans in the United States have embodied this concept in their way of life and their use of language, creating in the process a new Cuban American cultural and linguistic reality.

The new Cuban American identity is simply one more in the long history of transculturated Cuban identities. Transculturation, including neoculturation, has long been evident in Cuban music and religion. Cuban music is best known for its mixture of Spanish and African rhythms, which has given rise to the *rumba,* the *conga,* and the *guagancó,* sung in Spanish lyrics interspersed with words from African languages. Musical transculturation is even more noticeable in the work of the Cuban composer and pianist Ernesto Lecuona, known not only for *Siboney,* which evokes aboriginal sounds, but also for *Malagueña,* reminiscent of Peninsular Spanish rhythms, and *Canto Carabalí,* filled with African accents.

Religion in Cuba shows considerable evidence of transculturation. Although most Cubans are Catholics, there are also many believers in the Yoruba-based religion known as *Santería.* Significantly, many Cubans believe in both Catholicism and *Santería,* and the images of the mother of Christ and of the saints are also images of African *orichas.* For example, the image of the Blessed Mother that Cubans claim as their patron, the Virgin of Charity, known in Spanish as the *Virgen de la Caridad del Cobre,* is syncretized into the African goddess *Ochún.*[1]

1 The *Virgen de la Caridad del Cobre* derives her name from the sanctuary of Cobre in eastern Cuba. She is usually portrayed as a mulatto floating peacefully above a turbulent sea, looking down benevolently on a boat in which three desperate fishermen beg

Similarly, the patron of the port of Havana, the *Virgen de Regla,* is also the Yoruba goddess *Yemayá.* In neoculturated Cuba, the procession that takes place on her feast day in the town of Regla is led by a Catholic priest, but the faithful march to the tune of African rhythms produced on three *batás,* the Yoruba liturgical drums, and of *oriki* melodies sung in the Cuban variety of the Yoruba language, known as *Lucumí.*

Transculturation and neoculturation have also long been evident in the language Cubans speak. Throughout the colonial period but especially in the nineteenth century, Spanish in Cuba was in deep contact with a number of West African languages whose grammatical structures and sound systems were quite different from those of Spanish. Throughout the period, many Cuban Blacks spoke a form of Spanish known as *habla bozal,* which exhibited many African elements (Granda, 1971; Otheguy, 1973). Some of the features of *habla bozal* are still found in the speech of some Cubans (Ortiz López, 1998).

Speaking in Cuban in the United States today, then, has to be understood in the context of a process of Cuban transculturation that took place prior to and only partially connected with the contact between Cuban and North American societies and between the Spanish and English languages. As Cubans grow stronger and more rooted in the United States, especially in the South Florida area of Miami-Dade County, their centuries-old experience of transculturation has paved the way for the creation of an original and independent way of being that is distinct from its Cuban and American components and is expressed in more than simply Cuban Spanish or American English.

Cubans in the United States

Since the end of the eighteenth century, an important agent of Cuban transculturation has been U.S. society itself, whose impact on Cuban and Cuban American culture has long been considerable at all levels. (For a study of the presence of English in Cuba in the past and present, see Corona & García, 1996.) This impact stems not only from the extensive U.S. commercial and military presence in Cuba at a number of different points in the island's history but also from the continuous presence of Cubans in the United States since the nineteenth century.

The central works of early Cuban literature in the nineteenth century were written by Cuban exiles in the United States. The most important Cuban novel of the 1800s, *Cecilia Valdés,* was written by Cirilo Villaverde in New York. Much of the towering prose and exquisite poetry of José Martí, the famous patriot, prolific writer, and initiator of

to be spared the horrors of the storm. The three fishermen represent Cuban transculturation, one of them being Black and the other two, Indians.

the first independent Latin American literary movement, *modernismo*, was also written in the United States in the late nineteenth century. The cities that came alive in Martí's essays were not Havana or Santiago but Manhattan and Brooklyn. The beach in the famous verses of "Los Zapaticos de Rosa" was not Varadero, Santa María del Mar, or any other Cuban beach, but Newport, Rhode Island (Otheguy, 1990).

The years around the turn of the twentieth century were witness to the boom in the cigar-making industry in Tampa, the Spanish American War, the first occupation of Cuba by the United States, the first independent Cuban government, and the second North American occupation of the island. These events caused close to 56,000 Cubans to move to the United States between 1896 and 1910. By the latter part of the nineteenth century approximately 100,000 people of Cuban origin were living in New York and in the Florida cities of Tampa and Key West (Pérez, 1986).

Throughout the first half of the twentieth century, Cuban immigration to the United States was steady but slow, with an increase in the period 1951–1958, when 63,000 Cubans fled Fulgencio Batista's regime (Pérez, 1986). Another, even sharper, increase in the number of arrivals occurred after the revolution that gave Fidel Castro control of the Cuban government in January 1959.

The Cuban exodus to the United States since 1959 been highly episodic. Since Llanes (1982) described the three large waves of arrivals, there has been a significant fourth wave. The first wave, arriving between 1959 and the missile crisis of 1962, carried approximately 248,070 people who were mostly White and well educated. By 1961 the Kennedy administration had established the Cuban Refugee Program, providing these early-arriving Cubans with help in the form of food, clothing, resettlement services, and loans. In the aftermath of the Cuban missile crisis, from 1962 to 1965, only 56,000 Cubans arrived in the United States, coming mostly through third countries or clandestinely in small boats. Released prisoners from the failed Bay of Pigs invasion, and their families, made up another 6,000 arrivals during this interlude (Boswell & Curtis, 1983).

In September 1965, the Cuban government announced that it would allow Cubans in the United States to pick up relatives from the port of Camarioca. By December, both countries had agreed to an orderly airlift. The two daily Freedom Flights as they came to be known in the United States, carried approximately 302,000 Cubans (Boswell & Curtis, 1983). This second wave was racially and socially more heterogeneous than the first. It comprised many more working- and middle-class Cubans, 24% of whom were Black or Asian. By 1973 the Freedom Flights were brought to a halt. Between 1973 and 1980 only 50,000 Cubans arrived in the United States, mostly through third countries.

The third wave was initiated when thousands of Cubans took refuge in the Peruvian Embassy in Havana in April 1980. These events eventually led to the Cuban government's authorizing a boatlift from Mariel, a small port city west of Havana. The 125,000 Cubans who arrived in the United States during this episode included more Blacks, younger single males, unskilled and manual laborers, and many whom the Cuban government regarded as undesirable (mental patients, people with criminal records, and, according to some reports, homosexuals). Months before the boatlift started, the U.S. Congress had passed The Refugee Act of 1980, which required Cubans to prove that they were victims of political persecution before being granted automatic refugee status.

The fourth wave was initiated in July 1994 with the exodus of an additional 37,000 Cubans, known as *balseros* for the rudimentary rafts on which many of them sailed. Eighty-four percent of this group was male, and 31% was either Black or mulatto. During this episode, President Bill Clinton terminated a 30-year-old policy that had given Cuban immigrants preferential treatment, sending all rafters to camps in Panama and Guantanamo, from which they were not released until after 1995. To halt another massive influx of *balseros* during the summer of 1995, Cuba and the United States held extensive bilateral talks, leading to an agreement under which the United States committed to admitting 20,000 new immigrants from Cuba each year for an unspecified period.

Cuban Americans in the United States today are an extremely heterogeneous group, racially, economically, and linguistically. In October 1997, four Cuban Americans made national headlines, each representing one facet of the Cuban American community. The Florida Marlins won Major League Baseball's World Series behind their most valuable player, a Black Cuban named Liván Hernández, who at the time had been in the United States for only 2 years. In a televised interview after winning the first game of the World Series, Hernández spoke in Spanish through an interpreter. Just weeks before, Roberto Goizueta, the enormously wealthy and fabulously successful president and chief executive officer of the Coca-Cola Bottling Company, died of lung cancer. Goizueta had attended U.S. high schools and colleges in the 1950s and had lived in the United States since the early 1960s. That same week, Luis Felipe, a young Cuban who had come to the United States during the 1980 Mariel boatlift and who according to New York authorities had gone on to become the leader of the fearsome Latin Kings gang, was sentenced to solitary confinement for ordering murders from jail. And Gloria Estefan, the immensely popular lead singer of the Miami Sound Machine, who with her English-language *Conga* has contributed to the transculturation not just of Cubans and Cuban Americans but of the entire U.S. society, found herself embroiled in controversy for supporting

169

the right of artists residing in Cuba to perform in the United States. Hernández, Goizueta, Felipe, and Estefan all represent the cultural and linguistic continuum that embodies the transculturation of Cuban Americans.

Sociodemographic characteristics

In 1990 there were 1,053,197 Cubans in the United States, which means that in fact 1 of every 10 Cubans was a U.S. resident (Castellanos, 1990, p. 50). The characteristics of Cuban Americans reported in the 1990 census yield information of considerable relevance to the development of educational and social policy. Almost three fourths of Cuban Americans were born in Cuba (a small number were born in Spain or other countries), only 28% having been born in the United States. In 1990, 26% of those who were Cuban born had entered the United States in the immediately preceding decade. Almost 90% of Cubans spoke Spanish at home, and almost half (49%) claimed in 1990 not to speak English well. The majority of Cuban Americans, about 65%, lived in the state of Florida, most of them in Miami-Dade County (Boswell, 1994). The strength of Spanish among Cuban Americans thus stems from three factors: the predominance among them of the Cuban born, the continuous flow of immigration from the island, and the fact that Cuban Americans have congregated primarily in Miami-Dade County. This area was much smaller when Cuban Americans began settling, allowing them to become a significant proportion of the population and to turn Miami into a heavily Spanish-speaking area (U.S. Bureau of the Census, 1992).

The comparison with other Latino groups offered in Table 1 shows that in 1990 Cuban Americans were the oldest Hispanic group in the United States and the group with the highest median family income. More Cubans than Mexican Americans and Puerto Rican Americans were foreign born (i.e., Cuban born), and approximately the same proportion of Cuban Americans and of the more recently arrived Dominicans, Central Americans, and South Americans were foreign born. More Cuban Americans than Mexican Americans and Puerto Rican Americans spoke Spanish at home, and their English language ability was less than that of these two groups.

Although the Cuban American community still labors under serious economic difficulties, particularly when compared with the United States population as a whole, Cuban Americans have had more success than other Latinos in achieving economic incorporation into North American society. For the most part, this success stems from the greater racial, social, and class congruence between the Cubans of the early

TABLE 1. A COMPARISON OF NATIVITY, ENGLISH ABILITY, AGE, AND MEDIAN FAMILY INCOME OF CUBAN AMERICANS AND OTHER LATINO GROUPS IN THE UNITED STATES, 1990

Characteristic	Cuban Americans		Mexican Americans		Puerto Rican Americans		Dominican Americans	
	No.	%	No.	%	No.	%	No.	%
Native born	298,481	28	8,933,371	67	2,618,963	99	153,078	29
Foreign born	754,716	72	4,459,837	33	32,852	1	367,073	71
All	1,053,197		13,393,208		2,651,815		520,151	
Speak a non-English language	890,183	89	9,054,572	77	1,920,231	81	442,719	94
Do not speak English well	484,106	48	4,60,389	39	794,283	34	281,491	60
Median age (years)	39		24		26		28	
Median family income (dollars)	32,417		24,119		21,941		19,726	

Source: U.S. Bureau of the Census (1990).

waves and the power groups in the United States (García & Otheguy, 1985, 1988). There is also evidence that the economic success of Cuban Americans is due to the large number of workers per family. The percentage of Cuban American women in the labor force is higher than that of female workers in the U.S. population as a whole (Pérez, 1986).

Another important factor in the relative success of Cuban Americans has been their concentration in Miami-Dade County, where they have established enclaves that provide economic and social support. Cuban Americans of the first two waves quickly created their own Cuban-owned and Cuban-run enterprises, which provided jobs for other Cuban Americans, who in turn became the customers of these Cuban American businesses (Portes & Bach, 1985).

In addition, the evidence suggests that Cuban Americans owe a large part of their success to having turned a deaf ear to the notion that assimilation and dispersion are the keys to success. A comparison of Cubans with other Latinos, yields a telling negative correlation between English language skills and income levels (García, 1995) and an even more telling negative correlation between settlement outside the original ethnic enclave and economic success. Instead, Cuban Americans have been able to use their adherence to the Spanish language and to the Miami-Dade area to create a relatively successful group with, in Ortiz's terms, a *neocultural identity* in a United States context.

Despite their relative success, Cuban Americans have experienced downward occupational mobility (Fradd, 1983). Even though a higher proportion of Cuban Americans than of all other Latino groups work in managerial and professional occupations, the modal occupational status of Cuban Americans is still that of blue-collar workers. (Of all Cuban Americans in the labor force in 1990, 23% were working as managers, compared with 20% of South Americans, 17% of Puerto Rican Americans, 12% of Mexican Americans, and 11% of Dominican Americans.)

In short, Cuban Americans are a highly successful group relative to other Latinos but in many ways continue to be a struggling minority that is not completely incorporated structurally into U.S. society. Moreover, Cubans have succeeded in the United States in part simply because they are escapees from a Communist revolution that initially pushed out onto North American shores a large pool of highly educated, highly skilled professionals who, in the mostly small-town environment of Dade County, succeeded in exploiting to their advantage not only their skills but also their status as welcome allies of North American power groups.

Geographic concentration: Havana USA

Cuban Americans live mostly in four states. In 1990, 65% (674, 052) lived in Florida, 8% (85, 378) in New Jersey, 7% (74, 345) in New York, and 7% (71, 977) in California. Other states that had a significant number of Cuban Americans in 1990 were Illinois, with 18,204, and Texas, with 18,195. More than half of all Cuban Americans (56%) live in Florida's Miami-Dade County, and an additional 15% live in the metropolitan area of New York, New Jersey, and Connecticut (Boswell, 1994b).

In an effort to disperse the Cuban American population throughout the United States, the Cuban Refugee Program, established in February 1961 under the U.S. secretary of health, education and welfare, mounted a massive resettlement program. By 1978, approximately 470,000 Cubans had been resettled (Portes & Bach, 1985). The program turned out to be a failure, as the resettled Cubans worked their way back to the three focal points of Florida, New York, and New Jersey, which, when the dust settled, had ended up with close to 80% of the Cubans who had arrived in the country between 1970 and 1978. Of the 125,000 Cubans of the 1980 Mariel period, 60% settled in Miami-Dade County. The ingathering of the resettled Cubans has focused increasingly on Miami-Dade County. Since 1978 there has been a steady decline in the Cuban American populations of New York and New Jersey and a corresponding increase in that of Miami-Dade. About 40% of Cuban Americans in Miami-Dade County have lived in other parts of the United States (Boswell & Curtis, 1983).

The towns of West New York and Union City cover a large part of the northern section of New Jersey's Hudson County. The settlement of Cuban Americans in West New York started in the 1960s. By 1970 over a third of West New York's total population of 40,666 was of Cuban origin. In 1978, almost two thirds of the population was Latino, with Cubans constituting the vast majority (Rogg & Cooney, 1980). Although in 1990 West New York was three fourths Hispanic, with Cubans representing 32% of the total population, by 1998 Cubans were no longer the majority of the Hispanic population, representing only 45% of Latinos. Union City has experienced the same phenomenon. Although it was three fourths Cuban in the 1970s, in 1990 it was still three fourths Latino, but in 1998 Cubans represented only one fourth of that population.

Cuban Americans have thus reversed the dispersal experience of Mexican and Puerto Rican Americans, increasingly returning to what they perceive to be their home, a U.S. Cuban American city, Miami-Dade. In 1970 only 46% of all Cuban Americans lived in metropolitan Miami, but by 1994 that figure had increased to 54% percent (Boswell, 1994b).

Miami-Dade County, referred to by García (1996) as "Havana USA," has held a great deal of attraction not only for the nation's Cuban Americans but for other Latinos as well. In 1960, only 5% of Miami-Dade's population was of Latino descent, but by 1995 that proportion had risen to 55% (Fradd & Boswell, 1996, p. 285; García & Díaz, 1992 p. 15). The growth of the Latino population in Miami-Dade County, Florida, is displayed in Table 2.

Miami-Dade has the highest percentage of foreign-born residents among all counties in the United States and the largest metropolitan population density of Spanish speakers, being second in absolute numbers of Hispanic population only to Los Angeles (García & Díaz, 1992, p. 14). In 1990 the Hispanics of Miami-Dade were concentrated in the municipalities of Sweetwater (which is 93% Latino), Hialeah (88%), Hialeah Gardens (82%), West Miami (79%), and Islandia (77%) (U.S. Bureau of the Census, 1990).

Miami-Dade, with a Cuban-origin population of 563,979 in 1990, was second only to Havana in the number of persons of Cuban descent. Cuban Americans in Miami constituted two thirds of all Latinos and a fourth of all residents. In 1990 Cubans were followed in number in Miami-Dade by Nicaraguans and then Colombians (Castellanos, 1990 p. 50). Havana USA has had Cuban American mayors in all its large municipalities. The annual Calle Ocho Festival, a March carnival that takes place along the main street in the section of Miami known as Little Havana, attracts over a million revelers each year.

Despite the relative success of many Cuban Americans, there are many problems in Miami-Dade, including the feelings of animosity against Cubans felt by significant segments of both the White and Black population, feelings that often take the form of negative attitudes toward the Spanish language. Castro (1992) refers to Miami-Dade as "the birthplace of the contemporary English Only movement" (p. 151). In 1973, the Board of Commissioners for metropolitan Miami-Dade County passed a resolution that declared the county a "bilingual and bi-

TABLE 2. HISPANIC-ORIGIN POPULATION IN DADE COUNTY, FLORIDA, 1990

Year	Total Population	Hispanic population	% Hispanic
1950	495,000	20,000	4
1960	935,000	50,000	5
1970	1,268,000	299,000	24
1980	1,626,000	581,000	35
1990	1,937,000	953,000	43
1995	2,057,000	1,134,000	55

Source: U.S. Bureau of the Census (1990).

cultural county, where Spanish language is considered the second official language" (Castro, 1992, p. 173). But on November 4, 1980, more than 59% of voters approved an antibilingual ordinance barring the expenditure of county funds on Spanish-medium activities and requiring that "all county governmental meetings, hearings and publications" be in English. The referendum obtained a "yes" vote from 71% of Whites, 44% of Blacks, and 15% of Hispanics. In 1989 an amendment to Florida's constitution made English the state's official language (García & Díaz, 1992, p. 15).

The languages of Cuban Americans

The use of Spanish in Miami-Dade is widespread. Resnick (1988), Castellanos (1990), and Roca (1991) have shown that Spanish is prevalent in the public domain. Castellanos reports that in health settings, banks, government institutions, workplaces, and businesses Spanish is widely used. For example, more than 60% of second-generation Cuban Americans report speaking Spanish at least some of the time with doctors (p. 53). At work, bilingual communication is the norm with colleagues, with English spoken only to superiors. Although internal administrative functions take place in English, in banks and government institutions, services are offered in both English and Spanish (Castellanos, 1990). And even in schools, where Spanish is sometimes formally absent, there is a high frequency of bilingual usage among teachers and students, even those who are second-generation Cubans (p. 55).

An important study by Fradd and Boswell (1996) has shown the importance of Spanish as an economic resource in Miami. Ninety-six percent of the businesses surveyed indicated the need for a bilingual workforce, and more than a quarter claimed that their employees simply did not have the bilingual skills needed for future economic growth (p. 310).

The Spanish media boom in Miami is startling. There are more Spanish media in Miami than in Los Angeles and New York City combined (Fradd & Boswell, 1996, p. 290). *The Miami Herald* started a Spanish language supplement in late 1976, but in 1987 *El Nuevo Herald,* a distinct paper with professional editors and distinguished writers, came into being. By 1990 *El Nuevo Herald,* under Cuban American publisher Roberto Suárez, had a daily circulation of over 100,000. There are ten Spanish language radio stations in South Florida, among them WQAB, *La Cubanísima* (the Cubanest); WFAB, *La Fabulosa;* and WRHC, *Cadena Azul.* There are three Spanish language television stations in South Florida: WLTV, Channel 23, an affiliate of the Spanish

175

International Network, later renamed Univisión; Channel 51, the Miami affiliate of the Hispanic Broadcasting Network (now Telemundo); and Channel 40, an independent station known as TeleMiami (García, 1996, pp. 106–108).

In 1990, almost 90% of Cuban Americans spoke Spanish at home, and almost half of those who did claimed not to speak English very well. Although the Cuban American community uses Spanish at home more and is more monolingual than other Latino groups, it has clearly started to edge away from the Spanish end of the bilingual continuum, with the Dominican and Central American communities now showing more Spanish monolingualism (see Table 1).

The still-strong presence of Spanish among Cuban Americans has much to do with the economically viable ethnic enclaves in which they live and work. Because of the enclaves' unusual beginnings as beachheads for professional and entrepeneurial refugees rather than for poor immigrants, the Cuban *barrios* in Miami have generated the economic and personal resources that other Latino settlements have found difficult to produce. Castellanos (1990) gives the example of weekly credit meetings at a Miami bank that have to be translated into Spanish because the chairman of the board does not know English.

Nevertheless, a study of second-generation Cuban Americans reveals that 80% of them prefer to use English instead of Spanish in everyday conversation (Portes & Schauffler, 1993). And Castellanos (1990) reveals that over three fourths of second-generation Cuban Americans use both languages at home. Castellanos observes that second-generation Cuban Americans show a register restriction in Spanish that does not exist in English. García and Díaz (1992) show that among Cuban American youths, English is encroaching on Spanish even in the intimate family domain, especially among siblings.

Although Cuban American youths in Miami-Dade hear more Spanish in public domains than do other U.S. Latino youngsters, they seldom travel to Cuba or other parts of Latin America and are therefore seldom in situations in which they are forced to speak Spanish. For the most part, Cuban Americans interact bilingually in a bilingual city where they can usually be understood regardless of the language they use. Although their receptive bilingual ability may last longer intergenerationally than that of other Latino groups in the United States, their productive bilingual ability may indeed be even less stable than that of their Mexican American and Puerto Rican American counterparts.

The point is worth stressing. Cuban Americans, especially young ones born in the United States, have only in very few cases ever gone back to Cuba, since their families and often they themselves regard the present Cuban government as an illegitimate usurper and Cuba as a place to be avoided. The harsh U.S. government embargo on all types of transactions with Cuba, combined with entry visa requirements on the part of the Cuban government, makes travel to Cuba by Cuban Americans cumbersome. Therefore, even though constant waves of new arrivals replenish Miami's ranks of monolingual Spanish speakers, most young Cuban Americans have had contact with Spanish only in the United States and thus have never had the experience of being in a country where Spanish is the sole language of power and prestige. For them Spanish only is truly the language of the past, the language of *la Cuba de ayer,* in the familiar plaintive phrase of Miami exiles.

Speaking in Cuban

More than second- and third-generation Mexican Americans and Puerto Rican Americans, Cuban Americans see Spanish and English bilingualism as the norm. This is due to two factors. First, the greater socioeconomic power of Latinos in Miami-Dade gives the Spanish language a greater role in public and official life than in any other U.S. context. Second, these second- and third-generation Cuban Americans, isolated geographically in the Florida peninsula, have little familiarity with monolingual contexts of language use. They know neither the English monolingual context that is the norm in most settings in the United States nor the Spanish monolingual context that is the norm in their country of origin. Young Cuban Americans thus have little need to speak either solely in English or solely in Spanish.

The sociolinguistic context of Cuban Americans is therefore different from that of Mexican Americans, Puerto Rican Americans, and other language minorities in the United States. This context reinforces and assures maintenance of receptive bilingual ability across generations yet weakens productive ability in Spanish.

Reinforcing the sociolinguistic context are the stirrings of transculturation that animate the heart of Cuban identity. Just as those who arrived in Cuba centuries earlier through involuntary or voluntary immigration felt that they were transients in a place with no cultural definition, the Cubans who arrived in Dade County in the early 1960s felt that they were in the United States only temporarily. Dade County was then a rural and underdeveloped context, best known for Miami Beach, where the elderly gathered only for the summer. In over four decades, the process of transculturation has taken hold of Miami-Dade and its communities, not only those of Cuban American descent but also those of other Latinos, African Americans, Jews, and Anglos.

An understanding of intergenerational speaking in Cuban in Miami-Dade might require a reexamination of the traditional concept of *diglossia* (Fishman, 1967) in this special transcultural context.[2] Writing about the Indian subcontinent, Sridhar (1997) explains that code mixing with English, which is pervasive not only in speech but also in written documents, may actually serve to strengthen the other languages of the subcontinent. Most Indians are not literate in the languages they speak, and they do not use all their languages in their repertoire in all domains. Likewise, young second- and third-generation Cuban Americans are only partially bilingual, having better receptive than productive bilingual skills and often lacking literacy in Spanish. The transcultural and bilingual context of Miami-Dade may be enough to maintain this partial bilingual competence even though full bilingual maintenance and especially biliteracy cannot be supported intergenerationally.

The Spanish of Cuban Americans

The Spanish of Cuban Americans reflects the general characteristics of the Spanish of Cuba. It is usually classified by dialectologists as a form of Caribbean Spanish, a variety that includes the three Antillean islands as well as the coastal areas of Mexico, Panama, Colombia, and Venezuela.[3] Along with many other of what are sometimes called *coastal* varieties of Spanish, such as those of the River Plate area, Caribbean Spanish is noted for the word- and syllable-final pronunciation of the phoneme /s/ in alternants that include a glottal and a dentoalveolar realization, [h] and [s]. This phenomenon, widespread and widely noted in Spanish, is observed in the interior of such words as *esto* (this), *cuesta* (it costs), and *basta* (enough), and in nominal and verbal suffixes in words such as *casas* (houses) and *tienes* (you have). Caribbean Spanish is also noted for certain morphosyntactic phenomena, for example, the overt expression of subject pronouns at rates that are statistically higher than those observed in other regions, especially in first- and second-person contexts such as *yo tengo* versus *tengo* (I have), and *tú tienes* versus *tienes* (you have).[4]

---

2 Diglossia refers to the specialization of languages for different communicative domains and purposes in multilingual settings. In highly diglossic settings, one language is used for one purpose (say, family or church) and another language for a different purpose (say, business or commerce). In less diglossic settings, more than one language is used in the same domains and for the same functions (say, two languages used both at home and in public domains).
3 Surveys of Caribbean Spanish are available in López Morales (1992), Lipski (1994), and Zamora Munné and Guitart (1982). Discussions of the features of Cuban Spanish can be found in López Morales (1971), Ruiz Hernández and Miyares Bermúdez (1984), Paz Pérez (1988), and Valdés Bernal (1986).
4 For a discussion of this feature in the Caribbean in general, see Cameron (1996) and Morales (1997). For a discussion of this trait in Cuba and among Cuban Americans, see Lipski (1996).

Within the Caribbean, Guitart (1978) has distinguished four phonological phenomena that, though not exclusive to Spanish in Cuba, are often regarded as typical of Cuba and form part of the Spanish spoken by Cubans in Miami-Dade:

1. segment deletion, for example, [ma] for /más/, *más* (more)
2. segment-internal changes, for example, [sekka] for /serka/, *cerca* (near)
3. epenthesis or the addition of segments, for example, [fuistes] for /fuiste/, *fuiste* (you went)
4. metathesis or the transposition of segments, for example, [delen] for /denle/, *denle* (give him)

For the second generation of Cuban Americans, Varela (1992) has identified the following additional phonetic traits, which are generally not found among Cubans on the island:

1. the use of [v] as a variant of /b/, particularly in words spelled with a v, such as *vamos* (we go), a pronunciation not found in other varieties of Spanish
2. the pronunication of /r/ and /rr/ with a palatal point of articulation, as in English
3. the use of schwa, especially in the article *la,* and the use of /ae/ for /o/, for example, [l] for /la/, *la,* (the) and [aek-tu-bre] for /ok-tu-bre/, *octubre* (October)

With regard to morphosyntax, the Spanish of Cuba fits not only within the broad region of Caribbean Spanish but shares most of its features with the Spanish of wider areas of Latin American and Spain. Cuban Spanish is like that of Latin American but unlike that of Spain in its lack of a fifth person in the verbal paradigm, an innovation that is now centuries old. Cubans, like all Latin Americans, say *tienen* whereas Spaniards say *tenéis* (you [plural] have). Again in common with Latin America but in contrast to Spain, Cuban Spanish displays a conservative pronominal paradigm in the expression of direct and indirect objects, eschewing still-substandard innovations that are common in Peninsular dialects. Thus Cubans go along with the general standard in saying *le dije* (I told her) whereas many popular varieties in Spain commonly say *la dije.* And Cuba, along with the rest of the Caribbean, Spain, Mexico, and sections of the rest of Latin America, adheres to the general standard usage of second-person pronoun *tú,* as in *tú tienes* (you [singular] have) when many Central and South Americans use *vos,* as in *vos tenés* (you have).

Varela (1992) mentions several additional usages that are characteristic of Cuban Americans and that are generally not found in the Spanish of the island. Some of these usages, which in some cases may represent structural influences of English on the Spanish of Cuban Americans, are also in some cases parallel to usages noted in other U.S. Hispanic communities, such as those in the Spanish of Mexican Americans in Los Angeles (Silva-Corvalán, 1994). Among the most prevalent of the Cuba American innovations recorded by Varela are:

1. omission of the definite article, for example, *Carne es buena para la salud* where Cubans would say *La carne es buena para la salud* (Meat is good for your health);
2. addition of the indefinite article to the attribute, for example, *Es una cubana* where Cubans would say *Es cubana* (She's Cuban);
3. change in the order of the adjective and noun, for example, *La Suprema Corte* where Cubans would say *La Corte Suprema* (The Supreme Court);
4. lack of agreement of the adjective and the noun, for example, *El y ella están feliz* where Cubans would say *El y ella están felices* (He and she are happy);
5. confusion between the preterite and the imperfect, for example, *Era un placer conversar contigo el lunes* where Cubans would say *Fue un placer conversar contigo el lunes* (It was a pleasure speaking with you Monday);
6. the substitution of the indicative for the subjunctive, for example, *Espero que vendrá hoy* where Cubans would say *Espero que venga hoy* (I hope he will come today);
7. the idiosyncratic use of the gerund, for example, *La ley condenando el aborto* where Cubans would say *La ley que condena el aborto* (The law condemning abortion); and
8. the omission of, the addition of, and changes in prepositions, for example, *Se atreve mirarme* where Cubans would say *Se atreve a mirarme* (He dares to look at me).

Young Cuban Americans express a less strict attitude toward Spanish than the older, first generation does. Olimpia Rosado, author since 1977 of the well-known column in *El Diario Las Américas*, "¿Conoce Ud. su idioma?" is in her nineties and appears to have no successor of comparable status. Since 1980 many Cuban American writers have begun to write in both Spanish and English. Fernández, perhaps the best known of the new generation of Cuban American writers, published *La Vida es un Especial* (1981), *La Montaña Rusa* (1985), and *Raining Backwards* (1988). Ethnolinguistic identity and the use of language becomes the focus of the work of this generation of Cuban American writers. In a poem entitled "Dedication," Pérez-Firmat (1995) explains the subject of his poetry:

how to explain to you
that I
don't belong to English
though I belong nowhere else,
if not here
in English.

The bestseller by García (1992), *Dreaming in Cuban,* also displays features of the transculturation revealed by Pérez-Firmat's use of prepositions. In the words of the poet, Cuban Americans do not belong "to" English, although they are "in" English, an English that they, with sounds of Spanish, are making their own.

In general, speaking in Cuban involves speaking Spanish or English while transferring or replicating features of the other language. In addition to features associated with morphosyntax, such as those noted by Varela (1992), García and Otheguy (1988) identify three kinds of English-origin innovations in the Spanish of Cuban Americans.

1. *Loanwords* bring both a form and a meaning from the donor language, usually adapting the form of the word, to some degree, to the phonology and morphology of the host language. In the case of Cuban Americans, the donor language is usually English and the host language Spanish, but loans from Spanish to English are also found. Examples are *Tengo oportunidad de hacer overtime* (pronounced [*oBertain*]) (I have a chance to work overtime) and *I'm watching my libras* (I am watching my pounds).
2. *Code switches* involve the use in the host language of usually multiword sequences from the donor language, generally without adapting them to the phonology or structure of the host. That is, code switching does not involve the introduction of a linguistic element from one language into another but the alternating use of both.[5] The conversation in the following example has to do with cheerleading:

Porque unas veces nos fajamos, tú sabes, no somos we don't agree on one thing, y todo el mundo quiere ser lo que quiere, y no puede ser. Y si queremos be, to be good, we would have to agree on one thing, y no es así. (Because sometimes we fight, you know, we're not, we don't agree on one thing, and everybody wants to be the way they want to be, and that can't be. And if we want to be good, we would have to agree on one thing, and that's not the way it works.) (Otheguy, García, & Fernández, p. 43)

3. *Calques* are meanings taken from words in the donor language that have been borrowed without their corresponding word forms and

---

5 For a thorough study of code switching in another U.S. Latino community, see Zentella's masterful study of Puerto Ricans in New York, *Growing up Bilingual* (1997).

that have come to be lodged in word forms of the host language. Again, Cuban Americans usually calque the meaning of English words onto the forms of Spanish words, but the inverse process also occurs. Words that have suffered this kind of change are often said to have undergone a *semantic extension.* Examples are *Está corriendo para alcalde* (He's running for mayor), where Cubans on the island would be more likely to say *Se ha postulado para alcalde;* and *Is it my turn to rob?* (said during a card game), where monolingual English-speaking North Americans are more likely to say *Is it my turn to draw?*[6]

The particular pattern of appearance of loanwords, code switches, and calques in the Spanish of Cuban Americans gives some hint as to the future of Spanish in this community. Weinreich (1953/1974) suggested that whereas situations of language shift are characterized by loans and code switching (p. 109), stable bilingualism is marked by calquing. The importance of calques as a differentiating factor between the generations points to elements of stability in the bilingualism of the second-generation Cuban Americans. In a statistical study on the Spanish of the Cuban American community of West New York, Otheguy, García, and Fernández (1989) have shown that although loanwords are much more prevalent than calques in the Spanish of Cuban Americans, what distinguishes the Spanish of the second generation from that of the first is the increased use of calques in the second.[7]

A distinction that is relevant to an understanding of the Spanish of Cuban Americans is that between word-scope and phrase-scope calquing. Word-scope calquing refers to using words from the host lan-

6 García and Otheguy (1987) made reference to their New York–born 10-year-old son's using the calque in the last example, *Is it my turn to rob?* during a card game. Ten years later, the authors were faced with another 10-year-old, their third daughter, again born and raised in New York, who was recently heard asking the same question to a perplexed Anglophone uncle: *Is it my turn to rob?* Emma, our 10-year-old, often gets herself into trouble with that uncle. Once after having dinner at his house and while still sitting at the table, she asked him, "*Can I get up?*" He was totally confused. Of course, Emma is used to asking her parents in Spanish after dinner *¿Me puedo levantar?* in the context where an English-monolingual child might have said *May I be excused?* But Emma apparently wants to communicate something different that she has learned in Spanish, namely, that one doesn't ask to be excused but to get up from the table. The only trouble is that when trying this approach on someone who has never heard the Spanish language message, the communication does not always work out.

7 We heard an interesting exchange between our two daughters and their cousins that also involved the use of calques. After tasting some food, one of the cousins said, "It tastes like thunder" (calqued from Spanish, *Sabe a rayo* [It tastes like lightning]). Raquel, our 14-year-old, repeated it for her cousin and said, "It tastes bad," to which he replied, "No, it's worse than bad, it's like thunder." Bilingualism is in itself a transcultural experience, and most of what transpires linguistically has to do with this transculturation.

guage with meanings taken from words of the donor. And it is English-based calques that distinguish the Spanish of second-generation Cuban Americans from that of first generation. But these calques, which represent a true structural change in the meanings of words in the host language, are to be distinguished from the calquing of entire phrases, items that often go under the name of *loan translations*. Otheguy (1993, 1995) has shown that in most cases these phrasal calques are cases of cultural, not linguistic, contact. He shows that many loan translations, ranging from those that are highly acceptable, such as *El día de dar gracias* (Thanksgiving Day) to those that are highly stigmatized, such as *llamar para atrás* (call back), are in fact linguistically traditional rather than innovative from a structural point of view.

Loan translations of this type are rampant in the language of Cuban Americans, and they contribute to the mostly false impression that their Spanish is highly Anglicized and that their English is highly Hispanized. These loan translations show precisely the opposite, that is, they are examples of Cuban Americans incorporating American elements into their culture without bringing English elements into their language. The studies by Otheguy (1993, 1995) show that these loan translations in the Spanish of Cuban Americans are manifestations of a changing transcultural identity that makes use of a linguistic medium that is itself considerably more stable than it may at first appear.

Implications for teaching Cuban Americans

The Miami-Dade public schools have now been schooling language minority students since the 1960s. In 1963 Miami-Dade was the site of the first contemporary bilingual dual-language experience in the United States, the Coral Way School. This successful bilingual experience in U.S. schooling, a product of circumstances created by the unique characteristics of the early Cuban Americans, the specific social context of Dade County in 1960, and the national political context at that time, has consistently affected the way in which the school system educates language minority students in Miami-Dade County.

Today the language minority population in the Miami-Dade public school system constitutes 40% of its nearly two million students. Although Miami-Dade County has developed large programs in English for speakers of other languages (ESOL), it also provides native language instruction to all students who so desire. All elementary schools in Miami have 30-minute Spanish language classes after second grade for both Spanish and non-Spanish speakers. Recognizing the importance of a bilingual workforce for the multinational companies in Miami, Superintendent of Schools Octavio Visiedo issued a position paper in 1994 stating, "Foreign languages should be an integral part of the curriculum and full proficiency should be the goal of our teachers and students" (cited in Fradd & Boswell, 1996, p. 293).

In 1997 five public elementary schools used a bilingual curriculum in which 40% of classes were in Spanish, French, or German. Six other elementary schools offered $1\frac{1}{2}$–2 hours of daily instruction in academic subjects in Spanish. Besides the public schools, several Cuban American independent schools require Spanish language proficiency (García & Otheguy, 1985, 1988). Perhaps more than other U.S. cities, Miami-Dade schools provide many opportunities to develop bilingualism through schooling.

The concept of English language learners seems inadequate in the Miami-Dade County context, especially for Cuban Americans. English monolingualism is not the linguistic goal in this bilingual U.S. city, where schools and businesses actively promote bilingualism as a preferred goal. In Havana USA, *bilingual language learners* seems to be a more useful concept.

Yet, despite educational and business efforts, intergenerational maintenance of productive ability in Spanish, especially of full Spanish literacy, is difficult to achieve. A recent study showed that of one hundred secondary school students in Miami-Dade, only two could be considered native fluent Spanish speakers and biliterate (Barry, 1996). The school system has been faulted for its ineffectiveness in halting the language shift toward English monolingualism among Cuban Americans and other Miami-Dade Latinos.

The public school system not only has proven ineffective in promoting Spanish-English bilingualism but is starting to experience the same failure as other large urban school systems in educating second- and third-generation Latinos. The dropout rate for Miami-Dade's Latino population, most of whom are Cuban, neared 40% in the mid-1980s. The number of youth gangs has increased to more than sixty, and 80% of gang members are estimated to be of Cuban origin (Badía, 1994). Cuban American youths are showing the same discontent as other second- and third-generation immigrant youths (see Pedraza & Rumbaut, 1996; Rumbaut, 1997).

An analysis of the reasons for this discontent is needed, but clearly what we have described as "speaking in Cuban" may have something to do with the increased educational failure of second- and third-generation Cuban Americans. As gradual but persistent transculturation and language shift continue to mark the passage of the generations among Cuban Americans, the ways of speaking of this bilingual community become more distant from those of the monolingual communities that claim standard English or standard Spanish as their linguistic norm. In turn, the gap between the ways of speaking in Cuban of youths and the ways of speaking English and Spanish by teachers in school becomes greater. Unless teachers become sufficiently sensitive and learn to embrace rather than reject the ways in which bilingual communities use their languages, and unless they can apply this sensitivity to develop the standard languages of school and to educate their bilingual charges, it is likely that bilingual learners will fail.

The schooling needed in bilingual Miami-Dade County must build on the success of the 1963 Coral Way model and the ESOL programs, but it must go beyond them. There is a difference between teaching English as a second language to newcomers, or maintaining and developing the Spanish of Spanish-speaking students, and teaching English (or Spanish) to bilingual students. As experience with bilingual education increases and as the United States becomes more linguistically heterogeneous, twenty-first-century educators would do well to address the second task. In the context of Miami-Dade County, this will mean being able to develop a transcultural educational model that can build on the community's ways of speaking in Cuban to develop the community's success in using English as well as Spanish in complex academic tasks.

Suggestions for further reading

Boswell and Curtis (1983) and Llanes (1982) continue to be excellent accounts of the Cuban American experience, and García (1996) is a good recent account of Cuban Americans in South Florida. Still relevant as accounts of the schooling of Cuban Americans in Miami-Dade are García and Otheguy (1985, 1987). Important studies of language use in Miami-Dade are Castellanos (1990), Fradd and Boswell (1996), García and Díaz (1992), and Roca (1991). Otheguy, García and Fernandez (1989) look at language contact in a Cuban American community in West New York, and Lipski (1996) looks at the evolving Spanish of Cuban Americans. The most comprehensive treatment of Cuban American Spanish is that of Varela (1992).

References

Badía, A. (1994). *The academic performance of Hispanics in Florida public schools.* Miami, FL: Cuban American National Council.

Barry, J. (1996, June 14). Dade descuida dominio del español [Dade County neglects mastery of Spanish]. *El Nuevo Herald*, p. 1A.

Boswell, T., & Curtis, J. (1984). *The Cuban American experience: Culture, images and perspectives.* Totawa, N.J: Rowman & Allanheld.

Ricardo Otheguy, Ofelia García, and Ana Roca

Boswell, T. (1994). *A demographic profile of Cuban Americans.* Miami, FL: Cuban American National Council.

Cameron, R. (1996). A community-based test of a linguistic hypothesis. *Language in Society, 25,* 61–111.

Castellanos, I. (1990). The use of English and Spanish among Cubans in Miami. *Cuban Studies, 20,* 49–63.

Castro, M. J. (1992). On the curious question of language in Miami. In James Crawford, ed. *Language Loyalties. A source book on the Official English controversy.* Chicago: University of Chicago Press.

Corona, D., & García, O. (1996). English in Cuba: From the imperial design to the imperative need. In J. A. Fishman, A. W. Conrad, & A. Rubal-López (Eds.), *Post-Imperial English: Status change in former British and American colonies, 1940–1990* (pp. 85–111). Berlin: Mouton de Gruyter.

Fernández, R. G. (1988). *Raining backwards.* Houston, TX: Arte Publico Press.

Fernández, R. G. (1985). *La montaña rusa.* Houston, TX: Arte Publico Press.

Fernández, R. G. (1981). *La vida es un especial.* Miami, FL: Ediciones Universal.

Fishman, J. A. (1967). Bilingualism with and without diglossia; diglossia with and without bilingualism. *Journal of Social Issues, 32,* 29–38.

Fradd, S. (1983). Cubans to Cuban Americans: Assimilation in the United States. *Migration Today, 11*(4–5), 34–42.

Fradd, S. H., & Boswell, T. D. (1996). Spanish as an economic resource in metropolitan Miami. *Bilingual Research Journal, 20,* 283–337.

García, M. C. (1996). *Havana USA: Cuban exile and Cuban Americans in South Florida, 1959–1994.* Berkeley: University of California Press.

García, O. (1995). Spanish language loss as a determinant of income among Latinos in the U.S. In J. W. Tollefson (Ed.), *Power and inequality in language education* (pp. 142–160). Cambridge: Cambridge University Press.

García, O., & Otheguy, R. (1985). The masters of survival send their children to school: Bilingual education in the ethnic schools of Miami. *Bilingual Review/Revista Bilingüe, 12,* 3–43.

García, O., & Otheguy, R. (1987). The bilingual education of Cuban American children in Dade County's ethnic schools. *Language and Education, 1,* 83–85.

García, O., & Otheguy, R. (1988). The language situation of Cuban Americans. In S. L. McKay & S. C. & Wong (Eds.), *Language diversity: Problems or resource?* (pp. 166–192). New York: Newbury House.

García, R. L., & Díaz, C. F. (1992). The status and use of Spanish and English among Hispanic youth in Dade County (Miami) Florida: A sociolinguistic study, 1989–1991. *Language and Education, 6,* 13–32.

deGranda, G. (1971). Algunos datos sobre la pervivencia del criollo en Cuba. *Boletín de la Real Academia Española, 51,* 481–491.

Guitart, J. (1978). Conservative versus radical dialects in Spanish: Implications for language instruction. *The Bilingual Review, 5*(1), 57–64.

Lipski, J. (1994). *Latin American Spanish.* New York: Longman Group.

Lipski, J. (1996). Patterns of pronominal evolution in Cuban-American bilinguals. In A. Roca & J. B. Jensen (Eds.), *Spanish in contact* (pp. 159–186). Miami: Cascadilla Press.

Llanes, J. (1982). *Cuban-Americans. Masters of survival.* Cambridge, MA: ABT Books.

López Morales, H. (1971). *Estudio sobre el español de Cuba* [Studies on Cuban Spanish]. New York: Las Americas.

López Morales, H. (1992). *El español del Caribe.* [The Spanish of the Caribbean] Madrid: Editorial MAPFRE.

Llanes, J. (1982). *Cuban Americans: Masters of survival.* Cambridge, MA: ABT Books.

Morales, A. (1997). La hipótesis functional y la aparición de sujeto no nominal: el español de Puerto Rico [The functional hypotheses and appearance of the nominal subject: The Spanish of Puerto Rico]. *Hispania, 80,* 154–165.

Ortiz, F. (1978). *Contrapunteo cubano del tabaco y el azúcar* [Tobacco and sugar: A Cuban counter point]. Caracas; Venezuela: Ayacucho. (Original work published 1940)

Ortiz López, L. 1998. *Huellas etno-sociolingüísticas bozales y afrocubanas.* [African and Afro-Cuban ethno-sociolinguistics]. Madrid: Editorial Iberoamericana.

Otheguy, Ri., García, O., & Fernandez, M. (1989). Transferring, switching, and modeling in West New York Spanish: An intergenerational study. *International Journal of the Sociology of Language, 79,* 41–52.

Otheguy, R. (1973). The Spanish Caribbean: A creole perspective. In C.-J. N. Bailey & R. W. Shuy (Eds.), *New ways of analyzing variation in English* (pp. 323–339) Washington, DC: Georgetown University Press.

Otheguy, R. (1990). *Meditaciones interlinguisticas: Africa y Estados Unidos en la transculturación de la lengua y la identidad cubana* [A cross-linguistic meditation: Africa and the United States in the transculturation of Cuba's language and identity]. Keynote paper presented at the Conference on El Español en los Estados Unidos, Miami, FL.

Otheguy, R. (1993). A reconsideration of the notion of loan translation in the analysis of U.S. Spanish. In A. Roca J. M. Lipski (Eds.), *Spanish in the United States: Linguistic contact and diversity* (pp. 21–41). Berlin: Mouton de Gruyter.

Otheguy, R. (1995). When contact speakers talk, linguistic theory listens. In E. Contini-Morava & B. S. Goldberg (Eds.), *Meaning as explanation: Advances in linguistic sign theory* (pp. 213–242). Berlin: Mouton de Gruyter.

Paz Pérez, C. (1988). *De lo popular y lo vulgar en el habla cubana* [Popular and vulgar elements in Cuban speech]. Havana: Editorial de Ciencias Sociales.

Pedraza, S., & Rumbaut, R. (1996). *Origins, destinies, immigration, race and ethnicity.* Belmont, CA: Wadsworth.

Pérez, L. (1986). Cubans in the United States. *The Annals of the American Academy of Political and Social Science, 487,* 126–137.

Perez-Firmat, G. (1995). *Bilingual blues.* Tempe, AZ: Bilingual Press.

Portes, A., & Bach, R. (1985). *Latin journey: Cuban and Mexican immigrants in the United States.* Berkeley: University of California Press.

Portes, A., & Schauffler, R. (1993). *Language and the second generation.* Unpublished manuscript, Johns Hopkins University.

Resnick, M. (1988). Beyond the ethnic community: Spanish roles and maintenance in Miami. *International Journal of the Sociology of Language, 69,* 89–104.

Roca, A. (1991). Language maintenance and language shift in the Cuban American community of Miami: The 1990s and beyond. In D. F. Marshall (Ed.),

Language planning: Focusschrift in honor of Joshua A. Fishman. Philadelphia: John Benjamins.

Rogg, E. M., & Cooney, R. S. (1980). *Adaptation and adjustment of Cubans: West New York, New Jersey.* New York: Hispanic Research Center.

Ruiz Hernández, J. V., & Miyares Bermudez, E. (1984). *El consonantismo en Cuba* [Consonants in Cuban Spanish] Havana: Editorial de Ciencias Sociales.

Rumbaut, R. (1997). Assimilation and its discontents. Between rhetoric and reality. *International Migration Review, 31,* 923–960.

Silva-Corvalán, C. (1994). *Language contact and change: Spanish in Los Angeles.* New York: Oxford University Press.

Sridhar, K. K. (1997). The languages of India in New York. In O. García & J. A. Fishman (Eds.), *The multilingual apple: Languages in New York City* (pp. 257–280). Berlin: Mouton de Gruyter.

U.S. Bureau of the Census. (1990). *Census of population 1950–1990, summary tape file 1-A* [Computer file]. Washington, DC: Author.

U.S. Bureau of the Census. (1992). *1990 census of population and housing.* Washington, DC: U.S. Government Printing Office.

Valdés Bernal, S. (1986). *La evolución de los indoamericanismos en el español hablado en Cuba* [The evolution of indigenous loanwords in the Spanish of Cuba]. Havana: Editorial de Ciencias Sociales.

Varela, B. (1992). *El español cubano-americano* [The Spanish of Cuban Americans]. New York: Senda Nueva de Ediciones.

Weinreich, Ul. (1974). *Languages in contact.* The Hague: Mouton. (Original work published 1953).

Zamora Munné, J., & Guitart, J. M. (1982). *Dialectología Hispanoamericana.* [Spanish American dialectology] Salamanca, Spain: Editorial Almar.

Zentella, A. Ca. (1997). *Growing up bilingual: Puerto Rican children in New York.* London: Blackwell.

188

6 The linguistic situation of Central Americans

John M. Lipski

Introduction: Central Americans in the United States

Latin American immigration to the United States is certainly not a new phenomenon, but the geographical areas of Hispanoamerica that are represented by the major migratory trends have shifted over time, although always set against the constant background of immigration from Mexico. The major population shifts have come from Puerto Rico and Cuba, respectively, but in the 1980s and 1990s the immigration from Central America gave every indication of eventually attaining the same proportions as the Caribbean groups (Jamail & Stolp, 1985; Peñalosa, 1984; Wallace, 1989). Economic reasons were the original motivating factor, but political pressures in the convulsed the Central American region played an ever more important role in stimulating the northward migration of economically stable family units, particularly during the 1970s and 1980s. Since Central America and the United States share no common border and since many families arrive by air or by sea, immigrants have a greater tendency to settle in geographically delimited population clusters, which then form centripetal nuclei attracting further immigration. Like their fellow Latin Americans, Central American immigrants commonly settle in cities with large Spanish-speaking populations; this follows both from the geographical location of such cities, which usually represent the southern border of the United States or a major airline terminus, and from the desire to live in a minimally foreign environment. Although the Central Americans who have moved to established colonies at first interact principally with their compatriots, before long the inevitable contact with other Latino Americans and American-born Latinos takes place, with the resulting transculturation and expansion of social horizons of all groups involved. Traditionally (i.e., before the political turmoil of the past three decades), the majority of Central Americans immigrating to the United States represented the professional classes, those with funds to travel and establish themselves in the United States. The lower middle classes have also come in large numbers, particularly to the major cities, whereas members of the lower working classes, particularly from rural regions of Central America, were not as frequently represented. As a result of the

189

economic status of the Central Americans living in the United States, contact with their home countries was frequent and all-pervasive, and Central Americans routinely sent their children to be educated in the United States, often to live with family members already there.

The large-scale political turmoil in Central America that dominated the 1980s and extended into the beginning of the 1990s brought new waves of immigration to the United States, not only from the privileged classes but also in increasing numbers from members of the lower middle and lower working classes, including the peasantry, who by whatever means escaped the violence, destruction, and instability of their homelands, and sought a haven in the United States. By the end of the 1980s, as many as one million Central Americans lived in the United States, the majority of them undocumented refugees living in difficult conditions. Today, immigration from Central America has slowed considerably, and Central Americans in the United States are caught up in a tangle of conflicting perspectives on immigration reform and repatriation of former refugees. Although the lives of many Central Americans have stabilized, a cloud of uncertainty hangs over other Central American families in the United States. Because of the difficult conditions under which they arrived and lived, the language and culture of Central Americans in the United States have not received an acknowledgment proportional to the numerical strength of this population.

To date, no educational programs in the United States have targeted Central Americans. In each area in which they have settled, Central Americans have been lumped together with other Latino groups, and because of their Meso-American origins they have been identified with Mexican Americans. In general, the social services available in Spanish are as appropriate for Central Americans as for other groups, but in the bilingual classroom or school counseling office subtle differences between Mexican and Central American varieties can blossom into major sources of miscommunication. In addition to specific vocabulary items that may have substantially different meanings in each dialect group or be completely unknown to one group, young Central American children may not recognize the use of the familiar pronoun *tú* used by non–Central American Spanish speakers in the United States; conversely, school personnel may be baffled by Central Americans' use of *vos* and the accompanying verb forms. Central Americans use *hasta* to refer to the beginning of an event (*la maestra viene hasta las ocho* [the teacher will come at 8:00] whereas other U.S. Latino groups use the same word to refer to the end of an action (*estamos aquí hasta las ocho* [we will be here until 8:00]). These are but a few of the differences that teachers and counselors who deal with Central American students should be aware of.

Salvadorans in the United States

Demographics and history of migration

Beginning around 1979 and ending with the peace accords of 1992, El Salvador underwent one of the most bloody, prolongued civil wars in the history of Central America. During the worst of the violence, wealthy Salvadorans fled the likely possibility of death or injury and loss of their property; middle-class citizens fled to establish small businesses in other nations rather than risk certain ruin in El Salvador. Left-leaning intellectuals and professionals fled to avoid falling into the hands of the police intelligence system, aided by a program of anonymous denunciations and death squads, which cast a pall of uncertainy and fear over large segments of the citizenry. Peasants fled the country following destruction of their villages by Vietnam-style scorched-earth tactics after having had home and family destroyed by confrontations between military forces and guerrillas or after having failed to find a safe haven in neighboring areas of Honduras and Guatemala. Tens of thousands of these Salvadorans ended up in the United States. Although some Salvadorans have returned to their home country or have been deported since the end of the political violence, the majority of those who arrived in the United States during the 1980s still reside there. As a result, the cross-section of Salvadorans émigrés is very broad, as is the political spectrum, ranging from fierce right wing to revolutionary left wing and passing through a neutralist or isolationist desire for peace at any price. Salvadorans have made their presence felt as a social force, a refugee group to be dealt with, a political-action current that must be handled cautiously by government agencies, and a further source of Latino identity in the United States. At present, an undetermined but large number of Salvadorans are in the United States under questionable circumstances; immigration has dwindled from the huge influx during the 1980s, but small numbers of Salvadorans continue to enter the United States, both legally and illegally. Legislation (under the broad heading of immigration reform) that would mandate the forced repatriation of all illegal Central Americans in the United States has been temporarily put on hold at this writing, but the political future of Salvadorans and other Central Americans in the United States remains in jeopardy. Currently, the largest Salvadoran communities in the United States are found in Houston (Lipski, 1986a, 1989), Los Angeles (Peñalosa, 1984), San Francisco (Saragoza, 1995), Miami, and Washington, DC (Jones, 1994), with smaller groups scattered throughout the country, particularly in large cities with significant Spanish-speaking populations.

Even before the civil turmoil in El Salvador, which began around 1980, Salvadorans emigrated in large numbers to neighboring Central American nations as well as to the United States. El Salvador is the most densely populated nation in Central America, and its population density contrasts markedly with that of neighboring Honduras as well as with that of Belize, Guatemala, Nicaragua, and southeastern Mexico. By the 1960s, the population density of El Salvador, combined with landowners who devoted production to cash-crop agriculture, had forced thousands of Salvadoran peasants to seek opportunities elsewhere. Neighboring Honduras, whose population density was a fraction of that of El Salvador, was a natural destination, and by the late 1960s some 300,000 Salvadorans were squatting across the border in Honduras (Peterson, 1986, p. 6). Thousands of other Salvadorans worked in the banana plantations of northern Honduras. In 1969, smoldering resentment of Salvadorans within Honduras came to a head after a bitterly disputed soccer match, and for a brief but bloody period the two nations went to war. The outside world ridiculed the soccer war between two so-called banana republics, but the real cause had more to do with displaced workers and an increasingly difficult labor situation within Honduras. As a result of this conflict, thousands of Salvadorans were forcibly repatriated or coerced into leaving Honduras. Guatemala – El Salvador's other neighbor – became the next major destination, as Salvadoran agricultural workers flooded into southwestern Guatemala to work on coffee, sugar, and cotton plantations. These jobs had traditionally been held by laborers from northern Guatemala, but the Salvadorans were willing to work for less money. It is estimated that as many as 300,000 Salvadorans migrated to Guatemala in the 1970s, nearly all illegally since Guatemala did not grant work permits to foreign workers.

Mexico was also a favorite destination of Salvadorans, particularly after the Salvadoran civil war broke out, but Salvadorans in Mexico were never regarded as any more than transitory visitors en route to the United States. Despite the unfriendly, often brutal treatment afforded to them by Mexican authorities, thousands of Salvadorans settled in Mexico; in 1985 it was estimated that some 116,000 undocumented Salvadorans lived in that country (Peterson, 1986, p. 9). An estimate made the preceding year placed the number closer to 120,000 (Montes, 1986, p. 56), and as early as 1982 as many as 140,000 Salvadorans were estimated to be living in Mexico (Torres Rivas, 1986, p. 10). Of these, some 40,000 lived in the greater Mexico City area, with others found in Guadalajara, Monterrey, and towns along Mexico's northern and southern borders.

Salvadoran migration to the United States was already significant before the outbreak of civil war, considering the small size and relative distance of that country. Some 73,000 Salvadorans appeared in the 1980 U.S. census (a small fraction of the total number residing in the United States), nearly all of whom had migrated during the 1970s. However, not until the outbreak of civil conflict in the late 1970s did Salvadoran emigration reach staggering proportions. In 1980, the total population of El Salvador was approximately five million inhabitants; in 1980–1981 alone, more than 300,000 Salvadorans, or 6% of the total population, left the country. The trends were similar for most of the 1980s, so that by the end of the period, a third or more of all Salvadorans were living outside the country.

By the middle of the 1980s, some 500,000 Salvadorans had been internally displaced, and as many as 750,000 had fled the country (Ferris, 1987, p. 22); this figure represents well over 20% of the national population. Some took refuge in Guatemala (100,000), Nicaragua (21,000), Honduras (30,000), Costa Rica (23,500), Belize (2,000), and especially Mexico (150,000–250,000), and still others made the longer trek to the United States (Ferris, 1987, p. 35; see also Montes, 1986, pp. 56–57; Morel, 1991). By the middle of the 1980s, as many as 850,000 Salvadorans lived in the United States (Ferris, 1987, p. 121; Aguayo & Weiss Fagen, 1988, p. 58). The emigration can be broken down roughly as follows, using the time period 1941–1987 as representative of Salvadoran emigration to the United States (Montes Mozo & García Vásquez, 1988, p. 9):

Time period	Emigrants to the United States (%)
1941–1976	16.7
1977–1978	6.0
1979–1981	28.5
1982–1987	48.8

In the period 1941–1981, some 34% of the Salvadoran emigrants had entered the United States legally, 46% were undocumented, and 20% were attempting to obtain legal immigrant status. (Montes Mozo & Garcia Vazquez, 1988, 9 f). In the period 1982–1987, only 16% entered the country legally, 66% were undocumented, and 18% were applying for legal residence. Some more recent census figures for the Salvadoran population in the United States suggest that the numbers decreased following peace initiatives in El Salvador and the remainder of Central America, but given the undocumented status of most Salvadorans in the United States, the new numbers must be regarded cautiously. The 1990 U.S. census (Funkhouser, 1995, p. 29) shows the following breakdown of known Salvadoran immigrants by state (including some but not all those who entered the country illegally):

California	281,087
Texas	46,519
New York	38,365
Virginia	21,261
Maryland	13,619
Florida	9,991
District of Columbia	9,559
Massachusetts	6,954
Illinois	5,235
Total	464,798

Among cities with large concentrations of Salvadorans as of 1990 were the following:

Los Angeles	211,401
Washington, DC	43,730
Houston	30,834
San Francisco	27,934
New York	21,655
Nassau, Long Island	15,828
Anaheim	10,924
Dallas	9,942

Even if underreporting and return migration are accounted for, these figures clearly show the effects of the Salvadoran civil war, which began around 1979 and produced a mass exodus during the 1980s.

For most of the regions, the preceding figures are probably too low, since they include only immigrants who were identified by the U.S. government through census counts, use of social services, etc. Although some illegal immigrants are included in these figures, the true numbers have always been considerably greater, especially in major centripetal areas such as Houston and Los Angeles. Illegal immigration was spurred by the fact that very few Salvadorans have been able to achieve legitimate political refugee status, even during the height of the civil conflict in El Salvador. For example, of some 30,000 Salvadorans applying for political asylum in the United States from 1980 through 1985, only 3% of the cases were approved. In fiscal year 1980–1981, of 5,500 Salvadoran requests for political asylum, only 2 were granted (Suárez-Orozco, 1989, p. 55). With rejection rates this high, illegal entry and residence were the only option available to most Salvadorans.

Analyses vary as to the relative proportion of urban and rural emigrants to the United States among voluntary immigrants and displaced persons. Montes (1987, p. 56), who carried out a study in El Salvador among families of emigrants to the United States, discovered that 47% were from urban areas; the number was 53% among voluntary immigrants, but only 20% among displaced persons. A study carried out among Salvadoran immigrants in the United States gave similar results. Peasant farmers represented 12% of the reported immigrant population (9% among voluntary immigrants and 20% among displaced persons). According to Montes (1987, p. 84) breakdown of other occupations (as reported by family members remaining in El Salvador) was as follows:

Profession	Voluntary (%)	Displaced (%)
Professional	3.2	2.6
Laborer	9.7	9.8
Subordinate	25.5	9.4
Small business operator	13.1	8.5
Mechanical tradesperson	15.9	12.7
Domestic service worker	18.6	28.7
Farm laborer	9.4	19.9
Other	6.4	8.5

The figures are highly skewed according to gender. For example, domestic service represented 1.3% of the male immigrants but 35.0% of the females. Among laborers, 40.1% were male and 17.6% female. Educational levels varied widely, from illiterate rural residents to urban residents with the equivalent of a high school education. Taken as a group, the educational level of displaced Salvadorans ranged from 6 to 8 years (Montes, 1987 pp. 86–87; see also Suárez-Orozco, 1989, pp. 83–84).

The preceding data are quite limited as a result of the precarious situation of the Salvadoran community in the United States, the lack of viable background studies that may be used as a point of reference, and the constantly evolving nature of the political situation in El Salvador (Cabib, 1985; Peterson, 1986; Speed, 1992). Nonetheless, as is evident from the preceding remarks, the Salvadoran community in the United States is demographically and socially significant, particularly as more members acquire legal immigration status, learn English, become socially and economically more mobile, and begin to participate fully in the life of the United States outside limited Latino American neighborhoods.

Linguistic particulars

Salvadoran Spanish pronunciation shares with other Central American dialects the weak pronunciation of intervocalic /y/ and the velarization of word-final /n/ (i.e., pronounced as the -*ng* in English *sing*). Most Salvadorans, particularly from urban and rural working classes, strongly aspirate not only word-final /s/ but also word-initial /s/ (as in *la* [h]*emana, El* [h]*alvador*), in this distinguishing themselves from other Central

Americans except for some Hondurans (Lipski, 1983, 1985, 1986b). This trait alone, together with a tendency for many rural speakers to pronounce /s/ as interdental [Õ] (like English *th* in *thick*) and to speak nasally, makes colloquial working-class Salvadoran speech difficult for speakers of non–Central American varieties to understand. Like other Central Americans, Salvadorans use the familiar second-person pronoun *vos* and its accompanying verb forms to the nearly total exclusion of *tú*. Combinations with *hasta* are used to signal the beginning of an event: *¿Hasta cuándo viene el jefe?* (When will the boss arrive?). Salvadoran Spanish exhibits a construction also found at times in Guatemala, the combination *indefinite article + possessive adjective + noun: una mi amiga* (a friend of mine; normally *mi amiga/una amiga mía*). The tag *¿va?* (right, you know), probably derived from *verdad,* is often used to punctuate conversations.

Interaction with other varieties of Spanish

The largest Salvadoran communities in the United States are in contact with Mexican and Mexican American varieties of Spanish, and given the precarious situation of many Salvadorans (undocumented and fearful of arrest and deportation by immigration officials), Salvadorans sometimes attempt to attenuate strikingly Central American traits and even to imitate what are perceived to be Mexican features. On a personal level, Salvadorans of all socioeconomic groupings feel no negative emotions toward Mexicans or Mexican Americans but rather regard them as fellow Latinos. Some Salvadorans note that Mexicans and particularly Mexican Americans adopt an attitude of superiority and even hostility toward (illegally entering) Central Americans; this situation is likely to increase as the new immigration laws widen the social divions among Mexican Americans (U.S. citizens), Mexican nationals who qualified for amnesty under the 1986 Immigration Reform and Control Act (and who are already perceived by many Mexican Americans as undesirable competition for scarce jobs), and new arrivals, i.e., Mexicans and Central Americans who do not qualify for amnesty. At the same time, Salvadorans aspiring to acceptance in European American society are quick to perceive the stigma attached to being Mexican and spare no attempt to highlight the differences that separate Mexicans and Salvadorans. This has created considerable ambivalence among Salvadoran laborers who are working under illegal conditions; although many Mexicans in the southwestern United States work under similar conditions, the presence of Mexican workers is in itself not sufficient to trigger migratory investigations or raids (since Immigration and Naturalization Service officers in the Southwest often accept the de facto presence of illegal Mexican workers and intervene only randomly and sporadically), whereas a Central American may be singled out for presentation of documents and declarations of citizenship or migratory status. Therefore, most Salvadoran laborers, while trying to maintain their cultural identity as Salvadorans, try to fade into the background of the Mexican and Mexican American labor force in the hope that the current will carry them along; such is usually the case.

The questions of identification and differences vis-à-vis Mexicans are strongly felt in language usage. Salvadoran Spanish differs in several major respects from the dialects of Mexican Spanish most commonly heard in the United States. Numerous differences exist in the lexical dimension as well as in the countless idiomatic expressions peculiar to each group. In the syntactic dimension, Salvadorans share many of the peculiarities of Central Americans, whereas on a phonological level Salvadoran Spanish exhibits striking differences from the most common Mexican speech patterns. In reality, most Salvadorans' attempts at masking their regional origins or mimicking Mexican Spanish are only marginally successful. The most consistent strategy is avoidance of *vos* and obviously regional expressions. Few Salvadorans can or will modify their pronunciation.

Domains of language use

The vast majority of Salvadorans in the United States come from the poorest rural regions of El Salvador. Many are illiterate, and virtually none knew English before arriving in the United States (Nackerud, 1993, p. 211). Precariously finding employment in work sites staffed by other undocumented Spanish speakers and excluded through fear or by law from access to adult education programs, few Salvadoran adults have moved beyond the pale of Spanish-speaking neighborhoods. Most have acquired the rudiments of English, which allow them to conduct basic transactions in English, but at work and at home the Salvadoran community continues to be overwhelmingly Spanish speaking. With the coming of amnesty programs, a greater number of Salvadoran children are attending school, usually in bilingual education programs.

Educational needs

When Salvadorans first began arriving in the United States in large numbers, most were from rural regions and possessed little or no literacy in Spanish and no abilities in English. Given the undocumented status of the majority of refugees, many were reluctant to place their children in U.S. schools for fear of deportation. As Salvadorans discovered that most school systems accepted children without documentation of immigration status, larger numbers of Salvadoran children entered the U.S.

school system (Saragoza, 1995). These numbers increased even more after the amnesty of 1986, and even though many Salvadorans were excluded from amnesty or political asylum, today most young Salvadorans in the United States are receiving public education. Since the originally arriving Salvadorans spoke little or no English, the children were normally placed in transitional bilingual education classes, often surrounded by a cohort of Mexican children. Salvadoran children were at a disadvantage for several reasons. First, their predominantly rural upbringing in contrast to the increasingly urban origin of recent Mexican immigrants meant that they were less familiar with any sort of formal schooling; many were behind the grade level of their Mexican classmates. Furthermore, available bilingual education materials focused primarily on Mexican (or occasionally Caribbean) dialects of Spanish, particularly in vocabulary. Salvadoran children were at times alienated by these materials, and at other times they simply could not understand the items in question. Mexicans' *ándale* (let's go), *papalote* (kite), *güero* (blond, fair-skinned), *chamaco* and *huerco* (child), *lana* (money), and *popote* (soda straw), are as unknown to Salvadorans as the latter's *pupusa* (corn pancake filled with cheese or meat), *chele* (blond), *chucho* (dog), *pisto* (money), *piscucha* (kite), *cipote* (child), and *caites* (sandals) are to Mexicans. Small Salvadoran children unaccustomed to verb forms associated with the pronoun *tú* did not always make the transition from *sentáte* (*vos*) to *siéntate* (*tú*) (sit down), (*vos*) *sos* to (tú) *eres* (you are), and so forth. Few bilingual teachers were familiar with Central American dialects, and not all reacted favorably to the unexpected words and pronunciation. Although there is little hard evidence of specific educational differences occasioned by culture and dialect clash, anecdotal accounts suggest that matters were not always easy. Teachers who did not obtain the rapid acknowledgment that they expected sometimes attributed the children's silence as surliness or even cognitive disorders. At this writing there are no comprehensive accounts of Spanish dialect differences appropriate for bilingual education teachers, but as the number of non-English-speaking Salvadorans entering the U.S. school system diminishes, group-specific educational problems are also on the decline. Finally, and perhaps most important for school achievement, many Salvadoran children arriving in the 1980s had personally witnessed political terror, torture, and murder in their homeland and had been traumatized to the point where academic success was an unattainable goal (Arroyo & Eth, 1985). A number of students had been forced to leave school in El Salvador because of the fear of violence and death, which further hindered their entry into the U.S. school system. Currently, the number of Salvadoran children in U.S. schools who have personally experienced political violence has been significantly reduced, and their situation is falling into line with that of economic immigrants who have not lived under the shadow of terror in their homeland.

Nicaraguans in the United States

Demographics and history of migration

Nicaraguans have been present in the United States in small numbers since the early 1900s, but no large groups of Nicaraguans were to be found until the beginnings of the Sandinista insurrection against the Somoza regime began in the mid-1970s. The rebels used the name of Agusto César Sandino, a Nicaraguan patriot who had died while leading a resistance to the occupation of Nicaragua by the U.S. Marines in the 1930s. Sandino's capture and death was followed by the installation of Anastasio Somoza, a military officer with close ties to the U.S. occupation forces. Four decades of dictatorial Somoza rule ensued, including rule by the father, two sons (Luis and Anastasio Jr.), a grandson in training (Anastasio III), and interim puppet presidents. This situation created the inevitable exile population, but most were found in Mexico or neighboring Central American countries. When the Sandinista armed insurrection began to gather force in 1978, the increasing death toll, political repression, guerrilla warfare in both urban and rural areas, shortages and blackouts, and a general climate of insecurity prompted many Nicaraguans with the means at their disposal to leave the country temporarily or at least to send their children abroad. The United States was a favored safe haven for those who could afford it, since other Central American countries had problems of their own. Honduras openly supported the Somoza government, Costa Rica increasingly favored the Sandinistas, and El Salvador and Guatemala were rapidly sliding down the path to civil wars of their own.

    With the abdication of Somoza and the triumph of the Sandinista Revolution in July 1979, political violence temporarily stopped. However, the rapid social changes that accompanied the Sandinistas' rise to power provoked an almost immediate exodus of the wealthiest elements of Nicaraguan society, at least some of whom had actively contributed to the prosperity of the Somoza regimes and others who simply because of their socioeconomic status in this poor nation were regarded with suspicion and hostility by revolutionary supporters. Almost immediately after the Sandinista takeover, a counterrevolutionary movement was formed, spearheaded by former members of the Somoza National Guard and supported financially by Nicaraguans whose fortunes had diminished by the transition from *Somocismo* to *Sandinismo;* the U.S. government also provided crucial economic and logistical support through both public and clandestine channels. The *contras* began an active military campaign against the Sandinista regime, which in practice affected virtually all residents of the country. As a result of the intensified *contra* activity, together with the increasing Sandinista interference in all aspects of Nicaraguans' lives, the Nicaraguan exodus grew from a trickle to a torrent. Large numbers of Nicaraguans moved to the United States, especially Miami and Los Angeles, where they established small businesses or found other employment. Assuming at first that return to Nicaragua would be imminent, they soon felt the reality of exile, as matters in Nicaragua went from bad to worse. Stable Nicaraguan communities in the United States took shape, with an internal structure that duplicated patterns found in the home country. Particularly in Miami, the climate was favorable for educated, middle-class refugees from a leftist revolutionary government that also openly embraced Communist Cuban support. This is not to suggest that all exiled Cubans in Miami welcomed Nicaraguans with open arms, since both groups were often placed in competition for scarce resources, but the fact that the groups shared a common enemy served to smooth over many differences.

In response to international calls for elections, the Sandinistas held elections in 1984, which confirmed Sandinista rule. Although foreign observers reported no extraordinary irregularities, these elections were rejected both by the Nicaraguan opposition and, more important for the future of the country, by the U.S. government. A new round of elections, with rigorous supervision by invited observers as well as opportunity for the diffusion of opposition views, was scheduled for 1990. Much to the surprise of even the most anti-Sandinista hopefuls, the presidency was won by the candidate of an opposition coalition, Violeta Barrios de Chamorro. Although Chamorro had openly aligned herself with the political wing of the *contra* movements, headed by ex-Somocista National Guard officers, she was clearly not in favor of a return to *Somocismo,* since her husband, Pedro Joaquín Chamorro, a popular newspaper editor, had been assassinated in the later years of the last Somoza regime.

The Nicaraguan community in exile was jubilant over Chamorro's election, but, perhaps, predictably, this event did not spur a large-scale, permanent return of expatriots. Many Nicaraguans had lived in the United States for 5–10 years, had established successful business, were living in comfortable and safe neighborhoods, had children in American schools, and were little inclined to return to a chaotic post–civil war environment in which economic fragility and political uncertainty were the order of the day. Return migration was slow, and Nicaragua has not experienced the torrent of returning immigrants that the numbers of displaced persons during the Sandinista period would suggest (Ortega, 1991). Within the country, the return of displaced persons to their original homes has been much more extensive, as has the repatration of Nicaraguans from the neighboring countries of Honduras and Costa Rica.

In 1996, the second post-Sandista government, headed by Arnaldo Alemán, was elected in Nicaragua. This government adopted a more confrontational stance vis-à-vis the Sandinistas, and the result has been strikes, protests, and considerable civil unrest. At the same time, the U.S. government, having once admitted tens of thousands of Nicaraguans as de facto political refugees, decided that few Nicaraguans living in the United States would face political persecution if they returned to their homeland and passed repatriation laws that could theoretically result in mass deportations. In the face of protests from Nicaraguans in the United States and by the Nicaraguan government, U.S. authorities reacted cautiously, promising that massive eviction of Nicaraguans will not occur. As of mid-1997, the applicable laws had been stalled by court injunctions, but the future of Nicaraguans in the United States was more uncertain than ever before.

Emigration of Nicaraguans to the United States during the Sandinista period is better documented than that of other Central American refugees from the same time period, given the more preferential treatment afforded by the U.S. government. During the insurrection against Somoza, some 100,000–200,000 Nicaraguans left the country as refugees; another 800,000 were internally displaced (the total population of the country at the time was perhaps 2.5 million). In the first year of the Sandinista triumph (1979), many Nicaraguans most of whom had been directly implicated in the Somoza government or the Nicaraguan military, took refuge in the United States. By 1984, it was estimated that some 30,000 lived in the Miami area alone, with smaller numbers in Los Angeles, New York City, and New Orleans (Universidad para la Paz, 1987, p. 178). By 1985, some 50,000 Nicaraguans were estimated to live in the United States, undoubtedly a figure much lower than the true population (Ferris, 1987, p. 35). In 1984, some 25,000 Nicaraguans were known to have taken refuge in neighboring Honduras (including at least 14,000 Miskitos), and at least 4,000 in Costa Rica (Farías Caro & Garita Salas, 1985, pp. 43–59; Montes, 1986, p. 57). Some estimates place the total number of Nicaraguans in the two neighboring countries at more than 40,000 during the first years of the 1980's (Torres Rivas, 1986, p. 11). By 1986, more than 30,000 Nicaraguans lived across the border in Costa Rica.

Not all the Nicaraguans living in the United States come from the western, Spanish-speaking departments. The Caribbean or Atlantic coast of Nicaragua, whose residents are largely of African American or Native American descent, is the home to creole English, Miskito, and Sumu (together with a vanishingly small number of Rama speakers), to the almost total exclusion of Spanish except in official usage. Most post-colonial Nicaraguan governments, while commercially exploiting the natural resources of the Atlantic region, made little attempt to alter or even interact with the cultural and ethnic institutions of this area. Some government schools were always present, but the government tolerated the establishment and maintenance of schools by foreign-based missionary groups on a scale that would probably have been scrutinized if not curtailed had it occurred in the more densely populated, Spanish-speaking Pacific region. The Sandinista government, in power from 1979 to 1990, regarded the Atlantic region as a challenge to plans for social and political integration of the entire nation, and the Sandinistas apparently unaware of earlier, largely successful efforts by other groups, undertook a literacy campaign in the region at times. Alienation and direct conflict often resulted, leading to the presence of more Spanish-speaking government officials in the Atlantic region, in turn spurring a more negative reaction to the Spanish language and the creation of a vicious circle (Cayasso, 1995). One result was the immigration of many *costeños* to the United States, where the largest single concentration is found in Miami. Although most speak Spanish reasonably well, the Atlantic coast residents in Miami do not frequently interact or identify with Spanish-speaking Nicaraguans, except for some professionals and business owners aspiring to a Nicaraguan clientele. A significant concentration of English-speaking Nicaraguans live in Opa Loka, just to the north of Miami, in a neighborhood also inhabited by other Caribbean groups, mostly African American. Many *costeños* bring a knowledge of English sufficiently developed that they immediately secure desirable jobs, a situation not so often found among Spanish-speaking Nicaraguans, which adds to incipient resentment of the Atlantic-coast residents on the part of Spanish-speaking Nicaraguans. Miskito-speaking Nicaraguans, traditionally among the country's most marginalized citizens, are not common in the United States, although a small pocket of Miskito fishermen can still be found in Port Arthur, Texas. They also speak Spanish, most quite fluently, and use this language when interacting with the Mexican American population.

Linguistic particulars

Like other Central American dialects, Nicaraguan Spanish gives a weak pronunciation to intervocalic /y/ and velarizes word-final /n/. Word-final /s/ is aspirated to a much higher degree than in other Central American varieties, approaching the levels found in Caribbean varieties of Spanish. Nicaraguans share with other Central Americans the use of *vos* as the informal pronoun. Nicaraguans of all social classes are much more inclined to proffer *vos* to total strangers than other Central Americans are, a trait that has earned them the reputation of being overly familiar, or *confianzudo*. Among typically Nicaraguan words are the interjections *idiay* and *chocho*, the use of *chucho* for dog (the word means *light switch* to Cubans), *chavalo* and *chigüín* for small child, *chunches* for unidentified or unimportant objects, *reales* for money, *maje* for male friend, *chele* for blond, fair-skinned individuals, and numerous foods, including *gallo pinto* (dish of red beans and rice), *pinol* and *pinolillo* (drinks made of cacao and toasted corn) and *vigorón* (dish made of yucca and pork rinds).

Interaction with other varieties of Spanish

In Miami, Nicaraguan Spanish comes into contact with Cuban Spanish on a daily basis. Cuban Spanish, representing a variety of registers, generations, and degrees of bilingualism with English, defines the norms of Miami Spanish language broadcasting and journalism and is the de facto lingua franca in most parts of the city. It is nearly impossible for a Spanish speaker in Miami, particularly one who relies on Spanish more heavily than English, to avoid contact with Cuban Spanish, regardless of individual attitudes toward Cubans and their language. Less frequently, depending on personal circumstances, Nicaraguans, in South Florida, encounter other Spanish dialects, with Salvadoran, Colombian (of several regions), and Puerto Rican being the most common.

Virtually all Nicaraguans living in the greater Miami area have definite opinions and attitudes regarding Cuban Spanish, Nicaraguan Spanish, and the interface between the two. Those Cubans who are familiar with Nicaraguans and their speech have equally well-defined opinions. In a survey I conducted in 1991, a majority of middle-class Nicaraguans in Miami over the age of about 20 expressed at least some negative sentiments toward Cuban Spanish. Frequently, these feelings were vague and not associated with particular linguistic characteristics; they reflected cultural differences and perhaps concealed some resentment at the obviously dominant position enjoyed by Cubans in South Florida. Typical of these nonspecific negative comments (by no means characteristic of the entire Nicaraguan community) were the fact that Cubans speak "too loud," "too fast," "too nasty," and so forth. These are precisely the same unsubstantiated criticisms that neighboring Central American countries level against Nicaraguans and are typical of xenophobic attitudes worldwide. As with all stereotypes, there is always a kernel of truth. Compared with the baseline Central American varieties of Spanish, Cuban Spanish in the more emotionally charged registers is objectively marked by greater intonational swings, often perceived as absolute differences in volume. In animated conversations, Cubans (particularly Cuban men) tend to prefer simultaneous participation, with each intervention taking place at a successively higher volume level, instead of a greater emphasis on turn taking, which prevails throughout Central America. To the ear unaccustomed to such energetic exchanges, a Cuban conversation can seem impossibly rapid, deafeningly loud, and incredibly rude.

Claims of "vulgar" talking normally involve certain key lexical items that are inoffensive and common in one dialect but carry a heavy negative connotation in the other. Cuban Spanish is noted for the very frequent use of *coño*, an originally obscene epithet still very common in Spain but rarely heard in Latin America outside of the Caribbean. Nicaraguans are aware that *coño* is a "bad" word and are sometimes surprised at the ease with which well-bred Cubans, including women and children, employ this term. Even more shocking to the Nicaraguan ear is the uninhibited use of *comemierda* for fool or gullible person.

On a more specific basis, many Nicaraguans criticize Cubans for an excessive use of Anglicisms, particularly loan translations and slightly adapted borrowings. At the time of the survey, the Nicaraguan community in Miami had not resided in a bilingual environment long enough for this type of subtle syntactic Anglicism to penetrate vernacular speech. Nicaraguan adolescents picked these combinations up naturally, through contact with Cuban friends and simply by existing in the Miami Hispanophone environment. Older Nicaraguans are predictably dismayed when their children begin using constructions from other groups, particularly when in the parents' eyes the combinations are socially unacceptable.

Nicaraguans do not frequently comment on Cubans' pronunciation of Spanish except to note neutralization of preconsonantal /l/ and /r/, giving rise to forms such as *pocque* instead of *porque* (because) and *calta* in place of *carta* (letter). Objectively, the change from /r/ to [l] is rather infrequent in Cuban Spanish, compared, e.g., to Puerto Rican and even Dominican dialects. In Cuba, it is characteristic of the lower classes in the central and eastern provinces and was not widely found in the Cuban exile community until after the Mariel boatlift of 1980, in which large numbers of less educated, working-class or rural Cubans arrived in the United States.

Relatively few Cubans in Miami have close enough contact with Nicaraguans to have formed clear opinions regarding Nicaraguan Spanish. Among those Cubans who do mention specific features, the use of *vos* stands out as the most striking difference. Cubans' reactions toward this distinctly non-Caribbean phenomenon range from "strange" to "incorrect." A few Cubans comment on Nicaraguans' weak pronunciation of intervocalic /y/, especially in contact with /i/ and /e/, which can make *gallina* (hen) sound like *gaína* and *sello* (stamp) emerge as *seo*. Cubans also comment on the frequency with which Nicaraguans punctuate their speech with *pues* [pueh] (well), a trait of which Nicaraguans themselves are also aware. Among the more shocking differences is the use of *jodido* as a casual greeting among Nicaraguans of both sexes. To Cubans, use of this word in anything less than an insult would be unthinkable.

Nicaraguans are not exempt from feelings of linguistic insecurity, but the Nicaraguan community in the United States is less afflicted by such sentiments than other Central American groups are. A high level of education and a more comfortable socioeconomic status is probably the main contributing factor, aided by a certain smugness about being the bearers of a form of Spanish as yet unaffected by the overwhelming influence of English. Few Nicaraguans consciously alter their language when speaking to Cubans, and even fewer willingly adopt Cubanisms into their own speech. With regard to the characteristically Central American use of *vos*, a majority of Nicaraguans stated that they used such forms to Cubans who had attained a level of *confianza* which warranted such usage. A few confessed to employing *tú* so as to not shock or offend Cubans.

Nicaraguans in Los Angeles are primarily in contact with Mexican speakers of Spanish, together with smaller numbers of Salvadoran and Guatemalan speakers. To date there is no evidence of significant dialect clash between Nicaraguans and other Spanish speakers in the Los Angeles area, although individual incidents no doubt occur.

Domains of language use

In U.S. cities with large Nicaraguan communities, the Nicaraguans tend to cluster in ethnically homogeneous neighborhoods. The largest such colony is in far western Miami, where entire subdivisions and shopping centers re-create a Nicaraguan lifestyle. A smaller neighborhood in central Miami also contains a high concentration of Nicaraguans. Those Nicaraguans coming from middle- and upper-class backgrounds (a significant proportion of the total) learned some English before going to the United States; many sent their children to American schools in Nicaragua. In the United States, Nicaraguan children have been rapidly absorbed into the school systems, receiving bilingual education when necessary. There is a natural tendency for Nicaraguan children to cluster around other Spanish speakers, but the increasingly English-dominant young Nicaragan population is broadening its social networks. Nicaraguans who arrived as adults live in neighborhoods and frequent stores and businesses where all linguistic interchanges take place in Spanish. Most Nicaraguans also work in Spanish-speaking businesses, preferably owned or staffed by other Nicaraguans. There is interaction with the wider English-speaking community, but, particularly in Miami, the combination of recent immigrant status and the over-whelming presence of Spanish facilitates retention of Spanish as the main language for all domains.

Educational needs

The majority of Nicaraguans entering the U.S. school system after the immigration surge of the 1980s spoke little or no English and were placed in bilingal education classes. Most had attended school in Nicaraga and experienced little shock upon entering school. Linguistic diferences with respect to the prevailing Spanish dialects (Cuban in Miami, Mexican American in Los Angeles and most other cities) have been noted, but anecdotal testimony suggests that few Nicaraguans experienced educational difficulties due to dialect clash or the lack of bilingual materials that reflected Nicaraguan usage. The relatively high average educational level of their parents is one important factor in accounting for this difference, and it is not irrelevant that most Nicaraguan children have not been perceived as penniless refugees on whom educational resources need be spent. The current generation of Nicaraguan Americans entering the schools is proficient in English, and although some Nicaraguan children continue to be placed in bilingual programs, immigration from Nicaragua has diminished greatly. Nicaraguans from the creole-English-speaking Caribbean coast tended to enter English language programs, although the English spoken by these Nicaraguans differed from U.S. usage. In Miami, where the majority of Atlantic Coast Nicaraguans reside, local schools are accustomed to dealing with West Indian students, and English-speaking Nicaraguan children have largely been able to make a smooth transition to the U.S. educational system. There is no information on the Miskito-Spanish bilinguals residing in Texas; this population is marginal within Nicaragua and appears to have slipped between the cracks of bilingual programs in Texas.

Guatemalans in the United States

Demographics and history of migration

The total Guatemalan population in the United States is not large, even in comparison with other Central American communities. In some areas, however, significant groups of Guatemalans are concentrated, and it is feasible to speak of pockets of Guatemalan Spanish in the United States. These communities are typically formed of indigenous Guatemalans speaking a variety of Mayan languages, and in some instances these languages take precedence over Spanish, even in the United States. The largest Guatemalan community is located in Los Angeles. A smaller and locally almost unknown group lives in rural southern Florida (Miralles, 1986), where community members work in agriculture alongside immigrants from Mexico and the Caribbean. Smaller groups of Guatemalans are found in Houston (Hagan, 1990), New Orleans, the Pacific Northwest, and Washington, DC. An assessment of Guatemalan Spanish in the United States, requires a focus on bilingual indigenous communities, whose use of Spanish is often little studied and receives little prestige either in Guatemala or abroad.

Guatemalans in the United States are mostly refugees from the desperate political and economic situation that, though always difficult, reached crisis proportions by the late 1970s. It is estimated that between 50,000 and 75,000 Guatemalans died as the result of political violence between 1978 and 1985 alone; during the same period, the Guatemalan army admits to having destroyed more than 440 villages (American Friends Service Committee, 1988, p. 4). By the mid-1980s, some 80,000 Guatemalans lived in Los Angeles, with smaller groups in San Francisco, Chicago, Washington, DC, and Houston (Universidad para la Paz, 1987, p. 178). In 1985, it was estimated that 220,000 recent immigrants from Guatemala were living in the United Statzes (Suárez-Orozco, 1989, p. 57), and by 1988, at least 200,000 known Guatemalans were living there (Aguayo & Weiss Fagen, 1988, p. 23). Some 100,000–150,000 lived in Mexico as well (Aguayo & Weiss Fagen, 1988, p. 58; Ferris, 1987, p. 35; Montes, 1986, p. 56). Some 3,000 Guatemalan refugees lived in neighboring Belize, and at least 1,000 in Honduras. Internally, at least 400,000 Guatemalans were displaced during the first half of the 1980s (American Friends Service Committee, 1988, p. 5; Montes, 1986, p. 56). Like Salvadorans, few Guatemalans have been able to obtain legitimate immigrant or political refugee status. During the 1980s, only about 0.3% of Guatemalan requests for political asylum in the United States were approved (Suárez-Orozco, 1989, p. 57). A breakdown of the location of Guatemalans in the United States during the late 1980s follows (American Friends Service Committee, 1988, p. 24):

Los Angeles	60,000–100,000
Houston	10,000–20,000
Washington, DC	10,000–20,000
New York City	10,000–20,000
Chicago	10,000
New Orleans	1,000–5,000
Phoenix/Tucson	1,000–3,000
Miami	1,000–2,000

In Guatemala, Nahuatl-derived cultures and languages were not the primary indigenous force, although some Nahuatl and Pipil groups oc-

207

cupied the southwestern coastal regions. The principal indigeneous groups belong to the Maya-Quiché family, and given the cultural ascendency of these groups even after the decline of the Maya empire, Mayan languages were never displaced by Nahuatl, as occurred in El Salvador and Honduras. Among the languages still spoken in Guatemala are some four members of the Quiché group, six members of the Mam group, four members of the Pocomam group, two members of the Chol group, plus a tiny contingent of Pipil (Lipski, 1994). As a group, the Mayan languages have not contributed to Guatemalan Spanish in proportion to their numbers, but some lexical items of indigenous groups are in common use.

Linguistic particulars

Little research has been done on the linguistic peculiarities of the Guatemalan population in the United States; with the exception of a few sociological studies (e.g., Peñalosa, 1984), there is little accurate information on any aspect of the Guatemalan community within the United States. The majority of Guatemalans are undocumented political or economic refugees, usually from rural regions and almost invariably from an indigenous background. Some speak little or no Spanish, and those who speak Spanish most often do so with the linguistic characteristics of second language speakers. Most Guatemalans use *vos*, together with a very heavy reliance on *usted* in rural regions; *tú* is docmented as a legitimate variant in urban areas of Guatemala, especially among the middle class (Pinkerton, 1986), but few if any rural speakers use this form. The common denominators found among all Guatemalan Spanish speakers in the United States include a very strong pronunciation of word-final /s/ (similar to Mexican Spanish and different from Salvadoran and Nicaraguan varieties), velarization of word-final /n/, and weak intervocalic /y/. Many Guatemalans pronounce the trill /rr/ as a fricative, much like the *s* in the English word *measure*. Regional vocabulary items include *patojo* (small child) *canche* (blond, fair-skinned), *chompipe* (turkey), *chapín* (Guatemalan), and *chucho* (dog). Many Mayan speakers from the central highlands of Guatemala reduce or even eliminate unstressed vowels in contact with /s/, thus making *presidente* sound like *presdente*. This is a trait also found in central Mexico and accentuated among speakers of Nahuatl; in many ways, Guatemalan Spanish is similar to central and northern Mexican varieties.

Interaction with other varieties of Spanish

Most Guatemalans living in the United States live and work in contact with Spanish speakers, predominantly of Mexican origin. Although Spanish is not the native language of many Guatemalans, the majority of Guatemalans in the United States speak Spanish, often having acquired greater proficiency while living there. Superficially, Guatemalan Spanish might be mistaken for a Mexican variety, particularly as regards pronunciation; telltale vocabulary items clearly identify Guatemalans, but few observers from outside the Latino community possess this degree of sophistication. As with the Salvadoran community, many Guatemalans are undocumented and fear detection and deportation; in trying to blend in with the Mexican American population, occasional attempts to deemphasize Guatemalan traits or acquire Mexican traits can be observed. The strategies are normally quite superficial, such as suppression of the pronoun *vos* and the often exaggerated use of stereotypical Mexicanisms, such as *ándale, órale,* and the universal obscenity *chingar.* The film *El Norte,* which documents the struggle of Guatemalan refugees crossing Mexico and seeking entry into the United States, contains examples of the sort of informal dialect tutoring that goes on among the refugee community.

Educational needs

Of all the Central American groups in the United States, Guatemalan refugees are in the most precarious situation vis-à-vis the educational system. In addition to their dubious immigration status, most Guatemalans living in the United States are at best only recessive Spanish-Mayan bilinguals, and some speak no Spanish at all. A large number are illiterate, and many are unaware of even the most rudimentary aspects of U.S. immigration and refugee law (Nackerud, 1993, p. 211). In some areas (e.g., the state of Oregon), bilingual court interpreters who speak Mayan languages have been found, but more often than not Mayan-speaking Guatemalan children find no accommodation in bilingual programs and attend school only sporadically, exacerbating the already difficult situation of undocumented itinerant laborers in this country. Spanish-speaking Guatemalans fare little better, since the combination of low literacy rates and little familiarity with urban schools results in poor attendance and academic performance (Vlach, 1984).

Small Central American communities: Hondurans and Costa Ricans

Although the most prominent Central American varieties of Spanish in the United States are those of El Salvador, Guatemala, and Nicaragua, in descending number of speakers, there are significant Honduran communities in several cities. The most prominent is found in New Orleans, where the Honduran community first arose as part of the banana industry, which linked the northern Honduran ports of Tela and La Ceiba via maritime routes with the port of New Orleans. By the late 1980s an estimated 60,000–70,000 Hondurans lived in New Orleans (American Friends Service Committee, 1988, p. 24). Another large group of Hondurans (as many as 80,000), mostly from the central part of the country, is found in New York City, where they do not enjoy the same sense of community identity as in New Orleans (although they have published a small newspaper, *El centroamericano*). Los Angeles has more than 15,000 Hondurans, and smaller numbers are found in other large U.S. cities.

Costa Ricans have never emigrated to the United States in large numbers, since Costa Rica enjoys the highest standard of living and the lowest level of political violence and social unrest in all of Central America (González, 1989; Redden, 1980). The Costa Rican army was abolished in 1948 after a brief civil war, and during a time period when neighboring countries were beset by military coups, dictatorships, and counterrevolutions, Costa Rica devoted its resources to public education, health, and economic infrastructure. The price for demilitarizing the country has been a high level of political dependence on the United States, whose military forces stationed in the Panama Canal Zone have constituted a de facto deterrent to attacks on Costa Rica. The Costa Rican government openly sympathized with the Sandinista rebels during the insurrection against the Somoza dictatorship, but once the Sandinistas were in power, relations quickly soured. The United States pressured Costa Rica into allowing the breakaway ex-Sandinista *comandante* Edén Pastora to establish a counterrevolutionary force in the northern part of the country, and for several years Costa Rica was subject to the whims of Cold War politics in Central America. Despite this brief departure from the customary Costa Rican neutrality and political equanimity, the country has remained relatively prosperous, and those Costa Ricans emigrating to the United States usually come for higher education or as established professionals. The number of illegal immigrants from Costa Rica is vanishingly small; there are no political refugees, and there are no homogeneous Costa Rican neighborhoods in the United States.

General recommendations

Despite the fact that they come from a well-defined geographical region, Central American groups in the United States are sufficiently diverse – in language and personal background – to warrant individual consideration. The best tool a teacher of Central American students can bring to the classroom is knowledge of the culture, language, and recent sociopolitical history of the countries involved. This knowledge need not entail a major research effort, since the basic facts are available in most libraries. At issue is not so much mastering the peculiarities of individual Central American Spanish dialects but rather reaching out to students by acknowledging their unique background. Knowledge of specific linguistic differences among Spanish dialects, in particular those features that differ in the students' native varieties and textbook presentations, can help the teacher smooth over momentary misunderstandings, and the overwhelming mass of language shared by all varieties of Spanish will facilitate the remaining communication. However, a teacher can use awareness of the students' home language and culture in more subtle ways as a means for drawing the pupils more closely into the educational environment. Acknowledgment of regional words, foods, and cultural practices, accompanied by paraphrases of the remarks to the remainder of the class, goes a long way toward creating an inclusive atmosphere in which student responsiveness can be increased. Teachers who are pressed for time can consult regional glossaries (Lipski, 1994, provides references as well as samples of regional vocabulary). Those with more resources at their disposal can consult collections of folktales and customs from the countries represented by their students. Students themselves, their friends, and their family members are an invaluable resource in teaching the teachers; contacts ranging from brief conversations to extended interviews can provide teachers with the appropriate mix of words, phrases, and cultural referents to enliven the classroom and enhance the self-esteem of students.

Conclusion

The title of this chapter suggests that Central Americans are a homogeneous group, and, indeed, historical, cultural, and linguistic factors link the peoples of the isthmus. Within the United States, however, Central Americans find little unity in the midst of their great diversity, and a brief recapitulation of the salient social and educational needs of the various Central American groups is worthwhile.

Guatemalans in the United States are predominantly of indigenous background, and many speak Spanish only as a second language, if at all. At the poorest end of the spectrum, Guatemalans who arrived as refugees during the during the 1980s and 1990s represent the greatest challenge to educators, in view of the double language barrier, high illiteracy rate, rural upbringing, and great distrust of all official agencies.

Salvadorans in the United States represent a broader socioeconomic spectrum; semiliterate rural dwellers share social spaces with practitioners of skilled trades and professions, and lifestyles range from highly

211

marginalized to solidly middle class. As a group, Salvadorans are saddled with the common misperception that they are all maids and gardeners, occupations that have given prominence to thousands of needy Salvadorans in the nation's largest cities, and Salvadoran children can greatly benefit from explicit recognition of their language and culture as distinct from those of Mexicans and other Latino groups.

Although Guatemalans, Nicaraguans, and Salvadorans have immigrated to the United States in large numbers since the late 1970s, their true story is only now emerging, their language and culture remains as sidetracked by the American mainstream as ever, and when Central Americans make the headlines, it is only with respect to contentious legal battles over amnesty resulting from conditions most Americans only vaguely recall. As with other arrivals from Latin America, Central Americans have arrived to stay; the events that fueled the initial diaspora were only the final stage in a migratory pull whose roots go back over a century. The educational and social needs of the Central American communities in the United States may not be as acute today as during the worst moments of violence and desperation of the 1980s, but they have become a permanent part of the American fabric, and it is only fitting that their voices at last be heard.

Suggestions for further reading

Lipski (1994) provides detailed information on all Latin American Spanish dialects, including sample vocabulary items for each country; Lipski (1986a, 1989b) deals specifically with Salvadorans in the United States. Peñalosa (1984) provides (somewhat dated) information on Salvadorans and Guatemalans in the Los Angeles area. Saragoza (1995) and Suárez-Orozco (1989) comment on educational issues affecting Central Americans in the United States.

Most linguistic studies of regional Spanish dialects contain more detail than is required by classroom teachers. In addition to the general works mentioned above, the following are useful sources of regional vocabulary: Geoffroy Rivas (1978) for El Salvador; Mántica (1989) for Nicaragua; and Armas (1971) and Rubio (1982) for Guatemala. Good samples of folktales and popular beliefs are Lara Figueroa (1984) for Guatemala, Palma (1987) for Nicaragua, and Gutiérrez (1993) for El Salvador.

References

Aguayo, S., & Weiss Fagen, P. (1988). *Central Americans in Mexico and the United States*. Washington, DC: Georgetown University, Hemispheric Migration Project, Center for Immigration Policy and Refugee Assistance.

American Friends Service Committee. (1988). *In the shadow of liberty: Central American refugees in the United States.* Philadelphia: Author.

Armas, D. (1982). *Diccionario de la expressión popular guatemalteca.* [Dictionary of popular Guatemalan speech] (2nd ed.). Guatemala City: Tipografía Nacional. (Original work published 1971).

Arroyo, W., & Eth, S. (1985). Children traumatized by Central American warfare: In S. Eth & R. Pynoos (Eds.), *Post-traumatic stress disorder in children* (pp. 103–120). Washington, DC: American Psychiatric Press.

Cabib, C. (1985). *Salvadorans in the United States: A challenge to immigration and refugee policy.* Unpublished master's thesis, University of Florida, Gainesville.

Cayasso, B. (1995). The Afro-Nicaraguan before and after the Sandinista Revolution. In T. Saunders & S. Moore (Eds.), *African presence in the Americas* (pp. 163–198). Trenton, NJ: Africa World Press.

Farías Caro, O., & Garita Salas, A. T. (1985). *Características demofráficas, económicas y sociales de los inmigrantes centroamericanos por país de origin.* [Demographics, economics and social characteristics of Central American inmigrants by country of origin] Washington, DC: Georgetown University, Hemispheric Migration Project.

Ferris, E. (1987). *The Central American refugees.* New York: Praeger.

Funkhouser, E. (1995). *A profile of Salvadoran emigration* (Working Paper in Economics No. 4-95). Santa Barbara: University of California, Department of Economics.

Geoffroy Rivas, P. (1978). *La lengua Salvadoreña.* San Salvador: Ministerio de Educación.

González, P. (1989). *Intercultural adjustment problems of Costa Rican students in the United States.* Unpublished master's thesis, Portland State University, Portland.

de Gutiérrez, G. A. de. (1993). *Tradición oral en El Salvador* [Oral tradition in El Salvador]. San Salvador: Concultura.

Hagan, J. (1990). *The legalization experience of a Mayan community in Houston.* Unpublished doctoral dissertation, University of Texas at Austin.

Jamail, M., & Stolp, C. (1985). Central Americans on the run: Political refugees or economic migrants? *Public Affairs Comment, 31*(3), 1–8.

Jones J. (1994). *Political development of the Salvadoran community living in the Washington, DC, metropolitan area.* Unpublished master's thesis, University of Florida, Gainesville.

Lara Figueroa, C. (1984). *Leyendas y casos de la tradición oral de la Ciudad de Guatemala.* (2nd ed.) [Leqends and oral tradition of Guatemala City]. Guatemala City: Editorial Universitaria.

Lipski, J. (1983). Reducción de /s/ en el español de Honduras [Reduction of /s/ in Honduran Spanish]. *Nueva Revista de Filología Hispánica, 32,* 273–288.

Lipski, J. (1985). /s/ in Central American Spanish. *Hispania, 68,* 143–149.

Lipski, J. (1986a). Central American Spanish in the United States: El Salvador. *Aztlán, 17,* 91–124.

Lipski, J. (1986b). Instability and reduction of /s/ in the Spanish of Honduras. *Revista Canadiense de Estudios Hispánicos, 11,* 27–47.

Lipski, J. (1989b). Salvadorans in the United States: Patterns of sociolinguistic intergrantion. *National Journal of Sociology, 3,* 97–119.

Lipski, J. (1994). *Latin American Spanish.* London: Longman.

213

Mántica, C. (1989). *El habla nicaragüense y otros ensayos* [Nicaraguan speech and other essays]. San José, Costa Rica: Libro Libre.

Miralles, M. A. (1986). *Health-seeking behavior of Guatemalan refugees in South Florida.* Unpublished master's thesis, University of Florida, Gainesville.

Monks, S. (1987). *El Salvador 1987: Salvadoreños refugiados en los Estados Unidos* [El Salvador 1987: Salvadoran refugees in the United States]. San Salvador: Universidad Centroamerican José Simeón Cañas, Instituto de Investigaciones.

Montes, S. (1986). La situación de los Salvadoreños dsplazados y refugiados [The situation of Salvadoran displaced persons and refugees in the United States]. In *La migración centroamerica y la situación de los Salvadoreños desplazados y refugiados* [Central American Migration and the situation of Salvadoran displaced persons and refugees] (pp. 55–71). Mexico: Centro de Investigación y Acción Social.

Montes Mozo, S., & García Vásquez, J. J. (1988). *Salvadoran migration to the United States: An exploratory study.* Washington, DC: Georgetown University, Hemispheric Migration Project, Center for Immigration Policy and Refugee Assistance.

Morel, A. (1991). *Refugiados Salvadareños en Nicaragua* [Salvadoran refugees in Nicaragua]. Managuai: ACRES.

Nackerud, L. (1993). *The Central American refugee issue in Brownsville, Texas.* San Francisco: Mellen Research University Press.

Ortega, M. (1991). *Reintegration of Nicaraguan refugees and internally displaced persons.* Washington, DC: Georgetown University, Washington DC Hemispheric Migration Project, Center for Immigration Policy and Refugee Assistance.

Palma, M. (1987). *Senderos míticos de Nicaragua* [Mythic paths of Nicaragua]. Bototá: Editorial Nueva América.

Peñalosa, F. (1984). *Central Americans in Los Angeles: Background, language, education.* Los Alamitos, CA: National Center for Bilingual Research.

Peterson, L.(1986). *Central American migration: Past and present* (CIR Staff paper 25), Washington, DC: U.S. Bureau of the Census, Center for International Research.

Pinkerton, A. (1986). Observations on the *tú/vos* option in Guatemalan *ladino* Spanish. *Hispania, 69,* 690–698.

Redden, C. (1980). *A comparative study of Colombian and Costa Rican emigrants to the United States.* New York: Arno Press.

Rubio, J. F. (1982). *Diccionario de voces usadas en Guatemala* [Dictionary of terms used in Guatemala]. Guatemla City: Editorial Piedra Santa.

Saragoza, A. (1995). *Central American immigrant children in the classroom.* San Francisco: Many Cultures.

Speed, S. (1992). *The Salvadoran refugee experience: Humanizing our understanding of the migration process.* Unpublished master's thesis, University of Texas at Austin.

Suárez-Orozco, M. (1989). *Central American refugees and U.S. high schools: A psychosocial study of motivation and achievement.* Stanford: Stanford University Press.

Torres Rivas, E. (1986). Informe sobre el estado de la migración en Centroamerica [Information on the state of migration in Central America]. In *La migración Centroamericana y la situación de los salvadoreños desplazadios y refugiados* [Central American migration and the situation of Salvadoran displaced persons and refugees] (pp. 4–45). Mexico City: Centro de Investigación y Acción Social.

Universidad Para la Paz. (1987). *Los refugiados centroamericanos* [Central American refugees]. Heredia, Costa Rica: Universidad para la Paz, Universidad Nacional.

Vlach, N. (1984). *América y el alma: A study of families and adolescents who are recent United States immigrants from Guatemala*. Unpublished doctoral dissertation, University of California, San Francisco.

Wallace, S. (1989). The new urban Latinos: Central Americans in a Mexican immigrant environment. *Urban Affairs Quarterly, 25,* 239–264.

7 English language learners of Vietnamese background

Chuong Hoang Chung

During the second half of the 1970s and in the 1980s, many immigrants entered the United States from Southeast Asia, fleeing war, poverty, and destruction. This movement lasted well into the early 1990s with over one million refugees and immigrants entering the United States from Vietnam, Cambodia, and Laos (see Chapter 8). Vietnam itself contributed close to one million entrants (Office of Refugee Resettlement, 1995).

After more than 20 years of choosing the best approach to resettlement in new communities across the United States, Vietnamese immigrants still face many challenging issues in their arduous resettlement process. One of these issues involves the immigrant generation's desire to acquire English in a very short time for access to employment and education while seeing their children maintain their native language skills. Both of these tasks require tremendous efforts from parents and children. Whereas English language programs were at one time easy to enter, cutbacks have meant that many new immigrants face long waits for openings in the local adult schools.

The plight of the refugees once touched the hearts of many Americans, who were horrified by accounts of the tragic escapes of refugees. Now many Americans are experiencing compassion fatigue, and Vietnamese are often perceived as problem immigrants and are accused of producing unfair competition in the job market, creating overcrowding in urban centers, and contributing to the depletion of resources across the United States.

This chapter reexamines the language situation of the Vietnamese American community. In 1989, I explored this issue with a special focus on the characteristics of the Vietnamese language learners (see Chung, 1989). This chapter presents information on the language issues facing the Vietnamese American community after 20 years of adaptation to and integration into American society. I look specifically at demographics associated with the new immigrant movements and examine the various educational, sociocultural, and linguistic factors related to English language acquisition. Specifically, I outline the major

The research assistance of Michael Chang and Marie Lo, who worked graciously under time pressure, is greatly appreciated.

hurdles Vietnamese face on their way to becoming fully proficient English speakers and, given the lack of language training programs, the language problems these immigrants face and the resources that can assist newcomers in becoming proficient in English. In addition, I discuss ethnic language maintenance within the Vietnamese American community.

Background of the Vietnamese migration

Researchers of refugee movements have documented the Vietnamese migration since the first arrivals in the United States (Chung & Le, 1994; Haines, 1985; Kibria, 1993; Rumbaut & Ima, 1988; Strand & Jones, 1983). Although explanations regarding the causes of the entire migration process differ, by and large most researchers agree that the many distinct movements of refugees and immigrants from Vietnam were dictated by both internal factors and external conditions. Internal factors included the overall economic situation in Vietnam, persecution suffered by a specific population or group, and semiofficial policies of pushing out certain ethnic groups. External factors include a U.S. refugee policy that allowed the admission of up to fourteen thousand entrants a month during the Carter administration (see Office of Refugee Resettlement, 1981). Countries such as Thailand and Malaysia, although adopting tough positions at times with regard to the refugees, granted temporary asylum to boatloads of escapees from Vietnam and land refugees from Cambodia and Laos (Grant, 1979, Kelly, 1979; Wain, 1981). These countries also facilitated the establishment on their soil of operations by humanitarian organizations. These factors encouraged the exit of the refugees, who knew that they might receive assistance once they landed on shores of the asylum countries. Not until the late 1980s did strict screening processes limit the number of refugees. The goal of this stringent process was to determine whether asylum seekers were indeed true refugees and not economic immigrants, since the asylum countries were overburdened by the number of arrivals and the slow pace of resettlement.

The immigration of 1975

Based on available data on refugee admissions, statistics provided by asylum countries, and various pieces of legislation regulating the processing of the Southeast Asian refugees, one can distinguish four distinct movements of refugees and immigrants from Vietnam (see Table 1). The first movement began with the events of April 1975, when the government of South Vietnam fell under the advance of Communist troops,

217

TABLE I. VIETNAMESE ARRIVALS IN
THE UNITED STATES, FISCAL YEARS
1975–1989

Year	Arrivals
1975	125,000
1976	3,200
1977	1,900
1978	11,100
1979	44,500
1980	95,200
1981	86,100
1982	43,656
1983	23,459
1984	24,818
1985	25,457
1986	22,796
1987	23,012
1988	17,654
1989	22,664

Source: Office of Refugee
Resettlement (1989).

triggering the first major flow of refugees (Grant, 1979). Overnight, armadas of crafts and vessels ferried departing refugees out of Vietnam. The chaotic scene touched many hearts worldwide, and the United States quickly passed Public Law 94-25, also known as the Refugee Act of 1975, to allow the admission of at least fifty thousand Vietnamese characterized as at risk because of their affiliation with the United States or their having worked for the defeated South Vietnam government. Islands in the Pacific were used as staging areas, and after a short stay the refugees were ferried to the five major refugee centers located on the U.S. mainland.

In California, the marine base Camp Pendleton served as a major receiving center (Liu & Murata, 1979). Other military bases, such as Fort Chaffee, Arkansas, and Eglin Air Force Base, Florida, were also mobilized to accept the refugees on a temporary basis. Volunteer agencies and humanitarian organizations joined the government to find the best way to obtain private sponsorships for refugee families. A huge system of volunteer services was put into place to find sponsors for refugees, and in a matter of only a few months the first refugees were able to relocate in communities where they began to learn English and start a new life. This first movement of refugees brought 125,000 Vietnamese to the United States (Office of Refugee Resettlement, 1989).

Post-1975 immigration

After the first big push in 1975 came three other major movements that lasted until the first half of the 1990s. The years 1976 and 1977 saw very few refugees trying to escape the harsh conditions of the country after the war. However, in 1978 the number of refugees escaping from Vietnam suddenly increased. First, Vietnam experienced several years of bad crops, and the effects of the war were beginning to be felt. In addition, hostilities between Vietnam and its northern neighbor, China, flared up, and China readied itself to fight Vietnam. Preparing for the worst, Vietnam engaged in neutralizing Cambodia, which was waging a border war with Vietnam, and it was only a matter of time until the first exchanges of shelling triggered a new Southeast Asian confrontation (Chanda, 1979).

The volatile situation between Vietnam and China coupled with the banning of private enterprise by the Vietnamese government led to the disenchantment of ethnic Chinese Vietnamese, who were for the most part business owners and merchants (Amer, 1991; Tran, 1993). Faced with a difficult future, many chose to leave the country through arrangements made by both internal and external groups wanting to cash in on the refugee situation by charging transportation and exit fees. Within months, Southeast Asian countries experienced an outpouring of Boat People, who found sea routes to beaches and border towns. The movement started in 1978 and lasted until the early 1980s, when the new Orderly Departure Program (ODP) facilitated authorized departures from Vietnam (Grant, 1979; Strand & Jones, 1983). Faced with mounting pressures from the Boat People, the countries of Southeast Asia and others concerned with the refugee movements convened in Geneva and worked out the ODP, through which Vietnamese nationals could apply for immigrant visas to the United States. This program was sanctioned by the Vietnamese government, which cooperated in the paperwork. The ODP, the answer to clandestine exits and unauthorized departures, avoided the asylum countries and refugee camps. Waiting time increased, but the process was much safer. By 1982, U.S. volunteer organizations were faced with two types of Vietnamese entrants: those who came from the refugee camps in Southeast Asia and those who arrived straight from Vietnam. The ODP moved 600,000 Southeast Asian refugees to the United States. Many refugees chose to settle in the warm weather of California and Texas, and by the mid-1980s, the large Vietnamese concentrations in some cities had made news (see Phung, 1996).

In 1985, the U.S. news media were invited back to Vietnam for the tenth anniversary of the U.S. departure from Vietnam. There they found many children of Americans, known as Amerasians, who had been left behind. Thus, the final U.S. effort was a program designed to bring out the children of former U.S. servicemen and Vietnamese women. Under the Amerasian Homecoming Act of 1987, many Amerasian children and their parents were allowed admission to the United States. In addition, in 1989 the United States negotiated an agreement with the Vietnamese government that allowed political prisoners from reeducation camps to be settled in the United States. As of June 1992, an estimated fifty thousand former Vietnamese political prisoners and their families had been admitted to the United States; many of them were religious leaders, former government officials, and military servicemen (Le, 1993, p. 169). In addition, by the early 1990s around thirty thousand Amerasians and their close relatives had been admitted to the United States (see Chung & Le, 1994). However, after the renewal of diplomatic relations between the two countries, the official immigration of Vietnamese to the United States may fall under the jurisdiction of the U.S. Immigration and Naturalization Service, that is, immigration may take place through normal channels and not under refugee legislation.

The Vietnamese arrived in the United States during the Cold War, when their particular political position and affiliation fit well with U.S. foreign policy (see Scanlan & Loescher, 1986; Zucker & Zucker, 1987). The continual reauthorization of refugee programs helped Vietnamese immigrants for two decades. However, with the change in relations between the United States and the former Soviet Union, the issue of refugees has become less and less important. Hence, the United States cut down the number of admissions from Vietnam in the early 1990s, and currently there is very little immigration.

The refugee situation in the late 1990s

According to the U.S. Committee for Refugees (1997), the situation in Vietnam called for repatriation to be complete at the end of 1996. Thailand and other countries with refugee camps signed the Orderly Return Program, and Hong Kong, Thailand, Singapore, Indonesia, and Malaysia sent refugees back to Vietnam despite claims that forcible repatriation was in violation of the refugees' rights. In one case of violence, one hundred Vietnamese stabbed themselves to avoid repatriation and protest the actions of local authorities. Some Vietnamese on the way to the airport scuffled with security forces. By the beginning of 1997, very few refugees were left in Southeast Asian camps except for about two thousand Vietnamese who were to be resettled on the island of Palawan in the Philippines.

The United States and the government of Vietnam have agreed on a program, called the Comprehensive Plan for Action, that allows returnees to Vietnam from Southeast Asian camps to be reinterviewed for admission to the United States if they voluntarily returned to Vietnam during the program. Those who had close association with the U.S. presence in Vietnam or with the government in South Vietnam prior to 1975, those who are members of certain ethnic groups, and those who were involved in certain political or religious activities are given preference. Any person who was in an asylum camp in Southeast Asia as of October 1, 1995, and who either had returned to Vietnam or had applied and registered for voluntary repatriation by June 30, 1996, may apply in writing for consideration to be interviewed in Vietnam for possible admission and resettlement in the United States. Individuals accepted after the interview and screening process can start doing the paperwork for admission to the United States. This program could mark the final phase of the Southeast Asian refugee era. It is estimated that up to fifteen thousand slots will be made available for this special category, but exact number that will actually immigrate is hard to determine. Future immigrants from Vietnam will have to go through the usual immigration and naturalization procedures with the U.S. consulate in Vietnam.

Patterns of settlement and the Vietnamese speech community in California

Since 1975, the Vietnamese community has grown substantially. According to the 1990 census, there were 614,547 Vietnamese in the United States, some 60.0% of those who traced their ancestry to Southeast Asia (who in turn made up 13.0% of the total Asian American population). Vietnamese Americans represented 8.4% of the total Asian American population and 0.2% of the total U.S. population (Shinagawa, 1996, p. 86). Since a significant number of people from Vietnam, Cambodia, and Laos may have chosen to identify themselves as ethnic Chinese, these figures probably represent an undercount (Le, 1993, p. 171).

The greatest concentration of Vietnamese was found in California (40.9%), followed by Texas (9.8%), Washington (4.3%), New York (3.9%), and Massachusetts (3.2%) (Shinagawa, 1996, p. 90). In Texas, Vietnamese Americans were the largest Asian American group (Shinagawa, 1996, p. 71). Two other Gulf states, Louisiana and Florida, also had significant Vietnamese American populations (Le, 1993, p. 172).

The five U.S. metropolitan areas with the largest concentrations are Anaheim–Santa Ana (9.7% of the Vietnamese American population), Los Angeles (9.3%), San Jose (8.4%), Washington, DC (4.7%), and San Diego (3.0%) (Shinagawa, 1996, p. 91). Vietnamese are perhaps most visible in California, with many large concentrations in both the northern and the southern sections of the state. Westminster, San Jose, Sacramento, and San Francisco have experienced dramatic increases in the refugee population. In the downtown sections of these cities, new business centers advertise Vietnamese ethnic goods and services.

As mentioned, most of these immigrants are part of the four major movements from Southeast Asia since 1975. California attracted a large number of refugees for a number of reasons. First, the state has very mild weather. Second, there are far more Asians in California, so opportunities to locate within Vietnamese enclaves are greater. Third, California has very liberal refugee policies and many programs that help refugees resettle. Fourth, many jobs were available within the electronic industry in the 1980s. Finally, some refugees have joined family members who have settled in California. (See Chung, 1989, for a discussion of this phenomenon of secondary migration.)

Educational background

Education and literacy in Vietnam

According to reports provided by the United Nations Development Program (UNDP), in 1990 Vietnam, with a population of seventy-five million, had an adult literacy rate of 82%. Learning has always been important in Vietnam – its first national university, Quoc Tu Giam, was founded in 1070, around the same time as Oxford University in England. Vietnam also has a very long and rich literary tradition (Marr, 1989). Under the monarchy system, education was accessible only to the elite ruling class – a tiny proportion of the community – and remained so throughout the French colonial period. By 1945, around 90% of the population was still illiterate (Brazier, 1992).

Nationalists like Ho Chi Minh have always viewed education as important. In the struggle for independence and to rid themselves of colonialism, Vietnamese nationalist leaders believed that the more people understood, the less resigned they would be to their own exploitation. This is why one of the most important campaigns in the 1940s was to combat illiteracy across all classes in the Vietnamese community. The romanized form of Vietnamese, called Quoc Ngu, was supported and taught. This new script made the acquisition of literacy much easier. Education and the acquisition of literacy have remained a top priority for the immigrant community in the United States. Educational successes among the Vietnamese community in the United States are highly praised despite the community's short history there.

English language teaching in Vietnam

Unlike the first wave of refugees from Vietnam, many of whom were urbanized and had contacts with Americans, today's immigrants are often ill-equipped to adapt quickly to an English-speaking society. The large-scale teaching of English is a recent phenomenon. Between 1954 and 1971, in then – North Vietnam, all secondary- and tertiary-level students had to study Russian or Chinese as their foreign language (Sullivan, 1996, p. 94). In South Vietnam, residual French and American influences were strong. After the Vietnam War ended with the victory of the North Vietnamese, for a period Russian was the most important foreign language for the nation. However, after the policy of *doi moi* (renovation) was officially adopted by the government in 1986 (p. 99), Vietnam shifted from the socialist system of collectivization and central planning to an open-market economy, and English soon became the most important foreign language.

Sullivan (1996) notes that "English is seen as a basic necessity for well-paying city jobs" (p. 111), and hundreds of English language centers have sprung up in cities. At the secondary level, English is the most popular choice for the compulsory foreign language requirement (p. 114). However, despite contact with other English-speaking countries that had established relations with Vietnam earlier than the United States did, there is a shortage of well-trained teachers (many are retrained former Russian teachers), and teaching methods are often ineffective. The English skills of Vietnamese arrivals reflect their training at home. In Vietnam, many Vietnamese spent hours in English classes writing words, memorizing the spelling of those words, and studying English grammar. Shifting from a grammar-based approach to a more communicative approach, they experience difficulties in keeping up. In addition, if their instructor in Vietnam used a different variety of English, then they have to adjust to the pronunciation of American English.

Educational attainment in the United States

According to 1990 census figures, the educational attainment of Southeast Asian Americans was considerably lower than that of other Asian Americans. Among Southeast Asian Americans and Pacific Islanders, on average less than 10% had a bachelor's degree or higher (Shinagawa, 1996, p. 80). In comparison, some 40% of Asian Americans

223

TABLE 2. EDUCATIONAL ATTAINMENT OF VIETNAMESE AMERICANS AGED 25 AND
ABOVE (%)

	Less than a bachelor's degree	Bachelor's degree	Master's degree	Doctorate
Male (N = 155,403)	78.1	15.7	5.5	0.8
Female (N = 145,596)	88.7	8.9	2.3	0.1
Total (N = 300,999)	83.0	12.4	3.9	0.5

Source: Adapted from Shinagawa (1996, pp. 119–120).

aged 25 years and older had a bachelor's degree or higher (p. 79). Nevertheless, within the Southeast Asian population, the Vietnamese tend to be the best educated and most proficient in the English language (Le, 1993 p. 172). In a study conducted in California, Rumbaut (1989) found that by both local and national measures of school achievement, the Vietnamese did best among the Southeast Asians, followed by the Sino-Vietnamese (ethnic Chinese from Vietnam) and the Hmong, with the Khmer and the Lao ranking below the majority White population (cited in Smith-Hefner, 1995, p. 206).

Table 2 shows the educational attainment of Vietnamese Americans aged 25 and above, based on 1990 census figures. The gap between male and female educational attainment widens as one goes up the educational ladder.

Educational needs in the United States

Vietnamese Americans have great educational needs because they are a relatively young group. Ima and Rumbaut (1995, p. 180), using a 1986 source, note that the median age of Vietnamese Americans was 18, in contrast to 32 for the general U.S. population. Le, (1993) using more recent Office of Refugee Resettlement data from 1991, found that the median age of those arriving as refugees was 28, but 21% of the group was between the ages of 6 and 17 (roughly the K–12 population), and an additional 19% were between the ages of 18 and 24 (roughly the college-age population). Of all Southeast Asians, "close to one third . . . are of school age, indicating the tremendous impact this population has on the education system in their communities of residence" (Le, 1993, p. 173). For example, in California, which has the highest concentration of Vietnamese Americans, there are 43,008 limited English proficient (LEP) students of Vietnamese language background in the public schools, the second largest language group after Spanish speakers, who number over 1.1 million. Students of Vietnamese background are more numerous than Chinese (Cantonese and Mandarin speakers combined) (www.cde.ca.gov/demographics.htm). Thus the need for English language teaching services at the K–12 level is great, and the 18- to 24-year-old group may also "impact the vocational training or higher education systems" (Le, 1993, 173).

Ima and Rumbaut (1995), who studied Southeast Asian refugee youth in 1986–1987 in San Diego, California, point out that for young Vietnamese and other Southeast Asian Americans, "the acquisition of English-language competency is the principal obstacle they must overcome in their educational adaptation; it is also a major challenge for their teachers in American schools" (p. 180). They caution against conflating them with other Asian American groups because of "fundamental differences between the immigrant and refugee experiences" (p. 181). They add, however that the severity of problems associated with refugee traumas (e.g., posttraumatic stress disorder, disruption of schooling) varies greatly with period of arrival, social class, and other factors and that with time in the United States the differences between refugees and immigrants will lessen (pp. 182–183). Ima and Rumbaut's key findings regarding LEP and fluent English proficient (FEP) Southeast Asian students are that (1) Southeast Asian students are more likely to be LEP than those from other linguistic minority, groups are; (2) as expected, FEP students do better in all measures of academic achievement than LEP students do; (3) in spite of the disproportionate number of LEP individuals, Southeast Asians as an aggregate have above-average grades; (4) the level of academic achievement corresponds roughly to the socioeconomic composition of each group, such as the proportion of parents with more schooling; and (5) although the Southeast Asian students' CTBS (California Test of Basic Skills) mathematics scores are above average, their reading scores are significantly below average (p. 188).

Based on these findings, Ima and Rumbaut (1995) make a number of observations and suggestions that might be useful for classroom teachers. For example, they emphasize that the different cultural backgrounds of various groups of Southeast Asian Vietnamese and Sino-Vietnamese tend to have been influenced by the Chinese, especially the Confucian tradition, whereas the Khmer and Lao have been influenced by Indian civilization. The former's background may have been more congruent with the U.S. school system and may have led to more success (p. 194). Second, Ima and Rumbaut note that, based on their findings of the predictive power of various scores, "in assessing Southeast Asian students, practitioners who have access to test scores should pay special attention to mathematics achievement and to the more memorizable aspects of English language skills rather than to the more culturally problematic areas that test vocabulary, reading comprehension, and language expression," especially for newly arrived refugees (p. 192).

Contrastive features of Vietnamese and English

Besides the differences in teaching methodology, Vietnamese learners experience other problems in their efforts to acquire English. The following list of contrastive features is drawn from the California State Department of Education (1994) and my own knowledge of the Vietnamese language and culture. For one thing, the sound systems of English and Vietnamese differ greatly. Each tone in Vietnamese represents a completely different meaning. Most Vietnamese words are monosyllabic, and Vietnamese has fewer consonants and no consonant clusters. Thus, it is not uncommon to hear Vietnamese speakers drop consonant clusters in plural forms. In addition, English grammar is far more complex than Vietnamese syntax. Verb tenses, for example, have been identified as a major problem for Vietnamese learners.

Vietnamese use forms of address and formulas of politeness that could be confusing when used in an English setting. Repetition and formulaic sentences in specific settings are encouraged more than spontaneous responses and dialogues. As an example, Vietnamese learners are very embarrassed to call their teachers by their first names after just a few classes. Even with encouragement, they are likely to begin their sentences with such forms as *Mr. Mike, Miss Helen, Teacher Mike,* or *Teacher Helen.* In such sociolinguistic situations, the English teacher should not try to correct the students right away and should let them adjust as they go along.

Other situations could be very confusing for American interlocutors. For example, in yes-no questions, the Vietnamese response for *yes* often consists of repeating a question word in Vietnamese. For example,

Are you hungry?	Hungry.
Do you want to eat?	Eat.
Do you know how to drive?	Know.

Vietnamese speakers can confuse American interlocutors further by answering *yes* to every question even if they want to answer in the negative. *Yes* could mean "I hear you," I agree with you, or "I heard you, but I do not agree with you." Negative questions are answered differently than in English: For example, when asked the question, "Don't you have a place to stay?" the person without a place to stay can answer, "Yes, I don't have a place to stay," meaning "Yes, that is right, I don't have a place to stay." "Aren't you married? could elicit the reply, "Yes, I am not married."

A final factor is the variety of English spoken in some Vietnamese enclaves. Vietnamese children are quick to pick up English in the neighborhood in which they live, whether the South Side of Chicago or a mixed community in the Tenderloin in San Francisco. From this beginning, they pick up not only accents but also nonstandard forms of English. Hence, when they enter school, they may have a repertoire of spoken English that reflects the community or the neighborhood in which they live.

The challenge of maintaining Vietnamese

The prospects for maintaining the Vietnamese language depend to a large extent on the family. Except for cases of refugee trauma and family separation (e.g., due to obstacles in emigration and immigration rules), Vietnamese have arrived in the United States with their families. When the parents or grandparents speak limited or no English, interaction in the family is likely to be in Vietnamese. On the other hand, the difficulties of adjustment (especially those peculiar to refugees) as well as racism and racial conflict in the United States (Hein, 1995, pp. 69–91) may create severe stresses within the family – between husband and wife and in other gender relations (see, e.g., Hein, 1995, pp. 116–121; Kibria, 1993, pp. 108–143), and between elders and children (see, e.g., Hein, 1995, pp. 121–132; Kibria, 1993, pp. 144–166). These stresses compound other problems that cause a communication gap between elders and children, such as differences between Vietnamese and American culture, a home-school language discrepancy, and children's exposure to English language media, and together they contribute to the erosion of the Vietnamese language.

Second, the extremely high geographic mobility of the recent immigrants greatly limits the role of Vietnamese enclaves. In the mid-1990s, there were organized community efforts to help maintain the Vietnamese language and other cultural traits among the children of Vietnamese parents. Like many early European and Asian immigrant groups, the Vietnamese community has begun to take direct steps toward language maintenance and the enhancement of ethnic cultural identity by establishing numerous weekend schools in large urban communities. Daily Vietnamese newspapers with a relatively large circulation include a homeland section with current news and information on Vietnam so that readers can keep up with the major social and political developments there. The mass media have also shaped public opinion about the necessity and value of language and culture maintenance in the Vietnamese community (Nguyen, 1991).

In addition to an explicit emphasis on Vietnamese language maintenance, several hundred social, religious, and other community-based organizations, representing the local Vietnamese American community, provide a wide range of activities. In addition, various businesses, professional groups, community service organizations, cultural groups,

Buddhist temples, and Catholic churches validate the importance of Vietnamese in ethnic cultural life. Most meetings of such associations are conducted exclusively in Vietnamese. Recognizing the rapid growth in the Vietnamese population and the problem of language communication being experienced by most incoming Vietnamese, federal, state, and other public agencies have begun to assist community organizations by providing funds or special services, such as printing common forms in Vietnamese for a number of uses. For example, the San Jose City School District and San Francisco Unified School District have parent consent forms in Vietnamese.

In spite of various difficulties, the community's efforts to maintain its language and culture seem to be growing rapidly. Will such organized efforts bring about results that are different from what the other ethnic minorities with a longer immigration history have experienced? At present, the prospects for maintaining Vietnamese are uncertain. Bilingual education in California has been seriously curtailed by the passage of Proposition 227 (see Chapter 15). Although immigration from Vietnam has continued during the 1980s and 1990s, it is unclear how long the current immigration policy in the United States will remain unchanged.

The language maintenance efforts in the Vietnamese American community are relatively recent. To ensure a good beginning and to achieve the desired results, Vietnamese American community leaders must express their language maintenance goals in terms that are understandable and convincing to the first generation of immigrant parents and to their children, who are now entering college in large numbers. They must reevaluate the current language programs and their goals and pool their resources to come up with some serious language planning. Curriculum materials developed by a language-planning team could certainly attract commercial publishing houses that would see the investment as worthwhile. Along with these efforts, leaders must continue with research on the linguistic, psychological, sociological, and ethnological aspects of language maintenance in the Vietnamese American community. The language issue is still one of the most challenging that the Vietnamese American community has to face. For a smooth road to self-sufficiency, Vietnamese have to learn English while maintaining the Vietnamese language and ethnic heritage they hope the second generation will not forget. Only time will tell whether these two important objectives can be achieved simultaneously.

Suggestions for Further Reading

For general background reading on Vietnam and its culture, see Lam (1987), Ha (1989), and Jamieson (1991). Liu and Murata (1979) and

Kelly (1979) are older but frequently cited studies of early Vietnamese refugees and their adaptation. More recently, Rutledge (1992) provides an overview of the Vietnamese experience in America, combining first-hand interviews with historical and sociological information, and Haines (1987) and Hein (1995) both consider Vietnamese Americans alongside other Southeast Asian refugees.

Zhou (1998) examines the adjustment of refugee children, including their school experience, using a student survey, participant observation, and interviews in a low-income community in New Orleans as well as quantitative data sets such as the census. Kibria (1993) uses participant observation and in-depth interviews to examine the lives of Vietnamese immigrants in Philadelphia. Rumbaut and Ima (1988) deal with the adaptation of Southeast Asian youth; Ima and Rumbaut (1995) focus specifically on education, especially English proficiency. California State Department of Education (1994) publishes a handbook, updated from its 1982 edition, designed for teachers with Vietnamese students.

References

Amer, R. (1991). *The ethnic Chinese in Vietnam and Sino-Vietnamese relations.* Kuala Lumpur, Malaysia: Forum.

Brazier, C. (1992). *Vietnam: The price of peace.* Oxford: Oxfam.

California State Department of Education. (1994). *Handbook for teaching Vietnamese speaking students.* Sacramento, CA: Office of Bilingual Education.

Chanda, N. (1979). *Brother enemy.* New York: Free Press.

Chung, H. C. (1989). The language situation of the Vietnamese American. In S. L. McKay & S. C. Wong (Eds.), *Language diversity: Problem or resource?* (pp. 276–293). Rowley, MA: Newbury House.

Chung, H. C., & Le, V. (1994). *The Vietnamese Amerasians: A California study.* Rancho Cordova, CA: Southeast Asian Resource Center.

Grant, B. (1979). *The boat people: An age investigation.* Melbourne, Australia: Penguin Books.

Ha, V. T. (1989). Reflections on Vietnamese history and systems of thought. *Vietnamese Studies, 4,24,* 5–14.

Haines, D. (1985). *Refugees in the United States.* Westport, CT: Greenwood Press.

Haines, D. W. (Ed.). (1989). *Refugees as immigrants: Cambodians, Laotians and Vietnamese in America.* Totowa, NJ: Rowman & Lattlefield.

Hein, J. (1995). *From Vietnam, Laos, and Cambodia: A refugee experience in the United States.* New York: Twayne.

Ima, K., & Rumbaut, R. G. (1995). Southeast Asian refugees in American schools: A comparison of fluent-English-proficient and limited-English-proficient students. In D. T. Nakanishi & T. Y. Nishida (Eds.), *The Asian American educational experience: A source book for teachers and students* (pp. 180–197). New York: Routledge.

Jamieson, N. (1991). *Culture and development in Vietnam.* (Working Paper No. 1). Honolulu, HI: East-West Center.

Kelly, G. P. (1979). *From Vietnam to America.* Boulder, CO: Westview Press.

Kibria, N. (1993). *Family tightrope: The changing lives of Vietnamese Americans.* Princeton, NJ: Princeton University Press.

Lam, T. B. (Ed.). (1987). *Borrowings and adaptations in Vietnamese culture.* Honolulu: University of Hawaii at Manoa, Center for Asian and Pacific Studies.

Le, N. (1993). The case of the Southeast Asian refugees: Policy for a community "at-risk." In *The state of Asian Pacific America: Policy issues to the year 2020* (pp. 167–188). LEAP Asian Pacific American Public Policy Institute and UCLA Asian American Studies Center.

Liu, W., & Murata, A. (1979). *Transition to nowhere.* Nashville, TN: Charter House.

Marr, D. (1989). *Vietnamese tradition on trial.* Berkeley: University of California Press.

Nguyen, X. T. (1991). *Language, education, and culture: A Vietnamese perspective.* Melbourne, Australia: Philip Institute of Technology.

Office of Refugee Resettlement. (1981). *Report to Congress.* Washington, DC: U.S. Department of Health and Human Services.

Office of Refugee Resettlement. (1989). *Report to Congress.* Washington, DC: U.S. Department of Health and Human Services.

Office of Refugee Resettlement. (1995). *Report to Congress.* Washington, DC: U.S. Department of Health and Human Services.

Phung, N. (1996, April). Dan so cong dong [The total number of people in the community]. *Thoi Bao,* p. 2.

Rumbaut, R. G. (1989). Portraits, patterns and predictors of the refugee adaptation process: Results and reflections from the IHARP panel study. In D. W. Haines (Ed.), *Refugees as immigrants: Cambodians, Laotians and Vietnamese in America* (pp. 138–182). Westport, CT: Greenwood Press.

Rumbaut, R., & Ima, K. (1988). *The adaptation of Southeast Asian refugee youth.* (Report prepared for the Office of Refugee Resettlement). Washington, DC: U.S. Government Printing Office.

Scanlan, J., & Loescher, G. (1986). *Calculated kindness.* New York: Free Press.

Shinagawa, L. H. (1996). The impact of immigration on the demography of Asian Pacific Americans. In B. O. Hins & R. Lee (Eds.), *The state of Asian Pacific America: A public policy report: Reframing the immigration debate* (pp. 59–126). Los Angeles, CA: LEAP Asian Pacific American Public Policy Institute and UCLA Asian American Studies Center.

Strand, P., & Jones, W. (1983). *Indochinese refugees in the United States.* Durham, NC: Duke University Press.

Sullivan, P. N. (1996). *English language teaching in Vietnam: An appropriation of communicative methodologies.* Unpublished doctoral dissertation, University of California, Berkeley.

Tran, K. (1993). *The ethnic Chinese in Vietnam and economic development of Vietnam.* Singapore: ISEAS.

U.S. Committee for Refugees. (1997). *World refugee survey.* Washington, DC: Author.

Wain, B. (1981). *The refused: The agony of the Indochina refugee.* New York: Simon & Schuster.

Zhou, M. (1998). *Growing up American: How Vietnamese children adapt to life in the United States.* New York: Russell Sage Foundation.

Zucker, N., & Zucker, N. (1987). *The guarded gate.* New York: Harcourt Brace Jovanovich.

8 The language situation of the Hmong, Khmer, and Laotian communities in the United States

M. G. López

The year 2000 will mark not only the beginning of a new millennium but also the twenty-fifth anniversary of the resettlement of the first Southeast Asian refugees in the United States. Since the first refugees were airlifted out of Cambodia, Laos, and Vietnam in 1975, more than 1,187,000 refugees from Southeast Asia have been resettled in the United States. Although Southeast Asians are often described as a singular community – based principally on their common experience as refugees – this chapter explores the diversity that exists among the Hmong, Khmer, and ethnic Lao and in their experiences as refugees.[1] Though not exhaustive in its description of each community, the chapter is intended to provide educators with an understanding of how the historical and sociocultural contexts of immigration, resettlement, and adjustment shape the use, learning, and maintenance of languages within each of the three ethnic communities. Such an understanding will help educators – teachers, counselors, administrators, and researchers – see beyond the important, but largely symbolic, images of the of Southeast Asian refugee experience that have been made popular by the movie *The Killing Fields,* beautifully embroidered Homing story cloths (*paj ntaub*), or the news accounts of a Cambodian refugee youth's near victory as an American Spelling Bee champion. In the chapter, the term *Southeast Asian refugees* refers to persons originally from Cambodia and Laos. (Individuals from Vietnam are discussed in Chapter 7.) I recognize that this use of the term is imperfect in that, geographically, Southeast Asia also encompasses the nations of Indonesia, Malaysia, Myanmar (formerly known as Burma), the Philippines, Singapore, and Thailand. My use of the term reflects its prevalent use in the public and academic discourse to identify individuals from the nations of Cambodia, Laos, and Vietnam and the fact that the term is considered by many to be less offensive than the word *Indochina* or *Indochinese.* The term *refugee* is equally a problematic descriptor of the Cambodian, Hmong, and ethnic Lao populations in the United States (see the section "New Contexts, New Lives: The Southeast Asian Community in Transition"). I use the term refugee to highlight the fact that the first Cambodians, Hmong, and Laotians were initially admitted to

---

1 The discussion of the Laotian community throughout the chapter is comparatively shorter than that of the Cambodian and Hmong communities. This reflects the fact that the Laotian refugee community is perhaps the least well known and researched.

the United States as refugees. Therefore, their emigration from Asia differs from the immigration experiences of the majority of persons from other Asian nations, especially other Southeast Asians, such as the Thai (see Chapters 9 and 10 for a discussion of the immigration of other Asians to the United States).

The term *Khmer* refers to the language and persons of the dominant ethnic group of Cambodia. In addition to the Khmer, Cambodia is inhabited by ethnic Chinese and Vietnamese as well as by a number of ethnic minority populations. Throughout the chapter the term *Khmer* is used interchangeably with *Cambodian* to refer to persons who emigrated from, or were born to parents who emigrated from, the nation of Cambodia. The name *Cambodia* is used to refer not only to to the nation of Cambodia before April 1975 but also to Pol Pot's *Democratic Kampuchea,* the Vietnamese backed People's Republic of Kampuchea, the State of Cambodia, and the Coalition Government of Democratic Kampuchea.

The ethnic Lao, the politically and numerically dominant population of Laos, are also referred to throughout the chapter as the *lowland Lao,* a descriptor that differentiates them from the highland Lao. The term *Laotian(s)* is used also to refer to the ethnic Lao.

The essay is divided into five main sections. The first gives a brief history of the Hmong, Khmer, and lowland Lao communities in Southeast Asia and their subsequent immigration to the United States. The second part of the essay describes the settlement patterns of the Hmong, Khmer, and Lao across the United States. The third section reviews each community's educational attainment prior to resettlement, and the fourth section describes a few key sociocultural issues common to Southeast Asian refugees' adaptation experience in the United States. The final section examines the interplay of the issues examined in the first four sections in light of their influence on language use, maintenance, and learning within each ethnic community.

Hmong, Khmer, and Laotian immigration to the United States[2]

While the world's focus throughout the majority of the Vietnam War was on the military conflict in North and South Vietnam, the nations of

2 For more comprehensive accounts of the exodus of Hmong, Khmer, and Laotian refugees from Cambodia and Laos, their experiences in various Thai refugee camps, and their resettlement in the United States, see Bliatout, Downing, Lewis, and Yang, (1988); Chan (1994); Donnelly (1994); Dunnigan Olney, McNall, and Spring (1996). On the Hmong, see Hendricks, Downing, and Deinard (1987) and Koltyk (1998). On the Khmer, see Hopkins (1996); Mortland (1996); and Ouk, Huffman, and Lewis (1988). On the ethnic Lao, see Bounkeo, Inthavong, Luangpraseut, Phommasouvanh, Compton, and Lewis (1989); DeVoe (1996); and Thee (1973).

Cambodia and Laos were critical military theaters within the American effort to battle the rise of communism in Southeast Asia. Through the Central Intelligence Agency (CIA), the U.S. government conducted covert military operations in Cambodia and Laos throughout the 1960s and 1970s in an effort to defeat not only the Vietnamese Communist forces but also the Socialist Khmer Rouge and Pathet Lao armies.[3] With the victories of the Khmer Rouge and Pathet Lao in Cambodia and Laos respectively, hundreds of civil and military leaders of the defeated governments, along with their families, were evacuated from the capital cities of Phnom Penh and Vientiane as well as a number of key military sites, such as Long Tieng, from which the Hmong and other highland Lao (e.g., the Iu Mien) operated. By the end of 1975 approximately 130,400 refugees from Cambodia, Laos, and Vietnam had been resettled in the United States under the provisions of the Indochina Migration and Refugee Assistance Act of 1975 (Gordon, 1987). Of these first admitees, 95% were Vietnamese. Among the remaining 5% were roughly 300 highland Lao (principally Hmong), 4,600 Cambodians, and 500 ethnic Lao (see Table 1). These 5,400 Cambodians, Hmong, and ethnic Lao represented only a minor fraction of what by 1997 would total roughly 400,000 refugees from Cambodia and Laos.

Hmong immigration

In Laos, the Hmong were one of approximately sixty ethnic minority groups that made up about half of the four million citizens of Laos before 1975. Known as the Miao in China and the Meo in Vietnam, the Hmong were one of the largest ethnic groups. Bliatout, Downing, Lewis, and Yang (1988) note that the Hmong totaled three hundred thousand by 1972 and represented 10% of the entire population of Laos. Most often described as a primitive hill tribe or as highland Lao, the Hmong emigrated from China to Laos around 1810 to 1820 and settled along the borders with China and Vietnam. In Laos, the Hmong, as they had previously done in China, sought to maintain a lifestyle that was essentially independent from the political institutions of the country and to remain culturally distinct from the dominant ethnic Lao. For the Hmong, their residency in the mountainous northeastern provinces enabled them to remain geographically isolated and politically semiautonomous from the successive French and Laotian governments in Vientiane. During World War II and the subsequent struggle for independence, however, the Hmong, who by then were divided into the Ly and Lo clans – headed by Touby Lyfoung and Faydang Lobliayao, respec-

3 For a more detailed reading on the military conflict in Southeast Asia and the rise of communism in Cambodia and Laos read Adams and McCoy (1970), Chandler (1990), Shawcross (1979), Stuart-Fox (1982), and Thee (1973).

TABLE I. CAMBODIAN, HIGHLAND LAO, AND LOWLAND REFUGEE AR-
RIVALS IN THE UNITED STATES, 1975–1997

Year	Cambodian	Highland Lao	Lowland Lao	Total
1975	4,600	300	500	7,375
1976	1,100	3,100	7,100	13,276
1977	300	1,700	400	4,377
1978	1,300	3,900	4,100	11,278
1979	6,000	11,300	18,900	38,179
1980	16,000	27,200	28,300	73,480
1981	27,100	3,700	15,600	48,381
1982	20,200	2,600	6,800	29,600
1983	13,100	700	2,100	17,883
1984	19,900	2,800	4,500	29,184
1985	19,100	1,900	3,500	26,485
1986	9,800	3,700	9,200	24,686
1987	1,500	8,300	7,300	19,087
1988	2,800	10,400	4,200	19,388
1989	1,900	8,500	4,000	16,389
1990	2,200	5,200	3,600	12,990
1991	40	6,400	2,900	11,331
1992	140	6,800	500	9,432
1993	20	6,700	200	8,913
1994	10	6,300	20	8,324
1995	0	3,700	20	5,715
1996	0	1,700	500	4,196
1997	0	800	170	2,967
Total	147,110	127,700	124,410	399,220

Sources: Figures for Cambodians for 1975–1981, are from Gordon
(1987, p. 156). Figures for Highland Lao for 1975–1981 are from
Dunning, Olney, McNall and Spring (1996, p. 198) and are rounded to
the nearest hundred. Figures for Lowland Lao for 1975–1981 were
tabulated from totals for Lao in Gordon and for Highland Lao in
Dunnigan et al. The total for 1981 for Highland and Lowland is higher
than that reported by Gordon for refugees from Laos. This reflects the
fact that Dunnigan et al.'s total for Highland Lao was greater than the
number of arrivals from Laos reported by Gordon for 1981. Counts for
Cambodians, Highland Lao, and Lowland Lao for 1982–1997 are from
U.S. Committee for Refugee Concerns (1993, 1997).

tively – were drawn significantly into the Laotian political structure
(Yang, 1993). Touby Lyfoung's faction aligned itself with the French
and later with the Royal Lao government and the CIA. In contrast, Faydang Lobliayao and his followers gave their allegiance to the Japanese
during World War II, then to the Lao Issara (a force that sought inde-

pendence for Laos from France), and later joined forces with the Pathet Lao. Note that a great majority of the Hmong chose not to align themselves with either side during the First or Second Indochina War, but nonetheless became victims of the conflict, especially when it began to expand into their homeland areas in 1959.

Although the Hmong and other highland Lao, like the Iu Mien, had worked with the CIA in Laos since the early 1960s, not until the 1970s did the United States admit publicly that it had been conducting operations in Laos. Moreover, the relationship between the Hmong and the CIA was not fully understood until after the Pathet Lao victory (Dunnigan, Olney, McNall, & Spring, 1996). Lee (1982) estimates that about 12,000 Hmong were killed during the war between 1962 and 1975 and that by 1973 the Hmong represented roughly 30% of the displaced persons within Laos. As displaced persons (or internal refugees), the Hmong and other highland Lao became dependent on CIA provisions, or what is at times referred to as *rice from the sky* (Yang, 1993). Because of their association with the Royal Lao government and the CIA and because of their history of seeking to remain autonomous from the control of the leadership in Vientiane, the Hmong quickly became victims of various Pathet Lao campaigns for reeducation and military retribution. A Hmong refugee coordinator summarizes well the plight of the Hmong under the Pathet Lao:

Every family has lost at least one or two members. And it hasn't stopped. Because of the Hmong courage as fighters, they became the Communists' major enemy and suffer the most from reprisals. In three years since the war ended, Communists have killed more Hmong than during the 14-year war. (Miller, Kiatoukaysay, & Yang, 1992, p. 12)

Although General Vang Pao, the leader of the Hmong and other highland Lao forces, and most of his top military aides were evacuated from Laos and resettled in the United States in 1975 and early 1976, the majority of Hmong refugees arrived in the United States after 1979. As shown in Table 1, 127,700 highland Lao, the majority of whom were Hmong, were resettled in the United States as refugees between 1975 and 1997.[4] For the Hmong, refugee arrivals were the greatest during the period 1979–1980, when 38,500 highland Lao refugees arrived in the

4 The Office of Refugee Resettlement of the U.S. Department of Health and Human Services, which publishes the yearly *Refugee Resettlement Program: Report to the Congress,* the Immigration and Naturalization Service of the U.S. Department of Justice, which produces the annual *Statistical Yearbook of the Immigration and Naturalization Service,* and organizations like the U.S. Committee for Refugees, which publishes the monthly *Refugee Reports,* do not maintain separate tabulations for the different highland groups (e.g., Hmong, Iu Mien, Kammu, Lahu, Tai Dam). It is estimated that the Hmong represent the greatest cohort of highland Lao among those admitted to the United States as refugees (see, e.g., Gordon, 1987).

United States (representing 30% of all highland Lao arriving from 1975 to 1997). The 8 years from 1987 to 1994 also witnessed the arrival of an additional 58,600 highland Lao refugees (46% of all highland Lao arriving from, 1975 to 1997). These two periods of intensive resettlement of Hmong refugees collectively account for more than three quarters of all highland Lao resettled in the United States to date.

Khmer immigration

Cambodians have resided in Southeast Asia for more than 4,000 years and experienced their greatest region during the Angkorian period (802–1431 AD), when the temples of Angkor Wat were built. From that period until the arrival of the French in the mid-1800s, much of Cambodian history was marked by military conflict with Thailand (Siam) and Vietnam. In 1863, Cambodia became a French protectorate, a status that lasted until 1953, when Cambodia gained its independence under Prince Sihanouk. Though Sihanouk proclaimed Cambodia a neutral and non-aligned state throughout the Vietnam War, its strategic location along the border with Vietnam made it a vital military area to the United States and the armies of North and South Vietnam. On April 17, 1975, the Communist Khmer Rouge forces entered Phnom Penh and established Democratic Kampuchea. Phnom Penh, then a city of two million people, was emptied, as were other cities throughout Cambodia. Under Pol Pot's leadership the entire citizenry of Cambodia was imprisoned in a vast labor camp in the attempt to transform traditional Cambodian society into a communist agricultural state. An estimated one million to two million of the roughly eight million Khmer died between 1975 and 1978 as a result of the torture, execution, disease, and starvation brought about by Khmer Rouge policies (Mortland, 1996). During these same years, fewer than 35,000 Khmer were able to escape to Thailand.

In 1977, Vietnamese forces invaded Cambodia and in January 1979 established a new government the People's Republic of Kampuchea, in Phnom Penh. The Vietnamese invasion allowed thousands of Khmer who had survived under Pol Pot to seek refuge in neighboring Thailand. Ngor (1987) states well the significance of surviving the Pol Pot era: "Nothing has shaped my life as much as surviving the Pol Pot regime. I am a survivor of the Cambodian holocaust. That's who I am" (p. 1). By the end of 1979, more than half a million Khmer had entered Thailand or settled along the Thai-Cambodian border (Ouk, Huffman, & Lewis, 1988). The resettlement of the Khmer in the United States peaked during the 8-year period from 1979 to 1986, when more than 131,000 Cambodian refugees arrived in the United States, a number that represents almost 90% of the more than 147,000 Khmer who had been resettled as of the end of 1997 (see Table 1). As with the Hmong, the first

Cambodians resettled in the United States were those with political or military ties with the United States. On the whole, this group was highly educated, was fairly fluent in either French or English, had resided in urban centers, and had been exposed to the West as a result of the U.S. presence in Phnom Penh. In contrast, the Khmer who arrived in the United States after 1979 were less educated and came from the rural countryside of Cambodia. These characteristics of the post-1979 refugees not only reflect the different waves of refugees but, more important, the fact that Khmer with any education or ties to the West were the primary victims of Pol Pot's policy of ridding Cambodia of so-called enemies of the new Cambodia.

Laotian immigration

The ethnic, or lowland, Lao, arrived from China into Laos in the sixth or seventh century. The period 1637–1694 is often referred to as the golden age of Laotian history (Bounkeo et al., 1989). After this period, Laos split into three kingdoms and, like Cambodia, was often caught up in the rivalries between Vietnam and Thailand. In 1893, Laos fell under French control, and it was controlled by France until its independence in 1954. Like Cambodia, Laos sought to remain neutral during the Vietnam War. However, U.S. interests in Laos's strategic location between Thailand, its ally, and the North Vietnamese Ho Chi Minh Trail through Laos compromised the Royal Lao government's attempts to remain neutral. The United States, in its efforts to defeat communism, dropped more than two million tons of bombs on the Laotian countryside (DeVoe, 1996). U.S. bombing and the conflict on the ground between the Pathet Lao and the forces of the Royal Lao government resulted in at least one third of the entire Laotian population being displaced from their homes.

With the Pathet Lao victory, thousands of ethnic Lao fled into Thailand seeking shelter. Because of the close linguistic, cultural, and ethnic ties between the Lao and Thai peoples, many lowland Lao were able to blend into the Thai countryside (DeVoe, 1996). In terms of lowland Lao immigration to the United States, almost 125,000 refugees were resettled in the United States between 1975 and 1997. For the ethnic Lao, arrivals in the United States peaked during the period 1979–1982, totaling 69,600, or roughly 56% percent of all lowland arrivals to date.

Settlement patterns of the Hmong, Khmer, and Laotian communities

My review of past volumes of the *Refugee Resettlement Program: Report to the Congress* of the Office of Refugee Resettlement (U.S. Department of Health and Human services) and the 1990 U.S. census shows six key common patterns of settlement among the Cambodian, Hmong, and Laotian communities in the United States. First, from 1975 to 1990, California annually received the largest number of refugees from Cambodia and Laos. Second, from the late 1970s to 1990, the states of Texas and Washington, along with California, were consistently among the top five states nationwide to receive the largest number of refugees from Cambodia and Laos. Third, the 1990 census showed that more than 50% of all Cambodians, Hmong, and Laotians lived in the western United States (59.0%, 55.5%, and 52.5% respectively) (U.S. Bureau of the Census, 1992, Table 135).[5] Fourth, California was home to the largest collective populations of each of the three ethnic groups; in fact, 41.1% of all lowland Lao, 47.8% of all Khmer, and 52.2% of all Hmong resided in California. Fifth, Minnesota was the only state other than California that was home to populations of 3,000 or more of each of the three ethnic communities. Finally, in 1990 the largest individual Cambodian, Hmong, and Laotian communities, by metropolitan statistical area (MSA), were in California (Los Angeles-Anaheim-Riverside-Fresno and San Francisco-Oakland-San Jose, respectively).

Since the U.S. census figures are from 1990, they are actually significantly less than the current population totals for the Hmong, Khmer, and lowland Lao in the United States. Since 1990, additional refugees and immigrants have arrived in the United States, and additional Cambodian, Hmong, and Laotian children have been born. For example, 1990 census figures indicate that 1,968 Hmong resided in Wausau, Wisconsin. Koltyk (1988) reports that by 1996, the Hmong population in Wausau had grown to 4,200.

These six common settlement patterns reflect the outcomes of a combination of initial resettlement policies of the federal government, the policies and resources of various voluntary resettlement agencies, and secondary migration patterns among each of the Southeast Asian ethnic groups. Beyond these similarities, however, the geographic and demographic makeup of Hmong, Khmer, and Laotian communities nationwide varies significantly.

Hmong settlement patterns and demographics

Bliatout et al. (1988) report that the first Hmong refugees were scattered across the United States in communities of 200–500 persons in Philadelphia, Pennsylvania; Missoula, Montana; Santa Ana and Long Beach, California; St. Paul, Minnesota; Denver, Colorado; South Car-

5 See Map IV-3 in U.S. Bureau of the Census (1992) for the division of the United States into the Northeast, Midwest, South, and West.

olina; and Honolulu, Hawaii. After the 1979–1980 influx of Hmong refugees, the geographic distribution of the Hmong changed considerably. Whereas some Hmong were placed in many of these same communities, others were scattered to other locations as part of the federal government's dispersal policy. This policy was designed to lessen the impact that additional Hmong arrivals would have on the economic and social resources of local communities (similar policies were designed for Khmer and Laotian refugees). For many Hmong, the dispersal policy did not take into account the strong family, kinship, and ethnic ties that the Hmong saw as essential to their survival in the United States. Accordingly, many Hmong have migrated from their initial points of settlement, particularly to California, Minnesota, and Wisconsin (referred to as *secondary migration*).

The 1990 census shows that in addition to the large concentration of Hmong in the West, 41.1% lived in the Midwest, 2.1% in the Northeast, and 1.3% in the South (U.S. Bureau of the Census, 1992, Table 135). The Hmong constitute the greatest concentration of persons in the Midwest among all Southeast Asians. Even more significant, these statistics hide the fact that the Hmong reside almost exclusively in three states: California (49,343, or 52.2%), Minnesota (17,764, or 18.8%), and Wisconsin (16,980, or 18.0%). In total, these states account for 84,087 Hmong, or 89% of all Hmong nationwide. The remaining 11% of the Hmong live in twenty-eight other states. The large concentration of Hmong in a few states is repeated in Hmong residency patterns by MSA. The cities of Fresno, California (18,321), and Minneapolis–St. Paul, Minnesota (16,435), are by a large margin the two largest Hmong communities nationwide, collectively representing 37% of all Hmong in the United States. The Hmong community of Minneapolis–St. Paul represents 92.5% of all Hmong in the state of Minnesota. In California, the Hmong are located in two geographical areas: the Central Valley (54% of the California Hmong) – which includes the MSAs of Fresno, Merced, and Visalia-Tulare-Porterville – and the northern California communities of Sacramento, Stockton, and Yuba City, which collectively are home to an additional 26% of the California Hmong. In Wisconsin, there is no one single large community of Hmong; rather, there are a number of small of concentrations.

The growth of Hmong communities nationwide can been seen in the increase of the Hmong population in Fresno, California, and Wausau, Wisconsin. Biliatout et al., (1988) report that in July 1979 the Hmong population in Fresno was only about 300. By December 1980, the Hmong population had grown to 2,000, a year later it reached 7,000, and by December 1982 it totaled 12,000. Census data for 1990 indicate that Fresno was home to approximately 18,300 Hmong. Although much of the initial secondary migration to Fresno was due to the success that a few families had with farming (Bliatout et al., 1988), additional arrivals from Thailand and elsewhere in the United States reflect Fresno's status as a cultural center for many Hmong (Miller et al., 1992).

Similarly, in Wausau, the Hmong community grew from a few families resettled in 1976 to 1,800 by 1988, to 3,128 by 1992, and to roughly 4,200 in 1996 (Koltyk, 1998). Although the totals for Wausau are relatively small compared with the growth of Hmong community in Fresno, they do represent a rapid growth rate. Many Wausau residents have characterized this rapid growth as an "invasion" (Koltyk, p. 5) that is "spinning out of control" (Beck, 1994, p. 84). In addition, the growth of the Hmong community – which includes refugees, legal immigrants, and secondary migrants – has changed the racial, ethnic, and cultural makeup of the city. By 1996, Koltyk notes, the Hmong alone represented a full 10% of the city's population, a significant racial-ethnic transformation of a city that in 1980 was less than 1% non-White. In cultural terms, Koltyk notes, "At every level the community [of Wausau] has been faced with an immigrant group whose belief systems, in many ways, differ radically from their own" (p. 5). At times, she notes, these differences have "incited a host of emotional feelings, ranging from concern to prejudice, anger, bitterness, and hostility (p. 5).

Khmer settlement patterns and demographics

By the time the Khmer were being resettled in significant numbers (1980–1986; see Table 1), the federal government had initiated the Khmer Cluster Project (KCP, also referred to as the Cambodian Cluster Project or the Khmer Guided Placement Project). As with programs for the Hmong and Lao, the KCP was intended to disperse Khmer refugees geographically across the nation (U.S. Department of Health and Human Services, 1983). Beginning in 1980–1981, agencies at ten favorable sites received funds to assist in the resettlement and integration of new Khmer arrivals. Two principal aims of the project, as with Planned Resettlement Projects for the Hmong and Lao, were to stimulate self-sufficiency among the refugees and to protect highly affected locales from receiving additional refugees. The KCP sites had low levels of unemployment and thus held the promise of rapid economic integration and self-sufficiency for the new Cambodian arrivals. These sites were location in Arizona, Florida, Georgia, Illinois, Massachusetts, New York, Ohio, Texas, and Virginia; North Carolina was added in 1983 (Gordon, 1987).

Although many Khmer have migrated to other states since their initial settlement, the federal government's policies have led to a geographic and demographic distribution of Cambodians across the United States that is more even than that of the Hmong. In addition to the large concentration of Khmer in the West (59.0%), 19.7% of the Khmer live in the Northeast, 13.4% in the South, and 7.9% in the Midwest (U.S. Bureau of the Census, 1993b, Table 135). The concentration of Cambodians in the Northeast is the greatest among the three Southeast Asian communities. Census data indicate that in 1990 there were Khmer in every state except Montana (U.S. Bureau of the Census, 1993b). As noted, California led all states in the total number of Khmer residents. After California, Massachusetts and Washington had the largest Cambodian populations. Collectively, these three states accounted for 64.3% of all Khmer nationwide, a percentage that is significantly lower than the corresponding percentage for the states with the three highest Hmong populations (89.0%) greater than the corresponding percentage for the ethnic Lao (51.8%). An analysis of city-by-city counts for the Khmer reveals that, in 1990, the Los Angeles – Anaheim – Riverside MSA (which includes the city of Long Beach) was home to more than 34,400 Cambodians, almost half of the California Khmer population (48.4%) and nearly a quarter of all Khmer nationwide (23.1%). The Cambodian communities of the Boston-Lawrence-Salem MSA (which also includes the city of Lowell, Massachusetts) and the Seattle-Tacoma MSA represented a full 86.6% and 85.6% of the Cambodians who resided in the states of Massachusetts and Washington, respectively. As with the Hmong, more than half (51%) of all the Cambodians in the United States resided in five MSAs. In addition, the Khmer had the largest percentage (70.5%) of residents in concentrations of 3,000 or more Cambodians in individual MSAs (the rates for the Hmong and the Lao are 58.2% and 44.5%, respectively).

The large concentration of Khmer in a few cities across the United States, as described for the Hmong in Wausau, has created tension. Melnick (1988) writes that the choice of the Khmer to live near family, friends, ethnic markets, and a Buddhist temple in the cities of Lowell, Massachusetts, and the Bronx, New York, has "created some neighborhood frictions that, in several cases, ended in acts of violence against Cambodians" (p. 6). The sharp, often bitter responses of long-term residents, as toward the Hmong in Wausau, reflect both opposition to the rapid growth in the number of Cambodians in Lowell and the Bronx and misunderstandings of who the Khmer are. Melnick writes that the Khmer are seen as "competition for an already slim job and cheap housing market" (p. 5) and as "receiving special benefits from the federal government" such that they can "afford fancy sport cars" (p. 7).

Laotian settlement patterns and demographics

Like the Hmong and Khmer populations, the overwhelming majority of all ethnic Lao (41.1%) reside in California. The Lao resemble the Khmer more closely than they do the Hmong in that they are distributed more evenly across the United States. In the northeastern states in 1990, the Lao totaled 15,034 (10.2% of all Lao), 26,312 in the Midwest (17.9%) and 28,692 in the South (19.5%) (U.S. Bureau of the Census, 1992, Table 135). Comparatively, of the three Southeast Asian communities, the lowland Lao had the largest concentration of persons in the southern United States. A state-by-state analysis shows that in addition to the large Laotian population in California, there were Lao in every state. Specifically, 3,000 or more Lao lived in ten states, including California, extending from Texas in the South to Minnesota in the Midwest and from Oregon in the West to Massachusetts in the East. After the high concentration of Lao in California (60,627), the number of Lao in the other nine states ranged from 3,200 in Oregon to 9,494 in Texas. In all, 103,858, or 70.5% of all Lao nationwide, lived in these ten states.

The more even geographic and demographic distribution of Laotian communities across the United States relative to the Hmong and Cambodian communities reflects the federal government's greater measure of success in its efforts to disperse lowland Lao refugees. In addition, it reflects the government's sponsorship of multiple Planned Secondary Resettlement (PSR) programs that were aimed at resettling refugees from "areas of high unemployment and welfare dependency to communities with more favorable prospects for employment" (U.S. Department of Health and Human Services, 1983, p. 64). As noted, whereas the Khmer and Hmong reside principally in a few major MSAs (Los Angeles for the Khmer and Fresno and Minneapolis – St. Paul for the Hmong), the Laotian population does not. Thus, the five largest Laotian communities represent only 28.5% of all the lowland Lao in the United States, a percentage that is significantly less than the corresponding rates for the five largest Hmong and Khmer communities. Rather, the lowland Lao principally (55.5%) reside in a large number of communities in concentrations of less than 3,000, the highest percentage among the three Southeast Asian communities.

Educational opportunities for the Hmong, Khmer, and Lao before 1975

This section briefly reviews the educational opportunities of the Hmong, Khmer, and lowland Lao before the Khmer Rouge and Pathet

243

Lao victories of 1975. The focus on the premigratory educational levels of the Southeast Asian community reflects the fact that these levels are strong predictors of educational success and English language attainment among refugees in the United States (see, e.g., Caplan, Choy, & Whitmore, 1991).

Hmong education

For the majority of Hmong, the need to receive a formal education was of little importance to their everyday lives as farmers. In addition, because they lived in the mountainous regions of the northeast, few Hmong had access to schools – the majority of which were in the Laotian capital. Some Hmong, mostly males, did, however, venture to the provincial capital of Xieng Khoung City to receive a formal education (Bliatout et al., 1988). These were sons from wealthy families that could afford to pay the school fees and, more important, would not suffer from the loss of their child from the family's labor supply. The first reported school for the Hmong was established in 1939, in Nong Het. Additional schools were started after World War II. In 1960, the number of Hmong students nationwide totaled 1,500 in twenty village schools, and the number had climbed to 10,000 by 1969. Though rarely reported, 340 Hmong secondary students traveled to Australia, Canada, France, and the United States in 1971 to receive an education (Bliatout et al., 1988). In Laos, formal schooling included the Lao language, French history, and an emphasis on the memorization and recitation of set texts. In short, a formal education held few advantages for Hmong after their return to their native villages.

In the Hmong communities of Laos, children acquired the most important community knowledge from their parents, grandparents, older siblings, or immediate clan members. As Bliatout et al. (1988) note, "Although in traditional Hmong society most individuals did not attend school or formal classes, the Hmong culture had alternative standards for what was considered 'educated'" (p. 17). Most Hmong learned about important activities like farming, animal husbandry, child rearing, and performing the traditional arts (playing the *qeej* for boys and embroidering *paj ntaub* for girls) and ceremonial and religious rituals directly from family or clan members. In addition, the Hmong community placed an emphasis on the elders' telling Hmong legends and folktales, and recounting history to their children and grandchildren. From the elders Hmong youth also learned a variety of Hmong registers and learned to create verses that would often be used during the New Year season (Bliatout et al., 1988).

The lack of educational opportunity – or need – for the Hmong is reflected in data from the 1990 census. Among the three Southeast Asian communities, the Hmong had the highest percentage of persons aged 25 years and older with less than a fifth-grade education (54.9%) and the lowest percentage of persons with a high school degree or more education (31.1%; U.S. Bureau of the Census, 1993a). In sum, the fact that relatively few Hmong received a formal education in Laos, that the majority of Hmong culture was passed across generations via an oral tradition, and modern Hmong orthographies were developed only after the 1950s (Smalley, 1976) has led most scholars and writers to identify the Hmong as a preliterate society and to describe Hmong children as educationally at risk (Bliatout et al., 1988; Walker, 1987).

Khmer education

The educational system that Khmer refugees would have participated in before 1975 has its roots in the French occupation of Indochina. In 1917 the French established an educational system across Vietnam, Laos, and Cambodia. Although school was compulsory, less than half of Cambodian children attended French schools. For those who did attend school, the curriculum focused on French history and culture and was taught in French. Even after independence, the educational system remained virtually the same, changing only slightly in 1958, when instruction in the Khmer language was promoted (Ouk et al., 1988). Although Khmer was given greater attention, the majority of the curriculum continued to be taught in French until 1967, when the government substituted Khmer as the language of instruction. After 1970 the educational system, like most institutions in Cambodia, was heavily disrupted by the increasing military conflict within Cambodia's borders, especially as U.S. bombing of the country increased dramatically in the countryside. After 1975, education in the traditional use of the word came to a halt. Ouk et al. write, "During the four years that began with the year zero, there was no education. . . . Obviously, there was no opportunity for education, and Cambodians who were school-aged during this time were taught only allegiance to Angkar, and learned only how to survive" (pp. 41–42).[6] The difficulties that the majority of Khmer experienced in obtaining an education, before and after the Khmer Rouge victory, are reflected by the fact that according to the 1990 census half of the Cambodian population had less than an eighth-grade education (51.7%) (U.S. Bureau of the Census, 1993b). The percentage of Khmer in the United States who had

6 *Year zero* refers to the Khmer Rouge victory of 1975, when Pol Pot launched his attempt to return Cambodia to the glory of its reign during the Angkorian period. In instituting an agricultural economy, the Khmer Rouge sought to remake the Cambodian citizenry by purging the society of enemies of the state and seeking the unquestioned loyalty of the people to Angka, the faceless organization that ruled Cambodia from 1975 to 1978.

245

obtained a high school education or greater (34.9%) is similar to that for the Hmong, reflecting not only the limited opportunities of the Khmer to receive an education in Cambodia but also the fact that many educated Khmer were killed or died during the reign of the Khmer Rouge.

Laotian education

The majority of lowland Lao who received an education went to school in the *wat,* the Buddhist temple. In the urban areas the French established a secular elementary school system about 1940. As in Cambodia, the system was an imported version of the French curriculum and was taught in French. In general, most Laotians had very limited opportunities for formal education before and after World War II; secular education was not introduced in the rural areas until the 1950s. Even then, only wealthy families who could afford the loss of manual labor need to produce the families' goods and food supply educated their children formally. In the 1970s, only about 30% of the school-age population of Laos nationwide attended private or public schools. Bounkeo et al. (1989) report that in Vientiane, roughly 950 students were enrolled in secondary education, which followed the French *lycée* system and prepared students for college. Literacy rates for Laos, a proxy for educational attainment, before the war are at best estimates. One given by Christian linguists places the literacy rate at about 20%. Though the rate is lower than most cited for other Southeast Asian nations, the Lao valued literacy, particularly for the ability to read Buddhist scriptures. Among the rural population, Bounkeo et al. note, Laotians are often illiterate and rarely attend more than 3 years of school (p. 25). In contrast, they state, urban Lao may have more than 6 years of education and may speak French. According to the 1990 census, more ethnic Lao than Hmong and Khmer had a high school degree or more education (40.0%), and fewer had less than a fifth-grade education (33.9%) (U.S. Bureau of the Census, 1993b). This difference principally reflects the fact that a greater percentage of lowland Lao were urban dwellers with greater access to public schools in Laos.

New contexts, new lives: The Southeast Asian community in transition

For many Cambodians, Hmong, and ethnic Lao, the expectations that Americans hold for a positive adjustment – which at the federal level have often focused principally on measures of economic self-sufficiently and English language attainment[7] – are often very low or negative.

7 Though not an official policy of the federal government, this perspective does underlie the majority of programs aimed at assisting newly arriving refugees.

Daniels (1990), for example, who has written widely on immigration issues, writes in a chapter called "The New Asian Immigrants,"

Even poorer [than the Vietnamese], as groups, are the Laotians, the Cambodians, and such premodern peoples as the Hmong. Few Laotians and Cambodians and no Hmong were really equipped to cope with modern urban society before they left Southeast Asia, and the transition has been quite painful and difficult. . . . [and] many of those most directly involved with these refugees fear that they, or most of them, will become a permanent part of the other America where poverty and deprivation are the rule rather than the exception. (pp. 369–370)

In short, the fact that the majority of post-1979 Southeast Asian refugees came from rural backgrounds and had low levels of education is seen almost exclusively as a determinant of the refugees' inability to adjust economically and socioculturally to life in the United States. This has been particularly the case for the Hmong. Like Daniels, the majority of writers, especially in the mass media, focus on the so-called premodern or primitive cultural background of the Hmong, emphasizing that it is the most serious impediment to their ability to adjust to life in the Information Age of a postindustrial America (e.g., Mydans, 1990). To some degree, one could argue that Daniels and others are correct. For instance, 1990 census figures show that the Hmong, Khmer, and Lao had median family incomes of $14,327, $18,126 and $23, 101 respectively (U.S. Bureau of the Census, 1992, Table 111), the lowest among all Asian ethnic groups and less, or slightly greater, than those reported for Blacks ($22,429) and American Indians and Eskimos ($21,750) (U.S. Bureau of the Census, Table 48). Similarly, 32.2% of all lowland Lao families, 42.1% of all Cambodian families, and 61.8% of all Hmong families nationwide lived below the poverty line – the highest among all Asian subgroups. (U.S. Bureau of the Census, Table 112). These figures paint a statistical portrait of the Southeast Asian community that seemingly confirms Daniels's description of its the fall into "poverty and deprivation."

Unfortunately, these census figures and the common description of Cambodian, Hmong, and lowland Lao refugees as not "really equipped to cope with modern urban society" do not adequately portray the dynamic nature of the adjustment experience of each of these ethnic groups to life in America. In response, members of the Southeast Asian community have spoken out against the negative images of the refugee community that are commonly presented in the media. For instance, a Hmong reader of *The New York Times* wrote a letter to the editor critiquing the common description of the Hmong as "the most primitive refugee group in America," noting that "such characterizations are disturbing to those in and out of the Hmong community who recognize the strengths of our culture, history, and people" (Herr, 1990, p. A28). In the same fashion, educators working in the Southeast Asian community have challenged the validity of the negative descriptions commonly ascribed to the majority of the post-1979 Southeast Asian refugee community. Weinstein-Shr (1993), for instance, writes, "Hmong refugees from Laos are often portrayed in the American media as helpless peasants who have been thrust empty-handed into the brutal realities of civilisation," yet, she continues, these writers "are unaware of some resources such as kinship ties that Hmong bring to life in America, while they report primarily those areas that would seem to pose difficulty for living in the United States" (p. 272–273).[8] Moreover, the myriad statistics on the Southeast Asian community and the various interpretations do not sketch an effective portrait of the community's response to a multitude of new cultural and structural opportunities that life in America presents to them. In short, educators must examine the perceptions that mainstream American society holds, and continues to disseminate, about Southeast Asians; for, as Camino (1994) writes, "the characterization of dislocated peoples as helpless and needy leads to a very different set of policies and guidelines for intervention than one which emphasizes refugees as resourceful and competent" (p. 204).[9]

As recent refugees and immigrants, the Hmong, Khmer, and ethnic Lao experience of understanding and, in turn, participating in American society mirrors that of countless other immigrants and refugees who preceded them to the United States. At the same time, however, the Southeast Asian experience is different. For the Hmong, Khmer, and Lao, many of the transformation of their traditional cultural practices and family, clan, and community-based structures are not simply the result of living in the United States. Rather, many of the changes, which include changes in family structure, educational opportunity, and language use, began in the 1960s and 1970s with the encroachment of the Vietnam War on the Cambodian and Laotian countryside and continued as the Hmong, Khmer, and Lao experienced life in the Thai refugee camps (see, e.g., Smalley, 1986, for an excellent discussion of the changes within Hmong society from its traditional expression to its current representation in the United States).

Changing identities and opportunities

Any discussion of the sociocultural adjustment of the Southeast Asian community in the United States, especially in regard to language issues,

8 See López (1997) for a similar critique of the ways the popular media and educators commonly describe the Iu Mien as another primitive and preliterate highland Lao refugee community in the United States.

9 I argue elsewhere (López, 1997) that such descriptions of the Iu Mien have translated into low teacher expectations for refugees within the public schools.

must begin with an understanding of the complexity of the Hmong, Khmer, and Laotian communities in the United States. Though described in the media and academic press as refugees, not all Cambodians, Hmong, or Lao necessarily embrace this term. At times the refugee label has held positive associations (e.g., certain financial benefits), for Southeast Asians in the United States but the notion of being a refugee has also been seen as offensive. Mortland (1994), for example, notes from her work with the Khmer that a number of refugees insisted that they were not refugees. For others, Khmer, Hmong, and Laotian alike, the refugee identity is more complex. As Mortland writes, "Once identified as refugees, Cambodians bounce back and forth between attempts at Americanization and struggles to re-establish Cambodianness" (p. 5). Or, as one Cambodian responded when asked if he still saw himself as a refugee, "Well, yes, I do. I am a United States citizen now, but psychologically I still feel homeless. I dream in Khmer and talk in English. . . . I dream of the Khmer Rouge, killings and murder. I talk in a different language-English-about life in the suburbs" (Iep, 1991, p. 30). For still others, particularly older persons, the fact that they had to flee from Pol Pot or the Pathet Lao means that they will always be refugees (see Mortland, 1994). In short, many Southeast Asians – not just the Khmer – find their identities tied closely to both their countries of origin and their new homeland.

The Southeast Asian identity is made even more complex by the fact that the Southeast Asian community does not consist simply of persons who have arrived from Cambodia and Laos, through Thailand. Rather, of the more than 390,000 Hmong, Khmer, and lowland Lao enumerated in the 1990 census, a full 24.2% were born in the United States (U.S. Bureau of the Census, 1993a, Table 1). Among the Khmer and Lao, one in every five persons was native born; the percentage for the Hmong community is one in three persons. These individuals, the great majority of whom are children 9 years of age and younger, do not share with their parents and grandparents the experience of having lived in Cambodia or Laos. Moreover, the everyday world of these children and their foreign-born counterparts is a blending of cultures. At home, Southeast Asian children are exposed to forms of traditional Hmong, Khmer, and Laotian culture as embodied in their parents' and grandparents actions and beliefs. Simultaneously, these youth are also exposed, principally through the public schools, to the norms and expectations of mainstream American society. And others, chiefly those who live in the inner-city neighborhoods of America's cities, are exposed to a variety of cultural patterns of other ethnic and racial groups (see, e.g., Hopkins, 1996; Melnick, 1998).

Studies of the Southeast Asian community show clearly that this blending of new cultural backgrounds and opportunities since 1975,

249

particularly the opportunity to receive a free education, has created a number of changes and tensions within the Southeast Asian community. For example, because of the Khmer Rouge policies a larger number of Cambodian families are now matriarchal (Ouk et al., 1988). Similarly, the Hmong's high death rate during the war has left many families without fathers and older brothers. Since resettlement, the family structure has also changed; to negotiate many aspects of daily life in the United States, Southeast Asian parents and grandparents rely on their children because of the younger generation's fluency in English and their growing sense of independence (both usually gained in school). Thus, although elders in the Hmong, Khmer, and Laotian communities, as in many Asian cultures, are to be respected because of their wisdom gained through years of experience, they have instead found themselves dependent on their children or grandchildren. This new family structure, which is often termed *filiarchal* – in contrast to patriarchal or matriarchal – that is, headed by children, has at times lead to the displacement of the adult's traditional role in the family and community. Miller et al. (1992) provide a similar summary for the Hmong community: "Power struggles go on among Hmong leaders as new ways replace old. The younger generation is too Americanized to listen to their elders. The elders, on the other hand, feel left out of Western society" (p. 27).

For Cambodians, Hmong, and Laotians, life in the United States has also brought a number of positive opportunities for the collective community. Although the majority of Hmong, like many Khmer and ethnic Lao, historically did not have access to or the need for mass public education, each of these Southeast Asian communities evidenced a strong appreciation of education and educated people. This commitment to education, combined with free public schooling in the United States, has created new opportunities for Southeast Asians. Even though many school districts have been unprepared to meet, or even resistant to meeting, the educational needs of Hmong, Khmer, and Lao students, a greater percentage of Southeast Asian children can now attend school. Equally important, many Southeast Asian children are achieving, despite the labels of preliterate or rural that are often ascribed to them (see, e.g., Caplan, Choy, & Whitmore, 1991). For instance, McNall, Dunnigan, and Mortimer (1994) found that Hmong in St. Paul, Minnesota, graduated from high school and attended college at rates comparable to those of the general population. Koltyk (1998) concluded that the Hmong in Wausau were increasing their understanding of the importance of education and held higher and higher aspirations for their children to receive a better education and even to attend college. In fact, in Wausau, she reports, over 90% of Hmong high school graduates participated in postsecondary education compared with only 40% of non-Hmong graduates. Equally important, public schooling has increased educational opportunities for females. DeVoe (1994) found that Khmer parents held similar expectations for boys and for girls and that "females [were] not more likely to quit school before completing high school than their male counterparts" (p. 240). Thus, especially for the Hmong, the at-risk label applied to Southeast Asian school-age children because of their preliterate background, lack of education, and tendency to marry at relatively young ages does not mean that these children necessarily become part of Daniels's "other America," defined by a permanent cycle of poverty.

At the same time, however, some Southeast Asians encounter difficulty in schools. Despite studies documenting school success for Southeast Asians in terms of grade point averages and graduation rates, Hmong, Khmer, and Laotian schoolchildren still face a number of barriers in the public schools (see, e.g., Asian Americans/Pacific Islanders in Philanthropy, 1997; National Coalition of Advocates for Students, 1997). Barriers include a lack of trained staff who speak Hmong, Khmer, or Lao; the lack of a curriculum that reflects the ethnic background of Southeast Asian students; racism and violence; low teacher expectations; and a lack of support for parent involvement.

Language use, learning, and maintenance in the Hmong, Khmer, and Laotian communities in the United States

The multiple changes brought about by the Vietnam War and the exodus and resettlement of Southeast Asians in the United States have significant implications for language use, learning, and maintenance in each of the three ethnic communities. This section examines the common issues of native language use; English language acquisition; and the maintenance of Hmong, Khmer, and Laotian across generations in a society that again is seeing a rise in the push for monolingualism in the forms of campaigns for English only and against bilingual education.

Native language use: A view from the 1990 census

A review of the settlement patterns of the Southeast Asian community shows that the high concentrations of Hmong and Khmer have fostered the use of these languages within each community. Thus, for example, 96.6% of all Southeast Asians aged 5 years and over report speaking their native language in the home (U.S. Bureau of the Census, 1993a,

Table 3).[10] Of all Hmong, 97.4% reported the ability to speak Hmong. Among foreign-born persons, the percentage was 97.8%, and for native-born Hmong the percentage was only slightly lower at 96.1%. The extensive use of Hmong in the community is also evidenced by the fact that almost 59.8% of all Hmong live in what are defined as *linguistically isolated households*.[11] For the Cambodian community, the rate of usage of Khmer in the home was also very high – 96%. Like their Hmong counterparts, foreign-born Khmer exhibit the strongest use of the native language: 97.3% of all foreign-born Cambodians reported using Khmer whereas the percentage drops to 86.3% for native-born Cambodians – the lowest among native-born individuals in the three Southeast Asian communities. Of Cambodian households, almost 55% were categorized as linguistically isolated. As in the other two Southeast Asian communities, native language use in the Laotian community was high: 97% of all ethnic Lao reported speaking a language other than English. Within the Laotian community, 97.7% of foreign-born persons and 90.5% of native-born individuals spoke Lao. In terms of linguistically isolated households, slightly more than 50% of all Laotians resided in homes in which Lao was the predominant language of communication.

English language acquisition: Challenges and successes

The majority of Cambodians, Hmong, and ethnic Lao emigrated from multilingual societies, a condition that was replicated in the Thai refugee camps, where they were exposed to a variety of languages, including English and Thai, in the camp schools. This background has instilled within the Southeast Asian community an appreciation of the value of knowing two or more languages, so that on the whole Southeast Asians place great importance on becoming proficient in English. Although many older refugees have found it difficult or, to some degree, unnecessary to acquire English – expressing at times that they are "too old to learn a new language" (Bliatout et al., 1988, p. 45) – the majority of Cambodians, Hmong, and Laotians seek to learn English even if the process is difficult. In a number Southeast Asian anthologies (e.g., Howard, 1990; Tenhula, 1991), refugees recount that learning English

10 The census information described in this section refers to the ability of persons aged 5 years and over to speak a language other than English. The Bureau of the Census does not actually indicate what language is in fact spoken or what the level of fluency is in that language. I assume that the majority of Cambodians, Hmong, and Laotians do in fact speak Khmer, Hmong, and Laotian respectively as their principal native language.

11 The U.S. Census Bureau defines a linguistically isolated household as one in which "no person age 14 years or over speaks only English and no person age 14 years or over who speaks a language other than English speaks English 'very well'" (U.S. Bureau of the Census, 1992, p. B-250).

was one of the most difficult tasks for them as they adjusted to their new country. Tenhula summarizes the comments of the refugees he interviewed as follows:

The process of learning English elicited a great deal of discussion. From the interviewees' perspective, the quality of English language training received is seriously questioned. The method of instruction, usually ESL, varies greatly in the way it is taught. Too often, respondents report that the classes are not relevant to their needs, are poorly taught, and are held at hours that are not conducive to learning. (p. 113)

Refugees themselves best describe the process of learning English. Even among more fluent refugees, learning and using English in everyday contexts is more difficult than their previous experiences of studying and teaching English in Laos, Cambodia, or the various Thai camps. As Iep (1991), a Cambodian refugee, noted,

Language is a difficult thing. Imagine, I taught French and English for eleven years in Cambodia before I came here. I would guess I got maybe forty percent of what people were saying to me in my first two years here. Americans swallow their words. We learned British English. Imagine coming here, and you supposedly know the language but are not able to comprehend but less than half of what you hear. It hurts. (p. 29)

Part of the challenge of understanding how well members of the Southeast Asian community have acquired English is that no good measurement of English language attainment exists. For instance, census data reports the English language ability of the Cambodian, Hmong, and Laotian communities by tallying the number of respondents who reported that they "do not speak English 'very well'" (U.S. Bureau of the Census, 1993a, Table 3): 70.5% of all Southeast Asians aged 5 years and over. By individual community, the percentages were 67.8% for the Lao, 70.0% for the Khmer, and 76.1% for the Hmong. As one would expect, the percentage varied significantly by nativity. For the Laotian and Cambodian communities the variation is similar: 69.9% of foreign-born Lao and 71.9% of foreign-born Khmer reported that they did not speak English very well. For native-born persons, the rates were 53.1% and 55.3% respectively for Laotians and Cambodians. For the Hmong, the difference in English language ability by nativity was considerably less: 77% foreign-born and 72.8% of native-born Hmong reported speaking English less than very well. On the surface, the census figures collectively represent a picture of limited English language ability among the Southeast Asian community. Outside of this broad portrait, which itself reflects data from 1990, no accurate picture exists of English language proficiency among the Cambodian, Hmong, and Laotian communities.

A critical reason for this lack of clarity is the role of the mass media in portraying two often contradictory images of the Southeast Asian community. On the one hand, especially within the public discourse about refugee adaptation, a common perception – which, as noted, to some extent is true for older Southeast Asians – is that the refugee community refuses to learn English. This perception has been highlighted particularly in recent years as anti–bilingual education and English-only sentiments have grown nationwide (see, e.g., Beck, 1994; Kiang, 1994). As evidence of this position, proponents argue, for example, that the fact that many Southeast Asians work only within ethnic minority enclaves proves that they are too lazy to learn English or assimilate. Against this perspective, the refugee community argues, "It is not true to say that we do not learn English or speak English; we do" (Rim, 1991, p. 90). The need to acquire English is, in fact, very clear to the Southeast Asian community. As one Hmong refugee noted, "To become part of America is simple – you get a job and learn good English" (cited in Tenhula, 1991, p. 110).

Another, very different perception is at times attributed to the Southeast Asian community. There is a growing belief, in part supported by some statistical data, that Southeast Asians (especially the Vietnamese), like Chinese, Japanese, and Korean immigrants before them, are learning English quickly and becoming universally successful in school (e.g., Brand, 1987; Caplan, Choy, & Whitmore, 1991). Examples of success in learning English are applauded and highlighted in the news media. A writer for the *New York Times* described Linn Yann, a Cambodian refugee girl who arrived in the United States at the age of 5 years, as "a bona fide celebrity" for her near victory to advance to the finals of the National Spelling Bee (Rawls, 1983). Linn's efforts were spotlighted mostly because she had arrived in the United States knowing the English words only for the numbers one through ten. Linn's success not only led to her picture being printed in *The New York Times* but to a congratulatory phone call from then-President Reagan.

Language use, learning, and maintenance across generations

For the majority of Southeast Asians, the experience of acquiring English lies somewhere between these two common images and requires more attention on the part of educators. Nevertheless, English has had a significant impact upon the community. Even though most Southeast Asian children live in linguistically isolated households,[12] this exposure

12 Almost 63% of all Southeast Asian school-age children (5–17 years) live in homes in which English is not the dominant language of communication, that is, in linguistically isolated households. The percentages are 58.7% for the Lao, 64.3% for Cambodians, and 66.7% for the Hmong.

254

to their parents' first language does not necessarily mean that the children are fluent speakers, much less writers, of Hmong, Khmer, or Lao. Rather, through television, interactions with English-speaking neighbors, and English as a second language instruction in the public schools, Southeast Asian children are rapidly gaining at least verbal fluency in English. In addition, the pressures that children feel to adopt mainstream American culture have led to a growing resistance among Southeast Asian children to speaking Hmong, Khmer, or Lao, so as not to be different from their English-speaking, mainstream peers (Wong Fillmore, 1991). Parents are also concerned about Southeast Asian children's quick acquisition of English and a corresponding loss of the Southeast Asian community's native languages. Thus, for example, Mortland (1994) found that Khmer parents feared that their children would forget the Cambodian language and that many were "already dismayed that so many of their children, although they [could] understand Cambodian to a degree, [could not] speak it." She adds that many fathers made such comments to her as "I try to teach them, but they won't study. They're not interested." In short, she adds, "Parents speak of the embarrassment of having children who do not speak Cambodian. Cambodians told me with shame, that their children can neither write nor barely speak it" (p. 7). Ouk, et al. (1988) add, "As time passes, it seems that more and more children use Khmer only when communicating with elders, and if given a preference, will use English instead" (p. 61). Thus, as in other refugee and immigrant households (see, e.g., Chapter 9), in conversations between parents and children in many Cambodian, Hmong, and Laotian households, the parents speak Khmer, and the children respond in English. Despite the prevalence of this means of communication, it does not in itself foster high levels of English language learning for Southeast Asian children (Wong Fillmore, 1991).

Even though the Southeast Asian community values English and promotes its use among the community's youth, Hmong, Khmer, and Laotian children's relative fluency in English has brought changes to their families. For instance, Ouk, et al. (1988) write, "The children are also the ones who go to school and learn English very quickly. . . . The children act as interpreter and the parent is dependent on the child to find our what is happening. English speakers address the child who understands English, rather than the adults" (p. 47). The increasing use of English by Southeast Asian youth is also tied to perceptions of identity. For Southeast Asian parents and college students, for instance, a person's ability to speak the Khmer, Hmong, or Lao language is a critical attribute of being Cambodian, Hmong, or Lao (see e.g., Bosher, 1997). For many parents, their children's limited ability to speak Cambodian, Hmong, or Lao is symptomatic of the child's growing Americanness. As

Mortland (1994) writes, Khmer parents are concerned that their children "act more American than Cambodian" (p. 45). The loss of the native language among Southeast Asian children is poignantly captured in the English translation of a poem, "The Children Don't Know Khmer, the Parents Don't Know English," written by Chea (1991), a Cambodian refugee:

> The children have forgotten Khmer
> Because their parents
> Are shortsighted.
> They're afraid their children won't know
> How to speak English.
> They don't worry
> That they've already forgotten Khmer!

Additional perspectives from Southeast Asian community evidence the changes in family structure that have accompanied the strain of language discontinuity, or what is most often described as *language shift*, across generations. As a Cambodian community advocate noted, "You want to look up to someone, but your parents don't have so much to offer you. Most of the parents don't speak English; sometimes they have difficulty reading and writing, even in their own language. So kids think, 'My parents are very, very low people'" (National Coalition of Advocates for Students, 1997, p. 6). Another section of Chea's poem reflects the impact of children's limited ability to speak the same language as their parents on the Southeast Asian family:

> Their mothers can barely speak English.
> One day the child swears at her
> And she says 'Thank you!'
> . . .
> [The mother] scolds them in Khmer
> Because she can't speak English.
> But the children don't understand,
> They wonder what she's saying!

In sum, although both the Southeast Asian community and the surrounding society have emphasized that the acquisition of English is essential to the successful integration of the Hmong, Khmer, and Laotian communities into American society, less attention has been paid to the implications of such a perspective for the Southeast Asian community. As Wong Fillmore (1991) notes, the shift from the home language to English has effects that go far beyond the use of a particular language. Rather, she writes, "When parents are unable to talk to their children, they cannot easily convey to them their values, beliefs, understandings, or wisdom about how to cope with their experiences" (p. 343). The result, she states, is that "for Southeast Asian refugee families especially, the breakdown of family can mean a loss of everything" (p. 344).

Language maintenance in the Southeast Asian community

Against this backdrop of language shift, the maintenance of the Cambodian, Hmong, and Laotian languages is critical to the well-being of the Southeast Asian community. As is true of other immigrant languages, the maintenance of the various Southeast Asian languages centers on a number of factors, including its perceived usefulness to the community. Nationwide, the high concentrations of Southeast Asians in a few locations foster the ability of community-based organizations to produce various media in the native language. Thus, across all three ethnic communities, a variety of newsletters, newspapers, and particularly the use of literacy for the reading of the Bible and Christian hymnals, serve as essential resources, that expose Southeast Asians to their own language in print. For instance, the California Central Valley Hmong community supports *The Hmong Times,* and Koltyk (1998) reports that the Wausau Hmong Mutual Association produces both a quarterly newsletter and a weekly 1-hour radio broadcast in Hmong. Hopkins (1996) notes that in the Midwest city where she worked with the Cambodian community, the Khmer Christian church offered a number of services and literacy classes in the Khmer language. The diaspora of Cambodians, Hmong, and ethnic Lao across the world has also created a need for them to use the native language, especially the written language, to communicate easily with others, both within the United States and around the world (see, e.g., Bliatout et al., 1988).

An additional element that is critical to the maintenance of the Hmong, Khmer, and Laotian languages in the United States is the nature of the Southeast Asian family. As in other immigrant groups, the teaching and learning of languages within the Southeast Asian community is closely tied to the intergenerational continuity of the family. For instance, within the Hmong culture, grandparents have traditionally played an important role in the transmission of Hmong stories, legends, history, and songs to young children. Yet, as noted, a variety of factors have undermined this role since the 1960s. It is essential, then, to create programs and opportunities that will reestablish the role of the elder as a respected member of the community. As Miller et al. (1992) note, the programs developed in a few Missoula, Montana, public schools, which utilize grandparents within the classroom curriculum, provided Hmong children the opportunity to learn what is culturally significant to elders and to gain a sense of pride in their identity as both Hmong and Amer-

M. G. López

ican. In addition, Hmong elders were able to see their "Americanized grandchildren learn about their roots, be honored for their skills and knowledge, and gain respect from the young" (p. 29).

In addition to their important role in teaching English to many Southeast Asian youth, the schools can also be a source of native language support and maintenance. Despite the 1998 passage of Proposition 227 in California, which severely limited the use of languages other than English in the classroom, a body of research documents that the effective use of children's native languages in the classroom can serve a multitude of positive purposes (Wong Fillmore & Valadez, 1986). For Southeast Asian students, as for other language minority children, a teacher who uses the Hmong, Khmer, or Laotian language for instruction not only promotes the learning of content but also supports the children's development of language skills in the language in which they can most effectively communicate with their elders. For the Southeast Asian community, more than any other language community, however, this requires the development of a cadre of native language teachers. A number of schools have also played a significant role in native language maintenance by developing after-school literacy programs. For example, the Thermalito School District in northern California has developed a Hmong literacy class for students in Grades K–8.

In summary, although the maintenance of the Hmong, Khmer, and Laotian languages and cultures is actively being pursued within the various Southeast Asian communities, it is difficult to fully assess the vitality of these languages. Because the Hmong, Khmer, and Laotian languages are three of the less commonly spoken languages within the United States, educators must continue to explore, fully understand, and promote the use of these languages within the Southeast Asian community. What is required is the investigation not only of the interplay of the Hmong, Khmer, and Laotian languages with English but also of a host of cultural and structural factors that shape the Southeast Asian community in its new homeland.

Suggestions for further reading

Although the number of readings that focus solely on language issues within the Southeast Asian community is limited, a number of excellent works describe the experiences of Cambodians, Hmong, and ethnic Lao in Cambodia, Laos, Thailand, and now in the United States. For biographical accounts of Cambodians under the Pol Pot regimes, their exodus to Thailand, and their resettlement in the United States as refugees, see Criddle (1992), Criddle and Mam (1987), Howard (1990), May (1986), Noup (1988), and Welaratana (1993). For biographical accounts of the Hmong journey from Laos, through Thailand, and to the United States, see the work of Faderman (1998), Howard (1990), Miller, Kiatoukaysay, and Yang (1992), Moore (1989), Rolland and Moua (1994), and Vang and Vang (1988).

As for broader educational issues for the Hmong, Khmer, and ethnic Lao, Hopkins (1996) includes a list of practical ideas and suggestions for educators in her chapter on the education of Cambodians. The collective reports of Asian Americans/Pacific Islander in Philanthropy (1997) and the National Coalition of Advocates for Students (1997) provide excellent coverage of the educational needs and opportunities afforded Southeast Asians in the public schools. The latter report includes individual chapters on Cambodians, Hmong, and the ethnic Lao. Caplan, Choy, and Whitmore's (1991) well-referenced study of student success in the Southeast Asian community (including, in particular, the Vietnamese) is a significant volume on the role of culture in school performance. Smith-Hefner's work (1990, 1993) on the Khmer in Boston provides a good explanation of Cambodian parents' views about education and language for Khmer youth. Finally, the publications of the Southeast Asia Community Resource Center (Bliatout et al., 1988; Bounkeo et al., 1988; Ouk et al., 1988) are excellent resource books with a wealth of information on each community.

References

Asian Americans/Pacific Islanders in Philanthropy. (1997). *An invisible crisis: The educational needs of Asian Pacific American youth.* New York: Author.

Beck, R. (1994, April). The ordeal of immigration in Wausau. *The Atlantic Monthly,* 84–86, 88–90, 94–97.

Bliatout, B. T. Downing, B., Lewis, J. & Yang, D. (1988). *Handbook for teaching Hmong-speaking students.* Folsom, CA: Folsom Cordova Unified School District, Southeast Asia Community Resource Center.

Bosher, S. (1997). Language and cultural identity: A study of Hmong students at the postsecondary level. *TESOL Quarterly, 31,* 593–602.

Bounkeo, S., Inthavong, O., Luangpraseut, B., Phommasouvanh, B., Compton, C. & Lewis, J. (1989). *Handbook for teaching Lao-speaking students.* Folsom, CA: Folsom Cordova Unified School District, Southeast Asia Community Resource Center.

Brand, D. (1987, August 31). The new wiz kids: Why Asian Americans are doing so well, and what it costs them. *Time,* 42–51.

Camino, L. (1994). Implications for application. In L. Camino & R. Krulfeld (Eds.), *Reconstructing lives, recapturing meaning: Refugee identity, gender, and culture change* (pp. 203–206). Basel, Switzerland: Gordon & Breach Science.

Caplan, N., Choy, M., & Whitmore, J. (1991). *Children of the boat people: A study of educational success.* Ann Arbor: University of Michigan Press.

Chan, S. (1994). *Hmong means free: Life in Laos and America.* Philadelphia: Temple University Press.

Chea, C. (1991). The children don't know Khmer. Their parents don't know English. In G. Chigas (Ed.), *Cambodia lament: A selection of Cambodian poetry* (pp. 72–81). Millers Falls, MA: Author.

Criddle, J. D. (1992). *Bamboo and butterflies: From refugee to citizen.* Dixon, CA: East/West Bridge.

Criddle, J. D., & Mam, T. B. (1987). *To destroy you is no loss: The odyssey of a Cambodian family.* New York: Atlantic Monthly Press.

Daniels, R. (1990). *Coming to America: A history of immigration and ethnicity in American life.* New York: HarperCollins.

DeVoe, P. A. (1994). Refugees in an educational setting: A cross-cultural model of success. In L. Camino & R. Krulfeld (Eds.), *Reconstructing lives, recapturing meaning: Refugee identity, gender, and culture change* (pp. 235–249). Basel, Switzerland: Gordon & Breach Science.

DeVoe, P. A. (1996). Lao. In D. Hainese (Ed.), *Refugees in America in the 1990s: A reference handbook* (pp. 259–278). Westport, CT: Greenwood Press.

Donnelly, N. (1994). *Changing lives of refugee Hmong women.* Seattle: University of Washington Press.

Dunnigan, T., Olney, D. P., McNall, M. A., & Spring, M. A. (1996). Hmong. In D. Hainese (Ed.), *Refugees in America in the 1990s: A reference handbook* (pp. 191–212). Westport, CT: Greenwood Press.

Faderman, L. (1998). *I begin my life over again: The Hmong and the American immigrant experience.* Boston, MA: Beacon Press.

Gordon, L. (1987). Southeast Asian migration to the United States. In J. T. Fawcett & B. V. Carino (Eds.), *Pacific bridges: The new immigration from Asia and the Pacific Islands* (pp. 153–174). New York: Center for Migration Studies.

Hendricks, G., Downing, B., & Deinard, A. (Eds.). (1987). *The Hmong in transition.* New York: Center for Migration Studies.

Herr, P. P. (1990, November 29). Don't call Hmong refugees primitive. *The New York Times,* p. A28.

Hopkins, M. (1996). *Braving a new world: Cambodian (Khmer) refugees in an American city.* Westport, CT: Bergin & Garvey.

Howard, K. (1990). *Passages: An anthology of the Southeast Asian refugee experience.* Fresno: California State University. Southeast Asian Student Services.

Iep, S. (1991). Dreaming in my own language. In J. Tenhula (Ed.), *Voices from Southeast Asia: The refugee experience in the United States* (pp. 27–30). New York: Holmes & Meier.

Kiang, P. (1994). When know-nothings speak English only. In K. Aguila-San Juan (Ed.), *The state of Asian America: Activism and resistance in the 1990s* (pp. 125–145). Boston: South End Press.

Koltyk, J. (1998). *New pioneers in the heartland: Hmong life in Wisconsin.* Boston: Allyn & Bacon.

Lee, G. Y. (1982). National minorities policies and the Hmong. In M. Stuart-Fox (Ed.), *Contemporary Laos* (pp. 199–219). New York: St. Martin's Press.

López, M. G. (1997). *Educating children into literacy: A portrait of one teacher's work in a bilingual classroom.* University of California, Berkeley. Unpublished doctoral dissertation.

May, S. (1986). *Cambodian witness: The autobiography of Someth May.* New York: Random House.

McNall, M., Dunnigan, T., & Mortimer, J. (1994). The educational achievement of the St. Paul Hmong. *Anthropology & Education Quarterly, 25,* 44–65.

Melnick, L. (1988). Cambodians in Western Massachusetts and Bronx, New York. *Migration World, 18*(2), 4–9.

Miller, S. L., Kiatoukaysay, B., Yang, T. (1992). *Hmong voices in Montana.* Missoula, MT: Missoula Museum of the Arts.

Moore, D. (1989). *Dark sky, dark land: Stories of the Hmong Boy Scouts of Troop 100.* Eden Prairie, MN: Tessera.

Mortland, C. A. (1994). Cambodian refugees and identity in the United States. In L. Camino & R. Krulfeld (Eds.), *Reconstructing lives, recapturing meaning: Refugee identity, gender, and culture change* (pp. 5–27). Basel, Switzerland: Gordon & Breach Science.

Mortland, C. A. (1996). Khmer. In D. Hainese (Ed.), *Refugees in America in the 1990s: A reference handbook* (pp. 305–327). Westport, CT: Greenwood Press.

Mydans, S. (1990, November 7). California says Lao refugee group is a victim of leadership's extortion. *The New York Times,* p. A20.

National Coalition of Advocates for Students. (1997). *Unfamiliar partners: Asian parents and U.S. public schools.* Boston: Author.

Ngor, H. (1987). *A Cambodian odyssey.* New York: Warner Books.

Noup, C. V. (1988). House of donuts. In A. Santoli (Ed.), *New Americans: Immigrants and refugees in the U.S. today* (pp. 307–332). New York: Viking.

Ouk, M., Huffman, F., & Lewis, J. (1988). *Handbook for teaching Khmer-speaking students.* Folsom, CA: Folsom Cordova Unified School District, Southeast Asia Community Resource Center.

Rawls, W., Jr. (1983, April 30). Mexican food trips Asian refugee in spelling bee. *The New York Times,* p. A6.

Rim, C. (1991). Greensboro, North Carolina. In J. Tenhula (Ed.), *Voices from Southeast Asia: The refugee experience in the United States* (pp. 89–91). New York: Holmes & Meier.

Rolland, B., & Moua, H. V. (1994). *Trails through the mist.* Eau Claire, WI: Eagles Printing.

Smalley, W. A. (1976). *Phonemes and orthography: Language planning in ten minority languages of Thailand* (Pacific Linguistic Series No. 43). Canberra, Australia: Linguistic Circle of Canberra.

Smalley, W. (1986). Stages of Hmong cultural adaptation. In G. L. Hendricks, B. T. Downing, & A. S. Deinard (Eds.), *The Hmong in transition* (pp. 7–22). New York: Center for Migration Studies.

Smith-Hefner, N. (1990). Language and identity in the education of Boston-area Khmer. *Anthropology and Education Quarterly, 21,* 250–268.

Smith-Hefner, N. (1993). Education, gender, and generational conflict among Khmer refugees. *Anthropology and Education Quarterly, 24,* 135–158.

Tenhula Tenhula, J. (1991). *Voices from Southeast Asia: The refugee experience in the United States.* New York: Holmes & Meier.

261

Thee, M. (1973). *Notes of a witness: Laos and the second Indochinese war.* New York: Random House.

U.S. Bureau of the Census. (1992). *1990 census of population – General population characteristics: United States.* Washington, DC: U.S. Government Printing Office.

U.S. Bureau of the Census. (1993a). *1990 census of population – Asians and Pacific Islanders in the United States.* Washington, DC: U.S. Government Printing Office.

U.S. Bureau of the Census. (1993b). *1990 census of population – Social and economic characteristics: United States.* Washington, DC: U.S. Government Printing Office.

U.S. Committee for Refugee Concerns. (1993). Refugees admitted to the United States by nationality, FY 80–93. *Refugee Reports, 14*(12), 10–11.

U.S. Committee for Refugee Concerns. (1997). Refugees admitted to the United States by nationality, FY 84–97. *Refugee Reports, 18*(12), 10–11.

U.S. Department of Health and Human Services, Office of Refugee Resettlement. (1983). *Refugee resettlement program: Report to the Congress.* Washington, DC: U.S. Government Printing Office.

Vang, S., & Vang, N. (1988). The sacred drum. In A. Santoli (Ed.), *New Americans: Immigrants and refugees in the U.S. today* (pp. 207–233). New York: Viking Books.

Walker, W. (1987). *An introduction to the Hmong.* San Francisco: New Faces of Liberty.

Welaratna, U. (1993). *Beyond the killing fields: Voices of nine Cambodian survivors in America.* Stanford, CA: Stanford University Press.

Weinstein-Shr, G. (1993). Literacy and social process: A community in transition. In B. Street (Ed.), *Cross-cultural approaches to literacy* (pp. 272–293). New York: Cambridge University Press.

Wong Fillmore, L. (1991). When learning a second language means losing the first. *Early Childhood Research Quarterly, 6,* 323–346.

Wong Fillmore, L., & Valadez, C. (1986). Teaching bilingual learners. In M. Wittrock (Ed.), *Handbook of research on teaching* (3rd ed., pp. 648–685). New York: Macmillan.

Yang, D. (1993). *Hmong at the turning point.* Minneapolis, MN: World Bridge.

9 English language learners of Chinese background

A portrait of diversity

Sau-ling C. Wong and M. G. López

In 1977, in a review of Maxine Hong Kingston's best-selling fictional-ized autobiography of Chinese American life, *The Woman Warrior: Memoirs of a Girlhood Among Ghosts* (1976), *New York Review of Books* critic Diane Johnson (1977) wrote, "The Chinese-Americans are a notably unassimilated culture. It is not unusual in San Francisco to find fourth- or fifth-generation American-born Chinese who speak no English" (p. 20). Her description of the group immediately provoked scathing rebuttals from Chinese American critics (Chan, 1977; Tong, 1977). This minor anecdote in American cultural history, though in one sense merely a result of individual oversight, is in fact an apt encapsula-tion of the Chinese American sociolinguistic situation. Johnson's state-ments, if somewhat extreme in their ignorance, actually reflect a fairly common perception of Chinese Americans' relationship to the English language. Such a perception, in turn, embodies a complex set of as-sumptions about the group's place in American society: a legacy of his-tory. Contrary to popular belief, it is not only what the Chinese "bring with them" (often conceptualized as a mysterious language tied to an alien culture) that shapes Chinese American language use patterns. Rather, the experience of being Chinese in America has a transforming influence that sometimes neutralizes the ethnic heritage itself. Any ac-count of the Chinese American language situation must therefore be guided by an understanding of the sociohistorical context in which the community's main languages, Chinese and English, operate.

Immigration history

According to the 1990 census (U.S. Bureau of the Census, 1992, Table 4), the Chinese, numbering 1,648,700, made up the largest of the Asian American groups. However, the Chinese have not always been welcome in the United States. Since the mid-nineteenth century the size and com-position of the Chinese American community have fluctuated greatly as

We are most grateful to Him Mark Lai; Franklin Ng; L. Ling-Chi Wang; and Sandra L. McKay, I-Hui Su, and Hamilton Chang for generously sharing their research on Chinese language schools, Taiwanese Americans, overseas Chinese education policy, and English language teaching in Hong Kong and Taiwan respectively; and to Marie Lo for her re-search assistance.

a result of changing attitudes and policies toward the Chinese. The following is a brief account of Chinese immigration to the United States.

Early immigration

Although the Chinese presence in the United States dates back to the end of the eighteenth century (Lai, Huang, & Wong, 1980, p. 12; Chen, 1981, pp. 3–13), the Chinese did not begin emigrating in significant numbers until gold was discovered in California in 1848 and news of the "Gold Mountain" reached China, which at that time was plagued by political corruption under Manchu rulers, civil strife, domination by Western powers, and economic collapse. Guangdong (Kwangtung) Province in southern China, a densely populated, poverty-stricken area with a long seafaring tradition, became the main source of early Chinese immigrants. Surging in 1852, emigration from China subsided to an average of 8,000 annually during the next two decades (Lai, Huang, & Wong, p. 20). However, the Chinese were quickly driven out of the mines by an exorbitant, discriminatory tax, and a pattern of concentrating in noncompetitive, service occupations such as restaurants and laundries, which is still observable today, began (King & Locke, 1980, p. 17).

In 1865, Chinese laborers began to be hired to build the western section of the transcontinental railroad; eventually, some 12,000–14,000 Chinese worked on the project (Lai, Huang and Wong, 1980, p. 23). After the transcontinental line was completed in 1869, most workers made their way back to California (Chen, 1981, p. 75; Lai, Huang, & Wong, p. 25). There they played a key role in opening up the West, developing agriculture, fishing, and various light industries by providing not only labor but also expertise (Chen, pp. 79–116; Lai Huang, & Wong, pp. 26–33).

In 1868, the United States and China signed the Burlingame Treaty, allowing reciprocal free immigration (Chen, 1981, pp. 128–129). "In the next decade, immigration averaged more than 12,000 a year and the Chinese population steadily rose to over 105,000 by 1880" (Lai, Huang, & Wong, 1980, p. 25). However, when economic conditions took a turn for the worse in the 1870s (Chen, pp. 134–135), Chinese laborers, who had been subject to racism since mining days (Lyman, 1974, pp. 58–62), easily became the target for public discontent. An anti-Chinese movement swept the nation, resulting in riots and lynchings, restrictive legislation regarding the occupations and lifestyles of the Chinese, and, most important, exclusionary immigration laws (Chen, pp. 127–180; Lai, Huang, & Wong, pp. 38–39; Lyman, pp. 54–85).

In 1882, the Chinese Exclusion Act was passed, barring the entry of

Chinese laborers for 10 years and prohibiting the naturalization of Chinese. Only certain exempt classes, such as officials, teachers, students, merchants, and travelers, were allowed entry (Lai, Huang, & Wong, 1980, p. 39). The act was renewed in 1902 and extended indefinitely in 1904. In 1924, the National Origins Law, which favored northwestern European immigration, was passed; among other things, it barred all aliens ineligible for citizenship (Chinese included), from entry, redefined the provisions in the 1882 Chinese Exclusion Act even more stringently (Lyman, 1974, p. 111), and prohibited the entry of Chinese wives of U.S. citizens (Chen, 1981, pp. 144–171). In the words of a Chinese American leader, Exclusion, in effect, meant extermination (Chen, p. 171).

Although a substantial number of Chinese continued to enter by resorting to the fraudulent "paper son" system (Lai, Lim, & Yung, 1980, pp. 20, 22; Lyman, pp. 110–111),[1] the community during the Exclusion era was far from a growing one. It became a "bachelor society" with no family life to speak of; in 1890, the male–female ratio among the Chinese in America was almost as high as 27:1 (Lyman, p. 88). (See Yung, 1995, pp. 52–105, for an account of the small number of Chinese immigrant women up to 1929.) "Old-timers," immigrants from the Exclusionary period, were still part of 1970s Chinatowns (Lyman, pp. 86–92; Nee & Nee, 1972, pp. 13–122). The 1910–1943 period was one of "institutional racism" for the Chinese, who were confined to Chinatowns, the "legitimized ghettos" (Lyman, pp. 86–118).

In 1943, because of both China's role in World War II and the United States' concern for its credibility as a world leader (Chen, 1981, pp. 204–207), the Chinese Exclusion Act was repealed. The repeal did not lead to a sudden influx of Chinese immigrants. Rather, an annual quota of 105 came into effect and remained until 1965. However, during the 1943–1965 period, Chinese immigration was augmented by the presence of several groups entering on a nonquota basis. After the war, under the War Brides Act of 1945 and the Act of August 9, 1946, many Chinese women entered as alien wives of veterans and U.S. citizens (Lai, Huang, & Wong, 1980, p. 70; Yung, 1986, p. 80). When the Communists defeated the Nationalists in the Chinese civil war and established the People's Republic of China (PRC) on the mainland in 1949, some 5,000 "stranded students" and other intellectuals remained in the Unit-

1 Under the "paper son" system, a Chinese man with American citizenship, after visiting his wife in China, would later claim the birth of a child in China, thus creating a slot for a new U.S. citizen eligible for future entry into the United States. This slot could then be sold, usually to someone who wanted to join his or her family in the United States but was barred by law from doing so. During the Exclusion period, Chinese immigrants were subjected to detention and interrogation on a "guilty until proven innocent" basis (see Chen, 1981, pp. 189–190; Lai, Lim, & Yung, 1980, pp. 8–29; and, Chan, 1991).

ed States (Lee, 1960, pp. 103–112; Tsai, 1986, pp. 120–124). Chinese also entered as refugees under the Refugee Relief Acts of 1953, 1957, and 1959 (Chen, pp. 212–213); and as parolees under President John F. Kennedy's Executive Order of May 1962 (some 15,000 entered between 1962 and 1965; see Tsai, p. 152).

As more women entered the United States (between 1944 and 1953, some 82% of immigrants were women; see Yung, p. 80), the male–female ratio became more balanced, climbing from 2.9:1 in 1940 to 1.3:1 in 1960 (Yung, p. 80). As Wong (1995) reports, census data verify that by 1990 Chinese females outnumbered their males counterparts for the first time. In short, gradually the Chinese American community has become more of a "family society."

The 1965 immigration reform

As for other Asian American groups, for the Chinese the turning point in their recent immigration history was the 1965 Immigration and Naturalization Amendments, which took effect in 1968. They abolished the discriminatory national origins quota system based on race and established a preference system based on family reunification and occupational skills, permitting up to 20,000 entries per country per year (Chen, 1981, p. 216). Thus began an influx of Chinese immigrants of varied backgrounds, mainly from Taiwan and Hong Kong, which continues today. Between 1966 and 1974, an annual average of over 16,000 Chinese *quota* immigrants (i.e., subject to numerical limitations) plus roughly 4,000 *nonquota* immigrants (i.e., immediate relatives, including spouses, minors, unmarried children, and parents of adult citizens) entered the United States. In addition, the immigration reform allowed over 40,000 Chinese who were in the United States on a temporary basis to switch to permanent residency status (Tsai, 1986, pp. 152–153).

During the 1980s immigration counts for the Chinese rose to an annual average of 25,000 and reached 31,000 in 1990. As a result, Hing (1993) notes, roughly 237,800 Chinese immigrants entered the United States from 1970 to 1980, and census data record that an additional 649,200 arrived between 1980 and 1990 (U.S. Bureau of the Census, 1993a, Table 1). A sizable population of foreign students, scholars, and business representatives, many of whom reside in the United States with their families, also augments Chinese immigration totals. Hing reports that in 1988 these "nonimmigrant" Chinese from Hong Kong, mainland China, and Taiwan totaled 128,702 individuals (p. 111). Specifically, emigrants from Taiwan totaled 159,600 between 1980 and 1990, almost twice the number of all Taiwanese immigrants prior to 1980 (U.S. Bureau of the Census, 1993a, Table 1).

IMMIGRATION FROM HONG KONG

Immigrants from Hong Kong are not as numerous as those from Taiwan, but they have been no less instrumental in bringing about the transformation of the Chinese American community. Prior to the 1965 immigration reform, the number of immigrants from Hong Kong to the United States totaled less than 12, 004 (U.S Bureau of the Census, 1983, Table 254). Following the change in legislation, however, immigration totals began to increase, with 17,757 new arrivals during 1965–1970. Immigrants from Hong Kong numbered roughly 50,200 during the 1970s and slightly more than 65,000 individuals during the 1980s (U.S. Bureau of the Census, 1983, Table 254; 1993a, Table 1).

Until July 1997, Hong Kong was a British colony, ceded to Britain in 1842 after the Opium War. As a colony, Hong Kong had an annual quota of 600, which was charged against that for Great Britain (U.S. Immigration and Naturalization Service, 1981, p. 34). The 1986 immigration reform increased the quota for Hong Kong to just under 5,000 (P. L. 99–603, November 6, 1986), a total that was raised to 10,000 in 1990. This allotment was inadequate relative to the number of people in Hong Kong who wanted to emigrate because of both population pressures and apprehension about the tiny "city-state's" return to China. Hing (1993) reports that the Tiananmen Square massacre in Beijing in 1989 also accelerated interest in immigration to the United States among Hong Kong residents. Recent studies of Chinese communities across the United States have documented the significant role played by Hong Kong immigrants in the Chinese American community, a role that will certainly continue to grow in the next decade (Kwong, 1987; Wong, 1998).

IMMIGRATION FROM THE PRC

Another new and important source of Chinese immigration is the PRC. After the normalization of diplomatic relations between the PRC and the United States in 1979, population movement between the two nations, cut off for decades, resumed. In 1981, "the annual 20,000-per-country quota for immigrants from 'China' was changed to apply separately to the PRC and Taiwan, resulting in an increase in immigrants from the two countries from 25,800 in fiscal year 1981 to 35,800 in fiscal year 1984" (Gardner, Robey, & Smith, 1985, p. 37). During the 1980s, the PRC gradually relaxed its emigration policy (Zhou, 1992, pp. 56–58). Whereas during the Cultural Revolution (1966–1976) people in China with *haiwai guanxi* (overseas relatives) were persecuted, these people were suddenly "looked up to . . . envied and prestigious" (Zhou, p. 61) after the thaw in U.S.-PRC relations. Those with U.S. citizens as relatives not only began openly receiving remittances from them again, but their own emigration was facilitated by the U.S. family reunification provision. Between 1980 and 1990, more than 283,000 émigrés from Mainland China arrived in the United States (U.S. Bureau of the Census, 1993a, Table 1). Of these recent arrivals, almost 60% (168,800) arrived between 1985 and 1990 (U.S. Bureau of the Census, 1993b, Table 1).

Although the backgrounds of PRC immigrants to the United States vary greatly – for example, some are similar in background to Cantonese old-timers while others resemble the so-called stranded intellectuals in origin – Zhou (1992) warns against the stereotypical assumption that they must be driven by economic desperation. In fact, many of them "came from the more well-to-do segment of the population in the most economically prosperous regions of the country" (p. 59). Of the nearly 40,000 PRC students studying in the United States in 1988, "more than 40 percent depended for funding largely on family or kinship sources abroad" (p. 61). Immigration from the PRC is often a function of the desire to escape unstable political policies and to fulfill dreams of a better life. This is perhaps best evidenced by the recent immigration of documented and undocumented Chinese from the coastal province of Fujian (Kwong, 1997). As dramatized by the drownings of 10 Chinese and the arrest of almost 275 more illegal immigrants from the grounding of the ship *Golden Venture* off the coast of New York in 1993, numerous Chinese continue to seek economic opportunities in the United States. Although no definitive count of these Fuzhounese (Fukienese) exists, Kwong reports that roughly 150,000 immigrants from Fuzhou (Fukien),[2] a great percentage of whom lack official immigration papers, arrived in the New York City area between 1988 and 1993 (p. 37).

ETHNIC CHINESE FROM OTHER REGIONS

Adding to the Chinese population in the United States are ethnic Chinese from areas of political instability, including Cuba, Myanmar (formerly known as Burma), and in particular Indochina (Lai, Huang, & Wong, 1980, p. 79). The Vietnam-China border conflicts of 1979 led to the exodus of a large number of Chinese Vietnamese. López (1982) estimates that as many as 100,000–200,000 of the refugees from Vietnam are "essentially Chinese . . . in race and language" (p. 6). (See also Chapter 7.) These ethnic Chinese are, of course, not counted under the

---

2 Fuzhou is the capital of Fujian Province; Fukien is the older English rendition of Fujian. In English, the term *Fuzhouness* is used to refer to the people from Fujian. Kwong does not explain this distinction in his book but rather draws on the historical presence of Fuzhouren arriving in New York in the 1970s as seamen.

quotas for China and are overlooked in considerations of Chinese immigration, but their visibility in the community has been steadily increasing (see, e.g., Kwong, 1987).

Current demographics: Diversity in the Chinese American community

The "old" and "new" Chinese American communities

As the preceding review of Chinese immigration history suggests, it is much easier to generalize about the early Chinese American community than about the contemporary one. The "old-timers" up through the exclusion era shared a fairly uniform background. Most of them hailed from eight districts (a district is comparable to an American county) in southern Guangdong Province, a small region about the size of the San Francisco Bay area (see Lai, Huang, & Wong, 1980, pp. 16–17). The majority came from rural backgrounds, had little formal schooling, and were predominantly male; the community structure reflected their relative homogeneity and cohesiveness (Lyman, 1974, pp. 29–53; Tsai, 1986, pp. 33–55), characteristics that were further reinforced by the fact that so few children were born in the United States (Lyman, pp. 112–115).

In contrast, the contemporary Chinese American community defies ready generalization. A definition by negation – that it is no longer predominantly Cantonese, rural, and male – is the safest generalization but is hardly illuminating. It may be more useful to think of succeeding groups of immigrants as layers of deposit in a geological formation, discernible in any cross section, whether cut by settlement patterns, nativity, occupation, educational attainment, or, of course, language. (Even the ways surnames are spelled tell stories of dialect origin and adaptation, as pointed out in Louie, 1998.) In short, the vicissitudes of Chinese immigration and settlement may be viewed as leaving their mark on the community in many different ways.

Settlement patterns

According to the 1990 census, Chinese Americans are concentrated overwhelmingly in the West: 52.8% as compared to 26.9% in the Northeast, 12.5% in the South, and 7.8% in the Midwest.[3] The six states with the most numerous Chinese population (greater than 50,000) are, in descending order, California (713,423; 43.3%), New

3 See U.S. Bureau of the Census, 1992, Map IV-3, for the division of states into the Northeast, Midwest, South, and North.

York (285,144; 17.3%), Hawaii (68,769; 4.2%), Texas (63,227; 3.8%), New Jersey (58,080; 3.5%), and Massachusetts (53,545: 3.2%) (U.S. Bureau of the Census, 1992, Table 143). These six states alone represent 75% of all Chinese nationwide.

Like other Asian Americans, Chinese Americans tend to be urban dwellers. Census figures for 1990 show that 97.7% of all Chinese reside in urban areas (U.S. Bureau of the Census, 1992, Table 4). Specifically, over 45,000 Chinese live in the five metropolitan areas of Boston, Honolulu, Los Angeles, San Francisco, and New York, with Los Angeles, New York–New Jersey, and the San Francisco Bay Area topping the list at over 300,000 each (U.S. Bureau of the Census, 1992, Table 160). This settlement pattern reflects, among other things, the historical role of the Chinese in developing the West, the continuing importance for new immigrants of Chinatowns, which served not only as entry points for newcomers but also as refuges from persecution during the era of exclusion, and the development of "New Chinatowns" (Fong, 1994; Kwong, 1987; Wong, 1998; Zhou, 1992).

The importance of nativity

Immigration has played a vital role in the formation of the post-1965 Chinese American community: Of the more than 1.6 million Chinese in the United States in 1990, fully 69.3% (1,142,580) were foreign born (U.S. Bureau of the Census, 1993a, Table 1). Equally important, the majority of this foreign-born population (roughly 57%) entered the United States during the 1980s. Given this breakdown, generalizations about the Chinese community must be made cautiously. Often, as soon as the distinction between native born and foreign born is taken into account, the picture of a given demographic characteristic looks quite different.

ECONOMIC SITUATION

A good example of heterogeneity along nativity lines concerns the economic situation of Chinese Americans, who, along with other Asian Americans, are often portrayed in the media as a prosperous, model minority that has reached parity with Whites (Osajima, 1988). It is true that 1990 census figures show the median income for full-time Chinese American male workers to approach that for White males ($18,375 and $22,555) and to be slightly higher for Chinese females ($11,455 and $11,300) (U.S. Bureau of the Census, 1992, Table 111, Table 87). For entire families, however, a greater percentage of Chinese families lived below the poverty line: 11.1% as opposed to only 6.4% for White families. (U.S. Bureau of the Census, 1992, Table 93, Table 112). However, a closer look reveals that the Chinese American community actually had a significant bimodal economic structure, with high concentrations of both affluent and poor. The distinction between native born and foreign born proves crucial here: Foreign-born Chinese earned substantially less than their native-born counterparts. In fact, only slightly more than 3.0% of native-born Chinese families lived below the poverty line as opposed to 20.2% of Chinese immigrants who arrived in the United States during the 1980s (U.S. Bureau of the Census, 1993a, Table 5). The latter figure more closely approximates the poverty rate for African Americans (25.7%), American Indians (22.8%), and Hispanics (22.2%) (U.S. Bureau of the Census, 1992, Tables 94–97). Of course, even within the immigrant designation, there is great variation; for example, among the Hong Kong–born are a handful of wealthy investors who tried to protect themselves from uncertainty over Hong Kong's political future by emigrating and bringing capital to the United States before 1997. Among Chinese-Vietnamese immigrants, there is a mixture of successful entrepreneurs and welfare-dependent refugees (Gold, 1994). Still, on the whole, place of birth is a significant factor in income distribution among Chinese Americans.

OCCUPATIONAL PATTERNS

A similar picture obtains for occupational distribution, which also shows the effect of nativity. According to the 1990 census, foreign-born Chinese were heavily concentrated in service occupations (36.4%) whereas only 19.8% of the native born were similarly employed (U.S. Bureau of the Census, 1993, Table 4).[4] Within Chinatowns, where many of the foreign born (documented and undocumented) live, there is in fact a "subeconomy" heavily dependent on two industries: tourist restaurant operation and garment making (King & Locke, 1980, pp. 32–33; Kwong, 1987, 1997). According to Shinagawa (1996, p. 78), using 1990 census data, Chinese Americans are the second most likely Asian American group (after Indian Americans) to be in professional occupations (20.7% and 29.6%, respectively). However, as Wong (1995) notes, "despite the high proportion of Chinese in the professions, they are absent in executive, supervisory, or decision-making positions" (p. 78).

EDUCATIONAL ATTAINMENT

As their occupations do, educational attainment of Chinese Americans shows a pattern, albeit qualified, of success for the native born contrasting with the disadvantaged status of the foreign born. Chinese Americans receive frequent publicity for their outstanding achievements in ed-

4 Service occupations are compiled according to the following census categories: service occupations; farming, forestry, and fishing occupations; precision production, craft, and repair occupations; and operators, fabricators, and laborers.

271

ucation, especially high school and college students in the science and technical fields (e.g., Tsai, 1986, pp. 163–164). Taken as a group, Chinese Americans show a consistently higher rate of enrollment in school and college, from age 3 through age 34, than Whites do (Tsang & Wing, 1985, p. 18). According to 1990 census data, a higher percentage of Chinese persons aged 25 years and over than of Whites in the same age group had a bachelor's degree (21.6% versus 13.9%) or a graduate or professional degree (19.1% versus 7.7%) (U.S. Bureau of the Census, 1992, Table 42, Table 106). However, several qualifications are necessary. To begin with, many immigrants completed their schooling *before* immigration, thus inflating the figures for educational attainment for the group (Tsang & Wing, p. 16); the statistics do not prove success within the U.S. educational system. Second, as Wong's (1995) analysis of 1990 data shows, "a greater proportion of Chinese than whites were also at the lower end of the education spectrum" (p. 80). Almost twice as many Chinese as Whites (16.8% versus 8.9%) had less than a ninth-grade education (U.S. Bureau of the Census, 1992, Table 42, Table 106). Moreover, 12.8% of Chinese families with school-age children lived below the poverty line, compared with 8.8% of White families (U.S. Bureau of the Census, 1992, Tables 49, Table 112).

The effect of foreign nativity on education is modified by length of residence in the United States, however. The percentage of Chinese American families with school-age children below the poverty line decreases sharply with length of residence (Kan & Liu, 1986, p. 23). This accords with a pattern described by Tsang and Wing (1985) for Asian Americans as a whole, including Chinese: "Those who have lived here for five or fewer years scored substantially lower than white students in both verbal skills and sciences [though not in mathematics] (p. 12)." In contrast, those who were born in the United States or have lived there for at least 6 years equaled or surpassed Whites in mathematics, science, and verbal skills. However, this pattern might not describe recent arrivals who are children of the elite (businesspeople, executives, professionals working for multinational corporations, etc.), for they may have attended international schools in Taiwan, Hong Kong, or the PRC before entering the United States, or they may have visited the United States frequently or attended summer programs there. In other words, such students would face significantly fewer adjustment problems in American schools compared to the adjustments required by less privileged immigrant students.

Linguistic diversity in the Chinese American community

The historical legacy and current complexity of the Chinese American community are both reflected in linguistic heterogeneity. No single language situation is shared by all Chinese Americans; an adequate account must focus on each subgroup separately.

Adult Chinese American immigrants and their language situation

Because adult Chinese American immigrants do not go through the American public school system, they should be considered separately from school-age immigrants. Native language background plays a more important role in their language use patterns than in those of their children.

THE CHINESE LANGUAGE

Chinese is spoken by more than one billion people worldwide, the vast majority of whom reside in the PRC. Within the Chinese language there are seven major dialect families: Mandarin (spoken by 70% of the total population), Wu (8.4%), Xiang (5%), Gan (2.4%), Hakka (4%), Min (1.5%), and Yue (5%) (Li & Thompson, 1981, p. 3); within each dialect family are further varieties. (What is loosely called *Cantonese* in the United States is a group of Yue dialects.) The dialects are often mutually unintelligible. The Mandarin of the Beijing (Peking) area is the basis for the national language for both the PRC and Taiwan. For transcribing sounds (so-called romanization), the former uses the *pinyin* system, which has a Roman alphabet; the latter uses the *zhuyin* system, made up of non-Roman phonetic symbols.

Whereas spoken Chinese is varied, written Chinese is uniform, made up of characters each representing a sound. Modern written Chinese is largely based on Beijing Mandarin. In learning to read and write, speakers of other dialects not only have to learn the standard pronunciation of characters but also have to contend with differences in vocabulary and sometimes syntax. The PRC uses a simplified script, which the Chinese in Singapore have also adopted. Taiwan adheres to the traditional script, as do Hong Kong and most other overseas Chinese communities, including those in North America.

The PRC has been promoting the use of Mandarin (known there as *Putonghua*, "the common language") since 1955 (Barnes, 1983, p. 295); Mandarin is supposed to be the medium of instruction in school. However, it has been difficult to implement the policy fully, especially in rural areas (Barnes, 1983). Taiwan, with a much smaller area, has been more successful in promoting Mandarin (referred to there as *Guoyu*, the "national language") in both education and other areas of public life (Tse, 1982). Although the vast majority of Chinese immigrants to the United States, particularly from the PRC and Taiwan, speak Mandarin, many of these same individuals are in fact bidialectical or multidialectical (Pan, 1997, 243–244).

Sau-ling C. Wong and M. G. López

An immigrant's Chinese background depends on where he or she comes from. Despite the large number of dialects in the Chinese language family, only a handful have played key roles in the Chinese American community.

The term *Cantonese,* as used in the American context, is used to refer both to the immigrant's origin (Guangdong province) and the dialect. However, a single term is inadequate to describe the nuances in language use among Chinese Americans from Guangdong; in fact, the label "has projected over the course of time an artificial view of the unity of a diverse resident Chinese population" (Chan & Lee, 1981, p. 121). (In the following account, the Cantonese pronunciations of dialect and place names, which are often more commonly heard in the United States, are supplied in parentheses.) As mentioned above, early Chinese immigrants were mostly from a small region in Guangdong made up of eight districts: the Three Districts, the Four Districts, and Zhongshan (Chungshan). The Three Districts, Sanyi (Sam Yup), consist of Nanhai (Namhoi), Panyu (Punyu), and Shunde (Shuntak) and include the city of Guangzhou (Canton), the provincial capital (Chen, 1981, p. 16). The Four Districts, Siyi (or Sze Yup), consist of Enping (Yanping), Kaiping (Hoiping), Taishan (Toishan), and Xinhui (Sunwui) (Chan & Lee, 1981, p. 129; Chen, pp. 16–18; Lai, Huang, & Wong, 1980, pp. 16–17). Depending on the degree of precision desired, immigrants might identify themselves as simply "Cantonese," as "Sze Yup," or further as "Toishan," and so on.

In early Chinese American society, a dialect served as a strong unifying force among its speakers, representing not only linguistic but also territorial and even ethnographic distinctions (Chan & Lee, 1981, p. 122); certain trades were dominated by immigrants and their descendants from certain districts or dialect groups (Chen, 1981, p. 19). The American experience also had a transforming effect: Over time, the varieties of Cantonese as spoken in the United States have evolved to include terms about American life not heard elsewhere (see, e.g., T'sou, 1973, pp. 134–135), forming what some researchers call *Chinatown Chinese* (Dong & Hom, 1980; but see Chan & Lee, 1981). Since 1965, however, old dialect loyalties have been undermined by radical changes in the community's structure.

Immigrants from Hong Kong speak the standard variety of Cantonese – which is spoken in Guangzhou and is therefore a kind of Sanyi – as opposed to the rural varieties of many of the early settlers. Standard Cantonese (alongside English) is the medium of instruction in Hong Kong schools (see the section "English Backgrounds of Chinese Immigrants in America"), although some schools started teaching Mandarin in preparation for the reversion to PRC control in 1997. As a city dialect, standard Cantonese is more prestigious than the rural versions. In addition, Hong Kong Cantonese, having evolved in a modern, cosmopolitan city, has the image of being slangy and "hip"; it is the version used in the widely distributed popular songs and movies of Hong Kong. Standard Cantonese has become the lingua franca of some Chinatowns, sometimes causing resentment toward speakers of dialects such as those of Taishan, which once dominated the community (Guthrie, 1985 pp. 42–43).

The importance of Cantonese speakers is enhanced by the influx of ethnic Chinese from Vietnam, the majority of whom are Cantonese speakers (California State Department of Education, 1984, pp. 8–9), the rest being speakers of Chaozhou (Teochew) (Him Mark Lai, personal communication, June 5, 1987). In addition, many recent immigrants from the PRC sponsored by relatives in the United States are Cantonese speakers. The strength of the Cantonese dialect in major Chinatowns is documented by that fact that 31% of all New York Chinese surveyed by Pan (1997) used Cantonese as their first dialect. In California, another state with high Chinese concentration, Cantonese speakers make up the fourth-largest group among LEP students, and Mandarin speakers rank ninth ⟨www.cde.ca.gov/demographics.htm⟩.

However, not only has Mandarin been increasingly heard in Chinatowns (Guthrie 1985, pp. 43–44; Kwong, 1987), but according to Pan, "the widespread proficiency in Mandarin of the population has become a threat to the status of Cantonese as a lingua franca [in New York]. Mandarin is well on its way to replacing Cantonese" (1997, p. 243). As the national language of the PRC and Taiwan, on which writing is based and in which works of literature are composed, it has the advantage of greater prestige and wider currency over Cantonese. It is also used in popular songs and movies from Taiwan and the mainland. As increasing numbers of Mandarin-speaking immigrants of the middle class, residing in suburbs or distant towns with no Chinatowns, come into Chinatowns to dine and shop, Cantonese shopkeepers and waiters have picked up a functional command of Mandarin, however heavily accented, in order to deal with their customers (Guthrie, 1985; Pan, 1997).

It should be noted that the term *Mandarin-speaking* is by no means synonymous with being from Taiwan. The language situation in Taiwan is more complex than many Americans realize. The overwhelming majority of the population in Taiwan are native speakers not of Mandarin but of "Taiwanese" or "Southern Fukienese," a Min dialect (Kaplan & Tse, 1982, pp. 33–35; Tse, 1982, p. 2). In addition, roughly 30,000 Taiwanese natives speak languages belonging to the *Malayo-Polynesian* language family (Pan, 1997, p. 238). The native Mandarin speakers can

275

loosely be identified as the "mainlanders" who took over Taiwan from Japan at the end of World War II and who fled the Communists in 1949. Because of political oppression of the native Taiwanese by the Nationalists (Tsai, 1986, p. 180), Mandarin-speaking mainlanders are resented by some Taiwanese speakers. Although Mandarin education has been successful in Taiwan, so that an overwhelming majority of the population can speak it, in many ways it is a language imposed on the population (Tse, pp. 34, 37). For a long time Taiwanese was the dialect of private life, in a fairly stable diglossic arrangement (Tse, pp. 35–37; see also Van den Berg, 1986). With the decline in the Nationalists' control since the mid-1980s and a precipitous rise in Taiwanese nativism in both political and cultural matters, the Taiwanese dialect has become more and more visible in the public sphere. Within the United States, Taiwanese Americans have been recognized by some as an emergent ethnic group (Ng, 1998). For Taiwanese immigrants in the United States, many of whom are highly educated (Tsai, 1986; Ng, 1998), Taiwanese continues to be important. As mentioned, with the increased immigration of Chinese from the province of Fujian, the number of Fuzhounese or Min speakers has greatly increased. Pan (1987) found that speakers of Fuzhounese as a first dialect accounted for 36.6% of the New York City Chinese population, representing the largest percentage of speakers of the various Chinese dialects.

Among Chinese immigrants in the United States, "dialect can be viewed as a factor of both division and unity" (Chan & Lee, 1981, p. 127). Although dialect loyalties are no longer as strong as they used to be, they continue to play a role in the interactions within the Chinese-speaking segment of the Chinese American community.

ENGLISH BACKGROUNDS OF CHINESE IMMIGRANTS IN AMERICA

Depending on the background of adult Chinese immigrants to the United States, their initial command of English upon entry may vary from no knowledge whatsoever to native proficiency. After immigration, they acquire or improve their English, of course; however, compared with school-age immigrants, adults are probably influenced more strongly and more persistently by the degree of their preimmigration exposure to English. Prior exposure to English is often a function more of social class than of place of origin; still, some generalizations are possible because various Chinese communities have different foreign language policies.

HONG KONG

Hong Kong, a former British colony that reverted to Chinese rule in 1997, has had a longstanding relationship with English. Readers interested in the history of English language teaching and use can consult Gibbons (1979), Ho (1979), Johnson (1983), Cheung (1984), and Flowerdew, Li and Miller (1998).

Hong Kong is a linguistically homogeneous metropolis, with 98% of the population speaking Cantonese (Flowerdew, Li, & Miller 1998, p. 203). Cantonese is the "language of solidarity" (Cheung, 1984, p. 279); this was true even when English dominated formal domains and served as the "language of power" (Cheung, 1984, p. 276). (Chinese did not become an official language until as late as 1974 [Cheung, 1984].) The Chinese take a pragmatic view of English. It was "needed for success in the civil service, law, education, and business with expatriates," and "by the 1980s and 1990s it had come to be viewed as the international language, essential for success throughout Hong Kong's economy (Flowerdew, Li, & Miller, 1998, pp. 203–204).

The most momentous change concerning language policy in Hong Kong took place shortly before the political changeover in 1997 (Farley, 1998b), when the new Special Administrative Region government adopted a policy of teaching in the mother tongue (Gargan, 1997; Farley, 1998a), reversing a decades-old trend of English-medium instruction in many of Hong Kong's schools. This move represents a decolonizing gesture, a step toward a future more closely tied to China, and a policy based on second language acquisition research and theory. The goal is to create a population that is both biliterate (Chinese and English) and trilingual (Cantonese, Mandarin, and English; Wong 1996; cited in Chang 1997). Although it is meant to correct some of the inadequacies and absurdities of colonial language education – e.g., producing overall "dismal" English proficiency (Ho, 1979:45); and making limited-English proficient teachers teach in English (Johnson, 1983) – it has provoked a groundswell of opposition, in no small part because a number of elite schools are allowed to continue teaching in English. Parents and educators fear that instead of creating better access to education, the new policy will be discriminatory and hurt Hong Kong's future as an international city (Gargan, 1997).

The effects of the mother tongue policy are too new to be reflected in the English proficiency of immigrant students from Hong Kong in U.S. classrooms. In the meantime, effects of the old situation are expected to continue for a while. Thus Hong Kong immigrants form an elite background, benefiting from "additive bilingualism" (Johnson, 1983, p. 282), are likely to enter the United States with near-native or native command of English, and will make a relatively smooth transition into American society. As Wong and López (1995) note, 86.2% of all Hong Kong immigrants residing in California are reported to speak only English or to speak English "very well" or "well" (13). At the other extreme, though, are Hong Kong immigrants who remain very weak in

English after going through part or all of a supposedly bilingual school system.

TAIWAN

Because of American political, economic, and cultural influence since the 1950s, as well as the domination of English in international trade and technology (both of which are vital to Taiwan's economy), English is the most popular foreign language taught in Taiwan. According to the most recently passed education reform, the "Twelve Education Reform Mandates" of summer 1998, English teaching will be introduced in the fifth grade in elementary school starting in the year 2001. Also, instead of English textbooks being prescribed by the Ministry of Education, the private sector will be allowed to publish them (Su, 1998). At the tertiary level, English language instruction is currently mainly offered through English Programs for Non-English Majors, which include freshman English (required), ESP, literature, journalism, and other courses; however, as of 1995, only two programs required English courses beyond freshman English. Use of traditional audiovisual aid for English learning is common, but computer-assisted language learning is still limited (Huang, 1997a). At the tertiary level, ESP is gaining attention because of the widespread use of textbooks written in English (Huang, 1997b).

Like Hong Kong immigrants, adult immigrants from Taiwan exhibit a wide spectrum of English proficiency upon their entry into the United States, although the range is slightly less extreme. Whereas Hong Kong immigrants who reported speaking only English or speaking English very well represented 53.9% of all Hong Kong immigrants in California, the total for Taiwanese immigrants was substantially lower at 39% (Wong & López, 1995, p. 13). These fluent speakers often represent college-level or postgraduate students who came to the United States to study and subsequently adjusted their status (Tsai, 1986, p. 152) as well as those in the elite class before immigration (Chen, 1981, p. 223). Working-class immigrants from Taiwan would be expected to have problems with English similar to those of working-class, Cantonese-speaking immigrants from Hong Kong.

THE PRC

The vastness of the PRC makes it even more difficult to generalize about than Hong Kong or Taiwan. A history of China's early contacts with English given in Ford (1988, pp. 12–25) contextualizes English language learning in the PRC after its establishment in 1949. After 1949, the PRC went through a series of changes in foreign language education policy tied to ideological shifts (Adamson & Morris, 1997; Ford, 1988, pp. 27–62; see also Hou, 1987; Sovel, 1983; Wang, 1982). Since the mid-1970s, the waning of extreme leftist ideology, the normalization of diplomatic relations with the United States, and in general a comparatively more open attitude toward the West have led to nationwide interest in the study of English. In 1987 an estimated 50 million students were studying English in Chinese schools (Hou, 1987, p. 25). The figures must be considerably higher now.

In 1986 government guidelines were passed to require 400 class hours of English in 3-year junior secondary schools and 530 hours in 4-year ones. (In some elite urban schools, English teaching apparently starts at the elementary, level; see Education Office, California State Department of Education, 1984, pp. 18–19; Hu, 1990, p. 60). Greater emphasis was placed on learning English for communication, for knowledge about foreign culture, and for strengthening "international understanding" (Adamson & Morris, 1997, pp. 21–22). A revised English curriculum in 1993 allowed for more holistic, communicative, and flexible pedagogy. However, "while the better qualified teachers in more prosperous regions generally have reacted favorably to the pedagogical innovations, there have been complaints from less developed areas about the expense of the textbooks and the difficulties encountered by poorly qualified teachers in handling the materials" (Adamson & Morris, 1997, p. 24). Great unevenness in the quality of English language teaching has also been noted by Hu Yining (1990, p. 61; alphabetized under Hu), who points out that schools in the provinces often lack teachers and materials, and many "teach English simply by speaking Chinese," that is, explaining grammar and translating. On the other hand, there are special Foreign Language Secondary Schools affiliated with and staffed by well-trained graduates of China's teachers' universities, foreign language institutes, or key universities, where besides English language classes, subjects such as history, geography, and science are taught in English (Hu, 1990, p. 59). At the tertiary level, Dzau (1990) reports that despite the introduction of new methodology, grammar-translation is still widespread through the emphasis on intensive reading.

Wong and López's (1995) evaluation of California census data is again illustrative of the English background of mainland Chinese adult immigrants. Whereas over 80% of all Hong Kong and Taiwanese adults reported speaking only English or speaking English very well or well, less than 50% of adults from the PRC reported similar abilities. In fact, a full 19.8% reported no knowledge of English. Relative to Hong Kong and Taiwanese immigrants, this overall limited exposure to English represents a vastly different opportunity structure for mainland Chinese in terms of employment and language used with children at home.

In outlining the English language backgrounds of various groups of Chinese immigrants, we need to emphasize that place of origin is hardly the only determinant of English proficiency. There is tremendous variation within each broadly designated group.

School-age Chinese American immigrants and their relationship to English

Compared with their adult counterparts, the way school-age Chinese immigrants (5 to 17 years of age) learn and use English is influenced less by their language background in the home country. A more important though less commonly examined influence is the experience of relocation and going through the American educational system as members of a minority. Any account of foreign-born Chinese students that focuses solely on their linguistic and cultural influences will be incomplete, if not misleading. Of course, depending on when they enter the United States, school-age Chinese immigrants are affected to varying degrees by their prior exposure to Chinese and English. In this they are no different from adults, and the information in the previous section on the Chinese and English backgrounds of adults from different regions also applies to children. What one needs to guard against is generalizing about the immigrant children's English proficiency based on place of origin and length of U.S. residence alone without taking into account their socioeconomic background and the type of school they attended. A student from the elite class from Taiwan who has been in the United States only half a year may have better English skills than a working-class immigrant who has been living in San Francisco's Chinatown for 5 years.

Teachers often ask whether the Chinese language, which is so different from English, interferes with the immigrant student's learning of English. Based on the hypothesis that there must be interference, some well-meaning if insufficiently informed teachers and counselors have advised Chinese immigrant parents to stop using Chinese at home. Although the question admits of no simple answer (for a detailed analysis, see Wong, 1987), several points may clarify the issue. First, with regard to phonology and morphology, there is a fair amount of consensus among researchers on contrastive features of the two languages that tend to cause problems with English (e.g., Chen, 1979; Ho, 1973; Lay, 1975; Lee, 1976/1977). The picture is not so clear at the syntactic and discourse levels. Schachter and Rutherford (1979) and Rutherford (1983) have hypothesized that the topic-prominent nature of Chinese may be transferred to English, a subject-prominent language, but empirical evidence is still sketchy. A Chinese "written discourse accent" may also have been created by nonnativelike use of cohesive devices (Hu, Brown, & Brown, 1982; Johns, 1984). Kaplan (1966, 1968, 1976, 1986) has suggested that Chinese learners of English tend to use a deeply ingrained "cultural thought pattern" – one favoring circularity and indirection as opposed to English linearity – and to rely on the traditional eight-legged essay form when they compose. His theory, though well known, is flawed in both reasoning and evidence (Mohan & Lo, 1985). However, it seems to apply to the rhetorical organization of Chinese speakers negotiating face-to-face in English (Young, 1982).

Interesting as the question of possible linguistic transfer is, in the case of Chinese immigrant students in the United States, a focus on the sociolinguistic context of English learning is much more important. Both the immigrant situation and the Chinese ethnicity of the students have a bearing on their relationship to the English language (Wong, 1988).

Bouvier and Tong (1968), Leong (1972), Wang (1972), Chao (1977), Sung (1979), and To (1979) have pointed out that Chinese immigrant students, especially newcomers from low-income families, suffer a number of economic and emotional stresses peculiar to or accentuated by the immigrant situation. As Kleinmann (1982) suggests in a related context, such pressures of daily life could affect the ability to concentrate on language learning.

A review of 1990 census data reveals a few of the linguistic challenges that immigrant Chinese school-age children face. Among the roughly 280,800 school-age children of Chinese ancestry, 45.1% were foreign born (U.S. Bureau of the Census, 1993a, Table 3). Among this foreign-born contingency, 8 of 10 (103,400) individuals spoke a language other than English in the home (among native-born Chinese the figure is roughly 72%). The vast majority of these children spoke one of the Chinese dialects described in the section on Chinese background, but some may in fact have spoken an additional language, like Vietnamese or Cambodian, reflecting their country of origin. Moreover, among these foreign-born children who spoke a non-English language in the home, 42.6% were reported as not speaking English very well (the corresponding figure for native-born Chinese is only 23.4%). To add to the linguistic complexity of these homes, 41.9% of all foreign-born school-age children lived in what are defined as *linguistically isolated households* (U.S. Bureau of the Census, 1993a, Table 3).[5] In short, almost half of all foreign-born Chinese students relied heavily upon the public school sector, along with other English media of communication in the wider society, for access to the English language. Last, since almost a fourth of all foreign-born children lived below the poverty line, many attended schools that were less than ideal.

In addition, Chinese-immigrant students, being members of not only

---

5 The U.S. Census Bureau defines a linguistically isolated household as one "in which no person age 14 years or over speaks only English and no person age 14 years or over speaks a language other than English speaks English 'Very well' " (U.S. Bureau of the Census, 1992, Definitions of subject characteristics, B-25).

a visible minority in this country but also one with a long history of denigration and discrimination, are often made to feel their Chinese linguistic and cultural background as a source of shame. A Chinese accent, unlike a European one, is regarded as ugly (Wang, 1972, p. 55) and is made fun of by English-speaking peers or even teachers (p. 54). "Chinese English" is traditionally stereotyped as either ludicrously florid, like Fu Manchu's, or primitive and pidgin-like, of the "no tickee, no washee" variety (Kim, 1979, pp. 46–48; 1982, pp. 12–14). Thus, unless Chinese immigrant students come into an American school with an already native command of English, they will most likely feel a tremendous pressure to get rid of the traces of any Chinese background.

The results of the pressure toward linguistic assimilation as a badge of one's cultural assimilation vary according to the individual's coping strategies.[6] Some Chinese immigrant students lose their accent with astonishing speed and go on to master English fully with little trouble; others may acquire accent-free speech but continue for years to have difficulties with written English; still others may react to the hostility of the target language group by withdrawing and socializing primarily with other speakers of their Chinese dialect (see, e.g., Nee & Nee, 1972, pp. 331). In situations of linguistic discrimination that are, in the last analysis, racially motivated, high socioeconomic status does not necessarily afford protection. A recent account of the plight of so-called little foreign students from Taiwan (Lin, 1987) – minors sent to study in U.S. schools while their well-to-do parents continue to make a living in Taiwan, a post-1979 phenomenon caused by uncertainty over Taiwan's future (see Yuan, 1987, p. 84) – shows that, in both their English classes and the schoolyard, such youngsters endure prejudice from native English speakers very similar to that experienced by low-income Chinese immigrant students. The rapid linguistic and cultural assimilation of young foreign-born Chinese Americans, the subject of many a success story in the media, is often achieved at a high cost to self-esteem.

Monolingual English-speaking Chinese Americans and their language situation

For the foreign-born, bilingual Chinese American, knowledge of Chinese, though often a subject of ridicule by English speakers, can also be a source of ethnic pride, a kind of psychological cushioning against the shock of relocation and adjustment. For the monolingual English-speaking Chinese American of the second or third generation and be-

---

6 There has been little in-depth study of the process specifically focusing on Chinese immigrant students: the account given here is based on the authors' observations and on the theoretical and research literature; see Wong (1988a) and McKay & Wong (1996).

yond, however, the Chinese language and the traditional culture it embodies can be yet another instrument of oppression. At the same time that the environment urges a virtually inevitable shift to English, native-born Chinese Americans are told by their elders that losing their Chinese (which is not really theirs to begin with) makes them guilty of a crime of betrayal against their own kind. For the majority of the native born, who are descended from the Cantonese peasant-immigrants of the past (Lai, Huang, & Wong, 1980 p. 16; Tong, 1971, p. 4), the situation carries an added irony: Their ancestors were actually outsiders to the class that formed the "repository of thousands of years of sophisticated civilization" in China (Tong, p. 4).

One manifestation of the pressure that the English-monolingual Chinese Americans feel from their ethnic culture is the tension between the so-called ABCs (American-born Chinese) and FOBs (fresh-off-the-boat Chinese, i.e., recent immigrants). The former, growing up monolingual in English, are seen by the latter as having been "white-washed," "stupid fools who know little or nothing of the great Chinese traditions." "Even for those who grew up in Chinatown and learned Chinese as kids [see section on Chinese language schools later in this chapter], the dialect of Chinese spoken is different from that of Hong Kong immigrants"; further, most of them have "very limited Chinese vocabularies" and are unable to communicate well (Leong, 1972, p. 35). Conversely, the ABCs tend to see the FOBs as "stupid and ignorant because they can't speak English" and are "not sophisticated in American ways" (p. 36). The rivalry between the two groups is vividly portrayed in Hwang's play, *FOB* (1983), and in the emerging educational literature on Chinese students (Goto, 1997; Lee, 1994; Mckay & Wong, 1996).

Native English-speaking Whites also impose unreasonable expectations on monolingual-English Chinese Americans, based on a distorted understanding of Chinese American history and of the group's sociolinguistic situation. It is not uncommon for Chinese Americans speaking with obviously native ability to be complimented on how well they have learned English or to be offered explanations of English vocabulary thought to be too difficult for them. In answer to the question "Where are you from?" if they mention an American place name, the interlocutor often rejects it and insists on learning their *real,* i.e., foreign, place of origin. On the basis of nothing but their appearance, they are frequently asked to interpret Chinese language and culture (calligraphy, customs, cuisine, etc.) (e.g., Lincoln, 1976, p. 48; Nee & Nee, 1972, pp. 379–381). Exasperating or even funny on an individual level, such expectations from White English speakers are hardly innocuous on an institutional level. For example, when native-born Chinese were trying to break into the teaching profession in San Francisco, their "Chinatown accent" was routinely used as an excuse for excluding them – and even

283

candidates raised among Whites were alleged to have such an accent (Low, 1982, pp. 169–171).

The double pressure from Chinese speakers and White English speakers caused Chin (1976, p. 557) to lament that English-monolingual Chinese Americans are "a people born without a native tongue." The native-born Chinese American critics' outraged response to Johnson's (1977) remark on Chinese unassimilability, quoted at the beginning of this chapter, must be understood in this context. Because of the long history of Chinese settlement in the United States and the overwhelming pressure on Chinese to assimilate, English is in fact the only language – not the second language – of the majority of the native born (see the following section).

In recent years, more and more English-monolingual Chinese Americans are creating works of literature, both fiction and poetry, to give voice to their unique experience (Wong, 1997). The writers are asserting their claim as rightful heirs to the English language. It remains to be seen how long it will take mainstream society to recognize that, in spite of the number of Chinese immigrants, over half a million Chinese Americans were born and raised in the United States, the majority of whom are native English speakers.

Language shift among Chinese Americans

The overall picture of Chinese Americans that emerges is that the shift to English is taking place at a fast rate in the community. Such an impression is borne out by several studies.

Kuo (1974), in an early, small-scale study of Mandarin-speaking immigrant families in the Midwest, notes certain patterns of language use within the family that would sound familiar to many Chinese Americans. Although the parents spoke mainly Mandarin in the home, the children of preschool age were already shifting to English: Half of them spoke English all or most of the time when talking to their siblings and other Chinese children and when talking to themselves (p. 129). Because of the use of English among siblings, later-born children were losing Chinese faster than first-born ones (p. 130). One parent commented, "He [the son] didn't like to speak Chinese as soon as he picked up some English . . . unless he cannot express himself in English. We still speak to him in Chinese; he'll answer in English." Another parent said of his daughter, "[She] probably thinks there is no need for her to speak Chinese since we [the parents] know English too" (pp. 134–135).

Kuo's subjects were upper middle class, which suggests that the parents, having a better command of English than working-class immigrants did, were themselves partly responsible for accelerating language shift. This might lead to the hypothesis that socioeconomic status (SES) and language shift are positively related. Nevertheless, in an analysis of 1970 census data, Li (1982) shows that the relationship between SES and language shift is in fact quite complex: "There is a negative correlation between SES and language shift . . . although the relation may not be linear" (p. 118). "The lowest SES group has the highest propensity for language shift"; "among persons with less than a high-school education, the proportions are about 15 percent in the second generation and 51 percent in the third generation; but among those with more than a high-school education, the proportions are 9 percent in the second generation and 47 percent in the third generation." At the same time, the "more-than-high-school" group shifted to English more than the "high-school" (as opposed to the "less-than-high-school") group (p. 116). Thus middle-class Chinese Americans are most likely to retain Chinese.

Li (1982) further points out that an extensive language shift has been taking place. "Among second-generation Chinese Americans . . . the use of Chinese as the mother tongue was virtually universal 60 years ago, but not today" (p. 114). The 1920s fell within the exclusion period, when Chinese were segregated in Chinatowns and when very few children were born to Chinese in the United States; thus the shift to English was in fact actively prevented by mainstream society. In the post-1965 era, the picture has been different. In the second generation, almost 12% had English as their mother tongue; in other words, a significant percentage of the immigrants had ceased to raise their children in Chinese. "Moreover, it is doubtful that even half of the 88 percent [who had Chinese as their mother tongue] can communicate intelligibly in Chinese, since mother tongue has only a slight bearing on language proficiency" (p. 113). By the third generation, almost half, or 49 percent, were reared in English.

Li's (1982) picture agrees with Fishman's (1985). Fishman finds that in 1970 there were 337,283 claimants of Chinese as their mother tongue, of whom the overwhelming majority, 308,039, were of foreign stock, that is, foreign born (186,039) or of foreign or mixed parentage (122,000). Only 29,244 Chinese mother-tongue claimants were "native of native parentage" (p. 115), indicating a phenomenal shift to English between the second and third generations.

Veltman (1983, p. 48), using a different set of data for 1976, gives a similar picture about overall shift to English among Chinese Americans. Among the Chinese foreign born, 34.1% had made English their usual language (28.1% who were bilingual and 6% who were monolingual in English). Analyzing this number by time of arrival in the United States reveals that, of those arriving before 1960, 43.4% had made English their usual language; of those arriving in the 1960s and 1970s, somewhat less than 30% had.[7] For the last subgroup, length of residence in the United States would have been at most 6 years. Thus any shift to English as the usual language must be seen as extremely rapid (p. 56).

Finally, an analysis of 1990 census data reveals again the significant interplay of nativity and length of residency in the United States as indicators of use of either English or Chinese. Among native-born Chinese, only 52.7% reported using both English and Chinese in the home. For foreign-born Chinese the percentage rises to 95.2% (U.S. Bureau of the Census, 1993a, Table 3). Moreover, among the Chinese who reported living in households in which Chinese was used in addition to English, 85% of all native-born Chinese reported speaking English very well. In contrast, only one third (36.9%) of foreign-born Chinese reported similar English language abilities. In addition, among the foreign born, 37.8% of those who immigrated to the United States between 1980 and 1990 reported speaking English not well or not at all. This total is a full 10% higher than that for Chinese immigrants who settled in the United States during 1965–1979. Consistent with Li's (1982) and Veltman's (1983) work, 1990 census data suggest that a shift in language use has occurred from Chinese to English within the Chinese community as length of residency increases and particularly among the native-born sector of the community.

The Chinese language school: An evolving institution

Within the context of a rapid shift to English among Chinese Americans, it would be worthwhile to examine in detail a long-standing community institution, the Chinese heritage community language school (hereafter referred to as Chinese language schools), which, in theory, has the potential to arrest the erosion of the ethnic language. Such an examination would enable us to determine more precisely the dynamics of language change.

Early Chinese language schools

Ethnic language schools are by no means unique to Chinese Americans; many language groups throughout American history, such as speakers of German and Yiddish, have had such schools (Fishman, 1980). For

---

7 There is apparently an error in Veltman's (1983) tables, as identical figures are given for arrivals during the 1960s (p. 55) and during the 1970s (p. 57). From the text, it seems that the percentage of Chinese immigrants making English their usual language is below 30% in both cases.

the Chinese, the ethnic language school can be said to have a history of over 100 years, the first one having been established in San Francisco in 1886 (Liu, 1976, p. 355). Yet it would be misleading to portray Chinese language schools as forming a continuing and monolithic institution, for over the decades, depending on American attitudes and policies toward the Chinese and the changes in the composition of the Chinese American community, the role played by such schools has undergone constant revision.

The earliest Chinese school in San Francisco shared one crucial feature with its modern counterparts: It was supplementary to "regular school" and took place "after hours" (Liu, 1976, pp. 355–357). (Note, however, that at that time "regular schools" for Chinese were racially segregated; see Low, 1982, pp. 59–111). In most other respects, the school was very different: The curriculum was highly traditional, involving the Chinese classics. In 1908, an official of the Manchu government toured the United States and Canada and, with the help of local community leaders, established Chinese schools in San Francisco, Sacramento, New York, Chicago, Portland, Seattle, Vancouver, and Victoria (Liu, 1976, p. 361). The arguments given by the official for establishing Chinese schools were to reinforce sentiments of patriotism toward China, to retain trained people for China's benefit, and to ensure a smooth transition when Chinese Americans returned to work in China (p. 358). After the overthrow of the Manchus and the founding of the Republic of China in 1911, in which Chinese in America played an important role, more Chinese schools were founded, some under the auspices of the Kuomintang or Nationalists, in such places as Oakland, Stockton, Fresno, Boston, and Phoenix (p. 368). There were also church-sponsored private Chinese schools (p. 367) and schools operated by district associations (Jung, 1972, p. 310; Leung, 1975, p. 54).

The functions of the earliest Chinese schools, then, were not linguistic and cultural in the sense of preserving a threatened language and way of life. Rather, at the turn of the century, under Exclusion, the Chinese in America had no chance for integration into American life and were therefore seen as logical candidates for contributing to the development of China. Moreover, with the often arbitrary enforcement of harsh immigration restrictions on the Chinese, the prospects of returning to China someday, by choice or by necessity, were very real. Supplementing an American education with a Chinese one therefore made sense.

Chinese language school during Exclusion

A study published shortly before the repeal of the Exclusion Act (Tom, 1941) shows the changes that occurred during the Exclusion years. The

287

advantages cited in the schools' favor are that they facilitated parent-child communication in Chinese and helped solve family problems, prevented children from developing inferiority complexes as a result of ill treatment from mainstream society, provided social life and recreation, and were a kind of vocational preparation. "Many college-graduate American-born Chinese have no chance to get a satisfactory job in the Chinese community. Therefore, a good knowledge of the Chinese language is a help, and in many cases a necessity, in securing vocational opportunities" (p. 561). The Chinese language school evolved during the first half of the twentieth century into a community resource, functioning to enhance family and social life and to alleviate the effects of discrimination against the Chinese.

Post-1965 Chinese language schools

A post-1965 study of Chinese language schools (Leung, 1975) judged them to be on the decline because they had "outlived their usefulness" (p. 63): after the Communists took power in 1949, preparation for return to China was no longer a good reason to attend Chinese school (p. 8). Moreover, with decreasing discrimination and improved employment opportunities during the 1960s, Chinese Americans had been more integrated into mainstream society, making a knowledge of Chinese unnecessary and attendance at Chinatown schools difficult (pp. 63–65). The Chinese schools' ostensible raison d'être – to teach the Chinese language – was no longer seen as important by many parents. In fact, the language teaching capacity of the schools was undermined by a host of practical problems (p. 58).

Leung (1975) may have been too pessimistic in his assessment of the Chinese language school's future. After suffering from declining enrollment and community interest in the early and mid-1970s (Jung, 1972, p. 311; Leung, p. 72), Chinese language schools have experienced a revival and have undergone changes in enrollment patterns (Wang, 1995, pp. 362–365). Chinese language maintenance seems to have acquired more positive connotations for the dominant society, for Chinese immigrant parents, and for Chinese American children and youth. Changing material circumstances and changing cultural attitudes have intervened to create more favorable conditions for Chinese language schools.

Factors favoring Chinese language maintenance

On a global scale, the Asian economic boom, in particular the business successes of "Greater China" (usually defined as the PRC, Taiwan, and Hong Kong) and of "diasporic Chinese" with their networks of transnational capital, had for a number of years created attractive job opportunities for those with bilingual skills. In the 1980s, the phenomenon of "reflux" immigrants to the United States, Canada, Australia, and other countries returning to work in Asia was quite pronounced, and bilingual second-generation Chinese Americans often found better job opportunities there as well. This phenomenon gave immigrant parents an economic incentive to maintain Chinese in the home and to urge their children to persist in efforts to learn Chinese. In the larger U.S. society, Asian economic success and Pacific Rim discourse had also created, at least in some circles, a more open attitude about the need for a bilingual workforce to enhance its competitiveness in the global market. Although the Asian economic crisis of 1997–1998 will likely curtail the importance of these factors, and Asia's economic future is uncertain indeed, their influence will not evaporate overnight.

Within the United States, the use of native-language advertising to tap into the vast market potential of Chinese immigrants means that, in communities with large Chinese populations, the Chinese language has a presence outside the home. This presence is likely to instill a more affirmative attitude about the language in the second generation. Technological advances have made it easier for immigrant families to obtain TV programs, rental videotapes, newspapers, and other media from the land of origin and to have Internet access to Chinese language sites, which have been proliferating rapidly in the last few years. Children exposed to these may have a sense of a broader Chinese language culture and may be less likely to feel that native language maintenance is a family idiosyncrasy or an isolating experience. For many middle-class immigrant parents, Chinese language school is an important enrichment activity for their children, like piano or tennis, and their children's success in language school is a point of pride. And with international travel increasingly affordable, middle-class parents often send their children to Taiwan or the PRC for intensive summer language training, cultural activities, and sightseeing. Although generalization is difficult, it is safe to say that at least in areas with large concentrations of Chinese immigrants, over the 1980s a more positive, or less resigned, attitude toward Chinese language maintenance developed.

Additional factors favoring a revival of interest in the Chinese language, as noted in Wang (1995), include the rise of ethnic consciousness and cultural pride among Chinese Americans since the 1960s and mainstream society's recent emphasis on multiculturalism in education. A key event that is certain to cement these gains and enhance the attractiveness of the Chinese language among the second generation is the institution of the Chinese Scholastic Assessment Test (SAT). The Educational Testing Service began to develop the exam in 1992, pretested it in 1993 and 1994, and offered it for the first time in April 1994 (Lee,

1996). The result of years of lobbying by Chinese American community members and educators, the Chinese SAT, like the Japanese one before it and the Korean one after, erodes the Eurocentric tendency in U.S. language educational whereby only European languages were deemed academically respectable. As Wang notes, "The development of the SAT-II Chinese legitimizes the teaching and learning of Chinese at all levels of education throughout the U.S. and is bound to stimulate more Chinese classes in the [sic] elementary and secondary education in the mainstream" (p. 363). The possibility of receiving college credit for Chinese language skills provides a tangible and immediate incentive for the children of immigrants to keep their home language. Since its inception, more than 18,000 students have taken the Chinese SAT II. The hour-long exam includes a 20-minute listening section that assesses students' ability to understand everyday spoken Mandarin and a 40-minute reading section that tests students' knowledge of Chinese language usage and reading comprehension (Lee, 1996). Part of the appeal of the exam is that designers intentionally incorporated the simplified and traditional scripts as well as the *pinyin* and *zhuyin* phonetic systems as a way to respond to the diversity of pedagogical approaches used in Chinese language schools, public and private secondary schools, and immigrant students' knowledge of Chinese gained in their country of origin.

A resurgence in Chinese language schools

The recent resurgence in Chinese language schools is evident in the results of two surveys. One, conducted in 1995 by the National Council of Associations of Chinese Language Schools, is summarized in Chao (1996); a fuller version in Chinese is *Quanmei zhongwen xuexiao ziliao diaozha jianbao* (1996; hereafter *Quanmei*). The other survey was conducted in 1996 by the Chinese School Association in the United States and published in 1997; it usefully tabulates its results side by side with those from the 1995 survey (*Meiguo shequ zhongwen xuexiao diaozha tongqi ziliao* (hereafter *Meiguo*). Corresponding to the different memberships of these two organizations, the *Quanmei* survey covered mostly schools serving American-born children of immigrants from Taiwan (76.3% of all students), whereas the *Meiguo* survey covered schools serving mostly mainland-born immigrant children (64% of all students) and some American-born children of mainland immigrants (22%). Taken together, these two surveys provide a fascinating snapshot of the state of Chinese language schools in the 1990s.

The *Quanmei* survey found 82,675 students enrolled in 634 Chinese language schools in 47 states; the *Meiguo* survey found 13,000 students enrolled in 83 schools in 32 states. The numbers of teachers involved were 5,540 and 1,300 respectively, about half of whom held bachelor's degrees and 30% master's degrees, according to both surveys. The *Quanmei* survey further broke down the geographical distribution of the schools it investigated: California led all states with 223 schools enrolling 36,794 students, or nearly 45% of all Chinese language school students nationwide (Chao, 1996, p. 13). New York was second with 11,786 students enrolled in 71 schools. Other states with more than 15 schools statewide included Texas (44), Illinois (33), New Jersey (28), Maryland and Washington (19), Virginia (16), and Michigan and Pennsylvania (15) (p. 13). The actual number of schools and enrollees involved in Chinese language maintenance is likely to be much higher if one includes the many semiformal afternoon and weekend Chinese language classes run by small groups of concerned parents, which would not reach any official list, and short-term Chinese classes (e.g., summer-only programs; see the following sections), which were excluded from the *Quanmei* survey. For comparison, we give earlier figures on Chinese language schools nationwide: Fishman and Markman (1979) reported 127; Fishman (1980), 142; Fishman (1985), 172 (on the basis of a 1982 survey); and Lin (1986) received responses from 99 schools, about half of those surveyed. Thus the growth of Chinese language schools since the 1980s has been quite dramatic.

Influxes of immigrants, the proliferation of Chinese language schools, and the considerable easing of political tensions between the Chinese mainland and Taiwan have combined to allow for a pattern of peaceful coexistence in curricular decisions in Chinese language schools. Before, schools and the communities they served were often caught in difficult debates about which Chinese script system to teach (the mainland uses simplified characters; Taiwan, traditional characters); which romanization system to use (the mainland uses *pinyin*, Taiwan, *zhuyin*); and what materials to adopt. In contrast, the two recent surveys found schools serving different clienteles each to be following their own path. The schools in the *Quanmei* survey used mostly textbooks published in Taiwan and the *zhuyin* romanization system, and 94% of them taught traditional characters. Those in the *Meiguo* survey used mostly textbooks published on the mainland or teacher-written materials, and 97% taught the *pinyin* romanization system and simplified characters. Cantonese speakers are a group shown to be underserved by Chinese language schools in both surveys: Of the schools in the *Quanmei* survey, only 12.8% of teachers used Cantonese, and none in the *Meiguo* survey did. This is due to the smaller number of Cantonese speakers among Chinese immigrants as well as the discrepancy between Cantonese and Mandarin in pronunciation and lexicon (textbooks are written on the basis of Mandarin).

Sau-ling C. Wong and M. G. López

Linguistic and nonlinguistic functions of the Chinese language school

In an earlier version of this chapter, Wong (1988b) presents a composite list of formidable obstacles – linguistic, sociolinguistic, pedagogical, administrative, and logistical – to the maintenance of Chinese in the United States.[8] Our update in the previous section shows that some of the environmental obstacles, such as negative attitudes from mainstream society, have become less pressing. In addition, institutions have been making efforts to facilitate teaching and learning. One example is a set

8 We observed the following problems cited in Tom (1941), Jung (1972), Leung (1975), Fan (1981), Lin (1986), and Chao, Chen, and Chang (1996). (1) Dialect diversity: Sometimes there are not enough students of a single dialect group to form a class or school. (2) Age diversity and lack of correspondence between age and Chinese proficiency: This leads to the need to mix students, causing teaching difficulties and shame and resistance among older but less proficient students. (3) Divergence in pronunciation, syntax, and vocabulary between Mandarin and vernaculars: This causes the dilemma of choosing between students' home language and the national standard and a need to decide whether to emphasize speaking and understanding or reading and writing. (4) Choice of script. The traditional script is more difficult but is the one used in North America; the simplified script is easier to learn but will not give students access to Chinese materials available in the United States and will be resisted by anti-PRC parents. (5) The decision about whether to use romanization as an aid and, if so, whether to use *pinyin* (which is easier for students in an English environment but associated with the PRC) or *zhuyin* (which requires learning an additional system but is familiar to and favored by many parents from Taiwan). (6) Difficulty of obtaining consensus among parents concerning program goals, approach, etc., especially if they are from different places of origin, generations, and socioeconomic backgrounds. (7) Lack of appropriate materials: for propagandistic purposes, the Nationalist government's Overseas Chinese Affairs Commission prepares and disseminates language teaching materials, which are quite widely used (Leung, 1975, p. 51; Overseas Chinese Affairs Commission, 1982, pp. 519–528; Lin, 1986, p. 12). These, however, reflect the values considered by the Taiwan regime to be worth encouraging among overseas Chinese. Chinese language arts texts specially produced in the United States for Chinese Americans in bilingual programs (see Asian Resource Center, 1987) are few in number. Overall, parents and teachers have very limited choices in materials. (8) Lack of teachers trained in language teaching and high turnover among teachers. Many teachers are volunteers; others work part-time at a salary; most are not language teachers by profession (Lin, 1986, p. 9). The fact that many of them are highly educated in other fields does not mean that they are familiar with the language learning process or language teaching methodology. (9) Use of outdated methods such as rote learning and excessive homework. (10) Overemphasis on discipline. (11) Lack of student motivation as a result of the above problems plus fatigue after "regular school"; reluctance to attend school on weekends; competition from other extracurricular activities; perception of Chinese as irrelevant; unwillingness to be different from mainstream peers: All of the researchers cited report a high dropout rate by secondary students. (12) Lack of parental support: English-monolingual parents sending their children to get what they themselves missed cannot help their children with the Chinese schoolwork. In the case of parents who fail to maintain Chinese at home but expect the school to do the job, the home environment will undo the school's efforts. (13) Lack of support from the English-speaking environment: Many students, especially those from the suburbs, seldom see or hear Chinese outside school. Mainstream society's denigration of Chinese

292

of materials using simplified characters produced by the PRC authorities on overseas Chinese education (*Haiwai huawen jiaocai,* 1988), developed specifically for students in Chinese schools in the United States and in consultation with local teachers. Thus, on the whole, the prospects for Chinese maintenance have significantly improved.

Yet scrutinizing the actual setup of the schools might uncover serious questions about their effectiveness as language maintenance institutions. Of the schools surveyed by Lin (1986), 55% held classes on Saturdays, 56% on Sundays, and only 5% on weekday afternoons (p. 11). Of the schools in the *Quanmei* survey, 85.2% were weekend-only schools. (The *Meiguo* survey does not give percentages.) Given the picture of language shift outlined in the previous section, one might ask how well a class held 2 or 3 hours a week, a portion of which is devoted to cultural activities (p. 12), could be expected to counteract societal influences and instill a functional proficiency in Chinese. Only the handful of schools meeting after regular school on weekday afternoons are likely to succeed in teaching language. But as Wang (1995, p. 362) notes, such schools, typical of an earlier period of demographic concentration in Chinatowns, have been on the decline, replaced by suburban Chinese community schools.

Lin (1986, p. 14) found that fully 94% of the schools surveyed had not done any evaluation studies on the effectiveness of their programs. One wonders what any formal evaluations would have found. A survey study (Chuang, 1997) of thirty-two Chinese language school teachers in the upstate New York area found that the majority of teachers felt they were not successful in teaching students to speak Chinese. Moreover, only 22% of the teachers believed teaching the students to communicate in Chinese was the most important goal of the school. Judging from our extensive contact with college-level Chinese Americans, most of those who attended Chinese school did so because their parents made them or because they wanted to spend time with other Chinese friends, learned very little Chinese in school, and forgot most of it after discontinuing attendance.

We add, however, that these graduates of or dropouts from Chinese language school frequently express regret that they did not learn more Chinese and a desire to take Chinese again sometime in the future. This seems to suggest that as Chinese American young adults emerge from adolescence, many begin to shed the internalized negative perceptions of themselves and their language and feel a need to incorporate the eth-

causes students to dislike Chinese and to look down upon Chinese language teachers whose English is less native-like than theirs (Leung, 1975; p. 60). (14) Difficulty establishing and maintaining administrative structures and personnel (Chao, Chen, & Chang, 1996). (15) Other practical difficulties such as securing facilities, transportation to and from school, and finances.

293

nic language into their evolving identity. This is particularly the case as students attend university and enroll in Chinese language classes and courses on the Asian American experience in the United States.

Nonlinguistic functions: A closer look

If the maintenance of the Chinese language is, as Li (1982) describes it, "an uphill, if not an unrealistic, struggle" (p. 113), the interesting question is why Chinese language schools, taken as a group, have enjoyed such longevity in the community. One can only conclude that the schools are in fact not primarily language-teaching institutions; rather, they serve vital, *nonlinguistic* functions.

The most important function of contemporary Chinese language schools seems to be to create a sense of cultural and ethnic pride (see the responses in Lin, 1986, p. 7). In fact, this function seems to be the main connecting thread among the schools over the decades, unifying programs that have been highly disparate in subject matter and format. Lin's respondents cited none of the practical purposes served by earlier Chinese schools, suggesting that parents too see little use for the Chinese language but have decided, however implicitly, that the language is associated with many essential but intangible advantages. This view is supported by the fact that many modern Chinese language schools include a heavy cultural component, such as Chinese calligraphy, brush painting, crafts, folk dancing, and martial arts (p. 12). Apart from the explanation that such activities enhance student motivation and make the language-learning portion more palatable, one may also infer that Chinese Americans are increasingly seeing the Chinese language as only a part, and not necessarily an indispensable part, of their overall ethnic heritage. This perspective is affirmed by Chao (1996), who writes that many Chinese teachers are "[m]otivated by a strong desire to preserve their Chinese heritage and to promote the ethnic identity of second-generation Chinese-Americans" (p. 7). Similarly, teachers in Chuang's (1997) survey noted the following goals for students in Chinese language schools: be proud to be Chinese, have a deeper understanding of Chinese culture, and realize the benefits of relearning their mother tongue. Under the given circumstances, in the face of massive shift to English parents would be willing to give up insistence on functional proficiency in the Chinese language in order to preserve the children's interest and pride in being Chinese. The existence of summer Chinese language schools (Lin, p. 11), which of course are only nominally language-teaching programs, is further evidence that Chinese language maintenance is taking a new form and serves a new function in today's Chinese American society.

Other nonlinguistic functions of the Chinese language school include, in the case of Chinatown after-school programs, providing day care as well as a smoother educational transition for recent immigrant children; in the case of parent-supported weekend programs, providing an occasion for socializing and group involvement among the parents; and in general providing more opportunities for the children to interact with other Chinese, which may, indeed, prove to enhance ethnic pride as effectively as structured cultural activities do.

Besides after-hours Chinese language schools, the Chinese language plays a significant role in other educational settings, but they are insufficient to arrest the overall language shift of the Chinese American community. Chinese-English bilingual education programs in the public schools, besides sharing many of the problems (e.g., in materials and teacher training) of private Chinese language schools, also suffer from problems related to the educational bureaucracy; in any case, they are intended to be primarily transitional (Guthrie, 1985; Wong, 1980, pp. 15–18). Immersion (in Cantonese and English) has been implemented in some San Francisco public schools, such as West Portal Elementary and Herbert Hoover Middle School (Wang, 1995, p. 364) and in Mandarin and English in a few schools in Boston and in Washington, DC. As for private immersion efforts, we know of a few Mandarin-English elementary schools in the San Francisco Bay Area, one with its own worldwide Web site (Tri-City Chinese School). Although one school has opened a sister school in another city, the high tuition and the limitations imposed by demographics make it unlikely that the establishment of such schools will become a trend in the nation.

The Chinese language is also supported by a number of Chinese summer language camps for 8- to 18-year-old Chinese youth (Chao, 1996). Established in 1976, these camps enroll 500–700 students annually in instruction not only in the Chinese language but also in a variety of cultural classes. Universities across the nation have also increased the number of introductory courses in Mandarin and Cantonese to respond to the growing desire of Chinese and non-Chinese students to relearn or learn Chinese. In fact, the University of California, Davis, is one of a handful institutions that have created web pages to provide elementary lessons on the Internet (the University of California, Davis, supports web pages for both Cantonese and Mandarin).

Conclusion

If our assessment of the language-teaching efforts of Chinese language schools and related institutions is well founded, what is one to make of the promising prospects for Chinese maintenance that some researchers seem to suggest?

Although Veltman (1983) documents a rapid shift to English among Chinese Americans, he also notes repeatedly that the Chinese, both foreign born and native born, are the most language retentive of the non-Spanish groups. Fishman's (1985) national survey of community resources for ethnic language maintenance found, in addition to 172 schools, as many as 375 local religious units, 36 TV and radio broadcasting stations, and 42 publications, making a total of 625 resources nationwide, by far the highest number among Asian American groups. On the basis of these and other data and using a criterion combining several factors, Fishman places Chinese ninth among thirty-seven ethnic languages listed on a scale of survival potential, which would make it the most likely among Asian American languages to survive. These data seem to suggest bright prospects for Chinese language maintenance, prospects apparently at odds with our picture of language shift and apparently agreeing with the popular image of the Chinese American community.

On the other hand, a closer analysis reveals that the strength of the Chinese language group is actually more a function of continued immigration than of intergenerational transmission of the language. Fishman's (1985) data on community ethnic language maintenance resources provide tallies but not an in-depth study of how the resources function. As we have shown, a large number of Chinese language schools in itself does not mean successful teaching of Chinese to the children. As for local religious units, so-called Chinese churches often provide separate services in English and Chinese so that, strictly speaking, they are not maintaining the language between generations. Often Chinese language schools are sponsored by Chinese churches, so that the actual total number of resources may be lower. Although the Chinese language press in America has a long history (Fishman, 1985, pp. 88; Lai, 1987; Tsai, 1986, pp. 128–132), the current flowering of Chinese language publications is due mainly to a rise in immigrant readership (Lai, p. 37; Tsai, p. 132) and the influx of Hong Kong and Taiwan capital (Lai, pp. 38–39). This is evident in the growth of Chinese language newspapers and periodicals published in New York City from roughly forty in 1982 (Fishman, p. 88) to as many as eighty by 1994 (Pan, 1997, pp. 24–25). As Pan concludes, what is noteworthy about these publications is their immigrant orientation in that they have "detailed coverage of news and events happening in Taiwan, the People's Republic of China, Hong Kong, and Singapore. In the entertainment section, pictures and anecdotes of Hong Kong and Taiwan celebrities dominate entire columns" (p. 248). The electronic media, such as Chinese TV and radio programs and now videotapes, are perhaps the only truly useful instruments for teaching children Chinese, since they do not involve literacy; however, at present their availability is limited to urban or suburban centers with high concentrations of Chinese. In New York City, four radio and six television companies provide programs in Cantonese and Mandarin (Pan, pp. 248–249). As with the print media, the focus of these companies is overseas issues, with the majority of programs emanating from Hong Kong, Taiwan, or the PRC.

Moreover, a close examination of Fishman's (1985) criteria for language survival potential reveals that, by the criterion of institutional strength alone, Chinese ranked fifteenth, lower than Korean, Thai and Lao, Cambodian and Vietnamese, and Hindi; only because Chinese ranked high (sixth) by the criterion of number of claimants (165) was the group able to lead other Asian American groups on the combined criterion (pp. 163, 165). Finally, both Veltman (1983) and Fishman use parentage, rather than place of birth, in categorizing their data for speakers of Chinese and English. However, because of the practice of entry through the paper son system during the exclusion period, the category *native of native* actually contains an unidentified number of Chinese born and raised abroad. The presence of this group might have inflated the number of Chinese mother-tongue claimants in the native of native category, giving a misleading estimate of how many third-generation Chinese Americans continue to be raised in or speak Chinese (Him Mark Lai, personal communication, June 5, 1987).

The answer to the question, "What are the prospects for the maintenance of Chinese in America?" thus depends very much on how one defines maintenance as well as how the place of Chinese Americans in the United States changes in the future. If retention is taken to mean intergenerational transmission of the language, the evidence points to rapid shift to English between the second and third generations, resulting in loss of Chinese from the third generation on. This trend is expected to continue unless policy makers adopt a language-as-resource orientation and society as a whole ceases to denigrate the Chinese language and its users. However, if the term refers to a large Chinese-speaking population, it is safe to say that, barring major changes in public policy toward the Chinese, the presence of the Chinese language will continue to be strong.

Suggestions for further reading

Lai, Huang, and Wong (1980) and Chen (1981) both give highly readable historical overviews of the Chinese experience in America, accompanied by a wealth of illustrations. More recent data are provided by Tsai (1986). For accounts of the contemporary Chinese experience in the United States, see Fong (1994), Kwong (1987, 1997), and Zhou (1992). Sung's (1987) account of the Chinese in New York is the only published study focusing exclusively on immigrant Chinese children. Siu (1992) reviews the literature on the educational achievement of Chinese Americans.

As for the language situation of Chinese Americans, most available sources are articles scattered in such journals as *Language Learning and Communication* (now unfortunately defunct), *Amerasia,* and *International Migration Review.* López (1982) gives a concise overview of demographic and language shift patterns among Chinese Americans but is based on 1976 data. Guthrie (1985), who has written one of the few book-length studies, provides an in-depth ethnographic account of how a bilingual education program functions in a Chinese American community. Leung's (1975) dissertation and Wang's (1996) edited volume remain the only detailed accounts of Chinese language schools. Pan's (1997) work on the Chinese language in New York City is an excellent resource on this important Chinatown community.

Veltman (1983) and Fishman (1985) have written large-scale and rather technical studies of language shift and maintenance, which help place the Chinese American language situation in a national context.

References

Adamson, B., & Morris, P. (1997). Focus on curriculum change in China and Hong Kong: The English curriculum in the People's Republic of China. *Comparative Education Review, 414,* 3–26.

Asian Resource Center. (1987). *Catalog of curriculum materials.* Oakland, CA: ARC Associates.

Barnes, D. (1983). The implementation of language planning in China. In J. Cobarrubias & J. A. Fishman (Eds.), *Progress in language planning: International perspectives* (pp. 291–308). Berlin: Mouton de Gruyter.

Bouvier, P., & Tong, T. (1968). *Education in San Francisco Chinatown.* San Francisco: San Francisco State College, Intercollegiate Chinese for Social Action.

California State Department of Education, Bilingual Education Office. (1984). *A handbook for teaching Cantonese-speaking students.* Sacramento: Author.

Chan, J. (1977, May 4). Jeff Chan, chairman of SF State Asian American Studies, attacks review. *The San Francisco Journal,* p. 6.

Chan, M. K. M., & Lee, D. W. (1981). Chinatown Chinese: A linguistic and historical reevaluation. *Amerasia Journal, 8,* 111–131.

Chan, S. (1991). *Entry denied: Exclusion and the Chinese community in America.* Philadelphia: Temple University Press.

Chang, H. (1997). One country, two systems, three languages: Cantonese, English, and Mandarin in Hong Kong. Unpublished manuscript.

Chao, R. (1977). *Chinese immigrant children* (Preliminary report, Monograph No. 5). New York: City University of New York, The City College, Department of Asian Studies.

Chao, T. (1996). Overview. In X. Wang (Ed.), *A view from within: A case study of Chinese heritage community language schools in the United States* (pp. 7–14). Washington, DC: National Foreign Language Center.

Chao, T., Chen, L., & Chang, E. (1996). Administration and management. In X. Wang (Ed.), *A view from within: A case study of Chinese heritage community language schools in the United States* (pp. 15–20). Washington, DC: National Foreign Language Center.

Chen, C. C. (1979). *An error analysis of English compositions written by Chinese college students in Taiwan.* Unpublished doctoral dissertation, University of Texas at Austin.

Chen, J. (1981). *The Chinese of America.* San Francisco: Harper & Row.

Cheung, Y. (1984). The uses of English and Chinese languages in Hong Kong. *Language Learning and Communication, 3,* 273–287.

Chin, F. (1976). Backtalk. In E. Gee (Ed.), *Counterpoint: Perspectives on Asian America* (pp. 556–557). Los Angeles: University of California, Los Angeles, Asian American Studies Center.

Chinese School Association in the United States. (1997). *Meiguo shequ zhongwen xuexiao diaozha tonggi ziliao* [Research and statistical data on community Chinese language schools in the United States]. Author.

Chuang, G. (1997). *A survey of Chinese school teachers in suburban New York.* Unpublished manuscript, New York University.

Dong, L., & Hom, M. (1980). Chinatown Chinese: The San Francisco dialect. *Amerasia Journal, 7,* 1.

Dzau, Y. F. (1990). How English is taught in tertiary educational institutions. In Y. F. Dzau (Ed.), *English in China* (pp. 41–58). Hong Kong: API Press.

Fan, C. Y. (1981). *The Chinese language school of San Francisco in relation to family integration and cultural identity.* Taipei, Republic of China: Academia Sinica, Institute of American Culture.

Farley, M. (1998a, March 9). Sound of English fades in Hong Kong. *Los Angeles Times,* pp. A1, A8.

Farley, M. (1998b, March 15). 14 schools win appeal to retain English. *Los Angeles Times,* p. A17.

Fishman, J. A. (1980). Ethnic community mother tongue schools in the U.S.A.: Dynamics and distributions. *International Migration Review, 14,* 235–247.

Fishman, J. A. (1985). The community resources of ethnic languages in the USA. In J. A. Fishman (Ed.), *The rise and fall of the ethnic revival: Perspectives on language and ethnicity* (pp. 195–282). Berlin: Mouton de Gruyter.

Fishman, J. A., & Markman, B. (1979). *The ethnic mother tongue school in the United States: Assumptions, findings and directory.* New York: Yeshiva University.

Flowerdew, J., Li, D., & Miller, L. (1998). Attitudes toward English and Cantonese among Hong Kong Chinese University lecturers. *TESOL Quarterly, 32,* 201–231.

Fong, T. (1994). *The first suburban Chinatown: The remaking of Monterey Park, California.* Philadelphia: Temple University Press.

Ford, D. J. (1988). *The twain shall meet: The current study of English in China.* Jefferson, NC: McFarland.

Gardner, R. W., Robey, B., & Smith, P. C. (1985). Asian Americans: Growth, change, and diversity. *Population Bulletin, 40,* 4.

Gargan, E. A. (1997, December 6). A new lesson for students: Use the mother tongue. *New York Times,* p. H4.

Gibbons, J. (1979). U-gay-wa: A linguistic study of the campus language of students at the University of Hong Kong. In R. Lord (Ed.), *Hong Kong language papers* (pp. 3–43). Hong Kong: Hong Kong University Press.

Gold, S. (1994). Chinese-Vietnamese Entrepreneurs in California. In P. Ong, E. Bonacich, & L. Cheng (Eds.), *The New Asian immigration in Los Angeles and global restructuring* (pp. 196–228). Philadelphia: Temple University Press.

Goto, S. (1997). Nerds, normal people, and homeboys: Accommodation and resistance among Chinese American students. *Anthropology and Education Quarterly, 28,* 70–84.

Guthrie, G. P. (1985). *A school divided: An ethnography of bilingual education in a Chinese community.* Hillsdale, NJ: Erlbaum.

Haiwai huaren jiaocai zhongwen zhongguowei xianhuo [Vivid Chinese flavor in Chinese teaching materials for overseas]. (1998, July 9). *World Journal,* p. B3.

Hing, B. O. (1993). *Making and remaking Asian America through immigration policy, 1850–1990.* Stanford, CA: Stanford University Press.

Ho, D. Y. F. (1979). English language skills and academic performance. In R. Lord (Ed.), *Hong Kong language papers* (pp. 44–61). Hong Kong: Hong Kong University Press.

Ho, W. (1973). An investigation of efforts in English composition of some preuniversity students in Singapore, with suggestions for the teaching of written English. *RELC Journal, 4,* 48–65.

Hou, Z. (1987). English teaching in China: Problems and perspectives. *TESOL Newsletter, 21*(3), 25–27.

Hsia, J. (1988). *Asian Americans in higher education and at work.* Hillsdale, NJ: Erlbaum.

Hu, Y. (1990). Teaching English in Chinese secondary schools. In Y. F. Dzau (Ed.), *English in China* (pp. 59–67). Hong Kong: API Press.

Hu, Z., Brown, D. F., & Brown, L. B. (1982). Some linguistic differences in the written English of Chinese and Australian students. *Language Learning and Communication, 1,* 39–49.

Huang, S. (1997a). *English curricula and language learning resources for non-English majors in universities in Taiwan.* Dept. of Foreign Languages and Literature, Tunghai University, Taiwan.

Huang, S. (1997b). *The ESP component in English programs for non-English majors at universities in Taiwan.* Paper presented at the 14th TEFL Conference in R.O.C., National Taiwan Normal University, Taipei, Taiwan.

Hwang, D. H. (1983). FOB. In *Broken promises: Four plays* (pp. 1–57). New York: Avon Books.

Johns, A. M. (1984). Textual cohesion and the Chinese speaker of English. *Language Learning and Communication, 3,* 69–74.

Johnson, D. (1977, February 3). Review of *The woman warrior. New York review of books,* pp. 19–20, 29.

Johnson, R. K. (1983). Bilingual switching strategies: A study of the modes of teachertalk in bilingual secondary school classrooms in Hong Kong. *Language Learning and Communication, 2,* 267–285.

Jung, R. K. (1972). The Chinese language school in the U.S. *School and Society, 100,* 309–312.

Kan, S. H., & Liu, W. T. (1986). The educational status of Asian Americans: An update from the 1980 census. *Pacific Asian American Mental Health Research Center Research Review, 5,* 21–24.

Kaplan, R. B. (1966). Cultural thought patterns in intercultural education. *Language Learning, 16,* 1–20.

Kaplan, R. B. (1968). Contrastive grammar: Teaching composition to the Chinese student. *Journal of ESL, 3,* 1–13.

Kaplan, R. B. (1976). A further note on contrastive rhetoric. *Communication Quarterly, 24,* 12–19.

Kaplan, R. B. (1986). Culture and the written language. In J. M. Valdes (Ed.), *Culture bound: Bridging the cultural gap in language teaching* (pp. 8–19). Cambridge: Cambridge University Press.

Kaplan, R. B., & Tse, J. K. (1982). The language situation in Taiwan (the Republic of China). *The Linguistic Reporter, 25*(2), 1–5.

Kim, Elaine H. (1979). Asian American students and college English. *Education and Urban Society, 10,* 321–326.

Kim, E. (1982). *Asian American literature: An introduction to the writings and their social context.* Philadelphia: Temple University Press.

King, H., & Locke, F. B. (1980). Chinese in the U.S.: A century of occupational transition. *International Migration Review, 14,* 15–41.

Kingston, M. H. (1976). *The woman warrior: Memoirs of a girlhood among ghosts.* New York: Knopf.

Kleinmann, H. H. (1982). External influences and their neutralization in second language acquisition: A look at adult Indochinese refugees. *TESOL Quarterly, 16,* 239–244.

Kuo, E. C. Y. (1974). Bilingual pattern of a Chinese immigrant group in the United States. *Anthropological Linguistics, 16,* 128–140.

Kwong, P. (1987). *The new Chinatown.* New York: Hill & Wang.

Kwong, P. (1997). *Forbidden workers: Illegal Chinese immigrants and American labor.* New York: New Press.

Lai, H. M. (1987). The Chinese-American press. In S. M. Miller (Ed.), *The ethnic press in the U.S.* (pp. 27–44). New York: Greenwood Press.

Lai, H. M., Huang, J., & Wong, D. (1980). *The Chinese of America: 1785–1980.* San Francisco: Chinese Culture Foundation.

Lai, H. M., Lim, G., & Yung, J. (1980). *Island: Poetry and history of Chinese immigrants on Angel Island, 1910–1940.* San Francisco: HOC DOI Project.

Lay, N. D. S. (1975). Chinese language interference in written English. *Journal of Basic Writing, 1,* 50–61.

Lee, L. (1996). The College Board SAT II: Chinese subject test with listening. *CLASS Journal* (Chinese Language Association of Secondary-Elementary Schools), *2,* 23.

Lee, M. (1976/1997). Some common grammatical errors made in written English by Chinese students. *CATESOL Occasional Papers, 3,* 115–119.

Lee, R. H. (1960). *The Chinese in the United States of America.* Hong Kong: Hong Kong University Press.

Lee, S. J. (1994). Behind the model-minority stereotype: Voice of high- and low-achieving Asian American students. *Anthropology and Education Quarterly, 25*, 412–429.

Leong, J. (1972). Hong Kong immigrants and the public schools. Asian American Review. Berkeley: University of California, Asian American Studies Program.

Leung, E. C. (1975). *A sociological study of the Chinese language schools in the San Francisco Bay area.* Unpublished doctoral dissertation, University of Missouri, Columbia.

Li, C. N., & Thompson, S. A. (1981). *Mandarin Chinese: A functional reference grammar.* Berkeley: University of California Press.

Li, W. L. (1982). The language shift of Chinese-Americans. *International Journal of the Sociology of Language, 38*, 109–124.

Lin, J. (1987, April). Diary of a teacher of "little foreign students" [In Chinese]. *Jiushi Niandai.*

Lin, Y. J. (1986). *Survey of Chinese language schools.* Unpublished manuscript.

Lincoln, M. W. (1976, July). I'm very sorry, but I don't know Charlie Chan. *Bridge, 48.*

Liu, P. C. (1976). [In Chinese] *A history of the Chinese in the United States of America.* Taipei: Liming.

López, D. E. (1982). *Language maintenance and shift in the United States today: The basic patterns and their social implications: Vol. 4. Asian languages.* Los Alamitos, CA: National Center for Bilingual Research.

Louie, E. W. (1998). *Chinese American names: Tradition and transition.* Jefferson, NC: McFarland.

Low, V. (1982). *The unimpressible race: A century of educational struggle by the Chinese in San Francisco.* San Francisco: East/West.

Lyman, S. M. (1974). *Chinese Americans.* New York: Random House.

McKay, S. L., & Wong, S. C. (1996). Multiple discourses, multiple identities: Investment and agency in second language learning among Chinese adolescent immigrant students. *Harvard Educational Review, 3*, 577–608.

Mohan, B., and Lo, W. A. (1985). Academic writing and Chinese students: Transfer and development factors. *TESOL Quarterly, 19*, 515–543.

National Council of Associations of Chinese Language Schools. (1996). *Quanmei zhongwen xuexiao ziliao diaozha jianbao.* (1996). [Brief report on research data on Chinese language schools in the United States]: Author.

Nee, V. G., & Nee, B. D. (1972). *Longtime Californ': A Documentary study of an American Chinatown.* New York: Pantheon Books.

Ng, F. (1998). *The Taiwanese Americans.* Westport, CT: Greenwood Press.

Osajima, K. (1988). Asian Americans as the model minority: An analysis of the popular press image in the 1960s and 1980s. In G. Y. Okihiro, S. Hune, A. A. Hansen, & J. M. Liu (Eds.), *Reflections on shattered windows: Promises and prospects for Asian American studies* (pp. 165–174). Pullman: Washington State University Press.

Overseas Chinese Affairs Commission. (1982). *Fifty years of overseas Chinese affairs* [in Chinese]: Author.

Pan, S. (1997). Chinese in New York. In O. García & J. Fishman (Eds.), *The multilingual apple: Languages in New York City* (pp. 231–255). New York: Mouton de Gruyter.

Rutherford, W. E. (1983). Language typology and language transfer. In S. Gass & L. Selinker (Eds.), *Language transfer in language learning* (pp. 358–370). Rowley, MA: Newbury House.

Schachter, J., & Rutherford, W. E. (1979). Discourse function and language transfer. *Working Papers in Bilingualism, 19,* 3–12.

Scovel, J. (1983). English teaching in China: A historical perspective. *Language Learning and Communication, 2,* 105–109.

Shinagawa, L. H. (1996). The impact of immigration on the demography of Asian Pacific Americans. In B. O. Hing and R. Lee (Eds.), *The state of Asian Pacific America: A public policy report: Reframing the immigration debate* (pp. 59–130). Los Angeles: LEAP Asian Pacific American Public Policy Institute and UCLA Asian American Studies Center.

Siu, S. (1992). *Toward an understanding of Chinese-American educational achievement: A literature review.* Baltimore: Center on Families, Communities, Schools and Children's Learning.

Su, I.-H. (1998). *Current educational reform: Country profile: Taiwan, Republic of China.* Unpublished manuscript.

Sung, B. L. (1979). *Transplanted Chinese children.* New York: City College of New York.

Sung, B. L. (1987). *The adjustment experience of Chinese immigrant children in New York City.* New York: Center for Migration Studies.

To, C. Y. (1979). *The educational and psychological adjustment problems of Asian immigrant youth and how bilingual-bicultural education can help.* Paper presented at the National Association of Asian and Pacific American Education Conference.

Tom, K. (1941). Functions of the Chinese language schools. *Sociology and Social Research, 25,* 557–561.

Tong, B. R. (1971). The ghetto of the mind: Notes on the historical psychology of Chinese America. *Amerasia Journal, 1,* 1–31.

Tong, B. R. (1977, May 11). Critic of admirer sees dumb racist. *The San Francisco Journal,* p. 6.

Tsai, S. H. (1986). *The Chinese experience in America.* Bloomington: Indiana University Press.

Tsang, S., & Wing, L. C. (1985). *Beyond Angel Island: The education of Asian Americans.* New York: Clearinghouse on Urban Education.

Tse, J. K. (1982). Language policy in the Republic of China. In R. B. Kaplan (Ed.), *Annual review of applied linguistics* (pp. 33–47). Rowley, MA: Newbury House.

T'sou, B. K. (1973). Asymmetric bilingualism: A sociolinguistic study of Cantonese emigrants. *Journal of the Chinese Language Teachers Association, 8,* 134–144.

U.S. Bureau of the Census. (1983). Chapter D: Detailed population characteristics. In *1980 Census of population: Vol. 1. Characteristics of the population.* Washington, DC: U.S. Government Printing Office.

U.S. Bureau of the Census. (1992). *1990 census of population – Social and economic characteristics: United States.* Washington, DC: U.S. Government Printing Office.

U.S. Bureau of the Census. (1993a). *1990 census of population – Asians and Pacific Islanders in the United States.* Washington, DC: U.S. Government Printing Office.

U.S. Bureau of the Census. (1993b). *1990 census of population – The foreign-born population in the United States.* Washington, DC: U.S. Government Printing Office.

U.S. Immigration and Naturalization Service. (1981). Immigrants admitted by country or region of birth, fiscal years 1972–1981. In *1981 Statistical yearbook of the Immigration and Naturalization Service* (pp. 34–37). Washington, DC: U.S. Government Printing Office.

Van den Berg, M. E. (1986). Language planning and language use in Taiwan: Social identity, language accommodation, and language choice behavior. International *Journal of the Sociology of Language, 59,* 97–115.

Veltman, C. (1983). *Language shift in the United States.* Berlin: Mouton de Gruyter.

Wang, L. C. (1972). *The Chinese-American student in San Francisco.* In *Chinese Americans: School and community problems.* Chicago: Integrated Education Associates.

Wang, L. C. (1995). Integration or separation in a shrinking world: Overseas Chinese education policies and strategies in the Post–Cold War era. In *Proceedings on Chinese Education in Southeast Asia.* (pp. 351–372). National Pingtung Teachers College.

Wang, X. (1996). *A view from within: A case study of Chinese heritage community language schools in the United States.* Washington, DC: National Foreign Language Center.

Wang, Z. (1982). English teaching and English studies in China. *Language Learning and Communication 1,* 5–20.

Wong, A. (1980, October). *Chinese bilingual education: Current status and issues.* Paper presented at the National Conference on Chinese American Studies, San Francisco.

Wong, B. (1998). *Ethnicity and entrepreneurship: The new Chinese immigrants in the San Francisco Bay Area.* Boston: Allyn & Bacon.

Wong, J. (1996, January 16). Speech to The Employers' Federation in Hong Kong on "Enhancing Language Proficiency," http://www.info.gov.hk/emb/general/speeches.htm.

Wong, M. (1995). Chinese Americans. In P. G. Min (Ed.), *Asian Americans: Contemporary trends and issues* (pp. 58–94). Newbury Park, CA: Sage.

Wong, S. C. (1987). The language needs of school-age Asian immigrants and refugees in the United States. In W. A. Van Horne & T. V. Tonnesen (Eds.), *Ethnicity and Language* (pp. 124–159). Milwaukee, WI: University of Wisconsin System Institute on Race and Ethnicity.

Wong, S. C. (1988a). The language learn situation of Asian immigrant students in the U.S.: A socio- and psycholinguistic perspective. *NABE Journal, 11,* 203–234.

Wong, S. C. (1988b). The language situation of Chinese Americans. In S. L. McKay & S. C. Wong (Eds.), *Language diversity: Problem or resources? A social and educational perspective on language minorities in the United States* (pp. 193–228). Cambridge, MA: Newbury House.

Wong, S. C. (1997). Chinese American literature. In King-Kok Cheung (Ed.), *An interethnic companion to Asian American Literature* (pp. 39–61). Cambridge: Cambridge University Press.

Wong, S. C., & López, M. G. (1995). *California's Chinese immigrant students in the 1990s*. San Francisco: Zellerbach Family Fund and New Faces of Liberty.

Young, L. W. (1982). Inscrutability revisited. In J. J. Gumperz (Ed.), *Language and social identity* (pp. 72–84). Cambridge: Cambridge University Press.

Yuan, J. (1987, April). Taiwan's "little foreign students" in the U.S. [in Chinese] *Jiushi Niandai*, 84–85.

Yung, J. (1986). *Chinese women of America: A pictorial history*. Seattle: University of Washington Press.

Zhou, M. (1992). *Chinatown: The socioeconomic potential of an urban enclave*. Philadelphia: Temple University Press.

10 Korean Americans' language use

Pyong Gap Min

Korean Americans, numbering approximately 1.2 million in 1997, consist largely of post-1965 immigrants. In 1990, they were the fifth largest Asian American group, after Chinese, Filipino, Indian, and Japanese Americans. The number of Korean immigrants has gradually decreased annually since 1988 whereas immigration from other Asian countries – China, the Philippines, India, and Vietnam – has increased. Consequently, as of 1997 Korean Americans were outnumbered even by Vietnamese Americans, becoming the smallest among the six major Asian ethnic groups. However, Korean Americans have attracted a great deal of media and scholarly attention – probably more than any other Asian group – because of their unique cultural and religious characteristics and mode of economic adjustment. Since many Confucian customs and values have been weakened in China by a half-century of Communist rule and since not many Japanese have immigrated in the post-1965 era, Koreans are the only major Asian immigrant group with a strong Confucian cultural tradition. They also compose the only Asian immigrant group with a heavy Protestant background. A combination of Confucian traditionalism and Protestant modernism, of Oriental and Western cultures, makes their lifestyles interesting to the American public. Moreover, Korean immigrants' concentration in small businesses and many Korean merchants' intermediary economic role (connecting corporations run by European Americans to minority customers) have intensified their intergroup conflicts and thereby ethnic solidarity. The 1990 Brooklyn boycott of two Korean stores, the victimization of many Korean merchants during the 1992 Los Angeles riots, and the Koreans' reactive solidarity have attracted national and international media attention.

For several reasons, Korean immigrants are culturally and socially insulated from other groups and the larger U.S. society. Whether settled in a Korean enclave or in a predominantly White, middle-class neighborhood, most Korean immigrants are involved in strong ethnic networks. They speak the Korean language and practice Korean customs most of the time outside as well as inside the home. However, second-generation and U.S.-1.5-generation, educated Korean Americans[1] show a high lev-

---

1 The term *1.5 generation* has been widely used by social scientists to refer to people who were born in a foreign country but who immigrated as preadolescents or adolescents.

el of cultural assimilation. And their coming of age is gradually changing the structure of the Korean community.

Immigration history

The old immigration

The approximately 7,200 Koreans who moved to Hawaii to work on
sugar cane plantations between 1903 and 1905 constituted the first
wave of Korean immigrants in the United States (Choy, 1979; Patterson, 1987). The Hawaiian plantation owners' need for cheap, non-
White laborers was the pull factor for the immigration of Koreans in the
beginning of the twentieth century, whereas economic difficulty in Korea caused by droughts, floods, and the ensuing famines was the push
factor. Despite these factors, the immigration of Koreans to Hawaii at
the turn of the century might have been impossible without the important intermediary role played by Horace Allen, then the U.S. government's delegate to Korea. Ninety percent of the 1903–1905 Korean immigrants to Hawaii were unmarried young males, with children
constituting only a small proportion. Approximately 40% of the pioneer immigrants had converted to Christianity in Korea, and the majority attended Christian churches in Hawaii. Many Korean Christians decided to emigrate to Hawaii for religious freedom as well as for a better
economic life.

Early Korean immigration to Hawaii came to a sudden end in the
summer of 1905, shortly after the Korean Foreign Ministry instructed
the mayors of the port cities to stop issuing passports. Pressure from the
Japanese government, which felt that an end to Korean emigration
would protect Japanese workers in the Hawaiian islands from competition (Patterson, 1987, Chap. 13), to halt Korean emigration to Hawaii
played a major role in the government's decision. In 1905, Korea became Japan's protectorate as a result of Japanese victory in the Russo-
Japanese War, putting Japan in a position to strongly influence Korea.

Approximately 2,000 additional Korean immigrants came to Hawaii
and California before the Asiatic Exclusion in 1924 completely banned
Asian immigration. The Korean immigrants admitted to the United
States during this period can be grouped into two categories: "picture
brides" from Korea invited by pioneer bachelor immigrants via the exchange of pictures and political refugees or students. After Japan an-
nexed Korea in 1910, many Korean intellectuals and politicians engaged in anti-Japanese agitations. Under surveillance by the Japanese
police, many anti-Japanese Korean patriots, most helped by American
missionaries, moved to the United States via Shanghai. These people

constituted the core of Korean community organizations in Hawaii and California, directing activities to promote Korean independence and the anti-Japanese movement.

The intermediate period

Korean immigration to the United States steadily increased between 1950 and 1964. The McCarran-Walter Act of 1952 allowed an annual quota of one hundred immigrants from each of the Pacific and Asian countries. This moderation of the exclusion partly contributed to the increase in Korean immigration in the 1950s, but a more important factor was the close U.S.-Korean relationship associated with the Korean War. The Korean wives of U.S. servicemen constituted the largest category of Korean immigrants during this period. During and after the Korean War, a large number of U.S. soldiers stayed in South Korea, and many married Korean women and brought them to the United States. Korean children adopted by U.S. citizens constituted another major category of Korean immigrants admitted to the United States between 1950 and 1964. During and after the Korean War, many U.S. servicemen stationed in Korea brought home Korean war orphans as their adopted children. Later, U.S. nonmilitary citizens began to adopt Korean orphans. Finally, Korean students who came to the United States to study and later changed their status to permanent residence were the third major category of immigrants in the intermediate period.

The new immigration

The Hart-Celler Act of 1965 abolished discrimination in immigration quotas based on national origin. More important for the immigration of Asians, the new immigration law abolished the Asian Exclusion, which had been in effect since 1924. This liberal immigration law led to a drastic shift in the major source countries of immigrants from European to non-European and has significantly affected Korean as well as other Asian immigration. As shown in Table 1, Korean immigrants numbered less than 2,000 annually in the early 1960s but gradually increased in the late 1960s and the early 1970s, reaching nearly 30,000 in the latter half of the 1970s and maintaining an annual flow of more than 30,000 in the 1980s. Korea was the third largest source country of U.S. immigrants in the 1980s, following Mexico and the Philippines.

Even though Koreans were greatly undercounted in the 1970 census (69,130),[2] the Korean population in 1970 still did not reach the

2 According to Yu (1977), the gross underestimation was due to "sampling biases, misclassification, and the systematic omission of certain persons of Korean origin (p. 122)."

308

TABLE 1. KOREAN IMMIGRANTS, 1965–1994

Period	Total	Average per year
1960–1964	9,521	1,904
1965–1969	17,869	3,374
1970–1974	93,445	18,689
1975–1979	148,645	29,729
1980–1984	162,178	32,436
1985–1989	175,803	35,161
1990–1994	145,843	29,169

Sources: U.S. Immigration and Naturalization Service, *Annual Report* (1965–1978); *Statistical Yearbook* (1979–1994).

100,000 mark. However, as shown in Table 1, nearly 700,000 Koreans immigrated between 1970 and 1995. The Korean American community consequently witnessed a radical growth. The 1990 census estimated the Korean population to be close to 800,000. The Korean American population as of 1997 was likely to be over 1.2 million, constituting 20% of over 5.2 million overseas Koreans. The 1990 census showed that the native born made up only 27% of Korean Americans, but as of 1997 American-born Koreans may have accounted for over 30% of the Korean American population.

The lack of economic opportunity, social and political insecurity, and the difficulty of sending children to higher education institutions pushed many Koreans to immigrate to the United States in the 1970s and the early 1980s. However, economic, political, and social conditions in Korea have improved substantially since the late 1980s. First, South Korea's economy had improved greatly before the economic crisis of 1997. Also, South Korea held a popular presidential election at the end of 1987, putting an end to the 16-year-old military dictatorship and reducing social and political insecurity. In the 1992 election, Kim Young-Sam was elected the first civilian president since Rhee Syngman was ousted by a student uprising in 1960. In the 1997 election, Koreans chose as president Kim Dae-Joong, the long-time opposition party leader, recording a peaceful transfer of power for the first time in Korean history.

These significant improvements on the one hand and the increasing publicity about Korean immigrants' adjustment difficulties in the United States on the other have mitigated the influx of Korean immigrants since the late 1980s. The annual number of Korean immigrants has gradually decreased since 1988, falling to below 30,000 in the first half of the 1990s. In contrast, the numbers of Filipino, Chinese, Indian, and

Vietnamese immigrants have increased greatly since the late 1980s. The reverse trends in Korean and other Asian immigration patterns are likely to continue until the current immigration law is revised, meaning that Koreans will make up an increasingly smaller proportion of the Asian American population in the future. As the annual number of Korean immigrants has gradually decreased, the proportion of native-born Korean Americans has increased substantially. Major Korean communities are gradually experiencing generational transitions as descendants of post-1965 immigrants are reaching adulthood.

In 1997, several Asian countries, including South Korea, underwent a major economic crisis. In South Korea the crisis resulted from a short-term deficit of foreign exchange reserves, which in turn was caused by long-term structural problems inherent in South Korea's "high cost, low efficiency economy" (Ahn, 1998, p. 2). The failure of Kim Young-Sam's government to manage the currency crisis helped the opposition party leader get elected president in December 1997. With "promoting democracy and market economy simultaneously" as his catchphrase, President Kim Dae-Joong restructured the Korean economy following the dictates of the International Monetary Fund to restore Korea's confidence and competitiveness. The restructuring temporarily resulted in closure of many companies, which had led nearly two million workers to lose their jobs as of July 1998. The economic crisis may push more Koreans to immigrate to the United States and discourage Korean immigrants from returning to Korea permanently.[3] The economic problems in South Korea have also had negative effects on Korean immigrant businesses that serve mainly tourists from Korea, as the number of Korean tourists to the United States was drastically reduced.

Korean immigrants' backgrounds

Historical and cultural background

Koreans share physical as well as cultural characteristics with the Chinese and Japanese. China has had a great cultural influence on Korea, particularly through Confucianism, whose powerful influence on Korea began during the Chosun dynasty (1391–1910), when the government adopted it as the familial and political philosphy (Pak, 1983; Park & Cho 1995). Today, Confucianism is important in Korea not as a formal religion but as a code of ethics and values that regulate people's social and familial relations. Five categories of interpersonal relations form

3 Beginning the late 1980s, a large number of Korean immigrants returned to Korea for good as an advanced Korean economy absorbed U.S.-educated or -trained professionals and managers.

the basis of Confucius's teachings concerning the duties and obligations of each individual: between king and people, parents and children, husband and wife, older (brother) and younger (brother), and friends. For the benefit of social harmony, Confucius envisioned a hierarchical society in which people would be subordinate to the king, children to parents, wife to husband, and younger (brother) to older (brother).

Historically, Korea influenced Japan culturally during Japan's several invasions of Korea. Most recently, between 1910 and 1945 Korea was under Japan's colonial rule, and as a result there are still strong anti-Japanese sentiments in Korea. As soon as Korea became liberated from Japan's colonial rule in 1945, Korea was divided into two halves by both internal political conflicts and U.S.-Soviet ideological conflicts. South Korea has been under the strong influence of the United States whereas North Korea maintained close political and military ties with the former Soviet Union and China until recently. The division of Korea led to a civil war, known as the Korean War, in 1950, in which the United States and other anti-Communist allies supported South Korea and the former Soviet Union and China supported North Korea. Although the Korean War ended in 1953, Korea has been permanently divided into two opposing political and economic systems, with millions of family members separated by the boundary between North and South. The Cold War period ended with the reunification of Germany in 1990 and the dissolution of the former Soviet Union in 1991, yet Koreans still suffer national division, a legacy of the Cold War.

The United States began to influence Korea culturally at the end of the nineteenth century, when American Protestant missionaries established Christian schools and modern hospitals there. However, it was during the Korean War that the United States came to maintain close political, military, and economic ties with South Korea. The United States sent over half a million soldiers to South Korea during the Korean War. It has maintained sizable military forces – approximately 45,000 – in South Korea, many of whom have brought Korean wives to the United States. The presence of U.S. servicemen and of a U.S television station (AFKN) in Korea also has exerted a strong American cultural influence. This cultural influence, in turn, encouraged many Koreans to immigrate to the United States when U.S. immigration law was relaxed in 1965.

Religious background

Several religions have coexisted in modern Korea without significant conflicts. In 1991, *A National Survey on Korean Religion* (National Statistical Office, 1991, p. 300) showed that Buddhism was the largest religion in Korea, with 29% of the population affiliated with it, and that two Christian religions, Protestantism and Catholicism, are the second (19%) and third (6%) largest religions, respectively. Christians, though outnumbered by Buddhists, are more active in social, political, and educational activities and services. In addition, Christian religions are over-represented among urban middle-class people, whereas Buddhism is strong in rural areas.

Korean immigrants have been overwhelmingly from the Christian population in Korea. Although Christians make up only 25% of the population, more than 50% of Korean immigrants were affiliated with Protestant or Catholic churches in Korea prior to immigration (Hurh & Kim, 1990; Park, Fawcett, Arnold, & Gardner, 1990, p. 60). A Chicago survey, for example, indicated that 40% of Korean immigrants had been Protestants in Korea and that another 14% were Catholics (Hurh & Kim, 1990). This heavily Protestant background clearly separates Korean immigrants from other Asian immigrant groups.

Christians are overrepresented among Korean immigrants for three reasons. First, Korean immigrants have been largely drawn from the urban, middle-class people, among whom the Christian religions are strong. For example, in a predeparture survey of the 1986 cohort of Korean immigrants conducted in Seoul, 59% of the respondents stated that they lived in Seoul, and 71%, that they lived in the four largest metropolitan cities in South Korea (Park et al., 1990, pp. 31–32). Second, North Korean refugees in South Korea, among whom Christians are overrepresented, have immigrated to the United States in a greater proportion than the general population in South Korea has (Kim, 1981; Yu, 1982). Initially, Christianity was stronger in the northern part of Korea, where the Confucian cultural tradition was relatively weak. However, many Korean Christians in North Korea fled to South Korea before and during the Korean War. North Korean refugees, who do not have strong kinship or regionalties in South Korea, emigrated to the United States more easily than other Koreans. Third, Korean Christians, who are more Westernized than other Koreans, are more likely to choose immigration to the United States than Korean Buddhists, Confucians, or those not affiliated with a religion.

Socioeconomic background

Post-1965 Korean immigrants, like other Asian immigrants, have come largely from the urban, middle-class segment of the population. The 1990 census showed that 34% of Korean immigrants 25 years old and over had completed 4 years of college education and that 80% had completed high school (U.S. Bureau of the Census, 1993a, p. 84). In contrast, 20% of the U.S. population had received a college education, and 75% had completed high school (p. 72). In general, the population in Korea has a much lower educational level than the U.S. population does. In 1990, only 14% of Koreans 25 years old and over had received 4 years of college or higher education, and 34% had completed high school (Yang, Kwon, & Hwang, 1997, p. 88).

Consistent with their high levels of education, an overwhelming majority of Korean immigrants held white-collar jobs in Korea, and a large proportion held professional and managerial jobs. For example, a 1986 survey of Korean immigrants in Los Angeles and Orange counties indicated that 54% of the respondents who had been working in Korea at the time of immigration had held jobs classifiable as professional, managerial, or administrative and that only 4% had been employed in blue-collar occupations (Min, 1989, p. 53). Korean professional immigrants include a significant proportion of medical professionals. The same survey also indicated that about one fourth of male immigrants were proprietors in Korea.

The significant improvements in economic, social, and political conditions in South Korea that have mitigated the influx of Korean immigrants since the late 1980s have also contributed to changes in Korean immigrants' socioeconomic status. The Korean immigrants admitted to the United States since the late 1980s represent a lower socioeconomic background than those admitted before, as middle-class Koreans have not been attracted to U.S. emigration recently. Earlier, the vast majority of Koreans who came to the United States for further study changed their status to permanent residence either before or after they completed their graduate education. Recently, more and more Koreans go back to Korea after finishing their education, as the highly industrialized Korean society absorbs American-educated professionals. Major private companies and government research institutes have recently hired a large number of American-educated technocrats in the fields of science, engineering, computer science, and business.

Settlement patterns

Koreans who immigrated before 1965 were heavily concentrated in the West Coast states, particularly in traditional Asian enclaves such as Honolulu, San Francisco, and Los Angeles. However, post-1965 Korean immigrants have been more widely scattered throughout the United States. Approximately 33% of Korean Americans resided in California in 1990 (U.S. Bureau of the Census, 1993b, Table 276). Nevertheless, their level of concentration in this traditionally Asian American state was much lower than that of other Asian groups. In 1990, 39% of Asian Americans resided in the West, including 50% of Filipino Americans and 52% of Japanese Americans. About 70% of Koreans in California were concentrated in Los Angeles and Orange counties. As of 1997, the Los Angeles metropolitan area, including the two counties, was home to approximately 250,000 Koreans, the second largest overseas Korean center next to the Yanbian Korean Autonomous Prefecture in China, with 800,000 Koreans.

The presence of Koreans in Los Angeles is more clearly discernible in Koreatown, located 3 miles west of downtown Los Angeles. Koreatown, which covers approximately 25 square miles, is the residential and commercial center for Los Angeles Koreans (Min, 1993a; Yu, 1985). Approximately 35,000 Koreans, one third of the Koreans in the City of Los Angeles, live there, although Mexican immigrants and illegals compose the majority of the residents in Koreatown. The Korean residents of Koreatown consist mainly of new immigrants, elderly Koreans with severe language barriers, and many illegals who find employment in Korean-owned stores. In the approximately 3,500 Korean-owned businesses with Korean language signs located in Koreatown, coethnics find Korean food, groceries, books and magazines, and other services with distinctive cultural tastes. As the social and cultural center for Los Angeles Koreans, Koreatown is home to the Los Angeles Korean Association, several Korean business associations, dozens of Korean social service agencies, and other Korean social and cultural organizations. Korean ethnic organizations hold meetings at Korean restaurants and offices in Koreatown at night, and Koreans from all over the Los Angeles–Orange Country area go there to eat traditional Korean food and celebrate important family affairs at Korean restaurants. Several Korean motels located in Koreatown accommodate many Korean tourists from Korea and other parts of the United States.

In 1990, 12.0% of all Korean Americans lived in New York State, a significant increase from 9.6% in 1980 (U.S. Bureau of the Census, 1983, Table 63; 1993a, Table 276). Between 1980 and 1990, its neighboring state, New Jersey (along with Orange County, California), experienced the highest growth (200%) in Korean population in the United States. As of 1997, over 150,000 Koreans lived in the New York–New Jersey metropolitan area, which has emerged as the second largest Korean center, next to the Los Angeles–Orange Country area. This northeastern area is attractive to other Asian immigrant groups as well; it is the largest population center for Chinese and Asian Indians (see Min, 1995a, Chapter 2). After Chinese and Indian groups Korean Americans are the third largest Asian group in New York.

Approximately 70% of the 100,000 Koreans in New York City are concentrated in several areas of Queens, particularly in Flushing, Elmhurst, Woodside, Bayside, and Little Neck. Koreans in New York have created another Koreatown in downtown Flushing. Although the

Flushing Koreatown is much smaller than the one in Los Angeles, it possesses many characteristics of a typical ethnic ghetto. First, it is the area of Korean immigrants' residential concentration, as about one fourth of the Koreans in New York City and more than three fourths of the Koreans in Queens live in Flushing. They are heavily concentrated within a dozen blocks with their core at the intersection of Roosevelt Avenue and Union Street. Second, it is a commercial center: Several hundred Korean stores bearing signs in Korean are located along the Union Street *Hanin Sangga* (Korean Business District) between Roosevelt Avenue and Northern Boulevard. Flushing is also Koreans' social and cultural center, home to two dozens of Korean social service agencies, including the Flushing Korean Association, the Korean YMCA and YWCA, and the Korean Senior Citizens Society.

In addition to Los Angeles and New York, such metropolitan areas as San Francisco, Chicago, Washington, Philadelphia, Atlanta, and Honolulu have sizable Korean populations. Koreans in these cities have established a residential and commercial center similar to Koreatown in Los Angeles and New York. However, most Korean immigrants consider a Korean enclave, which has a high crime rate and poor schools, at best a temporary home. Having lived in Koreatown long enough to acculturate, many Korean immigrants move to the suburbs (Min, 1993a). The radical Korean population growth in New Jersey and Orange County was caused mainly by the suburbanization of Korean immigrants originally settled in the City of Los Angeles and in New York City. Korean immigrants with school-age children are anxious to move to White, middle-class suburban neighborhoods particularly because of the educational benefits.

Korean immigrants' economic adjustments

Economic niches in small businesses

Probably the most interesting aspect of Korean immigrants' adjustments in the United States is their occupational concentration in small businesses. Census data from 1990 indicate that 35% of foreign-born Koreans 25–64 years old in the Los Angeles metropolitan area were self-employed (Light & Roach, 1996, p. 199), and Korean immigrants showed the highest rate of self-employment among all minority and immigrant groups in Los Angeles. The same data reveal that 30% of foreign-born Koreans in New York were self-employed. Public documents, based on respondents' self-reports, underestimate the self-employment rate of the general population and seem to underestimate that of Korean immigrants to a greater extent than they do that of the general population.[4] Independent survey studies conducted in Los Angeles and New York indicate that the self-employment rate of Korean immigrants is substantially higher than census documents suggest. For example, a survey of Korean married women in New York City conducted in 1988 showed that 49% of the respondents and 61% of their husbands were self-employed (Min, 1996, p. 48). The same survey showed that approximately 30% of the Korean workers in New York City found employment in Korean-owned businesses, with only 14% employed in the general labor market.

All major Korean communities contain a great concentration of four types of small businesses: grocery and liquor retail stores, stores selling items imported from Asia (such as handbags, clothing, jewelry, and wigs), dry cleaning establishments, and garment subcontractors (Min, 1996, p. 54). Nationally, Korean immigrants own large numbers of small grocery stores and dry cleaning shops. These two groups established national organizations in the late 1980s and have coordinated their commercial activities to protect their common interests (Min, 1996, pp. 57–59). In addition, Koreans in Los Angeles have developed maintenance service, construction, and fast-food franchises, and produce retailing, fish retailing, and nail care are major Korean businesses in the Korean community in New York. Nearly 2,000 Korean-owned produce stores are located throughout the New York metropolitan area, symbolizing Korean immigrants' commercial activities in the city.

Situational, social, and cultural sources of Korean small businesses

Korean immigrants choose to start small businesses mainly because language barriers and lack of job information put them at a disadvantage for employment in the general labor market (Min, 1984). As I discuss in more detail in the following section, Korean immigrants with a college degree have more language barriers than other college-educated Asian immigrants. Many college-educated Korean immigrants have been unable to find professional occupations commensurate with their high educational levels and have started small businesses as an alternative to blue-collar employment.

Korean immigrants' ethnic networks and their middle-class back-

---

4 Many new Korean immigrants work as peddlers, and some may do so without a business license. Some Korean immigrants have two jobs, one in their own small business and the other working for someone else, and many may report only their work for other to the census. Most important, Korean husbands and wives often work in the same family business, but only the husband reports himself as self-employed to the Internal Revenue Service and the Bureau of the Census.

ground help them establish and operate their small businesses (Light & Bonacich, 1988; Min, 1988b; Yoon, 1991). Active ethnic networks, particularly through their affiliation with ethnic churches, help Korean immigrants with small businesses by means of private loans, business information and training, and access to cheap and loyal labor sources. Furthermore, Korean immigrants' class background is helpful to their commercial activities. A large proportion of Korean immigrant business owners operated businesses or held managerial occupations in Korea, which facilitates their business activities in the United States (Min, 1986–1987; Yoon, 1997, pp. 124–125). Many Korean immigrants, particularly recent immigrants, have brought a large amount of money with them to use as business capital.

Lacking business capital, training, and information, the Korean immigrants in the early 1970s took several years to establish their own businesses. In contrast, recent Korean immigrants have been better prepared, since they know before they leave Korea that self-employment is the only option for most of them and usually expect to run small businesses in the United States.[5] Once they arrive, Korean immigrants easily acquire business information and training through employment in Korean-owned businesses.

Koreans' intermediary role and intergroup conflicts

Korean merchants serve four groups of customers: Korean, White, Black, and Hispanic, yet they depend upon minority customers to a greater extent than might be expected. For example, Korean merchants own the majority of liquor, grocery, produce, and fashion retail stores in most Black neighborhoods in South Central Los Angeles; Brooklyn, New York; and South Atlanta (Min, 1988a, p. 69; 1996, Chapter 4). Korean merchants depend upon White wholesalers and manufacturers for the supply of many of the retail items they sell to minority customers – grocery, liquor, and produce in particular. In this sense, they play a typical intermediary role, connecting White corporations and low-income, Black and Hispanic customers (Min, 1990, 1996; Min & Kolodny, 1994).

Historically, intermediary merchants specializing in retail businesses in minority neighborhoods have met with hostility and rejection from minority customers in the forms of boycotts, arson, and riots (Bonacich, 1973; Zenner, 1991). Korean merchants in Black neighborhoods in New York, Los Angeles, and other major cities have been no exception. The 1990–1991 Black boycott of two Korean stores in Brooklyn, New

5 For example, in one predeparture survey conducted in Seoul in 1986, 61% of all respondents and 71% of male respondents reported that they would go into business when they came to the United States (Park et al., 1990, p. 86).

York, which lasted 1-1/2 years, attracted international media attention. In the 1992 Los Angeles riots, approximately 2,300 Korean-owned stores in South Central Los Angeles and Koreatown were burned or looted by rioters (Ablemann & Lie, 1995; Min, 1996; Yoon, 1997).

High ethnic attachment and social segregation

Cultural, religious, and even economic experiences unique to members of a particular group are the bases for their ethnic identity and group ties. Korean immigrants maintain distinctive characteristics in all three areas that have enhanced their own and even second-generation Koreans' ethnic identity and group solidarity (Min, 1991).

Korean immigrants are more homogeneous than any other Asian group, including the Japanese, in culture and historical experiences. This lack of diversity forms the cultural basis for Korean ethnic identity and group solidarity. Korean immigrants have a single language, probably the most significant element of culture. This monolingual background gives Korean immigrants a big advantage over other multilingual Asian immigrant groups, such as Indians and Filipinos, in maintaining ethnic attachment. For example, Korean immigrants, almost all of whom can speak, read, and write the Korean language fluently, depend mainly on Korean language ethnic dailies and Korean language TV and radio programs for news, information, and leisure activities (Hurh & Kim, 1988). Their almost exclusive dependence on ethnic media in turn has strengthened their ties to the ethnic community and the home country, although it has hindered their assimilation into American society.

Approximately 75% of Korean immigrants in the United States are affiliated with Korean immigrant churches (Hurh & Kim, 1990; Min, 1992). As noted previously, over half of Korean immigrants attended Christian churches in Korea prior to their immigration. Many Korean Buddhists or those with no religion in Korea participate in Korean Christian congregations in this country. Koreans' involvement in these congregations provides another cultural and social basis for Korean ethnic attachment partly by providing fellowship and ethnic networks. Although most Korean immigrants do not live in physically separate ethnic communities, they can make friends with other Koreans and maintain ethnic networks through church service and activities. Also, Korean churches help maintain Korean cultural traditions by providing Korean language and other cultural programs for children, teaching traditional Korean values, and celebrating important Korean holidays with a variety of Korean food.

In addition, Korean immigrants' segregation in the ethnic economy either as business owners or as employees of coethnic businesses facilitates their preservation of Korean cultural traditions and their social interactions with other Koreans (Min, 1991). The vast majority of Korean immigrants work with family members and fellow Koreans, speaking the Korean language and practicing Korean customs during work hours. Although most Korean-owned businesses serve non-Korean customers, they do so with limited language skills. Because they are segregated at the workplace, Koreans also have little opportunity to make friends with non-Korean residents; thus even during off-duty hours they socialize mainly with coethnics.

Korean immigrants' language use

Until very recently, English education was offered from the seventh grade in Korea.[6] Because the vast majority of Korean adult immigrants had completed high school, they learned English prior to their immigration. Nevertheless, Korean immigrants have difficulty speaking English – probably more than any other Asian immigrant group when education is controlled – for two major reasons. First, English education in Korea was grammar oriented until very recently. Although I taught English in a high school in Korea, for example, I myself had great difficulty communicating in my early years of graduate education in this country because I had taught grammar, translation, and composition, rather than conversation, in Korea. Second, unlike India, the Philippines, and Hong Kong, Korea has no history of colonization by a Western power, so Korean immigrants did not have much contact with English-speaking people prior to immigration. Although the United States has had a strong cultural influence on Korea since the Korean War, only a small number of American citizens are long-term residents there.

These considerations imply that Korean immigrants as a group encounter a greater language barrier than other Asian immigrant groups do. Both census and independent survey data support this conclusion. As shown in Table 2, 62% of foreign-born Koreans 5 years old and over reported in the 1990 census that they did not speak English very well. As expected, much lower proportions of Filipino and Indian immigrants indicated that they were not good at spoken English. Similarly, more Korean immigrants (40%) than other Asian immigrants lived in linguistically isolated households. Only Chinese and Vietnamese immigrants show levels of difficulty in spoken English and of linguistic isolation

6 As part of the effort to help Korean businesses compete successfully in the global market, Kim Young-Sam's administration took measures to enhance Korean students' English language skills in 1995. Beginning that year, English was offered from the third grade on in Korea and more emphasis was placed on spoken English and composition than on grammar.

TABLE 2. ENGLISH SPEAKING ABILITY AMONG ASIAN IMMIGRANTS AGED 5
YEARS AND OLDER, 1990 (%)

	Immigrant group					
Ability	Korean	Chinese	Filipino	Indian	Japanese	Vietnamese
Do not speak English very well	62	63	26	27	59	65
Speak a language other than English	93	95	88	84	88	96
Live in linguistically isolated households	40	42	12	12	36	43

Source: U.S. Bureau of the Census (1993a, Table 3).

similar to those of Korean immigrants. Of the three Asian immigrant groups, Vietnamese immigrants had a much lower educational level than either Korean or Chinese immigrants.[7]

The structure of the Korean immigrant community further discourages the use of English. As noted, by virtue of their group homogeneity and monolingual background, Korean immigrants have developed many forms of Korean language media. For example, the Korean community in New York has two Korean TV stations, two 24-hour radio stations, and four ethnic dailies. As a result, Korean immigrants in large Korean communities can survive without speaking English. Moreover, their religious and economic segregation provide them with little opportunity to interact with members of non-Korean groups. Thus the Korean language serves as the medium of communication not only in family and community settings but also at the workplace.

In 1996 and 1997, I surveyed patterns of ethnic attachment among Korean, Chinese, and Indian immigrants in Queens, New York, by randomly selecting prominent ethnic surnames from the telephone directory. As shown in Table 3, the results of the survey revealed that Korean immigrants used their native language both at home and at the workplace more frequently than Chinese and Indian immigrants did. Significantly, 95% of Korean respondents reported that they used Korean al-

7 According to the U.S. Bureau of the Census (1993b, Table 3), 80% of Korean immigrants completed high school, and 34% completed 4 years of college education. The respective figures for Chinese immigrants were 70% and 30%, and for Vietnamese immigrants, 61% and 17%.

TABLE 3. USE OF NATIVE LANGUAGE AND ENGLISH BY KOREAN, CHINESE, AND
INDIAN IMMIGRANTS IN QUEENS, NEW YORK (%)

Situation and language	Koreans	Chinese	Indians
Speaking with spouse or other family members			
Almost always or more often native language	97	86	54
Half native language, half English	3	7	6
Almost always or more often English	0	6	40
N	98	81	83
Speaking with children			
Almost always or more often native language	95	67	39
Half native language, half English	2	17	12
Almost always or more often English	2	17	49
N	83	60	66
Speaking at the workplace			
Almost always or more often native language	40	19	7
Half native language, half English	23	13	0
Almost always or more often English	37	69	93
N	62	64	61
Watching TV programs			
Almost always or more of the native language	65	26	7
Half native language, half English	18	23	42
Almost always or more often English	17	52	51
N	99	89	82

Source: Survey of Korean, Chinese, and Indian immigrants in Queens, New
York City, conducted by the author in 1996 and 1997.

most always or more often to communicate with their children. Forty
percent of them used the Korean language more often than English at
the workplace, in comparison to 19% of Chinese respondents and 7%
of Indian respondents. This great dependence on the Korean language
for communication even at the workplace is due to the fact that over
80% of Korean immigrants work for their own businesses or for coethnic businesses.

The data on Korean immigrants' language use in Tables 2 and 3 have
important implications for understanding the disadvantages of new Ko-

TABLE 4. KOREAN HIGH SCHOOL STUDENTS' USE OF KOREAN AND ENGLISH
WITH PARENTS AND KOREAN FRIENDS (%)

Language and Frequency	Second-generation children		Immigrant children	
	With parents	*With Korean friends*	*With parents*	*With Korean friends*
English always or most of the time	20.6	67.8	1.3	20.3
English more often	14.0	16.9	0.0	7.1
English and Korean half and half	42.5	13.6	17.3	30.5
Korean more often	7.9	0.0	11.4	9.3
Korean always or most of the time	14.9	1.7	70.0	32.6
N	237	237	238	239

Source: Survey of Korean high school children in New York conducted by the author in 1989.

rean immigrant children in learning English. Since the vast majority of Korean immigrant parents use Korean exclusively at home and watch mainly Korean language TV programs, new Korean immigrant children have difficulty in learning English at home. In a survey of Korean junior and senior high school students in New York conducted in 1989 (see Table 4), 68% of immigrant respondents (those who immigrated after the age of five) reported that they used Korean always or most of the time, and another 17% said that they used it more often than English.[8] New immigrant children usually settle in a Korean enclave where the Korean language is exclusively used, so the community setting does not facilitate their learning of English and American customs, either.

Language shift among second-generation Koreans

In his comprehensive examination of the use and maintenance of ethnic languages in Los Angeles, Lopez (1997) concluded that "Asian languages are hardly maintained at all beyond the immigrant generation" (p. 139; see also Chapter 2). The Korean language is no exception. Although Korean immigrants maintain a high level of residential and social segregation, Koreans of the younger generation have for the most part assimilated residentially, culturally, and socially and, by virtue of their school, their peers, and American media, have mastered spoken English.

8 For details on the data collection techniques, see Hong and Min (1999).

In the same survey of Korean junior and senior high school students in New York cited above, more than 90% of second-generation respondents (those who were born in the United States or those who immigrated at the age of 5 years or younger) reported that they spoke English fluently. Because of their monolingual background and the existence of many ethnic churches, Korean immigrants have greater chances than other Asian immigrant groups for passing their ethnic language on to their children. Nevertheless, in practice Korean immigrant parents find it difficult to teach their children the Korean language, particularly because in most cases both parents work long hours outside of the home. In the same survey of Korean youth in New York, only 9% of second-generation respondents reported that they spoke Korean fluently. Moreover, as shown in Table 4, second-generation Korean children used English almost exclusively to communicate with their Korean friends.

Even to communicate with their parents at home, second-generation Korean children used English more often than Korean (see Table 4). This finding conflicts with the results of a survey of Korean adult immigrants in Queens in which 95% of the respondents reported that they used Korean almost always or more often than English to communicate with their children (see Table 3). The discrepancy in the two sets of findings seems to be due mainly to the fact that Korean parents speak to their children in Korean whereas the latter often respond in English. The parents' effort to make their children speak the Korean language at home and their children's unwillingness to do so are a major source of intergenerational conflicts in many Korean immigrant families (Min, 1995b; 1998a, p. 78). In a 1991 survey, a large proportion of Korean mothers indicated that one of their three major complaints about their children was that the children had not learned the Korean language (Min, 1995b). Many Korean immigrant parents feel ashamed of their children's inability to answer the phone in Korean at home, and many second-generation Korean children are embarrassed to hear their parents use broken English with their American teachers.

Most second-generation Korean children are forced to speak the Korean language at home, as their parents have difficulty speaking English. Moreover, the majority of Korean children have the benefit of Korean language education through the ethnic church.[9] However, as they leave their parental homes to attend college and then establish their own families, they reduce their contacts with their parents and the community and thus have less and less opportunity to use the Korean language as they grow older, although their ethnic identity may even increase with age.

9 As noted, approximately 75% of Korean immigrant families participate in ethnic churches regularly, and the majority of Korean churches have Korean language schools (see Min, 1992).

In this connection, it is important to note that the vast majority of second-generation Korean adults participate neither in the ethnic church nor in the ethnic economy, the two major contributing factors of Korean immigrants' ethnic attachment. Their attendance at an ethnic church is likely to decline to an insignificant proportion when they move away from their parents.[10] Moreover, few second-generation Koreans are interested in opening businesses involving long hours of work. Instead, they move into the general labor market, breaking up the economic segregation of their parents. The 1990 census shows that only 11% of native-born Koreans in the Los Angles metropolitan area were self-employed,[11] a rate lower even than that of native-born White Americans (13%) and much lower than that of Korean immigrants (35%) (Light & Roach, 1996, p. 199).

Based on their high social and occupational integration and high educational level, one would expect only a small fraction of native-born Korean adults to use their mother tongue at home. A study of language use and maintenance based on the Public Use Microdata Sample of the 1989 Current Population Survey supports this expectation: Only 22% of native-born Korean adults aged 25–44 in Greater Los Angles used a language other than English at home (Lopez, 1996, p. 158). Comparable figures for their Vietnamese, Chinese, Filipino, and Indian counterparts were respectively 65%, 32%, 35%, and 36%. These results are surprising in light of the fact that Korean immigrants face a great barrier to learning English relative to other Asian immigrant groups and suggest that language shift over generations has been more pronounced for the Korean group than for other Asian groups.

Future prospects for retaining Korean language and culture

The 1990 census data on language use analyzed by Lopez (1996; discussed above) paints a gloomy picture of the possibility of immi-

---

10 There are several reasons for this decline. First, second-generation Koreans are more likely to lose their religious faith than their parents as they become more secularized through assimilation. Second, participation in church services is less meaningful to U.S.-born Koreans, who do not have the adjustment difficulties that Korean immigrants encounter. Many Korean immigrants attend the church as an aid to enduring the hardships of adjusting to an alien environment. Third, most native-born Koreans do not need to find social networks in a Korean church because they have already established networks, ethnic and nonethnic.

11 I thank Mehdi Bozorgmehr and Claudia Der-Matirosian of the University of California, Los Angeles, for analyzing the self-employment rate of native-born Koreans in the Los Angeles metropolitan area using the Public Use Sample Microdata of the 1990 census.

grants' passing Korean language and culture on to second- and third-generation Koreans. However, the 1990 census data should be interpreted with caution. Native-born Korean adults aged 25–44 in 1990 were born in 1965 or before; thus they were not children of post-1965 immigrants. The cohort of second-generation Koreans aged 25–44 in 1990 grew up when there was a small Korean population in the United States – one much smaller than the Chinese or Filipino population. Thus they had slight disadvantages relative to other Asian Americans at that time and huge disadvantages relative to today's second-generation Koreans for retaining their mother tongue. The Korean communities in Los Angeles, New York, and other major cities in the 1990s are much larger and much more tightly organized than those in the 1960s and the 1970s were. Accordingly, when the second-generation Koreans of the 1990s become adults, they are likely to retain the Korean language and culture more successfully than today's second-generation Korean adults have done. Further, the second-generation Koreans of the 1990s seem to have advantages over other Asian counterparts for retaining their language and culture as a result of their monolingual background and tight community organization.

Several mechanisms in major Korean communities that were not available earlier facilitate language retention on the part of second-generation Koreans. First, a large number of Korean language schools have been established in major Korean communities mainly to teach second-generation children the Korean language and culture. As indicated, most medium-sized and large Korean churches offer Korean language programs to attract members (Min, 1992). As of 1997, an estimated 250 church-related Korean language schools existed in New York alone. About two thirds of such programs offer a 1-hour session before the Sunday service; the other third hold a 3-hour session on Saturday (Min, 1998a, p. 71). Although I have no data on the number of ethnic language schools for other Asian immigrant groups, the Korean community seems to have far more ethnic language schools than any other Asian community mainly because of Korean immigrants' high level of affiliation with Korean churches.[12]

In addition, several major non-church-related Korean language schools in the Korean community in New York provide Korean language, history, and cultural education for local Korean children on Saturday. Each has one hundred or more Korean students at different levels. Nationally, more than 1,000 Korean schools teach second-gener-

---

12 In a survey of Asian immigrants in Queens, New York City, 68% of Korean respondents reported that they participated in an ethnic congregation once a week or more often, in comparison to 23% of Indian respondents and 11% of Chinese respondents. See Min and Chen (1997).

ation Koreans the Korean language, history, and culture. The associations of Korean schools in different cities established the National Association of Korean Schools in 1981,[13] which as of 1997 had approximately 800 members in twelve areas. The Association of Korean Schools in Southern California, the largest local association, has not joined the national association.

Second, partly because of a phenomenal increase in the number of Korean students and partly because of an increasing emphasis on multicultural education, many American high schools and colleges have recently begun to offer classes in Korean as a foreign language. For example, as of 1997, six public high schools in New York City and more than fifteen colleges and universities in the New York area offered such classes. Nationally, 3,343 college students took Korean as a foreign language in the 1995 fall term, which marked a twentyfold increase from 163 students in 1977 ("The Korean Language Has Become Popular," 1996). One reason that Korean has gained far more popularity in high schools and colleges than Asian Indian or Filipino languages is that Koreans use only one language. The sizable increase in the number of high schools and colleges adopting classes in the Korean language gives second-generation Koreans more opportunities to learn their mother tongue.

Korean community leaders in Los Angeles and New York, in close coordination with the Korean Association of Korean Schools and the Korean Consulates in the two cities, lobbied the College Board to include Korean as one of the foreign languages on the Scholastic Aptitude Test (SAT) II. In response, the College Board asked the Korean community to donate $500,000 toward the expense of processing the Korean language test. In 1995, the community leaders established the SAT-Korean Committee as a lobbying and fund-raising organization. While it was raising funds in the major Korean communities, Samsung, a Korea-based conglomerate, donated the entire amount. As a result, the SAT II included the Korean language for the first time in 1997 as one of nine foreign languages and one of three Asian languages (along with Chinese and Japanese). Kwang Ho Lee, the president of the Northeastern Association of Korean Schools, said that over 2,300 students took the SAT Korean language test in 1997, the third largest number of students who took any SAT II foreign language test, following Spanish and Chinese.

Encouraged by this high turnout, the National Association of Korean Schools and the Association of Korean Schools in Southern California, in close coordination with the SAT-Korean Committee, have contacted many high schools in the nation, offering financial support from the

---

13 The information about Korean schools in this paragraph and on the inclusion of Korean in the SAT II in the next paragraph was provided by Kwang Ho Lee, president of the Northeastern Association of Korean Schools and vice president of the National Association of Korean Schools.

funds collected by the committee as an incentive to offer classes in Korean as a foreign language. The two organizations have also published Korean language textbooks and held annual training seminars for Korean language teachers.

Korean immigrants' ties to their home country, which have been made possible by improvements in international travel and telecommunication (Min, 1998a, Chapter 7), also help second-generation Koreans learn the Korean language and culture. Many Korean immigrants can afford to send their children to Korea for language and cultural education during summer vacation. My 1989 survey of youth in New York showed that approximately 80% of American-born Korean children had visited Korea at least once and that 20% had visited twice or more. The Korean government, through the Ministry of Education, and many Korean universities have established summer programs for second-generation Korean students. In addition, most second-generation Korean children are familiar with certain songs popular among young people in Korea mainly because they listen to them on music tapes at home. Even children who do not know the Korean language well still enjoy Korean songs. Many Korean American children also enjoy watching videotaped Korean movies with their parents or with friends. Such activities teach children about Korean language and culture.

Summary and conclusion

Most Korean immigrants face a severe barrier to learning English. Their limited access to English-speaking people prior to immigration is one major contributing factor, and, because of their cultural homogeneity in general and monolingual background in particular, Korean immigrants – even highly educated ones – want to maintain their language and culture. In addition, Korean Americans maintain residential, religious, and economic segregation, which enhances their strong ethnic attachment but isolates them from the larger society. As a result, most Korean adult immigrants use Korean exclusively not only in the family and community contexts but also at the workplace, suggesting that Korean immigrant children have a difficult time learning English.

Although Korean immigrant parents use Korean as the main medium of communication with their children, almost all of their second-generation children are fluent in English by virtue of their school education, American peers, and the U.S. media. Further, as they leave their parents' homes for a college education and jobs, second-generation Korean adults have less and less opportunity to speak Korean and practice Korean customs. In addition, a small proportion of second-generation Korean adults participate in the ethnic church or in the ethnic economy, the two major contributing factors to Korean immigrants' social isolation from the larger society. As a result, the vast majority of second-generation Korean adults, like other the second generation of other Asian American groups, have lost their mother tongue, becoming English monolingual.

The current Korean community is much larger and much more tightly organized than the Korean community of the 1960s and 1970s and is more supportive of second-generation Koreans' retention of their ethnic language and culture. Consequently, when today's Korean children grow up, they are likely to retain the Korean language and culture more successfully than today's second-generation Korean adults. First, major Korean communities have established many Korean language schools to teach second-generation children Korean language, history, and culture. Second, partly because of a phenomenal increase in the number of Korean students and partly because of an increasing emphasis on a multicultural education, many U.S. high schools and colleges have begun to offer classes in Korean as a foreign language, which encourages second-generation Korean students to learn the Korean language through their school curriculum. Third, Korean immigrants' transnational ties with their home country, along with their highly developed ethnic media, help second-generation Koreans learn the Korean language and culture. An emphasis on multiculturalism and transnational ties helps other second-generation Asian Americans preserve their language and culture as well. However, relative to other Asian groups, second-generation Koreans seem to have a slight advantage because of their monolingual background and cultural homogeneity.

Suggestions for further reading

For Koreans' immigration to Hawaii at the turn of the century, see Choy (1979) and Patterson (1987). Patterson's book in particular analyzes in detail a series of historical events in Korea and Hawaii in the late nineteenth century that caused Koreans to seek emigration to Hawaii.

For the contemporary migration of Koreans to the United States and their cultural, social, and economic adjustments, see Hurh (1998), Hurh and Kim (1984), Kim (1981), Light and Bonacich (1988), and Min (1996). Hurh's book, prepared for non-Korean lay readers, gives comprehensive and general information about the Korean community in the United States, whereas the others are sociological studies of Korean immigrants' social and economic adjustments. Hurh and Kim's book is good especially for understanding Korean immigrants' cultural and so-

328

cial assimilation, and the last three are useful for understanding their economic adjustments. Min's book shows how Korean immigrant merchants' intermediary role has contributed to business-related intergroup conflicts with both their minority customers and White suppliers, which in turn has solidified the Korean community.

Min (1998a, 1998b) provide a comprehensive analysis of Korean immigrant families, focusing on the effects of changes in Korean women's gender role on their marriages. Min (1998a) includes a chapter on Korean immigrants' child socialization, including the emphasis on children's education and on the retention of Korean culture.

For information about Korean immigrants' language use, see Byun (1990), Golden (1979), Hong and Min (1999), and Yoon and Nussenbaum (1987). As for the linguistic characteristics of the Korean language, the following sources include useful information: California Department of Education (1984), Chu (1979), Chu-Chang (1981), Koo and Nahm (1997), and Taylor (1995).

References

Abelmann, N., & Lie, J. (1995). *Blue dreams: Korean Americans and the Los Angeles riots.* Cambridge, MA: Harvard University Press.

Ahn, B. (1998). Prospects for Korean under the IMF and Kim Dae-jung. *Korean Observer, 6* (3), 1–17.

Bonacich, E. (1973). A theory of middleman minorities. *American Journal of Sociology, 37,* 583–594.

Byun, M.-S. (1990). Bilingualism and bilingual education: The case of Korean immigrants in the United States. *International Journal of the Sociology of Language, 82,* 109–128.

California Department of Education, Bilingual Education Office. (1984). Linguistic characteristics of the Korean language. In *Handbook for teaching Korean American students.* Sacramento, CA: Author.

Choy, B. Y. (1979). *Koreans in America.* Chicago: Nelson Hall.

Chu, H. (1979). *A contrastive analysis between Korean and English for ESL teachers (K–12).* Arlington, VA: Arlington Public Schools, Bilingual Education Project.

Chu-Chang, M. (Ed.). (1981). *Asian and Pacific American perspectives in bilingual education: Comparative research.* New York: Teachers College Press.

Golden, J. (1979). Acculturation, bilingualism, and marginality: A study of Korean American high school students. *Journal of the National Association for Bilingual Education, 14,* 93–107.

Hong, J., & Min, P. G. (1999). Ethnic attachment among second-generation Korean adolescents. *Amerasia Journal, 25.*

Hurh, W. M. (1998). *Korean Americans.* Westport, CT: Greenwood Press.

Hurh, W. M., & Kim, K. C. (1984). *Korean immigrants in America: A structural analysis of ethnic confinement and adhesive adaptation.* Madison, NJ: Fairleigh Dickinson University Press.

Hurh, W. M., & Kim, K. C. (1988). Uprooting and adjustment: A sociological study of Korean immigrants' mental health. Final report submitted to the National Institute of Mental Health. Macomb, IL: Western Illinois University.

Hurh, W. M., & Kim, K. C. (1990). Religious participation of Korean immigrants in the United States. *Journal of the Scientific Study of Religion, 19,* 19–34.

The Korean language has become popular in American colleges. (1996, October 17). *The Sae Gac Times.*

Kim, I. S. (1981). *New urban immigrants: The Korean community in New York.* Princeton, NJ: Princeton University Press.

Kitano, H., & Chai, L. K. (1982). Korean interracial marriage. *Marriage and Family Review, 5,* 35–48.

Koo, J., & Nahm, A. (Eds.). (1997). *An introduction to Korean culture.* Elizabeth, NJ: Hollym.

Light, I., & Bonacich, E. (1988). *Immigrant entrepreneurs: Koreans in Los Angeles, 1965–1982.* Berkeley: University of California Press.

Light, I., & Roach, E. (1996). Self-employment: Mobility ladder or economic lifeboat? In R. Waldinger & M. Bozorgmehr (Eds.), *Ethnic Los Angeles* (pp. 193–214). New York: Russell Sage Foundation.

Lopez, D. V. (1997). Language: Diversity and assimilation. In R. Waldinger & M. Bozorgmehr (Eds.), *Ethnic Los Angeles* (pp. 139–163). New York: Russell Sage Foundation.

Min, P. G. (1984). From white-collar occupations to small business: Korean immigrants' occupational adjustment. *Sociological Quarterly, 25,* 333–352.

Min, P. G. (1986/1987). A comparison of Korean and Filipino immigrants in small business. *Amerasia Journal, 18,* 78–89.

Min, P. G. (1988a). *Ethnic business enterprise: Korean small business in Atlanta.* Staten Island, NY: Center for Migration Studies.

Min, P. G. (1988b). Korean immigrant entrepreneurship: A multivariate analysis. *Journal of Urban Affairs, 10,* 197–212.

Min, P. G. (1989). *Some positive functions of ethnic business for an immigrant community: Koreans in Los Angeles* (Final report submitted to National Science Foundation). New York: Queens College.

Min, P. G. (1990). Problems of Korean immigrant entrepreneurship. *International Migration Review, 24,* 436–445.

Min, P. G. (1991). Cultural and economic boundaries of Korean ethnicity: A comparative analysis. *Ethnic and Racial Studies, 14,* 225–241.

Min, P. G. (1992). The structure and social functions of Korean immigrant churches in the United States. *International Migration Review, 26,* 1370–1394.

Min, P. G. (1993a). Korean immigrants in Los Angeles. In I. Light & P. Bhachu (Eds.), *Immigration and entrepreneurship: Culture, capital, and ethnic networks,* (pp. 185–204). New York: Transaction Books.

Min, P. G. (1993b). Korean immigrants' marital patterns and marital adjustments. In H. McAdoo (Ed.), *Family ethnicity: Strength in diversity* (pp. 287–299). Newbury Park, CA: Sage.

Min, P. G. (Ed.). (1995a). *Asian Americans: Contemporary trends and issues.* New York: Russell Sage Foundation.

Min, P. G. (1995b). The relationship between Korean immigrant parents and their children. *The Academy Review of Korean Studies, 18,* 119–136.

Min, P. G. (1996). *Caught in the middle: Korean merchants in America's multiethnic cities.* Berkeley: University of California Press.

Min, P. G. (1998a). *Changes and conflicts: Korean immigrant families in New York.* Boston: Allyn & Bacon.

Min, P. G. (1998b). The Korean American family. In C. Mindel, R. Habenstein, & R. Wright, Jr. (Eds.), (4th ed., pp. 223–253). *Ethnic families in America: Patterns and variations,* New York: Prentice Hall.

Min, P. G., & Chen, L. (1997). A comparison of Korean, Chinese & Indian immigrants in ethnic attachment. Paper presented at the Annual Meeting of the American Sociological Association, Washington, DC.

Min, P. G., & Kolody, A. (1994). The middleman minority characteristics of Korean immigrants in the United States. *Korea Journal of Population and Development, 23,* 179–202.

National Statistical Office. (1991). *A national survey on Korean religions* Seoul: Economic Planning Board, Korean Government.

Pak, C. H. (1983). Historical review of Korean Confucianism. In Korean National Commission of UNESCO (Eds.), *Main currents of Korean thought* (pp. 60–81). Seoul, Korea: Sisayongosa.

Park, I. H., Fawcett, J., Arnold, F., & Gardner, R. (1990). *Korean immigrants and U.S. immigration policy: A predeparture perspective* (Papers of the East-West Population Institute No. 114). Honolulu, HI: East-West Center.

Park, I. S., & Cho, L. J. (1995). Confucianism and the Korean family. *Journal of Comparative Family Studies, 26,* 117–134.

Patterson, W. (1987). *The Korean frontier in Hawaii: Immigration to Hawaii, 1896–1910.* Honolulu, HI: University of California Press.

Taylor, I. (1995). *Writing and literacy in Chinese, Korean, and Japanese.* Philadelphia: John Benjamins.

U.S. Bureau of the Census. (1983). *1980 census of population: General Population Characteristics – United States summary* (PC80-1-B1). Washington, DC: U.S. Government Printing Office.

U.S. Bureau of the Census. (1993a). *1990 census of population – Asians and Pacific Islanders in the United States.* Washington, DC: U.S. Government Printing Office.

U.S. Bureau of the Census. (1993b). *1990 census of population – General population characteristics: United States* (1990 CP-1-1). Washington, DC: U.S. Government Printing Office.

U.S. Immigration and Naturalization Service. (Various Years). *Annual Report.* Washington, DC: U.S. Government Printing Office.

U.S. Immigration and Naturalization Service. (Various Years). *Statistical Yearbook.* Washington, DC: U.S. Government Printing Office.

Yang, S. J., Kwon, S. J., & Hwang, J. I. (1997). *Statistical yearbook on women.* Seoul: Korean Women's Development Institute.

Yoon, I. J. (1991). The changing significance of ethnic and class resources in immigrant businesses: The case of Korean immigrant businesses in Chicago. *International Migration Review, 25,* 302–332.

Yoon, I. J. (1997). *On your own: Korean businesses and race relations in America.* Chicago: University of Chicago Press.

Yoon, K. K., & Nussembaum, G. (1987). Assessment of linguistic needs of Korean American students in northern New Jersey: Implications for future directions. *Journal of the National Association for Bilingual Education, 12,* 52–63.

Yu, E.-Y. (1977). Koreans in America: An emerging ethnic minority. *Amerasia Journal, 4,* 111–131.

Yu, E. Y. (1982). Koreatown in Los Angeles: Size, distribution, and composition. In E. Y. Yu, E. H. Phillips, and E. S. Yang (Eds.), *Koreans in Los Angeles: Prospects and promises.* Los Angeles: Center for Korean and Korean American Studies, California State University.

Yu, E. Y. (1985). Koreatown, Los Angeles: Emergence of a new inner-city ethnic community. *Bulletin of Population and Development Studies, 14,* 29–44.

Yu, E. Y., Phillips, E. H., & Yang, E. S. (Eds.). (1982). *Koreans in Los Angeles: Prospects and promises.* Los Angeles: California State University, Center for Korean-American and Korean Studies.

Zenner, W. (1991). *Minorities in the middle.* Albany, NY: SUNY Press.

11 The language situation of Filipina/os

Diversity and complexity

Joan May T. Cordova

The experiences of English language learners who are Filipina/o[1] reflect just one segment of a broad range of Filipina/o experiences rooted in an archipelago of more than 7,000 islands and some 110 languages. Unlike other Asian Pacific American groups, Filipina/o experiences are influenced by both Spanish and American colonization and a multilayered history of Filipina/o immigration from the Philippines. With an 80% increase in the U.S. Filipina/o population between 1980 and 1990 as well as the highest immigration rate of all Asian American groups, Filipina/o Americans constitute one of the fastest-growing groups in the United States.

History of Filipina/os in the United States

On October 18, 1587, the *Nuestra Señora de Buena Esperanza,* a 40-ton Spanish ship captained by Pedro de Unamuno, landed in what is now Morro Bay in California. In her account of this event, Gomez-Borah (1996) describes how Filipina/os (referred to as *Indios Luzones* [Luzon Indians]) led the landing party as scouts, lookouts, land explorers, and peacemakers: "It would be safe to conclude that upon reaching wading distance to the shore, it is the Filipinos who pull the small boat into the beach, perhaps carrying the priest to keep his long robes dry, and that Filipino footprints lay beneath those of the rest of the landing party" (p. 15).

More than 400 years later, Filipina/o Americans from throughout the United States would retrace these footprints. In October 1995 Filipina/os from Alaska, Michigan, Illinois, Massachusetts, Washington, and

1 To emphasize the presence of women in Filipina/o history and contemporary settings, I have chosen to use the term *Filipina/o* throughout this chapter. (This choice is consistent with the work of scholars Dorothy Fujita-Rony, Emily P. Lawsin, and others.) I use the term *Filipino* to refer specifically to men (i.e., to Filipino labor leader Manlapit).

Although some community members may use the term *Pilipino* to denote a 1960s shift in political identity, most national Filipina/o networks in the United States – the Filipino American National Historical Society, the Filipino Civil Rights Association, and the Filipino American Women's Network, among others – use the term Filipino. See the section "Current Multilingualism in the Philippines" on the difference between the Pilipino and the Filipino language.

333

California dedicated a historical marker to commemorate the 1587 landing of Filipina/os in Morro Bay, California. At this historic event, Jerry Paular, a 70-year-old second-generation Filipina/o American from Sacramento, said, "Finally, people are beginning to know our history." Recalling his experiences in California public schools, in which the school curriculum never mentioned Filipina/os, he emphasized the importance of continuing to claim the markers – both physical and symbolic – of the history of Filipina/os in the United States.[2]

Of significance is Espina's (1988) research of Filipina/o settlements, such as Manila Village in Jefferson Parish and the settlement of St. Malo near the mouth of Lake Borgne in St. Bernard Parish, both in Louisiana. Inhabited by about one hundred Filipinos, the latter is a fishing settlement believed to be the first Filipino colony established in the United States in the mid-eighteenth century. Espina reports that Filipina/os spoke Spanish, Cebuano, and Tagalog.

Other scholars believe that official U.S.-Philippine relations began after the Spanish American War of 1898, when the Philippines became a colony of the United States. Having successfully waged what was perhaps the first nationalist revolution in Asia beginning in 1896, Filipina/os did not passively accept U.S. declarations of sovereignty in the Philippines after the war. Guided by the doctrine of manifest destiny, which was based on economic, political, and military interests, the United States sent thousands of American soldiers to the Philippines. The subsequent conflict between U.S. and Filipino soldiers escalated, eventually killing an estimated one million Filipina/os. As one military strategy for the pacification of Filipina/os in the context of war, the United States established an educational system in the Philippines that would incorporate methods, texts, and curricula taught by American teachers in English (Cordova, 1998, p. 2).

The Spanish-American War and the eventual U.S. colonization of the Philippines stimulated Filipina/o immigration to the United States in a number of ways. First, America's first Asian war brides – the wives of Spanish American War servicemen – immigrated to the United States. Second, the Philippine Commission, through Act No. 854 in 1903, launched a *pensionado* system that enabled select, government-sponsored Filipina/os to study in colleges and universities in the United States with the goal of becoming professionals and government leaders upon their return to the Philippines (Bernabe, 1987). The success of returning *pensionados* encouraged even larger numbers of mostly self-supporting Filipina/o students to continue their education in the United States. In addition to the *pensionado* system, the U.S.-patterned educa-

---

2 This observation and others in the paper were gathered in my research on Filipina/o American communities.

tional system established in the Philippines succeeded in "educating a generation of Filipinos away from the Islands . . . and encouraged this generation to look toward the United States" (McWilliams, 1942, p. 233). One English language text (of 1904) used in the Philippines, for example, contains a sample letter written by a Filipino son who had recently traveled to America: "I hope to begin work in a few days. We shall study in the school here the rest of the year. . . ." (cited in Cordova, 1998, p. 46).

Responding to the Gentleman's Agreement Act of 1907, which limited Japanese immigration to Hawaii, the Hawaiian Sugar Planters Association (HSPA) brought two hundred Filipina/o laborers to work in Hawaiian sugar plantations. Large-scale recruitment followed as the HSPA enticed many with the promises of good job opportunities described in lectures and movies that actually misrepresented plantation life. In *Filipinos Fight for Justice*, Filipino labor leader Manlapit (1933) recalls how Filipinos' "glittering prospects . . . have vanished before the harsh realities of inflated prices and exorbitant profits" (p. 14). Of the HSPA, Manlapit writes, "The HSPA has failed. It has made terms with the laborer that are sufficient to attract him to Hawaii, but after he gets here the attraction ceases. . . . After a few months of struggle and privation on a 'dollar a day' he is ready to revolt" (p. 15).

When the Immigration Act of 1924 excluded Japanese and Chinese from immigration, no restrictions were placed on Filipina/os, who were classified as *nationals,* neither aliens nor citizens. In all, about 150,000 Filipina/os left the Philippines for Hawaii or the mainland United States from 1907 to 1930 (Lasker, 1931).

Although a significant number of Filipina/o immigrants became migrant farm laborers (as chronicled by Bulosan, 1990), many worked in Alaskan canneries; some worked in private homes as "schoolboys" and were able to complete their education; a few started small businesses, and others learned trades or engaged in other forms of labor. Despite the disproportionately high ratio of Filipina/o men to women – 14:1 and higher – a number of men were able to marry and raise families in the 1930s and 1940s. As a member of large, extended family rooted in Stockton, California, Angel Bantillo Magdael recalled how the homes of pioneering Filipina/o families often became havens of warmth and Philippine culture for a large number of single men in Filipina/o American communities (personal communication, July 1997).

After the stock market crash of 1929 and the ensuing Depression, Filipina/os became more of a threat to White labor. Although the scarcity of jobs during the Depression was often viewed as the source of anti-Filipina/o sentiments that led to eventual exclusion, anti-Filipina/o movements began years before the Depression. Incidents sparked by racist fears and economic factors occurred in Washington State in 1928;

Exeter, California, in 1929; and Watsonville, California, in 1930. As one example, Bogardus (1930/1976) described how Fermin Tobera was killed in Watsonville when some 700 people "attacked Filipino dwellings, destroyed property, and jeopardized lives" from January 19 to January 23, 1930 (p. 55).

As early as 1928, Congressman Richard Welch of California introduced a bill in the House of Representatives that prohibited further immigration from the Philippines by reclassifying Filipina/os as aliens. The bill failed since Americans were divided on the issue of Filipina/o exclusion: Some advocated Philippine independence so that Filipina/os could be legally excluded as aliens; others wanted the United States to retain possession of the Philippines to protect American commercial interests.

The Tydings-McDuffie Act (also known as the Philippine Independence Act), passed in March 1934, solved this dilemma. Under this law, the Philippines was granted a semiautonomous government by becoming a commonwealth of the United States for a specified 10 years, after which it would become an independent nation. At the same time, this act limited Filipina/o immigration to only fifty persons per year. Anti-Filipina/o factions that wanted the deportation of Filipina/os sponsored the Repatriation Act, which allowed Filipina/os to return to the Philippines with transportation expenses paid by the U.S. government. Those who took advantage of this act – only 2,190 – could not return to the United States.

Though exploited by racist legislation and victimized by anti-Filipina/o sentiments at times, Filipina/os did not remain passive. A publication of the National Advisory Committee on Farm Labor (1967) documents that the Filipino Agricultural Labor Association (FALA) was the "first thoroughly modern farm labor union" (p. 17) in California. Organized in 1939 and composed almost entirely of Filipino farm workers around the Stockton-Sacramento area, FALA won a number of strikes and gained union recognition. The National Advisory Committee on Farm Labor also reports that FALA "saved thousands of dollars for its members by calling the authorities' attention to the practice of some farmers of deducting workmen's compensation payments from their employees' wages in defiance of statute" (p. 17). Additionally, FALA helped form the Philippine Mercantile Association, a cooperative in Stockton that sold groceries and products from the Philippines.

World War II changed the character of Filipina/o American communities. Thousands of Filipino immigrants and Filipino American men served in the United States during World War II. Those who served in the armed forces were allowed to become citizens in 1943. One other outcome of the war was that some 16,000 women, Filipina war brides of both Filipino and American veterans, immigrated to the United States. Lawsin (1996) documents how Filipina war brides created numerous community organizations and promoted Filipino culture for the next generation of Filipina/o Americans.

Passage of the Immigration and Naturalization Act in 1965 led to dramatic growth in the Filipina/o American community. Economic and political factors, including the U.S. military presence in the Philippines and ongoing Americanization through education, all contributed to Filipinos' positive response to changes in U.S. immigration policy.

Current U.S. demographics

From 1980 to 1990 the Filipino American population increased 80% – from 774,600 to 1.4 million – with the largest Filipina/o concentrations in California, Hawaii, Illinois, New York, New Jersey, Washington, Texas, Virginia, and Florida. Currently averaging about 40,000 admissions per year, Filipina/os now have the highest immigration rate of all Asian groups and are the second largest (after Mexicans) of all immigrant groups to the United States (Hodgkinson & Obarakpor, 1994).

In light of the number of Filipina/os who have overstayed their visas, a number of researchers present higher population figures. Montoya (1997) reports that as of 1995 there were 2.1 million people of Filipino ancestry in the United States. From 1985 to 1988, the Philippines averaged 14,800 visa overstayers per year. Sometimes referred to as *TNTs* (from the Filipino phrase *tago ng tago,* loosely translated as "keep on hiding"), these undocumented immigrants pay $7 billion per year in taxes, help support Social Security and unemployment insurance, and often accept jobs that legal immigrants and citizens shun. According to Montoya, "Filipina/o TNTs are constantly trying to find ways to legalize themselves" (p. 116).

Census figures do not accurately account for the growing number of Filipina/o Americans of mixed heritage. A host of factors contribute to the growth of Filipina/o–African, –Caucasian, –Mexican, –Hawaiian –American, and other families: U.S. military presence in the Philippines for more than a century, the repeal of (and Filipinos' frequent disregard of) antimiscegenation laws, and Filipina war brides.

Citing 1993 U.S. Department of Commerce reports, Lott (1997) reports that Filipina/o families – with 4.02 persons on average – are larger than the average 3.16-person U.S. family. Among Filipina/o families, 78% were headed by married couples, and the percentage of female-headed households – 15.4% – increased among Filipina/o families from 1980 to 1990.

Nearly two thirds of the Filipina/o American population is foreign born. Yet simple generalizations about either immigrant or U.S. born Filipina/os do not hold, for Filipina/o American experiences differ according to generation of immigration; class; regional and language backgrounds; interracial marriage; urban, suburban, or rural experiences; and other complex factors. Flores (1994), editor of *The Journal of the American Association for Philippine Psychology*, states that such "cultural dimensions as family, region, and social class, when applied to Filipina/os in America, actually are gross oversimplifications" (p. 56). Flores considers, for example, Filipina/os' close affinity to kin connected by both matrilineal and patrilineal lineage as well as the possible convergence of language, religion, and class issues. In her article, Flores uses empirical research findings to illustrate how complex layers of variables – including socioeconomic origins and multilingual background in the Philippines – of Filipina/os in the United States influence traditional Philippine parenting styles and the subsequent cultural dissonance Filipina/o American students experience in American schools.

The majority of adult Filipina/os in the United States have a high school degree and are part of the labor force. In 1990, among persons 25 years and older, about four out of five Filipino males (82%) and Filipina females (81%) were high school graduates, and 40% of Filipino males and 41% of Filipina females were college graduates. Fully 75% of the Filipina/o population participates in the labor force. Nearly two thirds (63%) of all Filipina/os in the labor force in 1990 were in managerial, professional, and technical occupations. Nearly 10% were in sales and clerical work. Service workers and farm workers had diminished to 18%; craftspeople, to 9%. Filipina/os' relatively high median family income ($46,698) was due in part to larger families and a greater number of workers per household. Among all Asian American groups, Filipina/os had the greatest proportion of families with three or more workers (29%; Lott, 1997).

Current multilingualism in the Philippines

Depending on how language is defined, some 75–150 languages are spoken in the Philippines. Grimes (1996) lists 171 languages for the Philippines. Ramos (1996) reports the following breakdown of languages spoken there: Tagalog (25%), Cebuano (24%), Ilocano (9%), Hiligaynon (9%), Bicol (6%), Waray (5%), and others (22%). Gonzalez and Romero (1993) also describe the popular use of *Manila Lingua Franca*, a variety of Tagalog used for communication between first- and second-generation immigrant speakers of Tagalog and native speakers of Tagalog in Manila. More specifically, Manila Lingua Franca may be characterized as the "common features between the mixed Tagalog language of immigrants on the one hand and the native Tagalog of locals on the other hand" (p. 35).

The use of Taglish – a combination of English and Tagalog words and sentences structures – continues to develop in both the Philippines and the United States. Campos (1998) refers to Taglish as *Engalog, Philippine English, Englipino,* or *Pinoy Tok.* He concludes, "Whether the language is legitimate is not the point for it seems to be the language of the people. And the bottom line is that Taglish will continue to evolve – as all languages do – to suit the intercultural communication necessary in a world that is getting smaller and smaller every day" (p. 5).

Language history of the Philippines

Scott (1984) notes that

When the Spaniards first arrived in Luzon, they found the Filipinos of the Manila Bay region so literate in an indigenous script called baybayin that the missionaries printed Juan de Plasencia's Doctrina in the Philippine script with wood-blocks in Tagalog in 1593. (p. 53)

Among the Mangyans of Mindoro and the Tagbanwas of Palawan, for example, this indigenous Philippine alphabet has been preserved and is still used.

Contrary to notions that the United States established the first schools for Filipinos, the first college in the Philippines – the University of Santo Tomás – had been established as early as 1611 (some 25 years before Harvard College was founded in the United States). Through a royal decree in Spain, an 1863 educational reform act systematized primary instruction in the Philippines and provided schools for secondary instruction as well as other colleges. By 1869, some 138,000 children attended 680 schools. Documents from this period reveal that teachers in normal schools studied the Spanish language among other subjects (Barrantes, 1894).

After the Spanish American War, the Philippines became a colony of the United States. Facing the resistance of Filipinos who had been engaged in their own struggle for freedom from Spanish and then U.S. sovereignty, Major General E. S. Otis, in charge of U.S. troops during the start of the Filipino-American War in 1899, also supervised the establishment of some of the first U.S. public schools in the Philippines. In his 1899 report to the United States Department of War, Major-General E. S. Otis noted that

where our troops are stationed to give inhabitants protection, schools have been established. Parents and children are eager for primary-school instruction and are very desirous to acquire a speaking knowledge of the English language. (cited in Cordova, 1998, p. 29)

By January 1901, in addition to formally establishing the public school

339

Joan May T. Cordova

system in the Philippines, Act 74 – "An Act Establishing a Department of Instruction in the Philippines" – officially declared that "the English language shall as soon as practicable, be made the basis of all public school instruction." Although most accounts of U.S. educational programs in the Philippines tend to describe favorable responses to the use of English in the Philippines, a number of references present a contrasting perspective. In a report to the Department of War (1900), Brig. General J. F. Bell noted, "All the people would like their children taught their own dialect" (cited in Cordova, 1998, p. 31). Filipino historian Salamanca (1984) also provides evidence of Filipina/os' resistance to the adoption of English as the official language of the Philippines.

In the Moro province, an area known for ongoing resistance to foreign influences, a 1909 edition of *The Mindanao Herald* reported that the Sulu and Magindao dialects were taught as subjects. Further south in Zamboanga, descendants of Visayan, Tagalog, Ilocano, and other immigrants from the north compromised on a form of Spanish as their common language. District Superintendent Cameron observed that "additional place may be given to the study of native dialects without injuring the effectiveness of our educational system" (cited in Cordova, 1998, p. 32).

In spite of such resistance, English remained the official language of the U.S.-modeled school system. Bernabe (1987) describes an American soldier-teacher's approach to teaching English to Benito Pangilinan, onetime director of the Bureau of Public Schools.

We talked English the best we knew how. . . . We were unaware that he must have been amused at our addressing him as a "dirty chair," for that was how we sounded "dear teacher". . . . There was communication because he understood the context of the greeting. Of course, one whose ears were not attuned to the peculiar expression of our thoughts was puzzled by what we said. That was when real misunderstanding came in. Unflaggingly, therefore, our teacher hammered correct speech and usage by the well-known expedient of unremitting drill, drill, and more drill. (p. 26)

For many Filipina/os, the imposition of English was not a neutral act. In his frequently cited essay, "The Miseducation of the Filipino," historian Constantino (1966) describes how learning English in U.S. schools was the first step in "miseducation." According to Constantino, "They learned no longer as Filipinos but as colonials" (p. 39). To challenge such colonizing processes, Enriquez and Protacio-Marcelino (1984) claim, "the struggle of the Filipino people to emancipate themselves from foreign domination, including the value-bias of the colonizer's concepts and postulates of reasoning must also encompass the liberation of their national language" (p. 5).

The 1935 constitution proclaimed Tagalog to be the basis of the

340

Philippine national language. Renamed *Pilipino* (note the *P* in the spelling) in 1959, this language and English eventually became the official languages of the Philippines as outlined in the 1973 constitution. After 1957, however, the vernacular was used as a medium of instruction in accordance with a 1950 UNESCO recommendation that the best beginning medium of instruction for children was the home language (Gonzalez, 1996).

In 1974 the Department of Education adopted a plan to switch from monolingual (English) to bilingual (English and Tagalog-based Pilipino) education at the elementary and secondary education levels, to be gradually implemented over a period of 10 years. Gonzalez (1991a) identified the following requirements for effective program implementation: (1) production of Pilipino texts and curriculum, (2) the modernization of the Pilipino language itself, and (3) a theoretical framework for teacher training.

Based on the 1987 constitution, the Philippine National Assembly was charged to create a national language called *Filipino* (note the *F* in the spelling). Various perspectives arose in regard to the form this new national language would take: Would the Filipino language be rooted primarily in Tagalog, borrowed from other Philippine languages, or adapted from English? The 1987 constitution mandated that the Filipino language include vocabulary from other Philippine languages.

Gonzalez (1996) points out that the use of Filipino as one of two media of instruction would be "a means of intellectualising Filipino and contributing to its cultivation as a language of scholarly discourse" (p. 216). With Filipino as a medium of instruction, policy makers and educators faced the need for textbooks in Filipino, standard word lists, newsletters, translation, and research. Using Filipino as a medium of instruction presumed that the teachers knew both language and content. Yet given that Filipino was not at the same level of modernization, particularly in subjects previously taught in English, teachers subsequently faced the challenge of having to reconceptualize content areas in Filipino. This was complicated by the fact that versions of the Filipino language were still in the process of standardization.

In 1994, Republic Act No. 7104 created a commission, to be known as the Commission on the Filipino Language, composed of representatives of varieties of ethnolinguistic groups and different disciplines. The commission was charged to promote research and formulate policies for the development and preservation of Filipino and other Philippine languages

In her studies of bilingual science learning in the Philippines, Alvarez (1991) concluded that students seemed to relate to and understand science better in Pilipino than in a foreign language. This study supported the position of Filipina/os who opposed the use of English as a medium

341

of instruction, claiming that since science could be taught effectively using the native language, using English as the language of instruction benefited only the elite. Although often inconclusive, studies like Alvarez's highlight the difficulty in formulating a single educational policy flexible enough for a country like the Philippines, where the vernacular seems to influence the learning of subjects like science. How and what languages to teach Filipina/o students would also become an issue in the United States.

Language issues of Filipina/os in the United States

In his novel *Rolling the R's,* Zamora-Linmark (1995) presents a humorous example of how one elementary school teacher attempted to teach standard English pronunciation to Filipina/o children in Hawaii:

Think three not tree. Watch the r's. Think think, not tink. Th. Th. Th, th. Da ink. No: Th, th, th, th-ink. Think. Prrreee. F's, not p's. Frrreee. Do not roll the r's. Free Three. Three. Free. Bery good. V. V. Very. I am Filipino, not Pilipino. Fil, pil. Fil. Fil. Fil, fil, filfilfilfil. Philippines, not Peelipines. My name is Plorante. Flo. Flo-rante. Florante. Prrrrom. Frrrrom. (p. 54)

Even though Zamora-Linmark's novel often elicits laughter when read aloud, this excerpt presents actual characteristics of Filipino English while prompting critical questions about the historical dominance (and privileging) of standard English. In 1991, prominent Filipino linguist Gonzalez (1991b) asked, "When does an error become a feature of the new variety of English?" (p. 86). According to research by Gonzalez and other scholars, studies of the speech of educated Filipina/os reveals that Filipino English has nearly become standardized. Gonzalez generated a list of what scholars refer to as *perduring features* of Philippine English – features of spoken and written English that are found across all generations of Filipina/os (from the American colonial period until now). Consistent with Zamora-Linmark's anecdotes, such perduring features include /b/ for /v/, /s/ for /z/, and distinctive uses of certain verb tenses in English as a result of the Philippine verb system, which is purely aspectual. For Filipino speakers of English, these features of the Filipina/o language often result in the following:

1. the overuse of the simple past tense
2. the use of the present perfect for the simple past (e.g., "I have visited Baguio last year.")
3. a lack of tense consistency (e.g., "He said he is making his homework.")
4. the nonnative use of verb + preposition combinations (e.g., "Turn out the light.")

342

5. nonuse of *the* in sentences (e.g., "Majority of the students favored the bill.")
6. the use of the simple past tense to denote two past actions (e.g., "I already ate dinner when you arrived.")
7. the use of the present progressive tense to indicate action begun in the past and continuing to the present (e.g., "I am standing here now for 2 hours.") (p. 88)

Given these perduring features of Filipino English, Strobel (1997) notes that, in light of the hierarchical status of standard English as a universal norm, those who speak variations of Filipino English often experience discrimination. Students interviewed by Strobel contended that "English be considered a Filipino language because Filipinos have nativized it and made it their own" (p. 74). To eliminate the false division in the U.S. Filipina/o community marked by language, students advocated eliminating the association of Filipino English with inferiority and "otherness." Acting on the need to challenge the flawed hierarchy of languages in the United States, the United Filipino Council of Hawaii, a statewide federation of Filipina/o community organizations, responded to a 1987 language-related discrimination case in Hawaii by issuing this statement:

Employers should not confuse the ability to communicate with accent. All too often, the fact that a job applicant speaks with an accent obscures the reality that he or she can actually communicate well, and sometimes in flawless English. However, some listeners immediately erect a mental barrier upon hearing an accent. . . . This case should serve as an example to others who may have been discriminated against to seek justice through the courts. (Forman, 1991, p. 6)

Language background of Filipina/os in the United States

In the United States, nearly two thirds of Filipina/os (aged 5 years or older in 1990) spoke a language other than English at home. More than half spoke Tagalog, the sixth most frequently spoken language in the United States.

More than 90% of Tagalos speakers in the United States claimed to be bilingual (in Tagalog and English) to some degree. Of the 843,251 speakers of Tagalog, for example, 66% indicated that they spoke English very well; 27% indicated that they spoke English well, but only 7% indicated not well, and less than 1%, not at all. Native speakers of Ilocano, however, expressed less confidence in their English-speaking abilities than Tagalog speakers did. Of the 41,131 speakers of Ilocano, 80% indicated that they spoke English either very well or well whereas

18% claimed not well. Still, only 2% indicated that they did not speak English at all.

In a study of 524 households in the Los Angeles area, less than 1% of Filipina/os noted language as a barrier; less than 1% attended ESL classes (DaVanzo, 1994).

Studies of Filipina/o language patterns

Actual case studies of experiences of second-generation Filipina/o Americans that I have gathered reveal the range of language abilities – in Filipino as well as English – of sons and daughters of Filipina/o immigrants. The late Mary Arca Inosanto, for example, reared on a plantation in Hawaii, spoke fluent Tagalog, Hiligaynon, Ilocano, and English throughout her life. Bern, born and reared in Daly City, California, sings in and speaks both Tagalog and English with the accent of a native speaker of both languages. In Connecticut, Ligaya, whose father can trace his ancestors to the *Mayflower,* has learned fluent Ilocano from her Filipina mother. Raymund, born and reared in Florida, understands conversational Aklanon yet speaks only English. Maria, at 5 years old, was considered for placement in English as a second language instruction because of the Tagalog accent she learned from the grandmother who had been her baby-sitter. John of New York speaks English and Ebonics.

Other second-generation Filipina/o children may view their parents' language the same way 5-year-old Buddy reflects on his father's words in novelist Bacho's (1997) *Dark Blue Suit:*

At almost five years old, I didn't know much about my father. He didn't talk much, at least not to me. Maybe it was the language. Mine was native English-fluid, made in America. His was borrowed and broken, a chore just to speak; Dad preferred Cebuano. The English I did hear from him I imagined he saved, hoarding words that twisted his tongue. To me, they came mostly in the form of monosyllabic blasts, barked commands to "do dis, Buddy . . . now." And of course, "dis" got done – now, never later (p. 5).

Little formal research exists on Filipina/o American communication patterns. In one study of the communication patterns of a Filipina/o American student organization at a private, urban university in the Midwest, Speicher (1994) observed "overlap and parallel talk" that she defines as "multiple voices vying for the floor, joking, cajoling, asserting, conversing, and suggesting" (p. 419). She notes that Filipina/o Americans represent a collectivist (placing family first and foremost) rather than an individualistic society and concludes that parallel talk "may indeed function to signal and promote solidarity between speakers" (p. 421).

Speicher's research is consistent with the work of other Filipino researchers. Strobel (1997) describes the Filipino indirect communication pattern of *pahiwatig* as "the evocative ways of expressing the need or want of something" (p. 74). She notes that *pahiwatig* is grounded in the value of *pakikiramdam* – keen sensitivity to a complex of verbal and nonverbal cues in a given communication context – and *pakikipagkapwa-tao* – to feel one with the other. Salvator (1996) cites Enriquez's *Sikolohiyang Philipino,* which states that shared identity and strong equivalence with one's fellows is the basic core value of all Filipino values. Enriquez refers to the following traditional values: interaction with others on an equal basis, sensitivity to and regard for others, respect and concern for helping out, understanding and making up for others' limitations, and rapport and acceptance.

Factors favoring the maintenance of Philippine languages

Like other immigrants to the United States second-generation Filipina/o American students experience the legacy of U.S. educational practices of regarding home language and culture as deficits rather than strengths. In schools that work to eradicate immigrant students' home language and culture, many second-generation Filipina/o Americans grow up speaking only English.

Yet a number of factors indicate potential shifts in this trend. One indicator of the U.S. Filipina/o community's potential for the maintenance of Filipino language is the small but growing number of colleges and universities that offer classes in Tagalog as a foreign language. In 1996 the University of California, Los Angeles; the University of California, Berkeley; San Francisco State University; City College of San Francisco; University of Oregon; University of Michigan; University of Wisconsin, Northern Illinois University; University of Pennsylvania; and Cornell University all offered such classes. By 1997, at least a dozen other colleges and universities – including Arizona State University, Southwestern College, and the University of Pittsburgh – were added to the growing list of campuses that offered Tagalog/Filipino Classes. At the University of Hawaii, which has the largest and most comprehensive Philippine language program in the United States, two hundred students were enrolled in four levels of Tagalog in 1996. Ramos (1996) reports that second-generation Filipina/os claimed to have enrolled in Tagalog class "to learn more about my roots, appreciate my Filipino culture and communicate with my parents" (p. 167).

Strobel's (1997) research on Filipina/o American identity formation documents a generation of second-generation (post-1965) Filipina/o youth who call themselves born-again Filipinos and study Tagalog and other aspects of Philippine culture. Kobylarz (1997) describes these born-again Filipinos:

They write in alibata, the ancient Filipino script. They print and wear shirts with indigenous images and proverbs and quotations from Jose Rizal. They don necklaces with metal etchings that say "Pinay Pride." In cyberspace, they've created dozens of home pages and developed their own Filipino community chat-rooms. (p. 23)

These and other born-again Filipinos contribute to the popularity of Tagalog television and music, Filipina/o newspapers and magazines, programs created by community-based organizations, and even the growth of Web sites that provide Tagalog poetry and language instruction. As one example of the growing interest in Filipina/o American history, language, and culture at the high school level, more than two hundred Filipina/o American students from five eastern states participated in "The Centennial Journey Through Filipino America," a Regional Youth Summit, in Virginia Beach, Virginia, in October 1997. During this educational workshop, nearly all students identified the need for courses in Tagalog as well as Filipina/o American history and culture.

Filipina/o bilingual education programs

Filipina/o Americans have a strong but often overlooked history in bilingual education. Filipina/o community leader Cordova (1989) notes that when the Maryknoll School in Seattle attempted to teach Tagalog in the 1940s, it didn't work because the school brought in a Filipina/o teacher to teach Tagalog to Ilocano children. In 1971, Cordova helped organize one of the first bilingual programs in the nation in collaboration with the Filipino Youth Activities of Seattle, Inc. When the National Advisory Council on Bilingual Education was formed in 1974, Cordova served on the board.

Another community-based organization, Iskwelehang Pilipino, was established in Boston in 1976 to provide a bicultural-bilingual education to Filipina/o American children. With one of the best children's rondalla string ensembles in the United States, Iskwelehang Pilipino hopes to expand its programs to include more Tagalog instruction. In a 1992 interview by Yeng Felipe, Cris Castro, one of the founders of Iskwelehang Pilipino, noted, "Once [Iskwelehang Pilipino students] leave the school, many become leaders at universities . . . in Asian programs. They are more proud in saying that, 'We are Filipinos; we want to show you what our culture is like.'"

Ramos (1996) reports that Tagalog and Ilocano were taught in

Hawaii public schools when a private, nonprofit educational project developed teleclass materials for these languages in an effort to help maintain community ethnic languages. The two Philippine languages were included among the eleven selected for the project. Unfortunately, the project ended in 1992 owing to lack of funding. As of 1994, only Tagalog continued to be taught at Radford High School with funding from the Hawaii Department of Education. Ilocano and Tagalog are occasionally taught in elementary schools.

The 1,600 Filipina/o students in San Francisco Unified School District constitute 7.6% of the 21,054 English language learners. As part of San Francisco's Language Academy, San Francisco's Filipino Education Center (FEC) maintains a goal of becoming a "nationally known Filipino/English late exit/two-way immersion demonstration school of Language Academy by the year 2000." The school's vision is to "start the newcomer Filipino American children . . . on their way to becoming bilingual/bicultural critical thinkers who validate their bicultural identity and respect the identities of others." The FEC is one of the only Filipino bilingual programs with its own Web site: ⟨http://sf.bilingual.net/action_plan/FEC/homepage.htm⟩.

Conclusion: A new educational perspective

Educators continue to explore the relationship between language maintenance and educational achievement. Research points to a constellation of factors that influence the education of Filipina/o Americans.

Since the mid-nineteenth century, a major goal of U.S. public education has been to Americanize immigrant students by distancing them from their home culture and language. Hence, any student who differed from a standard norm was viewed as deficient. Despite the symbolic violence of such practices, the legacy of deficit assumptions persists. Teachers, community leaders, parents, and students must continue to find ways to challenge ideas and practices that view Filipina/o and other students as deficient.

The 1996 edition of *Social Process in Hawaii*, organized around the theme of "Filipino American History, Identity and Community in Hawai'i," documents one example of challenging deficit assumptions. Agbayani (1996) cites a Hawaii Department of Education report that identified the following four problems facing Filipina/o immigrant schoolchildren: (1) English language deficiencies, (2) difficulty in socializing with local students, (3) lack of relevant schooling, and (4) difficulty understanding the value system of American society. Rather than accepting these issues as problems of the Filipino child as presented by the Department of Education report, Agbayani reframes them in ways that promote partnerships among educational institutions, students, and the community. With this shift in focus, the issues become lack of appreciation of the language of the immigrant child, lack of bilingual teaching staff, lack of relevant curriculum appropriate to the school attended by the student, and difficulty in understanding the value system of the child. Recognizing how one's own thinking may be (even unconsciously) influenced by biased assumptions of deficit and then reframing issues so that the Filipina/o student is no longer simply the problem are critical first steps in creating teaching and earning settings that maximize learning for English language learners who are Filipina/o.

Suggestions for further reading

Cordova, F. (1983). *Filipinos: Forgotten Asian Americans – A pictorial essay 1763–1963*. Dubuque, IA: Kendall/Hunt.
    Community-based historian Cordova combines photos, narratives, and excerpts from oral history interviews to create the most comprehensive presentation of the pre-1965 history of Filipina/os in the United States.
Gonzalez, A. (1996). Using two/three languages in Philippine classrooms: Implications for policies, strategies and practices. *Journal of Multilingual and Multicultural Development, 17,* 210–219.
    Currently secretary of education in the Philippines, linguist Gonzalez provides an overview of the complex factors involved in developing bilingual programs in the Philippines.
Flores, P. (1994). *Journal of the American Association for Philippine Psychology, 1* (1).
    The first volume of the *Journal of the American Association for Philippine Psychology* opens with a valuable introduction to the late Virgilio G. Enriquez's pioneering work as founder of Sikolohiyang Pilipino, traditional Filipina/o indigenous psychology. It also includes "The Cultural Identity of Third-Wave Filipino Americans," by Leny Mendoza Strobel, and "Philippine American Youth Between Two Expectations: Filipino and U.S. Parenting Standards," by Penelope Flores.
Ramos, T. V. (1996). Philippine languages in Hawai'i: Vehicles of cultural survival. *Social Process in Hawai'i, 37,* 161–170.
    Author of numerous Filipino language textbooks, Ramos provides an expert overview of Hawaii Filipina/os' linguistic backgrounds and the process of language retention or loss by various waves of immigrants. Ramos presents the push for the teaching Philippine languages as a vehicle for cultural strength and survival of Filip-

ina/os in Hawaii. Since this volume of *Social Process in Hawai'i* has as its theme "Filipino American History, Identity, and Community in Hawai'i," many of the other articles will be of interest to teachers of Filipina/o students.

Root, M. P. (1997). *Filipino Americans: Transformation and identity.* Thousand Oaks, CA: Sage.

This interdisciplinary resource on Filipina/o Americans includes various articles on demographics, identity, mental health, gay and lesbian issues, mail-order brides, education, community organizing, and other topics. Many of the contributors frame issues within the broader context of U.S. colonization of the Philippines and its subsequent influence on Filipina/o experiences.

References

Agbayani, A. R. (1996). The education of Filipinos in Hawai'i. *Social Process in Hawai'i, 37*, 147–160.

Alvarez, A. (1991, December). *Pilipino or English in science learning? The case of bilingual education in the Philippines.* Paper presented at the International Conference on Bilingualism and National Development, Bandar Sri Begawa, Brunei.

Bacho, P. (1997). *Dark blue suit.* Seattle: University of Washington Press.

Barrantes, V. (1894). *La instruccion primaria en Filipinas* [Primary instruction in the Philippines]. Madrid: Imprenta de La Iberia.

Bernabe, E. J. F. (1987). *Language policy formulation, programming, implementation and evaluation in Philippine education (1565–1974).* Manila: Linguistic Society of the Philippines.

Bogardus, E. S. (1976). Anti-Filipino race riots. In J. Quinsaat (Ed.), *Letters in exile* (pp. 51–62). Los Angeles: University of California, Asian American Studies Center. (Original work published 1930)

Bulosan, C. (1990). *America is in the heart.* Seattle: University of Washington Press.

Campos, D. (1998, January 5). Taglish to the max. *Hawaii Filipino Chronicle,* p. 5.

Constantino, R. (1966). The miseducation of the Filipino. In R. Constantino (Ed.), *The Filipinos in the Philippines and other essays* (pp. 39–65). Quezon City, Philippines: Malaya Books.

Cordova, D. (1989). Why they came. In Asian Women United of California (Eds.), *Making waves: An anthology of Asian American women.* Boston: Beacon Press.

Cordova, J. M. T. (1998). *Goals of U.S. Educational Programs in the Philippines 1899–1909.* Unpublished manuscript, Harvard University.

DaVanzo, J. et. al. *Surveying immigrant communities: Policy imperatives and technical challenges.* Santa Monica, CA: Rand.

Enriquez, V. G., & Protacio-Marcelino, E. (1984). *Neo-colonial politics and language struggle in the Philippines.* Quezon City: Philippine Psychology Research and Training House.

349

Espina, M. E. (1988). *Filipinos in Louisiana*. New Orleans, LA: A. F. Laborde & Sons.

Flores, P. V. Philippine American youth between two expectations. *Journal of the American Association for Philippine Psychology, 1,* 55–68.

Forman, S. M. (1991). Filipino participation in civil rights policies and practices in Hawai'i. *Social Process in Hawai'i, 33,* 1–11.

Gomez-Borah, E. (1996). The Filipino landing in Morro Bay. *Filipino American National Historical Society Journal, 4,* 15–18.

Gonzalez, A. (1991a). From English to Filipino: Training teachers for the great shift in social studies in the Philippines. In E. Sadtono (Ed.), *Issues in language teacher education* (Anthology Series 30, pp. 120–134. Singapore: SEAMEO Regional Language Centre.

Gonzalez, A. (1991b). The Philippine variety of English and the problem of standardization. In M. L. Tickoo (Ed.), *Languages and standards: Issues, attitudes, case studies.* (Anthropology Series 26, pp. 86–96). Singapore: SEAMEO Regional Language Centre.

Gonzalez, A. (1996). Using two/three languages in Philippine classrooms: Implications for policies, strategies and practices. *Journal of Multilingual and Multicultural Development, 17,* 210–219.

Gonzalez, A., & Romero, M. C. S. (1993). The Manila lingua franca as the Tagalog of first and second generation immigrants into metro Manila. *Philippine Journal of Linguistics, 24,* 17–38.

Grimes, B. (1996). *Ethnologue.* Dallas, TX: Summer Institute of Linguistics.

Hodgkinson, H. L., & Obarakpor, A. M. (1994). *Immigration to America: The Asian experience.* Washington, DC: Center for Demographic Policy, Institute for Educational Leadership.

Kobylarz, X. P. (1997, November). A hard look in the mirror. *Filipinas Magazine,* pp. 21–24.

Lasker, B. (1931). *Filipino immigration: To the continental United States and to Hawaii.* Chicago: Institute of Pacific Relations.

Lawsin E. (1996). 'Beyond hanggang pier only': Filipino war brides of Seattle 1945–1963. *Filipino American National Historical Journal, 4,* 50–56.

Lott, J. T. (1997). Demographic changes transforming the Filipino American community. In M. P. Root (Ed.), *Filipino Americans: Transformation and identity* (pp. 11–20). Thousand Oaks, CA: Sage.

Manlapit, P. (1933). *Filipinos fight for justice.* Honolulu, HI: Kumalae.

McWilliams, C. (1942). *Brothers under the skin.* Boston: Little, Brown.

Montoya, C. A. (1997). Living in the shadows: The undocumented immigrant experience of Filipinos. In M. P. Root (Ed.), *Filipino Americans: Transformation and identity* (pp. 112–120). Thousand Oaks, CA: Sage.

National Advisory Committee on Farm Labor. (1967). *Farm labor organizing: 1905–1967.* New York: Author.

Ramos, T. V. (1996). Philippine languages in Hawai'i: Vehicles of cultural survival. *Social Process in Hawai'i, 37,* 161–170.

Salamanca, B. S. (1984). *The Filipino reaction to American rule, 1901–1913.* Quezon City, Philippines: New Day.

Salvator, D. (1996). Filipino Americans. In P. Pederson & D. C. Locke (Eds.), *Cultural and diversity issues in counseling* (pp. 29–32). Greensboro, NC: ERIC Counseling and Student Services Clearinghouse.

Scott, W. H. (1984). *Prehispanic source materials for the study of Philippine history.* Quezon City, Philippines: New Day.

Speicher, B. L. (1994). Simultaneous talk: Parallel talk among Filipino American students. *Journal of Multilingual and Multicultural Development, 14,* 411–426.

Strobel, L. M. (1997). Coming full circle: Narratives of decolonization among post-1965 Filipino Americans. In M. P. Root (Ed.), *Filipino Americans: Transformation and identity* (pp. 62–79). Thousand Oaks, CA: Sage.

Zamora-Linmark, R. (1995). *Rolling the R's.* New York: Kaya.

12 Soviet immigrants in the United States

Issues in adjustment

Eli Hinkel

Since the collapse of the Soviet Union in 1991, immigration from the republics that composed it has increased rather dramatically. Because the immigrants often live in close-knit communities, the impression is often that their numbers are sizable, as may be the case in a particular geographical area. Nonetheless, relative to other groups of immigrants, speakers of Russian and other languages found in the former Soviet republics still represent a relatively small number of people. The specific characteristics of Soviet immigrants, such as a considerable level of education, determination, and the years of conditioning necessary to overcome the institutional obstacles inherent in the Soviet system, have led to their being noticed by U.S. educational, government, and other agencies.

An overview of immigration from Russia to the United States

In the 50 years between 1820 and 1870, approximately 8,700 Russian immigrants, a majority of whom were Jews, arrived in the United States. However, between 1880 and 1900, 600,000 entered the country, followed by another 1.5 million before the beginning of World War I. The dramatic increase in the number of immigrants was primarily caused by the assassinations of Czar Alexander II in 1881 and his successor, Alexander III, which resulted in changes in Russian internal policies toward Jews and other religious minorities.

In the United States, the new arrivals settled primarily in eastern and large midwestern cities. In 1911, over 550,000 Russian immigrants lived in New York City, and approximately 160,000 in Chicago. Although those who arrived at the end of the nineteenth century and in the early 1900s were primarily skilled or unskilled laborers (tailors, peddlers, clerks, laundry workers, and carpenters), in the 1920s and 1930s Russian immigrants and their offspring were college-educated lawyers, dentists, musicians, physicians, reporters and editors, architects, teachers, and engineers. These immigrants enrolled in universities in such high numbers that Columbia, New York University, Dartmouth, Princeton, and other universities introduced policies to limit the number of entrants who were first-generation American Jews or Russian Jews who were immigrants (Simon, 1997).

Whereas ethnic Jews from Russia settled primarily in New York, Philadelphia, Boston, Chicago, and Milwaukee, Slavic and other ethnic immigrants commonly moved to California and established communities in San Francisco and Los Angeles. Between 1918 and 1924, prior to the onset of World War I and immediately following the Communist Revolution in Russia in 1917, a relatively large number of Russian immigrants arrived in the United States and Western European countries. Subsequently, however, emigration from the newly formed Soviet Union became severely restricted. In fact, no exit visas were granted to Soviet citizens of any ethnicity until the 1960s. However, some Russians who served in the Soviet armed forces during World War II and who were members of the troops occupying the territories of what were then Poland, Czechoslovakia, and Germany remained in Europe after the war ended and eventually settled in the established Russian communities in large California cities.

In the wave of immigration between the late 1960s and the 1990s, the majority of the new immigrants from the former Soviet Union and its republics have also been Jews who had been substantially assimilated into the Russian culture. As a result of severe restrictions on emigration imposed by the Soviet government throughout its history, the number of people allowed to leave the country prior to the 1970s was small. For example, during the entire decade of the 1960s, only 2,465 Soviet immigrants entered the United States. On the other hand, since the collapse of the Soviet Union, immigration policies have been liberalized, and at present almost half a million recent immigrants reside in the United States. In general terms, because of the immigration restrictions placed by the Soviet government, the numbers of people allowed to leave the Soviet Union and arrive in the United States have followed the variability of U.S.-Soviet relations and Soviet foreign policy.

Approximately 90,000 Jews, Russians, Ukrainians, and Armenians arrived in the United States between 1975 and 1980. However, following the Soviet invasion of Afghanistan, the Soviet government drastically reduced the number of exit visas issued to members of the numerous ethnic and religious groups who expressed their desire to leave the country. In 1983, only 1,400 visas were granted. In the mid-1980s, immigration from the Soviet Union to the United States declined to fewer than 1,000 per year. After 1988, when the liberalization of emigration from Russia and the other former republics began, small groups of non-Jews, e.g., evangelical Christians, Armenians, Baptists, Pentecostals, and Ukrainian Catholics, began to emigrate because of religious persecution. With the onset of the movement toward greater openness and the freedom to emigrate, the numbers of new arrivals rose dramatically, and in 1989, slightly over 11,000 immigrants arrived in the United States. The number of exit visas granted by the Soviet government continued to rise with the collapse of the regime in the early 1990s: 25,479 individuals immigrated in 1990, and 57,104 in 1991 (U.S. Immigration and Naturalization Service [INS] 1992). Another important change that occurred during this time is that the number of ethnic Slavs, e.g., Russians, Ukrainians, and Byelorussians, rose to a new high and represented approximately 50% of all arrivals from the three republics. Between 1992 and 1994, 36,185 immigrated from Russia, and 53,709 from Ukraine.

The increasing numbers of immigrants and the liberalization of emigration from the former Soviet Union led the U.S. Congress to impose a 50,000-immigrants-per-year cap in 1993. Although Congress recognized that certain minorities, such as Jews, evangelical Christians, and Ukrainian Autocephalous Orthodox Christians and Catholics are often subjected to religious persecution in their homelands, members of these groups are no longer considered refugees when they have relatives residing in the United States. All those who want to emigrate from the former republics can do so relatively freely, but U.S. immigration quotas have placed constraints on the numbers who are allowed to enter. According to the *INS Fact Book* (INS, 1997), in 1994, 17,432 immigrants from Ukraine and 14,560 from Russia arrived in the United States, and in 1995, 21,010 and 14,349 arrived, respectively. To put these numbers in perspective new arrivals from Vietnam numbered 41,752 in 1994 and 41,345 in 1995; entrants from the Dominican Republic numbered 38,512 in 1994 and 51,189 in 1995.

By 1995, the total number of immigrants from the former Soviet Union who had resettled in the United States had grown to approximately 454,000. The neighborhoods populated by these immigrants fall into distinct geographical patterns, and by far the largest group (about 258,000) live in the Northeast (New York, New Jersey, Pennsylvania, and Massachusetts). The second largest population center is in the western states, such as California and Oregon (slightly over 97,000), followed by the Midwest (approximately 80,000) and the South (fewer than 20,000) (INS, 1996). The majority of Soviet-born immigrants arrived from large urban areas and thus probably prefer to live in cities. Fewer than 2,000 have chosen to live in rural areas, whereas approximately 285,000 reside in center cities and metropolitan areas and nearby suburbs (167,000). Another reason that new immigrants have traditionally settled in large urban centers is that they provide a high concentration of jobs and offer opportunities for employment.

Over 80% of all immigrants from the Soviet Union have settled in New York, California, New Jersey, Illinois, Florida, Pennsylvania, and Massachusetts. The U.S. census data that account for place of birth and ethnicity do not provide sufficient information to determine areas populated by specific ethnic groups and religious minorities. A large number of Soviet Jews live in New York City; however, many are listed simply as immigrants from Russia and Ukraine. On the other hand, ethnic Armenians have chosen Los Angeles as their preferred location, but many Jews from Armenia live in New York as well.

Immigrants from the former Soviet Union are distinct from many other groups in that they are generally well educated and urbanized. Among all immigrant groups in the United States, they report the second highest levels of education and professional training, superseded only by immigrants from India (INS, 1996).

Until the collapse of its economic and political system, the Soviet Union remained a closed country, in which information about the United States was not available. For this reason, many immigrants arrived with little knowledge of American government institutions, economy, culture, and social values (Gold, 1995). Because the picture of the United States was portrayed in the media by the Soviet propaganda machine, immigrants had only misinformation to draw on as a resource. In reaction to the negative portrayals of capitalism and the attendant social problems, many immigrants created an idealized image of the United States and its economic prosperity and political freedoms. Upon their arrival, however, they often have had to face the fact that the U.S. government institutions are not always very responsive to their needs, that economic resources available for immigration assistance are not as plentiful as they had imagined, and that American communities do not always meet them with open arms as long-lost relatives (Markowitz, 1988). As a result, their period of initial adjustment is often fraught with disappointments. Many have complained about government and institutional inefficiencies, their sponsors' unwillingness to provide appropriate job placement assistance, and American sociocultural values that often seem alien to them, especially because their expectations were based on idealized myths created in the absence of accurate information.

Current demographics: Group size and language background of Russian Americans

In 1990, 333,725 immigrants from the former Soviet Union resided in the United States (U.S. Bureau of the Census, 1993). Of this number, only slightly over 30,000 were school-age children. On average, Soviet immigrants are substantially older than other immigrant groups, with a median age of 37 (Gold, 1996). Of the total number, 327,635 (98%) indicated that they could speak English, but 316,439 (97%) stated that

355

they possessed sufficient language skills to speak English only in daily household activities. However, such self-reports also indicate that 170,556 (51%) of the total did not speak English very well. Among all school-age children (32,051), 19,877 (51%) noted that they did not feel fully proficient in English, and many were enrolled in additional English as a second language (ESL) classes offered in churches, community centers, and public schools (Simon, 1996).

During the early 1980s, the Soviet government frequently required that those who wished to emigrate also take their parents. In this manner, the burden of supporting the elderly was shifted from the Soviet government to immigrant families in the United States. This factor, in addition to the close ties characteristic of traditional Russian households, contributed to the formation of a large group of immigrants aged 65 and older. These individuals often have difficulty learning English and are thus restricted in their choice of neighborhoods. In most cases, they cannot obtain employment and rarely seek it outside the community (Gold, 1996).

Approximately 202,200 immigrants (67% of the total number) arrived in the United States before 1980 and, by 1996 in many cases, had attained the English proficiency necessary to secure employment. According to 1990 census data, 74,502 (22%) reported having earned a college degree (a bachelor's, master's or professional school degree) in the Soviet Union and 5,731 (2%) held doctorates. On the other hand, 99,006 (30%) had not completed the equivalent of a high school education in either the Soviet Union or the United States.

Like many immigrant groups before them, immigrants from Russia and the countries of the former Soviet Union quickly discovered that the road to prosperity in the new land runs through education. The values of Russian, Ukrainian, Armenian, Jewish, and other immigrant groups are often similar to those of European Americans, and they place a great deal of importance on language learning as a means for upward socioeconomic mobility. In her study, Delgado-Gaitan (1994) observes that among Russian immigrants residing in California communities, all had the equivalent of a high school education, and many had obtained additional technical and vocational training. Most dedicated their time to learning English in order to be able to obtain employment. Community- and church-sponsored English classes play the central role in providing immigrants the necessary language skills.

However, like other new arrivals, the new immigrants often find themselves in an economic conundrum – they require resources to obtain language training and schooling that will enable them to obtain employment, but few are available within the community. Welfare assistance and the support of the ethnic and religious community is often needed to allow new arrivals to learn English and attain skills essential for employment. During the initial adjustment period, Russian Orthodox, Armenian, Ukrainian Catholic, Baptist, and Pentecostal churches, as well as Jewish resettlement and religious organizations, such as the Hebrew Immigrant Aid Society (HIAS) and Chabad, provide the requisite assistance that allows immigrants from the former Soviet Union to dedicate their time to learning the language.

Family structure and characteristics

Soviet immigrants usually live in families that include three (and even four) generations. The elderly family members are expected to care for the children, and the breadwinners include both the husband and the wife in the "sandwich" age group. The divorce rate among immigrants is relatively low, and the number of children is frequently limited to one or two. Because the elderly often have difficulty learning the language, living in neighborhoods with other immigrants of similar ethnic origins is often a necessity rather than a choice. However, the support system within the family and within the neighborhood usually creates a strong, cohesive structure of mutual dependence and community. Although most of the elderly remain on government support throughout their lifetimes in the United States, the younger generations quickly acquire the language, technical, and social skills necessary to join the labor force.

In traditional Russian families, parents and grandparents have a great deal of influence on the young generation. Unlike their American counterparts, who are socialized in the peer group, Russian children and adolescents are socialized in their families. Parents retain a great deal of authority in the lives of their children even when children reach their twenties and thirties. Similarly, parents often provide advice, guidance, and social value orientations in such crucial decisions as the choice of marriage partners, education and professional training, and even careers. However, the closeness that serves as a positive factor in the families' coping strategies and the economic adjustment may become a hindrance in the adaptation and socialization processes in the United States when school-age children and adolescents enter schools and the peer group. Compared to their American counterparts, the young generation of émigrés often develops strong ties and, occasionally, dependencies on their parents (Gold, 1996). For example, unmarried young men and women date, socialize, and develop friendships almost exclusively within the community, and many indicate that they would not even consider marrying a native American (Simon, 1996).

Incidents of generational and other internal family conflicts arise frequently and can be attributed to a variety of issues. One is the gap in the level of adaptation to life in the United States that separates individuals with high and low levels of marketable skills and English language proficiency. Although immigrants from the Soviet Union are considered to be highly trained and well educated, this is not true of all (or even most) new arrivals. Young people, whose skills are more technically oriented than those of the older generation, are usually able to find stable and full-time employment within a relatively short period of time, ranging from 1 to 5 years. For example, the average educational level of the Soviet-born population between the ages of 24 and 65 is about 14.8 years; on the other hand, those older than 65 report an average of 8.7 years (Jacobs & Frankel, 1981).

Similarly, young, educated immigrants between the ages of 24 and 45 are able to learn English and achieve a level of proficiency sufficient to secure jobs that allow them to earn a living proximate to that of the American middle class. Data from the 1990 census indicate that those who immigrated between 1971 and 1985 earned an annual average of $32,000 in the New York area and $43,000 in Los Angeles. On the other hand, those who arrived between 1986 and 1990 reported an average income under $15,000 (Simon, 1997). The reason for this disparity in the income of the immigrant groups within the community lies in the fact that language learning, adjustment, and the acquisition of skills marketable in the new country take several years. Thus, those immigrants who arrived in the early 1970s and 1980s had a substantially higher income at the time of the census than those who had been in the United States for less than 5 years. In addition, the gap between the earnings of male and female Soviet-born immigrants appears to be somewhat wider than that among the native-born American middle class, and depending on location, women earned 58–68 cents for every dollar earned by men.

However, the elderly (aged 65 and over) rarely attain high levels of English skills and are thus limited in their options of residence and in quality of life. These immigrants can rarely find employment and are supported by government cash assistance and by their employed children. Most reside in Russian-speaking neighborhoods, where they can find the necessary services and develop the community essential for their social (and often economic) adjustment in the new land. Many elderly people, whose children have found employment and moved out of the neighborhoods, continue to depend on their children for transportation, emotional support, and interactions with government and other bureaucracies. The younger immigrants often find themselves in a bind created by the need to maintain full-time jobs and provide the care needed by their elderly parents (Kosmin, 1990).

Opportunities to acquire the language and technical skills needed to attain economic self-sufficiency are not without pitfalls. Delgado-Gaitan (1994) observes that in Russian immigrant communities family roles frequently undergo shifts that increase conflicts within family units and undermine parental authority. She notes that while in Russia, both men and women spent their days earning a living, but during the adjustment period in the United States, they are often unemployed and devote their time to learning English. This activity puts them on par with their children, who are also involved in learning the language. In their homelands, children saw their parents as breadwinners, authority figures, and decision makers. However, in the United States, parental authority frequently declines, particularly when a family is dependent on welfare or other forms of social assistance. In addition, watching the frustration of their parents often leads children and adolescents themselves to feel frustrated and helpless. Delgado-Gaitan and Trueba (1991) and Jacobs and Frenkel (1981) report that a lack of means to change their environment and an inability to support themselves often lead to feelings of isolation, helplessness, and apathy among immigrant groups that were economically stable and closely connected in their home countries. The decline of the family structure and the shifting social and economic roles within the families of Russian immigrants often lead to behavioral problems among some school-age children and teenagers and to passivity and resignation among others.

Teenage immigrants are often aware of the isolation and somewhat limited educational options that stem from the difficult economic situations in their families. Other factors that contribute to their feelings of exclusion often include a lack of fully developed English proficiency and shortfalls in the social skills requisite in their new environments. Some of the adolescents interviewed by Zamenova (1995) noted that they often felt alien in the peer group. For example, a 19-year-old commented that, following his immigration at the age of 12, he did not seem to fit in with his peers and had few friends: "From the first day I was an outcast. Locked out of most activities by the language barrier, unfamiliar with basic games and customs, I quickly acquired a reputation of a dummy who doesn't even know how to play baseball" (p. 58). Another one mentioned that "the hardest part of being a refugee is to find a job. This was particularly hard for my parents" (p. 45). However, in time, many young Russian immigrants develop the survival skills needed to overcome difficulties associated with immigration.

Johnston (1981) finds a high motivation to achieve among various groups of immigrants from the former Soviet Union. In his study, he identified many similarities in the socioeconomic, educational, and vocational values of European Americans and Soviet immigrants, regardless of their ethnic and religious affiliations (i.e., Jews, Russian Orthodox, and Russian and Ukrainian Catholics). He concludes that because these values and background appear to be congruous, the successful adaptation of Soviet immigrants is not surprising. For example, Johnston points out that Russian immigrants are one of the few groups who arrive from an industrialized country and often have technical skills that can help them acquire the new skills necessary to find better-paid employment. According to Johnston, other sociological factors seem to have contributed to the economic success of the Russian immigrants relative to that of other immigrant groups. For example, he specifies that children's aspirations generally increase with their "father's occupational and educational level" (p. 17; 24% of Russian immigrants report having earned university degrees) and that the social class of the immigrants in their homelands has a direct effect on parental encouragement of children to perform. In the former Soviet Union, individuals with university degrees not only earned a higher income than those without them but also enjoyed a higher social standing. However, Johnston cautions that sociological values associated with achievement appear to have a limited predictive power when it comes to the individual performance of a new arrival. Other value orientations specific to Soviet immigrants, such as close family ties, culturally based socialization processes, and issues of personal identity, may come into play and work to reduce the rate of integration among immigrants.

Note, however, that Soviet immigrants often desire to become naturalized U.S. citizens and do so when this option becomes available to them (Gold, 1996). For example, between 1980 and 1990, over 59,000 Soviet immigrants and refugees became naturalized and thus eligible to vote (Kosmin, 1990). One of the primary reasons for their high rate of naturalization is that as U.S. citizens they can accord their immediate and distant relatives greater opportunities to immigrate to the United States.

Demographics and types of employment

With the exception of those who are 65 and over, approximately 70% of the Soviet born work full- or part-time. An additional 10–24% are actively looking for work. Because employment in the professions practiced in the former Soviet Union is not always available (for example, many immigrants are trained as concert musicians, specialists in the Soviet law, and Soviet management practices), a comparatively large number are unable to find employment in their former occupations. Furthermore, upon their arrival Soviet and Russian immigrants often discover that their English skills are not as good as they believed them to be (Kosmin, 1990).

As a result of these and other factors, many immigrants are underemployed, and the loss of status among them seems to be comparatively high. Individuals react to their unemployment and underemployment in various ways: Some become determined to regain their former professional status, level of earnings, and social prestige, and others may become angry and depressed. Nonetheless, within approximately 5 years of their arrival, a vast majority find stable employment, and about 90% of men and 70% of women find jobs that can meet their economic needs (Gold, 1996). According to U.S. census data, about 17% of Soviet immigrants were self-employed in 1990, but their businesses have not always been successful (Delgado-Gaitan, 1994). Shortfalls in their language proficiency and a lack of familiarity with U.S. business practices are often cited among the reasons for failures of small enterprises established by these immigrants (Simon, 1997).

The loss of employment status and social prestige, however, seems to be a prominent characteristic in the employment of women. Almost 70% had obtained some college training or graduated from colleges in their homelands. They report having been employed as professionals, engineers, teachers, medical doctors, and technicians. On the other hand, only 16% are able to reenter these occupations in the United States. In contrast, approximately 60% of the men list their former employment as professional or technical, but 26% are able to regain the social status similar to that accorded to their occupations in the former Soviet Union (Gold, 1994).

Resettlement and views on organizations and institutions

Throughout their resettlement and adjustment process, Jews from the former Soviet Union are supported by several private agencies, such as HIAS and the Council of Jewish Federations, that have long and established histories of immigrant assistance. These charitable agencies have developed community networks that include language classes; employment and retraining services; day care centers; summer camps for children and adolescents; and recreation, cultural, and religious centers. In addition, a number of other local volunteer assistance groups in various locations with sizable Jewish populations contribute to the successful resettlement of Jewish immigrants in the United States (Simon, 1997).

Church-affiliated and community organizations provide support for Russian Orthodox, Pentecostal, and Ukrainian Catholic immigrants. These organizations, however, are fewer and generally less well funded, in part because they are newer and serve fewer immigrants than those devoted to Jewish resettlement in the United States. Also, whereas HIAS and the Council of Jewish Federations are integrated and centralized resettlement agencies, church-based organizations are often established locally by ministers in the Baptist, Pentecostal, Orthodox, and Armenian churches. These ethnic and religious minorities often rely on the social services and retraining and employment agencies that provide assistance to other Americans in the area where they live. Although language classes are often offered in the resettlement organizations, these groups of immigrants attend ESL classes in local public schools and 2-year colleges.

In their homelands, Slavic immigrants usually worked as bookkeepers, farmers, drivers, mechanics, cooks, miners, construction workers, and tradespeople, although a few received training as dentists, electricians, and teachers. However, because they are often unable to reenter their former occupations, they also seek retraining in 2-year vocational schools and community colleges. Some entrepreneurs open small businesses in automobile repair, house cleaning, carpentry, and child care. Immigrant families devote a great deal attention and effort to their children's language learning, but, unable to prepare their youngsters for school, they seek assistance from community volunteers, home-study specialists, and school tutoring programs (Delgado-Gaitan, 1994). In general, because education has a high social value in the Russian, Ukrainian, and other Slavic cultures, and because parents understand the importance of language skills in their children's ability to secure jobs, the children are strongly encouraged to use English as much as possible (as is the case with many immigrant families).

Soviet immigrants usually have positive views of the centralized and community resettlement agencies and services. However, about one third of a sample of nine hundred noted that expectations of the adjustment processes and the quality of services, cultural differences, and American views on immigrants often create obstacles in their interactions with such organizations (Simon, 1985).

In general terms, Soviet émigrés are highly skeptical about institutions, organizations, and organizational activities and are accustomed to relying on their friends and relatives for help. For example, Delgado-Gaitan (1994), Gold (1994), Kosmin (1990), Markowitz (1988), and Simon (1985, 1997) recount the confrontations and problems experienced by the Soviet immigrants who deal with government, community, and social organizations in the United States. Culturally based views on welfare assistance, retraining and employment services, mental health issues, and community and religious socialization may come into play in the interactions between American service providers and immigrants who require their services. Occasionally, hostile relationships develop between these groups, which see one another as foreign and lacking an understanding of the adjustment process and appropriate ways of coping.

Another issue in the resettlement of Jews from the former Soviet Union seems to have exacerbated their attitude to American institutional practices. The majority of American Jews are descendants of immigrants from Germany and Russia who arrived in the United States in the 19th and the early 20th century. In most cases, they belong to religious congregations and social groups that encourage participation in temple activities, philanthropic institutions, and particular lifestyles. They often send their children to private Jewish schools and dedicate time to worthy causes, such as helping Jews emigrate or resettle in the United States. When Jewish emigration from the Soviet Union began in the 1970s, many American Jews saw this development as the fruition of their efforts to win the liberalization of restrictive Soviet policies and were willing to contribute their money, time, and other resources to facilitate the adjustment of the new arrivals. However, they also expected that the Soviet Jews would follow a resettlement path similar to that of their grandparents, i.e., accept any job offered to them, join religious congregations, gratefully participate in social gatherings, and become a part of the American Jewish community (Simon, 1997). American Jews often believed that theirs was the appropriate way to be Jewish in the United States and that Soviet Jews who lacked religious aspirations were "really not 'Jewish' after all" (Markowitz, 1988, p. 88).

However, the Soviet Jews were not very similar to the Russian immigrants of almost a century ago. Many were educated and urbane professionals who were not at all religious. They had successfully overcome many obstacles in the Soviet Union, where they had achieved a relatively high socioeconomic status, and expected to be treated according to their talents and accomplishments, regardless of whether or not they were willing to join the temples, social groups, and charitable undertakings. In addition, they expected American Jews to treat them as a part of the family instead of as "poor relatives"; they often looked down on American Jews whom they perceived to be materialistic and "soft" because they themselves (unlike their predecessors) would not have been able to overcome the adversity associated with Soviet anti-Semitism, immigration, and resettlement (Gold, 1995).

Because American Jews often sponsored the resettlement of the Soviet Jews in the United States, the resulting tension often led to disappointment and anger on the part of the former and withdrawal from the community (and even hostility) on the part of the latter. One of the outcomes of the conflict between the American and the Soviet Jews appears to be a strengthening of the social ties and self-reliance within the immigrant group, and the new arrivals often set out to assist one another through informal social organizations. For example, literary discussion clubs and magazines writers' groups, and musical performances devoted to Russian culture and artistic ventures have been flourishing in New York and Philadelphia. These undertakings represent an "integral part of the identify of most of the members of this network" (Markowitz, 1988, p. 89), and some of the members explicitly avoid any Russian resettlement programs sponsored by American Jews and affiliated with the American Jewish establishment.

Current research on language use in the community

As Delgado-Gaitan (1994) points out, "little, if any, research literature exists on the current Russian refugees" (p. 151), and relatively little information is available on language use in the Soviet immigrant community, Jewish, Russian, Ukrainian, and Armenian alike. Like other immigrant groups, the new arrivals from the former Soviet Union and the republics often live in neighborhoods where Russian is the language of daily interaction and business. Three Russian language newspapers are published in New York, and Russian radio and TV stations are also available. Younger immigrants between the ages of 5 and 19 usually attend public schools, where they receive ESL instruction (Delgado-Gaitan, 1994; Gold, 1994). In general, Soviet immigrants consider themselves highly literate in Russian, rating themselves 4.95–4.97 on a scale of 1 to 5 (Simon, 1985). Their children usually excel in American schools, where in mathematics and sciences classes they are 2 or 3 years ahead of American children of the same age (Delgado-Gaitan, 1994; Gold, 1996).

Language maintenance and shift

Soviet immigrants are relative newcomers among the many immigrant groups in the United States. In fact, in 1988 fewer than 3,000 individuals immigrated to the United States, and between 1990 and 1995, the annual number of arrivals ranged from 25,000 to 63,000. Because a majority of immigrants have not lived in the United States longer than 6–10 years, no substantial language shift has occurred in the community (Chaika, 1994). A vast majority report speaking their first languages at home and developing friendships within the group (Gold, 1996). Like those in other immigrant groups, teenagers and young adults are frequently involved in many family interactions with bureaucracies and institutions outside the immigrant community because their English skills are better than those of their parents and grandparents.

Educational alternatives

Outside of New York, the number of speakers of Russian has not been sufficiently large to warrant creating separate ESL or bilingual programs. Usually, school-age learners attend ESL classes in public schools together with other groups of immigrants, such as Chinese, Vietnamese, and Polish.

According to their self-reports, many immigrants make substantial strides in improving their language skills after arrival. In surveys of language learning efforts of immigrant groups from the Soviet Union,

50–75% reported attending ESL classes (Simon, 1985, 1997). Nonetheless, many immigrants seem to be dissatisfied with the quality of their language instruction (Gold, 1994) and often believe that the language instruction offered to them by Jewish organizations and ESL classes in public schools does not help them progress at an adequate pace.

Conclusion

The majority of Soviet émigrés state that despite their difficulties in finding appropriate employment, learning the language, and adjusting to the American way of life, they prefer living in the United States to living in the countries of the former Soviet Union. Highly literate and skilled, they have been able to succeed in their economic transition to the United States. The younger generations of immigrants have learned English sufficiently well to achieve many of their employment and academic objectives.

On the other hand, Soviet immigrants largely remain outside the mainstream of American social and political organizations and do not seek active involvement in organized activities sponsored by religious, political, and social institutions. Even though they naturalize in proportions greater than some other immigrant groups, naturalization is seen as a way to facilitate subsequent immigration of members of their families to the United States rather than an indication of a desire to take part in American political affairs. Whereas Soviet Jews usually do not have religious affiliations and consider themselves to be members of the Russian culture, ethnic Russians, Ukrainians, Byelorussians, and other Slavic minorities often have strong ties to various Christian communities. These religious minorities often cherish the freedom of practicing their faith without religious persecution. The church represents the focus of their social networks, commitments, and support systems. Their religious communities provide them with a social code of values for behavior and adjustment to their new life.

Jewish and Slavic families alike see members of their communities as a primary source of assistance in finding jobs, and of support in health, legal, and financial crises. Regardless of ethnicity, Soviet immigrants see the learning of English as an essential step in their ability to secure economic stability for their families. In general, they dedicate a great deal of family resources to the education and training of their children. These families are characterized by closeness and a multigenerational structure, with its attendant dependencies and conflicts often exacerbated by the immigration. Because a high proportion of the elderly (slightly fewer than two thirds of the total) are often unable to learn the language, many seek government assistance.

Soviet immigrants care deeply about maintaining their cultural identities and are unlikely to be pressured into Americanization, as sponsoring and resettlement agencies expected of them in late 1980s and early 1990s. Although individualism represents an important social value among these new arrivals, their collective sense of community often stems from belonging to their immigrant groups, with a shared language and cultural orientation. This prominent characteristic, which is common among Jewish and Slavic adult immigrants, is unlikely to change in the near future. The process of their children's adaptation to life in the United States and the adjustments they make as they enter adulthood remain to be seen.

Suggestions for further reading

Research devoted to Soviet immigrants has been carried out by anthropologists predominantly focusing on Jewish communities in the United States. Fewer than two dozen articles and books dealing with Soviet immigration to the United States have been published since the mid-1970s. Of this number, at least five are out of print. The following short bibliographical list is included to help those who are interested in additional information.

Delgado-Gaitan (1994) focuses on the role of religious and social organizations in the adjustment of Russian refugees in a California city. The development of coping strategies in families, as well as new approaches to dealing with the cultural and economic realities in the United States, are discussed, and their accomplishments and difficulties are highlighted. The Russian refugees' experiences with the American educational system – the schooling of youngsters and adult literacy programs – speak to their mixed success in adapting their cultural and community values to new environments.

Gold's (1995) in-depth ethnographic study of Soviet Jewish immigrants to California presents many aspects of their life in their new homeland. As an anthropological case study, this work covers many facets in the life of the community: the reasons for their immigration to the United States, their family structures and changes, economic survival and social mobility, the search for a new identity, the formation of new communities, and adaptation to American life.

Markowitz (1988), in her article about the most recent groups of Russian and Soviet Jewish immigrants to the United States, addresses their search for identity in the American Jewish community. The established American Jewish views on what it means to be Jewish and how to manifest Jewish attributions often conflict with those of the new arrivals, who are ethnically Jewish but culturally Russian. The author notes cultural and social rifts between these two divergent populations and describes the coping strategies of immigrants whose identity is challenged in the face of their adjustment processes.

Simon's (1997) work represents an anthropological analysis and historical and sociocultural overview of Jewish immigration from Russia and other countries of the former Soviet Union. The issues of Jewish religious and Russian cultural dichotomies are addressed as the new immigrants face them in their interactions with the American Jewish communities and with U.S. socioeconomic and political frameworks. The author concludes that although it may be too early to provide definitive assessments of the experiences of the Russian and Soviet Jews in the United States, they appear to have changed the long-standing belief that it takes three generations for immigrant families to achieve educational and economic parity with the native population; this group of immigrants attained it in one.

Zamenova's (1995) short book includes interviews with six teenagers, who together with their families immigrated from the Soviet Union in the 1980s. Some of the interviews are devoted exclusively to the teenagers' lives in their former homelands, and others focus mostly on their own and their families' adaptation to their new life in the United States. Although this volume is not designed to be a study, it presents interesting and sometimes touching testimonies on the difficult adjustment process of former Soviet families in the United States.

References

Chaika, E. (1994). *Language: The social mirror* (3rd ed.). Boston: Heinle & Heinle.

Delgado-Gaitan, C. (1994). Russian refugee families: Accommodating aspirations through education. *Anthropology and Education Quarterly, 25,* 137–155.

Delgado-Gaitan, C., & Trueba, H. (1991). *Crossing cultural borders: Education for immigrant families in America.* London: Falmer Press.

Gold, S. (1994). *Soviet Jews in the United States.* Newbury Park, CA: Sage.

Gold, S. (1995). *From the workers' state to the golden state: Jews from the former Soviet Union in California.* Boston: Allyn & Bacon.

Gold, S. (1996). Soviet Jews. In D. Haines (Ed.), *Refugees in America in the 1990s: A reference handbook* (pp. 279–304). Westport, CT: Greenwood Press.

Jacobs, D. & Frankel, E. (1981). *Studies of the third wave: Recent migrations of Soviet Jews to the United States.* Boulder, CO: Westview Press.

Johnston, B. (1981). *Russian American social mobility: An analysis of the achievement syndrome.* Saratoga, CA: Century Twenty-One.

Kosmin, B. (1990). *The class of 1979: The "acculturation" of Jewish immigrants from the Soviet Union.* New York: Council of Jewish Federations.

Markowitz, F. (1988). Jewish in the USSR, Russian in the USA. In W. Zenner (Ed.), *Persistence and flexibility* (pp. 79–95). Albany, NY: SUNY Press.

Simon, R. (1985). Soviet Jews. In D. Haines (Ed.), *Refugees in the United States* (pp. 181–193). Westport, CT: Greenwood Press.

Simon, R. (1997). *In the golden land: A century of Russian and Soviet Jewish immigration in America.* Westport, CT: Praeger.

U.S. Bureau of the Census. (1993). *1990 census of population – The foreign-born population in the United States.* Washington, DC: U.S. Government Printing Office.

U.S. Immigration and Naturalization Service. (1992). *Immigration from the former Soviet Union* (Bulletin No. 10). Washington, DC: U.S. Government Printing Office.

U.S. Immigration and Naturalization Service. (1996). *INS statistical year book.* Washington, DC: U.S. Government Printing Office.

U.S. Immigration and Naturalization Service. (1997). *INS fact book.* Washington, DC: U.S. Government Printing Office.

Zamenova, T. (1995). *Teenage refugees from Russia speak out.* New York: Rosen.

13 At home with English

Assimilation and adaptation of Asian Indians in the United States

Kamal K. Sridhar and S. N. Sridhar

Introduction

The study of the language and communication patterns of the *New Ethnics* (the educated, mostly professional, post-1965 immigrants) in the United States is interesting and important for a number of reasons. It raises and can potentially throw a new light on what are, to our mind, central theoretical and practical issues in how languages are used, preserved, and transmitted across generations in a multicultural society. Of these New Ethnics, the Asian Indians in particular are an especially promising case to study because their complex linguistic background, impressive achievements, and interesting reaction to assimilation provides insights into major issues of language maintenance, including the following:

- What is the nature of language use in the first and second generation of immigrants?
- Is there any difference between the patterns of language use and maintenance and of assimilation and socialization in immigrant communities that comes from traditionally multilingual and multicultural societies and the patterns of those who come from monolingual societies?
- What role does internal-linguistic diversity play in the language maintenance of a community? What limitations does it impose on the community's ability to influence public policy and obtain community services?
- What is the impact of extensive prior (that is, premigration) familiarity with the host language on the immigrants' ethnic language maintenance and assimilation?
- What is the impact of relatively high education, economic status, and family cohesion on language maintenance?

In addition, as part of the post-1965 New Ethnics, the Asian Indian community in the United States can contribute to the study of a number of equally fascinating contemporary issues:

We would like to thank Tony Polson and Soma Phillipos for help in collecting the Malayali data and Hema Shah for help in collecting the Gujarati data.

- How do the availability of instant and affordable global communication and travel affect patterns of language maintenance and loss?
- How have post–Civil Rights movement cultural values, in particular the greater tolerance of diversity, affected language maintenance?

Finally, the complex multilingual background of Asian Indians in the United States makes us rethink some fundamental theoretical constructs, including the very definition of a bilingual and the dichotomous conceptualization of language maintenance and shift.

Despite the potential significance of these and related issues, little systematic research has been done on the language patterns of Asian Indians in the United States. Our account is, therefore, based largely on our own pilot studies and informal observations and represents preliminary findings and hypotheses, which need to be supplemented by a large-scale empirical study with proper controls.

Asian Indians in the United States: Early history of migration

A colonial diary from the year 1790 records the first arrival of an East Indian in North America, a man from Madras (South India) who settled in Salem, Massachusetts. He had come to America with a colonial sea captain and with a desire to expand trade (of silk, linens, spices, and other goods) between New England, Britain, and South Asia (Helweg & Helweg, 1990, pp. 45–46). The numbers that followed him were not substantial. Only six Asian Indians participated in Salem's Fourth of July celebration in 1851. Most of the Asian Indians who came during this period were merchants who traveled to Chicago and San Francisco for trade but returned to India. In the late 1800s and the 1900s, a number of Indian men from Punjab migrated to the United States. Several were hired to work in the lumber mills in Bellingham, Washington. Others moved to the San Joaquin Valley in central California. Each group suffered a different fate.

The Indian laborers in Bellingham became targets of racism and violence. The laborers worked hard for minimum wages, angering the American and European workers, who belonged to organized labor movements that wanted to maintain higher wage levels in the lumber and railroad industries. To vent their frustration and anger, on September 5, 1907, a mob of over five hundred angry men kicked open the doors of the "Hindoo" laborers' homes. They beat them, looted their property, and burnt their bunkhouses. The police stood by and did not attempt to stop the mobs. The Bellingham riots triggered similar riots and expulsions elsewhere, e.g., in Everett, Washington. Bewildered by the intensity of the hatred, the Indian laborers left to find work elsewhere.

A larger number of Asian Indians came to the United States through Vancouver, Canada. The first Asian Indians in the United States, most of whom were farmers from the state of Punjab, probably never exceeded six thousand during the period 1904–1923. They settled in California, forming little communities in Yuba City. Their farming background in Punjab made them well suited for agricultural work, and they found jobs as farmhands. They worked hard, saved money, and eventually became farmers and landowners in the Sacramento, Imperial, and San Joaquin valleys. The land in these areas was "unfit for the white man," but the Indian farmers thrived there. According to the 1919 land census in the state of California, Indians owned 88,000 acres, 52% of which was in the Sacramento Valley (Koritala, 1998).

Between 1902 and 1910, a small group of students came to pursue higher education in the United States. They joined the other expatriates and became active in the Ghadhar Party, a movement established to support India's struggle for freedom from British colonial domination. They also faced hardships, for it was not just the labor movements that were creating problems for the Asian Indians. The colonial British government that ruled India also pressured the U.S. government to put an end to Indian students' support for the Indian freedom struggle. Unfortunately, the political forces in the United States supported racism and British colonialism. President Theodore Roosevelt called for an American conquest of the Philippines in 1903 because it was an "inevitable march of events" where the "dominant race" was the conqueror (Koritala, 1998, p. 4). While addressing Congress in 1904, he legitimized British colonial rule in India by comparing it with U.S. rule in the Philippines. It is unfortunate that the U.S. government joined hands with the British to monitor and deport these politically active Indian students, for most of them were put to death by the British upon their arrival in India.

During this same period, a small group of educated Asian Indians who came to the United States also faced discrimination. Their increasing numbers created a clamor among the local residents. In response, the U.S. Supreme Court ruled in 1923 that East Asians were not eligible for citizenship because they were not White. (A 1790 naturalization law had restricted citizenship to free White people.) This law, known as the Indian Exclusion Act, was successfully challenged by an Asian Indian lawyer, Sakaram Ganesh Pandit, who argued that East Asians are Aryans (hence White). Pandit was allowed to retain his U.S. citizenship. In 1946 the U.S. Congress enacted laws allowing East Indians citizenship in the United States and allotted an annual immigration quota of one hundred people.

TABLE I. ASIAN INDIAN IMMIGRATION TO THE
UNITED STATES, 1901–1990

Decade	Immigrants
1901–1910	4,713
1911–1920	2,082
1921–1930	1,886
1931–1940	496
1941–1950	1,761
1951–1960	1,973
1961–1970	30,461
1971–1980	172,104
1981–1990	267,838

Source: U.S. Bureau of the Census (1990).

The Asian Indian community in the United States: A profile

Only in the post–Civil Rights movement era did the immigration of Asian Indians begin to go beyond a marginal status. The 1965 Immigration Reform Act allowed people of every nationality equal immigration rights and gave preferential treatment to professionals, increasing the immigration of Asian Indians to the United States. Thus, almost the entire population of Asian Indians in the United States (except for the Sikh communities in Yuba City) arrived after 1960. (For a more detailed history of the Asian Indians in the United States, see Gall, 1995; Gall & Gall, 1993; Helweg, 1997; Helweg & Helweg, 1990; Saran & Eames, 1980).

The Asian Indian immigration figures for the years 1901–1990 are given in Table 1.

As of August 1998, over one million Asian Indians were estimated to be in the United States. In 1990, the latest year for which detailed census figures are available, the total population of Asian Indians in the United States was 815,447. (The corresponding figure in the 1980 census was 361,500.) They are spread all over the country, with varying degrees of concentration (see Table 2). The largest numbers of Asian Indians are in California (159,973), followed by New York (140,985), New Jersey (79,440), Illinois (64,200), and Texas (55,795), which may be termed high-density states.

As post-1965 immigrants, Asian Indians are included in the group referred to as the New Ethnics (Saran & Eames, 1980 p. 1). "The new wave of Indian immigrants, which started in 1965, has brought mostly professional and middle class people from India. . . . Although no surveys are available, it is reasonable to assume that Indians are not con-

TABLE 2. DISTRIBUTION OF ASIAN INDIANS IN THE UNITED STATES

State	No.	State	No.
Alabama	4,848	Montana	248
Alaska	472	Nebraska	1,218
Arizona	5,663	Nevada	1,825
Arkansas	1,329	New Hampshire	1,697
California	159,973	New Jersey	79,440
Colorado	3,836	New Mexico	5,193
Connecticut	11,755	New York	140,985
Delaware	2,183	North Carolina	9,847
District of Columbia	1,601	North Dakota	482
Florida	31,456	Ohio	20,848
Georgia	13,926	Oklahoma	4,546
Hawaii	1,015	Oregon	3,508
Idaho	473	Pennsylvania	28,396
Illinois	64,200	Rhode Island	1,975
Indiana	7,095	South Carolina	3,900
Iowa	3,021	South Dakota	287
Kansas	3,956	Tennessee	5,911
Kentucky	3,922	Texas	55,795
Louisiana	5,083	Utah	1,557
Maine	607	Vermont	529
Maryland	28,330	Virginia	20,494
Massachusetts	19,719	Washington	8,205
Michigan	23,845	West Virginia	1,981
Minnesota	8,234	Wisconsin	6,914
Mississippi	1,872	Wyoming	240
Missouri	6,111		

Source: U.S. Census, 1990, Census of the Population, Population Division.

sidered 'colored' in the United States today as they are in Britain. In England, Indians are a racial category; in the United States they are an ethnic group" (Varma, 1980, p. 30). Asian Indians tend to live mostly in big cities and towns, a preference probably due to the fact that most lived in metropolitan areas prior to immigration. Mogelonsky (1995) confirms these observations, noting that New York City was home to 106,000 Asian Indians in 1990 (forming 1.2% of the city's population), followed by Chicago (54,000), Los Angeles–Long Beach (44,000), and Washington, DC (36,000). They made up 2.1% of the population of Jersey City, New Jersey, in 1990 (p. 1).

Unlike the earlier Asian Indian immigrants, the new generation of immigrants occupy mostly professional jobs. Among the Asian Indians in the U.S. workforce in 1990, 30% were employed in professional specialty occupations, compared with 13% of all U.S. employees. Among the foreign-born Indian professionals, 26% are engineers, 20% are physicians, and 12% are college and university teachers (a total of 58%). Unlike many other immigrant groups, Asian Indians, by virtue of an extensive knowledge of and fluency in the English language, can take up well-paying, prestigious, and influential white-collar jobs and directly enter the American middle class, economically speaking, without much hardship. "Asian Indians are slightly over-represented among managerial and sales/technical/clerical workers, and under represented among service and blue-collar workers, according to the 1990 census" (Mogelonsky, 1995, p. 2). The median income for Asian Indian households, at $48,320, is the highest among several other Asian groups, U.S.-born persons, and other foreign-born persons, as summarized in Table 3.

Of course, not all Asian Indians are affluent. Whereas the immigrants who came in the 1960s and 1970s are mostly professionals, the sponsored relatives of the naturalized citizens are less educated and are likely to run motels, small grocery stores, or gas stations or to drive taxicabs. In this connection, it is interesting to note that 40% of New York City's 40,000 licensed Yellow Cab drivers are South Asians from India, Pakistan, and Bangladesh (Mogelonsky, 1995, p. 2). In addition, Asian Indians are a dominant force in the U.S. hospitality industry today. "Asian Indian ownership of hotels and motels is the standout example of Indian penetration into the service segment. In 1994, 7,200 Asian Indian owners operated 12,500 of the nation's 28,000 budget motels and hotels, according to the Atlanta-based Asian American Hotel Owners Association" (p. 3). According to Eliot Kang of the New York City–based Kang and Lee Advertising, which specializes in marketing to Asian minorities, "Asian Indians dominate in some trades, such as convenience and stationery stores . . . large family networks and family fi-

TABLE 3. MEDIAN HOUSEHOLD INCOME, UNITED STATES, BY COUNTRY OF ORIGIN (U.S. DOLLARS)

Country of origin	Median household income
India	48,320
Philippines	45,419
Japan	34,999
United Kingdom	34,339
Guyana	34,243
United States	30,176
All foreign countries	28,314

Source: U.S. Bureau of the Census (1990), Social and Economic Characteristics.

nancing give these businesses a chance to grow and expand. And because so many family members are involved, Asian Indian businesses can flourish in labor-intensive service industries" (cited in Mogelonsky, p. 2). These patterns of occupational preference are important in interpreting findings on language maintenance and language shift.

Asian Indian immigrants in the United States define themselves in terms of several overlapping identities: regional; linguistic; social (caste, occupation, income); and religious (Hindu, Muslim, Christian, Sikh, Buddhist, Jain).

Premigration language experience

Asian Indians come from a traditionally multilingual and pluricultural country. The 1981 census of India reported 107 languages being spoken there (Krishnamurti, 1989). However, this figure is at variance with that of the 1961 census, in which 1,652 mother tongues were reported (Pattanayak, 1971; Srivastava, 1988). The figures vary for a number of reasons: A given language may be reported under as many as forty-seven different names, reflecting the respondent's ethnic, professional, attitudinal and other affiliations; several varieties of the same language exist, some mutually unintelligible, others not. Languages reported by more than one thousand persons, excluding foreign mother tongues (e.g., Portuguese, French), number approximately 400. These languages belong to four different language families: Indo-Aryan, Dravidian, Sino-Tibetan, and Austro-Asiatic. Complicating the linguistic scene is the presence and use of more than forty scripts (Daniels & Bright, 1996), religious and caste dialects, diglossic variation (high and low varieties of the language), and code-mixed varieties (the mixing of two languages; see B. B. Kachru, 1997; Kachru & Sridhar, 1978; K. K. Sridhar, 1989). After winning independence from British colonial rule in 1947, the states of India were reorganized into twenty-five major states and other union (federal) territories, most of which are identified by a distinct language spoken by the majority of the people in the region. Apart from the dominant regional language, every region is inhabited by several types of minority language speakers, e.g., speakers of tribal languages, migrant language speakers, religious minorities. The proportion of minority language speakers varies from one state to another, ranging between 5% in Kerala (south) to 84.5% in Nagaland (northeast). The educational system also promotes multilingualism, as is evidenced by the protection given to minority languages and the active promotion of the official language-in-education policy, the Three Language Formula, according to which all school-going children learn to read and write in their mother tongue (or the regional language, in the case of languages without scripts or literary traditions), Hindi (the official language of the country), and English (the associate official language of the country).

The salient features of Asian Indian bilingualism (for more details, see K. K. Sridhar, 1989) include

1. the fluidity of language identity, leading to the underreporting and variable reporting of the extent of bilingualism in the area (Khubchandani, 1983);
2. the high degree of societal bilingualism, not only in border areas and among the educated population but also on a very widespread scale among the population in general (*grassroots bilingualism*);
3. the widespread use of mixed language varieties;
4. the phenomenon of linguistic convergence, i.e., the tendency for languages in contact to adopt one another's formal features, resulting in the formation of a South Asian *linguistic area* (D'souza, 1987; Emeneau, 1956; Gumperz & Wilson, 1971; S. N. Sridhar, 1981); and
5. the tendency on the part of minority language speakers to maintain their languages, despite a low level of literacy and inadequate formal language instruction (Pandit, 1972).

For the purposes of this chapter, Factors (2) and (5) warrant a more detailed discussion. Pandit's (1972) profile of a hypothetical Gujarati spice merchant settled in Bombay typifies Indian bilingualism. This spice merchant, according to Pandit, can simultaneously control five or six languages. He speaks Gujarati in his family domain, Marathi in a vegetable market, Hindi with the milkman, Kacci and Konkani in trading circles, and English on formal occasions. Such a person may not have a lot of formal training in all the languages, but in terms of verbal linguistic ability, he can easily be labeled a multilingual, fairly proficient in controlling different life situations with ease and skill. This societal type of bilingualism-multilingualism has contributed to language maintenance rather than to language shift.

Another distinctive feature of Indian bilingualism is its stability. Speakers of Indian languages tend to maintain their languages over generations and, often, centuries, even when they live away from the region where it is widely spoken. This phenomenon, so different from the norm in the United States, has been documented in a number of studies (e.g., Agnihotri, 1979; Bhatia, 1981; Bhatt, 1989; Gambhir, 1981; Ghuman, 1994; Mesthrie, 1992; Moag, 1978; Mukherjee, 1980; Rangila, 1986; Satyanath, 1982; Siegel, 1987). Although several exceptions exist, especially with reference to the loss of some tribal and minority languages (Chakledar, 1981; Ekka, 1979; Mahapatra, 1979; Srivastava, 1988), there is enough evidence of long-range maintenance to warrant a detailed study of this phenomenon. The migrant speech communities continue to speak their own language in the home domain, and through their mother tongues, they maintain their ethnic identities. Since diversity in food habits, dress, rituals, and languages is expected, and both the migrant community and the host community expect a limited degree of separation, the result is cultural pluralism. Thus, although the migrant speech community retains its native language as an effective device for ethnic separateness and survival, it may acquire the language of the host community as a job-specific language for a limited range of functions, e.g., in the workplace. Such cases of *limited functional shift* rather than total assimilation or loss are seen all over India. For example, in the state of Karnataka, large communities of Telugu, Tamil, Marathi, and Konkani speakers, as well as speakers of Marwari, Hindi, and other languages, have lived without conflict for centuries. Other examples include the Tamil-speaking Palghat Iyers settled in Malayalam-speaking Kerala (Subromoniam, 1977), the Saurarashtri-speaking Gujaratis settled in Tamil-speaking Tamil Nadu (Sharma, 1977), the more than 300-year-old Marathi community settled in Tamil Nadu (K. K. Sridhar, in press), the Tamil speakers settled in Marathi-speaking Bombay, the Telugu-speaking merchants and other Andhras from the neighboring Andhra Pradesh in Kannada-speaking Karnataka, the Bengalis settled in Hindi-Punjabi speaking New Delhi (Mukherjee, 1980), and the Kannada speakers in Hindi-speaking New Delhi (Satyanath, 1982).

Several explanations have been offered for this maintenance. As Gumperz and Wilson (1971) have noted, group-internal factors such as maintenance of social ties, kin relationships, and ethnic separateness of home life, that is, a strict separation between the public and private (intrakin) spheres of activity, are the central variable. The crucial question, as Southworth and Apte (1974) rightly point out, is why ethnic separateness is so critical in South Asia relative to other parts of the world. They also offer a partial answer by noting that the groups who have maintained their linguistic separateness are for the most part "rather small groups who could be said to have some particular reason for remaining separate" (p. 5), such as prestige (e.g., Brahmins), particular occupational identification (e.g., goldsmiths, tailors), or enforced separation (e.g., in the case of the so-called Dalits or formerly untouchables).

Empirical studies of Asian Indian languages in the United States

Asian Indian language groups are quite diverse and have settled in widely separate parts of the United States. Given this diversity and the salience of regional languages and cultures as rallying points, an initial research strategy is to study language maintenance and shift with reference to specific regional groups and to arrive at generalizations inductively. We therefore discuss a selected sample of three language groups among those reported on in earlier studies of language maintenance among Asian Indians in the New York–New Jersey area (K. K. Sridhar, 1988, 1993, 1997). We hope that with appropriate extensions and modifications, these observations can be generalized to other language groups within the Asian Indian community living in other parts of the United States.

Scope, data, and method

We began the study of language maintenance and language shift with speakers of Kannada (referred to as Kannadigas) and expanded the scope of the study to include speakers of Gujarati (referred to as Gujaratis) and Malayalam (referred to as Malayalis).

The Kannadigas were chosen for two reasons. First, our earlier studies of language use by Kannada speakers (K. K. Sridhar, 1982, 1988; S. N. Sridhar, 1978) gave us the background to interpret Kannada-English bilingualism, and, second, the existence of a systematic study of language maintenance and shift among Kannadigas in New Delhi (Satyanath, 1982) permits a comparison between patterns of language maintenance within and outside India.

The Gujarati community was chosen for several reasons, chief among them being, first, that it is one of the largest communities in the United States (it is the fourth largest Asian Indian community in New York State, with a population of 9,910 speakers); second, that it has been a pioneering migratory community both within India, e.g., the Saurashtris in Tamil Nadu, South India, and outside India – e.g., in Kenya (Neale, 1974), and Britain (Clark, Peach, & Vertovec, 1990) – and, third, that the members of this community are more widely distributed across a range of educational and socioeconomic status than are speakers of other Asian Indian languages.

The Malayalis were chosen for purposes of comparison and contrast. A large percentage of Malayalis in the United States are Christians, whereas the majority of Kannadigas and Gujaratis are Hindus. This contrast would allow us to see if religion is an important variable in the study of language maintenance. Both Hindus and Christians were included in the study. The majority (80%) were Syrian Christians, 4.7% were Catholics, and 14.4% were Hindus. All the three language groups in the study speak major regional languages in their respective geographical areas in India, e.g., Kannada in the state of Karnataka, Malayalam in Kerala, and Gujarati in the state of Gujarat. Each of these languages has a rich literary tradition, with Kannada dating back at least to the ninth century. The state of Kerala, in southern India, has the highest rate of literacy, followed by Karnataka, also in southern India. Gujarat, a state in the northwestern part of India, also has a relatively high level of literacy.

The study of the three groups is part of a longitudinal project. Our hope is to be able to document the use of the native language in the first and second generations so that future comparisons can be made in diachronic, cross-generational studies. Part of the problem in studying populous communities such as the Hindi- and Bengali-speaking communities is that they do not represent a homogeneous group. For example, in addition to the immigrants from India, a large number of Hindi speakers come from Guyana, Trinidad, Fiji, and other countries, and a substantial number of Bengali speakers are from India as well as Bangladesh. We hope to study these communities in the future.

The theoretical model of language maintenance and language shift employed in this research is based on the work of Fishman, Nahirny, Hofman, and Hayde (1966), which involves analysis of data on three topical subdivisions:

1. habitual language use at more than one point in time or space under conditions of intergroup contact;
2. antecedent, concurrent, or consequent psychological, social, and cultural processes and their relationship to stability or change in habitual language use; and
3. behavior toward language in the contact setting, including directed maintenance or shift efforts.

Although comparison across time (across generations) is not possible in the Asian Indian community because of its relatively short span of stay in the United States, we attempt comparison across space with reference to the three communities' migrations within India and to other parts of the world (e.g., Kannadigas in Karnataka and New Delhi, Gujaratis in Kenya and the United Kingdom).

The primary data for this study come from a fifty-five-item questionnaire administered to a randomly selected set of twenty-one Kannadiga families, twenty-one Malayali families, and ninety-one Gujarati families between 1985 and 1989 in the New York City metropolitan area. Compared with the Kannadigas and the Malayalis, who are mostly professionals, the Gujaratis pursue a wide range of professions and occupations and have a relatively lower educational level. Keeping this in mind, we wrote the questionnaire for this group in Gujarati. Whereas most of the Kannadiaga and the Malayali respondents were from Queens and Manhattan, several of the Gujarati families included in the sample were from New Jersey. The questionnaire elicited information pertaining to the following: (1) demographic details; (2) opportunities for use of their respective native language(s); (3) indicators of rootedness in the ethnic tradition; (4) parents' use of languages in different domains; (5) children's proficiency in their respective ethnic tongues; (6) children's use of and attitude toward their ethnic language; (7) parents' efforts at language maintenance; and (8) parents' attitude toward the future of their ethnic tongue in the United States. Data from the questionnaire were supplemented by interviews and (participant) observation in the home, in the community (during picnics, concerts, meetings, and religious celebrations), and in the school and school playground.

Major findings

The families included in the study represented a fairly young group. Most of the parents were in the range of 31 to 50 years old. The average length of their stay in the United States ranged from 6.4 years to 16.3 years. The educational qualifications of men and women for the three groups are shown in Table 4.

The respondents' occupations correlate well with their level of education. Most of the males and the females among the Kannadigas and the Malayalis were engaged in a professional job (e.g., doctors, lawyers, company and bank executives). Relatively smaller number of Gujaratis were employed as professionals. The employment pattern of women varied greatly, often reflecting the influence of networking on new immigrants. Approximately 36% of the women in the Gujarati sample with a bachelor's degree were employed as factory workers, machine operators, filing clerks, and so forth; 43% of the Malayali women with similar qualifications were employed mostly as nurses in area hospitals, and 62% of the Kannadiga women were employed in white-collar jobs such as those in banks and in information technology.

Most of the respondents (95% of both Malayalis and Kannadigas) received their college education through the medium of English. Among the Gujaratis there was a substantial difference between the males and

TABLE 4. HIGHEST EDUCATIONAL QUALIFICATIONS OF RESPONDENTS

	Kannadigas[a]		Malayalis[a]		Gujaratis[a]	
	Males	*Females*	*Males*	*Females*	*Males*	*Females*
Professional degree	76	33	76	43	35	17
Bachelor's degree	24	62	24	43	47	36
High school	–	–	–	14	18	41
Grade school	–	–	–	–	–	6
Total	100	95[b]	100	100	100	100

[a]Immigrants from the states of Karnataka, Kerala, and Gujarat respectively.
[b]Some respondents did not answer this question.

380

the females. Approximately 94% of the males but only 30% of the females were educated through the medium of English at the college level, and more than 60% of the women in this group reported Gujarati as their medium at college level. In high school, 96% of the males and females in the Gujarati group were educated in their mother tongue, whereas 48% of the men and 71% of the women in the Malayalam group and 20% of the men and 18% of the women in the Kannada group had been. In other words, the Gujaratis, especially women, on account of their education through the Gujarati medium, had had the least amount of exposure to English.

Another differentiating factor is the respondents' patterns of residence before emigrating to the United States. Most of the Malayalis and the Kannadigas lived in metropolitan cities, where English often is the common medium of communication, but only 27% of the men and 37% of the women in the Gujarati group came from cities. These data are significant because they relate to the degree to which the respondents used the ethnic language and their familiarity with English. As indicated in Table 5, in the 1990 census, a sizable number of Gujarati speakers rated their proficiency in English as not good or indicated that they did not speak English at all. The ratings of some of the other languages are also provided for purposes of comparison. The next set of questions solicited data regarding opportunities for the use of the ethnic language in the New York–New Jersey area. Extensive support networks exist for the three communities. Families in all three groups have friends and relatives in the area, anywhere from twelve to thirty-four families each. As for the frequency of interaction among the families, they stay in touch with other members of their ethnic group. The families get together often on weekends and during Indian festivals. They attend social events organized by their respective cultural organizations,

TABLE 5. ENGLISH-SPEAKING ABILITY AND HOME LANGUAGE OF INDIAN IMMIGRANTS TO THE UNITED STATES

Rank[a]	Language	No. of speakers	Very well	Well	Not well	Not at all
14	Hindi	331,484	234,705	67,276	24,365	5,138
26	Gujarati	102,418	67,704	22,657	8,998	3,059
39	Panjabi	50,005	31,837	10,448	5,616	2,104
44	Bengali	38,101	25,417	9,808	2,578	298
48	Malayalam	33,949	21,131	10,039	2,006	719

Column header spanning "Very well / Well / Not well / Not at all": *Self-rating of ability to speak English*

[a]Based on number of speakers in the United States.
Source: USA Today, April 13, 1993.

which are active. These data are significant in that they indicate a high degree of social interaction that often results in the use of the ethnic tongue. The respondents visit India at least once a year, the parents sometimes take their children to India for the summer or the winter, and most of them entertain relatives and friends visiting from India on a regular basis. Given the extended family structure of the Indian society, hospitality is extended to even distant relatives and acquaintances, who often stay as long as 3 to 6 months with the families. It is also fairly common for the immigrants' parents to spend an extended period of time taking care of their grandchildren in the United States. The native language tends to be used more if the visiting relatives are of an older generation.

Regarding interaction and socialization patterns, the three groups were asked how often they got together and whether they invited mixed groups of people or mostly members of their own regional language group. Most of the respondents indicated that they got together with friends and relatives at least once in 2 weeks (see Table 6). This indicates that the groups are very much rooted in their ethnic culture and traditions, with the Gujaratis and the Malayalis being more traditional. There seems to be relatively less interaction with Americans outside of the work domain, which indicates that the groups are self-contained to a certain extent. Ethnic enclaves of Punjabis, Gujaratis, and other groups are found in several neighborhoods in the borough of Queens, such as Jackson Heights and Flushing. People tend to interact socially on a regular basis primarily with members of their own language groups. During these get-togethers, the language of conversations is usually the ethnic tongue. Hegde's (1991) study of the patterns of interaction of 133 Asian Indian immigrant families in the New York–New Jersey area supports these findings. She observes that the immigrants in her study maintained two distinct interpersonal networks, intraethnic (between members of the same language group) and interethnic (between speakers of different Asian Indian languages). Similar findings are reported in Alexander (1990) and Gibson (1988) for earlier settlements of Asian Indians in California.

TABLE 6. INTERACTION AND SOCIALIZATION PATTERNS (%)[a]

Groups invited	Kannadigas	Malayalis	Gujaratis
Own group only	43	74	77
Own group and other Indians	67	24	28
Mostly Americans	0	0	0
Own group, Indians, and Americas	19	4	4

[a]Some people checked more than one response; hence the figures do not add up to 100%.

These patterns of interaction are consistent with other data, e.g., lack of interest in American sports, neighborhood activities, and local politics. (Note, however, that during 1992, an election year, there was more, though still quite marginal, involvement at both the local and the national level.) The immigrants are still heavily rooted in their home culture, as is evidenced by the data indicating their preference for Indian food, especially at dinners and on weekends. Most respondents indicated that they ate mostly Indian food. The younger generation also reported eating Indian food, although there was quite a bit of interest in American fast food, such as pizza, hot dogs, and hamburgers. Most of the Gujaratis in the study indicated that they were vegetarians and that their children ate mostly Indian vegetarian food.

Although most people reported using their mother tongues in social get-togethers, a pattern of code mixing, or mixing of the home language and English within sentences, was also reported. Most parents were categorical in their support for maintaining their languages, but the data in Table 7 present a different story. Parents tended to use a mixed language, as is evident from the data on phone conversation.

So far, we have discussed the patterns of language interaction among parents. Notably, it is in the nature and amount of exposure to Indian languages available to the younger generation that one notices some mismatch. Most parents agreed that, in conversing with their friends, they tended to mix their language somewhat with English. The Gujarati community is the only exception (see Table 8), but even here, about 33% of the parents report using a variety of language mixed with English. English is often used along with the native language in order to accommodate members of the younger generation, who are sometimes not as fluent as their parents in the ethnic language. These findings are consistent

TABLE 7. LANGUAGE OF PHONE CONVERSATIONS (%)

Language	Kannadigas	Malayalis	Gujaratis
Native language	43	40	57
Native language and English	57	60	43
Only English	0	0	0

TABLE 8. PARENTS' USE OF ETHNIC LANGUAGE (%)

Language	Kannadigas	Malayalis	Gujaratis
Native language	19	14	56
Mostly native language	24	57	16
Native language and English	57	48	33

Kamal K. Sridhar and S. N. Sridhar

with studies of Kannadigas in New Delhi (Satyanath, 1982), and Gujaratis in England, Kenya, Uganda, and other places. The pattern in contemporary urban India is mostly the same as well, with most groups using a code-mixed variety with English, which is slowly moving into the home domain (Mukherjee, 1980). As noted, English is the second language used most often among the educated in India. These data are significant in that they indicate the use of English in the home domain for all three groups. Considering the high level of education and the fact that they tend to use mostly English in their job-related conversations, this intrusion of English into the home domain is not surprising.

PARENTS' EFFORTS TO MAINTAIN THE LANGUAGES

The responses indicate that the Asian Indian parents were strongly committed to the maintenance and use of the ethnic tongue. Their efforts ranged from "insisting on children speaking only the native language at home" to "driving children to the local temple(s) and church(e) for native language instruction." These classes, taught in local temples, churches, and other community centers, are mostly run by concerned parents. They are usually held during weekends and are taught mostly by untrained people. However, there are no bilingual education programs for Asian Indian language speakers in the state of New York, though at one time there were some Gujarati-English bilingual schools in New Jersey. Most parents made an effort to keep the language alive by reading stories to the children in their native language and ensuring that the children were familiar with nursery rhymes, religious verses and hymns (*slokas*), and popular folk songs or songs in films from their language area.

We now turn to patterns of language use among the children. Our discussion is based on the parents' report rather than on observations of the children's actual language use. We confirmed the validity of the parents' reports in informal observations, though a more direct study is certainly needed. A distinctive feature of the present study is the attempt to present a more detailed description of the nature and extent of the children's proficiency in the ethnic tongue than is normally found in studies of language maintenance and language shift.

LANGUAGE USE BY THE YOUNGER GENERATION

Several questions related to the children's proficiency in the native tongue. First, the parents were asked whether their children understood the (variety of the) native language spoken in everyday conversations (e.g., when discussing foods, friends, holidays). All the parents reported that their children could understand the ethnic tongue in discussions of day-to-day matters. However, according to the majority of the parents,

TABLE 9. CHILDRENS' COMPETENCY IN THE NATIVE LANGUAGE (%)

Competency	Kannadigas	Malayalis	Gujaratis
Can read	24	0	66
Can write	14	0	90
Can recite poetry	48	5	58

the children responded to them in a variety mixed with English. The only sizeable figures for use of the native language came from the Gujarati parents (see Table 9). This result could be due to the fact that the mothers in this language group tended to be less educated (and therefore to speak less English) than the mothers in the other two groups. When visiting India also, parents reported, the children tended to use a mixed variety (with English) and not the native language except marginally with grandparents (who may have been monolingual).

The true measure of maintenance is, of course, the use of the ethnic tongue by persons of the younger generation among themselves. A few questions attempted to explore the children's attitude to the ethnic tongue. Not surprisingly, the children's pattern of socialization was much more assimilatory than that of their parents. The children socialized with children from different language and cultural backgrounds. When the children shared a native language background, the Gujarati children tended to use more Gujarati, though the Malayali children did not use Malayalam much. Across the groups, however, English seemed to be the preferred language among the second generation. The use of more English by Kannada children is consistent with the findings in Satyanath's (1982) study, in which Kannada children growing up in New Delhi tended to use the language of the majority (in this case, Hindi). The Gujarati children used more Gujarati, which is supported in the studies on this community in different parts of the world by Neale (1974), Clark et al. (1990), and others. The children did have a positive attitude about being spoken to in the native language, as the majority of the parents (Kannadigas, 95%; Malayalis, 48%; Gujaratis, 66%) said their children did not mind it. The sometimes-observed pattern of children asking their parents to speak to them in English was more attested among the Malayalis (78%) than the Kannadigas (5%) or the Gujaratis (11%).

PARENTS' ATTITUDE TOWARD THE NATIVE LANGUAGE

We also elicited the attitudes of the parents toward the future of their native language in their adopted land. Whereas 86% of Gujarati parents and 100% of Kannada parents felt that "it [would] be maintained

Kamal K. Sridhar and S. N. Sridhar

by a small number of people," the Malayali parents were more pessimistic: They felt that "it [would] disappear in the next generation." Parents were not comfortable with the possibility of their language not surviving them. They wished that their children would learn the language and use it for interethnic communication. Whereas 80% of the Malayali parents felt "children would be better off with English," 36% of the Kannadiga parents, and only 19% of the Gujarati parents felt this way. The parents were realistic, realizing that complete maintenance was not feasible. About 70% of the Gujarati parents and 64% of the Kannada parents pointed out that although they did not expect their children to be fluent in the native language, they hoped that the second generation would be aware of its roots and make an effort to maintain the culture if not the language.

Conclusions and implications

This set of studies of the patterns of language maintenance among the Asian Indian communities is an initial attempt to document and analyze the patterns of language use among the New Ethnics. In future observations of the use of the language in the first generation, the interaction between the first and second generations, and the interaction among the second-generation Asian Indian children and youths, several differences need to be kept in mind. First, whereas the older generation still professes loyalty to the language, members of the younger generation do not identify as much with their respective language groups. The children from all three groups tended to identify themselves as Indian Americans and not so much as Gujaratis, Kannadigas, or Malayalis unless pressed to do so. In fact, in the Malayalis group, 40% of the children labeled themselves Asian Indians, 30% claimed themselves to be Americans, only 10% identified themselves as Malayalis, and 20% did not respond to this question.

Second, the children of Asian Indian immigrants may not be fully bilingual in the usual sense of the term, i.e., full receptive and productive competence in all skills. Nevertheless, they are not completely monolingual either. Code mixing is a prime example of a group or individual's bicultural identity (see Dubey, 1991; B. B. Kachru, 1983, 1990; S. N. Sridhar, 1978; Sridhar & Sridhar, 1980; and others). Most of the parents who grew up in urban India use a code-mixed variety of their language, even in the intimate domain. Code-mixed songs are on the rise, and many musical groups that have emerged in India, the United Kingdom, and the United States capitalize on this mix. Parents and children alike watch and enjoy popular movies, such as *Bhaji on the Beach*. Although some elders lament the loss of "pure Hindi," code mixing is a way of life

386

for all Asian Indian immigrant communities. The youth show the same enthusiasm for Western pop music as their other American counterparts do, but they are equally enthusiastic about attending Asian Indian pop music concerts, especially the Hindi music concerts organized at Madison Square Garden and Nassau Coliseum, and watching Hindi movies screened in Hicksville, Queens, and New York City. All this suggests that these communities are best described in terms of Gibson's (1988) characterization of second- and third-generation Punjabi Americans in Valleyside, California, involving "selective adaptation" or "accommodation without assimilation," in which "parents firmly instruct their young to add what is good from majority ways to their own but not to lose what is significant about their [ethnic] heritage. Young people, for their part, adopt more of the majority group's values than their parents would like, but still they resist assimilation . . ." (p. 198).

The foregoing discussion on the Asian Indian communities in the United States emphatically demonstrates that the earlier stereotypes of bilingualism as the root cause of socioeconomic stagnation, poor educational performance, and low level of intelligence are, to say the least, groundless. None of these stereotypes fits the Asian Indian communities in the United States. On the positive side, this study has several implications for classroom teachers, including language teachers and teachers of English as a second language:

1. Minimally, not only educators in the United States but also professionals of various types, e.g., social workers, health care providers, and legal service professionals, need to familiarize themselves with the complexity of the linguistic background of Asian Indians. In the course of her 18 years' experience evaluating the language proficiency of South Asian children in American schools, the first author has noted several problems in the way children's native languages are identified and evaluated there. For example, many of the children identified as Hindi speakers were in reality speakers of Urdu, Punjabi, or Sindhi and often were from Bangladesh and Pakistan rather than India. The Asian Indian community, for its part, needs to make information about itself more readily available to those who need it. The establishment of outreach programs at pioneering institutions such as the Center for India Studies in Stony Brook, New York; many regional, civic, and religious associations of South Asians; and women's organizations, such as Sakhi, in major metropolitan areas is an attempt to meet this need.

2. Teachers need to become more aware that bilingualism and multilingualism are the norm in the world and that they are independent of intelligence and consistent with the highest educational and socioeconomic achievement.

387

3. The role of English vis-à-vis other languages in the learner's and the community's verbal repertoire should be reassessed. Teacher and policy makers need to recognize that English, despite its undoubted importance, may be only one of the languages in the learner's repertoire. The learner's other languages have distinctive and valued social and cultural roles to play in the learner's community. Ignoring the existence of these languages or negating their values by insisting on a maximal or exclusive use of English in the home domain (as many teachers routinely advise newly arrived and anxious immigrant parents to do) runs contrary to the dynamics of bilingualism and is detrimental to the learner's self-respect and cultural identity. Teachers need to recognize that children as well as adults are capable of adding new languages to their existing verbal repertoire. What is called for is an additive model of bilingualism, not a replacive one.

4. Language teachers who have been trained in a monolingual, monocultural paradigm have often been needlessly harsh toward minority students who switch and mix languages. They need to recognize that code mixing and switching are natural outcomes of bilingualism and do not preclude achievement of excellent proficiency in either language. This recognition will help minority students feel secure in their new and unfamiliar surroundings.

5. Teachers also need to be aware of the fact that, in bilingual settings, there is a great deal of give-and-take between languages. It is unrealistic for the language teacher to expect learners to keep their languages compartmentalized and thus devoid of any trace of mutual influence. Transfer from one language into another is not all negative. Unfortunately, second language acquisition theorists have looked at transfer as undesirable interference. Although some types of transfer can lead to loss of intelligibility and pragmatic failure, other types can actually enhance the communicative resources of the target language, adding color, charm, and variety to it. Creative writers from Shakespeare and Milton to Tolstoy, Achebe, Raja Rao, and Rushdie have exploited this strategy to great effect. This positive role of transfer in bilingual communication (B. B. Kachru, 1990; Y. Kachru, 1997; S. N. Sridhar, 1980; Sridhar & Sridhar, 1986) needs to be studied and promoted, for this is what multiculturalism is all about.

6. Since English is the most widely learned second language in the world today, the wide range of variation in the use of the English around the world needs to be recognized. Besides the native varieties such as British and American English, there are a number of extensively used nonnative varieties of English, such as Indian English, Filipino English, Singaporean English, and Nigerian English, that differ

considerably from native varieties (Kachru & Nelson, 1996). These nonnative varieties have acquired their distinctive characteristics because of their use as a second language by people with different mother tongues and for the expression of distinct (non–European American) sociocultural content. These varieties are neither acquisitionally deficient forms nor fossilized interlanguages but rich and functionally viable sociolinguistic varieties that follow different but productive formal processes of grammar and usage. These facts need to be kept in mind in evaluating the English language proficiency of children of Asian Indian immigrants and their parents as well as international students from countries where English is the most commonly used second language.

Suggestions for further reading

Bacon (1996) focuses on the Asian Indian community in Chicago. Using materials from extensive interviews with six families, the author points out that "this study is concerned not with the process of assimilation but with the interpersonal interactions that provide the mechanism for assimilation and community formation" (p. 11). The process of assimilation is rather universal, and the issues and the experiences are not very different from those that have been brought up by successive generations of immigrants to the United States.

Gibson's (1988) book is about an Asian Indian immigrant community in the United States, the Sikhs in Valleyside, California. The focus is on the youth, and the dilemma of the parents is not unlike that of earlier immigrants, namely, how to maintain one's ethnic roots while adopting the ways of the Americans. This book explores the strategies they use, which the author appropriately terms *accommodation and acculturation without assimilation.*

Helweg and Helweg (1990) present an ethnographic study of Asian Indian communities in the United States. The authors use materials from census reports, case studies, personal interviews, and observations in both formal and informal settings to describe this group. Theoretical issues are considered minus the jargon, making the book an informative text.

Saran and Eames's (1980) volume is one of the first edited studies on Asian Indians in the United States. A collection of eighteen chapters offers insights into the New Ethnics, the post-1965 immigrant group. A wide range of topics are addressed, including sociocultural, educational, political, and demographic profiles of this community; ethnicity and ethnic identity; issues surrounding health care; and psychological adaptations of Asian Indians in the United States.

Kamal K. Sridhar and S. N. Sridhar

References

Agnihotri, R. K. (1979). *Process of assimilation: A sociolinguistic study of Sikh children in Leeds.* Unpublished doctoral dissertation, York University, England.

Alexander, G. P. (1990). *Asian Indians in the San Francisco Valley.* Unpublished doctoral dissertation, Fuller Theological Seminary, San Francisco, CA.

Bacon, J. (1996). *Life lines: Community, family, and assimilation among Asian Indian immigrants.* New York: Oxford University Press.

Bhatia, T. K. (1981). Trinidad Hindi: Three generations of a transplanted variety. *Studies in the Linguistic Sciences, 11,* 135–150.

Bhatt, R. M. (1989). Language planning and language conflict: The case of Kashmiri. *International Journal of the Sociology of Language, 75,* 73–86.

Chakledar, S. (1981). *Linguistic minority as a cohesive force in Indian federal process.* Delhi, India: Associated Publishing House.

Clark, C., Peach, C., & Vertovec, S. (Eds.). (1990). *South Asians overseas: Migration and ethnicity.* Cambridge: Cambridge University Press.

Daniels, P., & Bright W. (Eds.). (1996). *The world's writing systems.* New York: Oxford University Press.

D'Souza, J. (1987). *South Asia as a sociolinguistic area.* Unpublished doctoral dissertation, University of Illinois, Urbana-Champaign.

Dubey, V. S. (1991). The lexical style of Indian English newspapers. *World Englishes, 10*(1), 19–32.

Ekka, F. (1979). Language loyalty and maintenance among the Kuruxs. In E. Annamalai (Ed.), *Language movements in India* (pp. 99–106). Mysore, India: Central Institute of Indian Languages.

Emeneau, M. B. (1956). India as a linguistic area. *Language, 29,* 339–353.

Fishman, J. A., Nahirny, V. C., Hofman, J. E., & Hayde, R. G. (1996) (Eds.). *Language loyalty in the United States.* The Hague: Mouton.

Gall, S. (1995). *The Asian American almanac: A reference work on Asian Americans in the U.S.* Detroit, MI: Gale Research.

Gall, S., & Gall, T. (Eds.). (1993). *Statistical record of Asian Americans.* Detroit, MI: Gale Research.

Gambhir, S. (1981). *The East Indian speech community in Guyana: A sociolinguistic study with special reference to Koine formation.* Unpublished doctoral dissertation, University of Pennsylvania, Philadelphia.

Ghuman, P. A. S. (1994). *Coping with two cultures: British Asian and Indo-Canadian Adolescents.* Clevedon, England: Multilingual Matters.

Gibson, M. A. (1988). *Accomodation without assimilation: Sikh immigrants in an American high school.* Ithaca, NY: Cornell University Press.

Gumperz, J. J., & Wilson, R. (1971). Convergence and creolization: A case from the Indo-Aryan Dravidian border. In D. Hymes (Ed.), *Pidginization and creolization of languages* (pp. 151–167). Cambridge: Cambridge University Press.

Hegde, R. S. (1991). *Adaptation and the interpersonal experience: A study of Asian Indians in the United States.* Unpublished doctoral dissertation, Ohio State University, Columbus.

Helweg, A. W. (1997). Asian Indians in the United States. In S. N. Sridhar & N. K. Mattoo (Eds.), *Ananya: A portrait of India* (pp. 881–896). New York: Association of Indians in America.

Helweg, A. W., & Helweg, U. M. (1990). *An immigrant success story: East Indians in America.* Philadelphia: University of Pennsylvania Press.

Kachru, B. B. (1983). *Indianization of English.* Delhi: Oxford University Press.

Kachru, B. B. (1997). Languages of India. In S. N. Sridhar & N. K. Mattoo (Eds.), *Ananya: A portrait of India* (pp. 553–586). New York: Association of Indians in America.

Kachru, B. B. (1990). *The alchemy of English: The spread, functions, and models of non-native Englishes.* Urbana: University of Illinois Press.

Kachru, B. B., & Nelson, C. L. (1996). World Englishes. In S. L. McKay & N. H. Hornberger (Eds.), *Sociolinguistics and language teaching* (pp. 71–102). New York: Cambridge University Press.

Kachru, B. B., & Sridhar, S. N. (1978). (Eds.). Aspects of sociolinguistics in South Asia [Special issue]. *International Journal of the Sociology of Language, 16.*

Kachru, Y. (1997). Culture and communication in India. In S. N. Sridhar & N. K. Mattoo (Eds.), *Ananya: A portrait of India* (pp. 645–663). New York: Association of Indians in America.

Khubchandani, L. M. (1983). *Plural languages, plural cultures.* Honolulu, HI: East-West Center.

Koritala, S. B. (1998). *A historical perspective of Americans of Asian Indian origin.* ⟨http:/www.trac.net/users/koritala/india/history.htm⟩.

Krishnamurti, B. (1989). *A profile of illiteracy in India: Problems and prospects.* Unpublished manuscript.

Mahapatra, B. P. (1979). Santali language movement in the context of many dominant languages. In E. Annamalai (Ed.), *Language movements in India* (pp. 107–117). Mysore, India: Central Institute of Indian Languages.

Mesthrie, R. (1992). *Language in indenture: A sociolinguistic history of Bhojpuri-Hindi in South Africa.* New York: Routledge.

Moag, R. F. (1978). Linguistic adaptations of the Fiji Indians. In V. Mishra, (Ed.), *Rama's banishment: A centenary volume on the Fiji Indians* (pp. 112–138). Melbourne, Australia: Heinemann.

Mogelonsky, M. (1995, August). The Indian Tower of Babel. *American demographics.* ⟨http:/www.demograpics.com/publications/ad/95_AD/_AD/ad781.htm⟩.

Mukherjee, A. (1980). *Language maintenance and language shift among Panjabis and Bengalis in Delhi: A sociolinguistic perspective.* Unpublished doctoral dissertation, University of Delhi, India.

Neale, B. (1974). Language use among the Asian communities. In W. H. Whiteley (Ed.), *Language in Kenya* (pp. 263–318). Nairobi, Kenya: Oxford University Press.

Pandit, P. B. (1972). *India as a sociolinguistic area* (Gune Memorial Lecture). Ganesh Khind, India: Poona University Press.

Pattanayak, D. P. (1971). *Distribution of languages in India, in states and union territories.* Mysore, India: Central Institute of Indian Languages.

Rangila, R. S. (1986). *Maintenance of Panjabi language in Delhi: A sociolinguistic study.* Mysore, India: Central Institute of Indian Languages.

Saran, P., & Eames, E. (1980). *The New Ethnics: The Asian Indians in the U.S.* New York: Praeger.

Satyanath, T. S. (1982). *Kannadigas in Delhi: A sociolinguistic study.* Unpublished doctoral dissertation, University of Delhi, India.

Kamal K. Sridhar and S. N. Sridhar

Sharma, B. G. (1977). Indian bilingualism. In B. G. Sharma & S. Kumar (Eds.), *Indian bilingualism* (pp. 3–16). Agra, India: Central Hindi Institute.

Siegel, J. (1987). *Language contact in a plantation environment.* Cambridge: Cambridge University Press.

Southworth, F. C., & Apte, M. L. (1974). Introduction. *International Journal of Dravidian Linguistics, 3*(1), 1–20.

Sridhar, K. K. (1982). English in a South Indian urban context. In B. B. Kachru (Ed.), *The other tongue: English across cultures* (pp. 141–153). Urbana: University of Illinois Press.

Sridhar, K. K. (1988). Language maintenance and language shift among Asian Indians: Kannadigas in the New York area. *International Journal of the Sociology of Language, 69,* 73–87.

Sridhar, K. K. (1989). *English in Indian bilingualism.* Delhi, India: Manohar.

Sridhar, K. K. (1993). Meaning, means, maintenance. In J. E. Alatis (Ed.), *Georgetown Roundtable on Languages and Linguistics, 1992: Language, communication, and social meaning* (pp. 56–65). Washington, DC: Georgetown University Press.

Sridhar, K. K. (1997). Languages of India in New York. In O. Garcia & J. A. Fishman (Eds.), *The multilingual apple: Languages in New York City* (pp. 257–280). Berlin: Mouton de Gruyer.

Sridhar, K. K. (in press). *Three centuries of language maintenance:* Marathi in Tamil Nadu.

Sridhar, S. N. (1978). On the functions of code-mixing in Kannada. *International Journal of the Sociology of Language, 16,* 109–117.

Sridhar, S. N. (1980). Contrastive analysis, error analysis, and interlanguage: Three phases of one goal. In K. Croft (Ed.), *Readings on English as a second language for teachers and teacher trainers* (pp. 91–119). Cambridge, MA: Winthrop.

Sridhar, S. N. (1981). Linguistic convergence: Indo-Aryanization of Dravidian languages. *Lingua, 53,* 199–220.

Sridhar, S. N., & Sridhar, K. K. (1980). The syntax and psycholinguistics of bilingual code-mixing. *Canadian Journal of Psychology, 34,* 409–418.

Sridhar, S. N., & Sridhar, K. K. (1986). Bridging the paradigm gap: Second language acquisition theory and indigenized varieties of English. *World Englishes, 11,* 2–3.

Srivastava, R. N. (1988). Societal bilingualism and bilingual education: A study of the Indian situation. In C. B. Paulston (Ed.), *International handbook of bilingualism and bilingual education* (pp. 247–274). Westport, CT: Greenwood Press.

Subromoniam, V. I. (1977). A note on the preservation of the mother tongue in Kerala. In P. G. Sharma & S. Kumar (Eds.), *Indian Bilingualism* (pp. 21–38). Agra, India: Central Hindi Institute.

Varma, B. N. (1980). Indians as new ethnics: A theoretical note. In P. Saran E. Eames (Eds.), *The new ethnics: The Asian Indians in the United States* (pp. 29–41). New York: Praeger.

III *Investing in English language learners*

The key concept in Part III, *investing* or *investment*, represents our borrowing and elaboration of Bonny Norton's term (Chapter 16), which she uses to replace the more established and (in her view) narrower notions of *attitudes* and *motivation*. The three chapters in this section explore how investment in English learning differs among individual learners and examines what educational, legal, and community support is needed to ensure that English language learners attain their particular language goals. In Chapter 14, "English Language Learners and Educational Investments," Sandra McKay argues that quality education for English language learners demands the commitment of language educators and administrators as well as family and community members. Beginning with a description of current program models for English language education, McKay maintains that an overemphasis on program design has tended to minimize the complexities of the individual language learner's experience. She summarizes a variety of current research that demonstrates how an individual's learning experience can be affected by the way the learner is treated in the classroom and by the degree of support the learner receives from family and community members. She emphasizes that language learning takes place not just in the classroom but also in the home, community, and workplace and urges language educators to draw on every available resource both within and outside the school to make certain that individual language learners' investment in acquiring English is met with equal investment on the part of those with whom they interact.

In Chapter 15 "Legal Investment in Multilingualism," Rachel Moran emphasizes that law and politics often set the parameters for program options and available resources. As Moran points out, "the politically naive run the risk of seeing their pedagogical options shrink in an ideologically charged policy-making environment." Moran illustrates the manner in which two states with large immigrant populations, California and New York, proceeded to make educational decisions regarding English language learners in the absence of strong federal mandates. In light of the failure of both states to provide high-quality education for English language learners, she argues, federal intervention is necessary to assist states in developing high-quality programs when levels of immigration are high. She urges language educators to consistently remind the public of the complexities of educating English language learners so that the necessary state and federal support is available for effective education programs.

Although Chapter 15 is a case study of the enactment of educational services for English language learners in two states in the United States, it offers a number of important observations for language educators everywhere. First, it highlights the way educational policies are often implemented against the backdrop of power disputes between various levels of government. Second, it demonstrates the need for countries that open their doors to immigrants to financially support high-quality language instruction. Finally, it emphasizes the need for language educators to become fully aware of how government decisions influence local educational policies and, where necessary, to take action to change government policies that undermine the delivery of effective educational programs. In short, the chapter shows that farsighted language policies depend upon a philosophical commitment of an entire community to a language-as-resource perspective, accompanied by adequate economic support.

In Chapter 16, "Investment, Acculturation, and Language Loss," Bonny Norton draws on her research with immigrant women in Canada to illustrate how individuals differ dramatically in their investment in learning English and maintaining their mother tongue. She also demonstrates how individuals' investment in language learning can be affected by those with whom they interact and shows that in many instances race, class, gender, and age affect an individual language learner's right to be heard. In light of her research, Norton argues convincingly that current theories of second language acquisition do not pay sufficient attention to inequitable relations of power in a society, noting that "such theories need to recognize that attitudes and motivation are not inherent properties of language learners but are constructed within the context of specific social relationships at a given time and place."

The three chapters in Part III highlight the fact that language learning is a social process affected by federal and local governments, the community, and the school. McKay demonstrates how the institutional divisions of learners into classes and classroom interaction patterns can influence language learning; Moran shows that the larger political and legal process has a direct effect on available resources. Norton, on the other hand, illustrates how the social context (such as racism) affects family and personal relationships, often dramatically influencing learners' investment in acquiring English. Taken together, the chapters emphasize the need for second language educators to recognize that schools are just one forum of language learning and that, ultimately, for successful English language learning to occur, educators must mobilize supportive forces in the larger social context – political and social leaders, school administrators, and the community – while remaining sensitive to individual variation in investments in language learning.

14 English language learners and educational investments

Sandra Lee McKay

In this chapter I argue that the attainment of effective educational programs for English language learners requires long-term material and intellectual investment on the part of the their teachers, administrators,
family, and community. Central to the chapter is the assumption that
schools alone have never had and never will have the ability to meet the
needs of English language learners in isolation. As Paulston (1981)
points out, "[e]ducational institutions have limited power in dealing
with language acquisition or the lack thereof, a learning process which
is primarily the result of social factors" (p. 476). Indeed, many chapters
in this book clearly demonstrate that a variety of social and cultural factors strongly affect the learning of English and the maintenance of the
mother tongue. What is particularly encouraging regarding the education of English language learners is the recent recognition among educational leaders that the family and community must be involved in the
educational process.

A second assumption made in this chapter is that, to be effective, educational programs must be designed to meet the particular needs of the
English language learners, families, and communities being served. As I
show in this chapter, successful language programs have typically been
characterized by great flexibility in design so as to meet local educational needs. My final assumption is that multilingualism is an important resource for a country. In supporting the value of multilingualism, I do
not mean to suggest that the promotion of English language learning
should in any way be neglected. Rather, what is needed is the promotion
of a multilingual and multiliterate citizenry.

To begin, I analyze the assumptions regarding language learning and
the value of multilingualism underlying various approaches to the
teaching of English to language minorities. I then describe prevalent
models for English language programs and summarize the existing evaluative research on these models. I maintain that a focus on program design fails to provide insight into the individual experiences of language
learners, and I suggest that educators need to examine the language
learner as a multifaceted individual who assumes a variety of roles in
the classroom, the educational institution, the home, and the community. As a way of demonstrating this point, I summarize current research
on the English-learning experience of language minorities.

Sandra Lee McKay

Assumptions underlying current program models for English language learners

Existing programs for English language learners in the United States can be distinguished on two primary levels: their assumptions about the value of mother tongue education and their assumptions about the relationship between first language and second language literacy.

The value of mother tongue education

In 1957 the United Nations Education, Scientific, and Cultural Organization issued a formal declaration on the right of all children to be educated through their mother tongue. Supporting this declaration, Skutnabb-Kangas (1994) argues that

> in a civilized society there should be no need to debate the right to maintain and develop the mother tongue. It is a self-evident human right. . . . Observing linguistic human rights implies at an individual level, that all people can identify positively with their mother tongue and have that identification accepted and respected by others whether their mother tongue is a minority language or a majority language. (p. 625)

Sridhar (1994), on the other hand, while wholeheartedly supporting the right to mother tongue education, points out various practical obstacles to its implementation. For example, members of the language community may be scattered geographically, the language may not have a script, there may be a lack of printed materials in the language, and speakers of the language may hold a variety of attitudes toward their mother tongue.

The valuing of mother tongue education represents what Ruiz (1988) terms an *orientation,* which refers to a "complex of dispositions toward language and its role, and toward languages and their role in society" (p. 4). Ruiz goes on to distinguish three prevalent orientations toward multilingualism: language-as-problem, language-as-right, and language-as-resource. In the first orientation, language-as-problem, members of a society see multilingualism as a problem that on a political level often results in a lack of social cohesiveness and on an individual level may result in cognitive deficiencies. In the second orientation, language-as-right, the promotion of bilingualism is viewed as a legal mandate involving the right of individuals to use their mother tongue and not to suffer discrimination for this use. Finally, in a language-as-resource orientation, multilingualism is viewed as a social and individual resource that can reap economic, political, social, and individual benefits.

These perspectives lead to different views on whether or not English language learners in the United States should receive instruction in their mother tongue. Proponents of a language-as-problem orientation argue that those in the United States who do not speak English must learn the language as quickly as possible as a way of both assuring national cohesiveness and avoiding what they view as the cognitive and developmental problems that can arise from bilingualism. Hence, they advocate English language–medium educational programs. Those who support a language-as-right perspective highlight the legal basis for individuals in the United States to use their mother tongue in a public educational context. In the United States these rights reside in the Fourteenth Amendment, Title VI of the Civil Rights Act of 1964, the Equal Educational Opportunities Act of 1974, and Title VII of the Elementary and Secondary Education Act. (See Wong, 1988, for a full description of the legal basis for special educational programs for English language learners.) Finally, those who hold a language-as-resource orientation emphasize the benefits of bilingualism for individual development and social advancement. Proponents of the last two perspectives support educational programs that seek to develop bilingualism. Frequently, those who support the maintenance of the mother tongue through some type of bilingual education program argue that the literacy and skills learned in the mother tongue will promote the learning of English.

The relationship between first language and second language literary

Cummins (1979, 1981) was the first to posit that literacy abilities acquired in the mother tongue will transfer to the second language. Central to his theory is the idea that a bilingual child must acquire a certain threshold level of linguistic competence in order for bilingualism to provide beneficial cognitive growth. Hence, in Cummins' view, acquiring strong skills in at least one language is a necessary though not sufficient condition to avoid deficits in the cognitive development of bilinguals. If this hypothesis is accurate, then bilingual children must be provided with the opportunity to develop at least one of their languages to this threshold level of proficiency. Cummins further argues that acquiring literacy skills in the mother tongue facilitates the acquisition of literacy in a second language since learners transfer these skills across languages. Cummins terms this idea the *developmental interdependence hypothesis*.

Whereas some research supports this notion of transfer (Collier & Thomas, 1989; Ramirez, 1992; Skutnabb-Kangas, 1979), much more research is needed to determine if the notion holds true regardless of the level of second language proficiency and the similarity of the structure and script of the two languages. In other words, how much proficiency in a second language must individuals have before they can apply the literacy skills and knowledge acquired in their first language to their second language? Furthermore, if students need a certain level of second language literacy, should they develop this proficiency by focusing on language instruction, particularly grammar instruction, or should they start using the second language to discuss content knowledge? Finally, must two languages be similar in their grammar and their script for this transfer to occur? As August and Hakuta (1997) point out,

> an insufficient attempt has been made to understand the cognitive processes underlying successful transfer of first-language literacy skill to the second language, the limitations of that transfer, the conditions that optimize positive and minimize negative transfer, or the difference between children who manage learning to read in a second language well and those who do not. Such information would make English literacy training for both child and adult immigrants much more efficient and effective. (p. 72)

Existing programs for English language learners in the United States reflect these different assumptions regarding the value of mother tongue education and the transfer of literacy skills from one language to a second. What follows is a description of common models for second language education in the United States and a discussion of the assumptions they make about the value of bilingualism.

Program Models

Submersion

In submersion programs, English language learners are placed in classrooms with native English speakers for the entire school day with no additional language support.[1] Supporters of this so-called sink-or-swim method argue that children will learn English faster if they are exposed to English for the entire school day and that, furthermore, children naturally pick up a language quite quickly and easily. This program reflects a language-as-problem perspective insofar as it seems to suggest that the primary need of the language minority student is to learn English. In addition, this approach obviously does not support the right of children to receive initial education in their mother tongue. Although this approach is not in keeping with the Supreme Court's 1974 decision in *Lau v. Nichols* (see Wong, 1988, for a discussion of this decision), some school districts nevertheless implement it. The rationale given is typically the lack of feasibility of offering mother tongue support, but the pro-

---

1 Submersion programs are not to be confused with what some refer to as *mainstreaming*, in which English language instruction is integrated into the mainstream classroom with the aid of special support services. See Clegg (1996) for examples of various types of language support provisions.

gram nevertheless is not in keeping with the legal rights of English language learners in the United States.

Pull-out English as a second language

In pull-out English as a second language (ESL) programs, English language learners are given separate classes in English language development for part of the day and spend the remainder of the day in English-only classes with native speakers. The number of children in the pull-out class, as well as the number of hours of instruction per week, can vary greatly. In addition, the instructors of these special classes typically have been trained in ESL rather than bilingual education. Various models of pull-out ESL exist in U.S. schools. In some cases the primary focus of these classes is on grammar and vocabulary rather than on academic content areas. In other cases, the students receive instruction in content areas, termed *content-based ESL*. When the content instruction is modified so that it is accessible to the students' level of English proficiency, the instruction is termed *sheltered instruction*. When such instruction is conducted by a bilingual teacher in a self-contained classroom, but all of the instruction is conducted in English for the entire day, the program is termed *structured immersion*. However, none of these variations of ESL programs give any attention to mother tongue education, suggesting that bilingualism is a problem rather than an asset.[2]

Bilingual education

Bilingual education in the United States includes an immense array of programs, some of which offer a good deal of instruction in the mother tongue and some of which, ironically, offer instruction only in English.[3] The great range of types of programs, reflecting the lack of a coherent philosophy underlying bilingual education, makes it difficult to assess these programs as an educational alternative.[4]

One of the main controversies surrounding bilingual education has been whether such programs should exist solely to provide a transition to English-only instruction (commonly termed *transitional bilingual education* or *early exit programs*) or whether they should support the de-

2 At present, 42.7% of public schools in the United States offer some type of ESL program (National Center for Education Statistics, 1993/1994).
3 In 1984, funding under the Bilingual Education Act was made available for special alternative instruction programs, termed SAIPs, which were in fact English-only classrooms. At present 23% of bilingual education funds are used for such programs (see McKay, 1997).
4 Currently, 17.8% of public schools in the United States offer some type of bilingual education program (National Center for Education Statistics, 1993/1994).

Sandra Lee McKay

velopment of the mother tongue (termed *maintenance bilingual education* or *late-exit programs*). Underlying the latter model particularly is a belief in the value of mother tongue education and in multilingualism as a resource. Proponents of maintenance bilingual education also support the notion that the literacy skills learned in the mother tongue will transfer to English. On the other hand, those who oppose bilingual education assume that the time on task is a key factor in promoting language learning. Hence, they believe that the time spent on developing the mother tongue detracts from the time spent directly on learning English.[5]

Two-way bilingual programs

In two-way bilingual education programs, sometimes referred to as *dual-language immersion programs,* native English speakers and English language learners are placed in the same classroom with the goal of making them proficient in two languages.[6] In some cases, the two groups of students receive separate instruction through the second or third grade, developing initial reading skills in their mother tongue. In other instances, students are initially separated but gradually do more and more tasks together until they are integrated into one classroom.

Variations of this model include *partial immersion* and *early total immersion.* In the former, students in Grades K–5 receive academic instruction for half the day in one language and half the day in the other. In the latter, students in Grades K–1 receive 90% of their academic instruction in the second language; this amount is gradually reduced so that in Grade 6, 40% of the instruction is in the second language. Immersion programs were originally developed in Canada as a way for Anglophone students to acquire fluency in French. Some educators interpret the success of immersion programs in Canada as support for placing English language learners in English-only classrooms from the time they enter school. In fact, in the popular press the terms early total immersion program and submersion program as defined here are often used interchangeably. Yet there are some important differences in the social context of language learning in Canada and the United States. In Canada, the participating students (typically Anglophone students) speak the language of higher prestige and widespread use, thus getting a good deal of support for the maintenance of their mother tongue in the larger community, whereas in the United States the school typically provides one of the only public contexts where English language learners can receive mother tongue support. In terms of assumptions regarding

5 See Rossell and Baker (1996) for a full discussion of this debate.
6 See Valdés (1997) for a discussion of the possible negative effects of dual-language immersion programs on language minority students.

bilingualism, two-way bilingual programs and immersion programs reflect a value placed on mother tongue education and a view that multilingualism is a personal and social resource.[7]

Program evaluations

What is known about the effectiveness of these various program models? An answer to this question comes from two sources: large-scale national evaluations of programs for English language learners in the United States and empirical studies that seek to identify school- and classroom-level factors that are related to effective education for English language learners. The following is a brief overview of the findings from these two strands of research.

National evaluations

The most recent national evaluation was a longitudinal study conducted by Aguirre International (Ramirez, Yuen, Ramsey, & Pasta, 1991). This congressionally mandated study sought to determine which of three instructional programs – a structured English immersion program, an early-exit transitional program, or a late-exit transitional bilingual program – best met the needs of Spanish-speaking limited English proficient (LEP) students and helped them catch up to their English-speaking peers. The study was conducted over 8 years at nine sites, with five of these sites having only one of the three types of programs. The study concluded that

providing LEP students with substantial instruction in their primary language does not interfere with or delay their acquisition of English language skills, but helps them to "catch-up" to their English-speaking peers in English language arts, English reading, and math. In contrast, providing LEP students with almost exclusive instruction in English does not accelerate their acquisition of English language arts, reading or math, i.e., they do not appear to be "catching-up." The data suggest that by grade six, students provided with English-only instruction may actually fall further behind their English-speaking peers. Data also document that learning a second language will take six or more years. (Ramirez, 1992, p. 1)

The study recommended that English language learners be provided with language support services for at least 6 years and that they have content instruction in their primary language until they are able to prof-

---

7 According to Christian (1996), two-way immersion programs appear to be gaining popularity in the United States. In 1995, 182 schools located in eighteen states and the District of Columbia reported operating some form of two-way bilingual program including more than 25,000 students. The vast majority of these programs offered instruction in English and Spanish on the elementary-school level.

it from English-only instruction (Ramirez, 1992). The study has been criticized on a variety of issues. For example, Rossell and Baker (1992) though noting that the study's design is quite impressive, point to the study's failure to directly compare the achievement of children in late-exit bilingual education programs with those of children in the immersion and early-exit bilingual education programs; its definition of programs by nominal type rather than by the extent of English actually used in the programs; and its failure to evaluate the most widely implemented program for English language learners, ESL pull-out instruction.

Several smaller-scale evaluations of programs have also been undertaken. Willig (1985), for example, conducted a meta-analysis of selected studies on the effectiveness of bilingual education in comparison with no program at all. She concluded that

> when statistical controls for methodological inadequacies were employed, participation in bilingual education programs consistently produced small to moderate differences favoring bilingual education for tests of reading, language skills, mathematics, and total achievement when tests were in English, and for reading, language mathematics, writing, social studies, listening comprehension and attitudes toward school or self when tests were in other languages. (p. 269)

In contrast to Willig's findings, Rossell and Baker (1996) reviewed 300 studies of bilingual education programs, selecting 72, or 25%, of these studies that they considered to be methodologically sound in that they included treatment group, a control group, and a statistical control for pretreatment differences when groups had not been randomly assigned. They concluded that "the research evidence does not support transitional bilingual education as a superior form of instruction for limited proficient children" (p. 7). They point out, however, that one of the serious limitations of research on bilingual education, one well worth highlighting, is that

> no one looks at the future educational success of graduates of bilingual or immersion programs, as well as their life chances. . . . It is quite possible, for example, that *maintenance* bilingual education, that is bilingual education for an entire school career, reduces English language achievement in comparison to educating a child in the regular English language classroom or structured immersion but increases life chances for these students. This is because it might better maintain an adequate ability in the native tongue, which might result in greater economic gains in later life than would be predicted from the English language achievement of these students. (p. 41)

In evaluating recent program evaluation research like that cited above, August and Hakuta (1997) point out that "it is difficult to synthesize the program evaluations of bilingual education because of the extreme politicization of the process. Most consumers of research are not researchers who want to know the truth, but advocates who are convinced of the absolute correctness of their positions" (p. 138). Based on the studies they evaluated, however, they conclude that the beneficial effects of native language instruction are clearly evident in programs that are labeled bilingual education and programs labeled structured immersion appear to benefit students, although a quantitative analysis of such programs is still lacking. Their overall conclusion, however, is one that is worth emphasizing here:

There is little value in conducting evaluations to determine which type of program is best. The key issue is not finding a program that works for all children and all localities, but rather finding a set of program components that works for the children in the community of interest, given that community's goals, demographics, and resources. (p. 138)

Effective school studies

The second approach to discerning the effectiveness of educational alternatives for English language learners seeks to identify factors within the school and classroom that contribute to effective programs for English language learners. August and Hakuta (1997) distinguish four methodologies employed in such studies: effective-school research, nominated-school research, prospective case studies, and quasi experiments. Effective-school research typically identifies effective schools through an outcome measure, such as student achievement scores, whereas in nominated school research, knowledgeable professionals in the field identify effective programs. In prospective case studies, researchers describe changes in schoolwide programs or classrooms and document the effect of these changes on student achievement. Quasi-experiment studies start with a school or classroom that is generally less effective and then study a change or intervention predicted to contribute to student achievement. Because such studies include a comparison site, they have a strong basis for claiming that the intervention produced changes in student achievement.

One large-scale nominated-school study (Tikunoff, 1983), which sought to delineate the significant features of successful bilingual programs, was mandated by the U.S. Congress as an aid in its decision regarding the continued funding of bilingual education programs. The study involved fifty-eight classrooms and 232 students, Grades K–12, at six sites that had been nominated for their success in providing bilingual instruction to a variety of ethnolinguistic groups. Various qualitative and quantitative procedures were used to gather data on such matters as time allocation, teacher characteristics, and student participation. Based on an analysis of this data, Tikunoff concluded that teachers in what are perceived as successful bilingual education program typically exhibit the following five significant features.

1. *Congruence of instructional intent, organization and delivery of instruction, and student consequences.* The teachers in these successful bilingual classrooms typically created tasks and communicated the intent of these tasks in ways that promoted student participation. This involved clearly stating the desired outcome of the task, using the mother tongue where necessary.
2. *Use of active teaching behaviors.* Teachers at these sites communicated goals clearly, engaged students, monitored students' work, and provided their students with feedback.
3. *Use of students' native language and English for instruction.* Although English was used for approximately 60% of the observed time, the teachers frequently switched to the students' mother tongue when they perceived that students were not comprehending what was required or needed feedback to complete a task.
4. *Integration of English language development with basic skills instruction.* The teachers typically stressed language development during skills instruction, often using the mother tongue to clarify instructions and new information while encouraging students to use English.
5. *Use of information from the LEP students' home culture.* Teachers often made use of the students' native culture to communicate tasks; they integrated classroom rules of discourse from the students' native culture to encourage student participation; and they upheld the values and norms of both the United States and the native culture.

The value of studies like Tikunoff's (1983) is that they focus on the behavior of teachers and students in language-learning classrooms rather than comparing the results of program models like structured immersion or bilingual education. The danger of the latter approach is that it can obscure the fact that the actions of the teachers and students in a particular program greatly affect its outcomes. Effective school studies, on the other hand, provide insight into what administrators, teachers, and students need to do to contribute to successful second language learning.

In reviewing thirty-three studies that utilize one of the four methodologies described,[8] August and Hakuta (1997) conclude that effective schools and classrooms tend to have the following characteristics:

8 For studies included in this review of the success of early childhood education programs, see Mace-Matluck, Hoover, and Calfee (1989), Pease-Alvarez, Garcia, and Espinosa (1991), and Wong Fillmore, Ammon, McLaughlin, and Ammon (1985). For investigations of school reform, see Berman et al. (1992) and Berman et al. (1995). For studies on content learning and language development, see Chamot, Dale, O'Malley,

a supportive school-wide climate, school leadership, a customized learning environment, articulation and coordination within and between schools, some use of native language and culture in the instruction of language-minority students, a balanced curriculum that incorporates both basic and higher-order skills, explicit skills instruction, opportunities for student-directed activities, use of instructional strategies that enhance understanding, opportunities for practice, systematic student assessment, staff development, and home and parent involvement. (p. 171)

Several of these characteristics are worth elaborating on here. First, although the schools included in these studies differed in their manifestation of a supportive schoolwide climate, typically such schools valued the linguistic and cultural background of the students, had high expectations for the academic achievement of the students, and sought to involve the students in the overall school operation. Second, the staff members at these schools typically coordinated their efforts, demonstrating close collaboration between content and second language teachers. Third, teachers involved the students in a great variety of meaningful activities and not just basic skills instruction. Finally, at most of these schools there was a strong commitment to school-home communication, and parents were involved in some type of formal support activities. In general, much of the research also pointed out that there is no one right way to educate English language learners. Rather, "different approaches are necessary because of the great diversity of conditions faced by schools" (August & Hakuta, 1997, p. 174).

An important challenge to this latter claim is presented by the Success for All studies (Slavin, Madden, Dolan, & Wasik, 1995), whose developers claim that programs with specific materials, manuals, and structures can be successfully exported to a wide range of school situations. Success for All is a schoolwide restructuring program designed to meet the special needs of disadvantaged students. The fundamental assumption of the program is that, given appropriate instruction and adequate support services, every child can learn to read in the first grade or shortly thereafter. The model was applied to English language learners in a 3-year evaluation of Cambodian students in an inner-city Philadelphia school (Slavin & Yampolsky, 1992). Special adaptations for the English language learners included the following. First, English instruction was not a separate program but was "an organic part of a coordinated approach" (p. 1) in which ESL staff and services were integrated into the regular classroom program. When English language learners received separate instruction, the focus was on supporting students' success in the regular reading program. Second, tutors worked one-to-one with

and Spanos (1992) and Short (1994). For studies on literacy instruction, see Gersten (1996).

students who were having difficulties keeping up with their reading program. Third, in Grades 1–3, students were regrouped for a 2-hour reading and language arts period according to reading level rather than age. Fourth, older students worked for 45 minutes 2 days per week tutoring kindergarten students in their reading. Those students who had older Cambodian students as tutors benefited from their tutors' ability to read to and with them in English, translating into Cambodian when necessary. The program proved to be highly successful in accelerating the reading and English language performance of the English language learners at the school.

Although program evaluation research and studies of effective schools provide important insights into the kind of investments necessary for high-quality second language education, typically they have not investigated how language learners' experiences in the classroom, the home, and the community affect their success as language learners. What information is available in this regard? As a way of gaining insight into the overall language learning experience of language minorities, I next examine the available research on English language learners in the classroom, the educational institution, the home, and the community.

The language learning experience of language minorities in the United States

To begin, I emphasize that language learning does not occur only in the educational context. The home and the community provide important contexts for both mother tongue maintenance and English language learning. Recent research, much of it qualitative, provides useful information for teachers wanting to gain a fuller understanding of the language-learning experience of their students.

The classroom

One of the central settings for language learning is, of course, the classroom. In this context the dynamics between the teacher and language learner and between language learners and their peers can have a major impact on language learning. Several studies have documented that the experiences of English language learners in this regard can differ significantly from those of native English speakers

In a review of the research on the differential treatment of Mexican American students in classroom interaction, Losey (1995b) concluded that Mexican American students may

receive differential treatment not only because of ethnic differences but also as a result of language differences and ability grouping within the bilingual

406

classroom. These studies also . . . revealed the interactive and reactive nature of the classroom, reminding teachers that student behavior is as much a reaction to teacher behavior as teacher behavior is a response to student behavior. (p. 304)

For example, in one of the seminal studies cited by Losey, the researchers found that teachers initiated significantly fewer of the following behaviors with Mexican American students than with Anglo students: "(a) praising and encouraging, (b) accepting and/or using students' ideas, and (c) questioning" (p. 297). In addition, Mexican American students talked significantly less in the classroom, both in responding to and in initiating interactions with the teacher. Another study of a K–12 school noted that teachers regularly called on

Anglo students to "help" Mexican students if the Mexican students showed any sign of hesitation in responding to a question. . . . [The study] also found that teachers asked general questions of the class and allowed class members to shout out answers whenever they thought of them. However, the Mexican children did not participate in this type of interaction; only the Anglo students did. (p. 298)

In a study of Mexican American students in a community college setting, Losey (1995a) found that whereas 55% of the students in a class were Mexican Americans and 45% European Americans, European American students carried out 81% of the student initiations and 82% of the student responses – twice as many interactions as their numbers in the classroom would suggest. An interesting aside is that a gender analysis of the interaction of the Mexican Americans revealed that Mexican American men, though very few in number, responded nearly as frequently as the European Americans. Thus the relative silence of the Mexican Americans in the class was actually the silence of women.

In summarizing the research on the differential treatment of Mexican Americans, Losey (1995b) points out that with the aid of ethnographic methods, the studies have

revealed the cause of this [differential] treatment as inappropriate assessment of students' abilities, largely because of the structure of the classroom and students' responses to it. These studies have emphasized the importance of assessing students on a number of skills and abilities in a number of different contexts. (p. 304)

Hence it is extremely important for teachers to adequately assess the language proficiency and abilities of English language learners so that these students experience equal treatment in the classroom.

An equally important factor in successful language learning is the amount of teacher talk that occurs in language classrooms. Ramirez (1992), in the large-scale evaluative investigation of structured-English

407

immersion programs and early-exit and late-exit bilingual programs summarized in the section on program evaluations, concluded that teachers in all three programs failed to provide an ideal language learning environment in that they tended to limit their students' opportunities to produce complex language. Based on direct observations of teachers, Ramirez notes that teachers did most of the talking in all three types of classrooms, producing about twice as many utterances as their students. In general, students produced language only when working with the teacher and then only in response to the initiations of the teacher. Even more unfortunate is that when students did respond, they provided only simple recall information. In summary, the classroom observations in Ramirez's investigation show that "teachers in all three programs do not teach language or higher order cognitive skills effectively. Teachers in all three programs offer a passive language learning environment, limiting student opportunities to produce language and develop more complex language and thinking skills" (p. 10).

Findings such as these suggest that often students do not participate equally in classrooms because teachers treat students differently based on the students' ethnic and linguistic background. In addition, frequently the type of interaction promoted in second language classrooms may not encourage students to use English in ways that develop complex language and cognitive skills. Such findings are particularly disturbing in light of the fact that the studies on effective classrooms cited previously emphasize the importance of using instructional strategies that promote opportunities for involvement and practice.

The school or institution

Another significant factor that can influence the effectiveness of the educational experience of the English language learner is the school structure itself.

TRACKING

One way in which schools can affect the quality of education that learners receive is through the grouping of the students. A very common feature of U.S. schools is *tracking*, or forming classes based on the supposed ability of the student population, resulting in high-track and low-track classes. Harklau (1994a), in her study on the effect of tracking on language minorities, points out that

tracking in high school institutional contexts is perhaps best understood as the tension between two powerful but inherently conflicting ethics in American society. One is to provide equal educational opportunities to all American citizens, and the other is to reward individual competitiveness, initiative, and talent. (p. 219)

Tracking is highly relevant to the education of English language learners in the United States because frequently a high proportion of these students are placed in what are termed *low-track* classes. Of course, this situation can be attributed partly to the type of assessment that is used to place students in these classes, in which English language ability may not permit students to demonstrate their knowledge of content.

To determine the effect of tracking on English language learners, Harklau (1994b) followed several English language learners for 3 1/2 years in an urban U.S. high school, which, like most, employed a tracking system. The school population was ethnically diverse, consisting of 50% African American, 30% Asian American, 20% White, and 3% Latino students. She found that the activities used in low-track classes differed dramatically from those in the high-track classes. The low-track classes used primarily material from the textbook or from simplified readings that often lifted a part of a text from its total context, making it more difficult to comprehend. High-track students, on the other hand, were assigned extensive reading from a variety of authentic sources – novels, short stories, poetry, news magazines, and so on. There were also differences in how the students responded to the assigned readings. In the low-track classes, students were involved in silent reading, reading aloud, or answering comprehension questions, but students in high-track classes were asked to do the reading at home, and class time was spent discussing the readings. Students in low-track classes were also rarely required to write compositions; rather, they completed sentence-level writing activities. Students in the high-track classes, on the other hand, received formal instruction in developing expository texts and were asked to write extended compositions. The so-called critical thinking skills that were necessary to function in high-track classes were, as Harklau points out,

not innate to high track students. Rather, in a vivid illustration of self-fulfilling prophecy, they were given explicit instruction in valued analytical skills simply because, as high track students, they were already assumed to be capable of such analysis. (p. 227)

The interaction that occurred in low-track classes also differed dramatically from that in high-track classes. In low-track classes, because of what the teacher viewed as potential discipline problems, students were asked to work on their own with little opportunity for peer interaction. High-track classes, on the other hand, often featured group work allowing interaction with peers. Hence, students in these two types of classrooms had very different learning experiences. As Harklau

(1994b) points out, in effect, tracking polarized instructional environments, and created vastly different second language learning experiences for students in high and low tracks. This analysis illustrates how
the language learned by linguistic minority students in mainstream
classroom contexts is inextricably woven into the instructional environments in which they are submersed. Because of the curriculum differen-
tiation practiced in a tracked system, they are socialized into different
discourse practices and literate behaviors (p. 229).

ESL CLASSES

The institutional division of language minorities into separate ESL
classes can also affect the type of interaction that occurs in the classroom and hence the extent of content and language learning. In her 3-
year ethnographic study of ESL classes, Harklau (1994a) focused on the
experiences of four Chinese immigrant English language learners in ESL
versus mainstream high school classes. Whereas in both types of classroom the predominant activity was teacher-led discussion, Harklau
found that in the ESL classes the teacher tried to make the input more
comprehensible and create more opportunities for students to interact
and participate. Harklau also found that the mainstream curriculum
was often constrained by state and curriculum guidelines, making it relatively static. On the other hand, the curriculum in the ESL classes tended to change depending on the particular makeup of the student population, which often varied in level and linguistic background throughout
the semester. In response to this changing population, the teacher often
used a spiral syllabus featuring a similar format and a good deal of review. This led some students to feel that the class was not challenging.
As one student put it, "ESL is kind of like re – I mean, every time is review. I mean every year is the same thing" (p. 258). Another student
pointed out that in the ESL class "it's going very slow, and the language
seems kind of like emergency things. If you don't learn it, you can't –
you have to be stupid" (p. 259). Harklau concludes that both the mainstream and the ESL classroom have certain strengths and drawbacks for
the English language learner. She maintains that

a systematic integration of content and language, might well serve students
best. ESL and mainstream teachers might, for example, work collaboratively
to develop a curriculum for language minority students that parallels the
regular curriculum. In some programs, collaboration might lead to the
formation of interdisciplinary teams of ESL and content-area teachers who
instruct both learners and native speakers of English. (pp. 268–269)

These studies vividly demonstrate that educational decisions made on
the institutional level, such as tracking or placing students in separate
ESL classes, can significantly affect the type of education that students

receive. Hence, if educators are to design locally appropriate educational options, they need to seriously consider how institutional decisions on such matters as ability grouping and curriculum development will influence the language development of their students, particularly those who come from language minority backgrounds. It is interesting to note that one central factor in the effectiveness of the Success for All program cited in the section on program evaluation was that the ESL and the regular staff worked together closely to design an organic, coordinated approach to English learning. Indeed, staff coordination seems to be an educational investment that is essential to ensure high-quality education for English language learners.

Home

Another important context that must be considered in promoting English language learning is the home environment, which is after all a key context for both acquiring knowledge and learning how to learn.

CULTURAL MISMATCH STUDIES

One type of research regarding language minority education has sought to ascertain to what extent the culture of the school, which is frequently based on White, middle-class standards, differs from the home culture of language minorities. The focus of these studies is on differences in home and school ways of speaking and interacting.

A common approach in this kind of research has been to focus on mother-child interaction patterns. One limitation of such studies is that most do not collect data from real-life interactions in actual settings. Rather, they provide experimental tasks for mother-child teaching in experimental settings. Summarizing the findings of such studies with Mexican American children, Losey (1995b) states that one "can tentatively conclude that there are differences in the interactional patterns of Mexican American and Anglo American mothers and that these vary based on such factors as the educational attainment of the mothers and the language of interaction." She continues, however, that "these conclusions must be tentative, however, as the validity of the studies – that is the degree to which they are actually measuring what they claim to be measuring – may be questioned" (p. 292). Auerbach (1989), for one, challenges the common approach of using the framework of school for defining the activities that parents should conduct at home. Instead, she suggests that researchers study the activities in the home that may promote school achievement. Hence, the question is not whether home practices match school practices but what home practices foster children's academic development.

411

Sandra Lee McKay

Other studies investigating the match between home and school patterns have attempted to account for the classroom interaction patterns of language minorities based on general home interaction patterns rather than merely mother-child interactions. Again in reference to Mexican Americans, the largest U.S. language minority group, Losey (1995b) notes that several such studies "have found that there is a difference between the home interaction patterns of many Mexican Americans, which could be described as cooperative, and the prevalent interactional patterns in mainstream classrooms, which is competitive" (p. 292). A major limitation of these studies, however, is that even though they document common interaction patterns in the school context, they often fail to fully examine the homes of the Mexican American students that are studied. One major exception is a study by Delgado-Gaitan (1987), who focused on seven Mexican children (Grades 1–3) for 18 months, observing the interactional styles of Mexican children at home and at play as well as at school. She found that

children engaged in collective work at home but that work was organized in a competitive way at school. Likewise she found the authority structure of the home different from that of the school. Though home and school were alike in that parents and teachers both assigned tasks to the children, children in the Mexican homes were allowed to decide how to carry out a task and when it should be done. They were given a great deal of responsibility and relatively little direction in how to carry out those responsibilities. But in school. . . . teachers not only assigned tasks but also controlled how those tasks were carried out. (pp. 295–296)

One way, then, that schools might be more responsive to the educational needs of language minorities is to investigate the type of learning that occurs in the home and use it as a basis for school learning and interaction. A collaborative project of educators and anthropologists is attempting to do this in its study of household and classroom practices within working-class Mexican communities in Tucson, Arizona (Moll, Amanti, Neff, & Gonzalez, 1992). This project attempts to coordinate three interrelated activities: "the ethnographic analysis of household dynamics, the examination of classroom practices, and the development of after-school study groups with teachers" (p. 132). The goal of the ethnographic analysis of homes is to ascertain what the researchers term the *funds of knowledge* of the home environment, that is, "historically accumulated and culturally developed bodies of knowledge and skills essential for household or individual functioning and well-being" (p. 133). As part of their study, the researchers examine how household members use their funds of knowledge to deal with changing and often difficult social and economic circumstances.

The research group is particularly interested in how families develop

412

social networks that help them deal with their environment and develop and exchange resources. They note two aspects of these social networks that contrast sharply with typical classroom practices. The first is that these networks are flexible and active and may involve persons from outside the home. The person from whom children learn carpentry, for example, may be the uncle who celebrates parties with them. Hence, the "teacher" knows the child as a whole person. Second, these networks are based on reciprocal practices in which the practices establish obligations and develop an enduring social relationship.

In order to draw on home funds of knowledge and social networks, the project actively involves classroom teachers in ethnographic investigations of children's homes and communities. Teachers then meet to share what they have seen and use these insights to develop classroom activities. For example, in one instance, several teachers noted that children were involved in buying and selling activities, some of them selling candies and other sweets that they had gotten in Mexico. This observation led to an activity that involved investigating the differences in the ingredients in candies produced in Mexico and the United States as well as various aspects of buying and selling this candy. The class thus investigated areas of math, science, health, consumer education, cross-cultural practices, advertising, and food production. Projects such as this then strive to design effective programs for English language learners by more closely linking the home and school environment. In contrast to the approach of much of the existing research, they do not emphasize the mismatch between the home and school culture; rather, they seek to integrate the learning experience of these two contexts.

SCHOOL-FAMILY PARTNERSHIPS

School-family partnerships are another way to more closely link the home and the school. One of the most active researchers in this area is Epstein (1992, 1995), who maintains that theoretical perspectives on schools and families have tended to be based on one of four perspectives: separate influence, sequenced influence, embedded influence, or overlapping influence. In the separate-influence perspective, educators contend that schools and families are most efficient and effective when they assume independent goals and activities. In the sequenced-influence perspective, on the other hand, educators argue that the parents and teachers contribute to children's development at various stages of their life. An underlying assumption of this model is that the early home years determine children's success in school and life. The third perspective, the embedded-influence theory, approaches the spheres of influence as a set of concentric circles, each contained within the next, but does not encourage explorations of developmental change nor of

413

the cumulative influence of these environments over time. In the final perspective, that of overlapping influences, Epstein (1992), who espouses this view argues that the spheres of influence overlap and can be pushed together or pulled apart:

The extent of overlap is affected by time – to account for changes in the ages and grade levels of students and the influence of historic change on environments – and by behavior – to account for the background characteristics, philosophies, and practices of each environment. (p. 1140)

Epstein (1995) argues that the family and school can be brought closer together through school-family partnerships.

In a partnership, teachers and administrators create more *family-like* schools. A family-like school recognizes each child's individuality and makes each child feel special and included. Family-like schools welcome all families, not just those that are easy to reach. In a partnership, parents create more *school-like* families. A school-like family recognizes that each child is also a student. Families reinforce the importance of school, homework, and activities that build student skills and feelings of success. . . . Communities also create *family-like* settings, services, and events to enable families to better support their children. (p. 702)

Epstein goes on to outline six types of involvement that can occur in partnerships, namely, (1) helping families establish home environments to support children as students, (2) designing effective forms of school and home communication, (3) recruiting parents' help and support, (4) providing information to families about how to help students at home with homework and other school activities, (5) including parents in school decisions, and (6) identifying and integrating resources from the community to strengthen the school programs and family practices. The recent interest in school-family partnerships is encouraging in light of the fact that home and parent involvement is one of the key factors that August and Hakuta (1997) maintain effective schools promote. Indeed, one area of educational investment that appears to be essential to providing English language learners with high-quality education is a commitment to creating strong links between the home and the school environment.

The community

A final sphere that needs to be considered in designing effective programs for English language learners is the larger community. Heath and McLaughlin (1994) investigated the influence of community activities on the learning experience of language minorities. This study, which involved 5 years of field research in more than sixty youth organizations in three major urban communities, recognized that community-based organizations (CBOs) "have been creating and maintaining institutions that are, on the one hand, highly educational, and, on the other, keenly oriented toward preparation for employment" (p. 279). As one example of the type of language learning that can occur in such organizations, Heath and McLaughlin recount the experiences of young people in a CBO named Liberty Theater, in which the mayor's office paid students between the ages of 14 and 18 the minimum wage for 6 hours daily for 6 weeks to produce plays that were performed before the city's various parks and recreation programs. Heath and McLaughlin document that, in the course of scripting and practicing these plays, the young people learned literacy skills and work skills (e.g., they had to show up daily and participate) as well as learning how to interact with one another.

Heath and McLaughlin (1994) point out that many of the CBOs they observed offer a great deal to young people – "they work them hard, teach them much, and encourage them to stick to school and to build a belief that dedication will help move them along toward the job or work they all covet eventually" (p. 289). Based on their investigation, Heath and McLaughlin argue persuasively for closer linkage between CBOs and schools. As they point out, the two have much to offer each other. Whereas CBOs often provide the students with work-related skills and personal encouragement and support, the schools have other resources critical to youth's productive learning and development: (1) numerous teachers and administrators dedicated to the education of youth and (2) the material resources essential to learning (e.g., libraries, computers, laboratories). As Heath and McLaughlin note,

both schools and community-based youth organizations are institutions dedicated to the healthy development, accomplishment, and achievement of young people. Yet each generally operates in isolation, separated by policies that bundle "education" into school and by professional boundaries. . . . These distinctions represent more than wasted resources and opportunities for youth; they fail to recognize the sizable body of evidence that shows young people learn not only in school, but also in their neighborhood, in the experiences they have and the people they meet in their discretionary time. (p. 292)

Investigations such as this one highlight the fact that English language learning is not the exclusive domain of the language classroom. Rather, it is a multilayered experience that involves learners in a multiplicity of roles in a variety of contexts. Given this fact, an educational investment that is essential to the provision of high-quality education to English language learners is for educators to actively seek ways to integrate these learning environments. Educators must achieve this integration both bureaucratically by establishing formal links between the school, home, and community and informally by drawing on home and community resources in the classroom experiences of English language learners.

Conclusion

Traditionally, much of the research and literature on the language education of English language learners has centered on which educational program models are most productive for developing English language and literacy abilities. Although such an approach clearly has its benefits, the danger of focusing on program models is that the complexity of the learning experiences of English language learners may be overlooked. Indeed, the research cited in this chapter demonstrates that English language learners interact in various language learning contexts with a variety of individuals. In light of these multiple roles, the educational investments required to achieve high-quality education for English language learners clearly needs to involve members of the school, home, and community. Specifically, the studies suggest the need for the following educational investments.

1. Classroom teachers need to make certain that they treat all learners in their classroom equally both in terms of their ability to participate in the class and in terms of the kinds of activities and tasks they are asked to undertake.
2. The entire school staff needs to coordinate efforts so that language learning is a schoolwide endeavor resulting in a well-integrated approach to promoting English language and content learning.
3. Schools need to encourage the investment of parents and family members in the education of English language learners. This involvement should focus on finding out not how the learning experiences in the home can better match the school's but rather on how the school enviorment can value and encourage the learning experiences of the family.
4. Educators and community leaders need to work together to directly link community-based organizations and activities with public education so that each context can share its valuable resources and reinforce the learning that takes place in the other.

Ultimately, educators must recognize that even though schools have a public mandate to develop English language and literacy abilities, in reality language learning takes place in a variety of contexts – the home, the community, and the workplace. What we as language specialists need to do is to encourage the families and communities of English language learners to invest their resources in English language learning and to make the classroom a place where this learning comes together in ways that promote the integrity of the learner as an individual with a variety of personal resources and multiple roles.

Suggestions for further reading

August, D., & Hakuta, K. (Ed.). (1997). *Improving schooling for language-minority children*. Washington, DC: National Academy Press. This book represents the work of a blue-ribbon committee that sought to investigate the needs of English language learners in the United States. The book carefully documents existing research in the following areas relevant to English language learning: bilingualism and second language learning, cognitive aspects of school learning, the social context of school learning, student assessment, program evaluation, school and classroom effectiveness, the preparation and development of teachers, and education statistics. After reviewing and summarizing significant research in each of these areas, the authors elaborate on present research needs in the area. The book's critical and comprehensive summary of the research, as well as its clearly specified recommendations for future research, makes it a valuable resource for second language educators and researchers.

Garcia, O., & Baker, C. (Ed.). (1995). *Policy and practice in bilingual education: Extending the foundations*. Clevedon, England: Multilingual Matters. This reader is a collection of influential papers on bilingualism and bilingual education organized into four sections: "Policy and Legislation on Bilingualism in Schools and Bilingual Education"; "Implementation of Bilingual Policy in Schools"; "Using Bilingualism in Instruction"; and "Using the Bilingualism of the School Community." The book contains articles on topics ranging from educational planning to dual language programs and process approaches to literacy and school-family partnerships. The book is particularly valuable in its inclusion of articles dealing with English language education in Anglophone countries other than the United States (i.e., Wales, England, and Canada) since these papers provide a basis for comparison and possible innovations in the U.S. context.

Minami, M., & Kennedy, B. (Eds.). (1991) *Language issues in literacy and bilingual/multicultural education*. Cambridge, MA: Harvard Educational Review. This book contains articles published in the *Harvard Educational Review* dealing with second language acquisition, literacy, and bilingual and multicultural education. The book is divided into three sections: "Classical Theoretical Approaches to Language Acquisition, Literacy, and Bilingual education"; "Literacy as a Social Product: A Sociocultural Approach"; and "Multicultural/Bilingual issues in Literacy." In light of the topics introduced in this chapter, the collection's particular value is its recognition of the social dimensions of language learning, as evidenced by the inclusion of articles on sociocultural approaches to family literacy, frameworks for empowering minority students, and immigrant socialization.

Wiley, T. (1996). *Language and literacy in the United States.* McHenry, IL: Center for Applied Linguistics and Delta Systems.
   This book is one of the first devoted entirely to the topic of the literacy of language minorities in the United States. A major focus of the book is to critique the widely held belief in the "cognitive great divide" between literates and nonliterates. The book contains a review of major scholarly orientations toward the study of literacy as well as an overview of common measures of literacy. One of the most valuable chapters in the book in terms of understanding the situation of English language learners in the United States is Chapter 2, which introduces and critiques commonly held myths and assumptions about literacy and language diversity in the United States.

References

Auerbach, E. (1989). Toward a social-contextual approach in family literacy. *Harvard Educational Review, 59,* 165–181.

August, D., & Hakuta, K. (Ed.). (1997). *Improving schoooling for language-minority children.* Washington, DC: National Academy Press.

Berman, P., Chambers, J., Gandara, P., McLaughlin, B., Minicucci, C., Nelson, B., Olsen, L., & Parrish, T. (1992). *Meeting the challenge of language diversity: An evaluation of programs for pupils with limited proficiency in English* (Vols. 1–3). Berkeley, CA: BW Associates.

Berman, P., McLaughlin, B., McLeod, B., Minnicucci, C., Nelson, B., & Woodworth, K. (1995). *School reform and student diversity: Case studies of exemplary practices for LEP students.* Berkeley, CA: National Center for Research on Cultural Diversity and Second Language Learning and BW Associates.

Chamot, A. U., Dale, M., O'Malley, O., & Spanos, G. (1992). Learning and problem solving strategies of ESL students. *Bilingual Research Journal, 16,* 1–33.

Christian, D. (1996). Language development in two-way immersion: Trends and prospects. In J. E. Alatis (Ed.), *Georgetown University Round Table on Languages and Linguistics* (pp. 30–42). Washington, DC: Georgetown University Press.

Clegg, J. (Ed.). (1996). *Mainstreaming ESL: Case studies in integrating ESL students into the mainstream classroom.* Clevedon, England: Multilingual Matters.

Collier, V. P., & Thomas, W. P. (1989). How quickly can immigrants become proficient in school English? *Journal of Educational Issues of Language Minority Students, 5,* 26–38.

Cummins, J. (1979). Linguistic interdependence and the educational development of bilingual children. *Review of Educational Research, 19,* 197–205.

Cummins, J. (1981). The role of primary language development in promoting educational success for language minority students. In California State Department of Education (Eds.), *Schooling and language minority students: A theoretical framework* (pp. 3–49). Los Angeles: California State University, Evaluation, Dissemination, and Assessment Center.

Delgado-Gaitan, C. (1987). Traditions and transition in the learning process of Mexican children: An ethnographic view. In G. Spindler & E. Spindler (Eds.), *Interpretive ethnography of education at home and abroad* (pp. 333–359). Hillsdale, NJ: Erlbaum.

Epstein, J. (1992). School and family partnerships. In M. Alkin (Ed.), *Encyclopedia of educational research* (pp. 1139–1151). New York: Macmillan.

Epstein, J. (1995). School/family/community partnerships: Caring for the children we share. *Phi Delta Kappan, 76,* 701–712.

Gersten, R. (1996). Literacy instruction for language-minority students: The transition years. *The Elementary School Journal, 96,* 228–244.

Harklau, L. (1994a). ESL versus mainstream classes: Contrasting L2 learning environments. *TESOL Quarterly, 28,* 241–272.

Harklau, L. (1994b). Tracking and linguistic minority students: Consequences of ability grouping for second language learners. *Linguistics and Education, 6,* 217–244.

Heath, S. B., & McLaughlin, M. W. (1994). The best of both worlds: Connecting schools and community youth organizations for all-day, all-year learning. *Educational Administration Quarterly, 30,* 278–300.

Losey, K. (1995a). Gender and ethnicity as factors in the development of verbal skills in bilingual Mexican American women. *TESOL Quarterly, 29,* 635–663.

Losey, K. (1995b). Mexican American students and classroom interaction: An overview and critique. *Review of Educational Research, 65,* 283–318.

Mace-Matluck, B. J., Hoover, W. A., & Calfee, R. C. (1989). Teaching reading to bilingual children: A longitudinal study of teaching and learning in the early grades. *NABE Journal, 13,* 187–216.

McKay, S. L. (1997). Multilingualism in the United States. *Annual Review of Applied Linguistics, 17,* 242–262.

Moll, L. C., Amanti, C., Neff, D., & Gonzalez, N. (1992). Funds of knowledge for teaching: Using a qualitative approach to connect homes and classrooms. *Theory Into Practice, 31,* 132–141.

National Center for Education Statistics. (1993/1994). *School and staffing survey.* Washington, DC: U.S. Government Printing Office.

Paulston, C. B. (1981). Bilingualism and education. In C. A. Ferguson & S. B. Heath (Eds.), *Language in the USA* (pp. 469–485). Cambridge: Cambridge University Press.

Pease-Alvarez, L., Garcia, G., & Espinosa, P. (1991). Effective instruction for language-minority students: An early childhood case study. *Early Childhood Research Quarterly 6,* 347–361.

Ramirez, D. J., Yuen, S. D., Ramsey, D. R., & Pasta, D. J. (1991). *Final report: National longitudinal study of structured-immersion strategy, early-exit, and late-exit bilingual education programs for language minority children: Vols. I and II. Technical report*. San Mateo, CA: Aguirre International.

Ramirez, J. (1992). Executive summary. *Bilingual Research Journal, 16*, 1–61.

Rossell, C. H., & Baker, K. (1996). The educational effectiveness of bilingual education. *Research in the Teaching of English, 30*, 1–74.

Ruiz, R. (1988). Orientations in language planning. In S. L. McKay & S. C. Wong (Eds.), *Language diversity: Problem or resource?* (pp. 3–26). New York: Newbury House.

Short, D. J. (1994). Expanding middle school horizons: Integrating language, culture, and social studies. *TESOL Quarterly, 28*, 581–608.

Skutnabb-Kangas, T. (1979). *Language in the process of cultural assimilation and structural incorporation of linguistic minorities*. Arlington, VA: National Clearinghouse for Bilingual Education.

Skutnabb-Kangas, T. (1994). Linguistic human rights and minority education. *TESOL Quarterly, 28*, 625–628.

Slavin, R., Madden, N., Dolan, L., & Wasik, B. (1995). Success for all: A summary of the research. Papers presented at the annual meeting of the American Educational Research Association. San Francisco: Center for Children Placed at Risk of School Failure, Johns Hopkins University, San Francisco.

Slavin, R., & Yampolsky, R. (1992). *Success for all: Effects on students with limited English proficiency: A three-year evaluation, Report No. 29*. Baltimore: Johns Hopkins University, Center for Research on Effective Schooling for Disadvantaged Students.

Sridhar, K. K. (1994). Mother tongue maintenance and multiculturalism. *TESOL Quarterly, 24*, 628–631.

Tikunoff, W. J. (1983). *An emerging description of successful bilingual instruction: Executive summary of Part I of the SBIF study*. San Francisco: Far West Laboratory.

Valdés, G. (1997). Dual-language immersion programs: A cautionary note concerning the education of language-minority students. *Harvard Educational Review, 67*, 391–429.

Willig, A. (1985). A meta-analysis of selected studies on the effectiveness of bilingual education. *Review of Educational Research, 55*, 269–317.

Wong Fillmore, L., Ammon, B., McLaughlin, B., & Ammon, B. (1985). *Learning English through bilingual instruction: Final report*. Berkeley: University of California Press.

Wong, S. C. (1988). Educational rights of language minorities. In S. L. McKay & S. C. Wong (Eds.), *Language diversity: Problem or resource?* (pp. 367–386). New York: Newbury House.

15 Legal investment in multilingualism

Rachel F. Moran

Language educators are experts in how children learn to speak, read, and write in a native language or a second one acquired in school. Their principal preoccupation is with how to choose among programmatic options based on available research and classroom resources. Yet law and politics often set the parameters of these choices. In the United States, federal, state, and local policy makers make critical decisions about whether to support research on and development of programs, mandate particular instructional approaches, and fund direct delivery of services to linguistic minority students. The politically naive run the the risk of seeing their pedagogical options shrink in an ideologically charged policy-making environment. For that reason, an exploration of how law and policy have affected pedagogy is critically important to language educators.

In many ways, this chapter illustrates the adage "Be careful what you ask for in youth; you may get it in old age." In 1988, I wrote an article entitled "The Politics of Discretion: Federal Intervention in Bilingual Education," in which I chronicled the rise and fall of strong federal leadership in shaping educational programs for non–English proficient (NEP) and limited English proficient (LEP) students. During the 1970s, the federal government invested in the problems of linguistic minority children by promulgating standards of nondiscrimination, enforcing these standards through guidelines and compliance reviews, and funding the delivery of bilingual programs. By the 1980s, however, federal officials had substantially reduced their commitment to interpreting and enforcing a principle of nondiscrimination and to funding special programs for NEP and LEP students. One rationale for this federal retreat was that too many uncertainties surrounded these programs to provide clear guidance to state and local educational authorities. In my 1988 article, I suggested ways in which the new federalism, which reduced national oversight and returned discretion on language policies to state and local education officials, might play a useful role in revisiting the debates about the values behind and efficiency of bilingual education programs.

With nearly 10 years of experience to gauge how the experiment with the new federalism has worked, I cannot paint an encouraging picture. Based on experiences in California and New York, two states with substantial populations of NEP and LEP students, I have concluded that relocating discretion to state and local authorities has neither mitigated ideological conflict nor led to a clearer picture of which programmatic strategies work and why. The new federalism was doomed to fail because bilingual education was characterized as a civil rights and pedagogical issue without taking account of the impact of high levels of immigration. The federal government adopted immigration policies that dramatically increased the number of NEP and LEP students in states like California and New York. However, these shifts did not trigger any obligation to assist the states in dealing with the needs of newcomers. On the contrary, federal officials reduced both regulatory oversight and fiscal support of bilingual education programs as the number of linguistic minority students soared. As a result, states like California and New York have faced a large influx of NEP and LEP immigrant students without federal guidance or financial assistance. The predictable result has been a system of public education in crisis as it struggles to meet the burgeoning needs of linguistic minority students.

From federal reform to federal retreat: The rise of the new federalism

When the modern Civil Rights movement began to mobilize in pursuit of racial equality after World War II, its focus was on an officially sanctioned caste system that subordinated Blacks by denying them access to facilities, such as schools, municipal parks, and public transportation, that were earmarked for Whites. The doctrine of *separate but equal* endorsed by the U.S. Supreme Court in *Plessy v. Ferguson* in 1896 ushered in an era of state-mandated segregation that harmed Blacks' life chances. When the Supreme Court finally disavowed these practices in *Brown v. Board of Education* in 1954 by declaring state-mandated segregation of public elementary schools unconstitutional, the lawsuit was framed by the Court's concerns about how an official doctrine of White superiority harmed the hearts and minds of Black children.

The Civil Rights movement succeeded in implementing *Brown* only after Congress expressed its support for the Court by enacting statutes like the Civil Rights Act of 1964. The Act provides that "[n]o person in the United States shall, on the ground of race, color, or national origin, be excluded from participation in, be denied the benefits of, or be subjected to discrimination under any program or activity receiving Federal financial assistance." By embracing a principle of nondiscrimination that would be federally enforced, the act enabled Civil Rights activists to enlist the support of powerful federal agencies, such as the Office for Civil Rights (OCR), in efforts to undo discriminatory practices. Meaningful desegregation initiatives ensued. The act's implications for other forms of discrimination against groups who were not Black remained unclear. Perhaps this lack of clarity should not be surprising. According to 1960 census data, only one in ten Americans identified themselves as non-White, and of these, 90% were Black (Ramirez, 1995).[1] As a result, addressing the problems of non-Whites and addressing the problems of Blacks probably did not seem to be very different propositions.

After 1960, however, the demographics of the United States began to change. In particular, there was dramatic growth in the Asian and Latino populations. In 1968, Congress enacted the Bilingual Education Act to fund research and experimentation on programs that would meet the needs of NEP and LEP students. Funding was minuscule under the act, but it did put bilingual education on the national reform agenda (Moran, 1988, pp. 1264–1265). Two years later, the OCR drafted a memorandum on the relevance of Title VI of the Civil Rights Act of 1964 to linguistic minority students. The memorandum states that "[w]here inability to speak and understand the English language excludes national origin-minority group children from effective participation in the educational program offered by a school district, the district must take affirmative steps to rectify the language deficiency in order to open its instructional program to these students (OCR, 1970)." Although the OCR did not aggressively enforce its 1970 interpretation, the memorandum made clear that civil rights concerns were not limited exclusively to Blacks (Moran, 1988, pp. 1267–1268).

In 1974, the U.S. Supreme Court upheld the OCR's 1970 interpretation in *Lau v. Nichols*. In that case, NEP Chinese students challenged the San Francisco school district's decision not to provide them with supplemental instruction of any kind. Relying on Title VI and the OCR interpretation, the Court concluded that the district was bound to take some steps to remedy the language barrier, although it did not specify what these steps might be. Following *Lau*, the federal government assumed a far more visible role in setting programmatic guidelines for linguistic minority students than it had before. The OCR adopted the *Lau* Guidelines, which expressed a strong preference for programs that relied on some native language instruction, such as transitional bilingual education or bilingual-bicultural education (OCR, 1975, § IX).[2] Under the Guidelines, intensive English instruction, such as English as a second language (ESL) programs and structured immersion, was to be used only when a child had an urgent need to learn English rapidly. For example,

---

1 For additional discussion of the demographic changes that occurred during this period, see Chapter 1.

2 Transitional bilingual education relies on a child's native language as a bridge to learning English, while bilingual-bicultural education is designed to produce students proficient in both English and their native language (OCR, 1975, § IX).

an older student who had only a short time remaining before high school graduation might receive intensive English instruction (§ III).[3]

At about the same time that the OCR was providing more centralized guidance to state and local educators, Congress passed the Equal Educational Opportunities Act (EEOA) of 1974, which codified *Lau*. According to the act, "No State shall deny equal educational opportunity to an individual on account of his or her race, color, sex, or national origin, by . . . (f) the failure by an educational agency to take appropriate action to overcome language barriers that impede equal participation by its students in the instructional programs." President Richard Nixon considered the EEOA a way to trade off "quality education" remedies against the increasingly unpopular use of busing to achieve racial integration (Haft, 1983). Along with greater federal constraints on state and local decision making about bilingual education came greater federal funding. Congress increased appropriations for bilingual education programs and earmarked the lion's share of the money for programs favored under OCR's Guidelines (Moran, 1988, pp. 1272–1280).

In the late 1970s and early 1980s, however, federal leadership in the field of bilingual education began to falter. An Alaska school district challenged the *Lau* Guidelines in federal court, arguing that they were applied so rigidly that they were tantamount to rules. However, federal officials had not notified the public of the proposed rules so that comments could be submitted and considered as required by the Administrative Procedure Act a federal law that regulates how federal agencies make and apply rules. Joseph Califano, then secretary of health, education, and welfare, signed a consent agreement that promised to replace the Guidelines with new rules that satisfied these procedural requirements (Northwest Arctic School v. Califano, 1978). Efforts to replace the Guidelines became mired in controversy about the ideology and effectiveness of bilingual education. The Guidelines eventually were withdrawn without any new provisions to replace them (Moran, 1988, pp. 1294–1296). As the controversy surrounding bilingual education grew, Congress began to withdraw financial support for the programs. Between 1982 and 1989, federal funding levels fell below the level of support in 1981. Since 1990, appropriations for bilingual education have grown modestly. Despite the increasing size of the NEP and LEP student population, funding levels are not substantially larger than they were in the late 1970s. However, the federal government has projected major increases in program support in the future.[4]

---

3 ESL programs often pull NEP and LEP children out of a regular English-speaking classroom to offer them instruction in English. In immersion programs, instruction is primarily in English but is specially structured to take account of the child's limited facility in the language (OCR, 1975, § IX).

4 Although the National Center for Education Statistics (1996) reports a dramatic drop

As a result of federal retrenchment in bilingual education, state and local educational agencies are now governed by Title VI as interpreted in *Lau* with the help of the 1970 OCR memorandum and the EEOA of 1974. In short, these agencies must comply with a general principle of nondiscrimination, but they are not bound to adopt any particular programmatic choice. A federal court of appeals decision in *Castaneda v. Pickard* (1981) makes plain that a program must be based on sound pedagogical theory, properly implemented, and monitored for its effectiveness. Still, these requirements leave state and local educators with considerable leeway to choose among competing approaches. Moreover, school officials must make programmatic choices with far less federal financial assistance. Because intensive English instruction is usually less expensive than programs that rely on native language instruction, fiscal constraints alone may tempt districts to prefer the former to the latter (Moran, 1988, p. 1304).

The impact of the new federalism on bilingual education

There is no reason to presume that the new federalism inevitably must lead to the deterioration of classroom instruction for NEP and LEP students. Indeed, local districts could be better able than the federal government to assess parental preferences about English acquisition, native language fluency, and cultural instruction when selecting a program. Freed of federal oversight, state and local educational agencies might experiment with instructional alternatives to find those that work best for their students. In fact, however, the experiences in two states, California and New York, suggest that the new federalism has neither mitigated disputes about instructional values nor enhanced experimentation to resolve pedagogical uncertainty.[5]

California

In 1976, when federal support for bilingual education was at its apex, California enacted the Chacon-Moscone Bilingual-Bicultural Education Act. The act endorsed programs that relied on native language instruction to meet NEP and LEP students' needs. In 1980, when federal lead-

---

in federal funding for bilingual education in 1993, other sources do not indicate such a decline. See Kindler (1996); Office of Management and Budget (1992, 1993, 1994, 1995, 1996, 1997, 1998).

5 This chapter focuses on California and New York for several reasons. Each state has dealt with the demands of a large and growing population of linguistic minority students. Whereas California has received national attention for its efforts to restrict the use of native language instruction, New York has touted its tolerance for and commitment to newly arrived immigrants. As a professor at the University of California at

ership was beginning to wane, California adopted the Bilingual Education Improvement and Reform Act. This new legislation emphasized the singular importance of learning English and allowed an expanded role for intensive English instruction in serving NEP and LEP students. In the mid-1980s, the State Board of Education, which is composed of political appointees chosen by the governor and approved by the state senate, acted to ensure that children in bilingual education programs were promptly reclassified and placed in English-speaking classrooms at the earliest opportunity (Cal. Admin. Reg. ch. 5, § 4306, 1985).

Despite these changes, bilingual education programs remained highly controversial. In November 1986, the California voters passed an initiative that amended the state's constitution to make English the official language of the state (Cal. Const. art. III, § 6, 1986). This constitutional amendment did not render native language instruction improper so long as it was designed to foster the acquisition of English. Still, the intensity of opposition to anything that sounded bilingual hit home when it came time to renew the Bilingual Education Improvement and Reform Act (1980). An expert panel recommended that new bilingual education legislation be enacted when the Act sunset in 1987, and California lawmakers did so. However, Governor George Deukmejian rejected the bill, and the state legislature was unable to muster sufficient votes to override his veto ("Bilingual Education Under Attack," 1997; Sunset Review Advisory Committee II, 1985). California, the state with the largest population of linguistic minority students in the country, had no bilingual education law.

To fill the gap, the State Department of Education continued to monitor and enforce programmatic requirements as part of its oversight role in dispensing state funds to local educational authorities.[6] In this guise, the department's personnel, most of whom were career professionals in the field of educational administration, successfully preserved a substantial number of the 1980 act's requirements. Even so, districts probably had more leeway than previously to use intensive English instruction. The department's role sparked new controversy. In 1993, the Little Hoover Commission, a panel of experts appointed by the governor, issued a scathing report that gave bilingual education in the state a failing grade. This failure was attributed to the overly prescriptive role of the State Department of Education. Characterizing bilingual education pro-

Berkeley, I have become deeply familiar with the politics of bilingual education in my home state. During a visit to the New York University School of Law, I had an opportunity to see firsthand whether the rhetorical differences in California and New York translated into meaningful distinctions in law and policy. This chapter provides an initial look at my findings.

6 For the original guidelines, see California Department of Education (1987); for the current guidelines, see California Department of Education (1996).

grams as "divisive, wasteful and unproductive," the commission recommended that local officials be given greater flexibility to experiment with alternative instructional approaches, most particularly intensive English instruction (Chavez, 1993).

With the commission's report in hand, the State Board of Education announced in 1995 that it would grant waivers to local districts that sought to use ESL or structured immersion rather than programs that rely more heavily on native language instruction.[7] A school district in Orange County, an area south of Los Angeles, took the board up on its invitation and successfully obtained a waiver from the Department of Education's guidelines. Subsequently, bilingual education advocates challenged the validity of the waiver, insisting that a statewide consent decree provided that only the department itself could grant waivers from its programmatic regulations (Anderson, 1997; Anderson & Wright, 1997; "Latino Activists Sue," 1997). Nevertheless, other districts in Orange County sought and received similar waivers. A federal district court refused to block the structured immersion programs because it found that the waivers did not violate federal nondiscrimination requirements regarding the instruction of NEP and LEP students (*Quiroz v. Board of Education,* 1997). Afterward, a state superior court judge held that state officials could not enforce standards under a bilingual education act that had sunset over 10 years before. The waivers were invalid because local districts should be free to choose programs without state interference (Chey & Love, 1998; Love, 1998). Shortly after the court handed down its ruling, the State Board of Education adopted a policy that gave local districts flexibility in adopting instructional methods (Anderson, 1998). The California legislature passed similar legislation, but Governor Pete Wilson vetoed it because he preferred to support an initiative that would mandate English immersion programs ("A Bilingual Bill at Last," 1998; Gunnison, 1998; Ingram, 1998; Matthews, 1998).

The battles over waivers and local flexibility became moot when Californians voted overwhelmingly for the "English Language in Public Schools" initiative in June 1998.[8] The initiative requires that all NEP and LEP children be given one year of intensive English instruction before being placed in English-speaking classrooms. The law permits waivers for children who already know English, who are 10 years or

---

7 Pyle (1995) notes that a state board committee member was concerned that waivers were needed to prevent "one-size-fits-all" education, whereas a bilingual teacher feared that the board would "go radical on us" by eliminating bilingual education altogether (p. A1).

8 Bruno (1998) reports that 61% of California voters supported the initiative to use English immersion rather than bilingual education in public schools; Purdum (1998) describes how the lopsided vote against bilingual education in California could "pav[e] the way for similar assaults on such programs around the nation" (p. A1).

older and require an alternate course of study, or who have tried immersion for 30 days and need a different approach. Parents must consent to any waiver. When a school has twenty or more students on waiver, it has to offer a program of bilingual education or some other alternative to English-language immersion (Proposition 227, 1998, §§ 310–311). Recently, a federal district court refused to halt implementation of the initiative, despite civil rights advocates' claim that it straightjacketed students in one-size-fits-all education. The court concluded that the initiative was based on a plausible educational theory and that there was no basis for finding that it would deny NEP and LEP students an equal educational opportunity under federal law (*Valeria G. v. Wilson*, 1998). Despite the judicial setback, some school districts insist that they will continue to offer programs that rely on native language instruction. These local educators say that the initiative simply imposes the additional burden of cumbersome paperwork to obtain waivers (Asimov, 1998).

The controversy surrounding the bilingual education initiative occurs against the backdrop of a growing crisis in the California public schools. The public school population has grown dramatically in part as a result of the heavy influx of immigrants into the state. Many of these children have special language needs, but there is a lack of qualified teachers and other resources to meet their needs. In part, this shortfall reflects a larger decline in the commitment to public education in the state, one that predates the recent controversies over language and immigration. During the early 1970s, the California Supreme Court was in the vanguard of school finance reform. In *Serrano v. Priest* (1971), the high court held that if schools funded through local property taxes faced substantial disparities in per capita revenues for student instruction, the financing system was unconstitutional. Equal protection under California's constitution required that local property taxes be pooled at the state level and allocated equally among schools in different districts, regardless of how wealthy they were.

The decision did not have the long-term impact that its supporters envisioned. Rather than lead to high-quality, equal education for all of California's schoolchildren, the case arguably precipitated tax reform. This reform led to caps on the local property tax, which have greatly eroded overall fiscal support for the public schools. The state is now among the least generous in funding its instructional programs (Asimov, 1997; "California: A State Slouching Toward Mediocrity," 1997; Fischel, 1989; Wolk, 1997). Efforts to supplement property taxes with other revenue sources, like the state lottery, have not staved off the decline. Urban schools with rapid population growth resulting from immigration have been especially hard hit. In a school finance case in Los Angeles, the proceedings did little more than demonstrate that funding could be equalized, but all students would then have a comparably inadequate education (Pyle, 1997; *Rodriguez v. Los Angeles Unified School District*, 1992). In light of these tight fiscal circumstances, intensive English instruction may seem attractive because it is a cheaper instructional method than programs that utilize native language instruction. The schools that have been most aggressive in pursuing waivers, for example, are in Orange County, an area that recently suffered a municipal funding crisis and must accommodate a substantial number of new immigrants (Grad, 1997). Immigrants have had little opportunity to express their views about education through California's majoritarian political process because noncitizens are ineligible to vote in state or local elections (Acuna, 1992).[9]

New York

On its face, the status of bilingual education in New York seems superior to its status in California. In 1972, Aspira, a group of middle-class Puerto Rican professionals concerned about access to education, filed suit against the New York City Board of Education, alleging that it was not meeting the needs of Puerto Rican students, particularly those who did not speak English (*Aspira v. Board of Education of New York*, 1973). Shortly after the *Lau* decision and just as the federal government was fashioning guidelines for bilingual education, the board entered into a consent agreement with Aspira. The decree provided standards for identifying students in need of bilingual services and regulated the programmatic offerings that the Board could utilize (*Aspira v. Board of Education of New York*, 1975). The Puerto Rican Legal Defense and Education Fund, which represented Aspira in the lawsuit, took primary responsibility for working with the board to implement the decree. After an initial period of bickering and conflict, the board adopted inclusive identification procedures and committed itself to native language instruction (Picard, 1992).

The board's increasingly cooperative stance derived in part from the deteriorating fiscal condition of New York City's schools. New York State's constitution does not require that schools be funded equally, and state funding formulas produce less generous allotments for students in the city than for those in the rest of the state (*Board of Education v. Nyquist*, 1995). In the early 1980s, the city's fiscal crisis left the public schools scrambling for funds. Indeed, the situation became so dire that in a 1995 lawsuit, a New York State court found that the underfunding of New York schools may have created such deficient conditions that children were being unconstitutionally denied even minimum access to

---

9 For a general discussion of the propriety of allowing noncitizens to vote in local elections, see Raskin (1993).

education (*Campaign for Fiscal Equity v. New York,* 1995). In the midst of this pressing need, one potential source of money for New York City schools was federal and state aid for bilingual education (Picard, 1992, p. 183).

As federal funding has declined, state aid has grown in importance. New York State's bilingual education act, which was passed the same year that *Lau* was decided, appropriates money on a per capita basis for children in bilingual programs. As a result, inclusive procedures for identifying eligible students maximize revenues for city schools (Picard, 1992, pp. 208–211). Moreover, the state's bilingual education act continues to prefer native language instruction (N.Y. Educ. Law §3204). In contrast to California, there has been little impetus to amend the statute to allow more use of intensive English instruction. Most affected children reside in New York City and are subject to the consent decree in *Aspira*. In 1993, for example, approximately 90% of the children eligible for state aid under the bilingual education act were in New York City schools (Office of Bilingual Education, 1995). Under *Aspira*, the city's Board of Education must, where possible, use native language instruction. So long as the decree is in effect, state funding for NEP and LEP children will be invested primarily in programs that have a native language component, no matter what the legislature does.

Opponents of the programs have cited the deleterious effects of the city's cash-starved approach to linguistic minority education. They contend that the push to maximize supplemental revenues has led to the warehousing of students in bilingual programs, regardless of whether the instruction is effective and whether the children are ready to enter an English-speaking classroom. In 1994, the New York City Board of Education issued a report indicating that whatever their original level of English proficiency, children in intensive English programs exited more quickly than those in transitional bilingual education programs that used a child's native language as a bridge to learning English. The more quickly the children exited the program, the better they performed in English-speaking classrooms. Most of the children in native language instructional programs were Spanish speakers, whereas those in intensive English instruction tended to be Korean, Russian, or Chinese students, whose small numbers did not support a full-scale bilingual program. Despite their small numbers, Haitian students also tended to be placed in transitional bilingual education programs. Despite these arguably negative findings, the board reiterated its support for programs that rely on native language instruction in a supplementary report the following year (New York City Board of Education, 1995).

In 1995, the New York Board of Regents, the state governing board, also issued a report on services for NEP and LEP children throughout the state. The Regents found that students in New York City remained in bilingual programs substantially longer than children elsewhere in the state. In 1992–1993, within 3 years after receiving special instruction, 95% of students outside the city had successfully met the criteria for entering English-speaking classrooms, but only 42% of students in the city had done so. Students in New York City programs systematically lagged behind those outside the city in making gains on English and mathematics tests. Moreover, statewide, only 43.2% of NEP and LEP students finished high school compared with 52.9% of non-LEP students. Of LEP and NEP students who graduated from high school, only 3.9% passed the examination leading to the prestigious Regents' diploma, which qualifies a student to compete for state financial aid for higher education. Of the remaining NEP and LEP students who completed high school, 91% received a local diploma, and 5.1% got a high school equivalency diploma (Office of Bilingual Education, 1995, pp. 6–27). (The equivalency degree is the least marketable way of completing high school, adding at best marginal value to the job opportunities available to high school dropouts; see Bracey, 1995; Cameron & Heckman, 1993; Murnane, Willett, & Boudet 1995). Significantly, the Regents have decided to mandate successful completion of standardized testing for all students to obtain a high school diploma. As a result, high schools will no longer be able to award local diplomas to students who attend but fail to meet minimum competency requirements. Implementation of the new policy has been delayed, in part because of concerns about the lack of tests in languages other than English ("Board of Regents Is Urged," 1997; "40,000 Exempted From Tests," 1997; Nelson & Terrazzano, 1997).

Confronted with this dismaying evidence about bilingual programs, particularly in New York City, an activist Catholic nun mobilized the Bushwick Parents Organization (BPO), a high school parent organization in New York City, to protest inadequate instructional methods for NEP and LEP students. Composed of mainly Latino parents, BPO went to the local school board to demand improved educational opportunities. In particular, BPO expressed concern that the board's programs were warehousing NEP and LEP children without enabling them to acquire English and other academic skills. BPO reflected the changing face of the Latino population in New York City. When *Aspira* was filed, Puerto Ricans dominated the city's Latino population; by the mid-1990s, Puerto Ricans represented slightly less than half of the population due to an influx of Dominican, Mexican, and South American immigrants.[10] These new constituents did not particularly identify with the bilingual education establishment that the Puerto Rican community had fought so hard to put in place.

---

10 For an analysis of the growth of the Puerto Rican and Central American communities in New York, see Chapters 4 and 6.

In the decentralized system of educational governance in New York City, each district elects its own officials to oversee the day-to-day operations of the school system. Instituted in the 1970s, local control is designed to give racial and ethnic communities a voice in the governance of their own educational institutions.[11] To maximize representativeness, noncitizens can vote in community board elections ("Noncitizens and Right to Vote," 1992).[12] Even so, BPO's efforts to gain the local board's ear failed. Fearful of the group's confrontational tactics, the community board broke off all relations with BPO. In fact, local control revealed the schisms in the rapidly changing Latino population. More established Latinos, such as school board chairman Tito Velez, rebuffed the emerging constituency of immigrant parents in Bushwick (Buettner, 1995; Moses, 1995).

As a result, BPO turned to the state court system for relief. Although the parents had been interested in quality education, Robert Smith, the partner from Paul, Weiss, Rifkind, Wharton & Garrison who offered his services on a pro bono basis, converted the lawsuit into a referendum on bilingual education. In the litigation, he contended that the state commissioner of education had abused his discretion by routinely granting waivers to New York City school districts so that students could remain in the programs for longer than the presumptive 3 years set forth in the state's bilingual education act. According to the complaint, the commissioner made no effort to determine whether the programs were effective in promoting the acquisition of English and other skills before awarding the waivers. Relying on the recent reports of the New York City Board of Education and New York Board of Regents, Smith argued on behalf of BPO that the programs were merely warehousing students and that the waivers therefore were inappropriate under state law (*Bushwick Parents Organization v. Mills*, 1995; "Lawsuit Is Filed," 1995; "Parents Bring Class to Lousy Schools," 1996).

Along with the State Attorney General's Office, the Puerto Rican Legal Defense and Education Fund assumed a leading role in defending the city's system of bilingual education services under the consent decree in *Aspira*. In the defendants' view, the statute permitted the commissioner to extend a child's stay in the programs for up to 5 years if a student did not meet the criteria for entering an English-speaking classroom. Thus, the legislature had expressly allowed for the possibility that, even in a well-run program, not all children would be able to exit in 3 years, and the commissioner's grant of the waivers was entirely jus-

---

11 For background and differing perspectives on the rise of community control, see Berube and Gittell (1969), Fantini, Gittell, and Magat (1970), Levin (1970), and Moynihan (1969).

12 All immigrants, whether legal or illegal, have been entitled to vote in New York City community school board elections since decentralization occurred in the late 1960s.

tified. Ultimately, the defendants' position carried the day (*Bushwick Parents Organization v. Mills,* 1996). Again, though, the conflict seemed to pit the old-guard Latinos (as exemplified by the Puerto Rican Legal Defense and Education Fund and Aspira) against the Latino newcomers (as exemplified by the Dominican parents in BPO). Despite BPO's lack of success before the courts, a group of Haitian parents subsequently filed another lawsuit challenging the adequacy of bilingual education programs in their New York City school district ("Haitians File Suit," 1997).

Why the new federalism has failed

The California and New York experiences represent different faces of the failed experiment with the new federalism. In California, efforts to use statewide regulations and constitutional requirements generated high-profile conflict. State agencies battled over the appropriate approach to use, and the legislature was so paralyzed by indecision and controversy that it was not able to pass a new bilingual education act (Bailey, 1997). With this highly visible breakdown of state decision-making processes, the California electorate took matters into its own hands by using the state's initiative process to mandate English immersion programs. The political controversy surrounding bilingual education in California has highlighted racial and ethnic schisms as a predominantly White electorate imposes policies on newly arrived, predominantly Latino immigrants, many of whom cannot vote.

Even at the local level, bilingual education controversies in California have taken on strong racial and ethnic overtones. With rapid immigration, many urban neighborhoods have undergone a turnover in their racial and ethnic composition. Yet immigrants, whether lawfully present or not, cannot vote in school board elections until they become citizens, even if their children attend public schools. Consequently, school boards seldom reflect the immigrant makeup of their student bodies. In Orange County, for example, White school board members sought waivers from bilingual education requirements over the protests of many Latino immigrant parents (Love, 1997). In Oakland, bilingual education programs have sparked intense disputes, in part because Black board members resent the fact that special treatment is given to immigrants' linguistic needs whereas Black English (or Ebonics) is treated as an object of ridicule (Colvin, 1997; Olszewski, 1997a, 1997b; "Schools Struggle," 1997).

In New York, there has been little statewide conflict over bilingual education because the bilingual education act is mainly a vehicle for

433

appropriating money to help students in New York City. These students are already subject to a consent decree that limits flexibility in setting criteria for student identification, program choice, and reclassification and exit. As a result, state officials have little reason to fight over bilingual education requirements, and racial and ethnic polarization is not as salient as in California. In New York City itself, the appearance of racial and ethnic conflict is further deflected by the role of the Puerto Rican Legal Defense and Education Fund in defending current programs from challenges by immigrant parents who are likely to be Dominican, Mexican, or South American. Whites may play a role in handling the immigrant parents' cases and may even set the agenda in these cases, but nominally at least, the battle seems to be one among Latinos over the best system of education for their children.

Community school boards provide an additional buffer against the emergence of racial and ethnic polarization. Community boards often oversee racially homogeneous communities because of pervasive residential segregation in the city. In contrast to California, in New York noncitizens can vote in school board elections. Even if Latino immigrants do not have the resources to run for a place on the community school board, they can at least support Latino candidates with whom they feel some identification. As a result, when school boards rebuff challenges to bilingual education, as in *Bushwick*, the conflict is apt to seem like a power struggle among Latinos rather than a battle between Whites and emerging non-White populations.

Although California's culture of governance is conflict maximizing whereas New York's is conflict minimizing, the two states face common problems that outweigh these differences. In both places, large numbers of immigrants have overwhelmed available municipal services, including the schools.[13] There has been little commitment to investing substantial resources in the education of immigrant children in either state. For the NEP or LEP child, the symbolism of the state and local political processes is undoubtedly less important than the day-to-day experience in the classroom. Whether in California or New York, a linguistic minority student is likely to be in an overcrowded, underfunded school with a teacher who may not be qualified to offer special instruction and who also may lack the necessary resources and materials to implement a high-quality program.[14]

13 To learn more about the growth in the school-age immigrant population in California and New York, see Chapter 1.
14 "Bilingual Education: A Squandered Opportunity" (1997) notes that only about 30% of NEP and LEP students receive instruction from qualified bilingual teachers; according to Wood (1997), fewer than one in five teachers of NEP and LEP students is certified to provide bilingual instruction; "Wanted Now in New York" (1997) and

This common failure of the new federalism in turn is a result not only of the federal government's retreat from leadership in the field of bilingual education but also its unwillingness to alleviate significantly the fiscal impact of immigration in states that have received large numbers of newcomers. California and New York are among the top five immigrant-receiving states. Neither state can control the influx of immigrants because the federal government determines immigration policy. Yet states must provide many of the services necessary to integrate new arrivals effectively into the population. Efforts by states receiving high numbers of immigrants to force the federal government to provide them with financial assistance have failed (*California v. United States,* 1996; *Chiles v. United States,* 1995; *Panavan v. United States,* 1996; *Texas v. United States,* 1997). Indeed, the federal government's main response has been to crack down on illegal immigration and to cut government benefits to immigrants, whether they are here lawfully or not (Illegal Immigration and Immigrant Responsibility Act of 1996; Personal Responsibility and Work Opportunity Reconciliation Act of 1996). These steps are not particularly well calculated to absorb long-term immigrants into the economic, social, and civic life of the states that they inhabit (U.S. Commission on Immigration Reform, 1997). The main appeal of these reforms appears to be that they reduce the states' fiscal burdens without requiring significant additional appropriations of federal monies.

Conclusion

In retrospect, it seems plain that the impact of the federal government's retreat from leadership in bilingual education can be understood only in relation to immigration policy. Had the population of NEP and LEP students been relatively stable, states might have been able to invest the resources to design at least some model programs, particularly if the federal government had continued to fund research and experimentation. However, the decline in federal funding and guidance coupled with the explosive growth in linguistic minority student populations made the grant of discretion to states under the new federalism an illusory one. At best, school officials were able to engage in triage to meet the needs of an increasing number of NEP and LEP children with a shrinking amount of resources. Unfortunately, the failure of bilingual programs in California and New York has no easy solutions at the state level. Whatever programmatic choice is made, it is unlikely to succeed in overcrowded, underfunded classrooms with teachers on emer-

"New Report" (1996) describe the burgeoning number of students and the teacher shortage.

435

gency credentials who must use outdated textbooks and inadequate materials.

Ultimately, federal intervention is necessary to assist states in coping with the impact of high levels of immigration, including the increased demands on the public educational system. The federal government should set minimum standards for nondiscrimination without being overly prescriptive about programmatic choices. Congress should support state and local discretion by funding research on language acquisition and disseminating the results. Part of this research effort should be devoted to identifying models of success in meeting NEP and LEP students' needs. Federal, state, and local agencies should develop strategies that provide fiscal stability in funding bilingual programs. Federal and state officials must work cooperatively with institutions of higher education to train second language educators and afford them ample opportunities to keep abreast of developments in the field. In addition, state and local educational agencies should create opportunities for second language educators to share their classroom experiences, including their most effective teaching strategies. Finally, state and local educators must work to inform all members of their communities about the programs offered to NEP and LEP children. Although the involvement of linguistic minority parents is important, reaching out to English-speaking parents and community members is also critical when bilingual education is so often vilified in ideological debates.

Rather than undertake cooperative initiatives with state and local educators, federal officials have increasingly disinvested in the public sector, as reflected in decisions to cut government benefits and services to the most vulnerable members of society. This disinvestment in turn derives from a growing willingness to tolerate economic, social, and political stratification. Public policy has increasingly drawn bright lines between citizens and noncitizens, between English speakers and non–English speakers, between Whites and non-Whites, between rich and poor. The bilingual education dilemma illustrates the perils of the politically voiceless under the new federalism. Although linguistic minority, immigrant communities may find it difficult to call attention to their needs, those who struggle daily to serve them can dramatize their plight. Few are closer to the challenges facing America's newcomers than second language educators. Educators must remind the public of the complexities of teaching NEP and LEP students, despite the political temptation to rely on simplistic, ideological slogans. The stakes in the debate are too important for them to remain silent. A policy of disinvestment threatens the egalitarian ethic at the very core of democracy, as the United States creates a socially and politically marginal population of immigrants who arrive in growing numbers to realize the uncertain promise of the American dream.

Suggestions for further reading

Bauer, C. (n.d.) *Resources: Bilingual education sites.* ⟨http://www.mind. net/pes/cuarto/bauer/bisites.html⟩.
This site provides links to Web sites for the National Clearinghouse for Bilingual Education, the Office of Bilingual Education and Minority Language Affairs, the National Association for Bilingual Education, the California Association for Bilingual Education, the New York State Association for Bilingual Education, and the New York State Bilingual/ESL Network, among others. These links offer an excellent way to stay abreast of developments in bilingual education law and policy.
Crawford, J. (1992). *Bilingualism and the politics of English only.* Reading, MA: Addison-Wesley.
This book takes an in-depth look at the effort to make English the official language at both the state and national level.
Crawford, J. (1995). *Bilingual education: History, politics, theory, and practice* (3rd ed.). Los Angeles: Bilingual Education Services.
This book provides a concise overview of the historical evolution of language policy in the United States, the politics surrounding the official English movement, the controversy over the effectiveness of different instructional approaches for linguistic minority students, and the challenges associated with implementing appropriate programs.
Hakuta, K. (1986). *Mirror of language: The debate on bilingualism.* New York: Basic Books.
This book reviews the evidence on the effectiveness of programs that rely on native language instruction, such as transitional bilingual education and bilingual-bicultural education, as well as those that use intensive English instruction, such as ESL and structured immersion. The book also addresses how efforts to incorporate objective research in the policymaking process have been hampered by ideological controversy.
Moran, R. (1987). Bilingual education as a status conflict. *California Law Review, 75,* 321–362.
This article argues that although bilingual education has been treated as just another instance of special-interest politics, it in fact reflects a struggle over intangible, symbolic attributes, not just tangible resources. To support this view, the article draws not only on the push to make English the official language of California but also the posturing in bilingual lawsuits, such as a case in Oakland, California.
Moran, R. (1988). The politics of discretion: Federal intervention in bilingual education. *California Law Review, 76,* 1249–1352.

This article chronicles the rise and fall of strong federal intervention in bilingual education beginning in the late 1960s and ending in the late 1980s. The article documents the roles of various players in the policy-making process, and it speculates on how the new federalism might play a constructive role in delivering services to linguistic minority students.

National Clearinghouse for Bilingual Education. *NCBE Newsline* [Online serial]. ⟨http://www.ncbe.gwu.edu/majordomo/newsline/⟩.

This on-line newsletter offers up-to-date information about educational research and policy in the field of bilingual education. Subscription is free.

Schneider, S. G. (1976). *Revolution, reaction or reform: The 1974 Bilingual Education Act*. New York: Las Americas.

This book offers a comprehensive, behind-the-scenes look at how Congress made bilingual education policy in 1974. The Bilingual Education Act of 1974 endorsed native language instruction to an unprecedented degree. This book tells how the ideological shift happened, not always in ways that one might have expected.

References

Acuna, R. (1992, December 27). Where are all the liberals when the city really needs them? *Los Angeles Times*, p. M6.

Anderson, N. (1997, September 11). U.S. judge lets Orange Unified go English-only. *Los Angeles Times*, p. A1.

Anderson, N. (1998, March 13). State overhauls rules on bilingual education: Districts no longer need waiver to abolish programs, but board does not rule out such instruction. *Los Angeles Times*, p. A18.

Anderson, N., & Wright, L. (1997, August 19). Judge halts Orange schools' English-immersion program. *Los Angeles Times*, p. A3.

Asimov, N. (1997, January 16). California schools rate D-minus in report: Exhaustive study blames Prop. 13 for the damage. *San Francisco Chronicle*, p. A2.

Asimov, N. (1998, July 31). Educators working around Prop. 227: Districts plan bilingual programs that don't violate law. *San Francisco Chronicle*, p. A1.

Aspira v. Board of Education of New York, 58 F.R.D. 62 (S.D.N.Y. 1973).

Aspira v. Board of Education of New York, 65 F.R.D. 541, 543 (S.D.N.Y. 1975) (describing August 29, 1974, consent decree in evaluating claim for attorney's fees).

Bailey, E. (1997, September 5). Panel blocks bilingual education compromise. *Los Angeles Times*, p. A3.

Berube, M., & Gittell, M. (Eds.). (1969). *Confrontation at Ocean Hill–Brownsville*. New York: Praeger.

A bilingual bill at last. (1998, April 22). *Los Angeles Times*, p. B6.

Bilingual education: A squandered opportunity. For the sake of youngsters, a 3-

year limit should be sought. (1997, October 26). *Los Angeles Times*, p. M4.

Bilingual Education Act, Pub. L. No. 90-247, 81 Stat. 783, 816-19 (1988) (codified as amended at 20 U.S.C. §§7401–7491).

Bilingual Education Improvement and Reform Act, Cal. Educ. Code §§ 52161–52179 (1980).

Bilingual education under attack: California ballot imitative backers hope effort will resonate elsewhere. (1997, July 21). *The Washington Post*, p. A15.

Board of Education v. Nyquist, 57 N.Y.2d 27, 439 N.E.2d 359, 453 N.Y.S.2d 643 (1995).

Board of Regents is urged to test in five languages. (1997, April 26). *The New York Times*, p. 1.

Bracey, G. W. (1995). To GED or not to GED. *Phi Delta Kappan, 77,* 257.

Brown v. Board of Education, 347 U.S. 483 (1954).

Bruno, F. (1998, June 14). The California entrepreneur who beat bilingual teaching. *The New York Times*, p. 1.

Buettner, R. (1995, May 19). Bushwick schools uproar: Political battle for control. *Newsday,* p. B19.

Bushwick Parents Organization v. Mills, No. 5181-95 (N.Y. Sup. Ct., Third Dept., 1995).

Bushwick Parents Organization v. Mills, 225 App. Div. 2d 104, 649 N.Y.S.2d 516 (Sup. Ct. 1996), aff'd, 89 N.Y.2d 816, 681 N.E.2d 1304, 659 N.Y.S.2d 857 (1997).

California: A state slouching toward mediocrity. (1997, September 17). *Sacramento Bee*, p. B9.

California Department of Education. (1987, August 26). Program advisory to county and district superintendents re education programs for which sunset provisions took effect on June 30, 1987, pursuant to Education Code Sections 62000 and 62000.2. Sacramento, CA: Author.

California Department of Education. (1996, September 19). Program advisory for programs for English learners. Sacramento, CA: Author.

California v. United States, 104 F.3d 1086 (9th Cir. 1996).

Cameron, S. V., & Heckman, J. J. (1993). The nonequivalence of high school equivalents. *Journal of Labor Economics, 11,* 1–47.

Campaign for Fiscal Equity v. New York, 86 N.Y.2d 307, 655 N.E.2d 661, 631 N.Y.S.2d 565 (1995).

Castaneda v. Pickard, 648 F.2d (5th Cir. Unit A June 1981).

Chacon-Moscone Bilingual-Bicultural Education Act, Cal. Educ. Code §§ 52100–52179 (1976).

Chavez, S. (1993, July 10). Panel assails state's bilingual education. *Los Angeles Times*, p. A19.

Chey, E., & Love, D. (1998, March 7). Ruling – just another day at Orange Unified: It becomes the fourth county school district to obtain the bilingual instruction waiver. *Orange County Register,* p. A8.

Chiles v. United States, 69 F.3d 1094 (11th Cir. 1995) (Florida).

Civil Rights Act, 42 U.S.C. § 2000d (1964).

Colvin, R. L. (1997, May 6). No "Ebonics" in new Oakland school plan. *Los Angeles Times*, p. A1. Equal Educational Opportunities Act, 20 U.S.C. §1703(f) (1974).

Rachel F. Moran

Fantini, M., Gittell, M., & Magat, R. (1970). *Community control and the urban school.* New York: Praeger.

Fischel, W. (1989). Did Serrano cause Proposition 13? *National Tax Journal, 42,* 465–473.

40,000 exempted from tests. (1997, April 18). *The New York Times,* p. B3.

Grad, S. (1997, September 7). Retiring debt is taxing topic for supervisors; Budget: More than a quarter of county spending goes toward paying creditors, but should priorities be elsewhere? *Los Angeles Times,* p. B1.

Gunnison, R. B. (1998, May 19). Wilson vetoes bill, pushes 227: Initiative's backer fears backlash, doesn't want his help. *San Francisco Chronicle,* p. A19.

Haft, J. (1983). Assuring equal opportunity for language-minority students: Bilingual education and the Equal Educational Opportunity Act of 1974. *Columbia Journal of Law and Social Problems, 18,* 209–293.

Haitians file suit against New York City and State schools. (1997, January 13). *NCBE Newsline,* ⟨http://www.ncbe.gwu.edu/majordomo/newsline/1997/ 01/13.htm#HAITIANS⟩.

Illegal Immigration Reform and Immigrant Responsibility Act of 1996, Pub. L. No. 104–208, 110 Stat. 3009, 104th Cong., 2d Sess. (1996).

Ingram, C. (1998, May 5). Legislators OK alternative to Prop. 227. *Los Angeles Times,* p. A1.

Kindler, A. L. (1996). *Title VII funding for states and territories from FY69 to FY95* (NCBE Policy Analysis Information Report). Washington, DC: National Clearinghouse for Bilingual Education.

Latino activists sue California educators for bilingual education. (1997, August 11). *The Washington Times,* p. A6.

Lau v. Nichols, 141 U.S. 563 (1974).

Lawsuit is filed accusing state of overuse of bilingual classes. (1995, September 9). *The New York Times,* p. B6.

Levin, H. (Ed.). (1970). *Community control of schools.* Washington, DC: Brookings Institution.

Love, D. (1997, August 6). English-only schooling to be on Orange ballot. *Orange County Register,* p. B1.

Love, D. (1998, March 7). Bilingual education faces test: Orange district officials say a judge's ruling allows California schools to scrap such programs without state approval. *Orange County Register,* p. A1.

Matthews, J. (1998, May 19). Unz fears Wilson's support: Governor endorses bilingual initiative. *The Oakland Tribune,* p. NEWS-1.

Moran, R. F. (1988). The politics of discretion: Federal intervention in bilingual education. *California Law Review, 76,* 1249–1352.

Moses, P. (1995, January 22). This parents group shut out. *Newsday,* p. A56.

Moynihan, D. P. (1969). *Maximum feasible misunderstanding.* New York: Free Press.

Murnane, R. J., Willett, J. B., & Boudett, K. P. (1995). Do high school dropouts benefit from obtaining a GED? *Educational Evaluation and Policy Analysis, 17,* 133–147.

National Center for Education Statistics. (1996). *Digest of education statistics 1996* (NCES Publication No. 96–133). Washington, DC: U.S. Government Printing Office.

Nelson, S. S., & Terrazzano, L. (1997, April 27). Regents in 5 languages? *Newsday,* p. A4.

New report: One in three city school students is an immigrant. (1996, December 17). *Newsday,* p. A7.

New York City Board of Education. (1994). Educational progress of students in bilingual and ESL programs: A longitudinal study, 1990–94. New York: Author.

New York City Board of Education. (1995). *Report of the chancellor's bilingual/ESL practitioners' workgroup and policy/research panels. New beginnings: Ensuring quality bilingual/ESL instruction in New York City public schools.* New York: Author.

Noncitizens and right to vote: Advocates for immigrants explore opening up balloting. (1992, July 31). *The New York Times,* p. B1.

Northwest Arctic School v. Califano, No. A-77-216 (D. Alaska Sept. 29, 1978).

Office for Civil Rights, Identification of Discrimination and Denial of Services on the Basis of National Origin, 35 Fed. Reg. 11,595 (1970).

Office for Civil Rights, Task-Force Findings Specifying Remedies Available for Eliminating Past Educational Practices Ruled Unlawful Under *Lau v. Nichols* (1975).

Office of Bilingual Education. (1995). Report on the implementation of the Regents policy paper and proposed action plan for bilingual education in New York State. Albany: New York State Education Department.

Office of Management and Budget. (1992). *Budget of the United States government, fiscal year 1993.* Washington, DC: U.S. Government Printing Office.

Office of Management and Budget. (1993). *Budget of the United States government, fiscal year 1994.* Washington, DC: U.S. Government Printing Office.

Office of Management and Budget. (1994). *Budget of the United States government, fiscal year 1995.* Washington, DC: U.S. Government Printing Office.

Office of Management and Budget. (1995). *Budget of the United States government, fiscal year 1996.* Washington, DC: U.S. Government Printing Office.

Office of Management and Budget. (1996). *Budget of the United States government, fiscal year 1997.* Washington, DC: U.S. Government Printing Office.

Office of Management and Budget. (1997). *Budget of the United States government, fiscal year 1998.* Washington, DC: U.S. Government Printing Office.

Office of Management and Budget. (1998). *Budget of the United States government, fiscal year 1999.* Washington, DC: U.S. Government Printing Office.

Olszewski, L. (1997a, June 26). Oakland parent calls for boycott of schools: Ebonics champion says blacks aren't being taught. *San Francisco Chronicle,* p. A17.

Olszewski, L. (1997b, September 18). Oakland schools may lose millions: Grants threatened over lack of bilingual teachers. *San Francisco Chronicle,* p. A15.

Panavan v. United States, 82 F.3d 23 (2d Cir. 1996) (New York).

Parents bring class to lousy schools. (1996, March 31). *New York Daily News,* p. 10.

Personal Responsibility and Work Opportunity Reconciliation Act of 1996, Pub. L. No. 104-193, 110 Stat. 2105, 104th Cong., 2d Sess. (1996).

Picard, W. G. (1992). Bilingual education and the bureaucratic creation of a linguistic minority in New York City. *Dissertation Abstracts International,* 54(04), 1553. (University Microfilms No. 9325816)

Plessy v. Ferguson, 163 U.S. 537 (1896).

Purdum, T. S. (1998, June 3). California passes measure to limit bilingual schools. *The New York Times,* p. A1.

Pyle, A. (1995, July 14). State panel OKs flexible bilingual education policy. *Los Angeles Times,* p. A1.

Pyle, A. (1997, July 28). Book shortage plagues L.A. Unified. *Los Angeles Times,* p. A1.

Quiroz v. State Board of Education, 1997 WL 661163 (E.D. Cal. Sept. 7, 1997).

Ramirez, D. (1995). Multicultural empowerment: It's not just black and white anymore. *Stanford Law Review, 47,* 957–992.

Raskin, J. B. (1993). Legal aliens, local citizens: Historical, constitutional, and theoretical meanings of alien suffrage. *Pennsylvania Law Review, 141,* 1391–1470.

Rodriguez v. Los Angeles Unified School District, No. C 611358 (1992) (consent decree entered August 25, 1992).

Schools struggle with shifting ethnic balance: Competing needs of Latino, black students put pressure on scarce funds. (1997, May 14). *San Francisco Chronicle,* p. A1.

Serrano v. Priest, 5 Cal.3d 584, 96 Cal. Rptr. 601, 487 P.2d 1241 (1971).

Sunset Review Advisory Committee II. (1985, September). *A report to the legislature on categorical programs scheduled to sunset on June 30, 1987.* Sacramento: California State Department of Education.

Texas v. United States, 106 F.3d 661 (5th Cir. 1997).

U.S. Commission on Immigration Reform. (1997). *Becoming an American: Immigration and immigration policy.* Washington, DC: U.S. Government Printing Office.

Valeria G. v. Wilson, 1998 U.S. Dist. LEXIS 10675 (No. C-98-2252-CAL)(July 15, 1998).

Wanted now in New York: 3,000 (or 9,000) teachers. (1997, August 10). *The New York Times,* p. 1.

Wolk, R. A., et al. (Eds.). (1997, January). *Quality counts: A report card on the condition of public education in the 50 states.* Washington, DC: Education Week.

Wood, D. B. (1997, April 29). Parents force schools to speak English-only. *Christian Science Monitor,* p. 1.

16 Investment, acculturation, and language loss

Bonny Norton

Introduction

In a recent longitudinal study of immigrant language learners in New-town, Canada[1] (Norton Peirce, 1993, 1995), I collected valuable data on what is often called *subtractive* and *additive* bilingualism, particular-ly with respect to language learning among children (Lambert, 1975; Swain & Lapkin, 1991). Subtractive bilingualism takes place when a second language is learned at the cost of losing the mother tongue, whereas additive bilingualism is associated with the development of sec-ond language proficiency with little loss to the mother tongue. In this chapter, I provide a detailed analysis of language practices in two of the families I studied – one in which subtractive bilingualism took place, and the other in which additive bilingualism flourished. This analysis will lead to a discussion of the relationship among investment, accultur-ation, and the development of bilingualism, focusing in particular on the insidious effects of racism on language loss. I make the argument that theories of acculturation in the field of second language acquisition (SLA) could have the presumably unintended and undesirable conse-quence of promoting subtractive bilingualism in children. I argue, specifically, that a major challenge for language teachers is to ensure that language learners have an investment in both the target language and the mother tongue.

I do not claim that this analysis is definitive. It is a window through which teachers and researchers can revisit some assumptions about SLA and the development of bilingualism. In particular, it provides some in-sight into the relationship among investment, acculturation, and lan-guage loss. In the following section, I introduce the notion of *investment* and describe how I use it in my work. I next describe the language pat-terns in the two immigrant families as seen, in particular, through the eyes of the language learners, Mai and Katarina, respectively, and ex-amine my data in light of theory on SLA, focusing on a central contra-

This chapter is a revised version of the article, "Rethinking Acculturation in Second Lan-guage Acquisition," *Prospect: A Journal of Australian TESOL,* Vol. 13, No, 2, pp. 4–19, 1998.
1 Names of places and people have been changed to protect the identities of partici-pants.

diction between acculturation models of SLA and models of bilingualism. I conclude with a discussion of the implications of my study for teachers and researchers.

Investment and language learning

In previous work (Norton Peirce, 1995), I have argued that theories of motivation in SLA do not capture the complex relationship among power, identity, and language learning that I have found in my research. I have argued that the concept of *investment* rather than *motivation* more accurately signals the socially and historically constructed relationship of learners to the target language, and their sometimes ambivalent desire to learn and practice it. The notion is best understood with reference to the economic metaphors that Bourdieu uses in his work – in particular the notion of *cultural capital*. Bourdieu and Passeron (1977) use the term to refer to the knowledge and modes of thought that characterize different classes and groups in relation to specific sets of social forms. They argue that some forms of cultural capital have a higher exchange value than others in a given social context. I take the position that if learners invest in a second language, they do so with the understanding that they will acquire a wider range of symbolic and material resources, which will in turn increase the value of their cultural capital. By *symbolic resources* I mean such resources as language, education, and friendship, whereas I use the term *material resources* to include capital goods, real estate, and money. Learners expect or hope to have a good *return* on the investment in that language – a return that will give them access to hitherto unattainable resources.

Thus the notion presupposes that when language learners speak, not only they are exchanging information with target language speakers, but they are constantly organizing and reorganizing a sense of who they are and how they relate to the social world. In essence, the notion attempts to capture the relationship between identity and language learning. It conceives of the language learner as having a complex identity and multiple desires, constantly changing across time and space. In this spirit, the central questions in my own work are not, Is the learner motivated to learn the target language? What kind of personality does the learner have? Instead, my questions are framed as follows: What is the learner's investment in the target language? How is the learner's relationship to the target language socially and historically constructed? It was by asking such questions that I was able to gain greater insight into the patterns of language use in Mai's and Katarina's families. Of particular importance, for the purposes of this chapter, was the question, What investments did Mai's and Katarina's families have in the mother tongue?

A tale of two families: Mai and Katarina

My case study of immigrant language learners took place over a 12-month period in 1991. The participants – all women – were Mai from Vietnam, Katarina and Eva from Poland, Martina from Czechoslovakia, and Felicia from Peru. A major source of data collection was a diary study in which the participants kept records of their interactions with Anglophone Canadians and reflected on their language-learning experiences in the home, workplace, and community. During the course of the study, we met on a regular basis to share the entries the participants had made in their diaries and to discuss their insights and concerns. I also drew a substantial amount of data from two detailed questionnaires I administered before and after the study as well as personal and group interviews and home visits.

Although the primary purpose of my original study was to come to an enhanced understanding of adult language learning, I gained insight into the language development of children in the immigrant families of my adult participants. What was particularly striking was the emergence of two very distinct and contrasting profiles in Mai's and Katarina's families. In Mai's extended family, I observed a breakdown of social relationships and a situation in which parents had difficulty conversing with their children. It was a family in which the children were monolingual speakers of English, having gradually lost proficiency in their mother tongue, Vietnamese. In Katarina's family, social relationships were strong, and the child in the family was learning English with no loss of her mother tongue, Polish. The central questions I address in this chapter are as follows: Why did subtractive bilingualism take place in Mai's family, while additive bilingualism flourished in Katarina's family? To what extent do theories of SLA and bilingual development account for these differences? How can teachers and researchers respond creatively to these findings?

Addressing these questions requires a comprehensive understanding of what could be called the *linguistic ecology* of Mai's and Katarina's families, respectively.

Mai's family

Mai was born in Vietnam in 1968 and arrived in Newtown, Canada, in October 1989, when she was 21 years old. She immigrated with her elderly parents "for my life in the future." Mai's father is Chinese, her mother is Vietnamese, and Mai is fluent in both Vietnamese and Cantonese. She had no knowledge of English before going to Canada. Mai has eight brothers and sisters, two of whom live in Canada. One of her brothers who lives in Newtown helped to sponsor Mai's immigration to

Canada in the "family" class. Before coming to Canada, Mai had not lived in any other country besides Vietnam.

Mai remained in her brother's home in Newtown for the duration of the data collection period – January–December 1991. The occupants of the house included her brother (Ming), her sister-in-law (Tan), three nephews, and her mother and father. Mai's nephews were Trong, born in Vietnam, age 14 at the time of data collection; Mark, Canadian born, age 12; and Kevin Canadian born, age 8. Mai's brother is at least 10 years older than she is. The family lived in an opulent neighborhood in Newtown. Mai's brother Ming worked in a government department and had been financially successful in Canada. Her sister-in-law Tan ran her own sewing business from home.

Significantly, three languages were spoken in Mai's home on a continual basis: Vietnamese, Cantonese, and English. Mai's parents spoke Vietnamese and Cantonese, but no English; her brother Ming and sister-in-law Tan spoke Vietnamese and Cantonese; Ming had a good command of English, but Tan spoke only limited English. Mai's nephews spoke English only. Mai's parents and Mai's nephews thus were unable to communicate with one another, and communication between Mai's nephews and their mother was limited. As Mai explained in her diary entry of March 5, 1991,[2]

1. It is funny when I think about my family. It's not too big but always had spoken by three languages.
   My parents can't speak English. I had to speak with them by Vietnamese or Chinese. I always spoke Chinese when my family's friends who are from Toronto came to visited us. They are all Chinese. With my brother and his wife, I spoke Vietnamese because they used to speak with each other by that language. And my nephews they didn't know any other language except English, so I spoke English with them although it is the language I spoke more than the other. For me it doesn't matter when people who speaks with me by Vietnamese, Chinese, or English. The only thing that I feel so sorry for my parents and my nephews because they can not talk with each other. It is very worst in the family. I think I won't let it happen to my children if I have in my future.

The most important set of relationships I examine consists of those between Mai's nephews and their parents. Extract 2 comes from a private interview with Mai in December 1990; Extracts 3 and 4, from my journal notes after diary study meetings on March 1, 1991, and February, 24, 1991, respectively.

2. (the author): B: You hear a lot of English here at home?

---

2 Punctuation, spelling, and grammatical errors that impede meaning in the written texts of participants have been corrected.

M (Mai):	Ya I do. For my nephews, they all speaking English, so I'm have to speak with them.
B:	Now do they speak any Chinese or Vietnamese?
M:	No they don't.
B:	Nothing? Nothing at all?
M:	No.
B:	Why not? Does your sister-in-law not speak to them in Chinese or Vietnamese?
M:	No. Because, um, for my sister-in-law she got this business, so she has to speak English, so she didn't want if she speaks Chinese with her kids, so she will lose her English. So she just try to speak English. My nephews speak better than her because they was born here and they go to school –
B:	But does she not speak Vietnamese to them?
M:	No. No. Not at all.

3. I asked Mai how her sister-in-law speaks to the boys if the boys do not speak Vietnamese and her sister-in-law's English is so poor. Mai said she hardly does speak to the boys. When she does, it takes a long time to make herself understood and the boys make fun of her efforts.
4. [Mai] says her brother and his wife are obsessed with making money. So much so that their children call the mother "Money" instead of "Mummy." Her nephews treat their mother with extreme disrespect because she doesn't know English. The boys say to the mother, "Shut up, Money."

With reference to these data, it appears that Mai's sister-in-law avoided speaking Vietnamese to her children because she thought her command of English would improve if she spoke English to the boys. Her desire to learn English was driven partly by economic need. Her children, however, who attended Anglophone schools, very soon became more competent in English than she was, and she began to lose her authority over them. The boys, in fact, seemed to exert power over their mother and used their English as a weapon against her: "Shut up, Money," they said. Mai's sister-in-law had no authority in the home and little relationship with her sons, and she spent her days and evenings in the basement making garments and drapes for clients. The father worked long hours every day.

There is another important point to note, however. At our diary study meeting on March 1, Mai discussed how the breakdown of the family structure and the use of English in the home were related to her brother's perception of Vietnamese and Chinese people in Canada. She said that her brother thought Vietnamese and Chinese people were "low" whereas Canadian people were "high." Even though he himself is Chinese and Vietnamese and his wife is Vietnamese, he didn't like Vietnamese and Chinese people and thought they were "bad people." Mai said that her brother tried to think he was Canadian but that other people didn't see him that way. He tried to have Canadian rather than Vietnamese friends – and treated the two groups very differently.

When she arrived in Canada, Mai was struck by the fact that her brother had "changed" so much and had little respect for his own parents. "You can't just throw away what has been passed down from generation to generation," said Mai at our June 7 meeting. Of particular significance to this chapter is the way in which Mai's three nephews were socialized – not only in the home but in the larger community. Mai said that her nephews had been brought up as Canadians and had never been encouraged to learn Vietnamese; only the eldest had any understanding of Vietnamese. They had no interest in finding out about Vietnam or Vietnamese people, and had said on occasion that they "hated" their appearance. When I was taking Mai home from a diary study meeting on March 1, Mai described the alienation that her nephews experienced as Chinese-Vietnamese people in Canada. The eldest child, Trong, for example, had chosen to change his name from a Vietnamese one to an anglicized one. Mai told her nephews that they should not reject their heritage, explaining, "With your hair, your nose, your skin, you will never be perfect Canadians."

Mai described herself as "always in the middle," meaning between her parents and her nephews and occasionally between her nephews and their mother. This earned Mai respect and authority in the eyes of her nephews, who were impressed because she could speak English better than their mother, who had been in Canada for more than 10 years. Mai's diary extract of February 21 illustrates this clearly: "One time Trong told me 'I hope you won't be like someone they just care about money then they forget about English. It's no good in the future.' I understood what he means." Mai's parents, furthermore, were not spared from social tensions both within the family and in the larger community. Mai said that her parents "have no voice" in Canada. Her non-English-speaking father was no longer the patriarch; Mai said he had no "power" in Canada. Mai's mother cleaned the house, did the cooking, and spent the rest of her time in her bedroom, alone and alienated from her extended family. Within a few months of her arrival, she took up a position as a childminder in a Chinese family and stayed with her employer's family. Before long she was hospitalized for depression. In Mai's diary entry of February 28, Mai described her mother's eviction from her brother's house and her own personal distress:

5. I am feeling so sad and very lonely now. Tonight will be the last night I can close to my mother. Then tomorrow she moves to someone's house and stays there all the time. She's going to take care of one child who is 6 months old.

 Since I was born until I came here, I used to stay with my parents. I couldn't miss them even ten days. But now, I can't help when something happens. It hurts me a lot come to think of it. Before we were living in Vietnam we always hoped that we could come here soon to see someone in family that we haven't seen for long time. Then we'll stay together and enjoy the time we have. But now so many bad things happened to us. It made my parents feel bad, because they never think about something like that happening to them. My parents didn't feel like staying in my brother's house any more. They tried to find some place to go. They don't care about that what's going to happen. At least they can get out of this house.

Two months ago my father already left. He went to Toronto to take care of one kid. Last month when he talked with me, his tears was dropping on his face. He said he never think that, at the last short time of his life, he can't have a good time. I just sat there and cried. And now my mother has to go too. For me, I can't move with my mother or my father and it is hard for me to find any place to take them go to stay with me. I feel so sorry for my parents and for myself. I think we are not supposed to be apart like that, but I can't do anything to make life of my parents any better. Even me, I don't know where to go now. I am confused. What's going to happen with my parents and I in the future? Around me now all storm and big windy. I am not sure if I am strong enough to stand up in this situation.

The frayed social fabric of Mai's home is starkly contrasted with the relatively cohesive structure of Katarina's home, a description of which follows.

Katarina's family

Katarina was born in Poland in 1955. She arrived in Canada in April 1989 with her husband and daughter, Maria. Her daughter, like Mai's nephew Kevin, was 8 at the time of data collection. Katarina, who had a master's degree in biology, had been a teacher in Poland. Her husband is similarly qualified. The family immigrated to Canada because they "disliked communism." Before going to Canada, the family spent a year in Austria. Apart from her mother tongue, Polish, Katarina knew some German and Russian when she arrived in Canada. Although Katarina had no knowledge of English, her husband was reasonably fluent as he had worked in international trade in Poland and had used English in his job. Katarina and her family's immigration, in the refugee class, was sponsored by the Catholic church, and she stayed at a sponsor's home on arrival in Newtown. Thereafter, Katarina and her husband looked for a two-bedroom apartment to rent. This apartment building, which tended to be less expensive than others in Newtown, was in a community that accommodated many recent arrivals in Canada. Little English was heard in this community.

Katarina said that she was happy she had come to Canada, a place where there is much diversity in the population. In her December 1991 essay she wrote,

6. Most people feel good in Canada. A great deal of people came here after the Second World War, but many came here in recent years. Most of them spent one or two years in Austria, Germany, Greece, or Italy. Austria is a beautiful country – but only to visit – not to live in. Other nationalities don't feel good in this country because most of people there were born there. Immigrants feel good in Canada because they are aware of various nationalities. In Canada life has a high standard. The Government gives possibilities for people to study. The mothers with children but without husbands have help from the government. People who aren't able to work or can't find jobs receive social welfare. I think that Canada is a "good country for immigrants."

At our diary study meeting on April 12, Katarina compared her experiences of living in Austria with her experiences of living in Canada. She said that in Austria, Polish people are "second category" people, whereas "in Canada they accept me." She said that a good education and knowledge of English give people options in life – the choice, for example, of doing a variety of jobs: "Life is easier when somebody can communicate with other people – can explain exactly what one thinks – can do another job than one has to do – because somebody has a good education and is a good speaker of English."

From the time of the family's arrival in Canada, Katarina was concerned that her daughter might lose command of her mother tongue, Polish. At a diary study meeting on March 1, Katarina said that when she arrived in Canada she cried every day because she realized that her daughter would "grow up speaking English." When asked to explain, she said that she was afraid Maria would grow up speaking a language that Katarina couldn't speak well. Katarina was afraid that she would lose contact with her daughter. The Polish priest at Katarina's church confirmed her fears. Katarina said that the priest had strongly urged all his parishioners to speak the mother tongue at home "not for patriotic reason, not for love of the language, but for the parents." He told them that when the children grow up, and the parents want to talk about things that mean a lot to them, the parents would not be as comfortable in English as they would be in their mother tongue. In order to keep contact with the children, he strongly encouraged them to speak their mother tongue in the home. The priest had said that the children would always be fluent speakers of English, so the parents did not have to be concerned about their integration into Canadian society.

When I interviewed Katarina in her home on a number of occasions, she clearly felt uncomfortable speaking English in front of her daughter. On one occasion when I was at Katarina's home, Katarina read an English text into the tape recorder. Her daughter walked by and said her mother sounded like a "child." This was very unsettling for Katarina. She was happy to watch English TV with her daughter, read English newspapers, and listen to English news programs, but she was adamant that the spoken language in the home should be Polish. She never spoke English to her daughter or husband, something she said was a "hard" thing to do.

Thus the Polish language meant more to Katarina than a link to the past – it was an essential link to her future and her identity as a mother. At our first diary study meeting on February 17, Katarina talked at length about her daughter, who was about to have her first communion. Katarina said that she wanted her daughter to have her first communion in Polish because "that's the way I did it. I remember it so well – in the long white dress." She also said that if the major communion texts, "Our Father" and "The Ten Commandments," were in Polish, she could help Maria learn them, but if they were in English, she could not. Maria learned both texts in Polish. In her diary, Katarina indicated the importance of motherhood to her when she expressed disapproval of women who had gone to serve in the Gulf War, leaving children with fathers. "Mothers have been at the war and children at home with fathers. I don't understand. What is more important – 'war' or 'children.'" Katarina strongly supported the heritage language classes run by the local school board and sent her daughter to learn Polish every Saturday morning.

Comment

It is instructive to compare the language patterns in Mai's household with those in Katarina's. In Mai's household, although three languages were spoken in the home – Vietnamese, Cantonese, and English – English was the language of power. The people who had access to this language had access to power. Conversely, those who did not have access to this language had, in Mai's words, "no voice." The effects on the family structure were devastating. It was a domestic situation in which the mother was almost at the mercy of her sons, in which the grandparents felt they had no place, and in which Mai survived by virtue of the fact that she could serve as an interpreter in the home, "always in the middle" between her parents and her nephews and occasionally between her nephews and their mother.

In Katarina's home, in contrast, Polish was the only language spoken. Katarina was aware that the use of English in the home may not have been in the best interests of the family unit and might drive a wedge between her daughter and herself. She actively sought to ensure that her daughter Maria maintained her mother tongue by sending her to heritage language classes, by speaking to her only in Polish, and by attending the Polish church. Despite occasional setbacks, Katarina indicated that Maria was successful in maintaining proficiency in the Polish language.

It could be argued that these are isolated cases in which, perhaps because of good but misguided intentions, Mai's nephews lost their mother tongue. The data paint a far more complex picture, however. They suggest that the language loss experienced by Mai's nephews can be partly explained by racist practices (either covert or overt) in Canadian society. Over time, Mai's brother grew to believe that Vietnamese people did not share equality with White Canadians and that the Vietnamese language had little value in Canadian society. Mai, herself, indicated that she would always feel like an immigrant in Canada. Apart from her accent, Mai said she did not have the features of a White Canadian and was immediately recognized as "different" by strangers. As she said in her final questionnaire,

7. I'm an immigrant in Canada, even if I'll be living in Canada for my whole life. Because I have a lot of things that are completely different – like the accent, customs. Even sometimes people ask when they don't know me too well "Are you Chinese? It makes me have more feeling that I'm immigrant, or Chinese Canadian citizen.

Under these conditions, it is not difficult to understand why Mai's nephews grew up despising their appearances, rejecting their histories, and eschewing their language. The ambivalence that Mai herself felt is eloquently captured in her comment to her nephews: "With your hair, your nose, your skin, you will never be perfect Canadians." Although Mai believed that one cannot dismiss one's history and your language, she did not actively resist the racist belief that perfect Canadians exist and that they are White. In contrast, Katarina's daughter, Maria, did not share the anguish experienced by Mai's nephews. Although she had been a "second-category" citizen in Austria, Katarina felt comfortable and accepted in Canadian society. Thus Maria grew up in a Polish-rich environment, in which her mother immersed her in the Polish community, sent her to Polish language classes, and took her to the Polish church. She had no need to feel ashamed of her "hair, her nose, her skin." She was, in Mai's words, a perfect Canadian.

Although Mai's extended family may have experienced overt or covert forms of racism in Canadian society, it would be simplistic to argue that such practices were solely responsible for language loss and social disintegration in Mai's family. Possibly, racist practices in Vietnamese society had had a deleterious effect on the family even before arrival in Canada, and identity conflicts were reinforced in Canada. Gender inequities may have also been more salient in Mai's family than in Katarina's family. Furthermore, the contrasting class positions of Mai's and Katarina's families may also be an important issue to consider. Following Connell, Ashendon, Kessler, and Dowsett (1982), I take the position that "it is not what people are, or even what they own, so much as what they do with their resources" (p. 33) that is central to an understanding of class. Even though Mai's family had every appearance of being middle class and Katarina's family was still struggling to regain the social status it had enjoyed in Poland, the ways in which each respective family chose to use its resources is significant. Mai's sister-in-law was under pressure to bring in as much money as possible in a full-time domestic business, a time-consuming activity that her sons greatly resented, whereas Katarina was better placed to meet her daughter's needs while upgrading her own professional skills for future gain.

At face value, then, an elementary school teacher encountering 8-year-old Kevin and 8-year-old Maria would probably be satisfied with their progress in learning the English language. Both children were excellent students and had no difficulty in communicating in English. What teachers might not have been aware of, however, was that Kevin was in danger of losing his mother tongue whereas Maria's Polish was flourishing; that Kevin had great difficulty communicating with his mother whereas Maria had a strong, productive relationship with her mother; that social relationships in Kevin's family were under great strain whereas relationships within the Polish family were secure. A complex intersection of race, gender, and class relationships, in which overt or covert forms of racism appear most salient, are implicated in the language loss experienced by the elementary school boy.

Rethinking acculturation

Having come to a better understanding of the situations of subtractive and additive bilingualism in Mai and Katarina's families, I now turn to theories of acculturation and bilingualism in the field of language education. To what extent do such theories predict the scenarios described in Mai and Katarina's homes?

In the field of SLA, the most influential model addressing processes of acculturation is that associated with the work of Schumann (1978a, 1978b, 1986.) I wish to examine his acculturation model of SLA in some depth for a number of reasons. First, the model was developed specifically with a view to explaining the language acquisition of adult immigrants: "This model accounts for second-language acquisition under conditions of immigration" (1978b, p. 47). As such, it is particularly germane to understanding the language practices in Mai's and Katarina's families. Second, the model is based on the premise that there is a causal link between acculturation and SLA: "SLA is just one aspect of acculturation and the degree to which the learner acculturates to the TL [target language] group will control the degree to which he acquires the second language" (1986, p. 384). Third, Schumann (1978b) states that

453

Bonny Norton

the model "argues for acculturation and against instruction" (p. 48). In other words, according to Schumann, if acculturation does not take place, instruction in the target language will be of limited benefit to the language learner. Finally, the model has been highly influential in the field of SLA, featuring prominently in the established literature on SLA theory (see, for example, Brown, 1987; Ellis, 1997; Larsen-Freeman & Long, 1991; McGroarty, 1988; Spolsky, 1989).

Drawing on his research with adult immigrants in the United States, Schumann (1978b) argues that certain social factors can either promote or inhibit the relationship between two linguistically distinct social groups that are in a contact situation. This in turn will affect the degree to which the second language group will acquire the target language. The first social factor is what Schumann calls *social dominance* patterns. Schumann argues that if the second language group is politically, culturally, technically, or economically superior (dominant) to the target language group, then it will tend not to learn the target language. Conversely, Schumann argues that if the second language group is inferior or subordinate to the target language group, then there will also be social distance between the two groups and the second language group will resist learning the target language.

The second social factor involves what Schumann (1978b) calls the *integration strategies* of assimilation, preservation, and adaptation. Schumann argues that if the second language group gives up its own lifestyle and values and adopts those of the target group, contact with the target language group will be enhanced and acquisition of the target language promoted. If the second language group chooses preservation as an integration strategy and rejects the lifestyle and values of the target group, there will be social distance between the two groups and less likelihood that the second language group will acquire the target language. If the second language group chooses adaptation as its integration strategy, then it adapts to the lifestyle and values of the target language group but maintains its own lifestyle and values for intragroup use. This will yield various degrees of contact with the target language group and thus varying degrees of acquisition of the target language. The last five social factors discussed by Schumann refer to enclosure[3] patterns of the two groups, cohesiveness and size of the second language group, congruence between the two cultures, attitudes of the two groups toward each other, and intended length of residence in the target language area. Specifically, second language learning is more likely to occur if there are positive attitudes between the two groups than if there are negative attitudes between them.

3 *Enclosure* refers to the degree to which the second language group and the target language group share the same churches, schools, clubs, recreational facilities, and so forth (Schumann, 1978, p. 30).

Apart from these social factors, Schumann (1978b) associates a second set of factors with acculturation and argues that they are causative variables in SLA: the affective variables of language shock, cultural shock, motivation, and ego-permeability.[4] Although Schumann associates the social factors with group behavior, he associates the affective factors with the behavior of individuals. Schumann argues that it is the affective variables that account for counter examples to his model. That is, individuals may learn under social conditions that are not favorable to SLA, and they may not learn when the conditions are favorable to SLA. In sum, Schumann's definition of acculturation is as follows:

I would like to argue that two groups of variables – social factors and affective factors – cluster into a single variable which is the major causal variable in SLA. I propose that we call this variable acculturation. By acculturation I mean the social and psychological integration of the individual with the target language (TL) group. I also propose that any learner can be placed on a continuum that ranges from social and psychological distance to social and psychological proximity with speakers of the TL, and that the learner will acquire the language only to the extent that he acculturates. (1986, p. 379)

The strength of Schumann's model is that it highlights the sociocultural context of language learning without neglecting the role of individuals in the language-learning process. It recognizes, furthermore, the importance of regular contact between language learners and speakers of the target language if successful language learning is to take place. However, with reference to data on Mai's and Katarina's families, I problematize a number of theoretical assumptions that are brought to the model:

Assumption 1: If a second language group is inferior or subordinate to the target language group, it will tend to resist learning the second language.

First, the acculturation model does not theorize inferiority and superiority with reference to inequitable relations of power, in which some immigrant groups are socially structured as inferior to the dominant group. The data from my study indicate that Mai's extended family did not arrive in Canada feeling inferior to Canadians; they were constructed as such by the signifying practices of Canadian society. As Bosher (1997) convincingly argues in the U.S. context, current theories of SLA "underestimate the challenges faced by racially and culturally distinct groups that choose to assimilate into U.S. society" (p. 594).

The second point to note in relation to Assumption 1 is that even though Mai's family felt marginalized in Canadian society, they did not resist learning English. On the contrary, they strongly believed that

4 *Ego-permeability* refers to the extent to which inhibition levels can be lowered (Schumann, 1978b, p. 33).

command of the English language would rid them of the Vietnamese-Chinese label and help them obtain the opportunities for which they had come to Canada. Indeed, research suggests that members of the dominant language group rather than immigrant language learners tend to resist interaction with the other group (Goldstein, 1996; Norton Peirce, 1995; Skutnabb-Kangas & Cummins, 1988; Smoke, 1998).

Assumption 2: Positive attitudes between the target language group and the second language group will enhance SLA.

Although positive attitudes between the target language group and the second language group will clearly enhance SLA, the acculturation model does not take into account that, in general, the second language group is far more vulnerable to the attitudes of the dominant group than is true in reverse. It is members of the second language group who need to make contact with the target language community if language learning is to improve, and they have a great deal more invested in this relationship than does the target language group. The model, in other words, does not address the fact that immigrant language learners are generally in a relatively powerless position with respect to the target language community and that their group identity, culture, and values may be under siege. Specifically, the model does not acknowledge that inequitable power relations based on race and ethnicity may compromise attempts by the second language group to maximize their contact with target language speakers, notwithstanding the positive attitudes of the second language group.

Assumption 3: If members of the second language learning group give up their lifestyles and values and adopt those of the target language group, they will maximize their contact with the target language group and enhance SLA.

Assumption 3 is described in the acculturation model as the integration strategy of "assimilation" (Schumann, 1986, p. 381) and refers to what Schumann calls "type two acculturation" (p. 380). This position takes for granted that the target language group is willing to accommodate attempts by the second language group to assimilate and that the target language group will reciprocate the positive attitudes of the second language group. More significantly, however, it does not consider the possibility that subtractive bilingualism in children can take place if members of the second language group give up their lifestyle and values in an attempt to assimilate.

Mai's brother and sister-in-law hoped that if they distanced themselves from the Vietnamese-Chinese history and culture, they would win greater acceptance in Canadian society. Notwithstanding the predictions of the acculturation model, the family's rejection of their lifestyle and values did not maximize contact with the target group and enhance

456

SLA. As Mai indicates, White Anglophone Canadians did not give her family the friendship and respect they hoped for. Furthermore, Mai's sister-in-law was still struggling to speak English after more than 10 years in Canada. Members of this family did not resist learning English, as the acculturation model might suggest, nor were they unmotivated or indifferent. Of even greater concern is that in attempting to become Canadian, Mai's extended family grew to despise its history and ethnicity, and a process of subtractive bilingualism took place among the children in the family. Mai was aware of this tragedy and, as indicated in Extract 1, vowed the following, "I think I won't let it happen to my children if I have in my future."

Crucially, the acculturation model does not acknowledge – or perhaps has not anticipated – the devastating linguistic and domestic consequences associated with giving up one's history, lifestyle, and language. The study indicates that situations of additive and subtractive bilingualism must be understood with reference to larger and frequently inequitable social processes in which racism and ethnocentricism can lead to language loss. Indeed, it is a tragic irony that in the only case in which a family rejected its own values and lifestyle in favor of the perceived values of White Anglophone Canadians, the social fabric of the family was destroyed, together with any hope of bilingual language development.

My study, conducted in Canada, supports findings from a large-scale study of children from linguistic minority families conducted in the United States. In this study, Wong Fillmore (1991) found convincing evidence of subtractive bilingualism in hundreds of families across the country, and argues as follows:

Second language learning does not result in the loss of the primary language everywhere. But it does often enough in societies like the United States and Canada where linguistic or ethnic diversity is not especially valued. Despite our considerable pride in our diverse multicultural origins, Americans are not comfortable with either kind of diversity in our society. (p. 341)

Implications for research and teaching

I have argued in this chapter that more textured theories of acculturation are necessary to understand and promote both second language acquisition among adult immigrants and mother tongue maintenance among their children. In previous research (Norton Peirce, 1995), I have drawn on Bourdieu (1977) to argue that language educators cannot take for granted that those who speak regard those who listen as worthy to listen or that those who listen regard those who speak as worthy to speak. Bourdieu argues persuasively that an expanded definition of competence should include the "right to speech" or the "the power to impose reception" (p. 648). Language educators must acknowledge the inequitable relations of power between target language speakers and second language learners so that they can support language learners in attempting to claim the right to speak. Furthermore, I take the position here that the right to speak refers not only to the target language but to the mother tongue. Much literature in the field of bilingual education (see Cummins, 1996; Genesee, 1994) demonstrates convincingly that the validation of an immigrant's language, culture, and history not only serves to maintain the mother tongue among children but can promote their learning of the target language, particularly with reference to the development of academic literacy.

Despite differences in their language-learning experiences, what both young and older immigrant language learners have in common is the struggle for identity in a new and sometimes threatening world (see Goldstein, 1996; Hunter, 1997; Martin-Jones & Heller, 1996; McKay & Wong, 1996; Morgan, 1997; Norton Peirce, 1995; Schecter & Bayley, 1997). Their investments in the target language and the mother tongue are no less fraught than their relationship to their past and their desires for the future. Teachers and researchers need to understand these multiple and sometimes conflicting investments in order to understand, for example, why the social fabric in Mai's family disintegrated, why Kevin experienced subtractive bilingualism, and how Maria became a successful bilingual. As Genesee (1994) notes, although researchers and educators recognize that children from minority sociocultural groups frequently experience academic difficulties, "they have had trouble understanding the precise nature of these children's backgrounds, and therefore the exact reasons for their academic problems" (p. 6). My research indicates that it is not enough to seek to understand "these children's backgrounds." Language professionals need to understand and address broader social inequities that have concomitant effects on the investments that immigrant families have in both the mother tongue and the target language. The implications of this study for teachers and researchers can be summarized as follows:

1. In the field of second language education there appears to be a fundamental tension between theories of acculturation in SLA and theories of bilingualism. Whereas theories of acculturation in SLA give implicit support to cultural assimilation, theories of bilingualism place greater emphasis on the importance of validating the histories, identities, and contributions of immigrant groups. It is appropriate, I believe, to revisit some of the assumptions about acculturation in the field of SLA.

2. Theories of acculturation in SLA do not pay sufficient attention to

inequitable relations of power between second language learners and target language speakers. Such theories need to recognize that attitudes and motivation are not inherent properties of language learners but are constructed within the context of specific social relationships at a given time and place. This study suggests that target language speakers and second language speakers often have unequal investments in their mutual relationship, which in turn affects opportunities for second language learning. It is both inaccurate and irresponsible to assume, for example, that immigrants such as Mai's sister-in-law, who have limited proficiency in the target language, are necessarily unmotivated or negative. Theories of acculturation in SLA should address the complex relationship among investment, language learning, and larger social processes.

3. The study suggests that the loss of the mother tongue among children can have devastating effects on the social fabric of the family. Children who are racial minorities may be particularly vulnerable to language loss. Teachers need to be proactive in bringing research on subtractive and additive bilingualism to the attention of immigrant parents. Subtractive bilingualism represents more than the loss of language; it puts identities into crisis.

4. Teachers should strive to encourage immigrant language learners to invest in both the target language community and the immigrant language community. Like Katarina's priest, teachers need to make parents aware that mother tongue maintenance has little to do with patriotism, nationalism, or love of the language but much to do with the very fabric of family life and productive relationships between parents, children, and the wider community.

Suggestion for further reading

Corson, D. (1993). *Language, minority education and gender: Linking social justice and power.* Clevedon, England: Multilingual Matters.
   This book examines three groups who seem most affected by unfair language practices in education: women and girls, minority cultural groups, and minority language groups. The author argues that reforms in language education policies can help address these inequities.

Cummins, J. (1996). *Negotiating identities: Education for empowerment in a diverse society.* Ontario: California Association for Bilingual Education.
   Cummins focuses on the way power relations in the broader society influence interactions between teachers and students in the classroom, arguing that culturally diverse students have been frequently

Bonny Norton

disempowered in North American society. The author challenges educators to resist historical patterns of disempowerment that frame bilingualism as a problem rather than a resource.

Fase, W., Jaspaert, K., & Kroon, S. (Eds.). (1992). *Maintenance and loss of minority languages.* Philadelphia: John Benjamins.

This edited volume includes papers from a wide variety of language contact settings in which one or more languages are in the process of shift. Data are presented from countries as diverse as Korea, Finland, and Tanzania. The focus of the book is on the precarious position of minority languages internationally.

Genesee, F. (Ed.). (1994). *Educating second language children: The whole child, the whole curriculum, the whole community.* Cambridge: Cambridge University Press.

This edited volume incorporates the work of fifteen elementary school educators who support an integrative approach to educating second language children. It goes beyond language teaching methodology to include a wide range of issues affecting both the social and the academic success of language minority children.

Norton, B. (in press). *Identity and language learning.* London: Longman.

The author makes the case that there is an integral relationship between identity, investment, and language learning. She argues that theories of second language acquisition need to pay greater attention to inequitable relations of power between language learners and target language speakers

References

Bosher, S. (1997). Language and cultural identity: A study of Hmong students at the postsecondary level. *TESOL Quarterly, 31,* 593–603.

Bourdieu, P. (1977). The economics of linguistic exchanges. *Social Science Information, 16,* 645–668.

Bourdieu, P., & Passeron J. (1977). *Reproduction in education, society, and culture.* Beverly Hills, CA. Sage.

Brown, H. D. (1987). *Principles of language learning and teaching.* Englewood Cliffs, NJ: Prentice Hall.

Connell, R. W., Ashendon, D. J., Kessler, S., & Dowsett, G. W. (1982). *Making the difference: Schools, families, and social division.* Sydney, Australia: Allen & Unwin.

Cummins, J. (1996). *Negotiating identities: Education for empowerment in a diverse society.* Ontario: California Association for Bilingual Education.

Ellis, R. (1997). *Second language acquisition.* Oxford: Oxford University Press.

Genesee, F. (1994). (Ed.). *Educating second language children.* Cambridge: Cambridge University Press.

Goldstein, T. (1996). *Two languages at work: Bilingual life on the production floor.* New York: Mouton de Gruyter.

Hunter, J. (1997). Multiple perceptions: Social identity in a mulilingual elementary classroom. *TESOL Quarterly, 31*, 603–611.

Lambert, W. E. (1975). Culture and language as factors in learning and education. In A. Wolfgang (Ed.), *Education of immigrant students.* Toronto, Canada: Ontario Institute for Studies in Education.

Larsen-Freeman, D., & Long, M. (1991). *An introduction to second language acquisition research.* New York: Longman.

Martin-Jones, M., & Heller, M. (1996). Introduction to the special issues on education in multilingual settings: Discourse, identities, and power. *Linguistics and Education, 8*, 3–16.

McGroarty, M. (1988). Second language acquisition theory relevant to language minorities: Cummins, Krashen, and Schumann. In S. McKay & S. C. Wong (Eds.), *Language diversity: Problem or resource?* (pp. 295–337). Cambridge, MA: Newbury House.

McKay, S. L., & Wong, S. C. (1996). Multiple discourses, multiple identities: Investment and agency in second language learning among Chinese adolescent immigrant students. *Harvard Educational Review, 3*, 577–608.

Morgan, B. (1997). Identity and intonation: Linking dynamic processes in an ESL classroom. *TESOL Quarterly, 31*, 431–450.

Norton Peirce, B. N. (1993). *Language learning, social identity, and immigrant women.* Unpublished doctoral dissertation, Ontario Institute for Studies in Education/University of Toronto.

Norton Peirce, B. N. (1995). Social identity, investment, and language learning. *TESOL Quarterly, 29*, 9–31.

Schecter, S., & Bayley, R. (1997). Language socialization practices and cultural identity: Case-studies of Mexican descent families in California and Texas. *TESOL Quarterly, 31*, 513–542.

Schumann, J. (1978a). *The pidginization process: A model for second language acquisition.* Rowley, MA: Newbury House.

Schumann, J. (1978b). The acculturation model for second-language acquisition. In R. C. Gringas (Ed.), *Second language acquisition and foreign language teaching* (pp. 27–50). Washington, DC: Center for Applied Linguistics.

Schumann, J. (1986). Research on the acculturation model for second language acquisition. *Journal of Multilingual and Multicultural Development, 7*, 379–392.

Skutnabb-Kangas, T., & Cummins, J. (1988). (Eds.). *Minority education: From shame to struggle.* Clevedon, England: Multilingual Matters.

Smoke, T. (1998). *Adult ESL: Politics, pedagogy, and participation in classroom and community programs.* Mahwah, NJ: Erlbaum.

Spolsky, B. (1989). *Conditions for second language learning.* Oxford: Oxford University Press.

Swain, M., & Lapkin, S. (1991). Additive bilingualism and French immersion education: The rules of language proficiency and literacy. In A. G. Reynolds (Ed.), *Bilingualism, multiculturalism and second language learning* (pp. 203–216). Hillsdale, NJ: Erlbaum.

Wong Fillmore, L. (1991). When learning a second language means losing the first. *Early Childhood Research Quarterly, 6*, 323–346.